NEW YORK: 15 WALKING TOURS
An Architectural Guide to the Metropolis

About the Author

Gerard R. Wolfe, Ph.D., is widely regarded as a leading authority on the history and architecture of New York. The author of books, articles, and book reviews on his native city, he has also lectured widely and conducted tours, not only in New York City and environs, but also in the Midwest and the Southwest. Among his publications are *The Synagogues of New York's Lower East Side*, *The House of Appleton: The History of a Publisher*, *Forty-Second Street: River to River Guide*, and the prize-winning *Chicago: In and Around the Loop*, as well as a series of essays for *The Encyclopedia of New York City*. He is a graduate of City University of New York, with a master's degree from New York University and a doctorate in American Studies from Union Institute and University in Cincinnati. He served for many years as a senior administrator at New York University's School of Continuing Education and, most recently, as Director of Arts & Liberal Studies at the University of Wisconsin—Milwaukee.

NEW YORK: 15 WALKING TOURS

An Architectural Guide to the Metropolis

Third Edition

by GERARD R. WOLFE

McGRAW-HILL
New York   Chicago   San Francisco   Lisbon
London   Madrid   Mexico City   Milan   New Delhi
San Juan   Seoul   Singapore   Sydney   Toronto

The **McGraw-Hill** Companies

Cataloging-in-Publication Data is on file with the Library of Congress

2   3   4   5   6   7   8   9   0   DOC/DOC   0   9   8   7   6

ISBN 0-07-141185-2

The sponsoring editor for this book was Cary Sullivan, the editing supervisor was Stephen M. Smith, and the production supervisor was Sherri Souffrance. It was set in Times Roman by Silverchair Science + Communications.

Designed by Philip Grushkin; maps by Henry Siwek.

Printed and bound by RR Donnelley.

McGraw-Hill books are available at special quantity discounts to use as premiums and sales promotions, or for use in corporate training programs. For more information, please write to the Director of Special Sales, McGraw-Hill Professional, Two Penn Plaza, New York, NY 10121-2298. Or contact your local bookstore.

This book is printed on acid-free paper.

Publication history:
    First New York University Press edition, 1975
    First New York University Press paperback edition, 1976
    First McGraw-Hill paperback edition, 1983
    New, revised McGraw-Hill paperback edition, 1988
    Second McGraw-Hill paperback edition, 1994
    Third McGraw-Hill paperback edition, 2003

To my students, colleagues, and friends,
whose insatiable curiosity about
New York's fascinating cityscape and history
was the inspiration for this work

Contents

Note: The following are the landmark symbols used in this guide:

 Designated Landmark by the New York City Landmarks Preservation Commission

 Listed on the National Register of Historic Places

Foreword

My goal in preparing this guide is to help you learn to look at buildings with a discerning and appreciative eye. New York City is a treasure house of architecture, with virtually every style—original or revival—represented in its varied repertory of public buildings, residences, and commercial structures.

With the passage of the Landmarks Preservation Law in 1965 and subsequent amendments, the city succeeded in stemming the relentless destruction of its heritage, although not before the tragic loss of such gems as Pennsylvania Station, the Produce Exchange, the Singer Tower, and the Jerome Mansion. Enough does remain, however, to provide miles of exciting discoveries, not only of our rich past, but also of the new and innovative building designs that have broken with the dull tradition of the glass box and are now offering bright punctuation to the changing skyline.

In selecting the walking tours, it was necessary to choose the most important areas, both architecturally and historically, and to keep the number to 15—the maximum if the book were still to be portable. Unfortunately, some interesting neighborhoods had to be omitted, which perhaps can be included in a forthcoming supplement. The tours begin in Lower Manhattan and are arranged to correspond with the northward growth of the city, ending uptown with the Upper East Side and Upper West Side. Unfortunately, there are no surviving examples of architecture from the Dutch Colonial period in Manhattan, as all vestiges of New Amsterdam were obliterated in the Great Fire of 1835. [*See* Chapter 2.]

The tours vary in length from two to five hours, and some, such as the Lower East Side, Brooklyn Heights, or Manhattan's Financial District, may be divided into two itineraries. The tours are all marked on accompanying maps, with travel directions included. Buildings or districts that have been designated as New York City landmarks by the Landmarks Preservation Commission are identified with a small black disk; those that are National Historic Landmarks—that is, listed on the National Register of Historic Places—are indicated with a star. Following the practice of the Landmarks Commission, no individual buildings within a historic district are identified separately, since technically all buildings within a designated district are landmarks. A glossary of common architectural terms is found at the end of Chapter 7. In some tours whose points of interest are at some distance from each other, key numbers have been used in the text and on the corresponding map.

This guide is designed not only for the out-of-towner, but for the usually blasé New York as well, who rarely, if ever, looks at buildings above the first floor. I learned to my surprise that my students, who were so enthusiastic about my New York University course, "The Many Faces of Gotham," were mostly native Gothamites themselves who were perpetually astonished at the beauty of the buildings they had passed every day without so much as an upward glance. I therefore earnestly hope that you will be encouraged to explore New York on foot and derive pleasure and satisfaction from the discovery of our great architectural and historical heritage...and at the same time become an outspoken and vigorous advocate of its preservation.

In this third, completely revised edition, many important additions to the cityscape have been included, although a number have been lost, among them, tragically, the World Trade Center complex. New in this edition are expanded tours of Battery Park City, Roosevelt Island, the Forty-Second Street–Times Square district, Bryant Park, South Street Seaport, St. Marks-in-the-Bowery Historic District, and Union Square, plus an overview of the outcome of September 11, 2001. In addition, the tours visit all the museums and significant historic sites in Lower Manhattan. The most recent New York City Landmark and National Historic Landmark designations are also included.

Enjoy exploring the city through these walking tours. By following the itineraries, you will gain an understanding of and an appreciation for the dynamic past and splendid architectural heritage of the greatest city in the world, while reliving and gaining new insight into New York's 375-year history.

GERARD R. WOLFE
March 2003

Acknowledgments

In writing a guidebook of this scope, I have had to call upon a number of people and institutions for information, recommendations, and advice. This third edition, because of all the changes that have taken place in the city, required a complete rewrite. Hence, the publisher thought that it would be appropriate to give the book a slightly altered title. This edition does, however, follow the format and style of the earlier editions of *New York: A Guide to the Metropolis*.

I am indebted to Justin Ferate, tour leader *par excellence* and director of Tours of the City, who not only is an acclaimed professional, but who also instructs aspiring tour leaders on the fine art of tour conducting, for giving freely of his time and advice; Joyce Mendelsohn, historian, author of a number of highly popular walking-tour guidebooks, distinguished teacher, and tour guide, whose scholarly research, suggestions, and encouragement proved invaluable; Jack Taylor, preservation activist, whose dedication helped save the Ladies' Mile Historic District, Union Square, and other East Side landmarks, for his personal interest, research, and suggestions; Richard McDermott, historian and publisher of the *New York Chronicle*, and the indisputable authority on the history of New York drinking establishments; and Patricia Myers, for her stacks of background information and for her uncompromising insistence on accuracy that helped keep me on track. Two others to whom I am very grateful are Joan Bielefeld and Nancy Falloon, without whose help during my weeks of rewrite on the streets of New York during the record, blistering summer heat wave of 2002 the task could not have been accomplished.

I must also acknowledge the guidance of Jeffrey Remling, Curator of Collections of the South Street Seaport Museum, for his many ideas; the Public Affairs Office of the Port Authority of New York and New Jersey, for necessary details on the aftermath of the World Trade Center tragedy; Bruce Parker, Director of Communications, General Theological Seminary; Sandra Bloodworth, Director, Arts for Travel, Metropolitan Transportation Authority; Bill Watson, Librarian, New York Yacht Club; Rosalind Muggeridge, P.R. and Program Coordinator, Mount Vernon Hotel Museum and Garden; Tama Starr, President of Artkraft Strauss Sign Corporation—the company that built most of Times Square's landmark displays; Barbara Bruer, for her suggestions and support; Ann Anielewski of the Municipal Art Society, for her invaluable background information; and Anne Guernsey, Rights and Reproduction Associate, Museum of the City of New York. I want to offer tribute to two distinguished publications that I relied on to double-check the accuracy of my architectural data: the *AIA Guide to New York City*, fourth edition, by Norval White and Elliot Willensky, and the *Guide to New York City Landmarks*, second edition, by Andrew S. Dolkart. I must also recognize *The Encyclopedia of New York City*, edited by Kenneth T. Jackson, for details on New York City theatre history and for biographical data. [*See* Recommended Reading.]

I also feel obliged to mention one of the outcomes of my teaching of New York history and architecture at New York University and the walking tours of the city that I conducted for many years. When I ultimately departed for an administrative post at the University of Wisconsin—Milwaukee, a group of loyal followers from those N.Y.U. seminars banded together to continue the architectural and historical walking tours and, much to my embarassment, called themselves the "Wolfe Walkers." These indefatigable veterans of my tours, some going back over 30 years, have been continuing the tradition, encouraging new participants, and even offering tours of discovery to far-flung points of interest beyond the borders of the city. Much of the organizational credit must go to committee members Bob Search and Sheila Heitner, Mimi Olanoff, Micki Watterson, and Lydia Latchinova; "walkers" Ida Schwartz, Deborah de Bauernfeind, Mary Lettieri, Adele Savodnick, Diane Rownd, Jack Taylor, Marjorie Berk, Johanna Sterbin, Stephen W. Schwartz, Patricia Schofield, Dr. Vera Schnelle, Dr. Esther Bearg, Elaine Elkind, Helen Ransower, Kay Blumberg, Ernst and Ellen van Haagen, Fern Treiber, Ruth K. Smith, Shirley Frank, Myra Mandzuk, Mimi Rothberg, Elizabeth Tom, Oliver Wayne, Joan Bielefeld, Bluma Cohen, Nina Lombardo, David Heerwagen, Colleen Floyd, Mary Helleis, Pete Salwen, Ann Stengel, Rita Panish, Milton and Lenore Norman, Pat Myers, Claire Wasserman, and Dr. Jack and Esther Traub—all alumni/alumnae of many years; and their superb tour leaders Justin Ferate, Joyce Mendelsohn, and Joseph Zito (a former N.Y.P.D. precinct captain, whose interest was kindled as a member of my very first tour in 1969); and a special acknowledgement to Marilyn Gross for valuable additional background materials.

I would be remiss if I failed to acknowledge the enthusiastic support of the McGraw-Hill editorial team: Cary Sullivan, Sponsoring Editor; Stephen M. Smith, Editing Supervisor; Sherri Souffrance, Production Supervisor; and Cathy Markoff in Marketing. A special note of thanks is also due to Brooke Begin, Production Editor, Silverchair Science + Communications, who helped me put the final touches on the manuscript.

Finally, I shall always feel a deep debt of gratitude to my late father, Samuel Wolfe, who, as a young immigrant to the Lower East Side in 1904, grew up in the teeming tenements, and, later, as an upwardly mobile City College graduate, helped raise his family in a "better" Brooklyn neighborhood. But he never forgot his youthful experiences and kept us entertained with endless tales about the trials and tribulations of growing up and working in the city. When I was old enough, he began taking me on my first-ever walking tours of the old neighborhoods and to the downtown Manhattan Financial District where he worked—fascinating walks punctuated with lively anecdotes, historical facts, and humor that awakened in me an intense curiosity about the city, an interest that grew into a passion, and ultimately became one of the paths that led to the writing of this book.

G.R.W.

NEW YORK: 15 WALKING TOURS
An Architectural Guide to the Metropolis

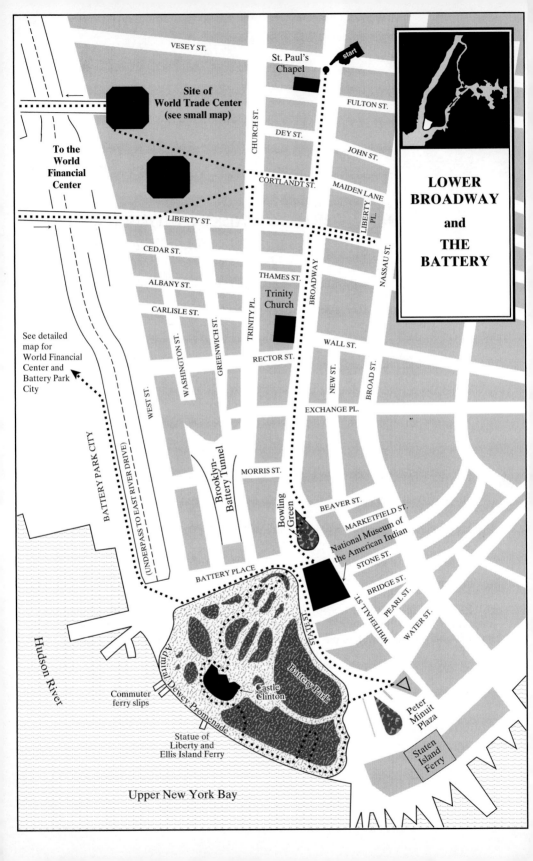

1. Lower Broadway, Battery Park City, and the Battery

[Subways: A, C to Broadway–Nassau; 1, 2, 4, 5, J, M, Z to Fulton Street.]

The walking tour begins at Fulton Street and Broadway.

St. Paul's Chapel is the oldest church in Manhattan (and its oldest public building as well). With its back to Broadway, it faces a peaceful churchyard, oblivious to the noise and clamor of the tumultuous thoroughfare. A branch of Trinity Church downtown, St. Paul's was completed in 1766, the tower and steeple in 1796. Architect Thomas McBean was undoubtedly influenced by London's St. Martin's-in-the-Fields when he designed this stately landmark. It is built of locally quarried Manhattan schist, and the tower (designed by James Crommelin Lawrence) is of brownstone. The church is an almost perfect example of the Georgian style, reflecting the tradition of the Colonial period. Much of the interior decoration of this National Historic Landmark was done by Pierre L'Enfant, the French-born architect who later became a Major of Engineers in the Continental Army, and who helped lay the plans of the city of Washington, D.C. His main work in the church is the altar, with its railing and sculptured "Glory" above it. Other splendid artifacts are the hand-carved and gold-leafed pulpit, 14 original Waterford cut-glass chandeliers, and the beautifully crafted organ case. The graceful columns are hollow and contain solid oak tree trunks which add support

---

Note: Since most of the points of interest on this tour are situated quite close to each other, the system of numbering each stop in the text and on the map will not be used; rather, the description and location of each point of interest will be a separate entry, indicated in bold-face type.

Broadway, 1850, at the foot of City Hall Park, looking south. Barnum's Museum, left, was destroyed by fire in 1865. The Astor House, the city's finest hotel at the time, is to the right, with the portico of St. Paul's Chapel adjoining. Trinity Church's spire dominates the thoroughfare. (The J. Clarence Davies Collection, Museum of the City of New York)

to the roof. The pew where George Washington regularly worshiped is in the north aisle, with the original seal of the United States on the wall behind. It was originally the canopied pew of the royal governor of the Province of New York. The pew of the first governor of the state, George Clinton, is in the south aisle. Among other distinguished worshipers were Prince William of Orange (later King William IV), Lords Cornwallis and Howe, Maj. John André, the Marquis de Lafayette, and Presidents Grover Cleveland and Benjamin Harrison.

The quiet churchyard with its numerous 18th-century headstones of prominent early New York families is well worth a visit.

Immediately after the September 11, 2001, disaster, St. Paul's Chapel became a respite center for construction workers, providing shelter, solace, and 3,000 donated meals a day. Miraculously, the church, situated only a block from Ground Zero, suffered only minor damage, although it was covered with two feet of dust and debris. For months after the tragedy the street sides of St. Paul's Chapel, as well as other locations nearby, displayed panel after panel of heartbreaking memorabilia: messages seeking information about missing family members (among whom were 2,749 missing or known dead, including 343 firefighters, 23 New York

City police officers, and 74 Port Authority police) plus photographs of loved ones, T-shirts, flags, teddy bears, fire department emblems nationwide, candles, poems, and countless personal notes in many languages from around the world containing prayers, expressions of grief, and words of condolence.

The former American Telephone & Telegraph Building, just south of St. Paul's, was built in 1917 from plans by Welles Bosworth. No other building in the city can boast so many columns; in fact, in its eight Ionic tiers stacked on a Doric base, it has more columns than the Parthenon. A gilt statue that once graced the tower (*The Spirit of Communication* by Evelyn Beatrice Longman) was removed and for a time was mounted in the lobby of AT&T's former corporate headquarters at 550 Madison Avenue. "Golden Boy," as the 10-ton statue is frequently called, now resides at the AT&T campus in Somerset County, New Jersey. A weekday visit to the marble colonnaded lobby reveals a sculpture of Alexander Graham Bell, and two lovely brass floor medallions, as well as a large marble and bronze sculpture, *Service to the Nation* by Chester Beach.

A dramatic exhibit of toxic dust–covered designer sweaters, shirts, and jeans—mute testimony to what was found after the smoke cleared at the WTC—was set up by the unfortunate owner of Chelsea Jeans, 195 Broadway, as a makeshift memorial shrine. In the year of its existence, the glassed-in display was seen by tens of thousands of visitors, many of whom left flowers and written tributes, before it was transported at considerable toxic hazard to a sealed, permanent 9/11 exhibit at the New-York Historical Society. The little shop, unable to recover, went out of business. (Photo by author)

Busy Broadway in the mid-1880s, lined with horse-drawn traffic. All the buildings on the right side, to the corner of Cortlandt Street, are still standing; but only one, the narrow, white Germania Building, erected in 1865, has not undergone a "face-lift." (American Telephone & Telegraph Company)

No. 195 Broadway was the site, until recently, of Chelsea Jeans, a clothing store situated only three blocks from Ground Zero and another victim of the fallout from the 9/11 disaster. After removing the pulverized debris and thick layers of toxic dust that had engulfed his merchandise, owner David Cohen reopened and set aside one glassed-in section as a memorial "against terrorism everywhere." In the months that followed, hundreds of thousands of visitors stopped by to gawk at the display of dust-covered designer jeans and sweaters, pay their respects, and leave mementos. In an unusual turn of events, the New-York Historical Society, which had preserved a number of Ground Zero memorabilia, undertook the unprecedented and daunting task of sealing and transporting the fragile and hazardous toxic shrine to the society's museum uptown. Mr. Cohen's business, however, never recovered, and one year after 9/11 it closed its doors.

No. 192 Broadway is an undistinguished survivor from the 1880s, somehow bypassed by the land developers. Interesting are the so-called Queen Anne cast-iron bay windows. A few feet around the corner was the **site of the John Street Theater,** from 1767 to 1798. During the British occupation of New York in the Revolutionary War, General Howe's army officers frequently would take part in the cast and production of plays. Later, Royall Tyler's play, *The Contrast*, opened as the first comedy work by a native author ever produced in America. George Washington was an often-seen theatergoer here.

No. 175 Broadway, the **Germania Building,** an even older survivor, is a typical commercial building, erected in 1865 in Italian Renaissance style. This was the style so often copied by the cast-iron architects and later recopied in stone. That this 1865 building remains at all is a minor miracle.

The twin Hudson Terminal buildings were razed to make way for the 110-story World Trade Center. Underneath was the terminal of the Hudson & Manhattan "Tubes," now called the PATH, and presently located about 100 yards west, beneath the site of the twin Trade Center towers. (Port Authority of New York & New Jersey)

Cross Broadway to the northeast corner of Maiden Lane.

Set in the sidewalk is a large glass clock. Dating from around 1925, it is said to have replaced an earlier model installed by the same firm of William Barthman just before the turn of the century. The timepiece is adjusted from the basement, and the protective glass, which had to be changed every few months because of the constant scuffing from millions of pedestrians' shoes, now has been supplanted by a type of quartz glass which lasts up to nine months. While the history of the earlier clock cannot be documented, a legend persists that in 1911 a runaway horse smashed into the store window, splintering the showcase and scattering a quarter-of-a-million dollars in jewelry across Broadway. Yet the street clock below the pavement survived undamaged.

Turn right (west) at Cortlandt Street.

Until the arrival of the World Trade Center, Cortlandt Street was the center of the amateur radio hobbyist. Rows of stores selling electronic gadgets, used parts, and an endless variety of radio hardware lined both Cortlandt Street and neighboring Church Street.

The former East River Savings Bank, now a Century 21 department store, at the northeast corner of Cortlandt and Church streets, is an almost perfect example of the Art Deco style of the 1930s. This was the approximate **site of a**

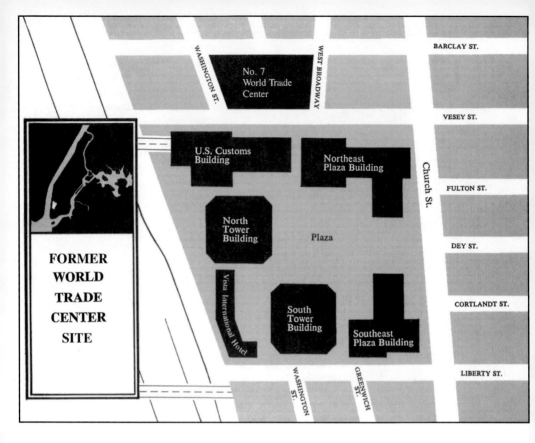

BARCLAY ST.

No. 7 World Trade Center

WASHINGTON ST.

WEST BROADWAY

VESEY ST.

U.S. Customs Building

Northeast Plaza Building

Church St.

FULTON ST.

North Tower Building

Plaza

DEY ST.

FORMER WORLD TRADE CENTER SITE

Vista International Hotel

CORTLANDT ST.

South Tower Building

Southeast Plaza Building

LIBERTY ST.

WASHINGTON ST.

GREENWICH ST.

New York became an important flour-milling center, and two flour barrels and a pair of crossed windmill arms are a part of the city's Great Seal.

The site of the World Trade Center is now under reconstruction following a design selected in early 2003 after considerable discussion and debate. The resultant project by Daniel Libeskind and David M. Childs, whose centerpiece will be the 1,776-foot-high Freedom Tower, will always remain a poignant reminder of the country's worst disaster in terms of human tragedy and economic loss.

The World Trade Center, a mammoth project that took more than ten years to complete, was designed by Minoru Yamasaki and Emery Roth & Sons, and construction was begun in 1962. The first buildings opened in 1970, but the towers and Plaza were not completed until 1976; the last building opened in 1988. Until its destruction on 9/11, the WTC had become an icon for New York City, and was considered the financial center of the nation, with links to the entire world. Created by the Port Authority of New York and New Jersey to be a center of world commerce, the site consisted of two 110-story towers—the tallest buildings in the nation—that rose 1,350 feet, and four low-rise plaza buildings (Nos. 3 through 6 WTC), plus No. 7 WTC. Alongside stood the Marriot Hotel (formerly the Vista International) and the diminutive St. Nicholas Greek-Orthodox Church. All were completely destroyed in the cataclysmic event. Every piece of public sculpture on the Plaza (with one exception) was likewise lost. [See the *Sphere* in Battery Park, Chapter 1.] On the lower concourse of the WTC an extensive mall, a subway station, a parking garage, and the PATH (Port Authority Trans-Hudson) Terminal were also obliterated.

Ground Zero, the site of the World Trade Center disaster, seen through its protective chain-link fence in late summer 2002. The removal of debris and the search for traces of the missing are virtually complete. All that remains of the WTC's 16-acre site is a six-story-deep excavation. In the rear is the Art Deco–style Barclay-Vesey Building, built for the headquarters of the New York Telephone Company, now Verizon Communications, 140 West Street (1923–27, McKenzie, Voorhees & Gmelin, with Ralph Walker). The façade suffered severe damage, and is being restored. The attractive skyscraper was the first in the city to follow the requirements of the 1916 zoning code. (Photo by author)

Buildings that collapsed:

1 World Trade Center
2 World Trade Center
5 World Trade Center (Credit Suisse First Boston)
6 World Trade Center (U.S. Customs Service)
7 World Trade Center
North Bridge
St. Nicholas Church

Buildings that suffered major damage:

3 World Trade Center (Marriott Hotel)
90 West Street
4 World Trade Center (Deutsche Bank) (scheduled to be dismantled)
140 West Street (Verizon Communications)
90 Church Street (U.S. Postal Service, Legal Aid)
South Bridge
Former East River Savings Bank

Most buildings surrounding the 16-acre Ground Zero site were severely damaged, and some, like 4 World Trade Center (Deutsche Bank), were scheduled to be demolished later. Efforts are under way to save and restore the magnificent landmark **90 West Street,** designed by famed architect Cass Gilbert in 1907,

Among the more heart-wrenching sights in the aftermath of the World Trade Center tragedy were the public displays of photos of missing loved ones, requests for information, letters from family members, prayers, flags, articles of clothing with personal messages, and fire department shoulder patches and memorabilia from around the country. This view of a display on the fence of St. Paul's Chapel is one of several near the WTC site. (Photo by author)

which incredibly, unlike its adjacent modern neighbors, withstood much of the force of the blasts and tower collapses. Other major buildings that suffered significant damage, but have been or will be reopened, are 1 through 4 World Financial Center, the Winter Garden, 130 and 140 West Street, 4 Albany Street, 1 Liberty Plaza, 101 Barclay Street, 90 and 100 Church Street, 22 Cortlandt Street, 75 Park Place, the Millenium Hilton, and the South Bridge. Destruction by the ensuing thick smoke and fallout of debris that blanketed much of Lower Manhattan caused economic losses in the billions. The total loss, however, in human terms, is beyond calculation.

Turn left on Church Street, then left again at Liberty Street, to Broadway.

   1 Liberty Plaza (Skidmore, Owings & Merrill, 1974) was designed to show the vertical faces of its steel structure. The 53-story tower occupies the site of the late lamented Singer (Sewing Machine Company) Tower as well as the ornate City Investing Building. When the Singer Tower was completed in 1908, it was

New York's skyline lost one of its great landmarks when U.S. Steel demolished the Singer Tower in 1968 to erect No. 1 Liberty Plaza on the site. The Tower was the crowning achievement of architect Ernest Flagg, and was completed in 1908. For a brief time it was the world's tallest building. The Singer Tower was the tallest building ever demolished.

Rebuilding Ground Zero. Plans for the 16-acre site call for a 1,776-foot skyscraper, called the Freedom Tower, to be erected on the northwest corner from plans by Daniel Libeskind and David M. Childs, with Skidmore, Owings & Merrill. The 70-story tower is expected to be the tallest in the world. Also underway is a Transportation Center, designed by noted Spanish architect Santiago Calatrava, to incorporate the PATH terminal and adjacent subway lines and bus routes, with both structures expected to be completed by 2006. Not yet approved at this writing is the design for the memorial to all who perished in the 9/11 disaster. Proposals for the rest of the site have included several high-rise commercial structures, a museum, a branch library, the New York City Opera, and public sculptures.

the tallest building in the world, until it was eclipsed by the Metropolitan Life Tower 18 months later. Architect Ernest Flagg's liberal use of metal and glass, incorporated into a graceful shaft in Renaissance Eclectic style, produced one of the most beautiful buildings ever to grace the New York skyline. Its replacement, built in 1974, adds nothing exciting to the cityscape and only heightens the feeling of loss. (The *AIA Guide* calls the building "a gloomy, cadaverous hulk.") The plaza area to the right was devastated in the 9/11 tragedy, but is being replanted and restored. It is hoped that the lifesize bronze sculpture, *Double Check*, by J. Seward Johnson will be returned to its original site.

Cross Broadway and continue east on Liberty Street.

The former Chamber of Commerce of the State of New York, now the International Commercial Bank of China (65 Liberty Street), is an attractive example of the French Beaux Arts style. Designed in 1901 by James Barnes Baker, it was built for the State Chamber of Commerce, which was founded at Fraunces Tavern in 1768. The solid Ionic columns seem to frame empty spaces. Originally there were three large sculpture groups, which did not survive New

York's air pollution (and pigeons) and suffered so much decay that they were removed some years ago. The impressive white marble edifice was dedicated by President Theodore Roosevelt in an elaborate ceremony witnessed by former President Grover Cleveland and several foreign ambassadors. In 1973, the Chamber of Commerce merged with the Commerce and Industry Association, and seven years later the organization moved to other quarters.

● **Liberty Tower** (55 Liberty Street) is a good example of the neo-Gothic style applied to commercial skyscrapers. It was designed by Henry Ives Cobb in 1909, and from 1919 served as the headquarters of the Sinclair Oil Company. The building, with its white terra-cotta walls, is now a cooperative apartment house. Step back a few yards down narrow Liberty Place, and observe the fantasy of Gothic reflections in the glassy façade of the Marine Midland Building. The building was erected on the site of the Manhattan home of poet William Cullen Bryant.

Return to the plaza in front of 140 Broadway.

The Marine Midland Bank Building, designed by Skidmore, Owings & Merrill in 1967, is one of the first New York skyscrapers to have its own plaza. The use of matte black spandrels between rows of glass gives an unexpected effect of sleekness, in sharp contrast to the ornamented façades of nearby buildings. The dark, smooth appearance is further offset by the orange, **cube-shaped stabile** in the plaza, by sculptor Isamu Noguchi. Before the Marine Midland Bank erected its tower, the site was occupied by the Guaranty Trust Company Building—a very impressive classic structure, designed by York & Sawyer in 1912, which received the American Institute of Architects Medal for Distinguished Architecture two years after its completion.

Continue south on Broadway.

●
● **The U.S. Realty Building** (115 Broadway) and its neighbor to the south, **The Trinity Building** (111 Broadway), are a delightful pair of early-20th-century skyscrapers. Both were designed in the year 1906 by architect Francis H. Kimball, in a modified Gothic style. There is an intimate quality about these narrow twins lacking in most modern buildings. Despite their height, they seem almost like charming residences. Look up at the catwalk connecting the two like a prop for a silent thriller movie. Diminutive Thames Street was originally an 18th-century carriageway leading to the DeLancey stables. Stephen DeLancey's home would later become Fraunces Tavern.

★ **The Equitable Building** (120 Broadway), designed by Ernest R. Graham in 1915, replaced an earlier Equitable Life Building that was destroyed by fire in 1912. Using every square inch of space, this blockbuster of a building rises 41 stories without setback for a total of 1,200,000 square feet of floor space on a site slightly under an acre! The result is a floor area of about 30 times the plot's. Present zoning laws allow less than 12. Upon completion of the building there arose such a tremendous clamor against the enormous building density that in 1916 new zoning laws were introduced, establishing the setback requirements that have been progressively tightened through the years.

● **100 Broadway,** recently the Bank of Tokyo, and originally the American Surety Building, was built in 1895 from plans by Bruce Price. The eight allegorical figures were sculpted by J. Massey Rhind. The building was sensitively remodeled in 1975 by the Japanese designers Kajima International with architect Herman Lee Meader, from designs by Nobutaka Ashihara.

● ★ **Trinity Church,** designed by Richard Upjohn in 1846, is the third church on the site. Its location at the head of Wall Street makes it one of the best-known landmark churches in the city. The original church was established in 1697 by Royal Charter of King William III of England, but it remained for Queen Anne to grant the land in 1705. The first church was destroyed by the Great Fire of 1776, and the second was demolished because of structural failure. Artistically, the most striking feature of Trinity Church is the three sets of huge bronze doors, designed by Richard Morris Hunt. They were a gift of William Waldorf Astor, and are patterned after the famous Ghiberti bronze doors of the Baptistery in Florence. The sculpture work for the main entrance doors was executed by Karl Bitter, the south doors by Charles H. Niehaus, and the north doors by J. Massey Rhind. The splendid stained-glass chancel window was designed by Upjohn himself. The building exterior is of brownstone. It was cleaned recently, and the church, once blackened by pollution and soot, is now a rosy pink (but for how long?). The 280-foot spire was for years a prominent New York landmark until it was dwarfed by the surrounding skyscrapers. The "ring" of ten bells in the steeple is played before services, and adds a quieting note to the commotion of the neighborhood. The side wall buttresses, while inserting a touch of Gothic glamour, are false, as the ceiling vaults are made of plaster and are hung for decoration

The classic Guaranty Trust Company Building, built in 1912, was awarded the AIA Medal for Distinguished Architecture. In its place at 140 Broadway stands the Marine Midland Bank Building. (Morgan Guaranty Trust Company)

only. The interior, however, is somber and majestic. To the left of the sanctuary is the lovely All Saints Chapel, built in 1913, as well as an interesting little museum of early New York history. (Hours: Mon.–Fri. 9:00 A.M. to 11:45 A.M. and 1:00 P.M. to 3:45 P.M., Sat. 10:00 A.M. to 3:45 P.M., Sun. 1:00 P.M. to 3:45 P.M.; free.) Short tours of Trinity Church are given daily at 2:00 P.M. by one of the vergers.

★ Surrounding the church is the **burial ground,** shaded by trees of many species. In the north section is the ornate Gothic-style Martyrs' Monument, a memorial to Continental soldiers who, during the American Revolution, died while imprisoned in a sugar house on Liberty (then Crown) Street. The various monuments read like a page from American history: Alexander Hamilton, Robert Fulton (whose steamboat *Clermont* set sail from the foot of Cortlandt Street), Captain James Lawrence (who, as commander of the ship *Chesapeake* in the War of 1812, immortalized himself with his dying command, "Don't Give Up the Ship!"), Albert Gallatin (twice Secretary of the Treasury under Thomas Jefferson, and a founder of New York University), Francis Lewis (signer of the Declaration of Independence), and William Bradford (early champion of freedom of the press, and editor of New York's first newspaper, the *New York Gazette*). In 1987 the Church constructed an ornate cast-iron footbridge across Trinity Place connecting the second floor of the parish building with the church complex. The churchyard is a favorite lunch-hour retreat in warm weather for office workers in the surrounding financial district; and the Church presents noontime concerts every Monday and Thursday.

The Bank of New York Building (formerly the Irving Trust Company Building) at 1 Wall Street is a massive limestone pile of Art Deco. An interesting touch by architects Voorhees, Gmelin & Walker in this 1932 building are the fluted walls and chamfered corners. An addition to the building was built in 1965. The attractive lobby is decorated with a polychrome mosaic design that gives a startling flamelike appearance. When seen from the street at night it literally glows in patterns of bright red and orange.

Wall Street is named for the original palisade fence or wall, built in 1653 on orders from Dutch Governor Peter Stuyvesant. Although generally believed to have been erected as a defense against hostile Indians, it was intended as a bulwark against an invasion by British colonists from New England. The wall stood from river to river for about 50 years. [For a tour of the Wall Street area and neighboring streets, *see* Manhattan's Financial District walking tour, Chapter 2.]

● **No. 71 Broadway,** the **Empire Building** (Renwick, Aspinwall and Tucker, 1894), at the southwest corner of Rector Street, was the headquarters of the United States Steel Corporation (now USX), until their recent move uptown. Converted to a residential building, it is now the Empire Apartments.

The **former American Express Company Building** (65 Broadway) was designed in 1917 by Renwick, Aspinwall and Tucker, and served as the New York headquarters of the worldwide firm that began as a one-man operation in 1839, when William F. Harnden made four trips by train to Boston every week to deliver parcels and make collections. In 1850 he merged with two other express companies, operating a fleet of delivery wagons. Under the leadership of president Henry Wells and secretary William G. Fargo, the American Express Company's new subsidiary, Wells Fargo, helped open the West. The novel "Traveler's Cheque" was introduced in 1891, but by 1918 express services were abandoned altogether. With its merger in 1981 with Shearson Loeb Rhoades, the company expanded its financial operations, which are now conducted at its new corporate headquarters at the American Express Tower in the World Financial Center at Battery Park City. Note the asymmetric eagle on the lower arch and a symmetric one at the top arch.

No. 55 Broadway, called **One Exchange Plaza,** at the corner of Exchange Alley, is in striking contrast to its neighbors. Designed in 1982 by Fox & Fowle, it is a 31-story office tower with buff-colored horizontal brick spandrels and clear glass bands, with radial corners. In the rear, facing Trinity Place, is a second-level shopping way, required by the City Planning Commission to provide appropriate pedestrian space and a continuous link with the street. Its neighbor down the street at No. 45, **The Broadway Atrium,** completed in 1983, is another Fox & Fowle–designed building, of the same height and color scheme, but set back, and with serrated corners in a sawtooth pattern. It, too, has a second-level shopping way on Trinity Place.

No. 50 Broadway marks the **site of New York's first skyscraper.** The Tower Building, designed by Bradford L. Gilbert, was an 11-story steel-skeleton building, completed in 1889. Gilbert had to occupy the topmost floor himself to dispel fears of New Yorkers that such a "tall" structure might collapse.

No. 39 Broadway has a plaque indicating the site of the Alexander McComb Mansion—George Washington's second presidential residence, occupied from February 23 to August 30, 1790.

No. 26 Broadway, the **former Standard Oil Building,** was the corporate headquarters of John D. Rockefeller's Standard Oil. Later, the company became SOCONY (*Standard Oil CO. of N.Y.*) when the government "trust busters" took action; then Socony-Mobil; and with a final simplification to Mobil Oil, the firm moved into new headquarters on East 42nd Street. The curved façade conforms to the principle of the "street wall"—so vital in good urban planning. The firm of Carrère & Hastings (which designed the New York Public Library at Fifth Avenue and 42nd Street, among other fine buildings) with Shreve, Lamb & Blake planned this imposing building in 1922 with the skyline in mind. Although the lower section of the building conforms to the path of Broadway, the upper tower coincides with the geometry of the Manhattan street grid. Atop the tower an appropriately symbolic oil-burning lantern (actually the chimney) crowns the massive structure. The building is best viewed from a distance. Before the rash of post–World War II boxlike skyscrapers obscured it from view, the Standard Oil Building formed an integral part of the lovely New York skyline, and was clearly visible from the harbor.

At No. 24, the side entrance of the Standard Oil Building, is the diminutive **Museum of American Financial History.** On display are artifacts and historical documents that relate to the story of the stock exchanges and various Wall Street brokerage houses. Founded by John E. Herzog in 1988, it opened here four years later. The museum portrays many aspects of the nation's financial history, including an array of beautifully engraved stock certificates, and a stock ticker. It probably is the smallest museum in New York. [Hours: Tues.–Sun. 10:00 A.M. to 4:00 P.M., (212) 908-4695, free.]

Across Bowling Green, the immense **Cunard Building** (25 Broadway) is a harmonious counterpart to the Standard Oil Building. Constructed in 1921 from plans by Benjamin Wistar Morris, when a transatlantic crossing by luxurious ocean liner was "the only way to travel," it is one of the finest office buildings in the world. The Cunard Line arrived in New York with the maiden voyage of Samuel Cunard's *Britannia* on July 4, 1840, and remained in the forefront in ocean travel until fairly recently. Merging with the White Star Line in the 1920s, it became the largest passenger ship company in the world. [The names of Cunard ships always ended in -*ia* (*Mauretania*, *Lusitania*, etc.), White Star's in -*ic* (*Britannic*, *Titanic*, etc.). Later exceptions were the great "Queens," including the *QE2*.] The building's ornate Renaissance façade is quite handsome with its three arched entranceways and second-story colonnade, but the charm of the impressive structure is in its vestibule and Great Hall—certainly one of the most beautiful interior spaces anywhere. Passing through one of the central bronze doors, the visitor enters the high vaulted vestibule whose ornament was created by artist Ezra Winter. Beyond high wrought-iron gates (by Samuel Yellin) is the *pièce de résistance*, the Great Hall. Now housing a post office branch, the octagonally shaped chamber measures 185 feet long by 74 feet wide, and the central section is surmounted by a dome 65 feet above the floor. Study the magnificent murals and pendentives covered in fresco. The walls and floor are covered with travertine with considerable detail, and the artistic maps of the world were executed by Barry Faulkner. The aesthetic climax of the great room is its groined, vaulted ceiling ornamented with arabesques and a multitude of design motifs. Ezra Winter and most of the artists who combined their talents here were winners of the Rome Prize. The four supporting pendentives created by Winter represent the ships of Christopher Columbus, John Cabot, Sir Francis Drake, and Leif Ericson. In the heyday of steamship travel, the rooms were called the Freight Distribution Hall and the Bill of Lading Hall. Thomas Hastings (of the firm of Carrère & Hastings) was a consultant to architect Morris, and is said to have suggested the plan of the Great Hall based on Raphael's Villa Madama in Rome. The Cunard Building is unquestionably one of the finest examples of the American Renaissance and, in the words of Henry Hope Reed, author of *The Golden City* and curator of Central Park, "Great art is to be found not in a glorified warehouse called a museum, but in such buildings as 25 Broadway."

Bowling Green was New York City's first park. It lay just beyond the original fort, and was merely an open space leading into *De Heere Wegh* (The Main Street, or Broadway). It served as a cattle market and also as a parade ground. In 1733 it was rented privately for "one peppercorn per year for the recreation and delight of the inhabitants of this city." An iron fence ornamented with crowns was erected in 1771 to protect the little park and its newly erected statue of King George III. A symbol of British tyranny, the gilt-lead statue was pulled down by patriots after General Washington ordered the Declaration of Independence read publicly on July 9, 1776. The crowns that topped the fence posts also were destroyed. Curiously, parts of the original statue still exist, and pieces later turned

Charging Bull, *by sculptor Arturo DiModica and cast by Domenico Ranieri, was originally placed (without permission) in front of the Stock Exchange in 1992. The Exchange, not appreciating the "bullish" implication, ordered it removed. Then one dark night it reappeared at the north end of Bowling Green, where, still without approval, it has become one of the most popular photo "op" spots in the city. Coming full circle, the bull stands today in the exact location of the Cattle Market of Dutch Colonial days. (Photo by author)*

up near the town of Wilton, Connecticut, where the pieces had been taken to be melted into musket balls. The **park** and **fence** have been restored recently as part of a major renovation of Bowling Green, which also included a pedestrian mall and a reconstructed subway station beneath.

Dominating Bowling Green is an enormous bronze **statue of a charging bull.** The work of sculptor Arturo DiModica, it was cast by Domenico Ranieri and placed here in 1992 after being removed from in front of the Stock Exchange. Strangely, the statue of the larger-than-life six-foot bull was installed without the required permission of the Parks Department, which is less than "bullish" about its being here. Whether it stays or not is uncertain, but what *is* certain is that the cost of removal is prohibitive. Meanwhile, it has become a favored photo spot for tourists who enjoy posing with it.

No. 11 Broadway, on the west side of Bowling Green, is an amusing hodge-podge of styles. Framing the entrances are "Egyptian" pylons, while above the third story the building takes on the bold look of the Chicago School of Architecture, with its glazed brick piers and articulated spandrels. It was designed in 1898

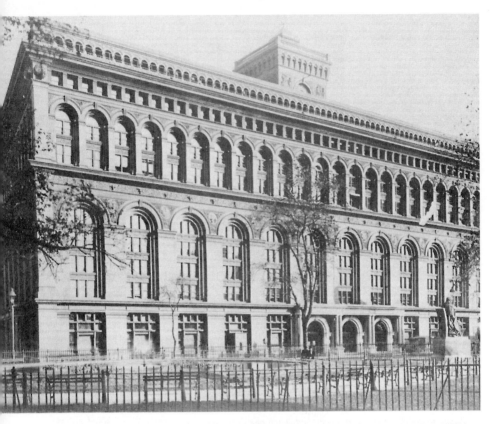

The Produce Exchange on Bowling Green was completed in 1884 and was replaced in 1957 by No. 2 Broadway. One of George B. Post's most notable works, the enormous red brick structure had a true iron skeleton and a main hall measuring 220 by 144 feet. At the right foreground is the statue of Abraham de Peyster, which has been moved to Hanover Square. (Museum of the City of New York)

by W. G. Audsley. Adjacent **No. 9 Broadway,** the Bowling Green Offices, is a continuation of the "west wall."

    No. 1 Broadway, formerly the United States Lines–Panama Pacific Lines Building, now the International Mercantile Marine Company Building, also hearkens to the days of sea power, when our country had at least some semblance of a respectable merchant marine. Built in 1921 from plans by Walter B. Chambers, the enormous structure is more famous for what used to be there. This was almost the southern tip of Manhattan Island and the site of the original Dutch fort that stood just a few yards to the south. During the late 18th century the Kennedy House was headquarters for Generals Washington and Lee. No. 1 Broadway was first called the Washington Building after its predecessor on the site with the same name, demolished in 1919.

    No. 2 Broadway (to the left of the Custom House), built in 1959 by Emery Roth & Sons, with a brand-new façade in 1999 by Skidmore, Owings & Merrill, marks the site of one of our most tragic building losses, the Produce Exchange. Designed in 1881 by noted architect George B. Post and completed three years later, it was a true iron-skeleton building, faced with dark red brick, and several years ahead of its time. The façade was adorned with terra-cotta motifs of the various products traded within. The second-floor Main Hall was an astonishing 220 feet by 144 feet, with a huge latticework skylight 60 feet above the floor. As Nathan Silver sadly comments in *Lost New York*, "The Produce Exchange, one of the best buildings in New York, was replaced after 1957 by one of the worst."

The former United States Custom House is considered the finest example of the French Beaux Arts style in the city. It is the new home of the **National Museum of the American Indian** under the aegis of the Smithsonian Institution. After a brief preview in 1992, it officially opened in 1994. The Museum, formerly on Audubon Terrace uptown, houses one of the most important collections of Native American art and artifacts. [Hours: 10:00 A.M. to 5:00 P.M., Thurs. to 8:00 P.M., (212) 514-3888, free.] The building, designed by Cass Gilbert and completed in 1907, is one of the city's foremost architectural treasures.

Spend a few minutes examining the superb façade and the exceptional collection of sculpture:

Contrasting with the dark gray granite of the building are four monumental white limestone sculpture groups by Daniel Chester French. Left to right, they represent the continents of Asia, America, Europe, and Africa. Above the cornice are statues symbolizing the 12 great mercantile nations of history: Greece, Rome, Phoenicia, Genoa, Venice, Spain, Holland, Portugal, Denmark, Germany, England, and France. The heroic cartouche atop the upper balustrade is by sculptor Karl Bitter. Ranged around the Custom House are 44 Corinthian columns.

The **interior's** second-floor rotunda has a splendid display of Reginald Marsh murals depicting early events on the site, and various seafaring themes.

The original nearby fortification called Fort Amsterdam was constructed in 1623 with the arrival of the first settlers. Then a more substantial fort was built in 1626, going through eight name changes until, as Fort George, it was demolished in 1787. Government House, intended as the presidential residence, replaced the fort three years later, but with the removal of the nation's capital to Philadelphia, it became the Governor's Mansion. It later became a boarding house, then the Custom House, and, after a fire, was razed in 1815. Subsequently, town houses lined the site, but by midcentury they were taken over as shipping offices and known as "Steamship Row," as the area became devoted entirely to commerce. (Detailed and colorful dioramas of the early Dutch fort and surrounding settlement are displayed at the Museum of the City of New York. The museum is well worth a visit.)

Facing the old Custom House is the colorful **"Buddy Bear"** statue, painted by Helga Leiberg in 2002, and presented to the city of New York by the city of Berlin as a symbol of friendship of the peoples of the two cities.

For almost three decades this sculpture stood in the plaza of the World Trade Center. Entitled
Sphere, *it was conceived by artist Fritz Koenig as a symbol of world peace. It was damaged during
the tragic events of 9/11, but endures as an icon of hope and the indestructible spirit of Americans.*
Sphere *was placed in Battery Park on March 11, 2002, in memory of all who lost their lives to the
terrorist attacks at the WTC. (Photo by author)*

**Enter Battery Park at the main entrance, directly to the right of the Custom
House, across State Street.**

Battery Park is named for the battery of cannon that, between 1683 and
1688, were mounted along what is now the sidewalk opposite the Custom House,
extending to just below the present Battery Place. From then until 1807 the area
was fortified with additional batteries of artillery pieces. Most of the park is built
on landfill added periodically through the years.

The tall flagpole and sculptured pedestal is the **Netherlands Memorial Monument,** inscribed in both English and 17th-century Dutch, giving a brief history
of the settlement of the Colony of New Netherland.

To the left is the huge bronze **Sphere,** by German sculptor Fritz Koenig, that
stood for three decades in the Plaza of the WTC. It was conceived as a symbol of
world peace but was damaged during the tragic events of 9/11. The sculpture was
placed here on the six-month anniversary in memory of all who lost their lives in
the terrorist attacks, and endures as an icon of hope and the indestructible spirit
of Americans. (It may be returned to the WTC site in the future.)

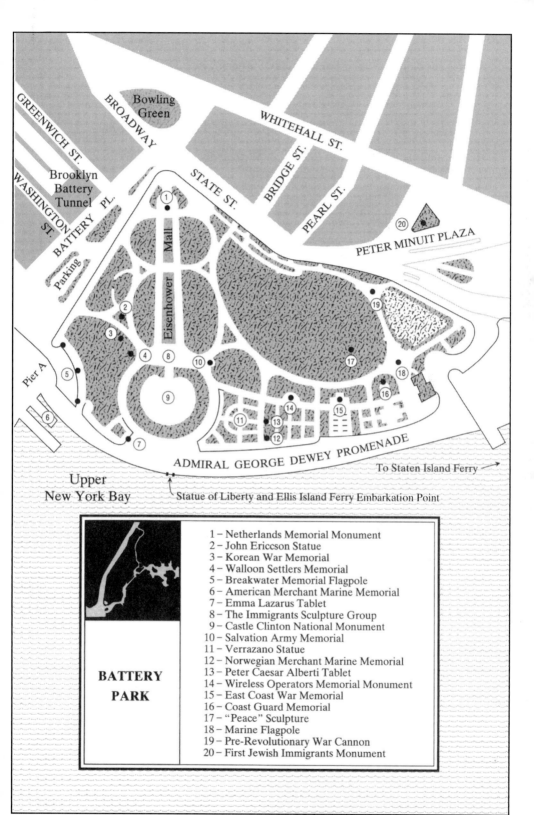

Bowling Green

GREENWICH ST.

BROADWAY

WHITEHALL ST.

WASHINGTON ST.

Brooklyn
Battery
Tunnel

BATTERY PL.

STATE ST.

BRIDGE ST.

PEARL ST.

Parking

Eisenhower Mall

PETER MINUIT PLAZA

Pier A

ADMIRAL GEORGE DEWEY PROMENADE

To Staten Island Ferry →

Upper
New York Bay

Statue of Liberty and Ellis Island Ferry Embarkation Point

**BATTERY
PARK**

1 – Netherlands Memorial Monument
2 – John Ericcson Statue
3 – Korean War Memorial
4 – Walloon Settlers Memorial
5 – Breakwater Memorial Flagpole
6 – American Merchant Marine Memorial
7 – Emma Lazarus Tablet
8 – The Immigrants Sculpture Group
9 – Castle Clinton National Monument
10 – Salvation Army Memorial
11 – Verrazano Statue
12 – Norwegian Merchant Marine Memorial
13 – Peter Caesar Alberti Tablet
14 – Wireless Operators Memorial Monument
15 – East Coast War Memorial
16 – Coast Guard Memorial
17 – "Peace" Sculpture
18 – Marine Flagpole
19 – Pre-Revolutionary War Cannon
20 – First Jewish Immigrants Monument

Bear to the right at the first path to the Statue of John Ericcson.

John Ericcson was the Swedish-born mechanical engineer who designed and built the first ironclad warship, the *Monitor*—the famous "cheesebox on a raft," which, on March 9, 1862, at Hampton Roads, Virginia, engaged the Confederate frigate *Merrimac* (renamed *Virginia*) and altered the course of naval history. The *Monitor*'s deck stood only 18 inches out of the water, while its revolving turret carried two 11-inch guns. Note the model in Ericcson's hand. The statue was executed by Jonathan Scott Hartley in 1893, and was replaced ten years later by the sculptor, who produced a better version.

Follow the numbers on the map of Battery Park for a tour of the park and its monuments.

Bear to the right before reaching Castle Clinton, to see the black granite obelisk that marks the **Korean War Memorial.** Installed in 1991, it has a rather unusual design with the outline of a soldier cut through the stone and highlighted with metal. Around the base are the flags of the allied nations that participated in the conflict, 1950–53. The figure represents the Universal Soldier, and is a silhouette that allows the viewer to see through the monument to the Statue of Liberty and Ellis Island. The sculptor, Mac Adam, designed the piece to function as a sundial. Every July 27 at 10:00 A.M., the exact moment in New York when hostilities ceased in Korea, the sun shines directly through the soldier's hand to illuminate the commemorative plaque installed in the ground near the piece.

At the water's edge, and located 40 feet offshore, is the striking **American Merchant Marine Memorial.** The sculpture group depicts four merchant mariners and their sinking ship—three still standing on the vessel as it slides under the waves, and a fourth in the water reaching up for assistance. The sculpture, by Marisol (1991), is based on a photograph taken during World War II by a U-boat officer whose ship torpedoed the vessel and watched it go down with all hands without attempting to rescue any of the crew. Adding to the emotional impact of the sculpture, the figure in the water is almost completely engulfed at high tide.

To the right is **Pier A,** renamed **Liberty Gateway,** built in 1886. It was built for the city's Department of Docks and Harbor Police (George Sears Greene, Jr., engineer). The last survivor of the early Hudson River piers, until recently it was a fireboat station. The clock on the 70-foot tower was donated in 1919 by Daniel Reed, a founder of the United States Steel Corporation, as a memorial to the 116,000 servicemen who died while serving in World War I. The clock peals the time on ships' bells. The city is planning to make the remodeled pier a visitors' center, with restaurants, shops, and an information bureau.

To the left of Liberty Gateway are the six ferry slips of the New York Waterway, which provides commuter service to various New Jersey points and Liberty State Park. Hopefully, they will replace the ugly Quonset-type building with a more appropriate structure, and one that does not provide an ugly backdrop to the Merchant Marine Memorial.

Walk left along the promenade to just before Castle Clinton. A few feet inside the park is the **Emma Lazarus tablet,** honoring the poet who in 1883 penned her immortal sonnet "The New Colossus" to help raise funds for the construction of the pedestal and the mounting of the Statue of Liberty. Her oft-quoted lines, "Give me your tired, your poor,/Your huddled masses yearning to breathe free..." are emblazoned on the base of the statue she helped secure.

Go around to the front of Castle Clinton, but, before entering, examine the impressive statue of **The Immigrants** (Luis Sanguino, 1981), which represents many of the immigrant groups that have come to these shores.

Castle Clinton National Monument. In 1807 it appeared that another war with England was imminent, and several fortifications were hastily erected to protect the unguarded harbor. Among them was Castle Williams on nearby Governors Island, and the West Battery (now Castle Clinton) on a small rocky islet connected to the tip of Manhattan by a 200-foot causeway. (The intervening land was not filled in until the mid-19th century.) Constructed from plans by John McComb, Jr., in a circular shape with red sandstone walls over eight feet thick, the battery's 28 guns never fired a shot in anger. Renamed in 1815 in honor of DeWitt Clinton, former mayor and later governor, the fort remained in the hands of the military until 1821, when Commanding General Winfield Scott moved the garrison to Governors Island. Two years later Castle Clinton was ceded to the city of New York.

In June 1824 the city leased it as a place of public entertainment, and, redecorated with a garden, shrubbery, a fountain, and a promenade above, it opened as **Castle Garden.** Among the variety of public events presented, including concerts, fireworks displays, and balloon ascensions, was Samuel F. B. Morse's demonstration in 1842 of his electric telegraph. Then, on September 11, 1850, P. T. Barnum, in the musical event of the century, presented Jenny Lind, the "Swedish Nightingale," in her American concert debut. At the close of the sellout performance at which more than 6,000 had paid the exorbitant fee of at least three dollars a seat, the audience broke into a "tempest of cheers."

In 1855 Castle Garden became the immigrant landing station, and for the next 34 years witnessed the arrival of over 8 million new Americans. With the closing of the Garden in 1890, the nearby Barge Office (now demolished) handled the growing tide of immigrants until the new immigration depot was opened two years later on Ellis Island.

The Garden was then remodeled by the architectural firm of McKim, Mead & White to serve as the **New York Aquarium,** opening on December 10, 1896, to a crowd of 30,000. In 1941 the Aquarium was closed, moving to new and spacious quarters at Coney Island, and the building was slated for demolition to make way for access roads to the new Brooklyn-Battery tunnel. However, public hue and cry saved it, and in 1946 Congress authorized the establishment of Castle Clinton as a national monument under the administration of the National Park Service of the Department of the Interior. It has been carefully restored as a fort, and provides a dramatic, if somewhat fanciful, link with the past.

Castle Clinton has a small museum, and in the center is the ticket office for the Ellis Island–Statue of Liberty boat. Check the schedules, as the last departure

The Lusitania *arrived on her maiden voyage to New York on September 13, 1907. Crowds jammed the waterfront between the Aquarium (formerly Castle Garden) and Pier A as the liner steamed up the Hudson, eight years before her ill-fated rendezvous with a U-boat off the English coast. (New-York Historical Society)*

for both islands is around 3:00 P.M. A visit to both is an absolute *must*…but on another day. There is also a small bookshop. The monument is open daily, 8:30 A.M. to 5:00 P.M.

On exiting Castle Clinton, turn right, past the Statue of Evangeline Booth, general of the Salvation Army, and along the path to the statue of Verrazano.

Giovanni da Verrazano was the first to sight these shores. Arriving in the small caravel *La Dauphine* in 1524, the Florentine merchant sailing for Francis I of France claimed the new land for the king, naming it *Terre d'Angoulême*. The French, however, did not follow up the claim, and Verrazano himself fell victim to cannibals on a voyage to the Caribbean four years later. The statue is the work of Ettore Ximenes, and was completed in 1909.

The same year, Esteban Gómez, a Portuguese mariner sailing under the Spanish flag, entered the harbor and named the mouth of the river Río San Antonio. It was not until 1609, however, that Henry Hudson, in his *Half-Moon,* actually sailed up the river that bears his name and brought back to Holland extensive reports on this "Great River of the Mountains." Four years later Adriaen Block, a Dutch trader, landed at the tip of Manhattan Island with a small group of men. When their ship *Tiger* caught fire and burned to the water, they were forced to spend the winter. The following spring they built a new ship, which they called the *Onrust* (Restless), and returned to Holland. One can only admire these stalwart men who with their bare hands were able to fashion a sea-

*An almost-deserted view of Broadway, looking north from Cortlandt Street in the mid-1880s.
Midday crowds often gathered in front of the tall Western Union Building to watch a ball descend
from the top of the pole precisely at noon. George B. Post's flamboyant Renaissance structure, built
in 1873–75—and considered one of New York's first skyscrapers—was demolished when the City
Investing Building was erected. After the Blizzard of 1888, the maze of telegraph wires was removed
and buried beneath the street. (New-York Historical Society)*

Not a view of the aftermath of 9/11—although strikingly similar—but a photo taken in the early 1960s during the deep excavation for the World Trade Center, when the two tubes of the PATH subway lines were exposed, and passers-by could hear the eerie roar of the trains in what at first glance seemed to be enormous sewer pipes. The eastbound tube is in the foreground; the westbound is just visible, passing to the right rear of the early framework of the WTC's North Tower. (Port Authority of New York & New Jersey)

The statue of stern-faced Abraham de Peyster, son of a leading Dutch burgher and mayor of New York from 1691 to 1695, was formerly situated in Bowling Green. After the renovation of the late 1970s, de Peyster was "banished" to Hanover Square. Except for the Bowling Green Offices at left, not one building survives from the time this photo was taken about 1900. (Museum of the City of New York)

A lithograph of Wall Street looking east from Trinity Church in 1834. In the distance is the cupola of the Merchants' Exchange, destroyed the following year in the Great Fire of 1835. (The J. Clarence Davies Collection, Museum of the City of New York)

Looking west on Fulton Street across Broadway in 1892, horsecars have been replaced by electric trolleys, but Dobbin still reigns. In the background are the Sixth and Ninth Avenue els. (American Telephone & Telegraph Company)

The former Equitable Building on Broadway, between Cedar and Pine streets. The Second Empire–style structure, built in 1872, was destroyed in a spectacular fire that burned for three days in January 1912. A replacement, completed in 1916, caused objections due to its sheer bulk, leading to a drastic revision in the building code. (King's Views of New York, 1909)

Firefighters work in vain to save the Equitable Building. The conflagration had begun in the basement Café Savarin and quickly engulfed the entire structure. (Museum of the City of New York)

Equitable founder Henry B. Hyde seems to be contemplating the destruction of the lobby. Only slightly damaged, the statue by J. Q. A. Ward now graces the lobby of the Equitable Center, 787 Seventh Avenue, uptown. (Equitable Life Assurance Society of the United States)

A mid-1880s advertisement for loft space in the headquarters of a predecessor of the New York Telephone Company (then located on the north side of Cortlandt Street between Broadway and Church Street). The Romanesque Revival–style building was one of several newly opened exchanges. (American Telephone & Telegraph Company)

etropolitan Telephone and Telegraph Company,
16, 18 & 20 COURTLANDT ST., NEW YORK.

rge STORE ROOM on ground floor, and rooms in suits or singly for OFFICES to suit tenants

FOR RENT.

For Diagrams showing location and prices, apply to
THE METROPOLITAN TELEPHONE AND TELEGRAPH COMPANY,
144 GREENWICH STREET.

Castle Garden in 1870 when it served as the State Emigrant Landing Depot. Millions of immigrants passed through its portals between 1855 and 1890, when a new center was opened on Ellis Island. (New-York Historical Society)

In this lithograph by Nathaniel Currier, "Swedish Nightingale" Jenny Lind makes her American debut on September 11, 1850, as P. T. Barnum inaugurates Castle Garden as the city's leading showplace. The structure has now been restored to its original appearance as Castle Clinton National Monument. (New-York Historical Society)

A Sunday promenade along the Battery in an 1830 engraving, depicting Castle Clinton to the right, and Castle Williams on Governors Island across the busy harbor to the left. (New-York Historical Society)

worthy vessel from the trees of the forest and sail it thousands of miles safely across the rough Atlantic.

Nieuw Amsterdam as a permanent settlement was established in 1625, and, one year later, Peter Minuit made his famous purchase from the Indians. In 1664 the Colony was captured by the English and named for the Duke of York. For a few months in 1673 the Dutch regained control, but they lost it again to Britain.

Several yards farther east and closer to the Promenade is the Norwegian Merchant Marine Memorial, consisting of a plaque and boulder. It honors the merchant mariners of Norway who served on ships of many nations during World War II.

A short distance to the east, and a bit farther into the park, is the **Wireless Operators Memorial Monument,** dedicated to those radiomen who went down with their ship. A new name is added with each tragedy, and some are quite recent. Note the name of Jack Phillips, the wireless operator of the *Titanic*, which struck an iceberg on her maiden voyage to America and sank on the night of April 14–15, 1912, with a loss of 1,517 out of 2,000 passengers.

Walk out on the **Admiral George Dewey Promenade,** at the water's edge. Considered the finest view in the city, the broad panorama includes (from left to right) Brooklyn Heights, Governors Island, distant Staten Island, the Statue of Liberty on Liberty Island, Ellis Island with its former immigration depot, and the New Jersey harborfront. And in the bay is the constant parade of ships of all types, which bring the harbor to life. Turning around, the view of the lower Manhattan skyline, now somewhat obscured by modern, and rather uninteresting, additions, is awesome. The finest view, of course, is from the Staten Island Ferry or from the Statue of Liberty excursion boat.

Facing the Promenade is the **East Coast War Memorial** (William Gehron and Gilbert Seltzer, 1960), which honors the 4,596 seamen, soldiers, and airmen lost in the American coastal waters of the North Atlantic during World War II. All the names are carved into the eight granite pylons. In the center is an immense sculpture of an American Eagle by sculptor Albino Manca, unveiled in 1963 by President John F. Kennedy.

Continuing to the east, the dramatic **Coast Guard Memorial** stands facing the bay. It depicts two men supporting a wounded comrade. The eight-foot bronze sculpture group was erected after World War II through one-dollar contributions from every Coast Guard member to help defray the $25,000 cost. There was some controversy at the time as to whether the work met the Municipal Art Commission's artistic standards, but, under pressure from then–Parks Commissioner Robert Moses, it was approved. Sculptor Norman M. Thomas was himself a Coast Guardsman and served in the war.

The American Park Restaurant is a pleasant and convenient amenity, where, until now, only hot dogs were the main bill of fare.

Follow the Promenade eastward to the end, and walk north on the park side of State Street.

A **new Whitehall ferry terminal,** to replace the one which burned in 1992, was completed in 1998. In a design competition for the new Staten Island ferry terminal, the winning entry was submitted by Philadelphia architects Robert Venturi and Denise Scott Brown, in association with the Manhattan firm of Anderson/Schwartz Architects. The plan called for a barrel-vaulted structure of green-tinted glass, and, in deference to the past, the south wall (facing the harbor) has a full-scale painted rendering of the adjacent 1907 Battery Maritime Building. The waiting room boasts a 125-foot ceiling with panoramic views of the bay, a SONY Jumbotron television sign, and direct connections to the Battery Maritime Building and Battery Park. An unusual addition is a typical Venturi touch—a 120-foot-high clock, the largest in the world—dominating the south side (twice the size of the Colgate clock on the Hoboken waterfront). Ferry commuters doubtless will be delighted to learn that they are late again as the ferry arrives in the morning mist.

To the left of the Staten Island Ferry Terminal is the **Battery Maritime Building,** originally Municipal Ferry Piers (Walker & Morris, 1907), the last surviving ferry building on the East River. It was the terminal for ferries to Brooklyn until 1938.

At approximately the site of the Battery Maritime Building was the point of embarkation in Dutch Colonial times for ships sailing to the mother country or to other distant points. The little wharf was soon called **Schreijers Hoek** (Weepers' Corner), since the perils of a long sea voyage threatened the safe return of loved ones. The name was taken from the *Schreijerstoren* (Weepers' Tower) on the Amstel River in Amsterdam, where relatives bade a tearful farewell to those departing on distant journeys.

Cross Peter Minuit Plaza.

The flagpole in the mini-park is New York City's tribute to the first group of Jews to arrive at these shores in 1654—23 men, women, and children, refugees from the Inquisition in Brazil. Attempting to return to Holland, their ship was taken by a Spanish pirate who in turn was captured by a French privateer. Pledging their possessions to the French captain, they were brought to Nieuw Amsterdam, where Peter Stuyvesant gave them a less-than-cordial welcome, but permitted them to stay. The townspeople paid off the captain, allowing the refugees to discharge their debt and keep the clothes on their backs. Practicing their religion privately, the small group of Sephardic Jews was later able to rent a room for services in a windmill, and ultimately built the first synagogue in America in 1730 on Mill Street (now South William Street), about one-quarter mile north.

Peter Minuit Plaza is named for one of the first Dutch governors, who purchased the Island of "Manhattes" in 1626 from the Reckagawawanc Indians (who didn't really own it anyway, as the concept of private land ownership was foreign to them), for an amount of trinkets valued at 60 guilders, or about $24.

At 7 State Street the **former James Watson House** is now the **Shrine of the Blessed Elizabeth Ann Seton,** the first American-*born* saint. Mother Seton (1774–1821) was the founder of the American Sisters of Charity, the first order of nuns in the United States. She is also credited with the establishment of the

American Catholic parochial school system. Mother Seton was elevated to saint-hood in September 1975. The house is a lone survivor of a magnificent row of elegant Federal mansions that lined State Street. Note the freestanding slender Ionic columns and the Georgian details. The building is completely original, and was built in the early 1800s, probably by John McComb, the architect of City Hall. What a splendid sight the long colonnade must have presented to approaching ships. The church of Our Lady of the Rosary, adjoining the shrine, occupies the site of a former residence of Mother Seton.

No. 17 State Street (Emery Roth & Sons, 1987) is a striking, if somewhat jarring, addition to the lower Manhattan skyline. In the shape of a quarter cylinder, its 44 stories of silver reflecting glass and anodized aluminum loom high over Battery Park. The building's curved contour was determined by its plot, which coincidentally follows closely the original 17th-century shoreline. It is another *tour de force* by developer Mel Kaufman, although less zany than his 127 John Street or his Disneylike setting for 77 Water Street. [*See* both in Chapter 2.] The site, until 1985, was occupied by the romantically designed and much cherished Seamen's Church Institute; and in 1819 it was the birthplace of author Herman Melville. Enter the shiny, hi-tech lobby where glass-enclosed elevator shafts disappear skyward—the first time this system was employed. Compare the bold design of this building with that of its bland, boxlike neighbor to the north, No. 1 Battery Park Plaza. Both were designed by the same architectural firm, but the latter was built 16 years earlier.

In the courtyard behind 17 State Street is **New York Unearthed,** a unique little museum dedicated to New York City's archaeological heritage; there, remains of the past tell the story of the city's history. The museum has two levels (one below ground), on one of which there is an interesting "time-line" depicting what was unearthed under the city's streets every few decades, eventually displaying artifacts excavated from the Dutch Colonial period. One can watch a conservator at work and even enter a darkened "elevator" and descend on an imaginary trip below Wall Street to experience an archaeological "dig." The museum, a program of the South Street Seaport Museum, was financed in part by the developers of 17 State Street, to compensate for their not having conducted the required archaeological study before excavations were begun on their building. (Open Mon.–Sat. 12:00 noon to 6:00 P.M.; free.)

Walk one short block down Pearl Street to Whitehall Street.

No. 33 Whitehall Street, to the left, is another behemoth, the 30-story **Broad Financial Center** (Fox & Fowle, 1986), its dark-blue reflecting façade described as "a two-sided butt-glazed curtain wall." The postmodern indented walls give welcome relief from the architectural doldrums of the 1950s and '60s that are so evident in the dull array of skyscrapers that mushroomed along the waterfront and obscured the picturesque New York City skyline. The lofty blue and gray granite lobby is stark and overwhelming, dominated by four tall stone pylons mounted on polished black granite spheres supporting gilt metal globes; on the bare stone wall is a clock of enormous proportions.

Much less interesting is its neighbor to the south, **No. 39 Whitehall Street,** a huge, unimaginative cube sheathed in dark-green reflecting glass. The building, in a new skin, is the 1880s' U.S. Army Building, remembered for its Induction Center and the anti-draft demonstrations of the Vietnam War era.

Return to State Street and turn right along Battery Park.

The little subway entrance building on the park side is one of the last remaining kiosks of the city's first subway system, and is known as the **Battery Park Control House.** The name derives from the original concept that once passengers had entered the building they were under the control of the transit company. The structure was built in 1904–05 in French Beaux Arts style from plans by Heins & LaFarge, the first architects of the Cathedral Church of St. John the Divine.

Walk briefly to the left (south) along the park fence to a small triangle. Among the vegetation is the **Oyster Pasty Mount Cannon,** a relic from English Colonial days that was uncovered during excavation. The "Oyster Pasty" was a derisive name given for incompetence to a group of artillerymen whose cannon had been banished to a pile of nearby oyster shells.

Turn around and walk back up State Street, past the subway kiosk to Battery Place, and turn left, but do not cross the street.

Just beyond the **Brooklyn-Battery Tunnel Ventilation Building** (1950, Aymar Embury II) is **The Whitehall Building,** No. 17 Battery Place (1902, Henry J. Hardenbergh; rear addition, 1910, Clinton & Russell), a huge early office building that was one of the first sights from the harbor. It still occupies an excellent vantage point. The front building is connected to the rear, which is now called the "Ocean," a condominium.

Turn right (north) on West Street.

Look north along West Street to the pair of buildings just ahead: **21 West Street** (1931, Starrett & Van Vleck), formerly an office building and now a residence, and the **Downtown Athletic Club** (1926, by the same architects), both displaying a brownish-orange façade of salt-glazed tile. These splendid Art Deco–style buildings have a certain Moorish quality—an architectural oasis in congested downtown.

Look back at 17 Battery Place and savor the unusual and attractive roofline.

Enter and continue along **Robert F. Wagner, Jr. Park** (1996, Olin Partnership, landscape architects, Machado & Silvetti Associates, and Lynden Miller, garden design). The park, which extends for about a mile along the Hudson River, is named for the former mayor of New York (1953–61). Among his many accomplishments was the inauguration of the largest public housing project in the nation. To the left along the waterfront is a sculpture called *Eyes* (Louise Bourgeois, 1995), a pair of huge, round, boulderlike stones with small dark "pupils."

Just ahead is the **Wagner Park Café and Viewing Platform** (1996, Machado & Silvetti Associates). Climb the Platform for a great photo opportunity of the

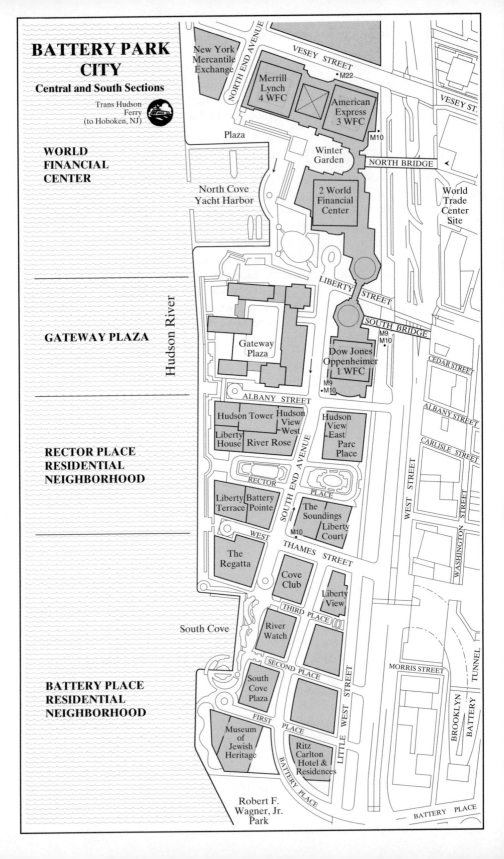

IN MEMORIAM. *The New York City skyline would never be the same after the savage destruction of the World Trade Center. The famed twin towers and several surrounding buildings are now gone, and the distinctive structures of the World Financial Center that complemented the WTC site now stand starkly alone. (Battery Park City Authority)*

harbor. Connecting the two-part structure is a wooden "gangplank." The Café, in front, is a convenient place for a harborside snack. Note the stylized bronze musical instrument sculptures.

Across West Street is the elegant 35-story **Ritz Carlton Hotel and Condominiums** (2001, Polshek Partnership with Gary Edward Handel & Associates), whose façade conforms to the curvature of the street. The management claims it is the only luxury hotel with panoramic views of the harbor, with each of its 288 rooms equipped with a telescope!

Within the hotel is the newly reopened **Skyscraper Museum,** which is dedicated to the study of high-rise buildings—past, present, and future—in New York City. Call (212) 988-1961 for hours, or visit its Web site, www.skyscraper.org.

A few steps farther is the **Museum of Jewish Heritage** (1996, Kevin Roche, John Dinkeloo & Associates), No. 18 First Place, Battery Park City. The museum is designed as a living memorial to the Holocaust to educate peoples of all ages and backgrounds about 20th-century Jewish history and the Holocaust. Its hexagonal granite-sheathed walls, topped by a stepped pyramid, are symbolic of the Star of David, as well as a visual reminder of the six million Jews who perished in the Holocaust. The three floors represent Jewish life a century ago, the war against the Jews, and Jewish renewal. A large east wing addition is scheduled to open in 2003. (Hours: Sun.–Wed. 9:00 A.M. to 5:45 P.M.; Thurs. 10:00 A.M. to

The Museum of Jewish Heritage, situated just north of Battery Park, is designed as a living memorial to the Holocaust. Its hexagonal walls, topped by a stepped pyramid, are symbolic of the Star of David, as well as a visual reminder of the six million Jews who perished in the Holocaust. (Photo by author)

8:00 P.M.; Fri. and evenings before Jewish holidays 9:00 A.M. to 3:00 P.M.; Sat., Jewish holidays, and Thanksgiving Day closed. Admission: $7.00 adults, $5.00 seniors and students; children 5 and under free.)

Ahead is **South Cove,** with a broad view of the apartment houses of the **Rector Place Residential Neighborhood** to the east, the first residential quarter built under the Battery Park City master plan. Unfortunately, space does not allow for a description of each of the residences, but do notice the variety of architectural styles that together create a harmonious totality.

For another superb view, walk out on unusual **Lookout, Bridge, and Circular Jetty** (1987, Mary Miss, sculptor, Stanton Eckstut, architect, Susan Child, landscaping). Designed as a park, a piece of sculpture, and a structure, it is "a reminder of the serious intent that has characterized every aspect of Battery Park City." Across the river is the burgeoning skyline of Jersey City and its landmark Colgate Clock.

At the foot of W. Thames Street is **Sitting Stance** (1988, Richard Artschwager), constructed of cast iron, granite, and redwood. A block farther north is Rector Place, with the aluminum towers of **Rector Gate** (1988, R. M. Fischer) guarding the entrance to the **Rector Place Residential Neighborhood** and its pleasant two-block-long **Rector Park** (1987, Innocenti-Webel and Vollmer Associates, landscape architects)—a highly successful urban design that is reminiscent of a small-town village green.

Follow the Esplanade a block farther to Albany Street and explore the startling **The Upper Room** (1987, Ned Smyth), a sculpture grouping evocative of ancient Egypt or Babylon, with stylized columns, a huge table, and stools on a grand scale, imbedded in red concrete.

Above Albany Street is **Gateway Plaza,** a cluster of drab high-rise residences set around a grassy plaza. These were the first buildings to be erected in Battery Park City (1982–83, Jack Brown with Irving E. Gershon). Since then much has been learned about quality urban design, as evidenced in the far superior planning, grouping, and general architectural harmony of the Rector Place and Battery Place neighborhoods. The north Gateway Plaza buildings closest to the WTC disaster suffered considerable damage, particularly by the enormous accumulation of debris. For months, residents were unable to return to their apartments until the repairs and cleanup were completed.

Along the Esplanade is **Steamer's Landing,** an attractive restaurant with a delightful panoramic river view.

Turn right at **North Cove Yacht Harbor,** marked by three tall flagpoles, into Monsignor Kowsky Plaza, and the sculpture **Ulysses** (1997, Ugo Atardi).

A few steps beyond is the **New York City Police Memorial** (1997, Stuart Crawford). On a polished granite wall are inscribed the names of all fallen police officers, from 1854 to 1999. At this writing there is a temporary tent set up to memorialize the police and fire rescue workers and others who died helping to save victims of the 9/11 tragedy. A variety of memorabilia from visitors adorns the site.

The World Financial Center, one of Manhattan's truly great architectural achievements, is a seven-million-square-foot commercial center designed by the firm of Cesar Pelli & Associates and developed by Olympia & York. The project, which occupies the center of Battery Park City, took six years to construct, and was completed in 1987. The WFC consists of four 34- to 51-story towers clad in sagami granite and reflective glass, each topped by a different geometrically shaped copper dome. Two nine-story octagonal gatehouses flank the project's entrance. It is an eight-million-square-foot mixed-use complex, and is the business and commercial hub of Battery Park City. Constructed on 13.5 acres of landfill, the buildings rise from a granite-sheathed base, and at each setback the proportion of glass to stone increases, until the walls at the top are made entirely of glass. The WFC houses in its four towers the world headquarters of American Express, Merrill Lynch & Co., Dow Jones & Co., Oppenheimer & Co., and the New York Mercantile Exchange, plus other major firms, restaurants, and upscale retail establishments. (*Note:* Although the events of 9/11 caused extensive damage to the east facades of the WFC and forced most commercial operations to cease for a time, at this writing it is business as usual in most of the offices, as well as in the splendidly restored Winter Garden.)

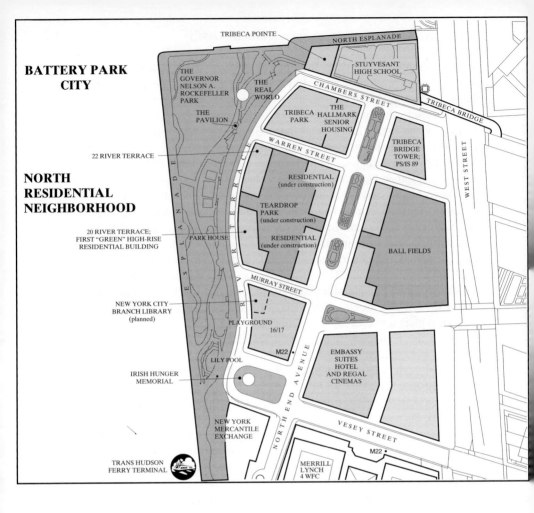

The Winter Garden—centerpiece of the World Financial Center—suffered severely, its 120-foot-high vaulted glass and steel roof shattered, and the inner court a state of ruin. This modern-day Crystal Palace had become one of the most popular attractions in the city. But with New Yorkers' typical energy and drive to rebuild, the Winter Garden has been restored to its former elegance—its hour-glass-shaped grand staircase rebuilt and cascading onto a marble floor below, together with a new grove of sixteen 45-foot-tall *Washington robusta* palm trees from California's Mojave Desert.

Walk around the North Cove, where ferries of New York Waterway carry commuters to Jersey City and Hoboken, and continue past a tree-lined platform on which sits **The Belvedere** (1995, Mitchell/Giurgola). The nearby **Pylons** (1995, Martin Puryear), a pair of stainless-steel mini-towers of differing styles, offer a welcome symbol to the yacht harbor. Continue past the west side of the

New York Mercantile Exchange, whose museum at this writing is temporarily closed. (Check for yourself.) Then proceed into the **North Residential Neighborhood** along River Terrace.

To the right is the **Irish Hunger Memorial** (2002, Brian Tolle, sculptor, with Juergen Riehm and David Piscuskas of 1100 Architects of New York) that commemorates Ireland's Great Famine of 1845–52. Set on a quarter-acre site, the entire memorial is constructed on a tilted concrete slab mounted on a wedge-shaped base, and duplicates an Irish hillside farm of that period. The base and surrounding plaza are paved with Kilkenny limestone imbedded with fossils from the ancient Irish seabed. The amazingly realistic replica consists of a genuine abandoned Irish fieldstone cottage, brought stone by stone from County Mayo, and is adjoined by potato furrows, transplanted native wildflowers and grasses, and a dirt path leading to the top. On the slope are 32 stones, one from each of Ireland's counties, plus an ancient pilgrim stone carved with a Celtic cross. Its location in New York is particularly appropriate, as a majority of the Irish immigrants fleeing the Great Famine arrived here and became integrated into all aspects of city life—including service in the police and fire departments. From the top of the slope, the Statue of Liberty and Ellis Island are clearly visible. The roofless cottage represents the actions of destitute farmers who tore off the thatch in a desperate act of poverty that they hoped would bring charity and relief. The limestone base of the memorial is surrounded by a series of printed texts mounted on Plexiglas strips, including reports from newspapers, parliamentary debates, and writings of parish priests, all of which provide poignant insight into the prejudice, suffering, and hopelessness of the times. Unlike other memorials in the city, this one must not only be studied, but also experienced.

Just to the west, along River Terrace, is the delightful **lily pool,** filled with colorful carp; it is a good place to relax.

Visible one block to the right is the **Embassy Suites Hotel** (2000, Perkins Eastman), now reopened after extensive fallout damage from the 9/11 disaster.

The apartment building at the northeast corner of Murray Street, **No. 20 River Terrace,** is the first "green" high-rise residential building. **No. 22 River Terrace** (2002, Gruzen Samton), unlike the apartment buildings in the southern residential neighborhoods, is a "blockbuster" and is typical of the new construction at the north end.

At the opposite end of Warren Street, at the entrance to **Gov. Nelson A. Rockefeller Park,** is another of the many surprises of Battery Park City, **The Pavilion** (1992, Demetri Porphyrios), a grouping of four brick columns on a stone platform covered by a wood roof supported by 12 smaller wooden columns. Nesting under the roof and oblivious to visitors are a number of barn swallows.

In the park, just to the north, and opposite the residential building called Tribeca Park, is yet another surprise, **The Real World.** Created in 2002 by sculptor Tom Otterness, this extensive collection of quirky bronze, mostly animal sculptures defies description. From the curving path of bronze footprints (a favorite with neighborhood children whose feet fit perfectly as they trot along the path), to the life-size bulldog chained to the water fountain, to the assortment of critters of all kinds, it is a visual adventure for kids of all ages. Other interesting examples of Otterness' work can be seen in the West 14th Street–Eighth Avenue subway station (A, C, E, and L lines), where more than 30 little bronze sculptures are distributed throughout the station. The exhibit is a feature of the Metropolitan Transit Authority's highly popular **Arts for Transit Program.** More Otterness figures can be seen in the Times Square Hilton Hotel, on West 42nd Street [*see* page 315].

Turn right (east) on Chambers Street.

To the north lies the enormous **Tribeca Pointe Tower,** 41 River Terrace (1999, Gruzen Samton). An interesting feature is how the building is divided so that the base matches the Chambers Street building line and the tower follows the Battery Park City grid to the south.

(**Tribeca,** often written as TriBeCa, is an acronym meaning "the Triangle below Canal Street." It was a slow-starting, but ultimately very successful ploy by real estate developers to stimulate interest in the then-available warehouses and loft buildings on the west side of Manhattan below Canal Street that could be converted to condominiums, hotels, and retail establishments. The "triangle" is really a trapezoid, with Broadway on the east, the Hudson River on the west, and Barclay Street on the south.)

On the right are **Tribeca Park,** No. 34 River Terrace (1999, Robert A. M. Stern and Costas Kondylis and Richard Cook), and, alongside to the east, **The Hallmark, Brookdale Senior Living Center,** No. 455 North End Avenue (2000, Lucien Lagrange and Schuman Lichtenstein Claman Efrom), offering senior housing exclusively. Across the North End Avenue mall is **Tribeca Bridge Tower** (1999, Costas Kondylis), a residential apartment house that embraces **Public School–Intermediate School 89,** 450 North End Avenue (1999, Pasanella + Klein Stolzman + Berg).

To the north is the massive **Stuyvesant High School** (1992, Cooper Robertson & Partners with Gruzen Samton Steinglass). The school is considered the city's finest academic high school and boasts extremely selective admissions policies. The school is connected to the "mainland" by **Tribeca Bridge** (1993, Skidmore Owings & Merrill), a dominant feature of the neighborhood with its arched bowstring trusses.

End of tour. Cross Chambers Street (carefully!) and continue east two blocks to West Broadway for the Nos. 1 and 2 lines, or one block farther for the A and C lines.

The towers of No. 2; No. 3; and, in the background, No. 4 WFC loom dramatically above Ground Zero in this photo taken nine months after 9/11. The severely damaged Winter Garden is barely visible between the towers. A year after suffering moderate-to-severe damage, the towers—each with its distinctive dome—were completely restored, the Winter Garden a few months later. During the final stages of the removal of debris from the fallen WTC towers, construction workers uncovered a remnant of the steel framework in the shape of a cross, which they mounted as a poignant temporary memorial. (Photo by author)

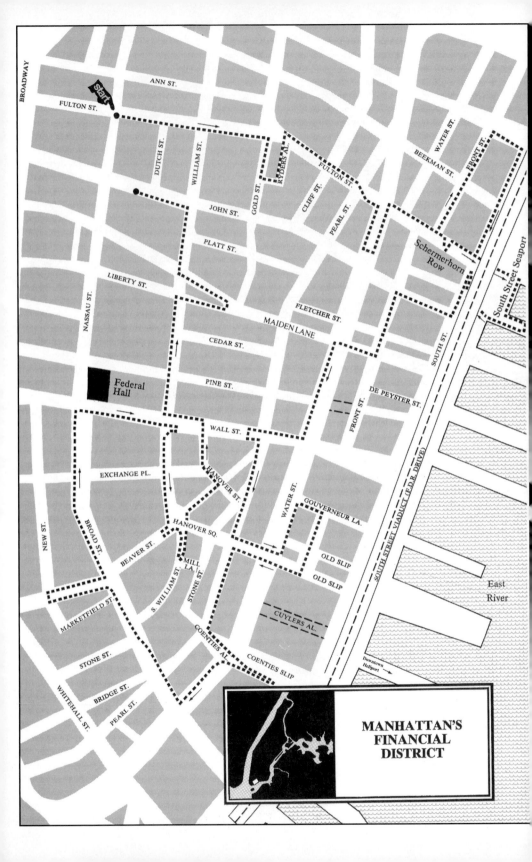

MANHATTAN'S FINANCIAL DISTRICT

2. Manhattan's Financial District

[Subways: A, C to Broadway-Nassau; 1, 2, 4, 5 to Fulton Street; J, M, Z to Fulton Street.]

The walking tour begins at the corner of Fulton and Nassau streets.

The Nassau Street Mall is a lively market with a variety of shops. In the years prior to World War II, Nassau Street was synonymous with philately, as most New York stamp dealers were located here. On the northwest corner is the startling, multicolor, cast-iron **Bennett Building,** erected in 1872 from plans by Arthur D. Gilman. Originally six stories high, it was raised to ten in 1888. Especially attractive is the texture of the façade with its recessed windows and curved glass corner windows. The building is named for the James Gordon Bennett family that published the sensationalist *New York Herald.* Their building stood to the rear.

Walk east on Fulton Street, past William Street—once known as "Insurance Row," where so many large insurance companies had their offices—to Gold Street.

Turn right on Gold Street.

A few yards down Gold Street, on the right side and almost hidden among its neighbors, is a surprising relic of the beginning of the mechanical age—the **Excelsior Power Company** building. Completed in 1888 from plans by William G. Grinnell, it was one of the city's first power houses. The whine of the huge dynamos has long been silenced, and the sturdy Romanesque Revival Industrial–style building has been converted into a co-op. Excelsior Power built the plant just six years after Thomas Edison inaugurated the world's first electrical generating station, a few blocks away at 225 Pearl Street.

Looking east on Fulton Street toward the Fulton Ferry Terminal about 1900. The Fulton Fish Market building, to the left, is long since gone, but the gabled-roof block across the street, known as Schermerhorn Row, survives from the first decade of the 19th century and is a designated landmark—the focus of the South Street Seaport Area. (South Street Seaport Museum)

Walk up the little lane paved with Belgian blocks, called **Eden's Alley,** which makes an abrupt left turn into Ryder's Alley, returning to Fulton Street. The street is named for Robert Ryder, an English surveyor during the Colonial Period.

The Southbridge Towers housing project was completed in 1972. The plans originally called for enormous high-rise apartment houses, but the city fathers felt that such height would overwhelm the adjacent South Street Seaport area. The modified plan by Gruzen & Partners is a pleasant blending with the surroundings, with considerable "breathing space."

At the corner of Water and Fulton streets is **127 John Street.** Walk around the building and into the lobby. According to the owners, it is designed "to create an atmosphere of pleasure, humor, and excitement for people." Note, too, the iron "bicycle rack" sculpture and *Telephone Booth,* by Albert Wilson. The clock at the south entrance was built as an extension of the wall to hide an old building whose owner would not sell to complete the land parcel. The imaginative building, with all its novel amenities, was designed by Emery Roth & Sons in 1972, and the amusing and creative sidewalk and ground-floor adornments with the pipe and canvas shelters are the work of developer Mel Kaufman, who also planned the pedestrian areas of 17 State Street and 77 Water Street (to be seen later). The lobby and plaza were designed by Rudolph de Harak. The site was occupied in the mid-19th century by the famous United States Hotel.

The Titanic Memorial Tower marks the entrance to the South Street Seaport. This memorial to the 1,517 victims of the *Titanic* who perished when the "unsinkable" liner struck an iceberg and sank on the night of April 14–15, 1912, was erected by public subscription in 1913 and stood atop the old Seamen's

Church Institute Building on South Street until 1967. The time ball at the top of the lighthouse would drop down the pole to signal the hour of twelve noon to the ships in the harbor, its mechanism activated by telegraph signal from the Naval Observatory in Washington, D.C.

The South Street Seaport Historic District is a 19th-century waterfront area that survives almost intact. The entire seaport area was redeveloped by the Rouse Company, whose restorations of Boston's Quincy Market and Baltimore's Harborplace have been highly acclaimed.

Begin your visit at the **Museum Visitors' Center** at 12 Fulton Street, where you can pick up the free *Map & Guide* to all points of interest, or better yet, if you have the time to explore, pick up a copy of *Walking around in South Street*, by Ellen Fletcher, in the Museum shop. You may explore the streets, markets, shops, and piers on your own, but to visit the historic ships and some exhibits, as well as boat tours, there is an extra fee. Museum admission: $5.00, under 12 free. [Hours: April 1–Sept. 30 10:00 A.M. to 6:00 P.M., Oct. 1–Mar. 31 10:00 A.M. to 5:00 P.M., closed Tues., (212) 748-8600.] There are also harbor cruises aboard the schooner *Pioneer*, which was launched in 1885.

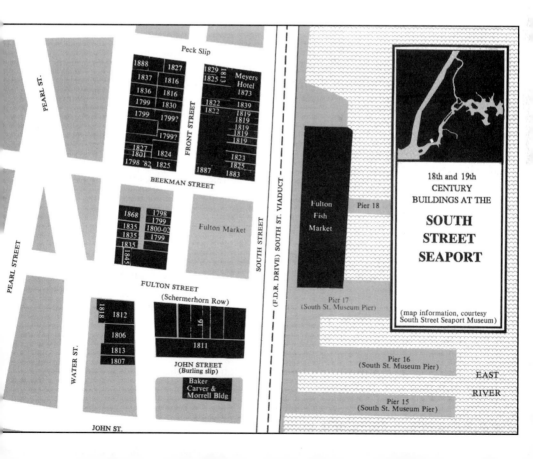

The following is a suggested itinerary: On leaving the Visitors' Center, stop at No. 207–211 Water Street, **Bowne & Co. Stationers,** a re-creation of a 19th-century printing establishment and a working commercial enterprise. Then browse in the adjacent **Book & Chart Store** with its fine collection of nautical literature and memorabilia. To the left is the **Museum Gallery and Museum Library.** The Museum features changing exhibitions on maritime New York, and a permanent ocean liner exhibit, including a 1/4-inch scale model of the *Queen Mary* that was formerly on display in the Cunard Building on Lower Broadway. A similar model of the *Titanic* is due soon.

Return to Fulton Street and turn left. In this same Museum Block is **Cannon's Walk,** a narrow court between the 19th- and 20th-century buildings, opened to the public in 1983, with a variety of shops. As you emerge on Front Street, turn right, back to Fulton Street.

The corner building of the same block is called the **New "Bogardus" Building.** It is a re-creation based on New York's first cast-iron building, the Edgar Laing Store of 1848. [*See* photo of the original on page 187.] To the left, across Front Street, is the huge **Fulton Market Building,** erected in 1983 on the site of three earlier markets, the first built in 1822. The present Market with its several floors of shops and restaurants recalls the time when the old market featured butchers, fishmongers, vegetable dealers, and dairymen.

Across Fulton Street is **Schermerhorn Row,** the heart of the Seaport. Built in 1811–12, this row of peaked-roof buildings, lovingly restored as the centerpiece of the Seaport project, is the only surviving block of Georgian-Federal–style and Greek Revival commercial structures in the city. When the area prospered in the Great Age of Sail, these structures housed a number of industries serving the sea, with ships' chandleries, sail and rope lofts, and naval-store warehouses. The Row is named for its original developer, Peter Schermerhorn.

At Water Street, turn right. Just north of Beekman Street is the **Seamen's Church Institute,** No. 241 Water Street, its fourth site since 1834, when floating chapels served originally as houses of worship for seamen. The Institute is affiliated with the Episcopal Church and is dedicated to safety at sea and the well-being of merchant seafarers. The building, formerly Schermerhorn Ship Chandlery, dates from 1800 and was remodeled authentically in 1989 by Polshek Partnership. Look up at the "Top Deck," a conference center and catering hall. The bell was rescued from the ill-fated steamer *Atlantic.* Go inside and see the fine collection of model ships and nautical memorabilia in the ground floor gallery. (Hours: Mon.–Fri. 9:00 A.M. to 5:00 P.M.)

Return to Beekman Street and turn left (east) to the corner of Front Street. At the northeast corner is an unusual survivor, **No. 142 Beekman Street.** It was designed by George B. Post (later architect of the Stock Exchange) and served the fish market area since 1885. Note the starfish tie-rod caps, the cockleshell cornice, and terra-cotta keystones adorned with fish.

Continue north on Front Street to Peck Slip, where on the north side of the street is a **Con Edison substation** disguised behind a fading trompe l'oeil by Richard Haas of a Greek Revival arcade through which the Brooklyn Bridge can be "seen." The adjacent building to the right is the **Jasper Ward Store,** built in 1807, ten years before Peck Slip's waterfront was filled in.

On the northwest corner and cleverly hidden behind a row of early 19th-century building façades is the **Best Western Seaport Inn,** No. 33 Peck Slip, a much-needed local hostelry, providing comfort and close proximity to the Seaport and the Fulton Fish Market.

Walk west on Peck Slip one block to **No. 257–259 Water Street** (also 21–23 Peck Slip), designed in 1873 by Richard Morris Hunt, the first American architect trained at the Ecole des Beaux-Arts in Paris. The six-story apartment building has its date of construction running vertically in iron numbers down the Peck Slip side. Note the polychrome brick and the star-shaped tie rods at each floor level that connect the timbers to the masonry, plus the shutter-pin hinges at each window frame. Nearby, **No. 251 Water Street** (Carl F. Eisenach, 1888) is distinguished for its elaborate terra cotta work, particularly in the tympanum over the stairway entrance that displays fancy sunflower motifs and the house number, while above the fourth floor windows are keystones carved with stern faces surveying the street below.

Continue up Water Street to No. 273, the **Joseph Rose House and Shop.** This Federal-style house, in seemingly pristine condition (although dating between 1773 and 1781), had suffered many disastrous fires and became a virtual ruin until 1998 when it was rebuilt and accurately restored by architect Oliver Lundquist with the Sciame Development Corp. Although little survives of the original structure, it is in reality the third oldest house in Manhattan (after St. Paul's Chapel and the Morris-Jumel Mansion). Few houses can boast such a colorful history. Built by Capt. Joseph Rose, whose ship was docked nearby, it later became an unsavory boarding house, a tavern, where, as Sportman's Hall, owner Kit Burns conducted dog fights, and later a house for fallen women.

A block farther north, at the corner of Dover Street, is the noted **Bridge Café** (No. 279 Water Street), in the shadow of the Brooklyn Bridge. It began its life as a food and drinking establishment in 1794, and according to noted tavern historian Richard McDermott, it is the **oldest continuous business establishment in the same building in New York City.** When built, the western shore of the East River was almost at its back door, and a wharf stood at approximately the site of the Café's present kitchen. The building has undergone many alterations through the years, although it has never yielded its primary function as a drinking establishment. The current owners purchased the building in 1979, upgraded the restaurant, and kept the charming 1920s interior. Former Mayor Ed Koch, an habitué, called it his favorite restaurant.

Turn right on Dover Street to South Street. The early 19th-century buildings on the right were once the Lydig Flour Warehouses. Turning south, the route passes Nos. 108–113, a row built in 1818–19 for various merchants. The granite piers and lintel above No. 115 are original to the building.

At the corner of Peck Slip is the 1873 **Meyer's Hotel,** named for Henry Meyer, a businessman of the 1880s, and renamed the Paris Café by the present owners. The noted prolific architect John B. Snook designed the building. Walk

The Andrew Fletcher, *an authentic replica of a 19th-century paddlewheel excursion steamboat, once sailed regularly from the South Street Seaport on tours of New York Harbor, but was scrapped in the early 1990s. (Photo by author)*

through the etched-glass panel doors to admire the dark-wood-and-mirrored bar, a splendid example of the Eastlake style.

Walk south to Fulton Street past the active Fulton Fish Market, cross left, passing beneath the South Street Viaduct, to the **South Street Seaport Piers.**

On Pier 16 is the **Pilothouse,** originally the pilothouse of the steam tugboat *New York Central No. 31,* built in 1923. The tug shunted barges loaded with railroad cars in New York harbor. Among the ships anchored at the piers are the lightship *Ambrose,* the fishing schooner *Lettie G. Howard,* the tugboats *W.O. Decker* and *Helen McAllister,* the schooner *Pioneer,* the 325-foot iron-hulled full-rigged ship **Wavertree,** and the 377-foot four-masted bark **Peking,** one of the largest sailing ships ever built. The *Pioneer* offers daily sailing trips. To the left is the multi-million-dollar **Pier 17 Pavilion,** erected in 1985. Standing on the site of the fish market's old piers, it boasts a variety of retail establishments and restaurants, and offers an absolutely super riverside panorama! (Go up to the third floor and out onto the deck!)

From this excellent vantage point one can appreciate the majesty and architectural brilliance of the **Brooklyn Bridge,** considered by many to be the most beautiful bridge ever built. [*See* Fulton Ferry Historic District in the Brooklyn Heights chapter, page 454, for a description.]

Return to South Street and walk south one block to John Street, originally called Burling Slip. To the right, at No. 171 John Street (1850), is the **former counting house of Abiel Abbot Low,** New York's first China Trade merchant. The building now serves as a research center of the Museum. Its iron front was

During the "Great Age of Sail" of the mid-to-late 19th century, South Street was lined with the tall masts of graceful sailing ships from all over the world. Here, near Burling Slip, are a four- and three-master, loading cargo for far-distant ports. (South Street Seaport Museum)

cast by Daniel Badger's Architectural Iron Works, and the façade is faced with brownstone.

Cross John Street (Burling Slip) to the south side.

Burling Slip, like so many former "slips" along the East River waterfront, is a reminder of the 18th and 19th century when they were docking areas. Other slips were James, Pike, Catherine, Beekman, Old, and Coenties. No. 170–176 John Street is the **former Baker, Carver & Morell Building,** erected in 1840. Originally a ship's chandlery, this attractive Greek Revival–style building, designed by Ithiel Town and Alexander Jackson Davis, may be the last commercial survivor of its type. It is faced with granite, with massive piers separating the windows. Since 1982 it has been a condominium.

Turn left (south) on Front Street.

Walking south on Front Street, we pass a trio of new skyscrapers begun in the winter of 1981–82. **One Seaport Plaza,** according to its architects, Swanke Hayden Connell, is designed as a "contextual" 34-story office tower with two distinctly different façades "in context" with its surroundings. The Front Street side is planned to be "reminiscent of another architectural era, echoing the mood of

Young boys enjoying an illegal dip "in the raw" at the Fulton Fish Market pier at the foot of Beekman Street, ca. 1892, apparently oblivious to the photographer, the man dragging the basket of fish, and the law banning swimming in the East River. Among the myriad sailing ships' masts in the background are the twin pilot houses of a Fulton Ferryboat. (New-York Historical Society)

the 19th-century seaport community," while the Water Street side, with its polished granite face and ribbon windows, "is designed to be totally modern and compatible with its neighboring high-rise buildings in an urban environment."

No. 175 Water Street, a 30-story office building designed by Fox & Fowle, was formerly the headquarters of the National Westminster Bank Group. During the excavation for the foundation, workers made a fascinating and important discovery. Buried in the mud only six feet below ground level they uncovered the complete hull of a mid-18th-century British merchant ship! The developer halted work and summoned archaeologists who, working under the supervision of the Landmarks Commission, rushed to learn as much as possible about the vessel. The 85-foot-long wooden hull belonged to a ship that had been scuttled some time between 1746 and 1755 to be used as part of a harbor landfill project extending Manhattan Island. The unexpected find attracted tens of thousands of visitors who waited in line for hours in the bitter cold for a view of the derelict ship, before it would disappear forever into the concrete foundations of the emerging skyscraper. The unusually shaped building is an example of the post-modern approach to high-rise construction, which offered a welcome relief from the ubiquitous "glass boxes" that dominated architectural thought beginning in the 1950s.

The Continental Center, 180 Maiden Lane, between Front and South streets, designed by Swanke Hayden Connell in 1982, is another example of post-

Archaeologists scramble over the hull of a derelict mid-18th-century British merchant ship, unearthed unexpectedly during the excavation for 175 Water Street, near the South Street Seaport. The ship had been scuttled and used for landfill, and remained undiscovered until the site was cleared in the late winter of 1982. (Fox & Fowle, Architects)

Charming Hanover Square was not enhanced by the Third Avenue El roaring overhead along Pearl Street. At the time this photo was taken in the early 1880s, India House was then the Cotton Exchange, and the lower level was rented to commercial tenants. (Museum of the City of New York)

Looking north on New Street the morning after the Great Blizzard of 1888. The storm wreaked such havoc with the overhead wires that the City thereafter required all utilities to run their wires underground. (Museum of the City of New York)

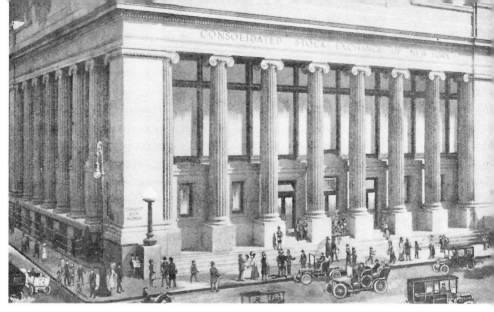

At the turn of the century, the Consolidated Stock Exchange operated briefly as a rival to the "Big Board," dealing mostly in mining stocks. The huge Greek Revival–style building stood at the southeast corner of Broad and Wall streets. (King's Views of New York, 1909)

Looking west on Wall Street, ca. 1890, from South Street to Trinity Church, with the Third Avenue El passing overhead at Pearl Street. To the right of the church is the cupola of the Gillender Building, now the site of the Bankers Trust Company Building at the corner of Nassau Street. (Museum of the City of New York)

modernism. A 41-story hexagonally shaped building, its blue-green reflective skin contrasts sharply with its neighbors.

Look up Pine Street to the towering **former Cities Service Building** (Clinton & Russell, Holton & George, 1932). When completed it was the third tallest building in the world (after the Empire State and Chrysler), and boasted novel double-deck elevators (since discontinued). Now called the American International Building, its 67 stories soar to a slender Gothic-style spire, illuminated at night.

At Maiden Lane, turn right to Water Street, then south (left).

Water Street once was the commercial hub of a thriving waterfront. The street was widened some years ago to provide a much needed traffic artery. In the process, however, many lovely old buildings were lost, and nothing now remains from the 19th century.

Maiden Lane, translated literally from the Dutch *Het Maagde Paatje,* was the site of a freshwater stream where young maidens in the 17th century did their laundry. Look up Maiden Lane to the fortresslike Federal Reserve Bank.

A refreshing change from the usual uninspired "glass box" is No. 88 Pine Street, now known as **Wall Street Plaza** (No. 88 Pine Street), a breezy, light tower of white-painted steel and large windows. Designed by James I. Freed of I. M. Pei Associates and completed in 1971, the building occupies a pleasant plaza, and with its see-through quality is ideally suited for a site close to the river. Look for the two-piece mirrored sculpture by Yu Yu Yang, just to the south.

On the southeast corner of Wall and Water streets was the **Merchants' Coffee House,** built in 1740. It was a popular gathering place for Revolutionary War plotters, and the area became known as Coffee House Slip.

The northwest corner was the site of the **Tontine Coffee House,** erected in 1792. It was here that the Stock Exchange had its beginnings, with transactions taking place on the street under a buttonwood (sycamore) tree and later within the Coffee House, the present site of No. 70 Wall Street. The building at the northwest corner (No. 82 Wall Street) commemorates the site in its name, Tontine House.

No. 100 Wall Street on the north side, and **No. 111** on the south, were built on landfill added in 1801. The Third Avenue El once followed the winding course of narrow Pearl Street.

Turn right on Wall Street to Pearl Street.

Pearl Street was originally the shore of the East River in Dutch Colonial times and is named for the mother-of-pearl oyster shells that were scattered along the beach.

Wall Street is the site of the original protective wall, built by order of Governor Peter Stuyvesant in 1653, at the northern limits of the town of Nieuw Amsterdam. At the site of Wall and Pearl streets, a blockhouse commanded the eastern end of the wall, and a large water gate was built between the blockhouse and the wall itself. It was called *'t Water Poort* to distinguish it from *'t Landt Poort* at

Broadway. The Dutch referred to the path along the wall as *de Cingel* (the Rampart). The wall was a fortified palisade fence, not, as is commonly believed, to keep out hostile Indians, but to prevent an invasion by the English from the New England colonies. The fortification gradually deteriorated (helped by colonists who "borrowed" planks for house repairs and firewood), and as the city grew northward, it was demolished around 1695. In 1709 the area became a slave market and later a grain market.

No. 72–74 Wall Street, at the northwest corner of Pearl Street, was built for the Seamen's Bank for Savings in 1926 from plans by Benjamin Wistar Morris, but at this writing remains unoccupied. The handsome building has an attractive façade of multicolored seamed-face granite blocks, and upon completion was cited by the Downtown League as "the finest building of the year." The tall structure with its artistic setbacks cannot be categorized as belonging to any particular style, but the huge entrance arch is Romanesque in character, while the graceful upper buttresses are vaguely Gothic. Stretching a point, it might be called a very early example of Art Deco. Attractive are the low-relief blocks around the arch, representing nautical themes. The Seamen's Bank for Savings was the city's second oldest, chartered in 1829. Its original charter restricted banking activities to seamen only, in the belief that too many sailors were losing their hard-earned wages, accumulated during long sea voyages, in waterfront saloons as soon as their ships returned to port. When the building was dedicated, the directors decided to change the street address from 76 to 74 Wall Street, as some "old salts" who had been longtime depositors suggested that the combination of numbers totaling 13 "was a thing to make good seamen wary." A plaque on the building marks the site of the home of Edward Livingston, Secretary of State in 1831, who may hold the record in number of public offices held: senator, mayor, congressman, and minister to France.

Across Wall Street is **Barclay's Bank Building,** No. 75 (Welton Becket Assocs., 1987). At the rear corner and facing the mini-park behind are archaeological window displays showing artifacts from Colonial days that were discovered at the site prior to excavation as part of an archaeological study undertaken by the developers to comply with New York City's environmental laws, and overseen by the Landmarks Preservation Commission. Among the finds were items from backyard privies, cisterns, and house and building foundations from the late 17th to late 19th centuries.

Turn back (east) and right into Pearl Street as far as Beaver Street.

Beaver Street honors the little furry rodent on which so much of early commerce depended. Beaver pelts were shipped in such large quantities, and figured so vitally in the early colony's business life, that the animal was incorporated into the seal of Nieuw Amsterdam and later into the seal of the city of New York. The corner building at **82–92 Beaver Street,** remodeled as "One Wall Street Court," was formerly the New York Cocoa Exchange. Designed in 1903 by Clinton & Russell, the 15-story office building incorporates Classical and Renaissance details. Note the polychrome-glazed terra-cotta ornamentation.

Turn right on Pearl Street to Hanover Square.

Hanover Square Park is an attractive oasis among the towering canyons of lower Manhattan. The intersection where Hanover, Pearl, Stone, and William streets meet Old Slip was originally a public common as far back as 1637, surrounded by elegant residences and situated very close to the river. At the site of nearby No. 119 Pearl Street, Captain (William) Kidd maintained a home. Captain Kidd was really not the pirate he was reputed to be. Although he was tried and hanged in England in 1701 for piracy, recent studies seem to indicate that he was an honorable sea captain who was the scapegoat of an unfair trial. Hanover Square, named for the royal house of England, is one of the few public places whose name was not changed during the Revolution, perhaps because George I was not disliked as much as his descendant, two Georges later. As the district became commercial, Hanover Square was the first "Printing House Square" of the city [*see* City Hall, "Old Newspaper Row," Foley Square, and "Five Points" Nos. 2, 3, 4]. It was here that New York's first newspaper, the *New York Gazette,* was published by William Bradford in 1725.

Dominating Hanover Square is the landmark **India House,** built in 1851–54 by Richard Carman, a carpenter, for the Hanover Bank. From 1870 to 1885 it housed the New York Cotton Exchange, and later W. R. Grace & Company. India House was organized as a private businessmen's club in 1914, and is dedicated to the furtherance of foreign trade. It contains a large collection of maritime artifacts and paintings in the charmingly reconstructed Marine Room. The lower floor of India House is occupied by *Harry's,* a restaurant popular with bankers and brokers. The brownstone exterior in Italianate style is reminiscent of a Tuscan villa.

Hanover Square was remodeled in 1978 and made into a pedestrian mall, and the **statue of Abraham de Peyster** (George E. Bissell, 1896) was moved here from Bowling Green. The carved legend in the base records the list of public offices held by de Peyster during his long career as a civil servant. (For some reason, de Peyster turns his back on the square, as he did at Bowling Green and Broadway.)

No. 7 Hanover Square, a 26-story office tower (Emery Roth & Sons, and Norman Jaffe, 1982), stands on the site of the old W. R. Grace & Company Building. Unable to find a tenant for its Florentine-style *palazzo* when the firm moved its headquarters uptown to 42nd Street in 1974, they demolished it, and the lot then lay "fallow" until later demand for office space brought a developer to the site. Had the need come a few years sooner, the lovely old predecessor might have had a new lease on life.

Walk east on Hanover Square to Water Street and turn left (north).

No. 77 Water Street, designed by Emery Roth & Sons in 1970, is another iconoclastic structure two years older than the same architect's 127 John Street building. Although the superstructure is not particularly engaging, the handling of the open lobby area and its "fantasies" is most pleasant, and is a credit to developer Mel Kaufman. Walk across the mini-stream's bridges with school of metal fish, examine the metal sculptures, including *Rejected Skin,* by sculptors Rudolph de Harak and William Tarr (and indeed made from rejected parts of the building's aluminum siding). Visit Ye Olde Time Country Candy Store, and in little Bennett Park to the north, note the modern sculptures *Helix* and *City Fountains,* by Victor Scallo. One unique bit of sculpture is *not* visible, except to tenants of nearby taller buildings. Perched on the roof is an almost full-scale **model of a World War II biplane,** designed by Rudolph de Harak and executed by sculptor William Tarr in 1969. Alas, it is not open to the public. Walk around to the rear of the building and turn right to Old Slip.

The flashy building to the left (32 Old Slip) is one of the newer additions to the skyline. **Financial Square,** a 35-story structure designed by Edward Durrell Stone Associates and completed in 1987, displays alternating gray granite bands that open on a gradually widening gray reflecting-glass curtain wall. A fire house that once blocked Old Slip has been incorporated, garagelike, into the ground floor, leaving a pleasant open space for pedestrians as one of the required zoning amenities. Financial Square occupies the **site of the United States Assay Building,** built in 1930 and demolished in 1985.

In the center of Old Slip, where sailing ships once docked, is the **former First Precinct Police Station (100 Old Slip),** once called the "Old Slip Station." Built in the style of an Italian *palazzo,* it is a trim, solid Italian Renaissance–style structure of pleasing proportion, and was designed by Joseph Howland Hunt and Richard Howland Hunt in 1909.

In 2001, the building was converted to **The New York City Police Museum.** Through a variety of exhibits, the Museum captures the rich history of the NYPD, from when "watchmen" patrolled the cobblestone streets of Nieuw Amsterdam to today's methods of crime prevention, law enforcement techniques, and weaponry. Visitors can play detective in the "Interactive Crime Scene," examine a display of vintage police vehicles, including an authentic 1972 Plymouth patrol car, and see the museum's Notorious Criminals Gallery, as well as the Hall of Heroes that honors the courageous men and women who gave their lives while protecting the city. A small gift shop sells police-related memorabilia. (Hours: Tues.–Sun. 10:00 A.M. to 5:00 P.M., Thurs. to 7:00 P.M. Closed Mon. and all federal and NYC holidays. Adults $5.00, seniors $3.00, children $2.00.)

Return to Hanover Square and turn left (south) into Pearl Street.

At the site of No. 81 Pearl Street, William Bradford (buried in Trinity Churchyard) installed **New York's first printing press** in 1693.

On the southwest corner of Pearl Street and Coenties Alley once stood the **Stadt Huys,** the first City Hall. Built originally as the *Stadt Herberg,* or City Tavern, by Governor William Kieft in 1641, it was an imposing five-story stone structure—the tallest in town—overlooking the harbor. When Nieuw Amsterdam was granted its municipal charter 12 years later, New York's first hotel was converted into the *Stadt Huys,* and remained the seat of city government until 1699. Two years later a new City Hall was built on Wall Street (on the site of the present Fed-

The Stadt Huys, the first New York City Hall, situated at the waterfront on Pearl Street and Coenties Slip, as seen in an 1869 print. (The J. Clarence Davies Collection, Museum of the City of New York)

eral Hall). Not long ago, when the buildings that occupied the site of Nos. 71 and 73 Pearl Street were removed, the *Stadt Huys*'s foundations were discovered underneath. A team of archaeologists studied and mapped the site before the plot was resurfaced. In addition to the foundation walls, the dig unearthed Delft and English pottery, fragments of Indian wampum, as well as clay pipes and wine bottles from Lovelace Tavern, built by Francis Lovelace, the second English governor of New York. The commercial building of the early 19th century that stood on the site of No. 71 was carefully dismantled, declared a landmark, and placed in storage pending re-erection at the South Street Seaport. The old *Stadt Huys* served a number of functions, including a jail and debtors' prison, a courthouse, and a public warehouse. In front of the building, at the river's edge, stood the gallows, a pillory and stocks, and even a ducking stool, in which violators of the strict Dutch Reformed moral codes were tied and plunged repeatedly into the cold water of the East River.

Turn right on Coenties Alley (now a pedestrian mall), and left into the arcade of towering **No. 85 Broad Street.** The building cuts off Stone Street, now a historic district, whose former path is marked by brown paving stones leading into the lobby. To the left, in the sidewalk of the arcade, is an excavation showing the **site of the General Lovelace Tavern** (1670–1706), which was owned by the British Crown, with its foundation walls and some bottles, and a nearby cistern. On the curb near the corner is a plaque describing in some detail the "Archaeology of the Stadt Huys."

Cross Pearl Street again into Coenties Slip.

Coenties Slip was one of the early city's largest wharfs, with a diagonally shaped breakwater projecting far out into the East River [*see* Great Fire map]; however, the inlet has been completely filled in, even out beyond the end of the old pier. Coenties (*pronounced* CO-en-teez) Slip is named for Conraet Ten Eyck, who operated a tannery on nearby Broad Street. ("Coentje" is the Dutch diminutive for Conraet.) At this point the old Third Avenue El made a dizzying zigzag turn as it twisted sharply east from its southward path down Pearl Street, over

The famous S-curve of the Third Avenue El, about 1879, at Coenties Slip. The serpentine structure was finally scrapped in 1950, depriving straphangers of a spectacular ride through the "canyons" of lower Manhattan. (The New-York Historical Society)

Coenties Slip, then south again into Front Street—on the last lap of its tortuous route to South Ferry. Built in 1879, the El survived until 1950.

Across Water Street is **Vietnam Veterans Plaza,** formerly Jeanette Park, a paved multilevel plaza made entirely of brick similar to adjacent No. 4 New York Plaza. Designed by landscape architect W. Paul Friedberg, it is terraced and equipped with an underground shopping mall, but is sterile in appearance. The mini-park's old name is a memorial to the sailing ship *Jeanette,* which met disaster on the George Washington De Long Expedition to the North Pole in 1881. The ill-starred venture was sponsored jointly by the U.S. Navy and James Gordon Bennett, publisher of the *New York Herald.* It was the *Herald,* in its tradition of sensationalism, which sent Stanley to Africa to find Livingstone. For years, Jeanette Park was a favorite port of call for unemployed seamen, and boasted a popular oyster bar in the middle of a shady mall.

In the center of the Plaza is the **New York City Vietnam War Memorial** (Peter Wormser and William Fellows, architects; John Ferrandino, writer), a wall of translucent green glass 14 feet high by 70 feet wide, on which are engraved letters to their families from servicemen and women who died in the conflict. The personal letters, moving in their honest simplicity, express their thoughts, hopes, and anxieties, perhaps epitomized by one letter at the top that asks: "One thing worries me. Will people believe me? Will they want to hear about it, or will they want to forget the whole thing ever happened?"

To the north of the Plaza is enormous **55 Water Street** (Emery Roth & Sons, 1972), a twin building connected by an exterior escalator bank. Take the escalator to the plaza level and enjoy the river views. To the south is **No. 4 New York Plaza** (Carson, Lundin & Shaw, 1968), one of the first of the behemoths to line Water Street. Note the old clock on the building's corner.

On the west side of Water Street, directly opposite No. 4 New York Plaza, is a **block of typical 19th-century commercial buildings** that survived because the street was widened on the east side only. It was later decided to save the entire block, which includes historic Fraunces Tavern, to re-create the atmosphere of the mid-19th-century commercial district. The group includes Federal, Greek Revival, and Victorian buildings, and has been designated the **Fraunces Tavern Block Historic District.** Unfortunately, the 19th-century atmosphere and scale is destroyed by the towering buildings that surround the block and overwhelm it.

Turn right at Broad Street to Pearl Street.

At the corner of Broad and Pearl streets is one of our most cherished landmarks, **Fraunces Tavern.** A handsome neo-Georgian building, it is a splendid re-creation of the Stephen DeLancey house, built in 1719. Except for some Dutch brick in the west wall, nothing remains of the original structure. Nonetheless, it is an excellent example of a formal English house of the 18th century. James DeLancey, a descendant of the wealthy merchant, lost all his family holdings by choosing the wrong side in the American Revolution, and suffered confiscation of his property. (Delancey Street on the Lower East Side is today the only physical reminder of the family name and the large estate he once owned in that part of Manhattan.) In 1757 the building became a warehouse, and five years later was purchased by Samuel Fraunces who converted it into the *Queen's Head Tavern.* Fraunces, a West Indian of French ancestry, operated the tavern successfully for a number of years and subsequently came into the employ of George Washington as his chief steward. What is now the New York State Chamber of Commerce was founded here in 1768, and just before the outbreak of the Revolutionary War, the Committees of Correspondence—soon to become the Continental Congress—held their first meeting at the tavern. On November 24, 1783, Governor Clinton gave a gala dinner here to celebrate the British evacuation of the city, and that December 4th, Washington bade his famous farewell to his officers in the Long Room on the second floor. During the 19th century, the tavern gradually deteriorated, suffered several fires, and fell victim to a number of unauthentic reconstructions. In 1904 the Sons of the Revolution of New York State purchased the building and spent three years restoring it to its present elegance. The **Fraunces Tavern Museum** conducts a wide variety of interpretive programs for young and old (phone 425-1778). There is also a library, a gift shop, and a charming ground-floor restaurant. (Open Tues.–Sat. 10:00 A.M. to 4:45 P.M., and Washington's Birthday and the Fourth of July. Admission: adults, $3.00; children and seniors, $2.00.)

Take a moment for a brief lesson in Georgian-style architecture by crossing the street and admiring the details: the slate hipped roof crowned by a balustrade, the tall chimneys, shed-roof dormers, a cornice set over a row of modillions, red brick walls with stone trim, and an ornate doorway flanked by classic columns and crowned by a pediment. The style was inspired by the north-Italian Renaissance as applied by the architect Palladio to many of the great Venetian and Lombardian villas.

On January 24, 1975, a bomb was exploded in the adjacent Anglers' Club, causing several deaths and many injuries. Allegedly placed by a Puerto Rican extremist group, the blast virtually destroyed the club, but luckily caused only minor damage to Fraunces Tavern.

Look back down Broad Street toward the river. At the corner of Water Street is the unusual and once controversial 50-story **One New York Plaza,** designed in 1969 by William Lascaze and Associates. Its novel façade with recessed picture-frame windows has been called derisively "the waffle iron." To its left, **No. 4 New York Plaza,** just seen close at hand, is another monolith that altered (but did not improve) the city skyline during the building boom of the 1960s and '70s. But even with its fortresslike proportions it is somewhat less overwhelming. Perhaps Manufacturers Hanover Trust was seeking an appropriate corporate symbol.

On the triangular plot across Broad Street, bounded by Pearl and Bridge streets (No. 100), is one of the offices of the **New York Clearing House,** erected in 1962. The institution oversees the daily clearing of billions of dollars of member banks' checks. To the rear is the blue-glass Broad Financial Center.

Continue north on Broad Street.

Broad Street in Dutch Colonial days was a wide canal, called the *Heere Graft* (Great Canal), which extended inland from the East River as far as the present Exchange Place, with a small side canal up Beaver Street. (The broad dimensions of the old canal account for the disproportionately wide size of Broad Street today.) By 1676, the canal became polluted and rather malodorous, and was filled in. In its place, *Brede Straet* survives in translation to the present. It is interesting to note that unlike other north-south streets, the numbers on Broad Street *decrease* in a northward direction.

No. 85 Broad Street (Skidmore, Owings & Merrill, 1982) rises 30 stories and occupies what was once several blocks of low-rise 19th-century commercial buildings. The rough-textured surface of the office tower is precast concrete exposed aggregate. In making way for this out-of-scale giant, it was necessary to close diminutive Stone Street at Coenties Alley. At its front and rear entrances are bronze plaques set into the sidewalk showing the early street pattern. As you reach South William Street, notice how the "street wall" of the 85 Broad Street building has been designed to conform to the curvature of the winding street.

No. 67 Broad Street, the **International Telephone Building,** was erected in 1930 from plans by Louis S. Weeks. When opened, the building housed ITT's world-wide communications headquarters, including a number of subsidiary cable and telegraph companies that comprised its vast network. Above the recessed corner entrance is a fine mosaic depicting the hemispheres linked by radio communication.

Directly across the street, a narrow trellised plaza leads to the rear of No. 2 Broadway, the **site of the first Huguenot church in New York.** Return to Broad Street and continue to Marketfield Street.

The entrance to tiny Marketfield Street marks the site of "the lost thoroughfare, Petticoat Lane." The diminutive street takes its name from the *Marcktveldt,* or Market Place, that once existed along the old canal. A market was held every Friday morning at the cattle bridge, one of several that crossed the *Heere Graft.*

Between Marketfield and Beaver streets stands the solid, Classic Revival–style former **American Banknote Corp. Building**, No. 70 Broad Street (Kirby, Petit & Green, 1908). The company, which has since moved uptown, was the major US security printer before the establishment of the Bureau of Engraving & Printing, producing paper currency, bonds, and postage stamps. It is still the largest in the world, and traces its origins to 1795. Since 2004 the building has been the headquarters of the **"Capital of the U.S. Peace Government,"** founded by Maharishi Mahesh Yoga, in Fairfield, Iowa.

Turn left on Beaver Street to New Street.

No. 18 Beaver Street is an ornate survivor of the "Elegant '80s"—probably a fancy restaurant of yesteryear, better known as a dining saloon.

Nowhere else in the city can the expression **"The Canyons of New York"** be more dramatically visualized than from this point looking north on New Street. (Return to Broad Street.)

Walking up Broad Street, observe the variety of early 20th-century office buildings: No. 50 (Willauer, Shape & Bready, 1911); No. 37; and the **Broad-Exchange Building,** 25 Broad Street (Robert Maynicke, 1899; remodeled by Clinton & Russell, 1900). When completed, it was the largest office building in the world. In 1998, it was converted by architect Costas Kondylis into a 345-apartment condominium, named The Exchange.

Exchange Place, named for a merchants' exchange located here during the Dutch Colonial period, is one of the city's narrowest streets. The surprising little hill leading to Broadway gives it the dubious distinction of being the steepest street in downtown Manhattan.

Across from the Broad-Exchange Building, on the northeast side of Broad Street and Exchange Place, stood the **Old Ferry House** from which boats to Long Island shore points departed down the "Great Canal." Passengers were sometimes forced to spend the night here waiting for fair winds to make the trip. Looking up Exchange Place with its massed skyscrapers, it is hard to imagine that the area during the mid-17th century was a sheep pasture.

Approaching the end of Broad Street is one of the most famous panoramas of the financial center (left to right): **The New York Stock Exchange** (southwest corner), the **Bankers Trust Company** with its gold stepped pyramid atop the tower (northwest corner), **Federal Hall National Memorial** (northeast corner), and the **J. P. Morgan & Company** (southeast corner).

The New York Stock Exchange (8 Broad Street), synonymous with Wall Street, is the largest securities exchange in the world. The "Big Board" lists more than 3,500 different stocks and bonds owned by about 30 million share- and bondholders. Transactions are printed on a nationwide ticker network, and activity is centered on the trading floor, two-thirds the size of a football field, where member firms' telephoned orders to buy and sell are handled by 22 horseshoe-shaped trading posts on the main floor and in annexes. The often hectic scene, which seems almost incomprehensible to the casual visitor in the gallery, is explained on the daily tours given by the Exchange. The enormous Classic-style building was completed in 1903 by George B. Post, with a 22-story addition in 1923 by Trowbridge & Livingston. The sculpture in the pediment is by John Quincy Adams Ward and Paul W. Bartlett. The busy Stock Exchange is a far cry from the old Tontine Coffee House and buttonwood tree of 1792, when 24 brokers drew up the original trading agreement. A reminder of those days is the little **buttonwood tree** planted in front of the Exchange in 1992 to mark the Exchange's 200th anniversary.

Until the opening of the American Stock Exchange on nearby Trinity Place, some stock transactions were conducted along the sidewalks of Broad Street, with brokers or their representatives waving frenetic hand signals signifying "buy" or "sell" orders to correspondents in adjacent buildings. This very active "Curb Exchange" is now housed in the much more modern "Amex."

Federal Hall National Memorial, built in 1842 as the U.S. Custom House, is considered the Parthenon of public buildings in the city and possibly its finest Greek Revival–style building. Its predecessor on the site was our second City Hall, which replaced the *Stadt Huys* in 1701. It was here that Peter Zenger, editor of the *New York Weekly Journal,* was tried in 1735 for "seditious libels" against the royal government, and particularly against Governor William Cosby. His acquittal for printing the truth was the first major victory in the battle for a free press. Thirty years later, the Stamp Act Congress met to draft a Declaration of Rights and Grievances in which the colonists strongly protested the imposition by England of the Stamp Act. After this first public protest by a colony against "taxation without representation" and a subsequent boycott of the hated stamps, the British government repealed the tax. On July 18, 1776, the Declaration of Independence was read here. During the Revolutionary War, the occupying British forces used the City Hall as their headquarters. After the war, The Second Continental Congress met here in 1785, and two years later passed the Northwest Ordinance (explained on the building plaque to the left). In 1789 the building was renovated under supervision of Maj. Pierre L'Enfant, and for a little over a year it served as the Capitol of the United States. Congress met here for the first time on March 4, 1789, and as its first official act, counted the electoral ballots for President George Washington's unanimous election. On April 30, Washington was inaugurated on the steps of the renamed Federal Hall. The **statue of Washington,** sculpted by John Quincy Adams Ward in 1883, stands at about the same place where Washington took his oath of office. Congress also adopted the Bill of Rights here on September 25, 1789, and sent it out to the states for ratification.

Unfortunately, the building later fell into disuse and was sold in 1812 for scrap for the sum of $425. In 1862, after 20 years as the Custom House, the present building became a branch of the Independent Treasury System. Of the six subtreasuries established, New York's was the most important and, as the Subtreasury Building, served until 1920. One of the old thick-walled vaults may be seen inside. Federal Hall was designed by Ithiel Town and Alexander Jackson Davis, under surveillance of John Frazee and Samuel Thomson, and is built of

In 1826, this charming Greek Revival structure was built by the government as the New York branch of the Bank of the United States. Later, it became the Assay Office, and upon demolition in 1915, its dignified façade was carefully dismantled and later re-erected in the American Wing of the Metropolitan Museum of Art. A subsequent Assay Office occupied the site briefly, and the building was acquired by the now-defunct Seamen's Bank for Savings.

Westchester marble. The rather incongruously shaped **interior rotunda** (a circular space in a rectangular building) forms part of an extensive museum, which should not be missed. (Federal Hall is open weekdays only, from 9:00 A.M. to 5:00 P.M.; enter on Pine Street.) It is one of nine national sites within the City of New York administered by the National Park Service of the Department of the Interior.*

J. P. Morgan & Company Building, across from Federal Hall, was formerly the offices of J. P. Morgan & Company, America's most powerful private bank. The austere building, completed in 1914 from plans by Trowbridge & Livingston,

*Castle Clinton National Monument, in Battery Park; **Federal Hall National Memorial,** Wall Street at the corner of Nassau Street; **Gateway National Recreation Area,** New York & New Jersey coastal environs; **General Grant National Memorial** (Grant's Tomb), Riverside Drive & West 122nd Street; **Governors Island,** Upper New York Bay; **Hamilton Grange National Memorial,** 287 Convent Avenue, between W. 141st and W. 142nd streets; **St. Paul's Chapel,** Broadway between Fulton and Dey streets; **Statue of Liberty National Monument,** New York Harbor; **Theodore Roosevelt Birthplace National Historic Site,** 28 East 20th Street.

was the assumed target of an anarchist's bomb. At about noon on September 16, 1920, a horse-drawn wagon parked in front of the bank exploded, killing 33 passers-by (and the horse), and injuring scores of others. The devastating blast occurred during the post-World War I period of anti-radical hysteria, and was said by some to be an act of violence against "one of the strongest bastions of capitalism." Another theory is that the wagon belonged to an explosives manufacturing company, and had been traveling on a prohibited street when the dynamite accidentally ignited. Numerous scars from the explosion are plainly visible on the bank's Wall Street façade—and for some reason, the bank has never made an effort to patch them up.

Continue east on Wall Street.

No. 30 Wall Street, formerly the Seamen's Bank for Savings, has an interesting architectural history. Its predecessor on the site, a lovely Greek Revival–style building designed by Martin E. Thompson, was built in 1826 as the New York branch of the Bank of the United States. After ten years the building was turned over to private banking interests, and in 1853 it was acquired by the Federal Government for the Assay Office. In 1915, the structure—by now the oldest federal edifice in the city—was demolished, but its charming Tuckahoe marble façade was carefully dismantled and stored away, to be re-erected in 1924 outside the American Wing of the Metropolitan Museum of Art. With the opening of the new American Wing in 1980, the lovely façade is now the centerpiece of the gallery. A new Assay Office was constructed on the 30 Wall Street site from plans by York & Sawyer, supervised by James A. Wetmore, and was completed in 1919, "designed to last a thousand years." However, it remained only until another Assay Office was constructed at Old Slip (demolished in 1986), where Wetmore's experience was again called on for the design.

In 1955 the handsome building was purchased by the Seamen's Bank for Savings, which found the five underground floors of bullion vaults in excellent condition and preserved them for the bank's archives. The 1919 Assay Office building was considered one of the best examples of Renaissance-style architecture. Because of its quality and beauty and the architectural harmony with adjoining Federal Hall, it was decided to preserve this historic landmark and retain its limestone façade while an eight-story addition was erected above it. Architects Halsey, McCormack & Helmer incorporated the superstructure most successfully, proving that a good building need not be demolished when more space is required. In the lobby, to the right of the main banking rooms, are the original marble cornerstones of the 1826 and 1919 buildings. The building now houses a branch of the N.Y. Sports Club.

Across the street, at **No. 37,** is the Renaissance Eclectic–style building designed by Francis H. Kimball in 1907 for the Trust Company of America. At the time of its completion, it was the tallest on Wall Street.

The Trump Building, 40 Wall Street, was built in 1929 for the Bank of the Manhattan Company. Designed by architects H. Craig Severance and Yasuo Matsui, it was planned to be the tallest building in the world. At the same time, Severance's former partner, William Van Alen, was completing the Chrysler Building uptown—also touted to become the world's tallest. The developing rivalry led Severance to add two feet to his 40 Wall Tower when it was announced that the Chrysler Building had reached its maximum height of 925 feet. To everyone's surprise (and Severance's chagrin), Van Alen's workmen secretly assembled a towering stainless-steel spire *inside* the building, and raised the Chrysler Building to a record height of 1,046 feet—the uncontested winner. Within nine months, however, Severance enjoyed the last laugh, as the newly completed Empire State Building rose almost 40 feet higher! The Bank of the Manhattan Company began its career as the city's first water supply company, a quasi-public utility known as **The Manhattan Company.** Founded by Aaron Burr in 1799, and chartered by the State Legislature, the company was the target of severe criticism from Alexander Hamilton, for the terms of the charter permitted it to engage in rather disparate financial pursuits, including banking. Hamilton saw this as an opportunity for Burr to gain banking privileges for his political party. This was one of the first confrontations between the two men that ultimately led to their tragic duel in 1804. The Manhattan Company did provide water to the growing city by means of pine-wood pipes bringing water from a reservoir on Chambers Street; however, banking became its primary interest. When the Croton Water System was opened in 1842, the Bank of the Manhattan Company became a financial institution exclusively. After many years in the banking business, it merged with the Chase National Bank, and in a later consolidation became the Chase Manhattan, whose innovative former headquarters skyscraper will be seen shortly. The bank recently joined with J. P. Morgan & Company to become the sprawling J. P. Morgan Chase, with headquarters next door at 30 Wall Street. Although no longer a water company, its assets are nonetheless still "liquid." The 40 Wall Street building was purchased and restored by Donald Trump in 1989.

An exciting addition to the block is the striking **60 Wall Street,** a 52-story tower, designed by Kevin Roche Dinkeloo & Assocs., and completed in 1989, replacing an earlier 60 Wall Tower designed by Clinton & Russell in 1932, built as an extension of the still-extant 70 Pine Street. (The owners at the time wanted the more prestigious Wall Street address.) The new building sports a huge block-through atrium with trees and shops, and is open to the public seven days a week, 7:00 A.M. to 10:00 P.M.—an amenity that offers a moment of respite and relaxation. Note how the imposing gray granite arcade relates to the multi-columned façade of the old Merchants' Exchange across Wall Street. The view is particularly impressive from inside the atrium.

The imposing Classic façade of the **former Citibank Building** at No. 55 (the southeast corner of William Street) is a dominant landmark on Wall Street. The original ground floor was built in 1836–42, from plans by Isaiah Rogers, as the Merchants' Exchange. An earlier **Merchants' Exchange** was destroyed in the Great Fire of 1835. From 1862 to 1907 it served as the Custom House after moving from its former Federal Hall site. When the Custom House at Bowling Green was opened, the vacant building was remodeled for the National City Bank by the firm of McKim, Mead & White [Stanford White was murdered the year before; *see* Madison Square, 11], and a second tier was added, doubling the size of the building. Note that the lower colonnade is Ionic, the upper, Corinthian. In designating the building a landmark, the New York City Landmarks Preservation Commission called it "a remarkable example of how a notable building can be sympathetically extended." The successor, the First National City Bank, now Citibank, chartered in 1812 and an outgrowth of the First Bank of the United States, vacated the venerable landmark building in the late 1990s for occupancy by the Regent Wall Street Hotel, and a masterpiece of adaptive reuse. Arguably the most luxurious hotel in the city at the time, it unexpectedly closed its doors in early 2004, an indirect victim of the WTC Disaster. The hotel's location, not far from the site of Ground Zero discouraged potential guests, and it was unable to attract enough business to support its lavish operation. A pity, as the Regent's elegant ballroom that occupied McKim, Mead & White's once great banking hall, is no longer accessible.

Turn right into William Street, to the corner of Exchange Place.

Named for William Beekman, who came from Holland with Peter Stuyvesant (not for King William of England, as is commonly believed), **William Street** forms another of the deep, winding canyons that give the neighborhood so much atmosphere. Beekman's descendants settled farther uptown in the area now known as Beekman Place [*see* East River Panoramas, 6].

Originally the City Bank-Farmers Trust Company Building, later the First National City Trust Company, No. 20 Exchange Place is generally known only by its street address. It is a striking 57-story limestone Art Deco shaft on an irregularly shaped base, designed by Cross & Cross and completed in 1931. The history of coinage is vividly displayed on plaques above the ground-floor windows (even our old Buffalo Nickel is there!). A "Bridge of Sighs" connects with the No. 55 Wall Street, now the Regent Wall Street Hotel, building. Although the street pattern is helter-skelter, the tower of the tall building conforms to the north-south city grid.

Turn right on William Street.

The famous **Delmonico's Restaurant,** at 56 Beaver Street, was founded in 1827 by Peter and John Delmonico, recent immigrants from Italy. In 1836 they built Beaver Street House for their establishment, which remained until the present building, designed by James Lord, replaced it in 1890. Although the original Delmonico's is long since gone, the present restaurant carries on the name and tradition. The establishment was always fashionable, and in Moses King's 1893 *Handbook of New York City,* it is described as "a familiar name among the epicures of two continents for nearly three-quarters of a century...where it will cost you from $3 upward for a good dinner" (a high price in those days!). The building was converted to residential apartments under the J-51 program, and Delmonico's was restored in 19th-century style.

No. 1 William Street, the building whose prominent cupola sits above an indented corner, was originally the banking firm of **J. & W. Seligman & Company** and later the house of Lehman Brothers. The Renaissance Revival–style edifice was designed by Francis H. Kimball and Julian C. Levi and completed in

1907. Both former banking tenants are still in business, and the present occupant is the **Banca Commerciale Italiana**—an appropriate neighbor for Delmonico's.

Continue down South William Street to Mill Lane.

South William Street was originally called Mill Street, and near this site in 1626, the Dutch West India Company had erected a large mill. Not only did it grind flour, but its large upper room served as a house of worship for the first settlers until their Reformed Church was completed within Fort Amsterdam (on the site of the former Custom House). The room later served the first Jewish immigrants, who had arrived in 1653 but were not permitted to hold services until several years later. Two millstones from the old mill are preserved in the Spanish & Portuguese Synagogue at 8 West 70th Street [*see* West of Central Park, 1]. It was here, too, that on August 29, 1664, the Dutch formally signed the document of surrender of Nieuw Amsterdam to the English.

The view down Mill Lane to Stone Street (seen earlier in the tour) is in sharp contrast to the surrounding tall buildings, and with a little squinting it is not difficult to imagine oneself back in the early 19th century.

Farther down South William Street, at No. 26, is the **site of the first synagogue in America,** built in 1730. A descriptive commemorative plaque on the building was stolen years ago and never replaced.

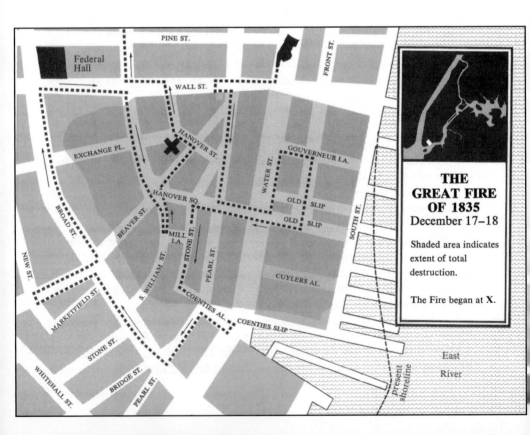

The Merchants' Exchange ablaze during the Great Fire of 1835, the worst conflagration in the city's history. A valiant attempt was made to rescue the statue of Alexander Hamilton (seen in this lithograph brightly lit by the flames) but the cupola, tilting dangerously, collapsed through the roof and shattered the sculpture. (New-York Historical Society)

Return to Beaver Street, and proceed to Hanover Street and turn left.

Note again the coin motifs on the 65 Beaver Street entrance of the 20 Exchange Place Building, this time Biblical coins, as well as the transportation motifs of the 1920s on the bronze doors. The corner of the building at the juncture of Beaver and Hanover streets is the **site of the Great Fire of 1835** [*see* map].

At nine o'clock in the evening on December 17, fire broke out in the store of Comstock & Adams at 25 Merchant Street (the street has since been demapped). The temperature had dropped to a near-record 17° and a howling gale was blowing. The fire, caused by a gas-pipe explosion, spread rapidly to adjoining buildings and within minutes the blaze raged out of control, fed by stores of dry goods and chemicals and driven by the wind. Fire companies fought desperately but ineffectively to stem the conflagration, hampered by frozen hydrants and hoses that became clogged almost instantly with ice. As the fire advanced in both east and west directions, whole blocks seemed to erupt spontaneously into flames. By the early morning hours the blaze had engulfed almost every block to the East River from Wall Street to Coenties Slip, and west nearly to Broad Street. Help was summoned from as far away as Philadelphia, and pump wagons were hastily put aboard freight cars of the newly built railroad and transported to New York. It is said that the flame-reddened sky was visible from as far away as Camden, New Jersey, and New Haven, Connecticut. By noon the following day, the fire had consumed all of Hanover

The corner of Broad and Wall streets in 1882. In the center, the former New York Stock Exchange Building dominates Broad Street, and to the left are the banking offices of Drexel, Morgan & Company (now the site of J. P. Morgan & Company). (The J. Clarence Davies Collection, Museum of the City of New York)

Square, including the merchandise that had been saved from threatened buildings and stacked for protection in the square. Adding to the horror were mobs of looters who converged on the area and overwhelmed the small police force in their mad scramble to steal what had not been burned. A supply of gunpowder was obtained from the Navy Yard in Brooklyn and rowed across the East River to blast a firebreak and hopefully to contain the still-roaring inferno. Fortunately, the masonry walls of the line of buildings along Wall Street helped contain the flames, although the magnificent Merchants' Exchange, one of the city's commercial and architectural showplaces, was itself completely destroyed. By late December 18, the fire burned itself out, leaving an area of 17 blocks—about 20 acres—a smoldering field of ashes, with the incredible loss of 674 buildings from the very heart of the financial district! The disaster was compounded by the total destruction of many fire insurance companies, which left their insureds with no chance of compensation. The 1835 fire was the worst in our young nation's history and completely obliterated every remaining Dutch Colonial building in the city. That is why there is not a single structure left in

Wall Street in 1864, seen from the Subtreasury Building. In the rear is the Merchants' Exchange, rebuilt after the Great Fire of 1835 (now sporting another story as the present Regent Wall Street Hotel), and the only building in the view still standing. (Museum of the City of New York)

A classic view of Wall Street, Trinity Church, and the Subtreasury Building (now Federal Hall), as seen in a magic lantern slide photo taken about 1875. (Author's collection)

Manhattan from the 17th century. As if this were not enough, another fire ten years later destroyed 345 buildings in the same general area.

Continue on Hanover Street to Wall Street.

The building on the right, **No. 63 Wall Street,** is also decorated with coin plaques—drachmas of Ancient Greece on large plaques above the fourth floor.

Turn left on Wall Street to the northeast corner of William Street.

The view to Trinity Church up Wall Street is one of the best known scenes of New York. [Trinity Church is described in the tour of Lower Broadway, Battery Park City, and the Battery.]

The oldest commercial bank in the country is the **Bank of New York Building,** No. 48 Wall Street, founded by Alexander Hamilton in 1784. Several plaques describe its history, including the story of its predecessor on the site, the United States Branch Bank. The original cornerstone of the Bank of New York has been reset several times for each new building in its history. A low-relief bronze plaque above the subway entrance, commemorating the famous Wall, includes an early map, and was placed there in 1909 during the Hudson-Fulton Celebration. The building, long a landmark in the lower Manhattan skyline, was designed in 1927 by Benjamin Wistar Morris. A graceful structure with a Georgian-style cupola and lantern, it is best seen at a distance. The building was converted to condominiums in 1999. Note the ornate roof with the huge bronze eagle.

Turn right (north) on William Street to Pine Street.

To the left soars the 60-story aluminum and glass **Chase Bank Building,** set on one of the largest plazas in the city. When completed in 1960 it was the trendsetter for the series of plazas to follow, conforming to the revised zoning regulations requiring more street-level space. The plaza is elevated at the William Street end due to the topography. Take a few minutes and climb the stairs to the plaza level. The sunken circular courtyard with its fountain is paved with basalt rocks from Japan in an unusual undulating form. It was originally planned to have fish and even dolphins, but the idea was quickly abandoned because of the dangers of pollution (by air and people). Sculptor Isamu Noguchi is responsible for the innovative design, and Skidmore, Owings & Merrill for the towering 800-foot aluminum and glass shaft. Stand beneath the edge of the lofty building and listen as the wind plays delicate tunes on the vertical metal strips.

Dominating the plaza is Jean Dubuffet's enormous free-form black and white sculpture, *Group of Four Trees,* constructed of 25 tons of fiberglass, aluminum, and steel. The group was fabricated near Paris and shipped to New York in 19 pieces and has been the subject of considerable comment since its installation in 1972. A weekday visit to the building's concourse reveals an atomic clock run by gamma rays from its cesium power supply; and to the left of the lobby a charming Japanese garden. The building houses the world's largest bank vault, five levels

The intersection of William Street and Maiden Lane, looking west, ca. 1760. The site is now occupied by The Home Insurance Company Building. In this E. P. Chrystie drawing, a beer barrel is being lowered from the third floor of Rutgers' Brew House. During the British occupation of New York, it was a storehouse. (The Home Insurance Company)

below ground. The vaults are reputed to hold over $40 billion in securities, and just a few scant millions in cash. The bank is the successor of the Bank of the Manhattan Company and the Chase National Bank. The latter was named for Salmon P. Chase, Secretary of the Treasury in Lincoln's administration, and founder of our national currency system and federal banking system. (There was no government-issued paper money prior to 1861.) The bank occupies the first 35 of the 60 stories above ground.

Continue north on William Street to Liberty Street.

The Federal Reserve Bank of New York, occupying the entire block between Liberty Street and Maiden Lane, is *the* great bank for banks—one of 12 of our Federal Reserve System. A Florentine *palazzo* that would have warmed the heart of Lorenzo de' Medici, it is actually based on the design of the Strozzi Palace of the Italian Renaissance. Completed in 1924 from plans by York & Sawyer, the Federal Reserve Bank is a dramatic and imposing structure with its massive walls of rusticated Ohio sandstone and Indiana limestone, fortresslike machicolations, and extensive wrought-iron ornamentation. The lovely triple lanterns and the window grilles in the great arched windows were executed by Samuel Yellin. An enormous subterranean vault five stories below street level and protected by 90-ton doors contains gold bullion stored for many foreign governments; when trade balances are settled, gold is moved from one nation's room to another,

rarely leaving the building. The tremendous volume of check handling and coin operations can be seen on visitors' tours, which begin in the impressive entrance lobby on
Liberty Street (telephone 720-6130 for reservations). All paper currency issued by the
Government through the New York branch of the Federal Reserve Bank bears the letter *B* on the face of each note. Bank notes issued by the Federal Reserve Bank in Boston have an *A*, Philadelphia, *C*, etc., through San Francisco, *L*. The Federal Reserve
System, our nation's central banking establishment, was organized in 1913. All
national banks must belong to a regional branch and keep a specific cash reserve on
deposit. It is said that the vaults here house more gold than does Fort Knox.

Louise Nevelson Plaza, the triangular plot where Liberty Street joins Maiden
Lane, and once the site of the Germania Life Insurance Building, was remodeled
into an outdoor gallery of the sculptor's work. *Shadows and Flags,* made of Cor-Ten
steel (1978), dominates the little plaza also known as Legion Memorial Square.

Directly opposite at No. 10 Liberty Street, is brand-new **"Liberty Plaza"** (Stephen
B. Jacobs Group, 2004), a graceful 287-unit residential tower overlooking Louise Nevelson Plaza and Chase Manhattan Plaza, funded in part by State-issued Liberty Bonds.

Back across William Street is the 44-story **Home Insurance Company
Building** (Office of Alfred Easton Poor, 1966) on a neat triangular plaza. A
plaque marks the **site of Thomas Jefferson's residence** while he lived in New
York City, serving as the nation's first Secretary of State. New York was the seat
of the federal government when Jefferson took office on March 21, 1790.

No. 100 William Street, on the northeast corner of Platt Street, is the city's
first building to take advantage of the special 1970 zoning resolution that encouraged builders to create a covered pedestrian space as an alternative to the open
plaza—outdoor space that was often uninspired and of minimal utilitarian design,
and, of course, subject to the vagaries of the weather. This 21-story building,
sheathed in green slate, was completed in 1972 from plans by Davis, Brody &
Associates with Emery Roth & Sons. Taking advantage of provisions of the new
law, the architects designed an impressive 80-foot *galleria,* cutting diagonally
through the ground floor of the building, providing an attractive arcade between
William and John streets. The arcade is lined with shops, lit in part by angular
windows and light troughs. The building received the Award for Excellence in
Design for 1973 from the New York Society of Architects. Walk through the
stainless-steel, black glass, and slate *galleria* (open weekdays only).

Continue on William Street to the corner of John Street.

About a hundred yards to the east, at the present corner of John and Gold
streets, was a small hillock covered with bright yellow flowers, which the Dutch
had called *De Gouwenberg,* or Golden Hill. On January 18, 1770, it was the site
of the first bloodshed between the colonists and the British army. Tempers had
been running high since the imposition of the hated tax on tea, and particularly
over the event of the previous night when soldiers knocked down a Liberty Pole
and deposited the remnants in front of a tavern that was the meeting place of the
Sons of Liberty. That afternoon several thousand citizens massed in "The Fields"
near Broadway to vow punishment to any soldiers caught armed in the streets.

on both sides, a running brawl broke out between the mob and 20 British soldiers. Both groups retired to nearby Golden Hill where they were met by a detachment of regulars who opened fire on the civilians, killing one and wounding several. The encounter, known as the **Battle of Golden Hill,** occurred two months before the Boston Massacre and five years before the first major hostilities at Bunker Hill.

Turn left on John Street.

The John Street United Methodist Church, 44 John Street, built in 1841, is the third on the site. The oldest Methodist church in America, organized by Irish Lutheran immigrants in 1761, was built on this site seven years later and traces its roots to John Wesley, the founder of Methodism. Under the leadership of Philip Embury and Barbara Heck, the congregation, which had been meeting in a rigging loft on Horse and Cart Street (now William Street), established the meeting house. Since that time, the building has been rebuilt twice, in 1818 and 1841, and was restored in 1965. Spend a moment and enjoy the intimate quality of the Georgian-style interior, including the original Wesley Chapel. Built in late Georgian style, the church is somewhat austere, yet cozy and inviting. Many of the original artifacts from the 1768 chapel still remain, including candelabra, John Wesley's great clock, foot warmers, and Embury's hand-carved pulpit. Climb the staircase to the gallery for a good perspective of the interior. There is a little museum that is open Mon., Wed., Fri., 11:30 A.M. to 3:00 P.M. The small brownstone church is a delightful surprise in the bustling financial district.

One Federal Reserve Plaza, officially 33 Maiden Lane, is a striking example of now-fading post-modernism; it was designed in 1984 by Philip Johnson and John Burgee to be contextual with the adjoining Federal Reserve Bank. The location had originally been set aside for an annex to the Bank, but plans changed, and instead, a massive overpowering 26-story "castle," dominated by four crenellated circular tan brick towers, arose on the site. The cavernous lobby, open only on weekdays, is worth a visit.

End of tour. The subway entrance is in the lobby. On weekends walk one block north on Nassau Street to Fulton Street, then left to Broadway.

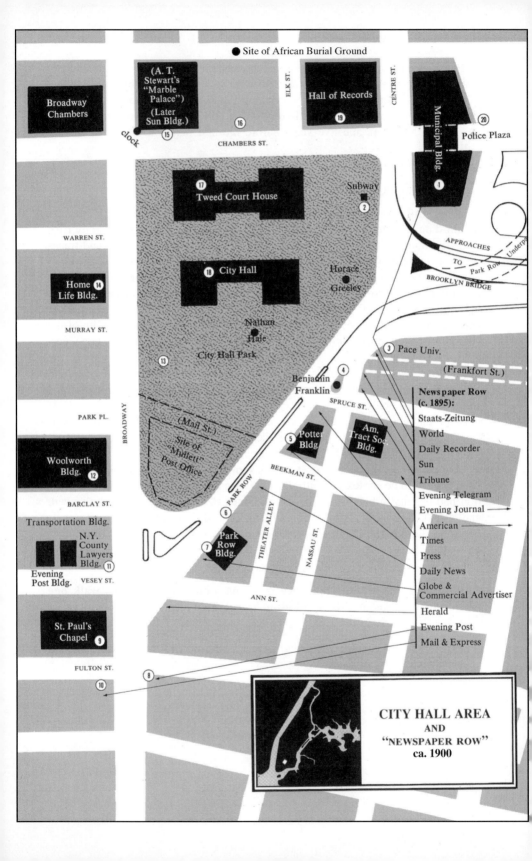

● Site of African Burial Ground

Broadway Chambers

(A. T. Stewart's "Marble Palace") (Later Sun Bldg.) ⑮

clock

⑯

ELK ST.

Hall of Records ⑲

CENTRE ST.

Municipal Bldg. ①

⑳

Police Plaza

CHAMBERS ST.

WARREN ST.

Tweed Court House ⑰

Subway ②

APPROACHES

TO

BROOKLYN BRIDGE

Underp

MURRAY ST.

Home Life Bldg. ⑭

City Hall ⑱

Horace Greeley

Nathan Hale

City Hall Park

⑬

③ Pace Univ.

(Frankfort St.)

PARK PL.

BROADWAY

Benjamin Franklin

④

SPRUCE ST.

Newspaper Row (c. 1895):

Staats-Zeitung

World

Daily Recorder

Sun

Tribune

Evening Telegram

Evening Journal →

American →

Times

Press

Daily News

Globe & Commercial Advertiser

Herald

Evening Post

Mail & Express

(Mail St.)

Site of "Mullett" Post Office

Potter Bldg. ⑤

Am. Tract Soc. Bldg.

Woolworth Bldg. ⑫

BARCLAY ST.

Transportation Bldg.

N.Y. County Lawyers Bldg. ⑪

Evening Post Bldg.

VESEY ST.

St. Paul's Chapel ⑨

FULTON ST.

⑩

PARK ROW

⑥

BEEKMAN ST.

THEATER ALLEY

NASSAU ST.

⑦ Park Row Bldg.

ANN ST.

⑧

CITY HALL AREA
AND
"NEWSPAPER ROW"
ca. 1900

3. City Hall, Old "Newspaper Row," Foley Square, and "Five Points"

[Subways: 4, 5, 6 to Brooklyn Bridge–City Hall; J, M, Z to Chambers Street; N, R to City Hall. Buses: M1, M6, M15, M22 to City Hall Park.]

The tour begins at Centre and Chambers streets.

1. Classic in style and original in design, the imposing **Municipal Building** is our greatest civic skyscraper and the focus of the new Civic Center plan. In scale it is complementary to nearby City Hall as well as to the modern counterparts mushrooming about it. Built in 1914 from plans by McKim, Mead & White, it now houses only a fraction of the city offices that oversee the functioning of the metropolis. Particularly attractive is the row of freestanding columns, the extensive sculpture work, and the lofty colonnaded tower topped by Adolph A. Weinman's 25-foot-high gilt statue of *Civic Fame.* Pause for a moment to examine the sculpture: on the north arch, *Progress*; on the north panel, *Civic Duty*; on the central arch, *Guidance* and *Executive Power*; on the south panel, *Civic Pride*; and on the south arch, *Prudence.* Between the windows on the second floor are symbols of the various city departments. Note the collection of plaques, among which is the "triple-X" emblem of the city of Amsterdam, Holland. A lavish subway entrance is incorporated into the south section, under a vaulted ceiling. Chambers Street, which originally passed through the building, is now closed to vehicular traffic and forms a part of a pedestrian mall leading to Police Plaza. (We will return later after a loop around City Hall Park.)

*The City Hall area from atop the American Telephone & Telegraph Company Building, ca. 1917.
In front of the lofty Woolworth Tower (the tallest skyscraper in the world at the time) is the Second
Empire–style "Mullett" Post Office, which virtually obscures City Hall from view. To the left rear
are the "Tweed" Court House and twin wings of the Emigrant Industrial Savings Bank. To the right,
the massive Municipal Building faces the diminutive Probate Court Building. Farther to the right
are the twin cupolas of the Park Row Building, just beyond the narrow St. Paul Building in the right
foreground. (American Telephone & Telegraph Company)*

Cross Centre Street to City Hall Park.

"The First Municipal Rapid Transit Railroad of the City of New York" was the brainchild of financier August Belmont, and took four years (and three mayors) to build (1900–04). The first station, City Hall, is no longer in service, although local No. 6 trains still rumble past it on a loop underneath City Hall Park. The original line followed the present Lexington Avenue route to Grand Central, swung west under 42nd Street to Times Square, along what is now the shuttle route, then north on Broadway to 145th Street. Down the subway stairs, in front of the change booth, is the startling overhead steel sculpture *Cable Crossing* by Mark Gebian (1996). (It won't cost you a token to see it.)

2. The statue of Horace Greeley in the park was executed in 1890 by John Quincy Adams Ward, and was moved here from its former site in front of the Tribune Building in 1916. Ward was the first American sculptor not trained abroad. His sculpture is typical of post–Civil War realism and captures the relaxed attitude, moon face, and odd beard of the *Tribune's* founder. The base is by Richard Morris Hunt. Horace Greeley (1811–72) founded the New York *Tribune,* which he edited for 30 years. The newspaper was published in a building across Park Row designed by Richard Morris Hunt in 1873 [*see* second photo in this chapter]. Greeley was an outspoken reformer and fighter for social justice. He attacked slavery, championed women's rights, promoted labor unions, fought railroad monopolies, promoted westward expansion ("Go West young man, go West!"), and waged an unsuccessful campaign for the presidency, losing to Grant in 1872.

Near Horace Greeley is a **replica of one of the original subway entrance kiosks,** although this one is designed to provide elevator service to the subway station below (4, 5, and 6 lines). Note the **bishop's crook lampposts** around and in back of City Hall.

Continue south about 100 yards.

3. Across Park Row (Centre Street joins it at this point), where modern Pace University is situated, was the beginning of the so-called **"Newspaper Row"** from the 1840s till after the turn of the century. In the year 1893, for example, there were 19 daily newspapers printed in the City of New York plus a score of foreign-language papers. In the year 1993, there were only four, yet the population of the city has grown from a million and a half in 1893 to almost five times that number!

Where the Municipal Building's south section is now was the site of the building of the *New-Yorker Staats-Zeitung,* the largest German-language newspaper in the country (and still publishing). To the right of the intertwining ramps of the Brooklyn Bridge stood the 26-story gold-domed *New York World,* the tallest building in the world when completed in 1890. Designed by George B. Post, the "World Tower" was a dominant feature of the lower Manhattan skyline. After Joseph Pulitzer purchased the *World* seven years earlier, the newspaper soon became one of the most literate and influential in the city.

Immediately to its right, across narrow Frankfort Street, stood the **Sun Building.** The *Sun* (not the present newspaper of the same name and logo) really

City Hall and its panorama of newspaper office buildings around 1910. Center to right, the domed World, *the diminutive* Sun, *and Richard Morris Hunt's Tribune Tower. The* Times *had moved uptown from the large building at the right. Between City Hall and the* World *is the Park Row terminal of the Second Avenue El, connected to a large iron train shed serving Brooklyn Bridge trains. Note the kiosk entrance to the now-abandoned City Hall subway station (although trains still roll by its darkened platform underneath). (New-York Historical Society)*

"shone" after its acquisition by Charles Anderson Dana, becoming the city's first penny newspaper, with a broad popular appeal. The paper lived out its remaining years in a building that will be discussed shortly.

Adjacent to the *Sun* stood the exuberant Victorian Gothic–style **Tribune Building.** The *Tribune* was acknowledged as New York's most important newspaper. When Greeley left the newspaper to help found the Republican party, he left the management to Whitelaw Reid, himself an active political leader (minister to France and unsuccessful candidate for vice-president in 1892). Reid was one of a line of distinguished journalists who began their careers on the *"Trib"*; others

Dominating the lower Manhattan skyline at the turn of the century was the 26-story gold-domed "World Tower," the tallest building in the world when it was completed in 1890. Designed by George B. Post for Joseph Pulitzer's Evening World, *it was demolished in the early 1950s to make way for new approaches to the Brooklyn Bridge. (New-York Historical Society)*

were Carl Schurz, William Dean Howells, Charles A. Dana, Henry James, Bayard Taylor, and Margaret Fuller, to name but a few. When the Tribune Tower was demolished in 1975, the city lost a great architectural treasure.

4. A bit farther to the left across Park Row, we see little **Printing House Square** with Ernst Plassman's statue of Benjamin Franklin, presented in 1872. Behind Franklin, at the corner of Spruce Street, is the **former American Tract Society Building.** Designed in 1896 by R. H. Robertson, it is a massive Romanesque Revival–style edifice that no longer houses any religious publishing concern, and is known merely by its address, No. 150 Nassau Street. It is now a condominium.

A block east of Printing House Square, on William Street, were William Randolph Hearst's *New York American* (an outgrowth of the earlier *Morning Journal*) and the *New York Evening Journal*. His *Journal* represented the archetype of "yellow journalism," as its rabble rousing and drum beating were held in great part responsible for our entry into the Spanish-American War.

To the right, at the corner of Park Row (No. 41), is the **former New York Times Building,** now an integral part of the Pace University campus. Designed in 1889 by George B. Post, and later remodeled by Robert Maynicke (1895), it housed the *Times* until its move to Longacre Square (now Times Square) in 1904. Note the plaque commemorating "Newspaper Row."

5. South of the former New York Times Building is the dazzlingly ornate **Potter Building** (38 Park Row), constructed in 1883. It was one of the first fireproof "skyscrapers," built with an iron framework encased in the then brand-new terra-cotta building material, and was the first major building to sport an ornamental terra-cotta façade in both cast and pressed forms. The fireproof quality of terra-cotta was appropriately chosen, as the predecessor on the site, the old New York World Building, was destroyed a year before in one of the city's most spectacular blazes. For a time, the *Press* was published in the Potter Building. It is now a luxury residence.

To the right rear, at 5 Beekman Street, are the twin pyramidal towers of the curious **Temple Court Building.**

6. "Newspaper Row" continued with a line of five-story brick buildings that housed a number of popular dailies. The *New York Daily News,* at 25 Park Row, was a relatively small evening paper at the turn of the century, and pro-Democratic at that. Adjoining was the *Morning Advertiser,* and two doors farther, the *Mail and Express.* Cyrus Field purchased the *Evening Mail* and the *Evening Express* in 1880 and 1882, respectively, and made them a financially successful enterprise.

The Park Theatre, ca. 1820, on Park Row, facing City Hall. One of the nation's first legitimate theaters, it was built at the time of the American Revolution. (Consolidated Edison Company of New York)

He later housed them in an interesting, rococo, T-shaped building near the corner of Fulton Street. The *Recorder* was at No. 21 and nearby, the *Evening Telegram.* Near Ann Street was the *Globe and Commercial Advertiser,* at the time the oldest newspaper in New York, dating from 1797.

7. When completed in 1899, the lofty **Park Row Building,** at No. 15, was the tallest in the world, and its twin cupolas added interest and variety to the growing skyline. The skyscraper was designed by R. H. Robertson, and the four caryatids (including the 16 figures on the cupola) are attributed to J. Massey Rhind.

Park Row during the late 18th century was the center of a lively **theater district.** The parallel street behind Park Row, between Beekman and Ann streets, is narrow Theater Alley. Although there is no theater there today, it was the site of the Park Theatre, New York's most famous playhouse from 1798 to 1848, and featured such notable actors as Edmund Keen and Edwin Booth. (Take a quick walk around the block.)

The southeast corner of Park Row and Ann Street has had a long and varied history. **P. T. Barnum's American Museum** delighted and deceived audiences from 1842 until it burned down in 1865 and featured such acts as Gen. Tom Thumb, a bearded lady, soprano Jenny Lind, and a variety of exotic animal acts. Who can forget Barnum's trick to persuade an oversized crowd to leave by announcing, "This way to the Egress"?

A year later, newspaper tycoon James Gordon Bennett erected his famous white marble French Second Empire–style **Herald Building** (No. 222 Broadway). The newspaper had been founded in 1835 and soon gained popularity for its frequent "scoops," as well as for printing news of the financial world. Although a penny newspaper, it made Bennett a fortune. His son, James Gordon Bennett, Jr., startled the "Fourth Estate" by moving the *Herald* uptown in 1894 to a magnificent McKim, Mead & White *palazzo* on what is now Herald Square. Although the Herald Building is now gone from the uptown square, the Bennett Clock still rings the hours while figures with hammers strike an enormous bell.

When the Bennett's Park Row building was razed early in the 20th century, it was replaced by the **St. Paul Building** (222 Broadway), which in turn was demolished and replaced by the present 25-story building, originally known as the **Western Electric Building.** It recently was remodeled for Merrill Lynch.

8. Occupying the same relative position one block south was the **Evening Post Building.** Founded in 1801 by Alexander Hamilton, the *Evening Post* was possibly the most conservative of all New York dailies. Under the leadership of editor William Cullen Bryant, the paper spoke out for free trade. Bryant, by the way, staunchly opposed allowing women to enter the journalism field. Later, under Carl Schurz, the paper adopted a more liberal attitude, both politically and toward women. In 1906 it moved to new quarters on Vesey Street (to be seen shortly).

9. The oldest church in Manhattan (and the oldest building as well) is magnificent **St. Paul's Chapel.** Turning its back on Broadway, it faces a peaceful churchyard, oblivious to the noise and clamor of the crowded thoroughfare. St. Paul's, a chapel of Trinity Church downtown, was completed in 1766, the tower and steeple in 1796. Architect Thomas McBean undoubtedly was influenced by London's St. Martin's-in-the-Fields when he designed this majestic landmark. It is built of locally quarried Manhattan schist, and the tower (by James Crommelin Lawrence) is of brownstone. The church is an almost perfect example of Georgian style, reflecting the elegant tradition of the Colonial period. Much of the interior decoration of this National Historic Landmark was done by Pierre L'Enfant, the French-born architect who later became a Major of Engineers in the Continental Army and helped lay out the City of Washington, D.C. One can still see the pew where Washington regularly worshipped. Among the list of distinguished worshippers were Prince William (later King William IV), Lords Cornwallis and Howe, Maj. John André, the Marquis de Lafayette, and Presidents Grover Cleveland and Benjamin Harrison. [*See* Chapter 1 for a description of the interior and its role in the World Trade Center disaster.]

The quiet churchyard is well worth a visit. Note the numerous 18th-century headstones with names of well-known families of early new York.

To the right of the churchyard on Vesey Street are two interesting landmark buildings. At No. 20 is the **Garrison Building,** formerly the home of the *Evening Post,* from 1907 to 1926. This is a rare example of Art Nouveau architecture. The bronze-finished cast-iron spandrels are decorated with the colophons of well-known 16th- and 17th-century printers, and the statues on the ninth floor represent "The Four Periods of Publicity"—the Spoken Word, the Written Word, the Printed Word, and the Newspaper, by Gutzon Borglum and Estelle Rumbold Kohn. The building was designed by Robert D. Kohn in 1906 (sculptor Estelle was his wife).

To its right, at No. 14, is the **New York County Lawyers Association Building**—"the Home of Law." Constructed in 1930 of Vermont marble and limestone, it was designed by Cass Gilbert in a neo-Federal style. Its auditorium is a reproduction of Independence Hall in Philadelphia. Vesey Street is named for William Vesey, first rector of Trinity Church.

10. Looking south from the churchyard, across Fulton Street, is the multicolumned **former American Telephone & Telegraph Building,** No. 195 Broadway, built in 1917 from plans by Welles Bosworth. It was formerly crowned with a gilt statue, *The Spirit of Communication,* by Evelyn Beatrice Longman; but the statue was removed and placed in the atrium of AT&T's former headquarters at 550 Madison Avenue. It has since been brought to AT&T's Somerset County, N.J. campus. A weekday visit to the spacious lobby reveals an interesting and educational display, including sculptor Chester Beach's marble and bronze statue, *Service to the Nation,* and the splendid bronze doors. Interestingly, the ex-American "Tel & Tel" Building, with its eight tiers of colonnades, has more columns than the Parthenon—or any other building, for that matter.

11. Turn north on Broadway to No. 255. **The Transportation Building,** designed by York & Sawyer in 1915, occupies the site of one of New York's most celebrated hostelries, the Astor House, which catered to affluent visitors from 1836 to 1913.

12. Possibly the most beautiful commercial building in the world is the dramatic Gothic Revival–style **Woolworth Building,** 233 Broadway. When dedicated in 1913, the Rev. S. Parkes Cadman, a famous New York clergyman, in a burst of enthusiastic rhetoric, referred to it as a "Cathedral of Commerce"—and the sobriquet still stands. Many believe it to be architect Cass Gilbert's greatest triumph. Ris-

The Federal Building at the intersection of Broadway and Park Row became the city's main post office in 1875. An elaborate Second Empire pile designed by government architect A. B. Mullett, it obstructed the view of City Hall until its demolition just before World War II. (Museum of the City of New York)

ing 729 feet (plus 1 inch!), the Woolworth Tower eclipsed the Metropolitan Life Tower to become the tallest building in the world for 17 years. The opening ceremony was climaxed when President Wilson pressed a button in Washington, illuminating 80,000 bulbs on the 60-story structure. Two years later, at the Panama-Pacific Exposition, it received a gold medal as the "most beautiful building in all the world erected to commerce." The observation deck on the 55th floor, which unfortunately is no longer open to the public, provided a breathtaking view, as visitors were whisked to the top at dizzying speed in the newest in high-speed electric elevators.

Frank Woolworth, the founder of the once ubiquitous five-and-ten-cent-store chain, paid the $15,500,000 cost of the building in cash! Note the typical Gothic elements: gargoyles, flying buttresses, arches, spires, traceries, trefoils, etc., all seen to good advantage after an extensive face-lift of the entire building. The style is followed in the interior as well. The lobby presents one of the most striking interior spaces in the city, with its vaulted, mosaic ceiling that sparkles in a jewellike effect; the delicate bronzework; the walls of veined marble; an imposing grand staircase; lacy wrought-iron cornices covered with gold leaf; polished terrazzo floors; and the amusing little sculptured caricatures of Mr. Woolworth (counting his nickels and dimes), Cass Gilbert (holding a model of his pet project), Louis Horowitz, the builder, and others involved with the construction of the "Cathedral."

13. Cross Broadway to **City Hall Park.** Called the Common in the 18th century, it was then at the northern edge of the city, a triangular plot formed by the confluence of the Bloomingdale Road (now Broadway) and the Boston Post Road (now Park Row and farther north, the Bowery). On the Common a prison was constructed, and nearby, a poor house, as well as a powder house and barracks as part of the city's defenses. A short distance to the west on the now demapped College Place was King's College (now Columbia University). As the city expanded northward, it became a popular public gathering place, and figured in a series of anti-British incidents for a ten-year period prior to the Revolution, in which patriots forcefully displayed their displeasure with the Crown by harassing the military post and erecting a series of Liberty Poles. After the Revolution, the city entered an era of prosperity and growth that required the construction of a new City Hall. In 1811 the present seat of town government was erected in what was the new City Hall Park. The park was enlarged to its present size in the late 1930s with the razing of the old Federal Building that occupied most of the southern corner of the triangle and housed a post office and court. The so-called "Mullett" (after the architect) Post Office was a massive granite pile of "wedding cake" built in 1878 in the French Second Empire style; its demolition provided light and space and a sweeping view of City Hall.

Recently renovated, City Hall Park is a pleasant oasis in chaotic downtown Manhattan. The highlights of the southern section are the 1871 **Jacob Wrey Mould fountain,** returned from "exile" in Crotona Park in the Bronx, and a new iron fence cast from an earlier one that had been sent to a cemetery upstate.

On the platform adjacent to the fountain is a large circular sculpture—a grand display of laser-cut pictures of Old New York, surrounded by a chronological sequence of city history from 1625 to 1999. Take a moment and walk around it.

Note: In recent times, tighter security needs, especially after the 9/11 disaster, forced the city to close the gates on the east and west sides of City Hall Park, as well as to restrict public access to City Hall. The southern portion of the park, however, is open and is very attractively landscaped. **The Statue of Nathan Hale,** by Frederick MacMonnies (1893), with base by Stanford White, which formerly graced the west side of the park and was a favorite with visitors and young schoolchildren, was moved deep into the park; alas, only its backside is visible through the gates.

Nathan Hale, a young school teacher captured by the British for spying early in the Revolutionary War, is depicted standing with hands and feet bound, with a disdainful look as he is about to be hanged. Legend has it that his last words were, "I only regret that I have but one life to lose for my country." On the lawn beyond, the flagpole commemorates the raising of the five **Liberty Poles** by Colonial patriots. Those poles were anathema to the British, not only for their symbolism, but also because they were cut from the prohibited white pine, a tree reserved exclusively for the masts of His Majesty's navy. The name Sons of Liberty was first applied to those who demonstrated against the hated Stamp Act by freedom-sympathizer Lt. Col. Sir Isaac Barré, a Member of Parliament, who is

The recently completed American Telephone & Telegraph Company Building dwarfs St. Paul's Chapel at Fulton Street and Broadway in this ca. 1919 view. Nestled in the T-shaped structure is the Victorian-style Evening Mail Building, which was later demolished when AT&T extended its building to Fulton Street. To the extreme left is the St. Paul Building, now the site of the Merrill Lynch Building. (The American Telephone & Telegraph Company)

The oldest German daily in the United States, the Staats-Zeitung, *began publishing in this Victorian pile on Park Row and Centre Street in the 1870s. Statues of Gutenberg and Franklin by Ernst Plassman adorn the third floor. To the right is the City Hall terminal of the Second Avenue El. The site is now occupied by the Municipal Building. (Museum of the City of New York)*

The buildings at Centre and Chambers streets represent a variety of styles. Note the pedestrian crossings, slightly elevated so rain could run off and vehicles would slow down, and also much easier on the feet than cobblestones. (Museum of the City of New York)

The Rhinelander Building at Duane and Rose streets was demolished in 1971. The marble entrance columns as well as the barred "Old Sugar House" window are now preserved on Police Plaza. (New York City Landmarks Preservation Commission)

Mulberry Street with its infamous "bend" between Park and Bayard streets in the early 1880s was, and remains, heavily Italian. Mulberry Bend Park (later Columbus Park) replaced the buildings on the left side of the street. (New-York Historical Society)

One of the few surviving photos (left) of the Beach Pneumatic Subway shows the approach to the Warren Street station in 1870. Below, the remains of the subway car found in a 1912 excavation. (New-York Historical Society)

remembered with a plaque on the far side of the lawn (beside City Hall) and also in the names of Barre, Vermont, and Wilkes-Barre, Pennsylvania. At the side of City Hall is a **bishop's crook lamppost.** Several more of these cast-iron relics have been rescued or replicated and placed around the building.

Located under Broadway, between Murray and Warren streets, was the **City's first subway.** In a short-lived experiment using compressed air for propulsion, Alfred Ely Beach constructed a 312-foot-long tube that was opened to the public in 1870. The subway was built in secret to prevent interference from corrupt "Boss" Tweed who had his own plans for mass transit. The passengers rode in a luxurious car, built to fit snugly against the tube's wall, and the "train" was propelled by air from a huge fan blowing through the tunnel. An elaborate waiting room was fully carpeted and furnished with paintings, a fountain, and even a grand piano. The entrance, waiting room, and ticket office were located at the southwest corner of Warren Street and Broadway. After his failure to secure adequate financial backing to extend the line, Beach abandoned the pneumatic underground railway a year later. In 1912, workmen excavating for the BMT subway came upon the old tube with its single car and lavish station.

14. No. 255 is the elegant former headquarters of the **Home Life Insurance Company.** Designed in Eclectic style by Napoleon LeBrun and completed in 1894, its pyramided gable atop the building is best seen from a distance.

At the northwest corner of Chambers Street, No. 277, the **Broadway Chambers,** designed by Cass Gilbert and completed in 1900, is a good example of "tri-

New York's first subway was the Beach Pneumatic Tube, built in 1869–70. It ran one block on Broadway from Warren Street to a point just south of Murray Street. In this rendering of the proposed car, the giant steam-operated fan that supplied the power through air pressure cannot be seen. (New-York Historical Society)

partite" skyscraper construction, where the building façade is divided into three basic sections, similar to the components of a Classic column.

15. Situated at the northeast corner of Chambers Street and Broadway is the **former A. T. Stewart "Marble Palace"** [*see* Ladies' Mile, 1]. Designed by John B. Snook and Joseph Trench, with marble cutting by Ottavino Gori, it was completed in 1846, and promptly became a trendsetter in American architecture. As the first commercial Anglo-Italianate–style building, its *palazzo* style was copied widely; and in this extravagant edifice, the tradition of the large retail emporium was firmly established. After Stewart moved his flourishing dry-goods business uptown in 1862, he retained the building as a warehouse. His later successor added two additional floors, and in 1884 the building was converted to commercial use. In 1917, the *Sun* moved in from across the Park, publishing here until its demise in 1952. The attractive **Sun Clock** on the corner of the building, bearing the motto "The Sun it Shines for All," has been preserved through the efforts of a local committee of businessmen and city employees who raised the funds to restore it, and it has become a kind of unofficial landmark. The *Sun*'s thermometer on the opposite corner, however, remains adamantly at 80°. In 1970, New York City acquired the building, and finally, more than three decades later, plans are under way to restore the exterior and renovate the upper floors.

In the Municipal Building, visit **Citybooks,** New York's municipal bookshop where you can purchase the *Green Book*, the official city directory, plus a selection of New York books, memorabilia, and souvenirs.

One block north of Chambers Street, between Reade and Duane streets, is the new **Federal Office Building,** 290 Broadway (Hellmuth Obata Kassabaum, 1993). Excavation for the structure was preceded by the required archaeological investigation, and it was then that about 400 graves were unearthed dating to the mid-18th century. Historians had long known that a "Negros Burial Ground" existed in this area, which in the 1750s was outside the city limits. The lands that encompassed what is now City Hall Park, the few blocks above, and part of Foley Square, had been set aside as common grounds by the Dutch colonial government of Nieuw Amsterdam. The northern part of the Commons was used as a graveyard for as many as 20,000 slaves and free blacks until the late 18th century, as well as a potter's field and a burial ground for American prisoners during the Revolutionary War. The discovery revealed the nation's earliest known African American cemetery (1712–13), and because of the site's historic significance, the Landmarks Preservation Commission designated the **African Burial Ground and the Commons** as an historic district. A design competition for a permanent memorial was announced by the government, but, to date, no action has been taken. The Burial Ground has the unique distinction of being the city's only underground landmark with no visible traces. Return to Chambers Street.

16. No. 51 Chambers Street is the **former Emigrant Industrial Savings Bank Building** (Raymond F. Almirall, 1908). Now owned by the city, its double towers, topped by spread eagles and globes, must have inspired confidence in the strength and security of the bank.

17. The Italianate "villa" back-to-back with City Hall, No. 52, is the famous (or infamous) Criminal Courts Building. Known familiarly as the **Tweed Court-**

Once faced with demolition as part of the projected Civic Center, the Criminal Courts Building on Chambers Street behind City Hall is a monument to civic corruption. Between $8 million and $12 million of taxpayers' money went into "Boss" Tweed's pocket. The building, now a designated landmark, serves as additional office space for City Hall. In the background, the ghosts of the former World Trade Center towers loom high above the former. (Photo by author)

City Hall, 1826, from a colored aquatint by W. G. Hall, Mangin and McComb's French Renaissance–Georgian–style building, completed in 1811, is considered one of New York's greatest architectural treasures. (The J. Clarence Davies Collection, Museum of the City of New York)

house, it stands as a monument to graft and corruption. Completed in 1872, it took nine years to construct, and the city's treasury found itself between $8 million and $12.5 million poorer. Approximately three-quarters of that amount was diverted into the pockets of "Boss" William Marcy Tweed and his Ring. Nevertheless, the city did inherit an attractive architectural addition. Its future, however, was in question, as the Mayor's Civic Center Task Force reported that the much needed renovation would be "substantially more costly" than building a new City Hall Annex. But considerable opposition arose from within the administration and from the public at large, and the historic Tweed Courthouse was spared. Subsequent landmark designation assured its future. A major renovation was undertaken in 1999–2001, returning the building to its original grand Italianate appearance.

18. The greatest architectural treasure in the city is palatial **City Hall,** built in 1811. The competition for its design was won by Frenchman Joseph F. Mangin and Scotsman John McComb, Jr., who combined their talents to produce a French Renaissance–Georgian–style building of consummate beauty. McComb remained the guiding hand throughout the period of construction, but Mangin seems to have slipped into obscurity.

City Hall has always been the nerve center and civic hub of the metropolis, the site of many public celebrations, and the traditional place of welcome for heroes. Noteworthy were the receptions given in honor of Lafayette, the opening of the Erie Canal, the state visits of a parade of royalty, the welcoming of Lindbergh in 1927, and, in more recent times, of the hometown winners of the baseball World Series. The rotunda of City Hall was also the laying-in-state site of a number of famous citizens: Maj. Gen. William J. Worth [*see* Madison Square, 18], Horace Greeley, John Howard Payne, President U. S. Grant, and Mayors Gaynor and Mitchell. Nothing, however, could equal the homage paid to Abraham Lincoln after his assassination, when his remains lay in the rotunda on April 24 and 25, 1865. In the following funeral procession, 60,000 New Yorkers joined in the mournful parade up Broadway.

The structure has undergone many renovations and repairs throughout its history. The first addition was an illuminated public clock—the first in the city—installed in the cupola in 1831. In the same year an ugly fire tower was erected on the roof, remaining for 34 years until the volunteer fire department was replaced by a paid staff. In 1858 City Hall suffered extensive damage in a roaring blaze resulting from a fireworks display on the roof during the Atlantic Cable Celebration. Following the fire, City Hall began to deteriorate, neglected through the years by many corrupt city administrations. Someone referred to those days as the "tobacco juice period," as the building became more and more decrepit and dismal. It was even suggested that City Hall be demolished in favor of a new, "more modern" municipal building.

In 1895 the Board of Aldermen declared that "…the present appearance and condition of the City Hall is an offence to the sight of the community and a menace to the health of those whose business necessitates their presence in the building." A minor renovation followed. During the next 20 years, additional restoration was conducted with outside philanthropic assistance. In 1917, fire struck again, this time from a workman's charcoal burner in the cupola. Major reconstruction was begun under the direction of Grosvenor Atterbury, who restored the copper dome to its original appearance. Little was done, however, to save the decaying exterior until 1954, when the Board of Estimate voted the necessary funds for a complete restoration of the building. The eroded Massachusetts marble façade was carefully cut away and replaced with Alabama veined limestone, the base with Missouri red granite. The north façade, which was originally faced with brownstone ("Who would see it, since nobody of importance in those days lived north of City Hall"), was also refaced with limestone.

The interior, too, was completely restored to what was believed to be its original elegance. Among the most attractive features are the double curved staircase, the colonnaded rotunda, the Office of the President of the City Council, the City Council Chamber, the Board of Estimate Chamber, the Mayor's Reception Room, the Committee of the Whole Room, and the Governor's Room (now a museum) with its famous Trumbull portrait of Washington and the desk used by Washington at Federal Hall.

The clock in the City Hall cupola has kept perfect time for many years, but the bells had been silent for a generation. Many may recall the old announcements on the municipal radio station, WNYC, giving the time "by the century-old bells of historic City Hall." The striking mechanism now has been repaired,

The elaborate City Hall subway station, closed to the public for many years, now serves only as a turnaround for the No. 6 trains after their last stop at the Brooklyn Bridge station. In this photo, taken in 1979, the last surviving set of old IRT subway cars snakes around the station's sharp curve on a final trip before being consigned to the NYC Transit Museum in Brooklyn. Note the impressive arches with their Guastavino tile vaults. The decorative chandeliers must have added a homey touch when this first subway station was opened in 1904.

thanks to the city's newly designated clockmaster, Marvin Schneider. He was appointed officially to the position after tending a number of old city clocks for 12 years, and once again the bells in the old City Hall clock ring out the hours.

In the sidewalk in front of City Hall is a tablet marking "the first shovelful of dirt" for the **construction of the New York City subway,** March 24, 1900 (unfortunately, it is not accessible now to visitors). The first line (now the Lexington Avenue subway) was opened four years later. A loop of that line passes directly underneath, and is used by the No. 6 trains to turn around at the end of the line. It passes through the **abandoned City Hall station,** which is still intact with its original Guastavino tile vaults and even chandeliers, but can be seen only by the motormen and conductors. [*See* photo on previous page.]

Return to Park Row, past the Horace Greeley statue, to the corner of Chambers Street.

19. Directly across Chambers Street is the city's second most splendid Beaux Arts–style building (after the old Custom House at Bowling Green), the **Surrogate's Court, originally the Hall of Records,** No. 31. The sculpture groups at the entrance represent "New York in its Infancy" and "New York in Revolutionary Times," by Philip Martiny. The eight cornice figures are: David Pietersen de Vries, Caleb Heathcote, DeWitt Clinton, Abram S. Hewitt, Philip Hone, Peter Stuyvesant, Cadwallader D. Colden, and James Duane, all by the same sculptor. In the attic are ten allegorical figures by Henry Kirke Bush-Brown. The building dates from 1901 and was designed by architects John R. Thomas, and Horgan and Slattery. On a weekday, visit the colonnaded rotunda. This is also the location of the **Municipal Archives,** an excellent collection of city history and an important resource for researchers.

20. Cross Centre Street to the Municipal Building, and walk left around the building into **Police Plaza.** As the first major accomplishment in the Civic Center plan, this enormous public space, together with its decorations and adjoining modern structures, is a tribute to the Office of Lower Manhattan Development, as well as to the architectural firm of Gruzen & Partners.

As you enter the Plaza, designed by landscape architect W. Paul Friedberg, turn right to the small **"prison window" monument** of the Rhinelander Sugar House, which commemorates the dismal Revolutionary War prison in which hundreds of American patriots died of starvation, neglect, and disease. When the Sugar House was demolished in 1892, a window from the prison was preserved and built into the Rhinelander Building, which occupied the site until it, too, was razed in 1968, to make way for the new Police Headquarters Building. The window was rescued again and mounted here in the Plaza.

In the center of the three-acre plaza—the city's largest public plaza—is the arresting **steel sculpture** by Bernard Rosenthal, *Five in One,* consisting of five 30-foot-high rolled steel discs painted bright red.

To the right are rows of honey-locust trees in front of the entrance to a five-tier **Municipal Parking Garage,** hidden beneath the Plaza.

Looking ahead, the dominant feature of Police Plaza is the red-brick-and-concrete **Police Headquarters Building.** Designed by Gruzen & Partners in

Rhinelander's "Old Sugar House," at the corner of Rose and Duane streets, was erected in 1763 and during the Revolutionary War served as a prison during the British occupation of New York. It was demolished in 1892 to make way for an office building, which kept the Rhinelander name. The building preserved a barred window of the "Old Sugar House" prison in its façade, and when the structure was razed in 1968 the window was removed and mounted on a special base adjacent to the Municipal Building, along with a commemorative plaque. (New-York Historical Society)

1972, this $58 million center for "New York's Finest" is a restrained and tasteful addition to the cityscape. Enter (ask permission at the desk), and enjoy the broad lobby with Josef Twirbutt's 20-foot-square brick sculpture, and the vista of the Municipal Building and the panorama of City Hall Park skyscrapers seen through the plate glass entrance windows.

Leaving Police Headquarters, turn left and walk down the staircase to the Madison Street entrance and the "Grecian Ruin." This **group of five Ionic marble columns** is a nostalgic artifact of the old Rhinelander Building, which stood on the site from 1892. [*See* photo on page 91.] To the east is **Murry Bergtraum High School** (Gruzen & Partners, 1976), named for a late president of the Board of Education; and behind it, a New York Telephone Company skyscraper, whose unusual height was achieved by "borrowing" the air rights from the adjacent high school.

Return to Police Plaza.

To the right is the **Federal Court House Annex** and the 12-story **Federal Metropolitan Correctional Center** (Gruzen & Partners, 1973), the lines of its gray split-faced concrete façade blending well with neighboring buildings. Note that the support columns are of the same height as those of adjoining St.

Andrew's Church and the Municipal Building. A special type of tinted shatter-proof glass with built-in alarm system has been installed in the prison section, replacing the traditional gloomy look of barred windows.

St. Andrew's Church was consecrated in 1939, replacing an earlier church, named Carroll Hall, built in 1842. Just before the Civil War when the City Hall area became the center of the printing and newspaper industry, the church received special dispensation to say a "Printer's Mass" at 2:30 A.M. for the night shift of newsmen and printers. It later became the first parish church to offer a noon mass for the growing number of businessmen in the area. The Latin phrase in the frieze means "Blessed are those who walk in the law of the Lord." The Plaza at this point is called St. Andrew's Plaza, although the church's address is 20 Cardinal Hayes Place.

Walk through to Centre Street and Foley Square.

A STROLL AROUND FOLEY SQUARE

Follow the route of the broken line on the Foley Square Area map, beginning (and ending) at St. Andrew's Plaza.

Foley Square, the irregularly shaped open space to the north, is named for Thomas "Big Tom" Foley (1852–1925), who operated a saloon on the site and

The original "Tombs" prison in an 1873 view. Built across Centre Street from the present "Tombs" site, this was the main city jail from 1838 to 1892. Compared to a pharaoh's tomb because of its columns, sun god motifs, and trapezoidal windows, this and the Croton Reservoir at 42nd Street were two examples of Egyptian-style architecture in the city. (Museum of the City of New York)

also held various political positions, including alderman, sheriff, and Tammany Hall political bigwig; he was also the guru of then Gov. Alfred E. Smith. A year after Foley died, the Board of Aldermen decided that the future "square" should be named for him.

U.S. Court of International Trade, 1 Federal Plaza (Alfred Easton Poor, Kahn & Jacobs, Eggers & Higgins, 1966). The customs court is an attractive glassy box set above ground level. Walk under it and explore its broad passageways and ceramic tile murals. During hot summer days, the neighboring community finds it a place of respite.

In the center of the Square is the unusual sculpture *Triumph of the Human Spirit*, by Lorenzo Pace. As the adjacent plaque explains, it is designed as a tribute to the 427 bodies of slaves excavated from the New York City African Burial Ground.

Jacob K. Javits Federal Office Building, 26 Federal Plaza (same architectural firms as above). Built in two sections, in 1967 and 1976, the whole appears to overwhelm the Foley Square complex. The eastern wing, built first, resembles a gargantuan checkerboard.

Department of Health, Hospitals & Sanitation Building (Charles B. Meyers, 1935), 125 Worth Street. Note the names of great men of medicine emblazoned around the frieze of this dignified but otherwise undistinguished civic building.

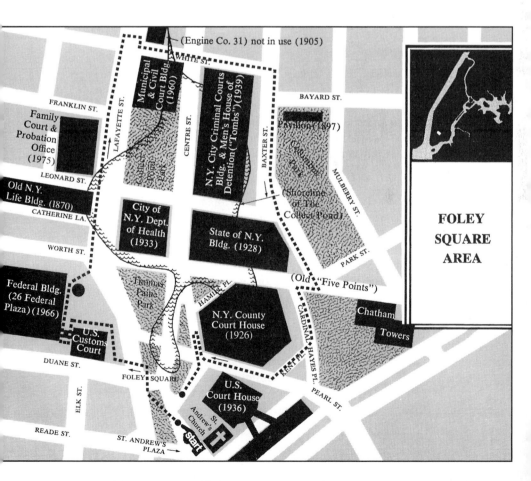

The most notorious section of the city in the mid-19th century was the festering slum and den of criminals called Five Points. In this 1859 print from Valentine's Manual *we see the crossing of three of the five streets: Baxter, Park, and Worth streets. (Museum of the City of New York)*

● **Old New York Life Insurance Company Building,** 346 Broadway (Griffith Thomas, 1870; remodeled and enlarged by McKim, Mead & White, 1896). Architect Thomas created a very imposing but appropriately sober headquarters for the company. Note the two clock towers, minus their cupolas, on this Renaissance Revival–style early skyscraper. The tower facing Broadway once sported a huge iron globe surmounted by an eagle. The company moved its headquarters to Madison Square in 1928, and the building is now temporarily used for government offices and the Clocktower Art Gallery. Cast-iron ornamentation on the Broadway side shows the New York Life Insurance monogram.

Family Court and Office of Probation, 60 Lafayette Street (Haines, Lundberg & Waehler, 1975). A polished black granite behemoth, it is overbearing and pretentious, and its angular façade is distracting rather than relieving.

Municipal and Civil Court Building (William Lascaze and Matthew Del Gaudio, 1960), 111 Centre Street. This undistinguished cubelike building houses the Small Claims Court and the spillover from the Criminal Courts' calendar, as well as the courts of civil claims.

● **Engine Company 31,** 87 Lafayette Street (Napoleon LeBrun & Sons, 1895).
★ This French Renaissance "chateau," no longer in use as a firehouse, is a delightful gem of a building—a pleasant surprise in this neighborhood of towering monoliths. The building is now occupied by Downtown Community Television Center, which provides, among other services, free media services to the community. DCTV claims to offer the most heavily attended media arts classes in the country, providing an opportunity for poor students to study the television arts without cost.

New York City Criminal Courts Building and Men's House of Detention, 100 Centre Street (Harvey Wiley Corbett and Charles B. Meyers, 1939; remodeled by Gruzen & Partners, 1986). The dramatic zigguratlike towers represent the height of the 1930s "moderne" or Art Deco style. Known familiarly as the **"Tombs"** since it incorporates the Men's House of Detention, it was built opposite the site of the original "Tombs" prison (so called because of its Egyptian-style architecture), which stood across Centre Street. The Men's House of Detention was moved in 1974 to Riker's Island, but reopened a few years later to relieve crowding at the island prison.

In the area encompassed by Franklin, Worth, Centre, and Lafayette streets was a small pond known as the **Collect.** A source of fresh water during colonial days, it became polluted as the city grew around it, and was ultimately filled in at the beginning of the 19th century. John Fitch tested his prototype of a steamboat on the Collect in 1796. Aboard was Robert Fulton, who received all the accolades for the invention some years later.

Columbus Park, formerly Mulberry Bend Park, was created just before the turn of the century after the razing of many of the Five Points slums. Its name was changed in 1911.

State of New York Building (1928), 155 Worth Street. Built on a wedge-shaped plot, this functional building is known by all as the location of the Motor Vehicle Bureau.

Five Points [*see* special map] was probably the worst festering slum in the history of this country. So named because of the intersection of three streets, it began as a district of cheap amusement at the beginning of the 19th century, but by 1840

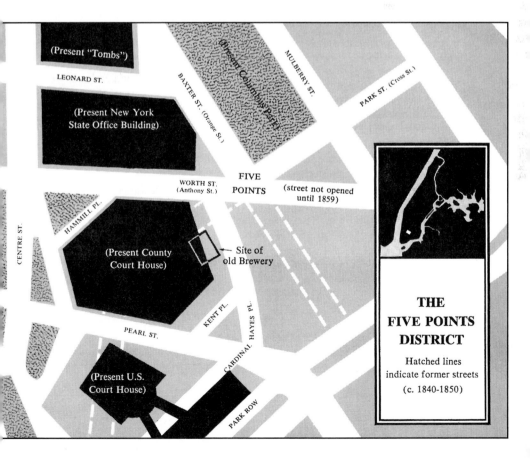

(Present "Tombs")

LEONARD ST.

(Present New York
State Office Building)

BAXTER ST. (Orange St.)

(Present Columbus Park)

MULBERRY ST.

PARK ST. (Cross St.)

CENTRE ST.

HAMMILL PL.

WORTH ST.
(Anthony St.)

FIVE
POINTS

(street not opened
until 1859)

(Present County
Court House)

Site of
old Brewery

KENT PL.

CARDINAL HAYES PL.

PEARL ST.

(Present U.S.
Court House)

PARK ROW

**THE
FIVE POINTS
DISTRICT**

Hatched lines
indicate former streets
(c. 1840-1850)

The Old Brewery at Five Points was the City's most infamous slum. Known locally as the "Den of Thieves," it is shown in this pen and ink sketch, just before its purchase and demolition by the Ladies' Home Missionary Society for the Construction of the Five Points Mission. (Museum of the City of New York)

it had become a foul, crime-ridden "rabbit warren" of the most depraved elements of the city. Centered about an old brewery, whose surrounding lane was known as Murderers' Alley, it housed over a thousand men, women, and children in filth, squalor, and crime. More than a murder a day occurred in the former brewery and its surrounding slums; the area was so dangerous that even the police shunned it. It was the hangout of such notorious gangs as the "Plug Uglies," "Shirt Tails," and "Dead Rabbits." By mid-century the brewery was finally demolished and many of the ramshackle Five Points houses were razed. With the completion of the Foley Square courthouse complex, not a trace remains of that infamous district.

● **New York County Court House** (1926), 60 Centre Street. The New York State Supreme Court occupies this hexagon-shaped building with an enormous Corinthian portico. Architect Guy Lowell won the competition for the unique design of a building to occupy the irregularly shaped plot.

● **United States Court House** (1936), 40 Centre Street. Designed by Cass Gilbert and Cass Gilbert, Jr., its gold pyramid set on a skyscraper shaft above a neo-Classic base is a familiar site on the city skyline. A pedestrian walkway has been created between the Court House and its brand-new Annex. Note the two connecting bridges in the rear. The old powerhouse was preserved, and can be seen nestled in the new addition.

United States Courthouse Annex (Kohn Pederson Fox Associates, 1995), 500 Pearl Street and 140 Worth Street. The contrasting convex and concave façades of this 27-story gray limestone and marble giant are a novel and more interesting addition to the Foley Square complex.

End of tour. Return to Foley Square, turn left (south) on Centre Street to the Municipal Building. Underneath and across the street are the subway entrances.

The Municipal Building is considered New York City's greatest civic skyscraper. As the winner of a design competition for a new city administration building, the firm of McKim, Mead & White, with partner William M. Kendall, planned the 25-story office tower in 1907, with construction completed seven years later. In this dramatic twilight view, it is an imposing presence, diagonally across from City Hall. The ornate limestone façade is topped by a lofty templed cupola, crowned by Adolph Augustus Weinman's gilt statue, Civic Fame. *To the left is the Surrogate's Court–Hall of Records and, visible at the rear, the gilt pyramid of the United States Courthouse on Foley Square. (Photo by Lisa Clifford)*

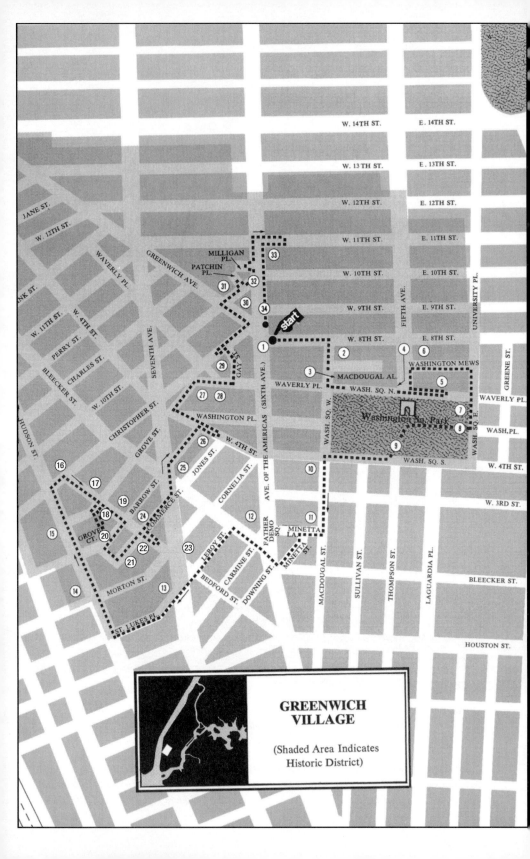

GREENWICH VILLAGE

(Shaded Area Indicates
Historic District)

4. Greenwich Village

[Subways: A, C, E, F, V, S lines to West 4th Street–Washington Square, PATH to 9th Street.]

Greenwich Village, a town within a city, has a unique character and personality of its own. Designated a **Historic District** of New York City, the Village dates back to an old Algonquin Indian settlement called Sapokanickan. When the Dutch arrived in 1626 they named it *Bossen Bouwerie* (Farm in the Woods) and developed it as a large tobacco plantation. After the British captured Nieuw Amsterdam in 1664, the plantation was purchased by naval squadron commander Sir Peter Warren, who then renamed it Greenwich. Gradually the settlement was transformed into a small town, and by the early 19th century, "Village" was added to the name. A series of smallpox and yellow fever epidemics in the lower city in the early 1800s drove thousands of city dwellers northward to the town of Greenwich, seeking the "healthful climate and quiet" of this distant suburb which somehow escaped these recurring plagues.

You may note that the streets of the Village do not conform to the orderly grid pattern of most of Manhattan, since the town of Greenwich had already been established with its own layout of streets before the city expanded northward. As the Village grew, its crazy-quilt pattern of streets spread from the banks of the Hudson River to what is now Broadway. Many of the winding streets were originally cow paths, or followed meandering brooks. One of these waterways, Minetta Brook, still causes problems far beneath today's busy streets, especially when foundations are dug for new buildings. The visitor may be flabbergasted to discover that West 4th Street, for example, runs west only briefly, then abruptly swings north to intersect West 10th, West 11th, and West 12th streets!

In the 19th century the Village began to attract writers and artists, and boasted such residents as O. Henry, Mark Twain, Edgar Allan Poe, Henry James, Stephen Crane, Winslow Homer, John La Farge, and Augustus St. Gaudens. Rents were low and the atmosphere was very attractive. After the turn of the cen-

Engraving of the Jefferson Market Police Court on Sixth Avenue looking north from 9th Street, showing the first train of the Gilbert Elevated Railway (ultimately the Interborough Rapid Transit's Sixth Avenue El), on April 29, 1878. (Museum of the City of New York)

tury, Greenwich Village began to earn its reputation as the cradle of bohemia in America. The rents are much higher now, and many of the *literati* have departed, but the Village still retains much of its charm in its narrow, winding streets, the houses of many architectural styles, the variety of curious shops, and an assortment of colorful Village "types." There are many boutiques, exotic food stores, coffee shops, fine restaurants serving food from many nations, art schools, and drama workshops, as well as the largest private university in the country.

1. The tour begins at the corner of **Avenue of the Americas and West 8th Street,** facing Village Square, the hub of the Village. All New Yorkers refer to Avenue of the Americas by its former (and more logical) name, Sixth Avenue. The sidewalk along the Avenue just south of 8th Street, once a gathering place for exponents of a wide variety of political and religious views, now is lined with street vendors offering books and a wide variety of mostly junk. Walk quickly down 8th Street, once the bustling "main drag" of the Village; now it is a dismal and seedy thoroughfare lined with shoe stores and cheap boutiques, with a number of establishments now boarded-up; however, in mid-block, the **Eighth Street Playhouse** still strives to maintain its tradition as the Village's avant garde movie house. Designed by Frederick Kiesler in 1928 exclusively for the showing of films, it opened as the Film Guild Cinema and was billed as "the first 100% cinema." Turn right at the first corner (Macdougal Street), and walk the short distance to the gates of Macdougal Alley.

● **2. Macdougal Alley,** with its picturesque and individually redesigned carriage houses, is a private dead-end street, of which there are several in the Village. The picturesque little houses were built as stables in the 1850s for the wealthy residents of 8th Street (then called Clinton Place) and Washington Square. Some residents claim that the two gas lamps are the last remaining in the city maintained free by the Consolidated Edison Company, but "'taint so!"

At No. 1, now a restaurant, poet Edwin Arlington Robinson wrote his famous *Tristram,* winning himself his third Pulitzer Prize. Facing the alley across Macdougal Street is the massive brick façade of the **Tenth Church of Christ Scientist,** remodeled in 1967. Turn left on leaving the Alley and walk to the corner of Washington Square.

3. Washington Square originally was a marshland teeming with wildlife and a favorite hunting ground of the colonists. In 1797 it became a municipal Potter's Field. Recent excavations during the park's renovation revealed skeletons of some of the 10,000 early New Yorkers buried here. Equally grim was the field's popularity as a dueling ground and its use as a site of public executions. Directly across from you is the famous (or infamous) **Hanging Elm,** said to be the oldest tree in the city. It is one of 27 varieties in the park. The public hangings drew large crowds in a festive mood from the downtown districts. It is said that in 1824, on his triumphal return to America, the Marquis de Lafayette was the honored guest at the hanging of 20 highwaymen. Two years later, the park was officially designated as the Washington Military Parade Grounds, and at its dedication, two oxen, 200 hams, and a quarter-mile of barreled beer were consumed in the largest public picnic ever held here. In 1831, the grounds became the unofficial campus of the newly established University of the City of New York—now New York University, the nation's largest private institution of higher education.

As you turn left and walk along Washington Square North, note the group of imposing town houses, Nos. 26–21. These elegant homes were built in the 1830s for the social elite, as were the houses farther down the street across Fifth Avenue. Known as **"The Row,"** they represent the finest group of Greek Revival–style houses in America. Henry James's novel *Washington Square,* written in 1881, had its setting at No. 18—his grandmother's house. Unfortunately, the building was demolished along with neighboring houses in 1950 to make way for the huge apartment house at the corner. The five-story annex in a pseudo-Georgian style is a sad replacement, but represents a compromise, as the builders of the huge apartment house originally intended to erect it directly on the square. Detour around the corner of Fifth Avenue for a moment, to the right side of the entrance to No. 2 Fifth Avenue, where through the plate glass you can see a small domed fountain that is **Minetta Brook** bubbling up from its meanderings way below. A descriptive plaque is affixed to the wall.

● **4. The Washington Memorial Arch,** designed by famed architect Stanford White, is one of the world's finest triumphal arches. Built of marble in 1891–92, it commemorates the centenary of George Washington's inauguration as first President. This arch replaced an earlier model constructed of wood in 1889 that spanned Fifth Avenue near the corner. The arch had proved so popular that the permanent stone monument was erected afterward by public subscription. The civilian statue of Washington was sculpted by Alexander Stirling Calder, the military statue, by Hermon Atkins MacNeil. The carved relief work on the arch was done by Frederick William MacMonnies, whose statue of Nathan Hale is in City Hall Park. At Christmastime, a tall fir tree is placed in front of the arch, illuminated with hundreds of colored bulbs. Neighbors gather to sing carols, often to the accompaniment of student musicians from N.Y.U., or even guitars. At night, the floodlighting on the arch can be seen from as far north as 42nd Street.

There is an interior staircase in the right section leading to the top, which figured in an unseemly escapade back in 1916, known as John Sloan's Revolution. Sloan, considered the father of the "Ashcan School" of painting, forced open the door to the stairs and led a group of slightly tipsy art students and fellow bohemians to the top of the arch on a cold January night. They built a fire in a large bean-pot, spread out food, and lit an array of colorful Japanese lanterns—all to the consternation and indignation of the very staid and proper residents of "The Row." The boisterous group read poems, fired cap pistols, and noisily declared the independence of the state of "New Bohemia." The arrival of a detachment of unsympathetic constabulary brought a quick end to the abortive "rebellion."

On weekends and during the warmer weather, the fountain and mall areas are a mecca for roller skaters, instrumentalists, frisbee "pros," speechmakers, and

Fifth Avenue just north of Washington Square in 1889, showing the temporary wooden arch built for the centennial of Washington's inauguration. A horse-drawn omnibus waits for passengers as a street vendor dispenses goodies to well-dressed youngsters on this once fashionable avenue. (New-York Historical Society)

Stereograph view of the Washington Arch, taken as it neared completion in 1892. The arch, larger than any in antiquity, is considered one of architect Stanford White's major achievements. (New-York Historical Society)

Celebrating the completion of the Washington Arch, community and civic leaders gather for their picture on the roof of the arch. William Rhinelander Stewart, one of the driving forces behind its construction, with ceremonial mallet and top hat, poses thoughtfully while architect Stanford White, to his right, looks down. In the rear is N.Y.U.'s neo-Gothic building. (New-York Historical Society)

Nos. 4, 6, and 8 Fifth Avenue, corner of 8th Street—stately town houses designed by Henry J. Hardenbergh (the Plaza Hotel, the Dakota, etc.). The photo was taken in 1936 by Berenice Abbott for the Federal Art Project "Changing New York." All three buildings were razed in the early 1950s for an enormous apartment house, No. 2 Fifth Avenue. (Museum of the City of New York)

exhibitionists of all kinds, as well as a gathering place for crowds of sightseers who come to watch them "do their thing." In June and September, the adjacent streets are host to the semiannual Greenwich Village Outdoor Art Show, where professional and amateur painters have the opportunity to "show and sell."

Cross Fifth Avenue and walk down Washington Square North to the lions in front of No. 6.

5. This magnificent **row of Greek Revival houses,** like their counterparts that you saw before, were built around 1831 for wealthy New York merchants. In later years, "The Row" was the residence of author John Dos Passos, and artists Rockwell Kent and Edward Hopper, all of whom lived in **No. 3**. Hopper's studio on the top floor is now maintained by NYU as a mini-museum. Former Mayor Stephen Allen lived in No. 1. Although the houses are similar (except for No. 3, rebuilt in 1884), each has its own minor architectural differences. The stately entranceways, graced by marble columns and carved wooden colonnettes, are evidence of the graceful style of living of the original owners. Observe the brickwork—an alternating long and short brick in each row. This arrangement is called Flemish Bond, and was used on the more expensive early houses. Nos. 7–13 are mere façade, as all were gutted in 1939 to make way for an apartment house, carefully hidden behind. Sacrificed was the elaborate cornice, which still remains on the houses to the right, to make way for a fifth floor. How different, and how much more aesthetic a treatment than the architectural vandalism committed on the previous block! The cast-iron fence, in a remarkable state of preservation, helps unify the row of houses. Note the honeysuckle adornments, called anthemions, the intervening obelisks, the fret design along the base, and the lyres at intervals. These are all Greek motifs so popular during the Greek Revival period. As for the stone lions in front of No. 6, they are copies of bronzes cast in 1883 by sculptor Samuel Kitson, which were said to be from the former William K. Vanderbilt Mansion on Fifth Avenue.

Return to Fifth Avenue, turn right, and stop at the arcaded entranceway to the apartment house masked by its Greek Revival façade. Peek into "Willy's Garden," named for the late gardener. Against the rear wall is a bronze statue of Cervantes, which was a gift to New York from the city of Madrid, and is a 19th-century replica of a monument in the Spanish capital's Plaza Mayor. The statue was originally intended for placement in Washington Square, but because of its fragility it was given to N.Y.U. A few steps up the Avenue is:

6. Charming **Washington Mews** was formerly a row of stables—in fact it was called Stable Alley until the 20th century. These converted carriage houses are

Stalled in the snow on University Place and 9th Street, the morning after the Great Blizzard of 1888, the horsecar's "motive power" is nowhere to be seen, in spite of the rush hour crowd aboard. In the rear is the Hotel Martin, an elegant French establishment with a famous basement restaurant. (Museum of the City of New York)

vaguely reminiscent of London's Chelsea district, and were the residences of such celebrities as Gertrude Vanderbilt Whitney (founder of the Whitney Museum), diplomat and writer Walter Lippmann, and former Official City Greeter Grover Whalen. Walk through the cobblestoned mews to University Place. No. 1 is now the Ireland House, and the last house on the right is the Maison Française of New York University, remodeled in an authentic rural French architectural style. Across from it is the Deutsches Haus. Turn right to the northeast corner of Washington Square.

7. Diagonally across the street (southeast corner) is the **Main Building of New York University.** Built in 1894, it replaced a handsome Gothic Revival structure completed in 1837, six years after the founding of the University. Then called the University of the City of New York, it had as one of its founders Albert Gallatin, Secretary of the Treasury under Thomas Jefferson, and boasted many creative teachers. Among them was a member of the art faculty who in his spare time changed the course of history by inventing the telegraph—Samuel F. B. Morse. Professor of Chemistry and Physiology John W. Draper made the first successful outdoor photographic portrait on the roof of his house adjoining the university building. Walt Whitman conducted classes in poetry, and Winslow Homer painted in a top-floor studio. Less academic perhaps was science professor Samuel Colt, who invented the "six-shooter." In later years, Thomas Wolfe gave courses in fiction writing.

The great neo-Gothic tower of New York University was completed in 1837, facing Washington Square, and was designed to resemble King's College Chapel in Cambridge, England. It is the first important example of the Collegiate Gothic style in America. It was in this building that Samuel F. B. Morse perfected the electric telegraph, Walt Whitman conducted classes in poetry, Winslow Homer painted in a top floor studio, and Samuel Colt invented the six-shooter. N.Y.U. demolished it in 1894 to build its present Main Building. (New-York Historical Society)

The construction of the original building in 1834 led to a riot that lasted for several days. It seems that some of the founding fathers thought they could save money by using inmates from the nearby state prison. This aroused the anger of guild laborers who demonstrated so forcefully that the local National Guard unit had to be summoned to quell the violence. The university gave in and peace was restored, and the incident became known as the **Stone Cutters' Guild Riot,** and is remembered as the first demonstration by organized labor in New York City.

Note the plaque honoring Manhattan's first schoolteachers; then walk south along the Main Building to Washington Place. Within the Main Building, around the corner at 33 Washington Place, is one of the University's major attractions, the **Grey Art Gallery and Study Center.** The frequently changing exhibitions of uncommon and unusual art are housed within white-painted Doric columns. [Hours: Tues., Thurs., Fri. 11:00 A.M. to 6:00 P.M., Wed. to 8:30 P.M., Sat. to 5:00 P.M., (212) 998-6780.]

Turn east to the northwest corner of Washington Place and Greene Street. Novelist Henry James was born on Washington Place near the northeast corner in 1843.

8. This is the architecturally undistinguished Brown Building of N.Y.U. Built in 1900 for commercial use and known then as the Asch Building, it was advertised as a fireproof structure. Nevertheless, on March 25, 1911, fire *did* break out in piles of discarded cloth in the ninth-floor workroom of the **Triangle Shirtwaist Company.** Efforts to extinguish the blaze were unsuccessful, and within minutes the eighth, ninth, and tenth floors became a roaring inferno. Although the building was equipped with fire exits, the terrified workers discovered to their horror that the ninth-floor exit doors had been locked by supervisors. A single fire escape was wholly inadequate for the crush of panic-stricken employees from the three floors, and the firemen's hastily stretched nets proved useless in breaking the fall from the upper floors of the dozens of workers who leaped—often hand-in-hand, and with their hair and clothing ablaze—to their death on the pavement below. In less than an hour it was over. One hundred forty-six young people, most of them recent immigrants living on the Lower East Side, had perished—and the city was in a state of shock! As a result of the tragedy, improved fire-safety regulations were quickly adopted by the City Council, and the newly organized International Ladies' Garment Workers Union succeeded in having labor laws enacted to improve working conditions for the tens of thousands still working in similar sweatshops. A plaque commemorates the sad event, and the site has been designated a National Historic Landmark.

Return to Washington Square and turn left (south). On the left, **No. 80 Washington Square East,** dating to the mid-1880s, was a private residence hall for men, called the Hotel Benedick. It is now one of N.Y.U.'s buildings. At the corner, turn right along Washington Square South. The **Elmer Holmes Bobst Library** (Philip Johnson and Richard Foster, 1972), No. 70 Washington Square South, is a mammoth presence that casts a long shadow on the Square. Its conspicuous red sandstone façade and concave "columns" characterize the lower section, while the interior contains an impressive spacious atrium. (Take a peek inside.)

Turn right (south) on LaGuardia Place and walk one block to West 3rd Street, to the east side.

Firemen pouring tons of water into the Asch Building at the corner of Washington Place and Greene Street on March 25, 1911, as the Triangle Shirtwaist Company burns in one of the worst disasters in the city's history. One hundred forty-six young garment workers lost their lives in this tragic fire that engulfed the upper three stories of the structure. The building still exists as the Brown Building of New York University. (Brown Brothers)

Burned out sewing machines are the only recognizable artifact in the charred debris of the 9th floor, the morning after the dread Triangle Fire. (Brown Brothers)

The attractive landscaped strip that extends to Bleecker Street, called LaGuardia Gardens, is a tribute to the efforts of the Friends of LaGuardia Place, a local civic group that solicited the funds to have the landscaping and lighting installed. The street, formerly called West Broadway, was widened in the 1870s. At the time, "Boss" Tweed planned an up-scale residential neighborhood, and even renamed what was then Laurens Street Fifth Avenue South, with the intention of slicing the thoroughfare through Washington Square. The plan failed, as did a similar project by Parks Commissioner Robert Moses in the late 1940s.

The centerpiece of the minipark is the imposing **statue of Fiorello H. LaGuardia,** the feisty reform mayor of New York from 1934 to 1945. LaGuardia, who was born on nearby Sullivan Street, also represented this district when he served several terms as U.S. congressman. The six-and-a-half-foot dark bronze figure, by sculptor Neil Estern, was cast in 1993, and is set on two bluestone platforms above a granite base. In a typical LaGuardia striding stance, the statue portrays the impetuosity and vigor of the "Little Flower."

Return to Washington Square South.

The building, which at this writing is nearing completion, will be the **Helen and Martin Kimmel Center for University Life,** 566–576 La Guardia Place, a new student center (Kevin Roche John Dinkeloo & Associates, 2001). The imposing structure replaces the 1959 Loeb Student Center. While it is too early to describe, one wonders what the ultimate outcome will be with its enormous glass mansard roof and concave façade. It will, however, provide a university-size auditorium, until now lacking, plus needed student services and athletic facilities.

Before the expansion of N.Y.U. to this site, the corner was occupied in the early 20th century by Mrs. Marie Blanchard's **"House of Genius,"** a boarding house that boasted among its guests Metropolitan Opera coloratura soprano Adelina Patti; Theodore Dreiser, who penned *An American Tragedy* in a tiny garret in 1915; Stephen Crane, whose *Red Badge of Courage* was conceived in an adjoining room; Gelett Burgess ("I never saw a purple cow..."); O. Henry; Eugene O'Neill; Frank Norris; and Maxwell Bodenheim. Mrs. Blanchard outlived most of her tenants and died just after her 81st birthday in 1937.

On the southeast corner of Thompson Street is the **Holy Trinity Chapel, Generoso Pope Catholic Center at N.Y.U.** (Eggers & Higgins, 1964), 58 Washington Square South. The church's exterior recalls the once popular A-frame style; while within, the walls display attractive stained glass windows.

9. Named for the first American Baptist missionary, Adinoram D. Judson, the **Judson Memorial Church and Tower** are fine examples of the Italian Renaissance style, designed by Stanford White and built in 1892 by his architectural firm of McKim, Mead & White. If the church is open, look inside at the splendid stained-glass work of artist John LaFarge, the painter who is credited with reviving the lost art of stained-glass making in this country. The tower now serves as a dormitory wing of the adjacent **Judson Residence Hall** of N.Y.U. Note the horse-watering trough on the corner of the church, a commonplace amenity for equine transportation in the days before the automobile.

In the annex of the Judson dormitory was the **studio of artist John Sloan.** Other painters of "The Eight" who rebelled against the sugary style of the National

Academy of Art, and who had studios on Washington Square, were Maurice Prendergast, Everett Shinn, Ernest Lawson, and William Glackens. The artists' own show, staged at the 69th Regiment Armory in 1913 together with others, became known as the "Armory Show," and is considered the birth of modern American art. Their realistic work was derided by critics who called it the "Ashcan School" because of their depiction of street life.

During the time when the Square was the site for public executions, the hangman's house was located where the Catholic Center is now. The shack later became a gathering place for early bohemians, and was known as Bruno's Garret, after the somewhat eccentric owner. Bruno would invite the public to visit (for a fee) to observe at first hand how his ostentatious tenants lived.

Walk west to Sullivan Street, and go around the corner to the entrance to the **Hagop Kevorkian Center for Near Eastern Studies** of N.Y.U. Designed by Philip Johnson and Richard Foster in 1972, the entrance hall contains a reconstruction of the interior of a 1797 house built in Damascus, Syria, for a merchant family, in whose possession it remained until the mid-1920s. The interior work was supervised by the late university architect Joseph Roberto.

Immediately to the left of the Kevorkian Center (No. 51) is N.Y.U.'s **Skirball Department of Hebrew and Judaic Studies.**

Continue west along the Square to N.Y.U.'s neo-Georgian–style **Vanderbilt Hall** (Eggers & Higgins, 1951), modeled after an English Inn of Court. Previously on the site was a rather pathetic structure known as "Papa Strunsky's," a rooming house for artists, most of whom could rarely afford the rent and who were subsidized by the beneficent Strunsky who never pressed them for payment. Among the threadbare boarders was the young writer Lincoln Steffens. The lease of the property was acquired by Columbia University, which was less charitable than Strunsky, and by the late 1940s they foreclosed. Knowing that N.Y.U. needed the space for its Law School, Columbia held out for a reported $1 million to close the deal so that Vanderbilt Hall could be erected.

A Fifth Avenue bus parked in Washington Square in 1936. These popular "double deckers" disappeared after World War II. In the rear is the Washington Arch and No. 1 Fifth Avenue. (Photograph by Berenice Abbott for the Federal Art Project "Changing New York," Museum of the City of New York)

Before leaving the Square, you should take a brief stroll around the Park to see its public art. (You have already seen the famous Arch.) Enter at the southwest corner and walk toward the center. One of the two main pieces of sculpture is the bronze portrait bust of **Alexander Lyman Holley,** by John Quincy Adams Ward (1888), which was recently restored. Holley, an engineer and inventor, improved the Bessemer process of manufacturing steel, and this figure by New York's most prolific public sculptor is considered one of his best. The marble base is by architect Frederick Hastings.

The center fountain, a 19th-century survivor, is the most popular gathering place in the park and site of all manner of side shows, lectures, political debates, folk music, and just people doing their thing.

Just beyond is the statue of Italian patriot and soldier **Giuseppe Garibaldi,** by Giovanni Turini. Garibaldi, who struggled for Italian liberty and unity, took refuge in Staten Island for a time after the failure of his Revolution of 1835. He later returned, joining forces with others, until the successful conclusion of his efforts in 1860. The statue was erected by New York's Italian community in 1888. A local myth claims that Garibaldi will draw his sword to protect any passing virgin in distress. Relax for a few minutes, feed the tame squirrels (but not the pigeons!), and return to the southwest corner. Turn south into Macdougal Street.

10. Macdougal Street and its adjacent blocks south of Washington Square are considered the "real Village" by the mobs of young people who throng here evenings and weekends. Before turning down Macdougal Street, make a short detour straight ahead along West 4th Street (the continuation of Washington Square South). John Barrymore, "The Great Profile," lived at No. 132; and at a former café at No. 148, Al Jolson and Grace Moore were discovered, while Norma Shearer worked as a hat-check girl. At No. 150, once "The Mad Hatter" Café, Hendrik Willem van Loon wrote his *Story of Mankind.* On the north side of the street is the neo-Gothic–style **Washington Square United Methodist Church,** built in 1860.

As you stroll down Macdougal Street, note the Provincetown Playhouse, Eugene O'Neill's theater. Nos. 127–131 (best seen from across the street) are little Federal houses that were built for Aaron Burr in 1829 and are among the oldest in the city. Notice the typical dormer windows in the peaked roof, and the pineapples on the cast-iron newel posts on No. 129—traditional symbols of hospitality. Around the corner at 106 West 3rd Street, Aaron Burr's ghost is reputedly still haunting the building. At No. 121 Macdougal Street is the famous Caffè Reggio, a Village landmark since 1927. Stop in for a cappuccino or luscious Italian pastry. At No. 130, south of West 3rd Street, Louisa May Alcott wrote her classic *Little Women.* Take an optional side trip one block farther to Bleecker Street and turn left. Try some of the exotic foods from around the world at the "hand held" food shops that line the street: souvlaki, tacos, sweet and hot sausage, empanadas, tandoori chicken, knishes, shish kebab, and Turkish coffee (but not all at once!).

11. Pause for a moment before turning the corner of Minetta Lane. The building on the southwest corner, No. 113 Macdougal Street, now the Minetta Tavern, was a speakeasy during Prohibition, and in the basement below, the *Reader's Digest* was born. Founded in 1922 by DeWitt Wallace, its first edition had a press run of only 5,000 copies. At narrow **Minetta Street** turn left. During the Prohibition Era, these narrow alleys were lined with speakeasies. Later those night spots became legitimate cabarets offering drink and amateur theatrical productions. Now, with stricter city licensing, few genuine cabarets remain, and the small theater groups have moved into their own "Off-Off" Broadway playhouses. Both streets follow the winding path of old Minetta Brook; and it is said that on a very quiet night, the gurgling waters can be heard below ground. However, there are very few quiet nights in this neighborhood. You will emerge at Sixth Avenue, on Father Demo Square. Before crossing Sixth Avenue, read the plaque on the fence of Minetta Triangle for interesting historical background of the neighborhood, then turn half right to the corner of Bleecker and Carmine streets.

12. The Italian Renaissance–style Roman Catholic **Church of Our Lady of Pompeii** (1926) is the parish church of the large Italian community in this part of the Village. Mother Francis Xavier Cabrini, the first American saint, often prayed here. (Mother Elizabeth Seton was the first American-*born* saint. *See* page 33.) Father Antonio Demo was its first pastor and the force behind the construction of the church. Walk along Bleecker Street, then turn west on Leroy Street and notice the variety of architectural styles, ranging from Federal-style houses to "Old Law" tenements. Cross Seventh Avenue (carefully!).

13. As you round the bend on Leroy Street, the atmosphere suddenly changes. You are now on **St. Luke's Place,** with its charming row of Italianate brownstone town houses of the 1850s. The gingko trees, which line both sides of the street, are particularly resistant to air pollution. A plaque on the Hudson Park Library tells of the residence of poet **Marianne Moore,** who moved from Brooklyn in 1918 and lived at No. 14, when she worked for a time in the predecessor library on the site. On the nearby fence of James J. Walker Park is another plaque describing the present playground's origins as the site of Trinity Cemetery and later, Hudson Park.

The twin lanterns on the stairway of No. 6 mark the former residence of Mayor James J. Walker—the popular "Jimmy" Walker of Prohibition days. Rampant corruption in municipal government forced his resignation, but he remained a beloved and colorful figure until his death in 1946. Until Gracie Mansion was made the official residence of all New York City mayors, a pair of lanterns customarily adorned the entrance to "his honor's" home. Across the street in James J. Walker Park, there is an interesting monument near the entrance, which honors two firemen from the Eagle Fire Company who lost their lives in a building collapse in 1834. The memorial is the lone surviving artifact from the former Trinity Parish cemetery that occupied this site before the park was built. Turn right at Hudson Street one block to Morton Street.

14. Had you stood on this spot 300 years ago, you would have been on the bank of the Hudson River. The land to the west was filled in gradually, until today the river is three blocks away. The tall building halfway down the block to the right is the former Federal House of Detention, now the New York State Manhattan Mental Development Center. Walk north one block to Barrow Street and make a brief detour west. On both sides of the street are typical early 19th-century houses. No. 97 was remodeled later in the century with the addition of ornate neo-Grec details on all the lintels.

Walk north to Barrow Street. Looking to the northwest, on Washington Street, is the enormous red brick **former U.S. Federal Building,** now a luxury condominium, The Archive. Completed in 1899 as the Customs Appraisers' Warehouse, it took seven years to build, and its style is the fortresslike Romanesque Revival. It once housed records from the National Archives and had a branch of the U.S. Post Office. The architect of this massive masonry building with its great brick arches is unknown; however, the designer of the lower two floors was Willoughby J. Edbrooke. Return to Hudson Street and turn left (north) one-half block to St. Luke's Chapel.

15. "St. Luke-in-the-Fields," as it was called when the cornerstone was laid in 1821, stood at the river's edge and overlooked small farms, wandering streams, and shady country lanes. In those days most visitors came from the lower city by boat, as the trip by carriage was very arduous, and the canal that bisected most of Manhattan island (site of present Canal Street) could be crossed in only two places. The first warden of St. Luke's was Clement Clarke Moore, who immortalized himself not with his dedicated church duties, but with the poem *A Visit from St. Nicholas* ("'Twas the Night before Christmas..."). The church, a branch of the downtown Trinity Parish, has always been dedicated to education, and today boasts an excellent elementary school, visible behind the church. A tragic fire in 1981 virtually destroyed the landmark church, but a generous outpouring of public support helped St. Luke's rise, phoenixlike, from its ashes.

To the left of the church are **Nos. 433–473,** and to the right, **Nos. 487–491 Hudson Street.** Observe how these restored Federal houses form a harmonious unit with the brick church. Built in 1825, they are the property of St. Luke's. Bret Harte, journalist, teacher, "gold rusher," and author of *Tales of Roaring Camp* and *The Outcasts of Poker Flat,* lived at No. 487 and maintained a steady feud with his contemporary, Mark Twain, also a Villager.

Continue to Christopher Street, turn right (north), then right again into Bedford Street.

16. As you rounded the corner, you probably noticed the **Lucille Lortel Theater** on Christopher Street, one of the oldest off-Broadway playhouses, formerly called the Theater de Lys, opened in 1954. Kurt Weill's *Three Penny Opera* had its New York premiere here and ran for nine years, with Weill's wife Lotte Lenya in a starring role.

You now are entering the most charming section of the so-called West Village. Homeowners take special pride in restoring and preserving their attractive houses. There are more original Federal-style houses in this neighborhood than anywhere else in the city. Note the **row of houses at Nos. 115–111 Bedford Street,** the plaque on **No. 113,** and **109–107,** the latter only two bays wide. Stop just before the next corner, which is Grove Street, and stay on the right side of Bedford Street.

17. The wooden house on your left, **No. 100 Bedford Street,** was originally the workshop of sash maker William Hyde, who lived in the corner house. The sash maker's trade has now been assumed by the glazier and carpenter. In the early 19th century, window making was an important craft. The workshop is now a private residence. **No. 102,** which you just passed, is best seen from a distance. It is no accident that it resembles a fairy-tale house. Although the building dates from 1835, it was remodeled extensively in 1926 by Clifford Reed Daily and financed by Otto H. Kahn, who sought to convert the decaying house into "an inspiring home for creative artists." When the city's Building Department approved the radical plans, **"Twin Peaks"** was born.

At the corner, **No. 17 Grove Street,** which dates from 1822, is the most complete wooden frame house in Greenwich Village. Turn right on Grove Street to No. 4.

18. The row of **Nos. 4–10** (1825–34) presents one of the most authentic groups of classic Federal-style houses in America. Unfortunately, No. 6's dormers have been "modernized" and the shutters have been removed. Note the charming oasis that is **Grove Court**—a secluded, shady mews. Now converted into triplexes, the row of old houses was built as laborers' quarters in 1854, and Grove Court was known by the not-so-charming name of Mixed Ale Alley. Return to Bedford Street and turn right, stopping opposite No. 95, once a winemaker's establishment. Note the goblet above.

19. Can you guess what **No. 86 Bedford Street** is (or was)? There are no visible signs of identification, but to Village *cognoscenti* it is Chumley's Restaurant. It was a notorious speakeasy during the Prohibition days, and patrons had to identify themselves at the little glass window in the door before being admitted. It was also a favored hangout for writers, and faded dust jackets of long-forgotten titles line the walls inside. The restaurant's popularity is so widespread in the Village, that former owner Lee Chumley never felt the need for a sign. During Prohibition, when the premises were raided by the police, patrons could beat a hasty retreat out a back exit in the rear of the restaurant, opposite the bar. This passageway, which leads through the courtyard of the adjacent building to Barrow Street, is still there. See for yourself around the corner!

Turn right on Barrow Street to No. 70.

20. No. 70 Barrow Street, when built in 1852, was Empire Hose Company No. 1. In those days each neighborhood had its own volunteer fire brigade. Look carefully and you will see where the old carriageway was bricked in.

Across the street is a rather large double house with mansard roofs, **Nos. 39 and 41 Commerce Street.** Both halves were built in 1831 for Peter Huyler, a milkman. "The Twins," as they are called, were built in Federal style with Second Empire roofs superimposed, and share a common garden. Walk ahead and around the bend into Commerce Street, to the little theater.

21. A group of local playwrights seeking a stage for their own works in 1924 converted an old brewery malt house into the **Cherry Lane Theater** (Commerce Street was then called Cherry Lane). Among some premieres were Samuel Beckett's *Waiting for Godot* and *Endgame,* as well as plays by Ionesco and Edward Albee.

22. At the corner of Bedford Street is the **Isaacs-Hendricks House,** built in 1799. Like the two wooden houses seen earlier, it is typical of the architecture of old Greenwich, and is the oldest surviving house in the Village, although a questionable restoration in the mid-1980s created a rather mysterious side wall on Commerce Street. Its entrance is in the rear, behind the fence. Around the corner at **No. 75½ Bedford Street** is the **narrowest house in the city,** measuring only 9½ feet wide! The first floor was formerly a carriage entrance, with living quarters above. A cobbler had his shop here, and later it was a candy factory. Between 1923 and 1924, poet Edna St. Vincent Millay lived here and won a Pulitzer prize

A row of pristine Greek Revival–style town houses, Nos. 3 through 6 Sheridan Square, was lost forever when an apartment was erected on the site in the early 1950s. The photo by Wurts Bros. was taken in 1915. A saddle and harness shop is barely visible at right. (Consolidated Edison Company of New York)

for *The Ballad of the Harp-Weaver* in 1922. Like the Isaacs-Hendricks House, this diminutive structure had its entrance facing the rear. Note the plaque on No. 70. Return to Commerce Street and turn right to No. 17.

23. Two years before killing Alexander Hamilton in that fateful duel in 1802, Aaron Burr lived briefly at the **site of No. 17. Nos. 16–18** across the street were built in 1830, as was No. 17. At **No. 11,** the plaque informs us that Washington Irving was a resident, where he was supposed to have penned his *Legend of Sleepy Hollow.* Continue to Seventh Avenue, turn right briefly to an abandoned gas station, which has been recycled as a residence, and has the distinction of being the **tiniest building in Manhattan.** Cross Seventh Avenue and walk north to Barrow Street.

24. At the corner of Barrow Street and Seventh Avenue is **Greenwich House, No. 27.** Originally a settlement house, it has expanded its services to the community with recreational facilities, arts and crafts studios, concerts, antique shows, and cultural programs for senior citizens. Proceed along Barrow Street. **No. 15** was once a stable. Note the horse heads indicating that it was a public livery stable; it is now a tavern. No. 17, a restaurant called One if by Land, Two if by Sea, is believed to have been a stable built on the site of Aaron Burr's carriage house.

25. At West 4th Street turn right briefly to Nos. 175–185, charming houses dating to the 1830s, then turn left at the Viewing Garden, past Washington Place to the corner of Seventh Avenue and Grove Street, and Sheridan Square.

26. Sheridan Square is shaped like a huge butterfly, with two distinct "wings." So many streets converge at this point that visitors often become confused (Villagers, too, for that matter). Because of heavy traffic at this intersection, the corner has been called "The Mousetrap." Pass through the second "wing" of the butterfly by walking along Grove Street, opposite the little park with the **equestrian statue of Civil War Cavalry General Philip Henry Sheridan** (Joseph Pollia, 1936). Actually, this half of Sheridan Square is called **Christopher Park,** but nobody ever calls it that. The Ellsworth Flagpole honors a 24-year-old colonel, the first of his rank to be killed in the Civil War. The Square figures in another aspect of the Civil War—the Draft Riots. In 1863, mobs of bloodthirsty rioters, in the worst civil insurrection in the city's history, gathered in the Square and attacked a number of freed slaves. They would certainly have hanged them from nearby lampposts, had not the residents of **No. 92 Grove Street** risked their lives to save them. The house has since been extensively remodeled, and is now called the Burges Chamber Studio. Its design won a prize from the American Institute of Architects.

A recent addition to the little park is the sculpture group by George Segal, in bronze with white patina, entitled *Gay Liberation* (1992). It is in a spot directly across Christopher Street from a former tavern called the **Stonewall Inn.** It was here in June 1969 that a large group of gays had a confrontation with the police, and for the first time fought back for what they considered their right to assemble peaceably. The event is commemorated every June by a large "Gay Pride" parade in the Village.

27. Grove Street now becomes Waverly Place, and as you stand before the **Northern Dispensary,** you are at the corner of Waverly Place and Waverly Place! Since the street divides at this point to meet Grove Street and also to swing northward, it has given rise to the saying that the Dispensary "has two sides on one street, and one street on two sides." Built in 1831 in Greek Revival style by Henry Bayard, carpenter, and John C. Tucker, stonemason, and surprisingly unchanged in appearance, the Northern Dispensary still functions as a public clinic. According to its records, Edgar Allan Poe was treated here (free) for a head cold in 1837.

Continue in the same direction, and turn left into narrow Gay Street.

28. Gay Street, probably named for a family that owned the property in the late 18th century, was the center of a small black neighborhood in the latter half of the 19th century. In the 1920s the street was lined with speakeasies. **No. 14** was the site of Ruth McKenny's play *My Sister Eileen.* Later, it was filmed here on location. Walk ahead to Christopher Street, and spend a few minutes window shopping in the curious shops to the left. Then turn right to Greenwich Avenue, and turn left, and walk to the corner of West 10th Street.

29. The delightful **Jefferson Market Garden,** supported by community volunteers, marks the **site of the former New York City Women's House of Detention** and an earlier police court, market, and firehouse. The massive orange brick Art Deco structure was demolished in 1973–74 after considerable community pressure, and the inmates were moved to Riker's Island. Turn east on West 10th Street to the entrance gates of Patchin Place. Illuminating the rear of this charming cul-de-sac is a cast-iron **bishop's crook lamppost,** of the type that first provided electric street lighting in the city in the 1890s.

30. The houses on quaint, private **Patchin Place** were built in the mid-19th century to house workers of the then-posh Brevoort Hotel on Fifth Avenue. The narrow street later became the residence of such famous authors as poet laureate

John Masefield, Theodore Dreiser, e. e. cummings (at No. 4), as well as Harry Kemp (the "Hobo Poet"), and William Brinkley, who wrote *Don't Go Near the Water.* Enjoy the peaceful atmosphere of this unusual cul-de-sac, away from the noise and clamor of nearby thoroughfares. Then walk ahead to Sixth Avenue (Avenue of the Americas) (we'll get to the "castle" across the street shortly), and turn left again. Watch carefully, or you'll miss the iron gates marking the entrance to Milligan Place.

31. Milligan Place, another private enclave, is named for the original landowner, Samuel Milligan, who settled here in 1799. His daughter married the surveyor of his property, Aaron Patchin. Perhaps part of the dowry was the small street named for him. Many native Villagers are unaware of this tiny, secluded mews. Walk ahead to West 11th Street, turn right and cross the avenue. Fifty feet down the street is a small cemetery.

32. The Second Cemetery of the Spanish & Portuguese Synagogue was one of three burial grounds of this first Jewish congregation in New York. The first cemetery, near Chatham Square, and the third, on West 21st Street, kept pace with the northward growth of the Jewish community from the 17th through the 19th centuries. The peculiar triangular shape of the cemetery resulted from the opening of West 11th Street through to Sixth Avenue in the mid-19th century, cutting off a substantial piece of the graveyard. As a result, it is the smallest cemetery in Manhattan. Return to Sixth Avenue, turn left, and stop at the "castle."

33. The Jefferson Market Library, the Village's most magnificent Victorian Gothic structure, was built in 1874–77 as a courthouse, with an adjoining jail, firehouse, and market. Designed by architects Frederick Clarke Withers and Calvert Vaux, it was listed among the ten most beautiful buildings in America at the time. (Vaux, by the way, worked with Frederick Law Olmsted on the design for Central Park.) Note the striking effect of the red brick and white stone, the Gothic motifs, stained-glass windows, and dramatic clock tower. The tower replaces an earlier wooden fire lookout, one of many throughout the city, long before the advent of the electric fire-alarm system. In 1967 the building was saved from the wrecker's ball at the eleventh hour by a dedicated committee of neighborhood residents, who not only saved it but convinced the city to restore it and make it a branch of the New York Public Library. Architect Giorgio Cavaglieri designed and supervised the restoration. The clock, known affectionately as "Old Jeff," was repaired and illumination for the dials installed. During the Christmas season the belfry is festooned with gaily colored lights. Read the plaques at the base of the tower and visit the library. Take the elevator to the third floor and walk down the intriguing spiral staircase to the dungeonlike basement, which houses the reference room. Finally, walk south one block to West 8th Street, where the tour began.

End of tour. The entrance to the West 4th Street–Washington Square subway station is a half-block down Sixth Avenue toward Waverly Place.

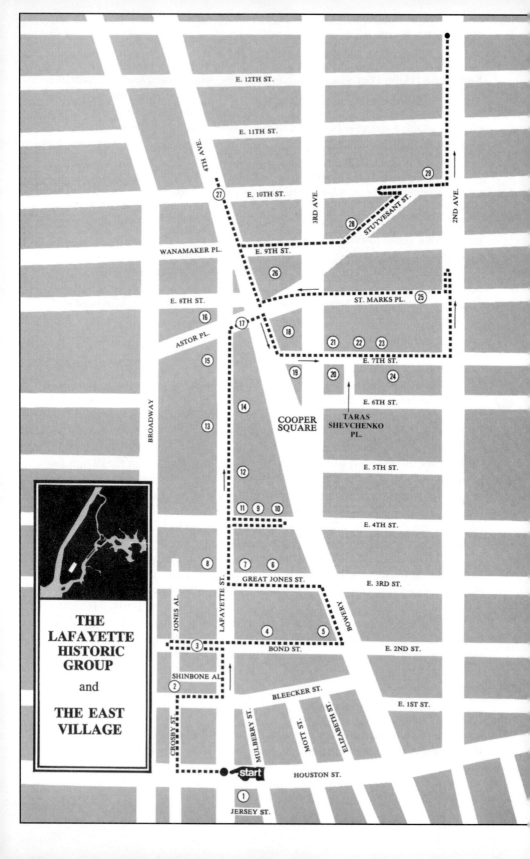

5. The Lafayette Historic Group and the East Village

[Subways: 6 to Bleecker Street; F, V, S to Broadway–Lafayette. Buses: M5, M6, M103 to Houston Street; M21 to Lafayette Street.]

With the end of the American Revolution, New York City, which had stagnated under years of British occupation, came alive again, regaining its position as an important port and commercial center. A burgeoning population began to push the city's frontiers northward, swallowing up the once-remote and peaceful farms of mid-Manhattan and crisscrossing them with a latticework of newly opened streets.

In 1811, the City Commissioners drew up their famous plan, laying out a gridwork street pattern for the entire island, numbering all east-west streets and north-south avenues, commencing roughly at the point of departure of this tour. By the end of the 19th century the last farms disappeared from Manhattan, yielding to the ever increasing needs for *lebensraum*.

By the 1830s this neighborhood became the "gold coast" of the city, boasting the most lavish residences—including that of the nation's wealthiest citizen, John Jacob Astor. Within 20 years the area gave way to commerce and public entertainment, and by the 1880s and 1890s it became a center for the printing trades. Light industry followed with factories, loft buildings, and warehouses.

Surprisingly, so many vestiges remain from each period of development that within the half-square-mile area can be found such diverse "artifacts" as opulent Greek Revival residences, Italian Renaissance cultural institutions, Romanesque Revival industrial structures, cast-iron commercial "palaces," plus a number of historic and architecturally unique buildings—most in an excellent state of preservation.

The tour begins at Houston and Lafayette streets. [For background information on Houston Street, *see* SoHo Cast-Iron District.]

1. On the southeast corner stands the **Puck Building** (295–309 Lafayette Street). Built in 1885, with an addition in 1892, it is a fine example of the industrial Romanesque Revival style. Architect Albert Wagner designed it for the publishers of the humor magazine *Puck*, whose Shakespearean character proclaimed "What Fools These Mortals Be!" across the magazine's cover. The publication lasted more than a "Midsummer's Night," entertaining New Yorkers for some 30 years, until it was absorbed by the now-defunct *New York Journal-American*, which kept only the old magazine's logo. Puck, however, lives on in two larger-than-life statues perched on a third-floor ledge at the northeast corner of the building and above the elegant polished-granite–columned entranceway, which opens on Lafayette Street. The gilt cherubic figures are by Bohemian immigrant Carl Buberl. The building now houses **New York University's Robert F. Wagner School for Public Service.**

Walk west on Houston Street to Crosby Street. Turn north (right), and stop about three-quarters of the way to Bleecker Street.

2. The startlingly ornate building directly ahead (65 Bleecker Street), almost hidden in the shadows of the dark narrow streets, is the **Bayard-Condict Building,** New York City's only building designed by Louis H. Sullivan. The guiding spirit of the "Chicago School," Sullivan was the teacher (and employer) of Frank Lloyd Wright. Ignore the altered ground floor and study the ornamented façade of this 12-story steel-frame structure, which is clad entirely in white terra cotta, noting the vertical clarity and romantic detail leading up to an astonishing cornice above six supporting angels. It is said that Sullivan objected strenuously to the figures, but placed them there at the insistence of Silas Alden Condict, the original owner. Architectural historian Carl W. Condit, commenting on the location of the Bayard Building, was heard to say, "Who would expect an aesthetic experience on Bleecker Street?" The building was erected 1897–99.

To the right, on the southeast corner, are the decaying remains of a once-proud Federal-style residence, with dormers in both the front and rear of its typical peaked roof. It was a Roosevelt family property and owned by FDR's great-great-grandfather. You are now entering the **NoHo Historic District.** (NoHo is the acronym for the district NOrth of HOuston Street.)

Turn east (right) to Lafayette Street, then left past Jones Alley, turning left into Bond Street.

3. In the 1830s Bond Street was one of the city's most fashionable. Lined with Greek Revival–style houses, it was a secluded, peaceful street whose most celebrated resident, Albert Gallatin, lived at No. 1. As Secretary of the Treasury under Thomas Jefferson and later minister to France, he helped reshape the financial structure of the country, and was a founder of the nearby University of the City of New York, later to be called N.Y.U. A few badly misshapen Federal-style

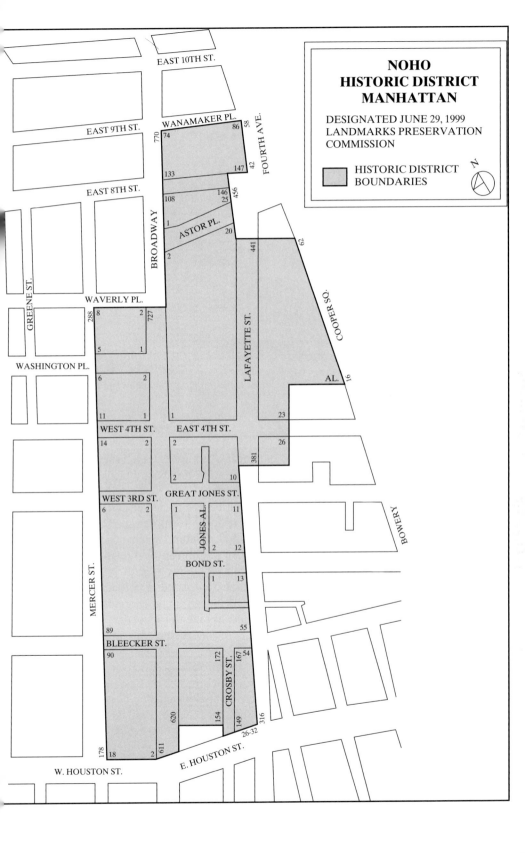

NOHO
HISTORIC DISTRICT
MANHATTAN

DESIGNATED JUNE 29, 1999
LANDMARKS PRESERVATION
COMMISSION

HISTORIC DISTRICT
BOUNDARIES

N

EAST 10TH ST.

WANAMAKER PL.

EAST 9TH ST.

770 74

86 58

FOURTH AVE.

133 147 42

EAST 8TH ST.

108 146
25

456

BROADWAY

1

ASTOR PL.

2 20

441

62

COOPER SQ.

WAVERLY PL.

GREENE ST.

288 8 2 727

LAFAYETTE ST.

5 1

WASHINGTON PL.

6 2

AL. 16

11 1 1 23

WEST 4TH ST. EAST 4TH ST.

14 2 2 26

381

2 10

WEST 3RD ST. GREAT JONES ST.

6 2 1 11

JONES AL.

MERCER ST.

2 12

BOND ST.

1 13

89 55

BLEECKER ST.

90

172 167 54

CROSBY ST.

BOWERY

620 154 149 316

26-32

178 18 2 611

E. HOUSTON ST.

W. HOUSTON ST.

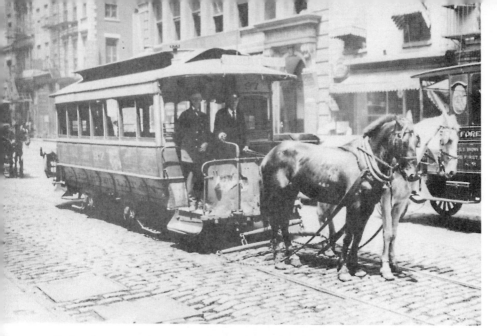

The last horsecar in the City of New York on the Bleecker Street Line, on its farewell trip on Bleecker Street, between Mercer Street and Broadway, July 26, 1917. Horse car service began in 1832. Although electrification was begun before the turn of the century, New York held on tenaciously to a number of its "horse power" lines long after most other cities had electrified theirs. (Museum of the City of New York)

houses survive on the north side of the street. Curiously, Jones Alley makes a right turn in the middle of the block, and goes north for about a block; its lower segment was once called "Shinbone Alley."

On the site of Gallatin's residence is one of the best preserved cast-iron buildings in the city. Built in French Second Empire style, it was designed by Stephen D. Hatch in 1879 for the firm of **Robbins & Appleton,** watchmakers. Shortly thereafter, the publishing house of D. Appleton & Company (no relation) moved into No. 1–3–5 Bond Street. The six-story office building, with floor upon floor of large recessed plate glass windows separated by graceful columns and surmounted at each level by a simple cornice, is topped by an enormous mansard roof with three ornate pavilions. The light and airy interior must have provided a relatively pleasant place to work. Adjacent No. 7–9, also in cast iron, has been joined to it as part of a new condominium.

At the northeast corner of Bond Street and Broadway is the very handsome red brick **former Brooks Brothers Store** (670 Broadway). Best viewed from across Broadway, this engaging 1873 Victorian pile, planned by George E. Harney, clearly shows the influence of English designer Charles Eastlake in its many decorative motifs. Find the date of construction in the ornaments on the four pilasters. This was Brooks Brothers' third location. An earlier site was at 466–468 Broadway [*see* Chapter 7].

Broadway, looking north from the old Broadway Central Hotel toward Great Jones Street, ca. 1895. Elegantly clad ladies and gentlemen walk by hansom cabs waiting at the curb, while horse-drawn traffic and Broadway cable cars clatter by. (Consolidated Edison Company of New York)

Return to Lafayette Street again, and continue east on Bond Street.

   4. No. 26 Bond Street is an unusually large late Greek Revival–style house that was probably the residence of an affluent early 19th-century family.

   5. At the northwest corner of the Bowery, the **former Bond Street Savings Bank** is pure wedding cake in cast iron. Built in 1874 from plans by Henry Engelbert, it is another attractive example of the French Second Empire style. With the influx of many German immigrants into the neighborhood, it later became the German Exchange Bank; and with its subsequent failure in the early 20th century, it ended its banking career as a deteriorating loft building. But in 1963, with the growing popularity of off-Broadway theater, it gained a new lease on life as a playhouse. The newborn **Bouwerie Lane Theater,** home of the Jean Cocteau Repertory Company, won additional recognition when it was designated an official New York City Landmark. Note the lovely façade with its rows of paired Corinthian and Ionic columns flanking the windows, the ornate modillions under the cornices of the roof and surmounting pediment, and the stately entranceway guarded by paneled cast-iron newel posts. Diagonally across the Bowery is the Amato Opera, long a cultural landmark in the East Village.

Walk north one block on the Bowery.

Originally **"Bouwerie"** in Dutch, the street's name hearkens back to the days of Peter Stuyvesant, when he had it built as a road from the lower city past the "bouweries," or farms, to his own estate a half-mile north. Although the Bowery is now synonymous with the less fortunate of society who inhabit much of this now-dismal thoroughfare in the many flophouses that line the street, it was for a time a lively center of entertainment. Music halls, theaters, and beer gardens were numerous in the late 19th century, and the street is recalled in the humorous lyrics of the Gay '90s song, "The Bowery—I'll Never Go There Anymore!"

Turn left (west) on Great Jones Street.

There never was anyone named "Great Jones"! The land for the street was deeded to the city by Samuel Jones, a lawyer and New York's first comptroller. The agreement called for the street to be named for him; however, there was already a Jones Street (in Greenwich Village), and it was named for his brother-in-law, Dr. Gardiner Jones. Neither would relinquish his prerogative, so for a time there were *two* Jones Streets. To resolve the dilemma, Samuel Jones suggested that *his* street be named Great Jones Street. (Logically, it should have been called East Third Street, which it really is, anyway!)

6. Midway down the block, at No. 44, is the home of **Engine Company 33 and Hook & Ladder 9.** Formerly the headquarters of the New York City Fire Department, it is a splendid example of the French Beaux Arts style and was

The Broadway Central Hotel, built in 1871 in Second Empire style by Henry Engelbert, on the site of an earlier hotel called the LaFarge House. A year after it opened, it witnessed the sensational shooting of Jim Fisk. The enormous hotel deteriorated badly in its last years and gave up the ghost in a spectacular cave-in of its north wing in 1973. The site is now occupied by an N.Y.U. Law School dormitory. (New York City Landmarks Preservation Commission)

designed by Ernest Flagg and W. B. Chambers in 1898. At the time of its construction, it was the headquarters of the chief of the Fire Department, so it is appropriately flamboyant in appearance. Imagine the excitement and thrill when the scarlet and gold horse-drawn engines, their steam boilers belching smoke, would dash out to answer the calls! Read the memorial plaques.

Across the street, at **Nos. 31** and **33,** are two mid-19th-century commercial buildings. A glance at the pediment reveals that they were once a pair of livery stables. Serving a similar purpose as today's public garage and rent-a-car establishment, Bienecke's (note name in the pediment) boarded horses and also rented various types of rigs to those who were unable to maintain their own private stable.

7. Reaching the corner of Lafayette Street, look through the parking lot on the northeast corner, approximately 75 feet east of Lafayette Street, and seek out the apse of an old neo-Gothic church protruding from the rear of a nondescript commercial building. About a hundred years ago, it was the **Mission Chapel of the Immaculate Virgin.** With the industrialization of the neighborhood, the congregation departed, and the building was sold. Don't look for the front of the church on the East 4th Street side…it isn't there any more.

8. No. 380 Lafayette Street, the Schermerhorn Building (on the northwest corner), is a solid and imposing Romanesque Revival–style loft building. It was built in 1888, from plans by Henry J. Hardenbergh, who designed, among others, the Plaza Hotel, the Dakota Apartments, and the Consolidated Edison Building. The ornamental detail is in brick and terra cotta—a remarkably handsome structure for an industrial building.

Turn right (north) on Lafayette Street, then right into East 4th Street.

9. The Old Merchant's House Museum, at 29 East 4th Street, is probably the only surviving Greek Revival–style house in the city—intact *within* as well as outside. Built in 1832 by Joseph Brewster from plans attributed to famed architect Minard Lafever, it was purchased in 1835 by Seabury Tredwell, a wealthy merchant. It remained in the Tredwell family until the last surviving member, Gertrude Tredwell, died in 1933. To save the house and its original furnishings from the auctioneer's block, the property was then purchased by George Chapman, a distant relative, whose sole interest was to maintain it as the only example of a New York City family's house and style of living. Among the furnishings are the original furniture, mirrors, carpets, draperies, chinaware, and a collection of dresses, shawls, and bonnets. The interior architectural elements also preserved are the mantelpieces, wainscoting, moldings, columns, banisters, and the kitchen. There is even a secret passageway that leads under the house from an upstairs closet. Chapman organized the Historic Landmark Society to maintain the Old Merchant's House as a public museum.

To protect and restore the house, which had suffered badly, the Decorators Club took it on as an official project, and a major renovation was undertaken in 1973–79 under the supervision of New York University's late architect Joseph Roberto. The Old Merchant's House, completely restored with all its furnishings,

Lafayette Place (now Lafayette Street) was an elegant, tree-lined cul-de-sac around 1870. Not visible on the left side of the street are the imposing façades of Colonnade Row, the houses of the wealthiest citizens in town. Note the raised pedestrian crosswalks and Greek Revival–style fence in front of old St. Bartholomew's Church. The view is north from Great Jones Street. (New-York Historical Society)

is open for all to enjoy. (Open for tours Thurs.–Mon. 1:00 P.M. to 5:00 P.M., adults $3.00, students and seniors $1.00.)

10. At 37 East 4th Street, a few doors east, is what remains of the **Samuel Tredwell Skidmore House.** Built in 1844–45 for a cousin of Seabury Tredwell, it is a late Greek Revival–style house, and much less imposing than its nearby neighbor. Unfortunately, its survival is uncertain. At one time the entire block was lined with similar houses.

Return to Lafayette Street.

11. On the northeast corner, at No. 393–399 Lafayette Street, stands the massive **De Vinne Press Building.** One of the great printing "giants" of the late 19th and early 20th centuries, Theodore L. De Vinne was the founder of the Grolier Club and the publisher of such popular magazines as *Scribner's, Century,* and *St. Nicholas.* The De Vinne Press was famous for its innovative typefaces and high-quality books. The architects, Babb, Cook, & Willard, designed this "Romanesque Utilitarian" structure in 1885, in a style reminiscent of the aqueducts of Ancient Rome. Notice how thick the masonry bearing walls are, since it was built before the advent of steel skeletons. The name of the old establishment is still visible on the upper façade. A restaurant now occupies the ground floor.

12. No. 411 Lafayette Street demonstrates how different building mediums can be employed together successfully (in this case, cast iron and brick) to produce a functional and aesthetic effect. Viewed from a distance, the ornate two-story-high cast-iron columns of the **Durst Building,** designed in 1891 by Alfred Zucker, are an imposing base for this former men's clothing store and factory. The "squared" style of the larger columns adds a feeling of strength, while lightness results from the beaded bands on all the columns, the ornate design on the spandrel panels above the ground floor, and the round-arch windows on the second floor; while slender iron columns divide the paired windows above.

13. The superb Corinthian colonnade across the street (Nos. 428, 430, 432, and 434) is all that remains of one of the most magnificent rows of Greek Revival town houses in America. On the site of John Jacob Astor's Vauxhall Gardens Amusement Park, and completed in 1833 by developer Seth Geer, probably from his own plans, **Colonnade Row** is an architectural treasure and an outstanding example of early urban design. Originally named LaGrange Terrace, after the Marquis de Lafayette's country estate in France, the group consisted of nine mansions on what was then Lafayette Place. (Lafayette Street was not opened till much later; Lafayette Place was a shady, cobblestoned cul-de-sac extending only to where Great Jones Street is now.) [*See* photographs below and on page 134.]

Constructed of Westchester marble and set back behind a 30-foot courtyard, the impressive row was separated from the street by an iron fence. The nine houses were reduced to four when the John Wanamaker Department Store callously destroyed them early in this century to make way for a garage for their delivery trucks. When he built the row, Geer was criticized for speculating "so far out in the country," but his plan was vindicated when possession was taken by such notables as John Jacob Astor, Cornelius Vanderbilt, Warren Delano (Franklin Delano Roosevelt's grandfather), and other wealthy citizens. Washington Irving stayed here for a time, as did two distinguished visitors from England, William Makepeace Thackeray and Charles Dickens. In 1844, then-President John Tyler secretly married the daughter

Colonnade Row, on the west side of Lafayette Street, was a group of nine Greek-Revival marble town houses built in 1833, which became the most fashionable addresses in the city. Today only four of these survive. (Museum of the City of New York)

of resident David Gardiner. John Jacob Astor died nearby in 1848 at the age of 85, leaving a fortune of $20 million. An interesting reminder of John Jacob Astor's lucrative fur business can be seen in the colorful ceramic panels depicting beavers, set in the tile walls of the **Astor Place subway station,** one block north.

The houses, now subdivided into apartments and commercial properties, are in a rather depressing state. The original stoops have been removed, outrageous disfigurements have sprung up on the roof, and many of the ornate details are either damaged or missing (observe what is left of the lovely row of anthemions on the cornice). In addition, a patina of a hundred years of neglect covers the entire façade. Some attempt at preservation and restoration is being undertaken by a few of the owners, which may possibly return this landmark to a modicum of its former opulence.

14. Facing the beautiful row is the **former Astor Library,** now the **Joseph Papp Public Theater.** Begun in 1849 as Astor's bequest to the City of New York, the library was built in three stages (south wing, by Alexander Saeltzer, completed in 1853; center wing, by Griffith Thomas, in 1859; and north wing, by Thomas Stent, in 1881). It was the city's first major library accessible to the public, and was combined in 1895 with the Tilden Foundation and the Lenox Library to form the nucleus of the New York Public Library.

From 1921 to 1965 the building was the headquarters of the HIAS—the Hebrew Immigrant Aid & Sheltering Society—which since 1884 has been a worldwide migration agency responsible for the rescue of almost four million refugees and their settlement in lands of freedom. When the HIAS moved uptown to larger quarters, the survival of this lovely Italian Renaissance *palazzo* was seriously threatened. Virtually at the eleventh hour it was saved through the efforts of impresario Joseph Papp and a group of concerned citizens who ultimately convinced a skeptical City Council to recommend municipal purchase of the building as a permanent home for the **New York Shakespeare Festival.**

Renovation began in 1967 under the supervision of architect Giorgio Cavaglieri (who restored the Jefferson Market Courthouse [*see* Greenwich Village, 33]), and was completed several years later. The Public Theater is an ideal example of adaptive reuse, proving that one can deal with old spaces and make them work. Contrary to the custom of gutting the interior and merely preserving the façade, Cavaglieri saved the elaborate interior, converting the two-tier skylit atrium of the former main reading room into the 300-seat Anspacher Theater. Two other large spaces were likewise made into theaters. The entrance and lobby remains a classic Corinthian colonnade. (Walk in, look around…and purchase a subscription to a performance series! Public restrooms are available.)

15. No. 436–440 is a large cast-iron commercial building in virtually pristine condition. Although no architectural beauty, it is typical of this type of construction [*see* SoHo Cast-Iron District walking tour]. It was designed by Edward Kendall in 1870 for Alfred Benjamin & Company, which manufactured men's clothing. Note their initials on the six escutcheons mounted on the pilasters. Interesting are the ram's horn volutes on the capitals, and full ram's horn on the shields.

Adjacent **No. 442–450,** occupying the corner lot, is maintained in almost original appearance by appreciative owners. Built in 1875 from plans by Griffith Thomas, it was for many years the headquarters of book publisher J. J. Little & Company (now Little, Brown & Co.), and is another example of the pleasing wedding of cast iron and masonry.

16. No. 13 Astor Place (formerly the District 65 Building of the Distributive Workers of America; earlier, Clinton Hall; originally, the Mercantile Library) (George E. Harney, 1890). It is also the site of the old Astor Place Opera House, "and thereby hangs a tale...."

A black page in New York City history was written on the evening of May 10, 1849, when a rampaging mob of thousands stormed the theater in one of the city's bloodiest outbursts of violence. **The Astor Place Riot,** as the event came to be called, stemmed from a bitter rivalry and ongoing feud between English tragedian William Macready and America's greatest actor, Edwin Forrest. Against a background of anti-British sentiment and a general antipathy toward foreigners as well as home-grown aristocrats, feelings had been running high for a number of weeks—spurred in great measure by rumormongers, know-nothings, and a sensationalist press.

That evening, when the curtain rose on the English actor's performance of *Macbeth,* a large and noisy crowd gathered in Astor Place, spilling over into the adjoining streets from Broadway to the Bowery. During the play, Macready was pelted with a steady stream of rotten eggs, copper pennies, and an assortment of vegetables. In the third scene a group of gangsters, led by small-time politician Isaiah Rynders, interrupted Macready's performance with screams and epithets, while a group of supporters of the English actor hurled back abuse with equal vigor. When the play was able to resume, the continuing commotion drowned out the stage. By the time the third act had begun, the mob outside started to assault the theater with bricks and stones. The police, although forewarned, were hopelessly outnumbered, and could do nothing to quell the screaming, cursing multitude that was now advancing on the theater's entrance. Estimates numbered the raging crowd at between 10,000 and 20,000.

In the meantime, the militia had been summoned from the nearby Tompkins Market Armory, but was restrained from action by nervous Mayor Caleb Woodhull, who feared the political consequences of any drastic action. Woodhull himself quietly fled the scene, leaving decisions to the unit's commanding officer. Finally, the order was given to fire, and after a warning volley over the heads of the rioters, the militiamen reluctantly fired volley after volley at point-blank range, killing 31 persons and leaving 150 wounded, putting an end to the worst theater riot in history.

17. At the time of the riot, Astor Place extended to where the "black cube" now rests, at the juncture with 8th Street (then called Clinton Place). Little St. Ann's Church occupied the site until Lafayette Street was pushed through to meet Fourth Avenue. Now occupying the traffic island is sculptor Bernard Rosenthal's stabile, **Alamo,** erected in 1967. Just north is the **subway entrance kiosk of the Astor Place Station.** Installed in 1986, it is an exact cast-iron replica of one of the 133 Interborough Rapid Transit subway entrances of the early 20th century.

18. Against the backdrop of a wide-open sky, the stunning **Cooper Union Foundation Building** stands as a most pleasing sight. Completed in 1859, this gift to the people by industrialist-engineer-philanthropist Peter Cooper played a significant role in the development of the city. The "Union" was established as the first free, private, nonsectarian, coeducational college. Dedicated to the fields of science and art, it occupies a special place of respect among American colleges and universities.

Peter Cooper (1791–1883), a self-educated "Renaissance Man," was responsible for the first successful American railway locomotive (the "Tom Thumb"); he worked with Cyrus W. Field in the laying of the Atlantic Cable, and, with Samuel F. B. Morse, developed the telegraph. Cooper also battled corrupt politicians and helped to improve the city's public school system. With the profits from his ironworks and a glue factory, he built Cooper Union. In 1876 he ran unsuccessfully for president on the Greenback ticket, although his son Edward was elected mayor of the city, as was his son-in-law, Abram S. Hewitt.

The building, designed in a kind of "Italian Renaissance cum Industrial" architectural style, is a unique achievement in itself, being the first to be constructed with wrought-iron beams as its framework. The exterior is of brownstone

Watercolor drawing of the Astor Place Riot of May 10, 1849, as militia from the nearby Tompkins Market Armory were firing into the crowd. A rampaging mob of between 10,000 and 20,000 stormed the Astor Place Opera House as the culmination of bitter feelings against English actor William Macready. When order was finally restored, 31 lay dead, and 150 were injured. (Museum of the City of New York)

and rough-hewn sandstone, with cast-iron columns, pilasters, and arches. It was originally a five-story building, but the "factory-roof" art studios were subsequently superimposed. The street level was built with rows of small shops to provide a steady source of revenue for the institution. On the south end of the roof, the cylindrical protuberance houses the shaft of the original circular elevator. Cooper anticipated a lift system and installed the shaft even before a practical elevator was available. The novel construction of the building, employing steel railroad rails produced in his Trenton foundry, demanded that the supported sections of the "Union" coincide in measurement with the standard length of these rails. The rails spanned the brick bearing walls and supported the brick floor arches. In a recent renovation, architecture students were fortunate in obtaining a first-hand view of the original rail placement, as the central section of the interior was literally jacked up several floors while the old masonry walls were replaced by more modern steel and reinforced concrete. Note the historical plaques on the north side.

The showpiece of the interior is the **Great Hall,** a magnificent auditorium, crisscrossed by arcades of supporting columns topped by granite arches. It was in

Diagonally across from Clinton Hall and the former Astor Place Opera House was Aberle's Theatre, previously St. Ann's Roman Catholic Church. The theater opened in 1879, changed its name to the Germania in 1894, and was demolished in 1903. St. Ann's, a national Catholic shrine, is now located at 110 East 12th Street. (The J. Clarence Davies Collection, Museum of the City of New York)

The Astor Place Opera House at the intersection of Astor and Clinton places (later 8th Street) was rebuilt after the riot of 1849 and later became Clinton Hall and the Mercantile Library. In this photo taken ca. 1868, the building also houses auction rooms and the Sixpenny Savings Bank. The present building on the site, No. 13 Astor Place, had also been called Clinton Hall. (New-York Historical Society)

the Great Hall that the Institution's inaugural lecture was given by Mark Twain in 1859. A year later Abraham Lincoln delivered his momentous "Right Makes Might" speech, establishing a Cooper Union lecture tradition followed by every president up to Woodrow Wilson.

The reconstruction, adhering essentially to the original plans of architect Frederick A. Peterson, was carried out by Cooper Union graduate architects under the direction of architecture department head John Hejduk.

Walk south along the Cooper Union Building to the small park called Cooper Triangle.

19. The statue of Peter Cooper was executed in 1894 by one of the country's foremost sculptors, Augustus Saint-Gaudens. Among his best known works

An engraving of Cooper Union, with the Tompkins Market (right) and Bible House (left), enlivened by prancing horses and richly clad citizens as seen in Valentine's Manual *of 1861, looking north from Fourth Avenue and 6th Street. (Museum of the City of New York)*

are the equestrian statue of General Sherman near the Plaza Hotel, the statue of David G. Farragut in Madison Square Park, the marble altar relief in the nearby Church of the Ascension, as well as the design of one of our former 20-dollar gold pieces. The base and canopy of the monument are by Stanford White.

Notice the attractive, and very visible, **Cooper Union clock** with its seven-foot frosted glass face. Once driven by an enormous weight and pendulum, it is now powered by a tiny electric motor.

The Bowery, which becomes Third Avenue at this point, was once darkened by the **Third Avenue El,** which rumbled by overhead from 1879 to 1950, on its way from South Ferry and Chatham Square to several points in the Bronx. Old-timers still look back with relish at the speedy, open-air ride provided by the old El. Although the Bowery and Third Avenue were never thoroughfares of scenic beauty, the exciting cityscape panoramas provided by these elevated trains cannot be duplicated by the much slower-moving ground-level buses of today.

20. The **Abram S. Hewitt Memorial Hall** of Cooper Union may by now be just a memory. Designed in 1912 by Clinton & Russell, and named for Peter Cooper's partner and son-in-law, it occupied the site of the Tompkins Market Armory. Before it burned down, the barn-like structure was a public market on the ground floor and an armory above. It was from here that the 27th Regiment, National Guard, was summoned to quell the Stone Cutters' Guild Riot in 1834 (*see* page 115), the Astor Place Theatre Riot in 1849, as well as the Civil War Draft Riots in 1863, in which the unit had to be recalled from Gettysburg. The regiment is now based in the Seventh Regiment Armory at Park Avenue and 67th Street. On the present site, to replace this dull 1950's structure will be

Cooper Union's nine-story engineering school and art studios by Thom Mayne, of Morphosis, whose revolutionary design calls for a shimmering metal façade resting on a base of retail stores, in scale with the CU's Foundation Building across Third Avenue.

Look south on the Bowery toward a house on the southeast corner of East 6th Street, where a huge colorful mural dramatically depicts the skyline of New York portrayed in flowers, and highlights the lost World Trade Center towers. (You may want to take a closer look.) The restored Federal-style house, dating from ca. 1835, now houses a restaurant.

Cross Cooper Square to the northeast corner of East 7th Street.

The area east of the Bowery, roughly between Houston Street and East 14th Street, and extending almost to the East River, is the **"East Village,"** formerly considered part of the Lower East Side.

From the early 19th century, successive waves of immigrants occupied the crowded tenements, leaving their individual ethnic stamp on the neighborhood. First came the Irish, followed by Germans, Jews, Poles, Ukrainians, and after World War II, the Spanish-speaking, mainly from Puerto Rico. In the 1950s and '60s the low rents attracted artists, writers, "beatniks," "hippies," and many who just liked the ethnic mix. During the 1980s, 1990s, and 2000s, the scene gradually changed. The new immigrants, who seem to prefer working to idling, are arriving in great numbers from Russia and Southeast Asia.

In the several-square-block area just east of the Bowery, centered on East 7th Street, there remains an active, tight-knit **Ukrainian enclave.**

21. The **former Metropolitan Savings Bank** is an ornate pile of marble, very similar in style to the cast-iron buildings for which it served as a model. Attributed to architect Carl Pfeiffer and built in 1868, its stately French Second Empire façade must have presented a convincing appearance of strength to its depositors, and it was one of the city's first fireproof buildings. It is now a church serving the First Ukrainian Assembly of God.

22. At 11 East 7th Street is **Surma's Ukrainian Shop**—a fascinating emporium offering Ukrainian books, music, records, colorful "peasant" clothing, painted (real) eggs, jewelry, and owner-cultivated honey.

23. McSorley's Old Ale House (No. 15) antedates the Ukrainian influx by many years, and claims to be the oldest saloon in the city, but it isn't! According to tavern-historian Richard McDermott, the site was an empty lot until 1860; nor is there any entry in business directories that lists a John McSorley until 1862. (But please don't mention it inside!) Incidentally, Pete's Tavern, on Irving Place, makes a similar inaccurate claim. [*See* Chapter 9.] Formerly a man's domain, it now permits women to share the authentic old-time atmosphere. In the dimly lit tavern, dozens of aging photographs and yellowing newspaper clippings hang on the grimy sheet-tin walls.

24. St. George's Ukrainian Catholic Church (Apollinaire Osadca, 1977) replaced an earlier church that was situated on an adjacent lot. St. George's, with its large school, is the religious and cultural center of the Ukrainian Catholic community. The adjacent short street, formerly Hall Place, has been renamed in honor of the 19th-century Ukrainian poet, Taras Shevchenko.

Continue toward Second Avenue.

At No. 31, on the north side, was the **Hebrew Actor's Union and Actor's Club,** which hearkens back to the golden age of the Yiddish theater at the turn of the century. At the height of the Jewish immigration, Second Avenue from Houston Street to 14th Street was known as the **Yiddish Rialto.** Little now remains of the once lively Yiddish theater except for an occasional on-Broadway production. The old playhouses that once lined Second Avenue were either demolished or stand vacant. One of a small handful of surviving buildings is the ornate little **Orpheum Theater,** around the corner at 126 Second Avenue. It still hangs in as a legitimate theater, but no longer as a Yiddish playhouse.

At Second Avenue, turn north to St. Mark's Place.

Side by side, at Nos. 135 and 137 Second Avenue, are the **Ottendorfer Branch of the New York Free Circulating Library** and the **Stuyvesant Polyclinic.** Both were donated by Ann and Oswald Ottendorfer, German-American philanthropists who were deeply concerned with the cultural and physical welfare of the large German community of the Lower East Side. Both buildings were designed by architect William Schickel and erected in 1883–84. The library and clinic, formerly the *Freie Bibliothek und Lesehall* and the German Dispensary, respectively, are a unified pair, the former in Victorian style, with some elements of neo-Italian Renaissance and Queen Anne; and the latter in an exuberant version of neo-Italian Renaissance, with innovative and decorative use of terra cotta. The Ottendorfer Library was the first free public lending library and the oldest branch of the New York Public Library system.

Turn around and walk west on St. Mark's Place.

25. St. Mark's Place is the "main drag" of the East Village and it was the center of New York City's "counterculture." It is difficult to conceive that this was a most fashionable residential block in the early 19th century, with rows of elegant Federal- and Greek Revival–style town houses. Vestiges still survive here and there along the block, covered by coats of garish paint and hidden by all manner of "improvements."

No. 20, the **former Daniel LeRoy House,** the last holdout of the former row of town houses on the south side of the street, was built in 1832, and shows many Greek Revival–style features. (Note the historic plaque.)

No. 12 was built for the **German American Shooting Society** in 1885. It was mainly a social club. (The beer drinking was done here, the shooting elsewhere.)

No. 4 (1830–31) still retains a few of its Greek Revival–style elements, including a stone molding and fanlight over the entrance.

26. Diagonally across St. Mark's Place, between 8th and 9th streets, is the modern **Cooper Union Engineering Building** (Voorhees, Smith, Smith, and Haines, 1961). It occupies the site of the old "Bible House," headquarters of the American Bible Society from 1852 to 1956, when it moved uptown to the Lincoln Center area—probably the last publishing house to move from the district.

Turn right (north) on 4th Avenue and walk one block north to just beyond 10th Street.

27. With the large number of local institutions dedicated to books and book production (Astor Library, Mercantile Library, Cooper Union, Scribner's, Bible House, the many publishing houses, as well as nearby New York University), it was no surprise that Fourth Avenue north to 14th Street became the second-hand book center of the city. The five blocks that once comprised **"Booksellers' Row"** boasted no fewer than two dozen book dealers. Sidewalk stands in front of the shops were always piled high with cheap books of every description, but the *cognoscenti* would seek out the real "finds" on the dusty shelves of the dark, labyrinthine interiors. Only one of the booksellers remains: Strand, at 828 Broadway. As in the past, browsers are always welcome.

On the west side of Fourth Avenue, between 10th and 11th streets, is the charming Gothic Revival–style **Grace Church Houses and School.** Enriching the appearance of the street, it was built in harmony with the landmark Grace Church, around the corner on Broadway. [For a description of Grace Church, *see* Ladies' Mile, Fashion Row, and Union Square, 2.] The attractive neo-Gothic–style group of buildings was erected in sections over a 35-year period: **The Clergy House,** No. 92 (Heins & LaFarge, 1892); **Grace Memorial House** (Huntington House), No. 94–96 (James Renwick, Jr., 1882–83); **Neighborhood House,** No. 98 (Renwick, Aspinwall & Tucker, 1906–07). In 1974–75 the church sought to demolish Nos. 92 and 94–96 to enlarge its school, and became engaged in a bitter struggle with preservationists. The matter was resolved by gutting the interiors but preserving the façades.

Return to 9th Street and turn left (east), cross Third Avenue (again), then half-left into Stuyvesant Street.

The corner of Third Avenue, East 9th Street, and Stuyvesant Street is bracketed by two university dormitories. On the southeast corner is Cooper Union's Undergraduate Dormitory (Prentice & Chan, Ohlhausen, 1996), and across Stuyvesant Street, New York University's Alumni Hall (Voorsanger & Mills Assocs., 1986). Note that the base of the N.Y.U. building matches the roofline of its neighbors, then leaps up 16 stories to its roof that is surmounted by what appears to be a blimp hangar.

Stuyvesant Street was originally designed to be the entrance to Governor Peter Stuyvesant's farm. The minipark, called the **George Hecht Viewing Garden,** pays homage to New York's Dutch heritage, according to the plaque on the fence, "by restoring a patch of greenery to what was in the 17th century part of Stuyvesant's *bouwerie,* or farm."

28. As you enter the **St. Mark's Historic District,** walk east along Stuyvesant Street to No. 21, the **Stuyvesant Fish House** (1803–04). The brick Federal-style house was built by Gov. Peter Stuyvesant's great-grandson Petrus as a wedding gift for his daughter Elizabeth, who was to marry Nicholas Fish, a young Revolutionary War officer. Their son Hamilton was born in 1808 and ultimately became Governor, U.S. Senator, and Secretary of State. The landmark house is considered a unique example of a fine New York urban dwelling of the period.

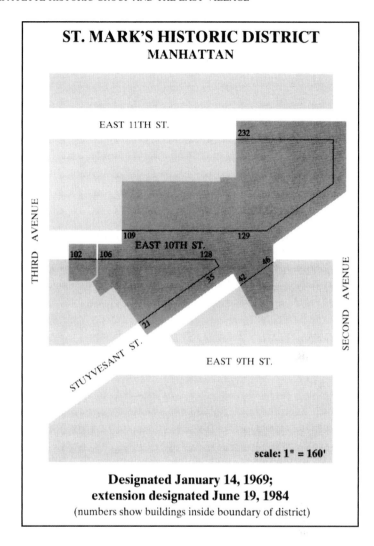

Across the street is the N.Y.U. **Edgar Starr Barney Building,** No. 34, originally the Hebrew Technical Institute. Founded in 1884, the mission of the Institute, one of the first technical high schools in the country, was to train immigrant youth in industrial arts. It graduated its last class in 1939.

Continue to where Stuyvesant Street meets East 10th Street at an acute angle. The houses numbered 21–35 and 42–46 Stuyvesant Street and numbered 106–128 and 109–129 East 10th Street are a unified group of Anglo-Italianate row houses that form part of the **"Renwick Triangle."**

These handsome brick houses were erected in 1861 by Mathias Banta, a well-known speculative builder, who had purchased the property, once the site of Elizabeth Fish's garden, from her son, Hamilton Fish. The restoration of the buildings, which had begun to deteriorate badly after years of rooming-house occupancy, began in the mid-1960s. **No. 118 East 10th Street** was the childhood home of Stanford White in the 1850s.

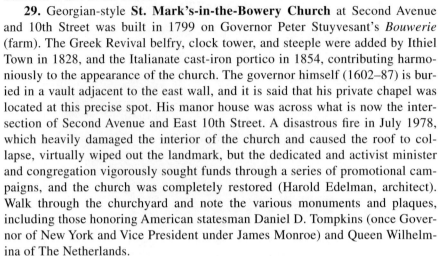

29. Georgian-style **St. Mark's-in-the-Bowery Church** at Second Avenue and 10th Street was built in 1799 on Governor Peter Stuyvesant's *Bouwerie* (farm). The Greek Revival belfry, clock tower, and steeple were added by Ithiel Town in 1828, and the Italianate cast-iron portico in 1854, contributing harmoniously to the appearance of the church. The governor himself (1602–87) is buried in a vault adjacent to the east wall, and it is said that his private chapel was located at this precise spot. His manor house was across what is now the intersection of Second Avenue and East 10th Street. A disastrous fire in July 1978, which heavily damaged the interior of the church and caused the roof to collapse, virtually wiped out the landmark, but the dedicated and activist minister and congregation vigorously sought funds through a series of promotional campaigns, and the church was completely restored (Harold Edelman, architect). Walk through the churchyard and note the various monuments and plaques, including those honoring American statesman Daniel D. Tompkins (once Governor of New York and Vice President under James Monroe) and Queen Wilhelmina of The Netherlands.

The flagpole on the sidewalk in front of the church was donated as a memorial by the Ukrainian-American Society in 1944. An adjacent plaque commemorates the career of community activist and business leader, Abe Lebewohl, who frequently expressed pride in his Ukrainian roots. Lebewohl, the owner of the nearby Second Avenue Deli, was the victim of an unsolved murder in front of his restaurant in 1996.

The Second Avenue Deli, 156 Second Avenue, a few steps south, has been a neighborhood landmark for over 70 years, as one of the few authentic remaining Jewish delicatessen restaurants. It became a popular gastronomic rendezvous for Yiddish Theater actors of the time, and on the sidewalk in front of the entrance are engraved the names of 60 of the most famous. (Those unfamiliar with the cuisine will find it a gustatory adventure.)

Continue north on Second Avenue to East 11th Street, cross, and walk east to No. 232.

The former Rectory of St. Mark's Church, now the **Neighborhood Preservation Center,** was designed by noted architect Ernest R. Flagg in 1900 and is built on part of the old Church graveyard. The attractive two-story house with a high metal roof was painstakingly restored in 1999 by Harold Edelman, architect of the Church's restoration. Note the handsome porch and cast-iron staircase that face the east side of the Church. The structure serves as home to the Neighborhood Preservation Center, an umbrella site for the Historic Districts Council, St. Mark's Historic Landmark Fund, and the Greenwich Village Society for Historic Preservation. Visitors welcome; (212) 471-9987.

Return to Second Avenue and walk north.

A famous survivor of the heyday of the Yiddish Rialto is the Moorish Revival–style **Louis N. Jaffe Art Theater,** formerly the Yiddish Art Theater/Yiddish Folks Theater, now The Village East City Cinemas, at the corner of Second Avenue and East 12th Street. The building was commissioned in 1925 by prominent Jewish civic leader Louis N. Jaffe as the permanent home for the Yiddish Art Theater, under the direction of preeminent Yiddish actor Maurice Schwartz. Yiddish theatrical performances continued until 1945, although there was a brief reprise between 1961 and 1965 and intermittently thereafter. With no fewer than 22 name changes through the years, including its longest tenure as the Phoenix Theater, it witnessed a variety of productions from burlesque to musicals and off-Broadway stage shows. The theater closed in 1988 and was converted three years later into a complex of seven movie theaters called the Village East City Cinemas. The interior has been designated a landmark because of its elaborate polychrome ornamentation (Harrison G. Wiseman, architect, and Willy Pogany, designer). The extravagant motifs of Moorish, Alhambraic, Islamic, and Judaic styles are splendid, particularly in the ceiling, which displays some of the most remarkable plaster craftsmanship in the city. The Jaffe Art Theater is listed on the National and New York State Registers of Historic Places.

End of tour. At 14th Street turn left to Union Square for the 4, 5, 6, N, Q, R, W, L subway lines, and the M1, M2, M3, M6, M7 buses.

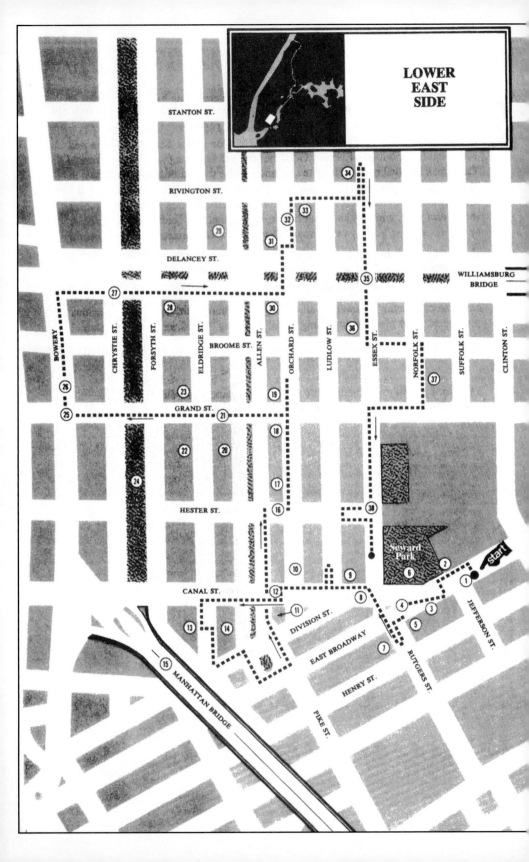

6. The Lower East Side

[Subway: F line to East Broadway, walk one block east on East Broadway to Jefferson Street.]

The first tides of mass immigration to this country began sweeping across our shores just before the mid-19th century, with millions of refugees, mostly from Europe, seeking a haven from famines, wars, economic and political repression, and religious persecution. In successive waves they came—Irish, English, Germans, Swedes, Jews, Italians, Slavs—from northern Europe to the eastern Mediterranean, enduring the hardships of a long steerage voyage in crowded, foul ships. Mostly poor and strange to our ways, they would frequently gather together in the larger cities, creating with their fellow countrymen sprawling ghettos that were to become a kind of staging area in the gradual process of assimilation into the new culture.

Among the largest of the immigrant groups were the Jews from eastern Europe, who after 1870 began arriving in ever increasing numbers, fleeing the widespread pogroms and economic restrictions that had become commonplace throughout Poland, Hungary, Bohemia, Russia, and the Balkans. Settling largely on the Lower East Side—a four-square-mile corner of Manhattan bounded roughly by 14th Street on the north, Catherine Street on the south, the Bowery on the west, and the East River on the east—they moved into the squalid, hastily constructed tenements that filled every block in the area. As new arrivals continuously swelled the teeming ghetto, it became the most densely populated district in the world. By 1894, the population reached an astonishing 986 people per acre—one-and-a-half times that of Bombay, India! The immigrant Jews, seeking to maintain their Old World ties, also tended to band together by country of origin, thus creating within the Lower East Side enclaves of Russians, Poles, Rumanians, Lithuanians, Hungarians, and Levantines. In common, however, they shared their religious beliefs and rituals, their miserable living conditions, and their hopes for a better life. Many of the immigrants were drawn to the needle trades, and eked out a meager existence working in the unregulated sweatshops, or laboring in their tiny, crowded cold-water flats in what soon became a cottage garment industry centered about the family sewing machine. Others were employed in the numerous small retail shops and factories that proliferated on the street floors of the tenements, while many chose "private enterprise" as pushcart vendors, hawking an endless variety of wares from these ubiquitous two-wheeled establishments that lined the main thoroughfares of the Lower East Side.

In spite of their grinding poverty, the struggle for survival, and the drudgery of daily life, Jewish institutions flourished. More than 500 synagogues and *talmud torahs* (religious schools) were constructed: a Yiddish theater was founded, Hebrew and Yiddish book publishers flourished, and more than a dozen Yiddish newspapers appeared on the newsstands. Rapid naturalization was the immediate goal of all immigrants, and evening classes in English and Americanization at the neighborhood public schools were always jammed to overflowing. Every newcomer dreamed of the day when, no longer a greenhorn, he could climb the economic ladder, become a "real American," and make a better life for himself and his children.

With the passage in the 1920s of restrictive laws, the great flood of immigration was finally halted and the growth of the ghetto stemmed. As families moved to better neighborhoods in the city, the "old neighborhood" began to decline, and the Jewish ghetto is now largely gone. The depressing tenements are being replaced by high-rise apartments; the small family-run shops are giving way to supermarkets and large retail stores; the hundreds of synagogues—many of them awesome architectural masterpieces—are reduced to a scant, crumbling handful; and the *lingua franca,* once exclusively Yiddish, is yielding to a babel of Chinese, Spanish, and Hindi.

The walking tour of the Lower East Side is largely an imaginative glimpse of the past through a number of the vestiges and surviving artifacts of that era of Jewish immigration—a sort of last look at the remnants of the old neighborhood, which in a few short years will be no more. It was a wonderfully rich and fruitful period of American history in which millions of Jews came to the United States through the port of New York and spread across the entire country making their contributions to the total fabric of American life.

Begin the Lower East Side tour at the corner of East Broadway and Jefferson Street (on the park side), one block east of the East Broadway subway station. (The tour is best made on a Sunday.)

1. The Educational Alliance (197 East Broadway) was known as the Hebrew Institute when the building was erected in 1891 from plans by the Jewish architectural firm of Brunner & Tryon. It was organized by a group of "uptown Jews" as an educational, cultural, intellectual, and social service center for the residents of the Lower East Side. It provided training in Americanization for the newly arrived immigrants, and is credited with helping speed up the immigrants' process of assimilation with its day and evening classes in English and citizenship. It housed a free library at a time when no public libraries existed in the city, and its classes were later used as models for the New York City Board of Education's citizenship program for the foreign-born. The Alliance also distributed clothing and food to the needy. Classes for children were also offered in Jewish religion and history, and the Alliance conducted free Sabbath and High Holy Day services for those too poor to be members of a synagogue congregation. It was also a pioneer in the concept of summer camp for children.

Through the years the Alliance has expanded its educational work, offering free courses in a wide spectrum of disciplines: art, music, philosophy, drama, science, and vocational skills. Although its original constituency is largely gone, it holds classes for Chinese and other children whose parents work during the day. It is also very active in community social service projects, and conducts many programs for senior citizens, including a daily lunch.

The Lower East Side's population is now approximately 50 percent Chinese, 25 percent Hispanic, 5 percent black, 10 percent other (South Asians, Koreans, Albanians, Italians, etc.), and only 10 percent Jews. The original East Broadway building of the Alliance was modernized in 1970–71 and renamed the David Sarnoff Building.

2. To the left (in the park) is the **Seward Park Branch of the New York Public Library.** Built in 1910, it was one of the early branches of the newly established free municipal library system. The public library was founded by Andrew Carnegie, who was instrumental in merging the Astor, Tilden, and Lenox Trust libraries—the three largest private collections in the city.

So great was this free library's popularity with the immigrants when it opened that it was not uncommon to see long lines of adults and youngsters patiently awaiting their turn to enter the crowded building. Until recently this branch had the largest Yiddish collection in the city. Next to the library, at the turn of the century, stood the office of _Der Groisser Kundess_ (The Big Stick), a popular Yiddish weekly that published humorous stories and cartoons, and offered a bit of comic relief from the grim realities of immigrant life.

3. Across the street, at 175 East Broadway, towers the ten-story **former Jewish Daily Forward Building** (George A. Boehn, 1911). The building is no longer occupied by the _Forward,_ as the newspaper has moved its offices uptown, where it continues to publish, with an annual deficit made up by contributions from loyal supporters. Founded in 1897 by Abraham Cahan, the _Forward_ became the most influential newspaper in the Jewish community, and was read with a dedication second only to that given to the religious books. As an ardent campaigner for the improvement of the human condition, Abe Cahan and the _Forward_ supported the labor movement, fought dishonest politicians, and led in the battle to eliminate the sweatshops, at the same time helping the immigrants adapt to the New World and encouraging them to become informed, loyal citizens. The _Forward_ always lent a sympathetic ear to the problems of its readers, and until 1982 conducted a daily column called the _Bintel Brief_ (Bundle of Letters), in which problems of readers were printed and answered by the editor. (The column has yielded to one on Social Security.) The paper has always provided a forum for the greatest Yiddish writers (Isaac Bashevis Singer was a regular contributor), and maintains a small staff of foreign correspondents who provide material not available from the usual wire services. Its present circulation is less than a fifth of the 1924 peak of 200,000, and it's now a weekly, published uptown, but there is still sufficient interest in Yiddish, with support from contributions, to keep it alive.

The building, which housed not only the *Forward* but also an active Yiddish theater and the offices of many Jewish labor organizations, is now in the hands of the Chinese Center. To the east of the Forward Building, at No. 183, in a structure that now houses the East Side Cafe, was the home of the large-circulation *Morning Journal–Day,* once two Yiddish dailies that merged in the late 1920s. Its closing in 1972 was mourned by many faithful readers. The *Tageblatt,* an even older daily, stood at the corner of Jefferson Street.

4. Triangular **Nathan Straus Square** (formerly called Rutgers Square) is named for the Jewish philanthropist who in 1919 sponsored a program of free sterilized-milk stations for children throughout the country. Nathan Straus, a partner in the R. H. Macy enterprise with his brother, Isadore, was active for many years in charitable causes. (Isadore and his wife went down on the *Titanic* in 1912.)

The circular marble shaft was erected in tribute to the servicemen of the Lower East Side who gave their lives in both World Wars.

5. At the corner of East Broadway and Rutgers Street is the **site of the former Garden Cafeteria.** A local landmark for many years, it had been a favored gathering place of the local "intelligentsia," especially for the staff of the nearby *Forward.* At the turn of the century when the immediate area was known as the "Athens of the Lower East Side" because of the number of newspapers, publishers, and bookstores located close by, an earlier restaurant on the site was the gathering place of journalists, authors, and celebrated actors of the then very active Yiddish theater. In its final years after the departure of the *Forward,* the "Garden" was just a popular and inexpensive dining spot, and a convenient place to meet for an assortment of East Side characters. Changing demographics and economic realities made it more and more difficult for the restaurant to survive, and as the last owner once commented dryly, "How can we stay in business when people come in and spend a whole day over one cup of coffee?" The present Chinese fast-food establishment, replete with typical roast fowls hanging in the window, is dramatic evidence of the changes that are taking place throughout the East Side. Note the many Chinese wholesale food distributors.

6. Seward Park, carved out of a former slum district, provides a pleasant retreat for the inhabitants of the surrounding crowded and shadeless streets.

7. St. Teresa's Roman Catholic Church, at the corner of Rutgers and Henry streets, was founded in 1863 to serve the growing Irish immigrant community that at the time occupied much of the Lower East Side. Built in 1841 as the First Presbyterian Church of New York, it was purchased through the efforts of then-Archbishop Corrigan, and now serves new immigrant groups. It is possibly the only trilingual Catholic church in the city, offering masses in English, Spanish, and Chinese. The church is typical of the Gothic Revival style that gained so much popularity in the decade of the 1840s. The adjacent apartment building was once the site of the Hebrew National *Wurstfabrik* (sausage factory).

Hester Street was the main shopping thoroughfare of the Lower East Side, with pushcarts, shops, and stalls lining both sides of the street. This view, looking east from Essex Street to Norfolk Street, was taken in 1899, at the height of Jewish immigration. (Museum of the City of New York)

Rutgers Street is named for the Henry Rutgers family, whose farm occupied much of the land from this point to the East River during the Colonial period. Their property bordered the James DeLancey farm, and the boundary, once a country lane, is now appropriately called **Division Street.** Division Street beyond the Manhattan Bridge was famous early in the century for its millinery district and its very aggressive "pulleresses"—women employees who stood outside the store and pulled in the unwary to get "bargains." From the 1920s until the early 1970s it was a well-known center for women's outerwear.

8. The nameless square (or triangle) formed by the confluence of Canal, Ludlow, and Division streets is particularly colorful during the Jewish festival of Succoth, or Feast of Tabernacles, which according to the lunar calendar can fall anywhere from late September to mid-October. The sidewalks are lined with vendors, many in Hasidic garb, selling myrtle leaves, palm fronds, and citrons imported from the Holy Land. These are bought by religious Jews to decorate their *Succah,* or outdoor lattice hut, where meals are taken during the holiday in celebration of the harvest, but with the fast-changing demographics, this colorful celebration will likely soon disappear.

9. Walk one block west on Canal Street, noting the large number and variety of Chinese establishments. Not a word of English can be heard. These blocks once boasted rows of Hebrew and Yiddish bookstores.

Turn right on Ludlow Street. On the right is the massive structure of the now-defunct **Loew's Canal.** When you return to Canal Street, see if you can discover the somewhat altered but still ornate former entrance to this defunct silent-film movie house. It is now occupied by a discount electrical appliance store, and the dark recesses of the theater are used as a warehouse.

At No. 5 Ludlow Street is the equally defunct **Independent Kletzker Brotherly Aid Society** building (1910), whose name and founding date may be read in the pediment. It was customary for newly arrived immigrant groups to maintain association with those from the same *shtetl*, or small town. If the group was large or wealthy enough, they might build a synagogue and a *talmud torah*, purchase a cemetery lot, and sometimes establish a benevolent or mutual-aid society, called a *landsmanshaft*, for their members. This is the only such surviving building in the neighborhood, and was constructed for an immigrant group from the Polish village of Kletsk. The L-shaped building was sold early in this century to Max Kobre's Bank, a private Jewish bank that failed after World War I. (Note the beehives on the second-floor ledge.) In more recent times it was the Zion Funeral Chapel; however, changing population patterns forced Zion to move and it is now a Chinese funeral parlor. The upper stories, which once housed the *landsmanshaft*'s synagogue, have been converted into apartments.

Return to Canal Street and continue west one block to Orchard Street.

10. Orchard Street for the seven blocks north of Canal Street has been the principal commercial thoroughfare for many years. For those living outside the neighborhood, Orchard Street, originally the location of the DeLancey estate's orchards, is now synonymous with the Lower East Side. Hectic, bustling, and noisy, it is the closest thing to a "native market." Before the pushcarts were ruled off the streets by city ordinance, it was even busier. Here on Sundays come bargain hunters from all over the New York metropolitan area, taking advantage of the discounts—real and fanciful—offered by the endless row of small retail shops. It is said that the Lower East Side is the only complete mercantile district in the city, where virtually anything can be purchased, and at a lower price than anywhere else. In recent years, there has been a noticeable decline in the busy commerce of Orchard Street, due to the popularity of the growing number of suburban "big boxes" that now offer similar (and sometimes better) discounts than the traditional Orchard Street bargains . . . and there is no bargaining. Yet the street hangs on, supported by loyal merchants' associations and community development organizations. (A stroll along Orchard Street comes later in the tour.)

11. On the southwest corner of Canal and Orchard streets looms the tallest structure on the Lower East Side—the **former Jarmulovsky's Bank** building (Rouse & Goldstone, 1912), now a multi-use loft building. Only a few old-timers remember that active financial institution, founded in 1873, which served as the local Baron Rothschild for more than 40 years, ultimately bringing grief to thousands of unlucky depositors when it collapsed in 1917. Federal banking regulations were quite lax in those days, and private banks flourished throughout the country. Sender Jarmulovsky, who died in 1912 and left the management to his sons, was a shrewd financier whose success climaxed in the construction of this imposing building at the height of the immigration period. However, mismanagement and a run on the bank by depositors wishing to send money to relatives as World War I threatened forced it into insolvency, owing its creditors millions and ruining thousands of trusting immigrants. The New York State Banking Department then took it over.

In 1991 the owner of the building demolished a circular, templelike structure which crowned the building, thus destroying what was once one of the neighborhood's most prominent skyline features and forfeiting any possibility for future landmark status.

12. Allen Street, one block west, was once a dark and dingy thoroughfare, echoing with the rattle of the former Second Avenue Elevated, and boasting one of the largest red-light districts in town. With the El gone and the street widened in 1930 (note the absence of building fronts on the east side), it is a main north-south artery of the city, and above Houston Street it becomes First Avenue. Little remains of its once lusty past. In recent times it was a popular center for copper-and-brass antique merchants, but now all have vanished—replaced by Chinese wholesale food dealers and restaurants.

Canal Street is named for the 40-foot-wide drainage ditch, or canal, that was dug in the late 18th century to drain the Collect (the fresh water pond on the site of Foley Square [*see* page 103], a former city water source that had become polluted). The canal emptied into the Hudson River and was crossed by a bridge at Broadway. The ditch was filled in by 1809 and Canal Street was laid out above it. Three years later, the foul-smelling Collect, no longer a viable drinking water source, was also drained and its underground springs filled in.

At Eldridge Street turn south (left).

13. On **Eldridge Street,** with its multitude of Oriental people, the proliferation of signs exclusively in Chinese, and the babel in Cantonese, Mandarin, Fukienese, and other dialects, one can easily envisage a busy side street in a major Chinese city. The street was named for Lieutenant Joseph C. Eldridge, killed in ambush by Canadian Indians in the War of 1812. At No. 20 is the **Pu Zhao Buddhist Temple.** Visitors are welcome to visit the diminutive incense-perfumed sanctuary and see the gilt statue of Buddha in a candlelit shrine surrounded by offerings of fruit and flowers. The Old Law tenement at **No. 19** is purported to be the birthplace of actor Eddie Cantor. Old Law tenements prevail throughout most of the Lower East Side. Prior to the passage of the "Old Law" in 1879, and modifications in 1887, there was little regulation of the construction of multiple dwellings. Houses were often built of wood, without fire escapes, toilets, or water supply; and there was no provision for the ventilation of interior rooms, as only the front and rear rooms had windows. The 1879 law corrected many of these evils, and included among its requirements that an airshaft be built between adjacent tenement houses to provide (some) light and air for inside rooms, that hallways and stairways be wider and constructed of fireproof materials, that water be piped into each apartment, and that there be a toilet for each two apartments. Thus backyard privies and curbside water pumps became a thing of the past, and the tenements became a bit safer, and possibly a trifle more comfortable. Another prohibition was the construction of the so-called "backyard houses"—multiple dwellings that were built behind other houses, without direct access to the street. The addition of the airshaft to the tenement changed the overhead shape of the building from a simple rectangle to that of an exercise dumbbell—and the name "dumbbell tenement" is still applied to those built under the Old Law. In 1901 the "New Law" was passed, further modifying the building code, widening the airshaft and including a provision that houses higher than five stories must be equipped with an elevator. Seven-story walk-ups were not uncommon in the old days!

Compare this row of Old Law tenements with the row of red brick buildings farther south (with curved lintels over the windows), built in the 1870s. These are without airshafts and have narrow hallways with sheet-tin walls and ceilings, and wooden floors and staircases. Fire escapes were added as mandated by the 1879 Law, otherwise these nonfireproof buildings would be frightening fire traps. Scores of pre–Old Law tenements still exist throughout the Lower East Side.

14. The imposing synagogue, **Congregation Khal Adath Jeshurun and Anshe Lubz, The Eldridge Street Synagogue,** at 12–14 Eldridge Street, was once the largest Jewish house of worship in the neighborhood. Erected in 1886 from plans by Herter Brothers, it is built mainly in Moorish Revival style with some Gothic elements. Except for missing finials on the cornice, the façade is in an excellent state of preservation. The interior is exceptional, with a hand-carved ark of Italian walnut, sculptured wooden balcony, enormous brass Victorian chandeliers and candelabra, high-quality stained glass, brightly painted wall murals, and a lofty, barrel-vaulted ceiling. The building had suffered years of neglect, and the effects of weather and vandalism had taken a dreadful toll. The Jewish population of the neighborhood had been declining through the years, and the congregation dwindled to the point where fewer than 20 active members remained to support this great house of worship. The magnificent sanctuary was abandoned in the mid-1930s, and services were held in the unheated basement whenever a *minyan,* or quorum of ten adult males, could be assembled.

The future of this magnificent synagogue appeared dim; but then a group of concerned citizens (including the author, who had discovered and publicized this hidden gem) organized an informal committee to help save the building. They offered tours of the building, accepted donations to make essential repairs, and then invited the New York City Landmarks Preservation Commission to visit the synagogue. The commissioners, impressed with its architectural beauty and its history as the first great house of worship built in America by Eastern European Jews, pushed through the synagogue committee's application for landmark status, and the Eldridge Street Synagogue was soon added to the list of official city landmarks. Shortly thereafter it was designated a National Historic Landmark.

It was soon apparent, however, that a more formal organization was required to assume responsibility for the restoration and maintenance. At this point the not-for-profit **Eldridge Street Project** was established to publicize the project and solicit funds and grants to preserve and protect the synagogue. The Project worked diligently, and within a few short years it accumulated donations and funds from city and state agencies, foundations, corporations, and thousands of individuals from across the country.

As a result, the building now has been stabilized, the plumbing and electrical work completed, and a very leaky roof replaced. Also continuing meticulous restoration of the stained glass, painting of the interior, and refinishing of the antique brass and elaborate woodwork are just a few of the gargantuan tasks faced by the Project. The Project has also been reaching out to the community at large by offering tours, lectures, literary and musical programs, and a variety of cultural events. They even offer Chinese-language tours for their local neighbors! And with the ongoing revitalization of the synagogue, it has become a more active house of worship with a growing congregation. But much still remains to be done, and the Project finds its work to be an ongoing day-to-day challenge. For information on tours or becoming a docent, call (212) 978-0083.

Continue south on Eldridge Street, turning left on Division Street to Pike Street.

Pike Street was named for the noted soldier and explorer, Zebulon M. Pike, for whom Pike's Peak is also named.

15. The Manhattan Bridge (Gustav Lindenthal and Carrère & Hastings, 1909) was the last-built of a trio of downtown bridges connecting Manhattan with Brooklyn. (The first, the Brooklyn Bridge, was completed in 1883, and was referred to in Yiddish as the *Alte Brick,* or Old Bridge. The Williamsburg Bridge, opened in 1903, was the *Naiye Brick,* or New Bridge.) A three-cent fare was charged on the creaky trolley that shuttled back and forth when the Manhattan Bridge was opened. In addition to four lanes of motor-vehicle traffic, it also carries several subway lines.

At the corner of Allen Street (called Pike Street as it curves toward the East River) is the **former power house of the Second Avenue El.** Note the old metal letters on the wall of the original Manhattan Elevated Railway building, as well as the row of holes for the power cables. Since the El made a sharp curve at this point to swing into Division Street, the corner of the power house was flattened. It is now a Chinese-owned warehouse.

Diagonally across the street at 15 Pike Street is the **former Congregation Sons of Israel Kalwarie synagogue,** built in 1903. This Classic Revival–style building also suffered from a dwindling congregation and was finally abandoned. In its place is the **Sung-AK Buddhist Association,** which remodeled the crumbling interior and established a temple and a bookstore (downstairs). Visitors are welcome, and as you climb the entry staircase, note the stone lions and other Buddhist artifacts.

Continue north on Pike Street (which becomes Allen Street as it passes Canal Street), to Hester Street.

16. By the 1880s **Hester Street** had become the busiest market in the Lower East Side. The street was named for Hester Rynders, daughter of Jacob Leisler, who in 1691 was wrongly hanged for treason. With both sides of the street lined with pushcarts and the wares of all the shops piled high on the sidewalks, the crowded street took on the atmosphere of an Oriental bazaar. Especially on Thursday evenings, the congestion and clamor reached its weekly peak, as Jewish housewives shopped for the Sabbath. Anything could be bought on Hester Street—dry goods, food, housewares, books, jewelry, furniture—and haggling was always the rule. On hot summer days the lack of refrigeration was very much in evidence, as fish peddlers pressed to sell out before nature took its course. Everywhere was the

The Police Court on Essex Street at the corner of Broome was replaced by Seward Park High School. In this view, taken in 1892, the high wall visible in the background was the Ludlow Street Jail, where corrupt "Boss" Tweed had died 14 years before. (New-York Historical Society)

The opening of the Manhattan Bridge in 1909 improved transportation to Brooklyn, and, to an extent, encouraged further emigration from the Lower East Side. The Manhattan Bridge Three Cents Trolley provided a cheap trip across the East River. (Brooklyn Historical Society)

smell of decay as the gutters and sidewalks accumulated "mountain ranges" of fruit peels, paper, fish scales, nutshells, rotting vegetables, and rubbish of all sorts. The horses that pulled the many wagons added an immense contribution, too.

Turn right on Hester Street and left on Orchard Street.

17. Note the **seven-story walk-up** on the west side of Orchard Street (No. 45), a short distance from the corner. One can only speculate on the number of unfortunate souls whose hearts were surely overtaxed by the wearying daily ascents to the upper floors. Jewish stars in terra cotta appear on the adjacent building to the right and on the façades of a number of tenements—no doubt a ruse by the builder to attract religious, but naïve, tenants.

18. At the southwest corner of Orchard and Grand streets is the **former E. S. Ridley Department Store,** painted a garish pink. Its imposing rounded corner and ornate cast-iron façade are all that remain of one of the most fashionable stores in the city during the Gay '90s. Together with competitor Lord & Taylor's, four blocks west on Grand Street, they presented an almost incongruous element of elegance in a neighborhood that could ill afford their wares.

Ridley's, established in the early 1870s, gave up the ghost in 1901, and a year later, Lord & Taylor's moved all of its retail operations to its main store at Broadway and 20th Street [*see* Ladies' Mile, 27]. A bizarre epilogue to the Ridley story took place in 1964, when the proprietor of the store occupying the old Ridley building was handed an envelope by the letter carrier who inquired if it was addressed to him. On examining the letter they were astonished to see that it was a Ridley business-reply envelope, recently postmarked, and addressed to the mail order department. On opening it they found a yellow slip of paper on which a message was scrawled from a man in Florida inquiring why Ridley's had not sent their catalog "for some time"—63 years after the firm went out of business!

Take a brief detour by continuing north on Orchard Street to No. 97, the **Lower East Side Tenement Museum.** Established in 1988 in a hundred-year-old typical tenement, the Museum conducts programs and tours, including a "living history" experience, with actors portraying the various immigrant nationalities that lived in the building.

Note: To visit the Museum, you will first have to go to the **Museum Shop & Visitor Center** at 90 Orchard Street (a half-block back) to purchase a ticket for a guided tour. A number of different tours are available, including walking tours, depending on the day, plus special tours for the physically challenged. The shop offers a large variety of books and gifts, all related to the Lower East Side immigrant experience. For information or tour brochures, call (212) 431-0233. Visitor center hours: Mon.–Sun. 11:00 A.M. to 5:30 P.M. Tickets: $9.00 adults, $7.00 students and seniors.

Return to Grand Street and turn west (right).

19. On the north side of Grand Street between Orchard and Allen streets, the large gray building was formerly a very popular **sports arena** when it opened in the mid-1880s. Indoor sports at that time were mainly confined to boxing.

portico recalls the days when this was primarily a seamen's house of worship. It is Manhattan's oldest Baptist church.

Turn left at Henry Street, named for Henry Rutgers—the second street in the neighborhood named for him. This block in the late 19th and early 20th centuries was known as "Doctors' Row," as so many physicians had their offices (and homes) in the buildings that lined the street, most of which have disappeared.

Grammar School No. 1, erected in 1897 in Flemish style, is an outstanding work of C. B. J. Snyder, who as Superintendent of School Buildings of the Board of Education for 30 years at the turn of the 20th century, was responsible for the design of some of the city's finest public school buildings. **St. Christopher's Chapel,** No. 48 Henry Street, now the Episcopal Church of Our Savior, was once an elegant Federal-style residence. At the site of No. 97, Beth Israel Hospital was founded in 1889 by Jews in a simple four-story building.

At the corner of Market Street is the landmark **Sea and Land Church.** Another "mariners' temple," it was built in 1817 of local Manhattan schist in Georgian style for the Northern Reformed Church, but with some elements that anticipated the later Gothic Revival period. In 1866 it became the Sea and Land Church, but now is the **First Chinese Presbyterian Church.**

Make a short detour to the right on Market Street to No. 51, the **William and Rosamond Clark House.** Built in 1824–25 in late Federal style for grocer William Clark and his wife, it retains much of its original detail, including a lovely entrance with fanlight, as well as window lintels and original ironwork. Two floors were added before the 20th century. The elegant house is typical of the former high quality of this residential neighborhood. Look up at the more-than-100-year-old wall sign painted on the adjacent building claiming that "Children Cry for Fletcher's Castoria." Whether or not they still cry for it is debatable, but that long-favored patent medicine (now with an altered formula) is still available in pharmacies. Return to Henry Street.

A cigarette factory sweatshop, ca. 1910. The worker in shirtsleeves at the extreme left is the author's grandfather. (Photograph courtesy of the author's late father, Samuel Wolfe)

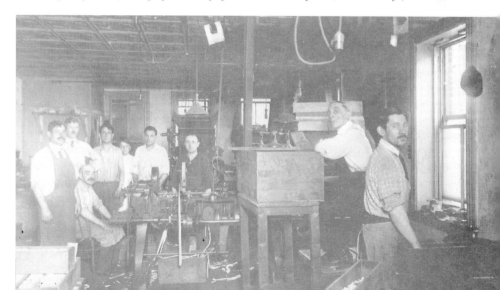

End of tour. Follow Henry Street, past Mechanics Alley (the origin of the name is unknown), **under the Manhattan Bridge to Pike Street; turn left one block to East Broadway, then right to where the tour began.**

SUPPLEMENTARY TOUR "B"
TO OTHER LOWER EAST SIDE LANDMARKS

From the original starting point, turn east on East Broadway (the opposite direction of Chatham Square), past the Educational Alliance building. [*See* main tour, No. 1.] In the block between Jefferson and Clinton streets are over a dozen small synagogues incorporated into the row of apartment houses that line the street. Some belong to small ultra-Orthodox congregations. **The Young Israel Synagogue** (No. 225) was founded in 1913 at the Kalwarier Synagogue on Pike Street, as an Orthodox movement for young people, with one of its main goals to combat the growing liberalization of the religion, as exemplified by Reform Judaism, and it is still very strong to this day. Many of these storefront synagogues belong to groups of common European origin, and are named for their hometown, or *shtetl.* There are at least eight in this one block. Others belong to Hasidic groups, of which there are two major communities, the Lubavitcher and the Satmar sects. The *Hasidim* are a very special ultra-Orthodox group (*hasid* means "pious one") who dress distinctively and stay apart from other Jewish groups, mingling with the outside world only when necessary. Modern Hasidism was founded in 18th-century Poland by Israel ben Eliezer, called *Baal Shem Tov* ("Master of the Good Name") by his followers. The movement began as a reaction to the overly academic attitudes of Jewish religious leaders at the time. The essence of the Hasidic spirit is in their intense concentration while performing religious acts and their unbounded joy in devotion—believing that to be truly religious, one must enjoy his relationship with God. The Hasidim frequently sing, sway, and dance during prayers. Although considered extremists by fellow Jews who do not accept their fundamentalist philosophies, dress, and attitudes toward worldliness and women, the Hasidic movement has nevertheless been growing in popularity since the arrival in this country of so many Hasidim after World War II. The Lubavitchers came mostly from Poland, while the Satmar Hasidim are Hungarians who fled their country after the 1956 Russian invasion.

While there are variations, the traditional Hasidic attire is adapted from the costume of the Polish nobleman of the 18th century, with a long black coat (*kapote*) and a broad-brimmed beaver or sable hat. Hasidim wear the traditional side locks and do not shave their beards. Married women shave their heads and wear a wig, and never expose bare arms or legs.

No. 235 East Broadway was until the mid-1970s the home of the *East Side News,* the Lower East Side's only newspaper. Today one of the tenants is the United Jewish Council of the East Side, a charitable organization which helps the aged sick and poor of the neighborhood. Across the street is the Art Deco–style Bialystoker Home for the Aged, erected in 1929.

At Montgomery Street, turn right to Henry Street, then left. Nos. 263, 265, and 267 are a trio of 1827 Federal-style houses and the home of the **Henry Street Settlement.** In 1893 when nurse Lillian Wald discovered the appalling conditions in the tenements, she devoted her life to caring for the sick and their families. She organized the **Visiting Nurse Service** and later, with the aid of philanthropist Jacob Schiff, the Henry Street Settlement. It was the pioneer social agency on the Lower East Side, and a model for later neighborhood settlement houses throughout the country.

The adjacent firehouse, now **Engine Company 15,** 269 Henry Street, has an interesting history. In 1854 a brownstone on the site was remodeled to be the home of a volunteer fire company known as Americus 6, **William Marcy "Boss" Tweed's own fire company.** His membership helped launch his infamous career, since city volunteer firemen were a potent political power. The fire engine sported a painting of a tiger, which political cartoonist Thomas Nast seized on to identify with Tammany Hall and the Tweed Ring. This successor Engine Company 15's building was rebuilt in the 1890s. Return to East Broadway, turn right to Grand Street.

The Classic Revival building at the intersection of East Broadway and Grand Street (311–13 East Broadway), formerly the Young Men's Benevolent Association (1904), is now a **ritualarium,** or *mikveh.* Among Orthodox Jews it is customary for the bride-to-be to take a ritual bath prior to the wedding ceremony, and for all women to go to the *mikveh* at least once a month. In former times, many synagogues had their own ritual bath chamber, although there were many nonaffiliated *mikvehs* such as this.

Turn west (left) on Grand Street to Willett Street (also Bialystoker Place), then right. (Marinus Willett was a patriot in the Revolutionary War and mayor of New York City in 1807–08). Standing alone in the middle of the block is the **Bialystoker Synagogue** (7 Willett Street). Built in 1826 in Federal style, its fieldstone construction gives it a simple but rugged appearance. Originally the Willett Street Methodist Episcopal Church, it was sold in 1905 to an immigrant Jewish congregation from Bialystok, Poland, which had arrived in the late 1870s. Still serving an active constituency mostly from the adjacent Sidney Hillman Houses, the East River Houses, and the Seward Park Houses, the synagogue is very active, well maintained, and has an impressive interior. A three-story-high carved wooden ark dominates the simple sanctuary. Colorful ceiling and wall paintings represent the signs of the zodiac and views of the Holy Land, while sparkling rays of blue and red stream down from a huge, arched stained-glass window. Contrary to the custom of facing east, the Bialystoker Synagogue must, because of its original design, face west.

Returning to Grand Street and continuing west, we pass the **Abrons Art Center and Neighborhood Playhouse of the Henry Street Settlement** (Prentice & Chan, Olhausen, 1975), and turning down Pitt Street toward the Williamsburg Bridge we see the **Police Station and Fire House,** completed in 1974. The 7th Precinct building replaced the former Clinton Street station house, which for over 70 years stood at the southeast corner of Delancey and Clinton streets, near the end of the Williamsburg Bridge. Walk one block west to Attorney Street.

Walk north on Attorney Street under the Bridge to Rivington Street, then turn left one block to Clinton Street, and turn right.

Clinton Street was named for Revolutionary War general, George Clinton, who became the first governor of New York State after independence. At the beginning of the century, Clinton Street was a busy commercial street and the center for religious-goods merchants. Store after store offered such articles as prayer books, prayer shawls, *yarmulkes, mezzuzahs,* phylacteries, torahs, candelabra, and ceremonial wine goblets. The street is now almost entirely Spanish-speaking. Walk north one and one-half blocks to the **Chasam Sopher** ("Seal of the Scribe") **Synagogue** (8 Clinton Street). Built in 1853 for the German congregation Rodeph Shalom, it is the second oldest surviving synagogue building in New York. Its design, rather unique for a synagogue, is of the Round-Arch Romanesque Revival style. In 1886, Rodeph Shalom moved uptown and sold the building to a Hungarian immigrant congregation which renamed the *shul* in honor of 19th-century religious leader Moshe Schreiber (1762–1839), a highly respected rabbi and talmudic scholar who traveled widely through eastern Europe founding religious institutions, and who left over 100 manuscript volumes of his writings. The exterior has suffered many alterations through the years, losing an ornate iron balustrade and the street-level doors that gave access to the women's galleries. The sanctuary, however, is virtually unchanged— spacious, bright, and unpretentious, its quiet atmosphere a relief from the tumult of busy Clinton Street. The design of the hand-carved ark is a model of the synagogue's front façade, with most of the architectural details faithfully reproduced in miniature.

Until recently the struggling congregation was too poor to afford a full-time rabbi or conduct badly needed repairs, and was sustained only through the dedicated efforts of Holocaust survivor, the late Moses Weiser, and his son Eugene. Fortuitously, at the last minute, a businessman, coincidentally named Hank Sopher, came to the rescue, contributing $3 million for the restoration of the building and to maintain a full-time rabbi.

Return to the corner of Stanton Street, and turn left.

Halfway down the block on the north side is **Congregation Bnai Jacob Anshe Brzezan** ("Sons of Jacob, People of Brzezan"; No. 180 Stanton Street). A synagogue built in 1913 to serve a small immigrant group from Brzezany, Poland, it is typical of the early "tenement synagogues" of the Lower East Side, and has served continuously since its founding. The simple brown-brick and masonry façade has three entrances, with the date of construction carved over the center door. Above the "star" window, a pediment bears the name of the congregation, and above, is a rose window between two round-arch windows. The narrow sanctuary has galleries on both sides and an ornate wooden ark at the end; on the walls, decorative murals portray the Hebrew months. In the basement "house of study" are 19th-century second-hand school desks with traditional inkwell holes.

Turn back, past Clinton Street to Norfolk Street, and turn right.

Halfway down the block, almost hidden by its taller neighbors, is the **former Congregation Anshe Chesed** synagogue (No. 172 Norfolk Street). Little evidence remains of the past glory of this, the oldest synagogue building in New York, and one of the oldest in the country! The smashed windows and doors, peeling stucco, broken fence, and overall state of deterioration presaged a melancholy end for such a historic building. Designed by architect Alexander Saeltzer in 1849 for the first

Reform Congregation in America, Anshe Chesed, it was for a time the largest synagogue in the city. Gone now are the polygonal pyramids that once graced the twin towers of this Gothic Revival–style building, as well as the elaborate windows, traceries, and other medieval details of the façade. It is said that the architect was influenced by Germany's Cologne Cathedral, which had just celebrated its 600th anniversary the year before. In any case, the decade of the 1840s *was* the period of the Gothic Revival. Saeltzer's reputation as an architect was assured two years later when he designed the famous Astor Library on Lafayette Street, later the Hebrew Immigrant Aid Society building, now the famous Joseph Papp Public Theater [*see* Lafayette Historic Group and East Village, 14]. As with nearby Rodeph Shalom, the German Anshe Chesed congregation also moved uptown, and the building eventually passed to a Hungarian Immigrant group, Ohab Zedek. Changing names several times as different congregations took over the building, it ultimately became Anshe Slonim in 1922, taking its name from a tiny village in Poland. By the early 1970s the neighborhood had declined badly; faced with unremitting vandalism and repeated violence, the members were forced to seek safer places for worship. The venerable building, abandoned and padlocked, and under a city demolition order, seemed doomed. Then in late 1986, as if by a miracle, Spanish sculptor Angel Orensanz, himself a Sephardic Jew, purchased the old synagogue from the city for use as an artist's studio. Shortly afterward, the Landmarks Commission granted it landmark status. Then, after several years of painstaking work, Angel and his brother Al, a sociologist and writer, created the **Angel Orensanz Foundation** and transformed the once decaying interior into a space for theatrical performances, gallery shows, special events, and weddings (Matthew Broderick and Sarah Jessica Parker were married here). Such luminaries as Nobel Prize–winner Elie Wiesel, poet Maya Angelou, and composer Philip Glass were among many who have appeared here. In 1999 a small congregation began worshipping in the basement. In an amazing coincidence, their search for a torah led them to one from the town of Slonim, in Poland, where the last congregation to use the synagogue had originated.

For a moment of amusement, walk north to Houston Street, and look across at the 13-story apartment house on the north side, No. 250 East Houston Street (Schuman, Lichtenstein, Claman & Efron, 1989). Although named **Red Square,** it is not an outpost of the former Soviet Union; rather, the funky title was aimed at those who enjoy being a bit contrary and who prefer "living on the edge." It was also an attempt to encourage living on the Lower East Side in a more-or-less luxurious style rather than in a dingy tenement. The developers correctly anticipated the influx of middle-class "twenty-plusers" that have been moving into the neighborhood. The roofline of the building is adorned with a series of street sculptures, a bronze statue of Lenin, by sculptor Yuri Gerasimov (brought here after the fall of the Soviet Union), and a large quirky clock with numbers arranged in random order. The whimsical timepiece is the work of Tibor Kalman, the iconoclastic designer whose ideas were influential in the remaking of Times Square.

End of tour. Walk west on Houston Street one block to Essex Street, then left three blocks to Delancey Street, for the F line.

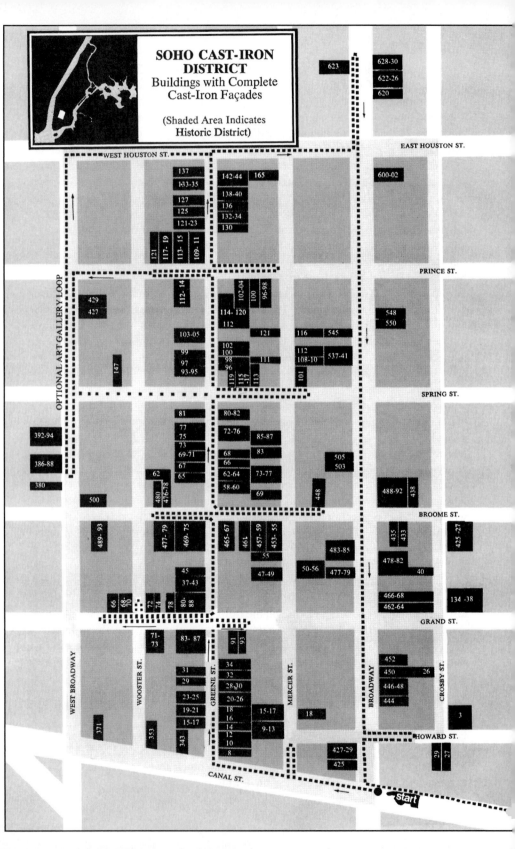

7. SoHo Cast-Iron District

[Subways: J, M, N, Q, R, W, Z, and No. 6 lines to Canal Street. Buses: M1, M6 to Canal Street.]

Cast iron as a building material had its origins in England in the mid-18th century. It was discovered that pig iron could easily be heated to the melting point by the use of coke, later coal, thus freeing it of impurities while maintaining the proper carbon content needed for strength. The molten mass could then be cast into sand molds of the desired size and shape. In 1779 a cast-iron bridge was completed in England over the River Severn, and in the last decade of the century a number of iron-framed buildings, mostly textile mills, demonstrated the feasibility of this type of construction. Subsequently, the use of cast iron to support large glass greenhouses became very popular, and in 1851 the world was treated to the awesome spectacle of architect Joseph Paxton's London Crystal Palace Exhibition Building. Two years later New York City was witness to another Crystal Palace Exhibition, which was built on the present site of Bryant Park on 42nd Street. The style lent itself successfully to the construction of the dome of the U.S. Capitol, completed in 1865, and to numerous railway train sheds around the world. A number of those expansive iron and glass stations are still in use today.

Cast iron, however, achieved its greatest popularity here in the United States during the period 1860–90, when more commercial buildings with iron fronts were built in New York City than anywhere else in the world! A surprising number of these structures still stand, the majority of which can be seen in the **SoHo Cast-Iron Historic District.**

Recognizing the importance of cast-iron architecture to the growth and development of the city, as well as its aesthetic and historic importance, the New York City Landmarks Preservation Commission in 1973 designated a 26-block area as a Historic District—the first such commercial district to be so named. "SoHo" is an acronym for the area SOuth of HOuston Street. Although still a commercial neighborhood, it has become in recent years a popular center for artists and sculptors who find the high-ceilinged loft buildings ideal for studios and workshops. The influx of these artists has given the area a new dimension, demonstrating that with imaginative zoning, industry and art can coexist successfully.

Until the end of the 18th century, the area was largely rural, difficult to reach by road from the lower city because of extensive marshlands. With the filling in of the Collect Pond (now the site of Foley Square), the draining of Lispenard's Meadow, and the subsequent paving of Broadway to Astor Place in 1809, the character of the area soon changed to middle-class residential.

By 1825, it had grown to be the most populous ward in the city, with a large freed-slave population. Large, fashionable retail emporiums with such familiar names as Arnold Constable, Lord & Taylor, and Tiffany's, established themselves along Broadway, while elegant hotels were soon erected alongside. For years to come, such hotels as the St. Nicholas, the Metropolitan, and the Prescott House would be synonymous with extravagance and luxury. An array of theaters and music halls soon followed, and by 1850, the Bowery was displaced by Broadway as the entertainment center of the city. And around it grew one of the biggest red-light districts in town.

But the glitter and gaiety lasted only ten years. Keeping pace with the north-ward growth of the city, the entertainment district moved up to 14th Street, and what was left of the former residential section gradually disappeared. In its place came large textile and other mercantile establishments, which commissioned the construction of new buildings, selecting for the most part the new cast-iron-front designs. For the next 30 years some of the largest and most prestigious textile firms in the country were housed side-by-side in those cast-iron "palaces" whose surviving rows of Renaissance Revival–style façades are reminiscent of Venice's Grand Canal. By the early 20th century, the industrial pattern changed again, as the district became New York's millinery manufacturing center. And with the felt hat makers came the fur and feather processors to add the essential details to milady's headgear.

Until recently, the area was devoted exclusively to diverse light manufactur-ing and warehousing; but with the rapidly growing colony of artists, it has achieved a new and charming atmosphere not seen in any of the city's other com-mercial districts. Many claim that SoHo has now replaced Greenwich Village as the center of artistic creativity. However, with the enormous popularity of SoHo as a place to live and work, there followed the usual skyrocketing rents, which have driven out young artists and craftsmen. In their place came the elegant gal-leries, "chic" bars, noisy discos, expensive restaurants, pretentious boutiques, so-called antique shops, and the usual health-food and fast-food establishments. The resulting "gentrification" of the artist community poses a serious threat to the future of SoHo as a center of creative inspiration. And while the area now houses the largest concentration of art galleries in the city, much of the talent that sup-plies the galleries has departed to less expensive and more distant neighborhoods.

The characteristics of cast-iron construction: in a masonry building, the weight (load) is borne by the exterior and interior walls, which must be built of a thickness corresponding to the height of the building. On the other hand, in pure

The aesthetics of cast-iron architecture are shown to advantage in the Dittenhoffer Warehouse, 427–429 Broadway, erected in 1870. (Photo by author)

iron construction, the load is borne by a skeleton of vertical and horizontal rolled iron beams, with the exterior brick walls attached to the framework, serving only as a "skin." The cast-iron parts making up the façade are then attached to the street wall. Cast iron, in effect, anticipated the principle of modern skyscraper construction, where similar "curtain walls" surround a structural steel frame.

Cast iron was employed not only functionally, but decoratively as well. Each foundry employed its own architect who designed the building details. At first, architects imitated the style of stone buildings, copying in cast iron the ornate French and Italian Renaissance motifs, which were so fashionable in the mid-19th century. Some went so far as to add sand to the beige-colored paint to give the finished product the look of rough stone. It is interesting to note that after cast iron achieved widespread popularity, many builders copied the ornate cast-iron fronts in masonry! It is therefore difficult at times to visually determine if a façade is of iron or stone—unless, of course, one has a magnet handy.

Most of the iron-front buildings erected from the late 1850s through the mid-1870s were essentially Renaissance in style, followed later by the influence of the French Second Empire. The French neo-Grec style, characterized by incised floral and geometric designs, using slender columns and mostly Ionic capitals, became popular in the 1880s. By the '90s, cast iron began to fall out of fashion,

Representation of the first cast-iron building erected in 1848–49 at the corner of Centre and Duane streets by James Bogardus for his Eccentric Grinding Mill. (Museum of the City of New York)

and only an occasional example can be found of that decade. With the introduction of structural steel, the skyscraper era soon followed.

There are many advantages to the cast-iron medium. In 1835 New York suffered a disastrous fire that literally burned off most of the buildings in the south end of Manhattan. Again in 1845 another conflagration occurred, this one consuming 300 buildings! Less combustible building materials were sought (masonry was expensive), and cast iron seemed to offer the solution. It could be melted only in a blast furnace. It was also lightning-proof—the iron framework, acting as a "Faraday's Cage," conducted the electricity safely to the ground. Cast iron was lighter and cheaper than stone, and much cheaper to erect. It could be mass-produced from standardized molds—the iron parts being interchangeable and easily replaced from the foundry's catalog. Cast iron, once painted, was weatherproof and required little maintenance. The building's appearance could be "renewed" with a different color paint. Iron's coefficient of expansion and contraction was similar to that of the brickwork to which it was attached, obviating the danger of separation under extremes of weather. In addition, an iron framework had greater structural integrity than other building materials, and could withstand stresses that would collapse wood or stone structures. A particular advantage was the space gained by the elimination of massive bearing walls. With a cast-iron façade, large windows were now possible for the first time, affording light and ventilation hitherto impossible. Finally, the simplicity of erection was such that an iron front could be raised almost overnight, with no more tools than a wrench, much like a child's Erector Set, since all parts were fastened together with nuts and bolts.

There were, however, some disadvantages. Although the builders described iron structures as fireproof, in reality they were not. Flooring, beams, joists, and staircases were frequently made of wood; and while a fire would not damage the cast-iron front, it could gut the interior. Cast iron, although highly compressible, was brittle, lacking the tensile strength of modern steel. Rusting was always a problem, as moisture frequently seeped into the iron sections. The iron panels, which could withstand the heat of a building fire, would often crack under the shock of cold water from the firemen's hoses.

The success of cast iron as a structural and architectural medium is credited to two contemporary engineers, **Daniel D. Badger** and **James Bogardus.** Badger's foundry mass-produced the first complete iron-front building. Bogardus, who invented the I-beam, designed the oldest surviving cast-iron building in New York, the famous Edgar Laing Store, which stood on the corner of Washington and Murray streets from 1848 to 1971, about a mile from the Historic District. The store was carefully dismantled when the neighborhood was urban-renewed, to be re-erected later on the new campus of the Borough of Manhattan Commu-

The former Edgar Laing Store, until recently the oldest surviving cast-iron building in New York. Built in 1848 at the corner of Murray and Washington streets, it was dismantled in 1971 for future re-erection. Thieves subsequently made off with most of the iron sections. (Photo by author)

nity College. Measured drawings were made by students in a Restoration and Preservation of Historic Architecture program of Columbia University, and the pieces were inventoried, all under the supervision of the Landmarks Commission. Unfortunately the remains fell to thieves, and most of the parts were stolen and sold as scrap iron! Hopefully, molds will be made from the drawings so that replacement parts can be recast and the landmark Bogardus Building erected again. Bogardus's original warehouse, however, still stands at 85 Leonard Street, a few blocks south of Canal Street. Badger and his Architectural Iron Works left us with possibly the finest example of commercial cast-iron architecture in America, the Venetian Renaissance–style Haughwout Building at Broadway and Broome Street [see pages 210 and 211]. Completed in 1857, it is the city's oldest surviving iron-front building, and a designated city landmark.

Within a few years, at least three dozen iron foundries were busily producing façades and decorations for the hundreds of new buildings going up in the area. The names of these iron works can be seen embossed in the base blocks of many of these structures: Aetna, Architectural, Atlantic, Cornell, Excelsior, Jackson, etc. With the lone exception of the Cornell Iron Works, which now casts other kinds of iron products, all the original building foundries are now gone. The advent of the "iron age" also brought immortality to such architects as Isaac F. Duckworth, Henry Fernbach, Robert Mook, Jarvis Morgan Slade, John Snook, Griffith Thomas, and Samuel Warner.

The walking tour map indicates *every* building with a complete cast-iron front; however, there are at least as many masonry buildings whose ground floors are full cast iron. Some stone buildings have only cast-iron ornamentation, such as columns, cornices or simply designs. Notice the iron loading docks, light platforms, and sidewalk vault covers.

Note: A glossary of architectural terms appears at the end of the chapter.

BROADWAY TO GREENE STREET (along Canal Street)

The tour begins at Canal Street and Broadway. Named for the drainage ditch that was built in the late 18th century to connect the old Collect Pond with the Hudson River, Canal Street was paved in 1820, and has grown to become one of the city's busiest crosstown thoroughfares. In recent years, Canal Street between Broadway and West Broadway has become one of the city's lively markets, specializing in such unusual used and surplus items as machinery, electrical supplies, hardware, and plastics of every description. The frenetic street scene reaches a fever pitch on weekends when the sidewalks are jammed with displays of merchandise and throngs of bargain hunters and sightseers.

Walk west on Canal Street to **No. 307–311.** Built in 1856–65 for the Arnold Constable "Marble House" [see Ladies' Mile, 29], this stone building is in a good state of preservation. It has an Italianate marble façade on Canal Street, and brick on the Mercer and Howard street sides. Note the second-story round-arched windows with decorative keystones, flanked by pilasters with Corinthian capitals. The windows on the third through fifth floors are topped by segmental arches.

The Arnold Constable Store, called the "Marble House," was erected in 1856 when the firm moved to Canal and Mercer streets to open one of the city's most elegant dry goods emporiums. Constructed of brick and stone, the Italianate building survives today in a surprisingly good state of preservation. (The Edward W. C. Arnold Collection, lent by the Metropolitan Museum of Art. Museum of the City of New York)

Above the fifth-floor windows, paired volutes rise toward the center, forming a modified pediment. The building is capped by a simple cast-iron cornice. Walk around this old department-store building and compare the three façades; then continue west on Canal Street to Greene Street and turn right (north), past one of the city's busiest weekend flea markets.

CANAL STREET TO WEST HOUSTON STREET (along Greene Street)

Greene Street, named after Revolutionary War General Nathanael Greene, hero of the Battle of Trenton, was opened just after the turn of the 19th century. It is still cobblestoned (they are actually called Belgian blocks), and boasts the largest aggregation of cast-iron buildings in the world! On a Sunday, when few automobiles are to be seen, the street is virtually the same as it was in the latter half of the 19th century. Even the street between Canal and Houston streets has been repaved with the original Belgian blocks, and the street lights are the old bishop's crook lampposts.

Another much-less-admirable feature that hearkens back to the turn of the century is the vast proliferation of sweat shops that can be seen throughout SoHo. These are mainly Chinese-owned, employing recent Chinese immigrant labor at minimum or below-subsistence wages.

The row of ten buildings on the east side of the street, from No. 8 through No. 32–34, is the **longest continuous row of such iron-front buildings anywhere. No. 8** dates from 1883, and **No. 10–14** from 1869—all four designed by architect John B. Snook. **Nos. 16** and **18,** built in 1882, and **No. 20–26,** built in 1880, were designed by Samuel Warner, and were joined together and converted into commercial condominiums in 1993. In front of No. 10–12 is the original iron stoop and light platform, which was converted into a loading platform.

Note the old paving of Greene Street with Belgian blocks (mistakenly called cobblestones), as well as the equally old "bishop's crook" lampposts, made of cast iron.

Warner also designed **No. 15–17,** across the street, in 1894. A rather late cast-iron building, its "flattened" façade shows the simpler style that supplanted the earlier ornate Renaissance motifs. There is a Cornell Iron Works trademark at the base. Adjacent **No. 19–21** is by Henry Fernbach, and was built as a warehouse in 1872.

No. 23–25, designed in a French Renaissance style by Isaac F. Duckworth (1873), is particularly impressive with its triangular pediment with delicate finials set over two central bays, its iron moldings, partially fluted columns, and stylized designs in the frieze panel and two flanking vertical rows of quoins that extend from the base of the building to the cornice.

The block, however, is dominated by **No. 28–30** on the east side of the street, designed in 1873 by Duckworth (who had a strong predilection for the French Second Empire style) for Picaut, Simon & Capel Company. Note the immense mansard roof with central pavilion, dormers, half-round attached columns, bell-shaped capitals, keystoned and segmental arches over wide windows, and projecting central bays that give a dramatic three-dimensional effect. Notice, too, the light disks in the iron vault covers surrounded by six metal studs. The risers have circle lights with hexagonal frames. These glass disks also permitted sunlight to illuminate the basement. The system was invented by Thaddeus Hyatt in 1845 for installation in sidewalk vaults, and is still to be seen throughout the city. What was formerly the stoop now serves as a loading platform. Except for the removal of the acanthus leaves from the columns' capitals, this imposing building is in as pristine condition as the day it was built, although lack of maintenance is beginning to show in the proliferation of rust, peeling paint, and graffiti.

No. 32, with a small bonnet cornice, is another Duckworth building (1873). Its neighbor, **No. 34,** by Charles Wright, and built the same year, continues the cornice line.

No. 31, across the street (George W. DaCunha, 1876), is interesting because of its neo-Grec details. Note the three square-topped windows on each floor, the freestanding Corinthian columns, flanking pilasters with neo-Grec designs on the terminal blocks at each floor's cornice level, and the repeating rosettes and concave brackets on the entablature. The building, unfortunately, is in a sad state of decay and its future is uncertain. There is another identical building by the same architect at 74 Grand Street (to be viewed soon).

Turn east briefly on Grand Street.

Grand Street got its name from its unusual width, as it was a major east-west thoroughfare when first laid out early in the 19th century.

Nos. 91 and **93** (John B. Snook, 1869), quite unusual in their façades, are not copied from the Renaissance or French Second Empire styles but cast in the appearance of ashlars (large masonry panels). At first glance one would take

Looking north on Greene Street near Broome Street in the heart of the SoHo Cast-Iron District where an almost unbroken panorama of cast-iron buildings presents itself. (Photo by author)

One of James Bogardus's only surviving iron-front buildings, his former warehouse at 85 Leonard Street, erected in 1862. (Photo by David Bishop)

The old New York Life Insurance Company building at 346 Broadway at Leonard Street, built in 1870 from plans by Griffith Thomas, still stands but is hardly recognizable from this early engraving. A turn-of-the-century addition by McKim, Mead & White added nine floors, a clock tower, and winged globe (now removed). The company moved to Madison Square in 1928. (New York Life Insurance Company)

An 1870s steel engraving showing the lavish interior of the New York Life Insurance Company building at 346 Broadway. (New York Life Insurance Company)

The Greene Street side of this neo-Grec–style cast-iron building at 112–114 Prince Street is an enormous trompe l'oeil *painting, by artist Richard Haas, simulating rows of windows—a pleasant solution to a blank brick wall. (Photo by author)*

An 1865 advertising poster for Daniel D. Badger's Architectural Iron Works, located between 13th and 14th streets, Avenues B and C. (Museum of the City of New York)

these for stone buildings. A dead giveaway is the tiny "J. L. Jackson & Bro. Iron Works" label at the base, to the right on No. 91.

Return to the corner of Grand and Greene streets.

No. 83–87 Grand Street (on the southwest corner) is a rather large structure in a modified neo-Grec style, designed in 1872 by William Hume. The date appears conspicuously over the central bays. The iron for this former silk warehouse was cast by the firm of Lindsay, Graff & Megquier (see label on base).

Across the street, No. 80–88 Grand Street (B. W. Warner, 1873) was built for a large importing and commission merchant. No. 78, alongside, was designed in 1882 by Robert Mook.

Nos. 72 and 74 (1885), as well as No. 68–70 (1887) on the northwest corner of Wooster Street, are by George DaCunha, who favored the neo-Grec style. In the latter building, a high cornice is set on paired concave brackets above three wide pilasters.

No. 71–73, on the southeast corner (Mortimer C. Merritt, 1879, corner section 1888), demonstrates how a cast-iron front permits the use of large plate-glass windows. Set between fluted Corinthian columns on paneled bases, the ground floor presents a light and expansive appearance. Each floor has its own cornice, partitioned by ornamental blocks. The bays are framed by smooth pilasters topped by stylized neo-Grec capitals with incised floral designs. The relief panels above the fourth floor serve as a transition to the splendid upper cornice with its paired elongated brackets above each column and similarly elongated modillions. Merritt was the architect of the great Hugh O'Neill Department Store, which still stands on Avenue of the Americas between 20th and 21st streets [*see* Ladies' Mile, 15].

Make a brief detour north on Wooster Street to No. 80 (Gilbert Schellenger, 1895). This seven-story former warehouse is considered to be the first conversion to artists' lofts in SoHo. In 1967 the new owner began selling co-ops to artists, before it become legal four years later. The building also housed Jonas Mekas's Filmmakers Cinematique and Richard Foreman's Ontological Hysteric Theater. Although many artists have left SoHo because of its skyrocketing rents and popularity as a tourist mecca, many still remain. Note the initials of the original developer, Boehm & Coon, in an escutcheon on the seventh floor. Return to Grand Street and turn left (east).

Return to Greene Street and turn left (north).

No. 37–43 (Richard Berger, 1884) is undistinguished and has lost its cornice.

No. 45 (J. Morgan Slade, 1882) is another typical neo-Grec–style iron front building. The pilasters and columns are topped by Ionic capitals. Note the egg-and-dart molding above the windows, the deep columnar base blocks and connecting panels, and the architrave above the ground floor in the form of a scrolled grillwork strip. The economy of cast-iron construction can be seen in the similarity of sections on each floor—all cast from the same mold.

Although **No. 49** is a stone building, its street number is a lovely cast-iron plaque set into a fluted iron column. Look for D. D. Badger's "Architectural Iron Works" label on the plinth, to the left of the entrance.

Across the street, **Nos. 42–44** and **46–50** are both masonry buildings that have attractive ornamental ironwork details. The former has an iron storefront with fluted columns and pilasters. Its neighbor to the north is far more ornate. Observe the twin iron pilasters on the ground floor with bolted-on scrollwork and medallions, and the small stone pediment on the second floor. With all the surviving details on the lower façade, one can only speculate on the appearance of the now-missing cornice.

Turn left (west) on Broome Street.

Broome Street is named for John Broome, the city's first alderman after the Revolution and lieutenant governor of New York State in 1804. He is also credited with initiating the lucrative China tea trade when he imported the first two million pounds of tea. Upstate Broome County is named for him.

One of the best-preserved cast-iron "palaces" in the city is the imposing Gunther Building, on the southwest corner, **No. 469–475** Broome Street. A Griffith Thomas masterpiece, it was built by the Aetna Iron Works in 1871–72 as a warehouse for William H. Gunther, a leading furrier. (The building that housed his old showroom still stands on the west side of Broadway just south of 23rd Street, near Madison Square.) Among its outstanding features are the impressive curved corner with unusual curved windowpanes flanked by columns of quoins, the bold cornice at each floor level, the rows of flat-arched windows, and a simple but firm roof cornice supported by heavy brackets over symmetrical rows of pilasters. The protruding pedestal blocks on both sides of the "Gunther Building" nameplate once supported life-size statues (draped in furs?). A balustrade, similar to the one on the second floor, once graced the roof cornice. A significant architectural feature—handed down by the ancient Greeks—is the foreshortening of each successive story. By progressively diminishing the height of each floor, an illusion of greater height is achieved. The Aetna Iron Works was located in former times at 104 Goerck Street, near the corner of Grand Street, on the Lower East Side. Goerck Street has long since disappeared, demapped for a large housing project.

The adjacent building to the west, **No. 477–479,** was erected in 1872–73 by the Excelsior Iron Works from plans by Elisha Sniffen. A very classical building in the French manner, it was built for the Cheney Brothers Silk Mills. While the neighboring Gunther Building has a uniform treatment of the windows, this building shows great variety. Some bays are flanked by engaged columns with Corinthian capitals, others are capped by keystones, and still others are decorated with balustrades. Twin pediments surmount a bracketed cornice, giving the structure an appearance of great width. No. 477 has a four-step iron entrance stoop while 479 has five steps. Note the circle lights surrounded by six raised metal studs, and the name of the iron works.

Across the street, **No. 470** is a typical Griffith Thomas building in stone, completed in 1867. The ground-floor columns and the entablature, however, are of cast iron.

No. 472–474 was designed by Thomas two years later, and was probably one of his last stone buildings, for from late 1869 on, he devoted himself exclusively to cast iron.

No. 476–478 is still another Griffith Thomas building (1872), now representing his cast-iron period. L-shaped, it wraps itself around No. 480 to become No. 62 Wooster Street, around the corner. Typical Thomas touches are a cornice line at each floor, flattened window arches, flanking three-quarter round Corinthian columns in the center section with connecting balustrades, and flat pilasters at the sides of the façade.

No. 480 was designed by Richard Berger in 1884.

Return to Greene Street and continue east on Broome Street.

Broome Street in former times was a major east-west artery, and is somewhat wider than its parallel neighbors. It is still a fairly busy thoroughfare, providing an alternate route to the nearby Holland Tunnel.

Situated in one of the finest cast-iron blocks in the district, **No. 465–467** Broome Street is another product of the Aetna Iron Works and was designed by Isaac F. Duckworth in 1872.

The stone building at the northwest corner of Broome and Greene streets, **No. 464–468,** designed in 1860 (architect unknown), was built for Aaron Arnold of the Arnold Constable emporium. Nine bays wide on Broome Street, it is divided into three sections of three windows each. The two-story-high columns flanking the windows are in the "sperm candle" style, for they resemble candles made from sperm whale oil. (More buildings, in both iron and stone, employing the "sperm candle" feature will be seen later on Broadway.) The graceful fluted iron columns on the ground floor were cast by the nearby Nichol & Billerwell Foundry on West Houston Street. The building is extremely handsome, and was a prototype for many later cast-iron copies.

No. 461 (1871) is another Griffith Thomas "iron-fronter."

Still in "Griffith Thomas Territory," **No. 457–459** (1871) is somewhat simpler than the adjacent corner building. Quoined pilasters are set at each end of this six-story, six-bay edifice. The windows are separated by modified Doric columns with egg-and-dart and floral-motif moldings above. Note the balustrade at the bases of the second-story windows. Above the cornice is a rather large pediment.

No. 453–455 (Griffith Thomas again, 1872–73) was built for the Welcome G. Hitchcock silk and veilings store. Two of Hitchcock's early partners were Aaron Arnold and James Constable. Five stories of foreshortened Corinthian columns, wide flat-arched windows, a cornice line at each floor, and quoined pilasters flanking the end bays give a bold look to this well-preserved cast-iron building. Lightness and charm result from the delicate Corinthian capitals, the second-story balustrade, the floral motifs and the intricate modillions and brackets under

The "Queen" and "King" of Greene Street cast-iron architecture: (left) No. 28–30, in Second Empire style; (right) No. 72–76 in Renaissance style; both designed by Isaac F. Duckworth in 1873. (Left, photo by author; right, New York City Landmarks Preservation Commission)

the ground-floor and roof cornices. Above the fifth floor is a classic attic that once sported finial-tipped cast-iron urns.

No. 448, on the north side of Broome Street, just beyond Mercer Street, is an outstanding cast-iron creation. Designed in 1871 by the firm of Vaux & Withers, it has a style of ornamentation not seen elsewhere in the city. Capped by delicately ornate friezes and outlined by pellet moldings, the windows with their flanking triple groups of colonnettes are the most unusual feature of the building. The fifth-floor windows are subdivided into round-arched groups of two, separated by colonnettes. The intervening spandrels repeat the floral motifs. Observe the striking entablature with its rosettes set in panels in a concave architrave and the upper frieze; while "sprouting" from the fifth-floor colonnettes are elaborate brackets. One cannot but condemn the first-floor alterations. Calvert Vaux and Frederick Clarke Withers designed the landmark Jefferson Market Courthouse (now Library) in Greenwich Village [*see* Greenwich Village, 33]. Vaux also teamed up with Frederick Law Olmsted to give us Central Park and Prospect Park.

Returning to Greene Street, note **No. 458,** a three-bay stone building between Mercer and Greene streets. Built in 1867 by David and John Jardine, who shortly thereafter were "converted" to the cast-iron medium, the structure has interesting molded drop-lintels over the windows whose keystones incorporate an incised fleur-de-lis. The ground-floor stone entablature, and its row of columns beneath, divides the building into two distinct sections. The decorative main entablature is of cast-iron capped by a raised, curved pediment. It appears that this former store and warehouse is a kind of structural parasite as it has no side bearing walls of its own, and relies on its two stalwart neighbors for support. D. and J. Jardine ten years later designed the palatial B. Altman store that still occupies the northwest corner of Avenue of the Americas and West 18th Street [*see* Ladies' Mile, 10].

Turn right (north) on Greene Street.

The block from Broome to Spring Street has no fewer than 13 full iron-front buildings, representing the height of cast-iron architectural development.

No. 58–60 (1871) is one of nine buildings in the block designed by architect Henry Fernbach.

No. 62–64, erected one year later, is also by Fernback. Observe how the first-floor columns are fluted on the lower section and topped by Ionic capitals. Each floor has its own entablature with Tuscan columns separating the four central bays. The ornamental double brackets in the roof entablature are a very dominant feature. The restrained curved pediment above the cornice shows the date of construction, 1872.

In front of No. 62–64 is a **"bishop's crook" lamppost.** The cast-iron lamppost weighs 835 pounds, almost twice that of today's modern aluminum tubular posts. The base shows the ornate fluting and the acanthus-leaf motif. In the "crook" above is the traditional curlicue known as a *feuille rinceau,* French for curling leaf. The next time you pass an older fire-alarm box, note the cast-iron flambeau above and the palmetto-leaf design of the shaft.

No. 66 (John B. Snook, 1873) was built as a store for the Lorillard (tobacco) Company. **No. 68,** identical in appearance, is also by Snook, and was built later in the same year.

Across the street, **Nos. 65** and **67** (1872) are another look-alike pair, although the former is by John B. Snook and the latter by Henry Fernbach. It appears that both buildings were ordered from the same catalog.

Looking to the east side again, we are confronted by the most regal cast-iron building in the block, **No. 72–76,** known as the "King of Greene Street." Considered to be the finest example of French Renaissance style in the district, this masterpiece was designed by Isaac F. Duckworth and completed in 1873 for the Gardner Colby Company, whose initials can be seen at the entrance. From its pedimented portico to its pedimented cornice, this stately "commercial palace" must have been considered the last word in cast-iron elegance. This ten-bay structure gives an imposing three-dimensional effect with its ranks of free-standing Corinthian columns—each group supporting its own cornice, with projecting centrally paired bays, as well as side bays that are set off on rusticated piers separated by Ionic pilasters. The broken pediments over the entrance and on the roof with their ornate iron urns further accent the central projection. In the roof pediment are decorative birdlike ornaments topped by a fleur-de-lis motif.

No. 69–71 on the west side (Henry Fernbach, 1876) is identical to **No. 73,** its next-door neighbor. Both were erected at the same time, were designed by the same architect, and were fabricated by the same Cornell Iron Works foundry...

and were built for the same owner! **No. 75** is another member of the family, with only minor differences in the façade. **No. 77** is a "younger brother," completed in 1878 as the office for the Jennings Lace Works, the firm that introduced Chantilly, Point d'Alençon, and Breton lace to this country. Unfortunately, the cornice on 69–71 has been removed. And **No. 81** is the fifth member of the Fernbach family, built in 1877.

No. 80–82, on the east side, was built as a store and warehouse (Griffith Thomas, 1872).

No. 84–86 (122–124 Spring Street) is a Henry Fernbach building in stone (1883), with brickwork trimmed with cast-iron ornamentation. It has an interesting, restrained façade, with such features as wide stone window lintels and sills, segmentally arched lintels with keystones on the sixth floor, with alternating soldier courses of brick under each window.

Turn right (east) on Spring Street.

Spring Street was named for a fresh-water spring that once flowed nearby.

On the north side of the street are a trio of late-1870s iron buildings. **No. 119** (1878) is by Robert Mook, **Nos. 115–117** and **113** (1878) are by Henry Fernbach. Typical of the Fernbach touch are the separate cornices on each floor ending in a heavy terminal block supported by double brackets, windows flanked by columns with egg-and-dart molding, plus paneled pilasters delineating the buildings. Note the Excelsior Iron Works plaque on No. 111, and the J. L. Jackson Iron Works plaques on Nos. 115, 113, and 109.

At the northwest corner of Mercer Street stands the **oldest house in the neighborhood, No. 107,** built *before* 1808! Its brickwork has been covered by stucco, but it shows its splayed lintels and keystones over the windows.

Across Mercer Street, on the northeast corner, is lovely **No. 101** (Nicholas Whyte, 1870). See how the expanses of plate glass, framed by slender columns, give it a light and airy look. Unusual decorative motifs appear in the clustered corner columns, which rest on piers with a unique rectangular design. Bizarre motifs also appear in the corners of the upper windows, while the ground-floor columns have leaf-ornamented capitals. The whole is an outstanding example of the success of cast iron as a functional and decorative medium.

Adjacent **No. 99** (D. and J. Jardine, 1871), a brick structure with an iron storefront, was built as a hotel. It has several architectural features worthy of note: all the windows have cast-iron drop lintels with a spiral molding and foliate design; above the storefront windows, two panels of stained glass still survive; and the roof displays an intricate iron cornice.

Return to Greene Street and continue west on Spring Street.

Wander down Spring Street to West Broadway to see the variety of new establishments that have taken root. West Broadway was once the heart of the art gallery district of SoHo, but high rents and high-priced boutiques have displaced many of them.

A 1912 American La France "Metropolitan" steam fire engine with front-wheel drive was one of the first steamers to replace the horse-drawn rigs in the city. Engines similar to this one were the first to respond in the tragic Triangle Shirtwaist Company fire of the year before. It is on exhibit at the New York City Fire Museum, 278 Spring Street. (Photo by Steven Scher)

An interesting and entertaining deviation from the tour can be made by walking a few short blocks west to 278 Spring Street to the **New York City Fire Museum.** The museum was opened in 1987 and occupies a former 1904 Beaux Arts–style firehouse, designed by Paris-trained architect Edward Pierce Casey. The collection was brought from the old Firehouse Museum on Duane Street and was augmented by the collection of the former Firefighting Museum of the Home Insurance Company, on Maiden Lane. The museum's highlights include beautifully preserved hand- and horse-drawn apparatus, fire buckets, helmets, trumpets (a kind of early megaphone for giving orders), toy and working models, portraits, prints, photographs, and an important collection of fire marks. The Museum also has displays and memorabilia on the 9/11 World Trade Center disaster. Another of the museum's functions is its Fire Safety Education Program. There is also a small gift shop. (Hours: Tues.–Sat. 10:00 A.M. to 5:00 P.M., Sun. to 4:00 P.M. $5.00 adults, $2.00 seniors, $1.00 children.)

Return to the corner of Spring and Greene streets and turn left (north) on Greene Street.

On the west side, **Nos. 93–95, 97,** and **99** all are neo-Grec–style buildings designed in 1881 by Henry Fernbach. At the base of the second-story windows is a row of vertically incised panels with a neo-Grec motif that, from a distance, simulates a balcony.

Across the street, **No. 96** is by Henry Fernbach (1879), while **Nos. 98** and **100** are by Charles Mettam (1880). The latter two are identical although built for different clients. The pair are flanked by two designed by Fernbach. Both Mettam and Fernbach were contemporaries, and quite similar in taste, but Mettam's work is lighter and somewhat more imaginative.

No. 103–105 (Fernbach again, 1879), occupying a double lot, was formerly one-third larger. **No. 101,** originally an iron-front building, was destroyed in a 1957 fire. The three central bays are framed by Corinthian columns, and each floor has a simple molded cornice. In spite of its present asymmetry it is a pleasing Fernbach building.

No. 112 across the street (1883) is another in the Fernbach line, but its neighbor, **No. 114–120,** is a superlative example of his work. Occupying four lots, it is six stories high and ten bays wide. It was built in 1881 as a branch of the Brooklyn-based Frederick Loeser Department Store (which went out of business shortly after World War II). This is an appropriately elaborate building with a typical Fernbach cornice and entablature. The ground-floor piers are quite ornate, as is the treatment of the broad square windows, which are separated by fluted Ionic columns. Note the different arrangement of the top floor, with segmentally arched lintels separated by columns with egg-and-dart motifs. Imitation fanlights appear between the cornice brackets. Dominating the cornice are stylized acanthus-leaf antefixes located above the pilasters in the middle and at the ends.

(For refreshment, there are a number of restaurants on Spring and Prince streets, and soon on West Broadway, running the gamut from prosaic diners to ethnic and organic food establishments.)

Turn right (east) on Prince Street.

The origin of Prince Street's name is unknown. It may possibly be a reference to Prince William, who later became King William III of England (with Queen Mary II) in 1689.

No. 102–104 (Henry Fernbach, 1881) was also built for Frederick Loeser & Company, and was connected to No. 114–120 Greene Street in the rear. **Nos. 100** and **96–98** were also designed by Fernbach and completed in 1882.

Cross to the northeast corner of Prince and Greene streets.

By now you must have noticed the astonishing *trompe l'oeil* painting covering the entire east wall of **No. 112–114.** The details are so accurate that passersby often fail to realize that an entire wall of windows has been painted, complete with all the traditional cast-iron details, where none exists. The painstaking work even includes a window air conditioner and a cat! The painting was done by illusionist artist Richard Haas, with the assistance of City Walls, Inc. Alas, this great deceptive mural is fading and losing its visual affect. Even the cat could use a bath! So don't look too closely. Much of the building is occupied by the SoHo Center for Visual Artists. This is a rather late cast-iron building on the south side of the block. Among its graceful elements are the banded pilasters at each end of

Iron foundries took pride in their prefabricated cast-iron buildings and frequently mounted a distinctive builder's plaque at the base. (Photos by author)

the building, fluted colonnettes with neo-Grec capitals flanking the windows, lintels with acanthus-leaf designs, an entablature dividing each story, and each cornice surrounded by incised terminal blocks and elaborate brackets. Above, the raised pediment encloses a fanlight motif. Continue west on Prince Street.

The corner building, **No. 109–111** Prince Street, is discussed later as No. 119 Greene Street. **Nos. 113–115, 117–119,** and **121** share a common façade. The three were designed by Cleverdon & Putzel for the Frank Seitz Warehouse in 1890. The whole is replete with French Renaissance designs in its frieze motifs, medallions, and leaf ornaments. Note how the design changes at each successive story. Only No. 113–115 retains its original entablature; nonetheless, the unity of the group is striking. A local landmark is the Prince Street Bar at the corner of Wooster Street.

If you would like to spend a little time exploring the **"art scene in SoHo"** before continuing the tour, walk one block west to West Broadway, where most of the galleries are located, and make a small loop by walking south almost to Broome Street, and returning on the opposite side, past Prince Street to Houston Street. Visit any gallery and pick up a free copy of the *Gallery Guide,* which has a map of the SoHo galleries and museums and lists current exhibitions throughout the city. If you are following the "Optional Gallery Loop," continue north on West Broadway to the northeast corner of Houston Street.

The quarter-acre plot of land, called **Time Landscape,** is a re-creation of a pre-Colonial mixed forest, showing Manhattan's topography and plant life as it would have existed before the arrival of European settlers 350 years ago. The landscaping and plantings, made possible through private and corporate contributions and the work of local artist Alan Sonfist, include oak, sassafras, maples, evergreens, and a variety of wild grasses and flowers typical of the dozens of plants that thrived in the primeval forest. Read the explanatory plaque.

You may either return to Greene and Prince streets (see below), or walk east to Broadway and resume the tour on page 204.

No. **119** Greene Street (Jarvis Morgan Slade, 1882) is beautifully adapted to its corner site. The diagonal bay was once the grand entrance. Slade used French Renaissance motifs very effectively. Note how the projecting cornices separate each floor, and how all architectural features are simply realized. The main cornice is plain, as are the pilasters and window groupings. A circular design appears in the paneled frieze in the entablature.

No. **121–123** (Henry Fernbach, 1882) is doubtless the most ornate structure in the block. With its fluted pilasters with acanthus-leaf design, its columns with ornamented capitals, an elaborate "Fernbachesque" cornice topping the whole, we have a wedding of the architect's skill with the founder's technique.

Nos. **125** and **127** are twins. The former was one of Fernbach's last works, completed in 1883. The latter is credited, however, to William Baker, and was not completed till the following year. Possibly Baker was an associate of Fernbach, carrying out the design after his death. Again we have the typical Fernbach style: pilaster moldings with egg-and-dart; fluting; acanthus-leaf and pellet details separating the two buildings; and the cornice above also ornamented with egg-and-dart, as is the upper frieze with rosettes.

Across the street, **No. 130** (Richard Berger, 1888) is an almost perfect example of the neo-Grec style. The designs on the pilasters and pier capitals are clear and precise. The colonnettes are delicate and topped by huge Ionic capitals with egg-and-dart motifs. They are attached to the building wall by means of a screen-like element, pierced with a stylized flower-and-leaf design. Each story is separated by a simple cornice, and even the upper cornice is simply detailed, supported by curved brackets above the colonnettes and pilasters with a row of dentils under its molding. The slender colonnettes emphasize the verticality of the building and demonstrate the decorative possibilities of cast iron.

Nos. **132–134, 136,** and **140** share a common façade. All are by Alfred Zucker (1885). **No. 142–144** (1871) is another by Henry Fernbach.

Back across the street, **Nos. 133–135** and **137** are others by Henry Fernbach (1882). Adjacent **No. 139,** a Greek Revival–style residence, dates from ca. 1835–40, and although its future survival is uncertain, it presents a picture of what the then–upper-middle-class neighborhood was like.

No. **143,** a brick, stone, and iron building, was designed by the architectural firm of DeLemos & Cordes in 1887. Nine years later they drew the plans for the famous Siegel-Cooper Department Store, the world's largest store at the time. Their professional skill can still be admired on the northeast corner of Avenue of the Americas (Sixth Avenue) and West 18th Street [*see* Ladies' Mile, 11].

GREENE STREET TO BROADWAY

Water tanks. By now you must have noticed the ubiquitous water tanks perched on the roofs of so many of New York's buildings. Since city water pressure is not great enough to rise more than six stories, most taller buildings require the installation of water tanks. Water is pumped up mechanically to fill them, and gravity then takes over and distributes it through the plumbing lines. Wood has been found to be the most durable and economical material. Since 1896 the Rosenwach Tank Company has built the greatest number of rooftop water tanks in the city. While other companies prefabricate their tanks, then hoist them up, the Rosenwach tanks are built on the roof in much the same way as a conventional wooden barrel—with tight-fitting staves held securely by encircling metal bands. The bands are closer together at the bottom because of the steadily increasing pressure of the liquid contents. The conical top usually contains electric heating coils to keep the water from freezing. Later in the tour, look for the conspicuous water tank atop the Haughwout Building (Broadway and Broome Street).

Turn right and walk two blocks to Broadway.

Houston Street was named for William Houstoun by Nicholas Bayard III (a street is named for Bayard, also, near Foley Square). His daughter, Mary, married Houstoun in 1788 after he served three terms as Georgia delegate to the Continental Congress. The current spelling is an error. Out-of-towners frequently associate the name with the Texas hero, Sam Houston, who was not even born when the Houstoun-Bayard wedding took place. And the street is pronounced HOUSE-ton! The buildings along the south side of the street were razed in 1963 when the thoroughfare was widened.

Broadway in the last few years has undergone a swift and dramatic metamorphosis. For nearly a century since the entertainment district moved uptown, it remained a manufacturing wholesale and warehousing area—dark and rather dingy. The lack of major development was fortuitous however, as the buildings were not "modernized," and the fine array of industrial architecture was preserved. The thoroughfare suddenly has come to life as a center for the arts, as many galleries found the loft space and rents attractive, and a spate of new museums opened their doors. And to feed the throngs of visitors, a variety of food emporiums offer many choices. Even new bank branches are taking advantage of the increase in economic activity.

The enormous building at the northwest corner of Broadway is McKim, Mead & White's **Cable Building,** 611 Broadway. Designed in 1894 by Stanford White, it was the headquarters of the Broadway Cable Traction Company, whose initials in wrought iron can be seen over the entrance. Also above the entrance are two relief sculptures, and topping the main cornice is a row of antefixes in the typical Greek anthemion design. For many years after horsecars were abandoned, Manhattan's streetcars were propelled by underground cables beneath the tracks, much like today's cable cars of San Francisco. The Cable Building not only housed the offices of the company, but also the steam-driven machines that controlled the cables. [*See* pages 227 and 228.]

Across the street, charming **No. 620** (John B. Snook, 1858) may be the second-oldest cast-iron building in New York. A gem of the Italian Renaissance *palazzo* style, this delightful former gaslight-fixture factory known as the "Little Cary Building" has somehow survived intact, except for some ground-floor modifications. The façade, in imitation of rusticated blocks, gives a three-dimensional effect behind the rows of paired, free-standing Corinthian columns. Each pair of fluted columns supports its own entablature and is joined to its neighbor by ornate semicircular arches rich in design. The structure is a tribute to Daniel D. Badger's Architectural Iron Works. A larger version of this delightful structure is the Cary Building, located at 105 Chambers Street, downtown. [*See* page 217.]

No. 622–626 (1882) occupies the site of the **former Laura Keene's Varieties Theater.** Laura Keene was one of the most popular actresses and theater managers of the day and is considered the first woman stage director. It was here in 1858 that *Our American Cousin*, with actor Joseph Jefferson, was first produced—the play that later was attended by Abraham Lincoln on that fatal day. The theater was renamed the Olympic and remained a popular entertainment spot until it was destroyed by fire in 1880. Two years later, the present commercial building was erected. Having suffered the ravages of "modernization," little remains except for the five floors of columns and a rather attractive upper story. Curved-arch windows with keystones and an intricate cornice give some idea of its original ornamentation. Oddly, the building is unevenly divided into two sections of four and six bays, possibly because it was first planned as two separate entities.

No. 628–630 (1882) was designed by Philadelphia architect Henry Schwarzmann, the supervising architect of the 1876 Centennial Exposition. Built for Henry Newman's **New York Mercantile Exchange,** it has a rather flat but pleasing façade, with bamboolike colonnettes and extensive floral designs. The firm name emblazoned across the front adds to the overall effect. The decorative cornice is made of galvanized iron, and the wrought-iron cresting has disappeared.

Return to Houston Street and continue south on Broadway.

HOUSTON STREET TO CANAL STREET (along Broadway)

Broadway, in the six long blocks south to Canal Street, offers as diverse an array of commercial architecture as can be found anywhere. Virtually every style is represented, in both cast iron and masonry, dating from the period of the late 1850s to the early 20th century. Although the tour is concerned primarily with cast-iron architecture, one should not overlook the great variety of brick and stone buildings—some of which were the forerunners in style of the early cast-iron edifices, as well as those later steel-framework behemoths whose over-ornateness often approaches decadence. As if searching for an architectural style of their own, the enormous commercial loft buildings of the 1890s through the 1900s cling tenaciously to all the old classic motifs, draping themselves in reckless abandon with a profusion of carved stone and terra-cotta adornments, apparently unwilling to face the stylistic demands imposed by the new "skyscraper" technology.

With the widening of Houston Street, **No. 600–602** Broadway is now the corner building. Built in 1882 from plans by Samuel Warner, each floor is built successively shorter to give the impression of greater height.

Across the street, **No. 597,** a marble building (John Kellum, 1867), looks so much like a typical early cast-iron building that one is tempted to test it with a magnet. **Nos. 593** and **591** are also an interesting pair. The former is an attractive Classical-style building dating from 1860.

No. 591, extensively altered about 1890, still has a great deal of charm. The iron arched doorways and ground-floor window seem to be original, and the window treatment is light and cheerful. Look up to the sixth floor with its attractive entablature and surmounting pediment.

No. 593 is the site of the **Museum of African Art,** which extends through to Mercer Street. The Museum, originally the Center for African Art, mounts two major exhibitions each year and a series of public programs. The interior was designed by Maya Lin, the architect responsible for the Vietnam Memorial in Washington, D.C. and the Martin Luther King Memorial in Atlanta, with designer David Hotson. [Hours: Sun. 12:00 to 6:00 P.M., Tues.–Fri. 10:30 A.M. to 5:30 P.M., Sat. 12:00 to 8:00 P.M., (212) 966-1313.]

No. 583, Astor Building (Cleverdon & Putzel, 1896; expanded and remodeled, 1998) houses the **New Museum of Contemporary Art,** which presents changing exhibitions of works of the past decade only. (Hours: Tues.–Sun. 12:00 to 6:00 P.M., Thurs. to 8:00 P.M. Admission: $6.00 adults; $3.00 seniors and students; members and children under 18, free.) John Jacob Astor died in his home that was on the site, in 1848.

No. 568–578, a typical structure of the mid-1890s, not unlike many in this four-block length of Broadway, was designed in Renaissance Eclectic style by noted architect George B. Post, who produced buildings of much greater interest: the New York Stock Exchange, City College north campus, the Brooklyn Historical Society, the Williamsburg Savings Bank, etc. On the northeast corner, from the mid- to late-19th century, stood the large and fashionable **Metropolitan Hotel,** one of the city's largest. Behind the hotel, extending to Crosby Street, was **Niblo's Garden Theater,** a popular entertainment spot—one of many Broadway theaters in the mid-19th century—whose entrance was through the basement of the Metropolitan Hotel.

No. 575 (Thomas Stent, 1881; remodeled 1996 and 2001) was originally the Rogers Peet Store and, until recently, housed the Guggenheim SoHo Museum. Now, in a remarkable renovation, the celebrated Dutch architect Rem Koolhaas has produced a dazzling, even iconoclastic bi-level interior design for the **Prada** women's and men's fashion and sports boutique. According to owner Muicca Prada, the goal was to bring a new era of chic and elegance to lower Broadway. Walk inside and see how the main floor, made of rare tropical hardwood, flows smoothly down to the lower level sales areas in a sweeping parabolic curve, then swings back up (in a shape that would warm the heart of any skateboarder). Converting the building from the former Guggenheim into this upscale and trendy establishment cost Prada in excess of $40 million.

(Look east on Prince Street to the diminutive red brick Federal-style house at the southeast corner of Crosby Street, a surprising remnant of the former residential district of the early 19th century.)

One of the outstanding architectural achievements of the early 20th century is **No. 561–563,** occupying an L-shaped plot on the southwest corner of Prince Street. Known as the **"Little Singer Building,"** it was designed in 1903 by architect Ernest Flagg as an office and loft building for the Singer (sewing machine) Manufacturing Company. Flagg was also responsible for their famous Singer Tower—once the tallest skyscraper in the world—which was located at the corner of Broadway and Liberty Street until its unfortunate demolition in 1967. One of the most avant-garde uses of iron, the "Little Singer" presents an innovative 12-story façade of cast iron, decorative terra-cotta panels, and broad expanses of plate glass. Delicate balconies and balustrades with wrought-iron traceries, supported by fragile cast-iron colonnettes, are surmounted by a graceful, lacy arch; while above, curved wrought-iron brackets support the 11th-story cornice. The Prince Street side has a narrower but similar façade.

No. 560–566 (Thomas Stent, 1883), a six-story brick and stone building, occupies the entire Prince Street side to Crosby Street. Heavy brick piers flank both the end and center bays; and at the first, second, fourth, and sixth floors, the piers are decorated with floral capitals. Foliated iron pilasters separate the windows, which have curved lintels, and the entablature between each floor has its own foliated frieze.

On the west side of Broadway, **No. 549–555,** in gray granite with cast-iron colonnettes and spandrels, is the massive **Rouss Building.** Designed in 1889 by Alfred Zucker for Charles Rouss, it stands as a symbol of success of the self-made millionaire who arrived penniless in New York from Maryland shortly after the Civil War. Making his fortune as a wholesale merchant, Rouss attributed his success not only to hard work, but to the opportunities afforded him by Broadway, and in gratitude, he took "Broadway" as his middle name, emblazoning it for all to see in the scrolled pediment above. When an identical section was built in 1900, the roof was altered and the triangular mansardlike attic dormers added. The windows of the façade are divided into groups of three by heavy quoined pilasters, each window grouping having a pair of intervening slender colonnettes. Cast-iron spandrels separate each pair of stories. Although the much-altered ground floor spoils the unity of the building, it is, nonetheless, a bold and impressive structure.

Nos. 552–554, across the street, are among the oldest on Broadway (John B. Snook, 1855). Both are of stone and have two-story iron fronts, joined together later in 1897. Note the wide central window on the second floor, the four large console brackets that support the second-floor cornice, the rounded window lintels with incised keystones, and the elaborate upper cornice with its modillions and decorated brackets.

No. 550, alongside, completed in 1854, was **formerly the Tiffany & Company store.** However, little can be seen of the original façade as it was refaced with cast iron in 1901, probably one of the last such fronts to be erected.

On the west side of Broadway, much altered **No. 545** (1885) is by Samuel A. Warner.

Just north of Spring Street, don't miss the attractive wood-and-glass store-front on **No. 546!** It is a replacement designed by Guy Lindsay Kohn in 1993 to lend authenticity to the Beaux Arts–style building, which had undergone a number of modifications. The structure dates from 1866 when it was built of brick and stone as a loft, replacing the Fourth Universalist Church on the site. In 1901 architect John Correja added a cast-iron front; then in 1930 it was "remuddled" with a sheet-metal ground-floor front. The new addition harmonizes with the Beaux Arts façade and is an asset to Broadway and the historic district.

In front of No. 542 is another "bishop's crook" lamppost.

Nos. 537–541 are a pleasing trio in cast iron (Charles Mettam, 1868). If one ignores the remodeled ground floor, the beauty can be seen in the harmonious treatment of the eight-bay façade set off by three-quarter round columns with Corinthianesque capitals and the flat arches with rope moldings. In the spandrels are rosettes above each column. The roof line, however, dominates the building. Above a paneled frieze are three pediments—two curved, and one triangular—supported by scrolled brackets and modillions. Ornate urns further highlight the intricate cornice.

Back across the street, **No. 542–544,** built of marble in 1864, has undergone several modifications; nevertheless the arrangement of the upper floors is quite eye-catching. The bays are separated by Corinthian columns, but on the very top floor they are separated by caryatidlike figures. The cornice, topped by two urns above the outer figures, is supported by large scrolled brackets.

No. 540 (D. & J. Jardine, 1867), built of marble, was once a store and warehouse. It has a most unusual two-dimensional effect created by the flatness of the pilasters, "capitals," window arches, lintels, and keystones—all with carved fleur-de-lis designs. Above the cornice, set in a small semicircular pediment, is the date of construction. Again, one can only speculate on how the motif was handled on the original ground floor.

The northwest corner of Broadway and Spring Street is the site of the luxurious Prescott House, built in 1852.

No. 521–523 is all that remains of the once opulent **St. Nicholas Hotel.** Completed in 1854 at a cost of over $1 million, it was one of the most elegant hotels in the city, competing in luxury only with the Astor House on lower Broadway. There is some controversy over who the architect was. Whether it was Griffith Thomas or John B. Snook, no one knows for sure. The 1,000-bed establishment occupied 11 lots from 507 through 527 Broadway, extending to the corner of Prince Street, opposite the Prescott House which was built two years earlier. During the Civil War, the St. Nicholas was taken over by the War Department as a headquarters, becoming one of the nerve centers of the Union Army. The life of the hotel, however, was relatively short. With the uptown move of the entertainment district, the plush hotels soon followed, and by the mid-1870s it closed its doors. This remaining section of the old hotel is faced with stone, showing only a trace of its former appearance. The old cast-iron Corinthian storefront has long

The remains of the once opulent St. Nicholas Hotel: a pair of stone buildings at 521 and 523 Broadway. Completed in 1854, the million-dollar hotel was second in luxury only to the Astor House downtown. The window lintels and ornamental cornices on No. 521 (left) were removed since this photo was taken in 1975. (Photo by author)

since been removed. Virtually nothing remains of the original façades of Nos. 521 and 523. [*See* photo on page 209.]

No. 513–519, designed by Lamb & Rich in 1884 (on the site of part of the old St. Nicholas Hotel), is a 13-bay-wide commercial building in the then-popular Queen Anne style. As the former DeForest Building it incorporated newly adopted terra-cotta elements into the building's polychrome façade. Heavy brick pilasters adorned with terra-cotta plaques and topped with ornate capitals divide the bays into three groups between the first, second, and fifth floors. The windows in the outer bays are separated by delicate cast-iron Ionic pilasters, while the center bay sections have iron columns with very ornate capitals. Scrolled brackets supporting the iron cornice alternate with terra-cotta plaques in the frieze. A half-story mansard roof is offset by three pediments—the center one enclosing an elaborate design. The dark red brick throughout is also typical of the Queen Anne style and became very popular in the contemporary Romanesque Revival style of the 1880s.

A "bishop's crook" lamppost stands in front of No. 515.

Nos. 503–505, 507–509, and **511** were all designed in cast iron by John B. Snook in 1878 to form a harmonious grouping, after the demise of the St. Nicholas Hotel. So many alterations have taken place that only the ornate entablature is really worthy of note. A row of vertical pseudo-brackets stretches across the broad concave frieze below the narrow cornice, with larger brackets topped by neo-Grec terminal blocks above the pilasters supporting the cornice.

Across the street, **No. 502–504,** designed by Kellum & Son in 1860, presents a striking façade with its "sperm candle" style. Named after the shape of old whale-oil candles, the motif is credited to Daniel D. Badger, whose Architectural Iron Works constructed the original storefront, and who used the design in full cast iron on a building erected in 1861 at 55–57 White Street (two blocks below Canal Street). The smooth white marble columns separate each window grouping into two-story units, forming a giant "double arcade." Under the cornice is a row of "inverse crenelation," and rising above the molded end brackets are small urns. Architecture buffs have long been arguing whether the "sperm candle" style originated in stone or cast iron.

Cross to the southwest corner of Broadway and Broome Street for the best view of the most beautiful commercial cast-iron building in the country, the

Haughwout Building (*pronounced* HOW-out), at **No. 488–492** Broadway. Referred to as the "Parthenon of Cast-Iron Architecture in America," this impressive building was one of the first designated New York City Landmarks. Architectural writer Ada Louise Huxtable said of it: "The Haughwout Store's iron elegance contained all the seeds of the future; its metal façade was to lead in turn to the metal frame; the elevator, combined with the metal frame, was to produce the skyscraper; and its repetitive Palladian rhythms were to become the basis of today's aesthetic of pre-fabricated, mass-produced structural units." In 1856 Eder V. Haughwout engaged architect John P. Gaynor to design an appropriate store and showroom for his china and glassware business. The result a year later was this superb Venetian Renaissance *palazzo*. The finely detailed iron façade was cast by Daniel D. Badger's Architectural Iron Works, and later appeared in his illustrated iron works catalog [*see* Recommended Reading]. Haughwout's chinaware was so highly esteemed that it was used in the White House and was displayed at New York's Crystal Palace Exhibition, 1853–54. He also commissioned Elisha Graves Otis to install a steam-driven passenger elevator—the first of its kind anywhere—which years later was to make skyscrapers feasible, at the same time launching the industrial empire of the Otis Company. The basic design motif, repeated on each level, is a keystoned round arch set on fluted Corinthian columns, flanked by taller columns supporting a full entablature, with an underlying balustrade in each bay. A delicate cornice rises above several bands of elaborate friezework; and in the center bay of the second floor hangs a large iron clock. The building is in virtually pristine condition, restored magnificently in 1995 by Joseph Pell Lombardi & Associates. Because of its architectural and historic significance, the Haughwout Building has been listed in the National Register of Historic Places.

Cross to the east side of Broadway to get a better view of **No. 491, The New Era Building** (Buchman & Deisler, 1897). Here is an unusual art nouveau variation on the turn-of-the-century industrial architecture theme. The building, with its short and stubby Doric columns and multistory verdigris copper mansard roof, was built for a printing firm, and simply exudes strength and solidity.

No. 477–479 (H. W. Smith and Sons, 1869) contrasts strongly with its neighbors. A center molded pilaster divides the bays into two distinct groupings. The bays themselves are separated by columns with hexagonal bases and stylized Corinthian

Considered to be the "Parthenon of Cast-Iron Architecture" is the landmark Haughwout Building at Broadway and Broome Street. This superb Venetian palazzo was cast by Daniel D. Badger's Architectural Iron Works in 1856, and was equipped with the first commercial steam elevator by Elisha Graves Otis. It is probably the oldest extant cast-iron building in the city, and certainly one of the best preserved. (Photo by author)

capitals. The windows have rounded lintels, and abstract geometric detail decorates the spandrels. Simple cornices separate the upper stories. Note the fine leaf-pattern design on the brackets of the upper cornice. And the storefronts survive intact.

The Roosevelt Building across Broadway, at **No. 478–482,** is the only surviving Richard Morris Hunt commercial building in New York. The Paris-trained architect also designed the Metropolitan Museum of Art, the base of the Statue of Liberty, the bronze doors of Trinity Church, and the lovely old New York Tribune Building, which dominated Park Row, downtown. This unusual neo-Grec–style building, owned by Roosevelt Hospital, was built as a store for income-producing purposes in 1873. The visual impact of this original statement in cast iron is often lost on the thousands of riders and pedestrians who pass it daily, as *few New Yorkers are in the habit of looking any higher at buildings than ground-floor level.* Built to utilize the advantages of iron architecture to the utmost, it resembles no masonry predecessor nor any other cast-iron building either. The enormous front is divided into three main sections by four fluted pilasters at the tall ground-floor level and continued by bold Ionic columns for the next three levels. Slender colonnettes separate the triple windows, disappearing behind a curved screenlike tracery arch set over each group. The top floor, which repeats the three-window pattern, is shaded by a broad projecting cornice, now minus much of its former decoration. On each incised pilaster is mounted a large circular escutcheon with the street address in bold numerals. A single section of the building extends back to Crosby Street (No. 40), where its one-third-smaller front is graced with a proportionately scaled version of the Broadway façade.

Nos. 466–468 and **462–464** (note the circular street number plaques) at the northeast corner of Grand Street combine to form a striking pair. Built from plans by John Correja in 1879, the pair was leased by the large textile importing firm of Mills & Gibb, specializing in linens and laces. An earlier tenant on the site was the **Brooks Brothers Store,** which during the Civil War had established its reputation by supplying uniforms for the Union Army. An interesting variation on the decorative theme is the sawtooth motif that embellishes the window lintels, and the rows of incised banding on the second- and fourth-story entablatures. On the third, fifth, and sixth floors, the pilasters have unique scallop-and-bandwork capitals, with a medallion motif halfway up the shaft. The cornice is rather heavy and is supported by brackets, while a row of modillions lines the architrave. [*See also* Chapter 5, 3, the Brooks Brothers Store.]

The parking lot across the street is the **site of an early Lord & Taylor department store** (1860–72). The original Griffith Thomas–designed building suffered a disastrous fire in 1967 and had to be demolished. During the Draft Riots of 1863, Lord & Taylor armed its employees for protection against the raging mobs that were surging down Broadway (the rioters were finally dispersed by Union Army artillery about a mile north, at what is now 3rd Street). In 1865, when President Lincoln's funeral cortege moved slowly up Broadway, the store was draped in mourning, with merchandise removed from the windows and seats installed for the viewing of the procession. [*See also* Chapter 8, 27.]

Midway down the east side of the next block are **Nos. 452, 450, 446–448,** and **444**—an interesting quartet in cast iron. The two outer buildings (Nos. 452 and

Now a vacant lot on the northwest corner of Broadway and Grand Street, the Lord & Taylor store occupied the site from 1860 until fire destroyed it a hundred years later. The firm sold the building shortly after the turn of the century when the retail district moved uptown to "Ladies' Mile." (The Edward S. C. Arnold Collection, lent by the Metropolitan Museum of Art. Museum of the City of New York)

444) are identical (by Schweitzer & Gruwé); while the inner pair (Nos. 450 and 446–448) share a common façade (John B. Snook). All were completed in the same year, 1877. The flanking outer buildings immediately bring to mind Richard Morris Hunt's Roosevelt Building (at 478–482 Broadway), with their pierced stylized arches and wide spandrel panels, together with the slim colonnettes separating the windows. Crowning the front is a bold projecting cornice decorated with anthemions alternating with raised circular motifs, with neo-Grec console brackets at the ends. Look for the foundry label, which unexpectedly gives the names of the architects along with the Long Island Iron Works. The inner group of buildings is distinguished by quoined pilasters at each end, Corinthian columns defining the window bays and ground floor openings; while above, the entablature is flanked by large console brackets topped by neo-Grec terminal blocks, a common cornice stretches above a paneled frieze, and additional concave brackets with their own incised terminal blocks alternate with frieze panels. The cast-iron fronts were supplied by the J. B. & J. W. Cornell Iron Works (see label).

A "bishop's crook" lamppost stands in front of No. 446–448.

Across the street, **No. 447** (architect unknown, 1860) has an iron storefront listed in D. D. Badger's Architectural Iron Works catalog of 1865.

No. 443–445 (Griffith Thomas, 1860): Although not of cast iron, the structure presents a very aesthetic appearance. Rows of pleasing round-arch windows are topped by individual projecting cornice slabs supported by brackets. A projecting balustrade runs along the second floor, with decorative urns at each end. Ornate scrolled brackets support the main cornice, above which a pediment adds the final touch.

Except for No. 441, built in 1876, the entire west side of the block dates from the 1860s.

"The Bank in the Park," No. 433, at the northwest corner of Howard Street (Eggers & Higgins, 1967) is now a sad relic. Once a branch of the Franklin National Bank (and successor banks), the fake Georgian-style octagonal structure with its 19 sycamore trees was planned to be an "oasis on dingy lower Broadway." Now more dingy than its surroundings, it stands forlorn, graffitied, and vandalized, with an uncertain future.

Howard Street is named for Harry Howard, a volunteer "fire laddie" of the early 19th century. It was called Hester Street until 1825, which, incidentally, is still the street's name after it makes a small zigzag at Centre Street on its way east toward the Lower East Side.

Turn left (east) on Howard Street for a brief glance at **Nos. 27** and **29.** The former, a modified neo-Grec–style building, was designed by Samuel Warner in 1888. No. 29, 20 years its senior, is by the firm of Renwick & Sands. One must look beyond the added fire escape and the dingy atmosphere, abetted by the narrow and dark street, to enjoy the profusion of decorative elements. The rolling iron shutter in the center window was a novelty introduced in the "iron age." Amazingly, both buildings' ground floors remain completely intact. In front of **No. 30,** on the northeast corner is a large **cast-iron sidewalk light vault** (bearing the mark of G. R. Jackson, Burnett & Co. Iron Works and Excelsior Iron Works). These sub-surface light vaults were fairly common before the advent of electric lighting and allowed sunlight to provide some illumination into the basement. See the **cast-iron shutter** (Excelsior Iron Works) on **No. 28** on the north side, also common in the mid-19th century, now rather rare.

Return to the northeast corner of Howard Street and Broadway.

Diagonally across the street is the exquisite **Dittenhoffer Warehouse, No. 427–429,** built (as emblazoned in the ornate triangular pediment) in 1870. The successive shortening of each story clearly creates a feeling of much greater height than would be expected from a five-story building. Architect Thomas Jackson used both Venetian and French motifs to highlight this palatial edifice. Particularly noteworthy is the beautifully ornate façade, as exemplified by the spandrels between the window arches, the decorated column shafts, the Corinthian capitals, the keystoned arches over the windows, and the frieze below the bracket-supported cornice, which repeats the florid details of the spandrels. Except for one remaining show window on the Howard Street side, most of the ground floor has been altered beyond recognition. The corner was the site of the City Hotel from 1852 to 1869.

Adjacent **No. 425,** erected in 1869, is one of architect Griffith Thomas's first full iron-front buildings (Aetna Iron Works). How different from its neighbor are the square-headed windows with curved corners, the unadorned entablatures, the almost bare columns, and curved broken pediments. Its most famous tenant was the LeBoutillier Brothers Store, which opened in 1898, but moved uptown in

1913, to establish one of the most fashionable women's wear emporiums during the gaslit era and for many years afterward. [*See* Ladies' Mile, 20.]

Continue west on Howard Street.

No. 48, a stone building with a cast-iron storefront, was built in 1860 as an annex to the Arnold Constable "Marble House" across the street. The façade with its rows of round-arched windows, pilasters, heavy entablature, and elaborate cornice is a typical example of the masonry prototypes of early cast-iron buildings.

No. 50–52 was built in 1860 as a store for a gun dealer. A stone building with a cast-iron storefront, it is more imposing than No. 48. The ground level has lovely fluted Corinthian columns, above which are rows of French-style segmental-arch windows in a kind of "recessed" style that creates a flat, two-dimensional effect. The overall restrained appearance ends at the cornice, which is disproportionately ostentatious. During the Civil War, the building became the **New York State Soldiers' Depot,** a rest home and hospital for troops on leave.

Howard Street ends at Mercer Street (named for General Hugh Mercer, killed in the Battle of Princeton in 1777). Return to Broadway, turn right, and walk one block south to Canal Street.

Turn left (east) one block on Canal Street to Lafayette Street.

On the southwest corner—in an appropriate climax to the tour—is one of the finest and oldest cast-iron-front buildings in the city, **No. 254–260 Canal Street.** The historic and well-preserved structure, formerly a loft and warehouse building, was remodeled for offices in 1987 and now has a branch of the HSBC Bank (Hong Kong Shanghai Banking Corp.). A splendid example of the highest quality of cast-iron architectural design, it was erected in 1857 from plans attributed to pioneer cast-iron architect James Bogardus.

End of tour. (An optional Supplementary Tour follows.) **The Canal Street station at the corner of Lafayette Street has entrances to the No. 6, J, and M lines, and, at Broadway, the N, Q, and R lines.**

SUPPLEMENTARY TOUR BELOW CANAL STREET

A short walk through the neighborhood from Canal Street to Chambers Street, using Broadway as an axis, reveals a number of additional cast-iron buildings of more than casual interest. A few are listed below. *Except where indicated, all cast-iron buildings are located in the one block west of Broadway.* [*See* street map.]

CANAL STREET:	**No. 268** (one block east) (Lansing C. Holden, 1886), and **No. 351–353** (two blocks west) (W. H. Gaylor, 1971).
LISPENARD STREET:	**Nos. 48–40.** See also cast-iron decoration on **No. 39–41,** Clark Building.

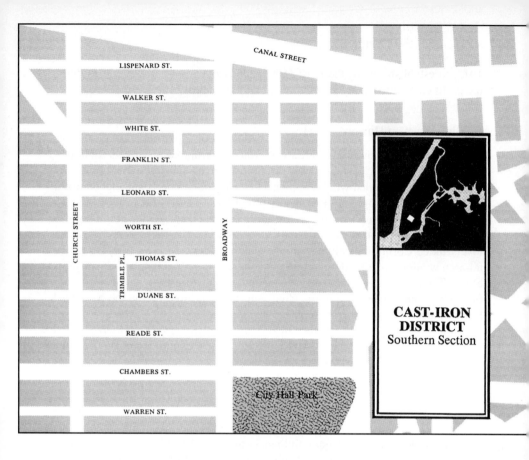

CAST-IRON
DISTRICT
Southern Section

WALKER STREET:	**Nos. 57, 49–43, 42.**
BROADWAY:	**No. 385–387** Grosvenor Building (Charles Wright, 1875).
WHITE STREET:	**Nos. 57–55, 60, 41, 37–35,** and the avant-garde **Civic Center Synagogue,** Congregation Shaare Zedek. Not cast iron, but astonishing! (William N. Breger, architect, and Paul Gugliotta, structural engineer, 1967).
FRANKLIN STREET:	**No. 81–83.** Only the lower part is cast iron (west of Broadway).
BROADWAY:	**No. 359,** originally Thompson's Saloon (1852); also the site (on the top three floors) of one of **Matthew Brady's photography studios.** Abraham Lincoln was photographed here the day after his historic Cooper Union speech in 1860. At this writing, the Brady studio sign is discernable on the upper south wall of the building.
	No. 361 James S. White Building (W. Wheeler Smith, 1881).
LEONARD STREET:	**No. 85 James Bogardus's former warehouse** (1860).
BROADWAY:	**No. 346** (east side). Not cast iron, this was the **former New York Life Insurance Company Building** (Griffith Thomas, 1870; enlarged by McKim, Mead & White, 1896).

● BROADWAY: **No. 319** (corner of Thomas Street) (D. & J. Jardine, 1869).
                           No. 287 (corner of Reade Street) (John B. Snook, 1871).

● THOMAS STREET: **No. 8** (Jarvis Morgan Slade, 1875).

● READE STREET: Walk one block farther to Church Street to admire the
● ...   splendidly preserved **Cary Building** at **No. 89–91** (Gam-
                           aliel King & John Kellum, 1856); castings made by
                           Daniel D. Badger's Architectural Iron Works.
                           No. 93.

● CHAMBERS STREET: **No. 105–107** (the rear façade of the Cary Building; King
                           & Kellum, 1857; Daniel D. Badger's Architectural Iron
                           Works).
                           No. 120 (just a bit farther west). Only the upper floors are
                           worth looking at; however, to get a good picture of its orig-
                           inal appearance, go around the corner to see the rear of the
                           building and its well-preserved façade at 50 Warren Street
                           (architect unknown, ca. 1860; cast by Daniel D. Badger).

GLOSSARY OF TECHNICAL TERMS USED IN THE SOHO CAST-IRON DISTRICT WALKING TOUR

ANTEFIX, an ornament projecting above a roof cornice, frequently incorporating an anthemion motif.

ANTHEMION, a conventionalized leaf motif based on a honeysuckle or palmette form, originating in Greek ornamental forms.

ARCHITRAVE [*see* ENTABLATURE].

BALUSTRADE, a row of baluster columns topped by a railing, forming a parapet, usually set on a cornice or in front of a window.

BAY, the general term for the window section.

BEARING WALL, a wall upon which the structural load of a building rests.

BRACKET, a projecting L- or S-shaped support used frequently in the form of an S-curve.

CARYATID, a decorative column in the form of a female figure.

CLASSICAL ORDERS. In discussing the buildings dating from the second half of the 19th century within the Historic District, references to the classical orders must be interpreted loosely. The architects of these buildings took great liber-ties in adapting Greek and Roman forms to commercial buildings. Reference to a specific order refers only to the capital (the design element at the top of the column shaft).

TUSCAN CAPITAL, a very simple unadorned capital, resembling the Doric, but frequently of heavier proportions.

DORIC CAPITAL, a relatively simple capital with a flat topmost member.

IONIC CAPITAL, a capital with spiral volutes beneath its topmost member.

CORINTHIAN CAPITAL, a capital embellished with carved acanthus leaves.

CORINTHIANESQUE CAPITAL, a capital incorporating stylized leaf forms.

COMPOSITE CAPITAL, a capital combining volutes and acanthus leaves (a composite of the Ionic and Corinthian orders).

CONSOLE BRACKET [*see* BRACKET].

CORNICE [*see* ENTABLATURE].

CORNICE SLAB, a cornicelike projection placed above a window.

CURTAIN WALL, an exterior wall, separate from the structural framework, that supports only its own weight.

DROP LINTEL [*see* LINTEL].

EGG-AND-DART MOLDING, a classical molding consisting of alternating egg-and-dart-shaped forms.

ENTABLATURE, the group of horizontal members directly above column capitals. It consists of:

ARCHITRAVE, the lowest member resting upon the column capitals. An architrave is also occasionally extended to enframe the sides of a door or window opening that is topped by an entablature.

FRIEZE, the middle member of an entablature, which in 19th-century architectural styles is frequently embellished by panels or medallions, and interrupted by large cornice brackets; 19th-century adaptations of classical orders often combine a frieze and cornice without architrave.

CORNICE, the horizontally projecting topmost member of an entablature. It is frequently found by itself as the crowning motif of a façade.

FANLIGHT, a semicircular window placed over a door, with bars radiating from its center like spokes of a fan.

FINIAL, an ornamental form at the top of a pediment, spire, pinnacle, etc.

FRIEZE [*see* ENTABLATURE].

IRON VAULT COVERS, a number of iron plates with lights (*see* below) that lie over the vaults, and are on the same level as the sidewalk.

KEYSTONE, the central voussoir (block) of an arch.

LIGHT, generally, a pane of glass, but in this district it refers to pieces of hardened glass of various shapes, sizes, and colors that are inserted in iron plates.

LIGHT PLATFORM, a flat, raised area in front of the façade of a building that is made up of a number of iron plates with lights, and which stands on the vault.

LINTEL, a horizontal member placed over a window or door to support the superstructure.

MODILLION, a small ornamental bracket used in a closely spaced, regular series below a projecting cornice.

PALAZZO, an Italian "palace," usually associated with those from the Renaissance. When referring to 19th-century styles, however, a *palazzo* can be any large, impressive building whose style was derived from the Italian Renaissance.

PEDIMENT, a low, usually triangular gable constructed in a classical style that is often filled by sculpture and usually framed by a cornice. It is used decoratively to crown central bays, porticoes, and important windows of a façade, and is sometimes segmental in shape or broken away in the center.

PIER, in masonry architecture, an upright supporting member carrying a structural load. When interpreted in cast iron, an exterior pier is, in most instances, merely a solid part of the curtain wall placed between the windows and/or on either side of a façade.

PILASTER, a shallow, flat engaged (attached) column, normally serving only a decorative function.

QUOIN, in masonry architecture, large stones used to reinforce a corner or salient angle of a building. When interpreted in cast iron, rusticated quoins were used decoratively to emphasize the flanking piers.

RISER, the vertical member between the treads of a stair.

RUSTICATION, in masonry architecture, an emphasis of individual (usually large) stones by recessing their connecting parts.

SEGMENTAL ARCH, an arch in which the curvature is a segment of a circle, but less than a semicircle.

SOLDIER COURSE, a course (row) of bricks set on their ends.

SPANDREL, the space between the outer curve of an arch and its rectangular enframement, or between two adjacent arches and a horizontal member above them.

SPANDREL PANEL, in skeleton-frame construction, the wall panel between the head of one window and the sill of a window directly above it.

TERMINAL BLOCK, a decorative block placed at the extreme ends of a cornice between floor levels, thus interrupting the quoin lines or flanking piers of a façade.

TREAD, the horizontal surface of a step.

VAULT, a cellar room used for storage, often extending under the sidewalk.

VOLUTE, a spiral or scroll-like form, as with the Ionic capital.

VOUSSOIR, a wedge-shaped stone forming part of a masonry arch.

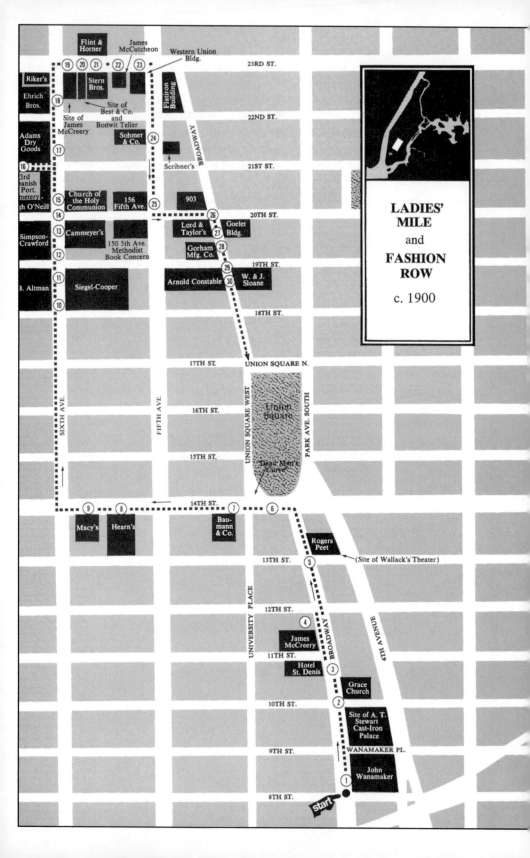

8. Ladies' Mile, Fashion Row, and Union Square

[Subways: N, R to 8th Street; 6 to Astor Place, walk west one block on 8th Street. Buses: M1, M2, M3, M5, M6 to 8th Street.]

The department store as we know it today had its genesis in the small wholesale and dry-goods shops that began to proliferate along the busier thoroughfares of lower Manhattan during the 1820s. With the upsurge of immigration in the following decades, and the rapid growth of commerce and industry, many keen merchants seized the opportunity to expand and diversify, making fortunes by catering to the changing tastes and increased demands of the burgeoning city. By the 1870s and 1880s, the main shopping center of the city had moved uptown, following the northward growth of the city, to an area between 8th and 23rd streets along Broadway, and also on Fifth and Sixth avenues. With women shoppers always in the majority, it did not take long before this bustling row of large retail stores was known as Ladies' Mile.

Today not one of those fine old establishments can be found on the Mile. The stores either relocated farther uptown to keep abreast with the inexorable northward tide, or, unable to update their merchandising techniques, closed their doors forever. Astonishingly, most of the buildings that housed those elegant department stores still remain intact, now the city's latest hot shopping spot.

Our itinerary takes us on a "shopping tour" of those glamorous "ghosts" of a bygone era, and using a little imagination, we can return to the bustling streets of those gaslit days. Listen carefully for the rhythmic clip-clop from the profusion of horse-drawn vehicles and the clatter of their iron-clad wheels on the cobblestoned street, the persistent bell-clanging of horsecars caught in the tangled traffic—their impatient conductors exchanging abuse with draymen and carriage drivers—and the shrill cries of "Extra! Extra!" from little boys hawking their penny papers at the street corners. When we reach Sixth Avenue, our walk will take us under the gloomy structure of the old El, whose wooden trains roar by overhead in an endless, ear-splitting clatter, their smoky locomotives spewing hot cinders and oil on the unwary below. Standing stiffly at the entrance portals to the fancy "magazines" that line the Avenue, liveried doormen await the arrival of the "carriage trade," and as a coach draws up, rush forward to escort the affluent patrons to the door. And clustered about the elaborate show windows, we glimpse elegantly clad women in trailing dresses, billowy hats, and frilly parasols, pressing to catch the latest fashions in furbelows, veils, shirtwaists, millinery, and high-button shoes.

1. The tour begins at 8th Street and Broadway, the southerly end of Ladies' Mile. The huge building at the northeast corner was formerly the **Wanamaker Department Store,** now known simply as 770 Broadway. Construction of this 16-story giant began in 1902 and took five years to complete. Designed by Daniel H. Burnham, architect of the Flatiron Building [*see* Madison Square, 24], the structure was planned as a modern extension to the older "Cast-Iron Palace" that occupied the block directly north. John Wanamaker came to New York in 1896 to open a branch of his Philadelphia store, and purchased the old cast-iron building from the successors of the faltering A. T. Stewart Company. Alexander Turney Stewart, who had been considered a merchandising genius, in 1846 opened New York City's first large department store, at Broadway and Chambers Street. Called "The Marble Dry-Goods Palace," the building still stands today [*see* City Hall, 15]. In 1862 he leased a portion of the old Randall Farm in Greenwich Village, and while maintaining his Marble Dry-Goods Palace as a warehouse, built the first large store in what was to become Ladies' Mile. His new emporium, employing the novel architectural medium of cast iron, occupied the entire block from 9th to 10th streets. Each of the six stories was supported by iron beams, the roof area enclosed by an enormous glass dome over a central court. Rows of cast-iron columns lined the façade, permitting sunlight to stream in through the wide intervening arched windows. A grand staircase and six steam-driven elevators provided easy access to all shopping floors. The exterior, painted a mottled white and sparkling like an architectural gem of the Italian Renaissance, was an immediate success.

When Stewart died in 1876, he was the second richest man in America, although his wealth had come mostly from real estate investments. His fashionable emporium, so successful during his lifetime, was now under the management of a former business associate, and the store was renamed Hilton, Hughes & Company. Later it was taken over by a firm called Dennings, and the once-great Stewart store began to founder. It would have gone under altogether were it not for an eleventh-hour reprieve from John Wanamaker, who purchased it in 1896. The establishment was completely reorganized, a new building erected alongside (connected to the "Cast-Iron Palace" by a double-decker "Bridge of Progress" and three subterranean passageways, as well as a direct entrance from the newly built IRT subway station at Astor Place). Business began to boom again, and for nearly half a century the name Wanamaker's was synonymous with the ultimate in department store merchandising.

The great Palladian cast-iron palace that had been the A. T. Stewart Store on Broadway at 9th Street was under the operation of Hilton, Hughes & Co. when this photo was made in 1889. In the distance is Grace Church, the Gothic-style landmark, which still stands at Broadway's bend at 10th Street. (New-York Historical Society)

By 1952, the center of retail trade had moved uptown, and patronage fell off rapidly. Although the southbound end of the Fifth Avenue Bus line was still called the Wanamaker Terminal, few customers were to be seen getting off. The older store building was vacated and all operations shifted to the newer facility next door. Time was running out for the once-popular Wanamaker Store. Two years later the end came, and all retail business was transferred to a small downtown shop and to Wanamaker's suburban stores. In a rather dramatic exit, the old cast-iron building, which occupied the entire block between 9th and 10th streets, fell victim on July 15, 1956, to one of New York's most spectacular conflagrations, blazing out of control for two days in a fiery farewell to the old merchant prince. The apartment building that now occupies the site of the "Cast-Iron Palace" is named Stewart House to recall the original merchant prince.

2. Grace Church, at the northeast corner of Broadway and 10th Street, is an outstanding example of the Gothic Revival style. This lovely church, built on land formerly owned by Henry Brevoort, was designed in 1846 by James Renwick, Jr., when only 23 years of age. Renwick was also the architect of St. Patrick's Cathedral and the Smithsonian Institution, but many consider Grace Church to be his crowning work. Renwick himself was a parishioner and later vestryman. Particularly beautiful are the 46 medieval stained-glass windows and the intimate Chantry. The garden beside the Chantry is the site of the former Fleischmann's Vienna Model Bakery, a popular continental café in the days of Ladies' Mile. Bought by Grace Church and named Huntington Close, after a former rector, the plot adds much charm to the setting. The steeple is illuminated at night and can be seen for miles down Broadway. Among the scores of architecturally notable structures of the city built before 1930, the Municipal Art Society places Grace Church in its first category of seven buildings "of national importance to be preserved at all costs."

Fleischmann's Vienna Model Bakery, at the northeast corner of Broadway and 10th Street, photographed in 1898 by Percy C. Byron. Conveniently located between Grace Church and the former A. T. Stewart Store, it was a European-style café that produced its own baked goods and was one of the most popular places of refreshment along Ladies' Mile. (The Byron Collection. Museum of the City of New York)

The view of Grace Church is a debt to early settler Henry Brevoort, whose family owned the lands where Grace Church now stands. He was so intent on preserving a much loved apple orchard that stood in the way of Broadway's northward march that he succeeded in forcing the city fathers to divert the street to the west, and blocked 11th Street from penetrating to Fourth Avenue.

3. On the southwest corner of 11th Street and Broadway stands a rather nondescript 19th-century building, whose extensively altered façade masks its former identity. **The Hotel St. Denis,** built in 1848 and renovated in 1875, was one of the more fashionable hostelries in the city. *King's Handbook of New York,* 1893 edition, praises the attractiveness of this 250-room hotel and adds, "The equipments of the house, as to steam heating, electric lighting, ventilating, and hydraulic elevators, are supplemented by a perfect corps of polite and well-disciplined attendants." In its heyday, it hosted Presidents Lincoln, Grant, and Arthur, as well as Sarah Bernhardt, P. T. Barnum, and Col. William "Buffalo Bill" Cody. Probably the most significant date in the hotel's history was May 11, 1877, when Alexander

The St. Denis Hotel and Taylor's Saloon at the southwest corner of Broadway and 11th Street, ca. 1875. It was in the corner parlor room on the second floor that Alexander Graham Bell demonstrated his "speaking telephone" to a group of prominent New York citizens May 11, 1877. The hotel closed in 1917 but the building, much altered, still stands. (Museum of the City of New York)

Graham Bell gave a preview demonstration of his telephone to a spellbound audience of prominent guests in the second-floor parlor room. The wire was strung from the hotel across the Brooklyn Bridge. The St. Denis closed in 1917, and shortly thereafter was converted to commercial use. At that time all the adornments were stripped from the façade. Enter at the 11th Street door, walk almost to the bank of elevators, turn right and admire the original cast-iron staircase.

4. Across 11th Street is the Palladian cast-iron establishment of the former **James McCreery & Co. Store.** Arriving in this country as a 20-year-old immigrant from Ireland in 1845, McCreery started in business opening a small shop selling Irish lace. Gradually expanding to larger quarters, and following the uptown tide, he commissioned architect John Kellum to build this large drygoods store in 1868. He was reputed to be a kindly, tolerant man, whose flowing white beard and long shock of hair, together with a thick Irish brogue, made him a very striking figure. He always showed great concern for the welfare of his employees in an era when social conscience in business was relatively unknown. McCreery, self-educated, became a patron of the arts and dedicated much of his later fortune to philanthropic and artistic causes, including helping to found the Metropolitan Museum of Art. [*See* page 240.]

In 1895 he moved to an even larger building at the northern end of Ladies' Mile, at Sixth Avenue and 23rd Street. The present building miraculously survived years of occupancy by a variety of users, but a few years ago suffered a disastrous fire, which all but sealed its fate. Demolition seemed the only alternative until a developer, sensing the value of such a rare example of cast-iron elegance, converted it into an apartment house. The interior was gutted, but the beautiful façade was restored to its original appearance. Except for the ugly two-story addition on the roof, it looks much the same today as when it was first built. Since the interior vertical iron beams had to be retained, a curious result is that many tenants have an ornate Corinthian supporting column adorning the middle of their living room! This creditable restoration is an excellent example of adaptive (and profitable) reuse.

5. On the northeast corner of Broadway and 13th Street was the location of the famous partnership of Marvin N. Rogers and Charles B. Peet. Although both gentlemen died before the firm moved here, **Rogers Peet Company** (Clinton & Russell, 1902) had been in business manufacturing men's clothing and army uniforms since 1874 at two previous lower Broadway addresses. [*See* No. 575 Broadway, SoHo Cast-Iron District.] A relative latecomer to Ladies' Mile, the company was the last to leave (1970), moving its executive offices to one of its Fifth Avenue stores uptown; now they, too, are gone.

From 1861 to 1881, the site was occupied by famed **Wallack's Theater.** John Lester Wallack, who managed the playhouse, was also a leading actor, performing in many of the old comedies and contemporary English dramas that were so popular in the late 19th century. When Wallack's moved to the new Rialto district on 30th Street, the house was renamed the Star Theater (1893) and continued to offer dramatic productions until its razing for the Rogers Peet building.

6. Turn west on 14th Street and pause briefly at **Union Square.** Called "Union Place" in the Commissioners' Plan of 1811, its present attractive layout was not achieved until 1831, a credit to Samuel B. Ruggles who planned nearby Gramercy Park [*see* Gramercy Park, 8]. The name "Union" derives not from Civil War days, nor from any association with the labor unions whose activities were later identified with the square, but merely from the fact that this was the "place of union" of the Bowery Road with the northbound Bloomingdale Road. Until the early 1860s it had been a beautiful residential district; then business took over the area. Gone from the west side of the square are the well-known establishments of Tiffany & Company and Brentano's, as well as the array of piano manufacturers that lined the north side of 14th Street east and west of Union Square, from Irving Place to beyond Sixth Avenue. [*See* the "Stroll around Union Square" at the end of the chapter.]

At the southeast corner of University Place was the **world's first nickelodeon,** the precursor of the moving picture theater. It burned down in 1923, whereupon **Nathan Ohrbach** and his partner Max Wiesen purchased the fire-ravaged building and rebuilt it as a fashionable clothing store for women. With the slogan "More for Less or Your Money Back" and a no-frills policy that offered stylish bargains with appeal to rich and poor alike, it soon was a highly successful enterprise. Through the years, Ohrbach's and Klein's maintained an ongoing cutthroat rivalry, but in the end, Klein's was the loser. In 1954, Ohr-

The equestrian statue of Washington, by Henry Kirke Brown and John Quincy Adams Ward, executed in 1856 and considered one of the finest in America, is seen here at the intersection of Fourth Avenue (now Park Avenue South) and 14th Street. With the advent of the motor age, it was moved into adjacent Union Square. (Museum of the City of New York)

bach's moved uptown to 34th Street to join other department stores that had abandoned Ladies' Mile, but in 1984, it closed its doors forever.

At the southwest corner of Union Square, on a small triangular plaza, is the **statue of Mohandas Gandhi,** executed by Kantilal B. Patel in 1986. Here we see Mahatma Gandhi dressed in his dhoti and carrying his familiar walking stick. The Parks Department chose this site because of Union Square's tradition of public protests.

For the Broadway horsecars and omnibuses, making the detour around Union Square presented no problem; but when the later cable cars were installed a major traffic hazard was created. The forward progress of the Broadway Cable Traction Company's cars was controlled by continuous sections of underground cable laid in a slot between the rails. To negotiate the sharp curve, the operator of the car, called the grip-man, had to get up speed, release his hold on the 14th Street cable section, stamp furiously on his warning bell as the car swung wildly around the bend, then catch the next underground cable section on Broadway. This repeated act of derring-do always attracted crowds of onlookers, and resulted in numerous accidents—some fatal—and the spot was soon called **"Dead Man's Curve."** [*See* Cable Building, page 204, and photo, page 228.]

7. Continue west on the north side of 14th Street, passing the **former Baumann Brothers & Co.** store, at 22 East 14th Street (D. & J. Jardine, 1881), a large, ornate, cast-iron edifice whose "modernized" ground floor belies its Classic-style upper façade. Baumann Brothers was a popular carpet store whose business lasted well into the 20th century.

8. Midway between Fifth and Sixth avenues, on the south side of 14th Street (No. 34–40), a small vestige remains of what was once a prosperous and dynamic enterprise, **James A. Hearn & Son.** Arriving on 14th Street in 1879 after a brief association downtown with his uncle Aaron Arnold (later of Arnold, Constable & Company), James A. Hearn built up a large dry-goods business, and soon became an aggressive rival of R. H. Macy, then at the corner of Sixth Avenue. The two merchants often indulged in cutthroat competition, to their mutual detriment and the customers' delight. It is said that Japanese silk, a favorite with the ladies of the day, was offered by Macy at 41 cents per yard, whereupon Hearn immediately dropped the price by a few cents; and Macy followed suit. Again and again the price was slashed, until at the next day's closing, the fabric was being "sold" at 11 yards for 1 cent!

Son George, who inherited the business on his father's retirement in 1886, followed the same merchandising path. He, like neighbor James McCreery, was very philanthropic and also became a benefactor of the Metropolitan Museum of Art.

The original building, with an immense cast-iron façade, was many times the size of the present relic. An apartment house to its left now occupies much of the old site, but still remains "tied" to Hearn's by a series of exposed reinforcing girders. For three-quarters of a century Hearn's remained a family "bargain" store. Older New Yorkers still recall the annual mini-riot at the Washington's Birthday Sale, when thousands of bargain-hungry shoppers pushed their way into the store, smashing plate-glass windows and doors, in their stampede to purchase a television set or major appliance for one cent! The store closed in 1955, although it did operate a liquor store for a brief period. Its name is still preserved in a store in the Bronx at East 149th Street and Third Avenue, now run by a department store chain.

9. No. 56 West 14th Street was one of a group of buildings that formed the **original Macy's department store.** This narrow Beaux Arts–style building (Schickel & Ditmars, 1898) is all that remains of a cluster of buildings that marked the early days of what was later to become the world's largest department store.

After a brief career as a whaler, Rowland Hussey Macy tried and failed three times to establish himself in the dry-goods business. His fourth attempt in 1858 with a small shop around the corner on Sixth Avenue, "buying and selling for

The perils of Dead Man's Curve at Broadway and 14th Street are depicted in this woodcut from Harper's Weekly *of March 27, 1897. (New-York Historical Society)*

A rare old photograph of Lord & Taylor's dry-goods store at 47–49 Catherine Street on the Lower East Side, just before the move to Grand and Chrystie streets. At this address, Samuel Lord founded the oldest retail store in New York in 1826, taking on partner George Washington Taylor in 1838. Judging from the "selling off" signs, the picture by an unknown photographer was probably taken in 1853. (The Consolidated Edison Company of New York)

Fourteenth Street decked out in patriotic bunting for the presidential election of 1892. The north side of the street, just west of Union Square, displays the signs for at least six different piano manufacturers as this was the music center of the city in the Gay '90s. Steinway Hall and the Academy of Music were just a few blocks east. (New-York Historical Society)

cash," met with more success; and within a few years he acquired several adjacent buildings, connecting them with passageways, and offering a wide selection of merchandise. The store prospered, and by 1877 when Macy died, it had grown to a row of 11 buildings, with an annual sales volume of well over a million dollars. The store's well-known emblem, a large red star, was adapted by Macy from his arm tattoo, a reminder of the sailors' navigation stars of his whaling days. The whale motif is still used to promote big sales.

After several changes in management, direction of the store was assumed by brothers Isadore and Nathan Straus who earlier had obtained from Macy a concession to operate a china and glassware department. Under their leadership business boomed, and R. H. Macy & Company became the city's largest department store. Its more than 500 red-and-black delivery wagons could be seen all over town. Using novel sales and advertising techniques, manufacturing many products under its own name, and offering a wide selection of merchandise sold at highly competitive prices, Macy's set the trend for the future retail industry. Its stock ranged in variety from five-cent ice-cream sodas, straw hats, fabrics of all kinds, furniture, and men's and women's clothing, to the newly popular bicycle. Bicycles, by the way, were demonstrated by professional riders on a specially designed track where customers could give their new "wheels" a trial spin.

Looking north from the 18th Street station of the Sixth Avenue El are Simpson, Crawford & Simpson (extreme left), the domes of Hugh O'Neill, and, to the right, Cammeyer's, all bedecked with flags. The El, which gave so much impetus to the growth of Fashion Row, had its origin in the Gilbert Elevated Railway, later the Metropolitan Elevated Railway, then the Manhattan Railway Company, and finally as part of the Interborough Rapid Transit. The photo, taken in 1899, shows a train approaching with its locomotive running backward. (New-York Historical Society)

Another innovation, soon copied by other stores, was the annual Christmas toy display—an event that attracted thousands of visitors.

By the turn of the century, it became evident that newer and larger quarters were essential. Fourteenth Street's popularity as a shopping center had begun to wane, and in 1901 a site was chosen for a new building. Purchasing Oscar Hammerstein's Manhattan Opera House, located on the north side of 34th Street west of Sixth Avenue, Macy's demolished the theater and erected the first of its present buildings, opening its doors three years later. Turn right (north) on Sixth Avenue (Avenue of the Americas).

Proceed north to the northeast corner of Sixth Avenue and 16th Street.

On the northeast corner, the four-story building **No. 574** (Simeon B. Eisendrath, 1903), sporting an excessively ornate cornice, was erected for what was then the elegant Knickerbocker Jewelry Company.

The old Sixth Avenue El, which cast its dark shadows from 1878 to 1938, is now just a memory. Its demolition, however, opened a vista not possible in the gaslit era. Lining both sides of the street in a five-block silent array from 18th to 23rd streets stand "The Ghosts of Sixth Avenue." Huge, overbearing, and pretentious edifices—in stone, brick, or iron—they evoke the spirit of another day.

10. On the northwest corner of 18th Street is the ornate gray cast-iron building that was once **B. Altman & Company**—"The Palace of Trade" (No. 621), erected from plans by D. & J. Jardine in 1876. Until 1906, Altman's was the trend-setter of women's fashions, specializing in the finest silks, satins, and velvets. Ceramics and sculpture, too, graced the show windows and shelves, for Benjamin Altman was not only a keen entrepreneur, but a lover of objets d'art. A collector himself, he presented his accumulation of art works, worth over $15 million, to the Metropolitan Museum of Art shortly before his death in 1913.

As the age of the sewing machine had just arrived, women flocked to his block-long emporium in quest of the high-quality dress goods that made Altman's famous. Benjamin Altman, a solitary man who remained a bachelor all his life, devoted himself exclusively to his enterprise. He took particular pride in appearances. His home-delivery wagons, seen in the more affluent precincts of the city, were rubber-tired, painted a shiny maroon, decorated with brass carriage lamps, and pulled by a matched team of horses driven by a pair of nattily uniformed men. Altman was a considerate employer who shortened the generally accepted 64-hour work week and installed restrooms and a subsidized cafeteria for his workers. In 1906 the store moved uptown, where "Ben" Altman built a striking Beaux Arts–style building on a full-block site between Fifth and Madison avenues, 34th to 35th streets. To the sorrow of many New York shoppers, B. Altman & Company, after enduring several acquisitions, and a leveraged buy-out, closed its doors forever in the late 1980s. The building now houses, among other tenants, the Mid-Manhattan branch of the New York Public Library. As for the old and neglected Altman "Palace of Trade" on Sixth Avenue, the attractive façade has been faithfully restored by its new owner and the interior remodeled for upscale retail establishments and a small shopping mall. Directly across the street stood one of Altman's biggest competitors—Siegel-Cooper & Company.

On the southeast corner is the **Price Building** (Buchman & Fox, 1910), No. 604. Built for small retail establishments and lofts, the neat white structure is very well preserved for its age. Look up at the carved lions' heads above the third floor.

Before continuing north, take a short detour west on West 18th Street to a **row of stables** (ca. 1865), where nearby affluent residents "parked" their carriages. Horses were boarded at larger neighborhood commercial stables. Five stables are remnants of the original row of thirteen, designed in a utilitarian round-arch style (Nos. 126, 128, 130–132, and 140).

11. New York was never the same after Henry Siegel arrived from Chicago! Fresh from successful participation in the 1893 World's Columbian Exposition, he joined with partner Frank H. Cooper to found a profitable department store in the windy city, and now sought to build the greatest one of them all in New York City—which he did in five short months! Six stories high and capped by a tall tower, the block-wide store extended back almost to Fifth Avenue. Designed by architects DeLemos & Cordes in a grandiose style reminiscent of the Exposition, the new store was unprecedented in proportions. With great fanfare and a record-breaking crowd of 150,000, **Siegel-Cooper & Company** (No. 616–632) opened its doors on Saturday evening, September 12, 1896.

Its motto "The Big Store—A City in Itself" was no exaggeration. Henry Siegel soon earned the reputation as "the father of merchants," for he was shrewd, innovative, and bold. Never before had such a variety of merchandise been seen under one roof. The central feature of the main floor, however, was the fountain. A circular marble terrace surrounded an enormous white marble and brass statue of *The Republic,* a replica of Daniel Chester French's towering sculpture at the Chicago Fair. Jets of water, illuminated by myriad colored lights, played around the granite pedestal; and from the open "well hole" in the second floor, protected

When the great Siegel-Cooper & Company opened its doors in 1896, it seemed that all of New York flocked to the event. In this Byron photo, overflow crowds jam Sixth Avenue between 18th and 19th streets, as El trains bring even more sightseers. (The Byron Collection. Museum of the City of New York)

by a mahogany balustrade, customers looked down in awe. The fountain was not only the prime attraction, but the major rendezvous place for shoppers, businessmen, lovers, and tourists. For Gothamites, "Meet Me at the Fountain" became an institution for years to come. To this day, old-timers will quote the slogan without hesitation when asked if they remember Siegel-Cooper.

Siegel showed great understanding of human nature when he introduced the "free sample," especially in his novel food department. After a round of taste-tempting goodies, people *did* buy. He also began the very effective demonstrator system, illustrating the possibilities of such disparate items as kitchen gadgets, wing collars, and sheet music. Among other revolutionary ideas, he installed an air-cooling system, which really brought in the masses on stifling summer days; he hired women in many of the sales departments; and he advertised widely in the daily newspapers and on billboards all over town.

So great was the variety of the store's inventory that one of its advertising slogans was "Everything under the Sun." In this connection there is a long-enduring legend that tycoon and inveterate gambler John W. ("Bet-a-Million") Gates made a wager with John Pierpont Morgan that Siegel-Cooper's boast was mere puffery. To prove his contention, he went to the store and asked a floorwalker if it sold elephants. He was directed to the fifth-floor toy department, but Gates

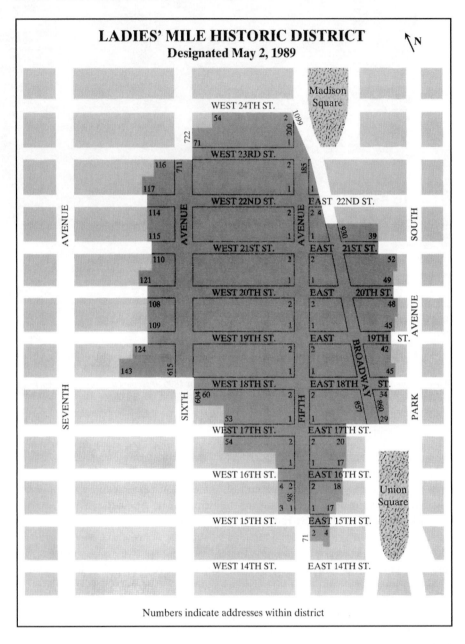

insisted that he wanted a *live* elephant. The unflappable employee then asked what color elephant he wanted. Gates, somewhat taken aback, replied "white." "Fine, sir, we'll let you know the delivery date."

Some weeks later, Gates received a telegram informing him that a freighter would be docking the next day with his order. He arrived at the pier in time to witness the unloading of an albino elephant from Ceylon. The chagrined Gates paid his debt to Morgan and ordered the pachyderm delivered to the Central Park Zoo.

The latest styles are worn by mother and children entering the Siegel-Cooper store. Elaborate bronze columns and lanterns flank the Sixth Avenue entrance. The imposing entrance remains unchanged today. (Photograph by Byron. The Byron Collection. Museum of the City of New York)

Siegel-Cooper advertisement in Pearson's Magazine *for September 1908 advertises the latest styles at prices that today seem unbelievable. Note the shirtwaists for only $1.00. (Author's collection)*

The business office of the Siegel-Cooper Department Store in a photograph taken ca. 1899 by Byron. (The Byron Collection. Museum of the City of New York)

The sales staff of Siegel-Cooper's sheet music counter poses for photographer Percy C. Byron with the latest tunes of 1899. (The Byron Collection. Museum of the City of New York)

An 1861 lithograph of Wallack's Theater, at the northeast corner of Broadway and 13th Street. The site was occupied until recently by the former Rogers Peet Building. (Museum of the City of New York)

The Eden Musée, an amusement hall and wax museum, stood in the middle of the north side of 23rd Street between Fifth and Sixth avenues. It was so popular in the gaslight era that all street cars made a special stop at the door. The Eden Musée was opened in 1884 and survived until 1916. Robert J. Horner's Furniture Store is at left, and is still there but no longer as Horner's. (The J. Clarence Davies Collection, Museum of the City of New York)

By the first decade of the 20th century, the inevitable uptown exodus of the shopping trade had begun again. Henry Siegel, however, had resolute faith in his magnificent palace of retailing. Surely the fountain would always remain the favorite meeting spot in town. Alas, time proved otherwise, for the crowds were now meeting at Macy's and Altman's, and the great empire was beginning to crumble. A reorganization with the backing of financier Joseph B. Greenhut failed to pump new life into the faltering enterprise, and by World War I, the great emporium, now called Greenhut-Siegel-Cooper, was no more.

A recent ground-floor tenant, Bed Bath & Beyond, has remodeled the interior and restored the front, including the splendid bronze portal. And to greet customers, the establishment has installed a *liveried doorman*—the first on Ladies' Mile since the heyday of the grand emporiums, almost 90 years ago!

The best view of the Big Store is from across Sixth Avenue. Note the intricately designed terra-cotta plaques with the firm's monogram, the huge bronze columns set in dramatic archways, and the overall effect of grandeur.

On the north side of West 17th Street, between Seventh and Eighth avenues, Siegel-Cooper's enormous wagon house and stable can still be seen. It, too, is heavily ornamented with distinctive terra-cotta S-C emblems and the company name in large letters on the parapet. During World War I, the store served for a time as a military hospital. And what of the famous statue of *The Republic* that graced the fountain? It now rests in Forest Lawn Memorial Park ("The Happy Cemetery"), in Glendale, California.

12. The large, somewhat restrained granite and limestone building occupying the whole block on the west side of Sixth Avenue between 19th and 20th streets reflects the type of establishment it was; for **Simpson Crawford & Simpson** (No. 641) catered exclusively to the "carriage trade." Partners Thomas and James Simpson and William Crawford opened their first retail store on the site in 1879, aiming for the patronage of the conservative moneyed classes, and dealing mostly in high-priced merchandise. A new building, designed by architects William H. Hume & Son, was opened in 1900—the first on the avenue with the newfangled Otis Escalators. It still shows evidence of the very large show windows, and even a trace of the mosaic floor (at the entrance). Price tags on the merchandise and in advertisements were considered superfluous, as the store's elite clientele would never think of asking anyway. This led to Henry Siegel's sarcastic comment that this was indeed a "priceless" store. Tailor-made dresses were a specialty of the house, with men tailors working overtime to make up the orders for delivery in 24 hours! After James Simpson died, the name was shortened to Simpson Crawford Company, and in the ensuing reorganization, Henry Siegel became president. After the demise in 1914 of the great Siegel-Cooper store across the street, Simpson Crawford limped on for another year, then expired.

13. The red brick and limestone Italianate building occupying most of the block across the avenue was built in 1893 for the largest shoe "department" store in town, **Cammeyer's** (No. 650). The stately, well-maintained *palazzo* remains as a tribute to the imagination and industriousness of Alfred J. Cammeyer and later partner Louis M. Hart. Together they raised the standard of the retail shoe business from the early custom of stringing up pairs of shoes on storefront poles to a distinguished and reputable enterprise on a scale comparable to their department-store neighbors. The store prided itself in its "standard of merit" slogan, which became synonymous with quality footwear. When the uptown exodus put an end to Ladies' Mile, Cammeyer's, still in the forefront of retail merchandising, moved to 34th Street in 1917, and four years later opened an elegant branch on Fifth Avenue. The pitfalls of specialization, however, ultimately doomed the firm, which disappeared after the Depression.

14. The **former Church of the Holy Communion,** on the northeast corner of 20th Street, dates from 1846, when the busy shopping center was a quiet and somewhat remote residential district. Architect Richard Upjohn, who designed the church—one of his lesser works—was one of the best-known advocates of the popular Gothic Revival style of the 1840s. The church was closed in the mid-1970s, and has seen a variety of uses—most recently as a disco!

15. When the **Hugh O'Neill store** (No. 655–671), designed by Mortimer C. Merritt, opened in 1876, it must have been a dazzling sight to its first visitors. With flamboyant round towers topped by huge bulbous domes, an imposing pediment rising high above five stories of Corinthian columns and pilasters, and a building almost unrivaled in size, O'Neill's began a tradition that was to cause amazement and surprise to patrons and competitors alike for years to come. Hugh O'Neill was no ordinary merchant, but an aggressive, extravagant, and colorful salesman. Hardly a week went by without a dramatic sale accompanied by much hoopla and publicity, for his appeal was not to the staid, conservative clientele of his neighbors, but to the working classes. With the advent of Elias Howe's great invention, the motto of O'Neill became "Put a Sewing Machine in Every Home!" He offered the machines as loss-leaders and was thus able to move his tremendous stock of piece goods at a healthy profit. His tactics of undercutting and doing battle with his competitors earned him the name, "The Fighting Irishman of Sixth Avenue." Although a bit crusty and brusque, he was a deeply religious man who commanded the love and respect of his employees. He always insisted that they observe their religious holidays, no matter what their faith, and would give them time off with full pay; nor was he ever above discussing their personal problems with them. A special source of pride to Hugh O'Neill was his shiny fleet of delivery wagons; he frequently would be seen making an early morning inspection round, like a general reviewing his troops, as the teams lined up for the day's deliveries. After he died, there was no one to carry on in the same spirit. To save the store, a merger was arranged with its neighbor to the north, the Adams Dry-Goods Company, resulting in a most unlikely partnership that was destined to last only for a few years. Adams had a different retailing style and an even more dissimilar clientele, so the O'Neill-Adams alliance disintegrated and collapsed completely in 1915.

16. On West 21st Street, just a few yards west, and seemingly hidden and protected by the L-shape of the Hugh O'Neill store, is the diminutive **Third Cemetery of the Spanish & Portuguese Synagogue, Shearith Israel.** This shady burial plot is the northernmost of three early cemeteries of this first Jewish congregation in America, and was in use between 1829 and 1851. [*See* Lower East Side Supplementary Tour A and Greenwich Village, 32.] Return to Sixth Avenue.

17. The ornate Beaux-Arts **Adams Dry-Goods Store** (No. 675–691), designed by DeLemos & Cordes, the architects of the Siegel-Cooper store, reflects the architectural style that came into vogue around the turn of the century. A relative latecomer to the avenue, A.D.G. tried to capture the fancy (and patronage) of the "carriage trade" through conservative merchandising and high-priced inventory. One of its novel offerings was men's ready-to-wear and made-to-measure clothing. Its founder, Samuel Adams, started in business much earlier, but did not erect this building until 1900 (note the date, set near the cornice). Since most department stores were family enterprises, Adams had no one to carry on the name. His only daughter, Eileen, showed no inclination for the retail trade, and married the son of march-king John Philip Sousa. When he sold out to Hugh O'Neill, the newly formed O'Neill-Adams Company made a desperate attempt to create a new image. The two firms now were connected not only by a hyphen, but also by a tunnel beneath 21st Street; and great sums were spent in promoting the new venture—but all in vain when it collapsed in 1915. The Adams Building was recently renovated; Barnes & Noble has moved in, opening another superstore. Owner Israel Taub received a special award for this restoration.

18. Ehrich Brothers (No. 695–709), the last of the old-timers in the Sixth Avenue row, was erected in 1889 from plans by Alfred Zucker, and stands dark and dingy, straddling much of the southwest corner of 23rd Street. The small corner plot, occupied by a polychrome cast-iron building that juts into the old department store, was always a thorn in the Ehrich Brothers' side—they were unable to acquire the property and had to build around it (much the same as the problem that later faced Macy's when they purchased the 34th Street and Sixth Avenue site in 1904). This corner building, recently restored almost to its original appearance after a destructive fire, shows what cast-iron structures looked like when new. It was formerly a branch of the **Riker's Drug Company,** later absorbed into the Liggett chain.

Ehrich Brothers (Julius S. and Samuel W.) was known as a "bargain store," perhaps even more so than Hugh O'Neill. The store was famous for its sales of manufacturers' closeouts and for its "omnibus advertising" (many categories of merchandise grouped into a single large advertisement). Saturdays were "Children's Days" at Ehrich's, when mothers could leave their young ones to enjoy specially provided entertainment and be free to shop at leisure. One of Ehrich Brothers' young trainees learned the trade quite well, and after the store ultimately closed, went into business for himself, establishing the name of **Nathan Ohrbach** as one of the city's successful retail merchants. [*See* page 226.]

In 1911 Ehrich's ceased operations for much the same reason as its neighbors. The brothers tried their hand briefly in a "horseless carriage" dealership, but that, too, proved a failure.

19. On the southeast corner of 23rd Street and Avenue of the Americas from 1869 to 1883 stood the **Edwin Booth Theater,** designed by Renwick & Sands, with Booth himself as manager and frequent star performer. When **James W. McCreery,** known as the "Dean of the Retail Trade," acquired the site, he demolished the theater, and in 1895 opened his second department store. In 1907 he joined his competitors in the great move uptown, building his newest emporium on 34th Street at Fifth Avenue. McCreery's went out of business unexpectedly in 1954 and the store was purchased by Ohrbach's. The 23rd Street structure survived until 1975 as a loft building. When McCreery opened the store in 1895 he

Simpson Crawford Company occupied the west side of Sixth Avenue from 19th to 20th streets and opened a new building in 1900. In this 1905 view of their unusually large show window, photographer Percy C. Byron captured the latest fashions of the day. The building is still there, although the company closed in 1915. (The Byron Collection. Museum of the City of New York)

The James W. McCreery store on the southeast corner of Sixth Avenue and 23rd Street, erected in 1895, replaced the Edwin Booth Theater. The company moved uptown in 1907, and in 1975 the building was razed. A mega-apartment house, "The Cardine," now occupies the site. (Photo by author)

installed a marble bust of Shakespeare into the façade—a memento from the Booth Theater, together with a bronze commemorative plaque honoring the theater. Both the bust and plaque were rescued by the author when the building came down and were donated by the former owner to New York University. It is said that Booth, dressed as Shakespeare, posed for the sculpture.

20. About 200 feet farther east on 23rd Street, and adjoining what was then the McCreery store, stood the twin buildings of **Best & Company,** which came to 23rd Street in 1881. Specializing in children's wear, it was known by its more popular name, "The Lilliputian Bazaar." The adjacent McCreery once boasted that he could easily take over Best by merely "punching a few holes in the wall." The store departed in 1910, moving to Fifth Avenue and 35th Street (the impressive building still occupies the southwest corner); and later to 51st Street, where, to the dismay of many New York shoppers, it closed its doors forever in 1970. The Olympic Tower now stands in its place.

Alongside, at what was 58 West 23rd Street, was the famed partnership of **Paul J. Bonwit and Edmund D. Teller.** "Bonwit's" began in 1895 at 289 Sixth Avenue, just south of 18th Street, selling fine-quality apparel for women. It opened its 23rd Street store three years later, then in 1908 Teller sold out to Bonwit, and three years later the store moved uptown to Fifth Avenue and 30th Street. In 1930 it moved again, into a large building at the corner of 56th Street. In the late 1970s, the firm almost disappeared, as its building had to be demolished; but phoenixlike, it arose again, around the corner on 57th Street in the Trump Tower next to Tiffany's, only to "give up the ghost" in the late 1980s.

The third member of the departed triumvirate was fashionable **LeBoutillier Brothers** (pronounced by all "Le-boo-ti-LEER"—even by founder Philip LeBoutillier himself). Arriving in 1898, the store soon became a mecca for the latest in women's styles. By 1913, hard times struck again, and Philip LeBoutillier, the only brother left in the business, closed his shop and joined Best's, ultimately rising to the rank of president of the company. [*See* pages 214 and 215.]

Across 23rd Street, No. 61–65 is another venerable cast-iron-front building, looking not much different from when it opened in 1877 as Robert J. Horner's Furniture Store. The store was designed by the noted architect of cast-iron buildings, John B. Snook, and later merged with the Flint Furniture Company, whose building still stands at 45–47, to become the once well-known **Flint & Horner Furniture Company.** Occupying the building until 1912, the firm moved uptown to 34th Street. Like Wanamaker's, Stern's, and Arnold Constable, the company abandoned the city and moved its operations to a suburban location, in this case, Manhasset. Cast iron was ideally suited to the retail trades, as the showrooms could be well illuminated by the large areas of window glass that an iron front permitted. Note the building's feeling of height created by the successive diminishing of each story—an illusive device credited to the architects of ancient Greece.

21. In the middle of the block is the gargantuan white cast-iron building of the **former Stern Brothers Department Store** (best viewed from the parking lot across the street). From humble beginnings when they arrived from Buffalo in 1867, the children of poor immigrants, Stern brothers Isaac, Louis, and Bernard, plus three sisters, opened a small dry-goods shop around the corner on 22nd Street. Business prospered, and in 1878 they engaged architect Henry Fernbach to design the original store, which in turn was greatly enlarged in 1892 by William Schickel, and extended through to 22nd Street. Until the opening of the Siegel-Cooper Store 18 years later, it was New York's largest. A far cry from the original little family shop, this was a luxury store, in front of which were posted blue-liveried doormen with top hats, giving the establishment a touch of class that it was to retain for years to come.

Although priding itself in its appeal to the carriage trade, Stern Brothers did not overlook the working classes, for their merchandise was priced for both extremes of the economic spectrum. Isaac, the guiding spirit of the firm, was frequently to be seen greeting customers by name; and it is said that on occasion he would make an urgent home delivery in his own carriage. A fourth brother, Benjamin, joined the partnership after Bernard's passing in 1884. A number of men working in the department stores of the gaslit era achieved later fame as merchandisers in their own right. One of them, a 13-year-old youngster starting as a stockboy, worked his way up in Stern's, eventually opening a store on 34th Street in 1902 bearing his own name, Franklin Simon.

By 1913, seeing the handwriting on the wall, Stern Brothers built a new store on 42nd Street and Sixth Avenue and joined the "uptown club." To the regret of many, the store ceased operations in 1970, leaving only its suburban branches to carry on the name.

Stern Brothers' original store, in an 1878 print, shares the south side of 23rd Street with residences, a church, and the Edwin Booth Theater, as well as the recently completed Sixth Avenue El. (Museum of the City of New York)

West 23rd Street looking east from Sixth Avenue, ca. 1905, shows the northern limit of Fashion Row. Right to left are the stores of Best & Company, Bonwit Teller, LeBoutillier Brothers, and the enormous white cast-iron front of Stern Brothers. The newly completed Flatiron Building appears in the distance. The Stern Brothers building still remains in a good state of preservation. (Museum of the City of New York)

Note the company monogram and the ornate design motifs in the well-preserved façade. It is apparent that the present owners of the building take pride in the historic and aesthetic value of this beautiful cast-iron front.

22. At 14 West 23rd Street is a small iron-front building, now rather woebegone in appearance, which was once **James McCutcheon & Company.** Known as "The Linen Store," it arrived in Ladies' Mile in 1886 after progressive moves uptown, having started 31 years before at Broadway and Astor Place. Dealing exclusively in fine linens, its tablecloths, napkins, doilies, sheets, pillowcases, and such were in great demand from the moneyed classes. In 1907 the store moved to more fashionable quarters on Fifth Avenue. Ultimately it merged with Plummer & Company, becoming Plummer-McCutcheon. More recently it was taken over by Hammacher Schlemmer on 57th Street, and for a time functioned as one of its departments. The building, incidentally, was the **birthplace in 1862 of novelist Edith Wharton.** It was then a brownstone, and was converted in 1882 to a retail store by architect Henry J. Hardenbergh (the Dakota, Plaza Hotel, etc.). The cast-iron front was installed ten years later by another architect, George H. Billings, for the new occupant, James McCutcheon's Linen Store.

23. Just before reaching Fifth Avenue, pause briefly at the red brick Queen Anne–style building also designed by Henry Hardenbergh that **The Western Union Company** built in 1883 as its uptown office. A terra-cotta plaque above the second floor bears the company name. Across the street is the unique **Flatiron Building,** erected in 1902 [*see* Madison Square, 24].

24. Turn south on Fifth Avenue to No. 170 (Robert Maynicke, 1897). The interesting cupola atop this narrow building, which can be seen from quite a distance, marks the location of the former offices and showroom of the **Sohmer Piano Company.** The building, painted white with its gilt dome, is floodlit at night, adding a delightful touch to the nighttime panorama of illuminated buildings. The former Sohmer piano factory on the East River shore in Ravenswood, Queens, is clearly visible from Roosevelt Island. [*See* Roosevelt Island tour at the end of Chapter 13.]

A few steps further, at the southwest corner of East 22nd Street, No. 935 Broadway, is the **former Glenham Hotel** (Griffith Thomas, 1861), an amazingly well-preserved neo-Renaissance survivor, now called the Albert Building. Its proportions give a good idea of the scale of the neighborhood in that era. Note the remains of the wood letters spelling the building's name and the clock (which should be repaired).

No. 166 (Parfitt Brothers, 1899) was an early retail establishment whose riot of terra-cotta ornament, particularly on the upper floors and roof, was doubtless an attraction for shoppers. The architects' work is better known in Brooklyn.

At No. 155 was the **former Charles Scribner's Sons** store, built in 1894 from plans by Ernest Flagg. Look for the "S" on the fourth-floor balcony. Not only was the firm a well-known book dealer, but the publisher of one of the most popular periodicals of the time, *Scribner's Magazine.* Scribner Publishing is now a division of Simon & Schuster, Inc. The building was purchased in 1973 by the United Synagogue of Conservative Judaism.

At the southeast corner of 21st Street (No. 141 Fifth Avenue) is the imposing **Merchants Central Building** (Robert Maynicke, 1897), a highly ornate Renaissance Eclectic structure with an enormous cupola.

25. No. 150 Fifth Avenue (southwest corner of 20th Street) is a particularly handsome building in a blend of Queen Anne and Romanesque Revival styles. Emblazoned on the cornice are the letters M.B.C., proclaiming the former home of one of the largest religious book publishers of the "Mauve Decade," the **Methodist Book Concern.** It was also the headquarters of the Methodist Church in New York. There were, in fact, so many publishers of religious books along the avenue that the district came to be known as **"Pater Noster Row"** from the first two words of the Lord's Prayer. Except for the dreadful "modernization" of the entrance, the building, designed by Edward Kendall in 1888, is in pristine condition. By contrast, note the splendid entrance to **No. 156,** on the northwest corner of 20th Street, the **former Presbyterian Building** (James Barnes Baker, 1894), built in Romanesque Revival style.

Turn left (east) to the corner of Broadway and 20th Street.

26. Both the northwest and southeast corners boast a Stanford White building! **No. 903 Broadway,** the **Warren Building,** in yellow brick and terra cotta, was designed in 1887 in Renaissance Revival style; while diagonally opposite is **No.**

900, the **Goelet Building,** built the year before in a "commercial eclectic" style. A rather unique structure, with a rounded corner and massive polychrome arches, it is missing its cornice and many decorative elements. This may be the only site where two such distinctly different McKim, Mead & White buildings stand face to face.

27. One of the most enduring partnerships in the retail trade was that of Messrs. **Lord and Taylor.** The spectacular structure on the southwest corner of 20th Street is a tribute to the courage and resourcefulness of these two English immigrants who together built one of the most respected fashion establishments in the trade. Opening a little shop on Catherine Street in 1826, Samuel Lord joined the growing number of dry-goods merchants; 12 years later he took on as a partner his wife's cousin, George Washington Taylor, and soon the firm of Lord & Taylor had the reputation for honest business practices and quality merchandise. A year after Taylor retired in 1852, the much-expanded firm opened its first "department store" on the corner of Grand and Chrystie streets, a large gray stone building capped by an imposing glass dome, which was a Lower East Side landmark for almost 50 years. Grand Street at the time was one of the busiest shopping streets and a major east-west thoroughfare whose crosstown horsecars connected with the New Jersey and Long Island ferries.

Rapid development of business encouraged the firm to open another branch farther west on Grand Street, at the corner of Broadway; however, it lasted only 12 years. During the 1863 Draft Riots, some 100 employees rushed to secure arms and ammunition from an uptown armory and barricaded the building, to discourage any attempt by the unruly mobs to sack the store.

This extraordinary five-story iron-front building, designed by James Giles in what was described as Bohemian Renaissance style, was opened to the public in 1869. Equipped with a steam elevator and other "modern" conveniences, it was an instant success. Surviving the Panic of 1873 four years later, Lord & Taylor continued to be one of the most fashionable women's stores on the newly developing Ladies' Mile [*see* pages 212 and 213]. When the store at Grand and Chrystie streets closed in 1902, the present building was greatly enlarged. Much of the elaborate emporium, however, has disappeared. An open lot on the 20th Street side now separates the main building from a segment that once extended to Fifth Avenue. (That amputated vestige is now a garishly painted cooperative apartment house, which, after conversion, has taken for itself a Fifth Avenue address.) Particularly attractive is the mansard roof on the corner pavilion, complete with dormers, and all in cast iron.

The year 1914, when so many of these great establishments either failed or departed, saw Lord & Taylor move to its present location at Fifth Avenue and 38th Street.

28. The building at the northwest corner of 19th Street, whose irregular and picturesque roof is reminiscent of an English Victorian castle, was the sales office of the **Gorham Manufacturing Company.** The name survives today and is still synonymous with fine silver. The structure, designed by architect Edward H. Kendall in 1883 in Queen Anne style, housed the company whose specialty was custom-designed silverware and a wide variety of ecclesiastical metalwork. The firm subsequently moved its operations uptown, erecting an appropriately impressive building on the southwest corner of Fifth Avenue and 37th Street.

29. A year after Lord & Taylor opened its magnificent store on 20th Street, its die-hard competitor **Arnold Constable** followed suit one block south. The saga of Arnold Constable, New York's oldest department store, began with Aaron Arnold, a young English immigrant, opening a small dry-goods shop on Pine Street in what is now the financial district. With business flourishing, he moved to progressively larger sites; and taking in two nephews, George and James Hearn, the partnership became Arnold, Hearn & Co. [*see* 8]. A recently hired friend of the Arnold family, James Mansell Constable—in typical Horatio Alger fashion— fell in love with the boss's daughter, married her, and was taken into the partnership. Apparently disgruntled by the sudden rise of Constable, the Hearn brothers left Arnold and went into business for themselves. After another change in location, the firm built a large establishment at the corner of Canal, Mercer, and Howard streets, with an impressive white marble façade, which Arnold referred to as his "Marble House." It was here that he renamed his firm Arnold, Constable & Company, and made his reputation selling luxury merchandise, soon becoming the darling of the carriage trade—with a customer list reading like the social register. The building, stripped of its fancy trappings, still stands. [*See* pages 188 and 189.]

In 1869 Arnold retired, leaving the reins of the company in the hands of James Constable. The same year marked the move to the 19th Street site. In a series of land acquisitions, the store, which was designed by Griffith Thomas, grew in size until 1877 when it covered the whole block to Fifth Avenue. The five-story brick and limestone structure, topped by an enormous French Second Empire mansard roof, was a sensation. Devoting itself exclusively to the sale of fabrics, carpets, and upholstery materials, it remained a prestige store for years to come. The vast selection of its dry goods, ranging from children's wear to mourning apparel, led to the comment that "Arnold Constable provides elegant clothing, from cradleside to graveside." The *New York Daily Graphic,* in its January 8, 1877, edition, described the store as "a new Emporium of Trade—a dominant and ornamental addition to the street architecture of New York."

In 1914, that famous "uptown moving year," the company abandoned its imposing building and moved to its final location at Fifth Avenue and 40th Street. It is interesting to note that from 1860 to 1975, the two fierce competitors, Arnold Constable and Lord & Taylor, had never been located more than two blocks apart! With the demise of Arnold Constable after 150 years, its die-hard rival survives as the oldest retail store in the city. (Cross Broadway.)

30. "The house of **W. & J. Sloane** stands indisputably at the head of the carpet and rug industry of this country," wrote Moses King in his *Handbook of New York* for 1893. Unlike the other department stores that had their origin in the dry-goods business, Sloane's dealt almost exclusively in rugs and floor coverings.

Arriving on a sailing ship in 1834, William Sloane, a young weaver from Scotland, found work in a Connecticut mill, learning American weaving techniques. Nine years later he established a small "Carpeting and Floor Cloth Shop" on lower Broadway, using the slogan "Dependable Merchandise at an Honest Figure." In 1852, brother John, the "J" of W. & J. Sloane, was taken into the business, but stayed with William for only nine years. At the closing of the 1876 Centennial Exposition in Philadelphia, William Sloane purchased a superb collection of Oriental rugs that had been a major display at the Fair, offering them to his growing list of wealthy clients. This marked the first time Oriental rugs were sold by a retail house. In the meantime, he had moved up Broadway twice, keeping abreast of the familiar northward push, and a few years later accomplished another "first," contracting with a weaving firm in India to become the only American rug store with its own Oriental source of supply.

William Sloane achieved fame of another sort a few years earlier, when the criminal jury of which he was foreman convicted "Boss" Tweed. While on the jury he learned that merchant-prince A. T. Stewart was about to foreclose a mortgage on the Alexander Smith Carpet Company in Yonkers, N.Y. Sloane raised the money, saved the Smith Company, and in return received an interest and became its exclusive agent for many years. On his death in 1879, the firm's direction was taken over by his eldest son, John II. It was under John Sloane that the company achieved its greatest growth, inaugurating in 1881 the large store across the street from Arnold Constable and an equally spacious outlet in San Francisco. W. & J. Sloane achieved national fame with a contract to carpet some of the swankiest hotels in the city, including the newly opened Waldorf-Astoria on 34th Street; and the company won international fame with the commission to supply all the carpeting for the coronation of Czar Nicholas II. At the same time, the store expanded its operations into home decoration, selling antiques, and manufacturing "registered reproductions" of antique furniture. The building was designed by W. Wheeler Smith and erected in 1881.

As the gaslit era waned, Sloane's moved in 1912 to Fifth Avenue and 47th Street, where they remained until 1962. In a subsequent move down the avenue to 38th Street, they sold their building to discount merchandiser E. J. Korvette, acquiring the store formerly occupied by Franklin Simon; and in a late 1982 move, Sloane's abandoned their Fifth Avenue address for an adjacent smaller location farther west on 38th Street. Two years later they closed their store and moved operations to the three W. & J. Sloane suburban stores. Interestingly, the present owner of the 881 Broadway store is also a rug and carpet retailer, and has restored the exterior and interior to re-create the aura of elegance of the 1880s.

Find the "S" monogram on a small cast-iron shield set high on the building, as well as the date of construction in terra-cotta Roman numerals.

At the northeast corner of Broadway and East 18th Street rises the rather unusual **McIntyre Building** (R. H. Robertson, 1890), a prominent feature in the area. Built as lofts and commercial space in this once-busy commercial neighborhood, the ten-story dark-red-brick-and-limestone Romanesque Revival–style building boasts a distinctive square tower topped by a pyramidal roof and sharply pitched gables.

End of tour. You may, however, want to enjoy the "Stroll around Union Square" that follows. The 4, 5, 6, L, N, Q, R, W subway lines are at 14th Street.

A STROLL AROUND UNION SQUARE

Union Square Park has recently undergone a complete renovation. It has now become one of the favored recreational and meeting places for the local community, as well as for countless visitors who enjoy its new landscaping and upgraded facilities. As mentioned earlier, the name derives neither from any Civil War reference nor from association with union labor activities; rather, it was the "union" or place of connection in the early 19th century between the Bowery Road and Bloomingdale Road (now Broadway). As the city grew northward, the better residential districts followed, and the Park was fenced in. Then came the theater district, whereupon the residents soon fled, and the area boasted many theatrical and entertainment centers. As they, too, followed the crowd uptown, the Park became the favored venue for union demonstrations and political rallies, and the annual May Day celebration attracted millions. Union Square Park became, in effect, New York's version of London's Hyde Park. In the 1960s and '70s, the Park fell victim to neglect, indifference, and a proliferation of drug dealers. In a concerted effort to take back the Park, local business and community groups banded together in 1987 with a number of municipal and private agencies, including the Department of Parks & Recreation, to plan a major redesign and renovation—a prodigious project that was not completed until 2002.

The tour around Union Square begins at the northwest corner and goes clockwise around the Square.

At the northwest corner, a highly popular **Greenmarket** is held four times a week, with farmers bringing fresh vegetables, fruits, and baked goods from as far as 100 miles away. The Greenmarket idea was conceived of by architect-planner Barry Benepe. To the east of the market and connected to the classical park pavilion is Café Luna, a pleasant and popular outdoor café/restaurant.

● Directly across the street is the **former Century Building,** 33 East 17th Street, now a **Barnes & Noble superstore** (William Schickel, 1880). The red brick, Queen Anne–style structure is one of the finest examples of the style and was built to house the many publishing activities of the Century Company. Among its imprints were the *Century* and *St. Nicholas* magazines and a host of fine books. It joined with D. Appleton & Company in 1933 and, after another merger, became Appleton-Century-Crofts.

● The adjacent **Everett Building,** 200 Park Avenue South (Goldwin Starrett & Van Vleck, 1908), was designed in simple classical terms and is an important link in the development of the high-rise commercial building through its use of open floor space, large windows, and fireproofing. Its functional simplicity can be attributed to the influence of famed Chicago architect Daniel Burnham, for whom Starrett had worked for several years.

● On the northeast corner of Park Avenue stands the former Guardian Life Insurance Company Building, now the **W New York Hotel,** 201 Park Avenue South (D'Oench & Yost, 1910). A magnificent presence on the Square for decades with its tall illuminated namesake sign above a towering mansard roof, it was a familiar sight in the city. With the departure of the insurance company, the building was converted into a hotel (Rockwell Group, 2001). Alas, the old sign is gone (despite a public outcry), replaced by the hotel's own. Interestingly, the former name of Guardian was the Germania Life Insurance Company, but anti-German sentiment during World War I resulted in a reshuffling of the letters of Germania to Guardian. The aluminum and glass annex to the east was designed in 1961 by Skidmore, Owings & Merrill.

Around the corner, the trim neo-Federal–style brick-and-limestone building, No. 100 East 17th Street (Thompson, Holmes & Converse and Charles B. Meyers, 1929), was the "final resting place" of **Tammany Hall,** the Democratic political machine that held the city in a corrupt stranglehold for almost two centuries. The club was founded in 1788 as an outgrowth of the patriotic Sons of Liberty and called The Society of St. Tammany or Columbian Order. According to local preservationist Jack Taylor, "the building is such a great example of Colonial Revival, of a time when a group tried to burnish its crooked reputation by linking itself to early American ideals," adding, "the history of Tammany Hall, shabby as it is, is also a big part of our past, and this building is the sole physical remnant of that." While awaiting the city's decision on landmark designation, it was suggested that the Tammany Hall building be converted into a "Museum of Political Corruption"; however, one wag observed that "it just wouldn't be large enough!"

By 1943, unable to meet its mortgage payments, Tammany sold the building to Local 91 of the International Ladies Garment Workers Union. In 2001, they, in turn, sold it to Liberty Theaters, who remodeled the union's former meeting hall—once called the Roosevelt Auditorium—into the present **Union Square Theater.** The building is also home to the **New York Film Academy,** a noted school for filmmakers.

At East 15th Street, look above the ground floor of No. 24–33 at the dingy cast-iron façade of the **former S. Klein-on-the-Square Department Store.** Klein's first opened on the Square in 1910, but by 1921 relocated to a rambling emporium that grew northward from 14th to 16th streets. For years, its huge distinctive neon "On the Square" sign atop the complex was a familiar city landmark. Klein's was a pioneer in discount merchandising, and its frequent sales would always attract hordes of bargain hunters. By 1975, however, competition from other discount stores and its distance from the city's new shopping centers, plus old-fashioned merchandising techniques and a rather decrepit interior, hastened its demise. The southwest corner of Klein's 15th Street building was earlier the site of the posh **Union Square Hotel,** a favorite with the Theater District celebrities of the Gilded Age.

At the northeast corner is the **former Union Square Savings Bank,** now the **Daryl Roth Theatre,** No. 20 Union Square East (Henry Bacon, 1905). Like a vestige of ancient Greece, the white granite–front structure boasts a façade of bold Corinthian columns, in a style favored by architect Bacon, whose major work is the Lincoln Memorial in Washington, D.C. The bank closed in 1992, but the venerable building is now enjoying a new life, with the former banking hall remodeled and converted for novel and unconventional theatrical productions.

Walk into the park to the bronze **Statue of Lafayette,** by famed French sculptor Frédéric Auguste Bartholdi (1876). While collecting funds for his later Statue of Liberty, Bartholdi offered the Lafayette statue as a token of French friendship with the American people in gratitude for their sympathy during the Franco-Prussian War. Lafayette, although an aristocrat, was sympathetic with the cause of the American Revolution and served as a Major General in the Continental Army. The pedestal is designed to resemble a ship's prow.

Facing Union Square between 14th and 15th streets is massive **Zeckendorf Towers** (Davis Brody & Assocs., William Zeckendorf, Jr., developer, 1987), a 670-unit condominium in four 29-story towers, topped by open framework pyramids. The towers are set on a seven-story base that fills a triangular plot while maintaining the orientation to the city street grid. Original plans called for much taller structures, but fierce community opposition forced the developer to scale them down, thus reducing the "darkening and overwhelming" effect on the park below and respecting Union Square's surroundings. The lower floors include retail establishments and also Beth Israel Medical Center facilities. At the very corner of the building at 14th Street was **Joe's Saloon,** rendered immortal by habitué Hugh A. D'Arcy, who, in 1887, penned the sentimental ballad *The Face on the Barroom Floor.*

Turn right (west) on Union Square South, but stay on the park side. The building complex on the block between Fourth Avenue and Broadway comprises Circuit City, a Virgin Megastore, and a United Artists theater, plus residential apartments (Davis Brody Bond and Schuman Lichtenstein Claman & Efron, 1999). The 15 changing illuminated five-foot-high numerals display "the hours, minutes, seconds elapsed in the day; and the hours, minutes, and seconds remaining, symbolizing the city's speed, frenzy, and fragmentation." Intrinsic in the display is the astonishing multimedia sculpture of brick, concrete, steel, aluminum, gold leaf, incandescent light, steam, and sound called **Metronome** (Kristin Jones/Andrew Ginzel, 1999). A gift to New York, it is intended as a "celebration of the energy and vitality of the city." From the five-foot circle *Infinity,* steam emanates at noon and midnight, while from the 67-foot-long cone, a low tone is produced to synchronize with the plume of steam. Among other features are a five-foot rotating sphere of gold and black that mirrors the phases of the moon and *Relic,* an enlarged replica of the right hand of George Washington from the equestrian statue in the Park. Occupying the mid-block from 1870 to 1936 was the (old) **Union Square Theatre,** which survived as a converted retail store until it was demolished in 1990.

Dominating the Park entrance is the historic bronze **equestrian statue of George Washington** (Henry Kirke Brown with John Quincy Adams Ward, 1856; granite pedestal by Richard Upjohn). The statue represents Washington entering New York City on Evacuation Day, November 25, 1783, marking the end of British occupation during the Revolutionary War. The sculpture is based on an earlier Houdon bust and is considered one of the finest equestrian statues in America. It was moved from its original location at the intersection of Fourth Avenue early in the 20th century. [*See* engraving, page 227.]

Turn right at the Gandhi statue (described earlier) and walk north on Union Square West; note the recent attempt to re-create an "old-time" atmosphere by paving the street with Belgian blocks. At the corner of 14th Street, the **former Lincoln Building,** No. 1 Union Square West (R. H. Robertson, 1899), is a typical example of a Romanesque Revival–style commercial building. Faced with gray granite, limestone, and brick and decorated with terra cotta, the building, considered a skyscraper when built, exemplifies the transition between masonry and later steel framework construction. Note the multiwindow cornice.

No. 5–9, the **Spingler Building,** faced with brown brick and ornate terra cotta, dates from the late 1890s and displays typical Romanesque Revival features. In the Gilded Age, many luxury establishments opened on the Square, particularly along the west side. **Brentano's**, one block north, called itself "New York's Literary Emporium," attracting a host of loyal readers. It is interesting to note that Agosto Brentano, who came to America as a poor cripple from Sicily, eked out a living selling newspapers and periodicals, and ultimately became the most famous book dealer in the country.

The 1960s modern "skin" of No. 11–15, the main office of the **Amalgamated Bank of New York,** hides a cast-iron structure within. The building, which was designed in 1869 by John Kellum, had housed the showrooms and silversmith operations of **Charles Tiffany**, who had moved up from lower Broadway in 1870. The famed jewelry and silver establishment remained on Union Square until 1906, when it relocated uptown. The bank opened on the site in 1923 under the auspices of the Amalgamated Clothing Workers Union and is reputed to be the only one in the United States owned entirely by a union. **No. 25,** the Carlyle Court, formerly an apartment building, is one of New York University's numerous far-flung dormitories.

No. 31, the **former Bank of the Metropolis** (Bruce Price, 1902), is a fine example of the architect's favored Renaissance Revival style. Although the building's front features polished marble columns, the entire structure is, in effect, columnar or tripartite in form, with a base, shaft, and capital represented by its three stone sections. The bank, founded in 1871, served local businesses until 1918, when it merged with the Bank of the Manhattan Company (now J. P. Morgan Chase). A restaurant occupies the main floor with residences above.

No. 33, originally the Decker Building, now the **Union Building** (Alfred Zucker, with John Edelman, 1892), displays the almost limitless possibilities of terra-cotta adornment, in this case with unusual Moorish Revival motifs. Built for the Decker Piano Company, its highly ornate façade was a singular attraction. Edelman, who was Zucker's designer, was influenced by his friend and teacher, Chicago architect Louis Sullivan, and the building exhibits many obvious Sullivanian touches. In the early 1990s, the building was renovated for condominiums by Joseph Pell Lombardi & Associates.

On the west side of the park stood a bronze **fountain sculpture group** on a tall pedestal, depicting a woman holding a baby in one arm and helping a child hold a water pitcher in the other, by German sculptor Adolf Donndorf and presented to the city in 1881. The large pedestal was festooned with lions' heads and a variety of animals, insects, and lizards. (Temporarily removed during park renovation.)

Enter the park, walk toward the center, and turn left to the heroic bronze **Statue of Abraham Lincoln** (Henry Kirke Brown, 1868). The statue was funded by popular subscription and shows the Great Emancipator in a pose as if address-

ing an audience. The work has been criticized for depicting Lincoln in unflatter-
ing baggy and wrinkled clothing (although he would doubtless win the approval
of today's teenagers). Brown's equestrian statue of Washington at the park
entrance is considered a far greater achievement.

Turn around and walk to the **Independence Flagstaff**—a drum-shaped granite pedestal 36 feet in diameter and 9 1/2 feet high that serves as a base for a tall
flagpole (Anthony De Francisci, sculptor, Peter Coke Smith, architect, 1926).
Formerly called the Charles F. Murphy Memorial after the last and most powerful
of Tammany Hall's bosses, it was built with Tammany-collected funds to commemorate the 150th anniversary of the signing of the Declaration of Independence. The high-relief figures represent the forward march of the pioneers, as
well as the forces of good and evil in our fight for independence.

End of tour. The subway entrances are at the south end of the park.

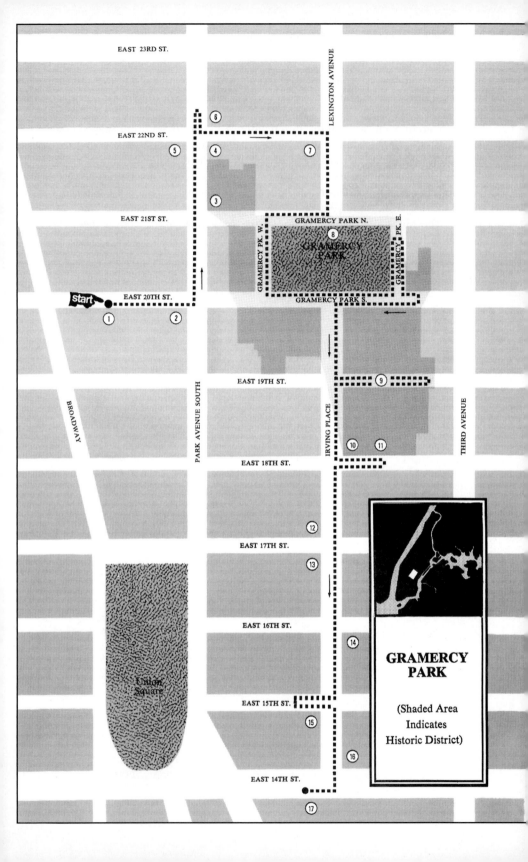

9. Gramercy Park

[Subways: No. 6 Lexington Avenue line to 23rd Street, R Broadway line to 23rd Street. Buses: Broadway buses M1, M6, and M7 to 20th Street.]

In Dutch Colonial days the locality was known as *Crommessie* (*krom* = crooked, *mesje* = small knife; the "knife" for the shape of a nearby brook), an area of woods and marshes situated just above the country estate of Governor Peter Stuyvesant. It later became the property of James Duane, mayor of New York City from 1784 to 1789, who named it Gramercy Seat. In 1831 land developer Samuel B. Ruggles purchased a substantial parcel from the Duane Farm and laid out the residential lots and park. Ruggles also laid out lower Lexington Avenue, naming it after the Revolutionary Battle of Lexington, and Irving Place, which he named for his friend Washington Irving. In spite of the growth of the surroundings and the encroachment of high-rise buildings, Gramercy Park has managed to remain one of the most charming residential districts of the city.

1. The tour begins at 28 East 20th Street, just east of Broadway, at the **birthplace of one of Gramercy Park's most illustrious residents, Theodore Roosevelt.** The original brownstone house in which he was born in 1858 was demolished in 1916 and replaced by a commercial building. After T.R.'s death in 1919, however, prominent citizens decided to purchase the site, raze the structure, and create a memorial by reconstructing Roosevelt's boyhood home as it appeared during the years 1865–72. The adjoining lot, No. 26, where T.R.'s uncle Robert had his residence, was also acquired and made into a museum. The birthplace was opened to the public in 1923, and in 1963 both sites were donated by the Theodore Roosevelt Association to the National Park Service. The rooms have been restored to the period of "Teedie's" boyhood. The parlor is furnished with crystal chandeliers, magnificent mirrors, and blue satin hangings, characteristic of the elegance of the day. The master bedroom in which he was born contains the original furniture and a portrait of his mother, Martha Bulloch Roosevelt. Next to it is the nursery and, beyond, the open porch that was used as a gymnasium. In addition to his widely known political accomplishments, Theodore Roosevelt was also an effective, reform-minded Police Commissioner of New York City. (The Birthplace is open Mon.–Fri. 9:00 A.M. to 5:00 P.M., closed federal holidays. Tours given hourly, 10:00 A.M. to 4:00 P.M. Admission: $3.00; under 17 and over 62, free.) Proceed east to Park Avenue South, known formerly by its more prosaic name, Fourth Avenue.

2. 250 Park Avenue South (Rouse & Goldstone, 1912) is a large industrial building in neo-Gothic style. But the most striking of these early 20th-century behemoths is No. 257, the **Gramercy Park Building** (Warren & Wetmore, 1912)—its façade divided into five sections by elaborate courses. The restored lobby is a gem!

3. Across the avenue, one block north, is **Calvary Church.** Designed in 1846 by James Renwick, Jr., architect of Grace Church and St. Patrick's Cathedral, it is in the tradition of the Gothic Revival so popular in the 1840s. The wooden steeples, however, were dismantled by the architect in 1860; the octagonal bases were removed in 1929. Eleanor Roosevelt was baptized here in 1884.

4. No. 281 is the **former Church Missions House** (R. W. Gibson & E. J. N. Stent, 1894), also the Protestant Welfare Agencies Building. A flamboyant Romanesque Revival–style edifice, it once housed the missionary societies of the Episcopal Church. Above the entrance, the reliefs in the tympanum depict St. Augustine preaching to the Barbarians of England, and Bishop Seabury preaching to the Barbarians in America.

5. Across the street, at the southwest corner of 22nd Street, in an odd reincarnation, is the **former Bank for Savings,** now the base of a 27-story condominium, Gramercy Place, with the old bank section converted into a supermarket! The original Classic Revival–style structure (Cyrus L. W. Eidlitz, 1894) was the home of the city's oldest savings bank, chartered in 1819 in Greenwich Village. With the bank's departure, the building was slated for demolition, but it was rescued at the eleventh hour by an association of Gramercy Park residents.

6. The **former United Charities Building,** at 105 East 22nd Street, was erected in 1891–93 from plans by R. H. Robertson and Rowe & Baker in a modified Romanesque Revival style, for the New York Association for Improving the Condition of the Poor, now the Community Service Society, "…to improve the condition of the working classes, and to elevate their physical state." It also houses the Children's Aid Society, The Associated Black Charities, and others. Turn east on 22nd Street to Lexington Avenue.

7. The lavish Renaissance-style *palazzo* on the southwest corner was originally designed for the **Russell Sage Foundation** in 1914 by Grosvenor Atterbury. Sage, a financier and philanthropist, died in 1906, leaving an enormous fortune to charity. Among the legatees was Russell Sage College, in upstate Troy, N.Y. He was known to be strongly opinionated, and it is said that upon being approached by August Belmont to share in the financial backing of the newly begun subway, he turned to the president of the Rapid Transit Construction Company and commented scornfully that "New Yorkers would never go into a hole to ride it." In more recent years the building was occupied by Catholic Charities, then in 1975 it was purchased by a developer who converted it into condominium apartments, called Sage House.

On the northeast corner of East 22nd Street and Lexington Avenue are a pair of buildings that served the Domestic Relations Court: No. 135, the former Fam-

The Abram Hewitt House at 9 Lexington Avenue, built in 1851 by Peter Cooper, and later occupied by his son-in-law Abram Hewitt, Mayor of New York, 1887–88. Hewitt commissioned his nearby neighbor Stanford White to redecorate the house and design the mayor's lamps in front. It was demolished in 1939. (Museum of the City of New York)

ily Court (Charles B. Meyers, 1938), and the adjacent Children's Court of New York City, No. 137 (Crow, Lewis & Wickenhoefer, 1912). The ten-story Art Deco corner building now serves as the **Administrative Building of Baruch College,** and the adjacent Italian Renaissance–style structure is Baruch's **School of Public Affairs.** When the new Family Court opened on Foley Square, ownership of these buildings went to Baruch.

The College is named for Bernard M. Baruch (class of 1889), economist, financier, and advisor to six presidents. It is a unit of the City University of New York and was originally the School of Business and Civic Administration of the City College of New York, founded in 1919, and opened in the tan-brick and limestone building that stands at 17 Lexington Avenue (Thompson, Holmes & Converse, 1928). The building also housed Townsend Harris High School, CCNY's high-standard academic preparatory school that closed in 1942. (Although beyond the scope of this tour, you might want to walk up to East 24th Street to see Baruch's **Academic Complex,** by Kohn Pederson Fox, 1997–2002. Called the "Vertical Campus" by some, it is an astonishing 200-foot, 14-story aluminum and black glass structure set on a red-brick base, with walls that curve sharply inward toward the top, and features a ten-story atrium.)

On the northwest corner of 22nd Street is the new **School of the Future,** part of the city's Collaborative High School Program. It was formerly the Mabel Dean Bacon Vocational High School, and originally the Manhattan Trade School for Girls. It was built in 1917 from plans by C. B. J. Snyder, whose Collegiate Gothic style for school buildings was very popular early in the 20th century.

Walk south one block to 21st Street. The northeast corner, No. 1 Lexington Avenue, is the **site of the Cyrus W. Field Residence.** Field, with help from Peter Cooper (who lived just a few doors north, at 9 Lexington Avenue), promoted the Atlantic Cable, which after some initial failures was laid successfully in 1866. He was also responsible for building most of the elevated railroads in the city during the late 1870s, only to lose them a few years later to railroad tycoon Jay Gould.

8. Gramercy Park, whose name, as mentioned, probably derives from the original Dutch *Crommessie,* is a tribute to Samuel B. Ruggles's foresight, and is an excellent example of urban planning. By taking the 42 lots that comprise the 1½-acre park and deeding the parcel to the 60 surrounding lot owners, he established, in 1831, the only surviving private park in the city. (An earlier private

Charming Nos. 3 and 4 Gramercy Park West still remain, adding to the pleasant atmosphere of the neighborhood. This pair of houses, built in 1847, are attributed to architect Alexander Jackson Davis. Twin lanterns in front of No. 4 denote the residence of former Mayor James Harper. (Photograph by Berenice Abbott. Federal Art Project "Changing New York," Museum of the City of New York)

plot, St. John's Park, owned by Trinity Parish, was destroyed by the takeover of adjacent land by the Hudson River Railroad, and ultimately obliterated by the entrance ramps to the Holland Tunnel.) The wrought-iron fence was erected soon after, with extensive planting undertaken thereafter. Although formerly restricted to adjacent property owners, this private park is now accessible to all who live close by and who pay the annual fee. The Park and surrounding lots, including Calvary Church and a stretch of property on 18th and 19th streets, were designated in 1966 by the Landmarks Preservation Commission as the **Gramercy Park Historic District.** (Note the plaque.)

The perimeter sidewalk of Gramercy Park itself has been restored to re-create the original bluestone paving. The repaving was done by the city using some of the original bluestones, plus some newly cut contemporary bluestones. Also, many of the ugly cobra-head lampposts in the historic district have been replaced by bishop's crook lampposts. Six of them were surplus and a gift from the city; about 18 additional were purchased by members of Gramercy Park Associates, Inc. and installed as gifts *to* the city. More are expected to be installed in the surrounding neighborhood.

Turning west at the Gramercy Park Hotel (1925), we pass the **site of Stanford White's residence** (at the corner) from 1901 until his untimely death in 1906. White was murdered by deranged millionaire Harry K. Thaw, who was jealous of his wife Evelyn Nesbit's former relationship with White. Stanford White is acknowledged not only as an exemplary architect, but as one who established the American tradition of art collecting. His private collection of paintings and sculpture is now distributed among several museums. The house was stripped of its art treasures and acquired by the Princeton Club. It was razed in 1923 for the construction of the hotel.

At what would be No. 55 stood the home of diarist **George Templeton Strong,** the peripatetic chronicler of mid-19th-century life and events, who was given the house as a wedding gift when he married Ruggles's daughter. One door east lived Robert "Bob" Ingersoll, orator and lawyer, who, because of his highly publicized lectures on religion, was dubbed "The Great Agnostic."

Rounding the corner, **Nos. 1 and 2 Gramercy Park West** date from 1849–50. Dr. Valentine Mott, probably the most renowned surgeon in the days just before the Civil War, lived in No. 1. He was responsible for the founding of the New York University Medical College and Bellevue Hospital.

The imposing iron fence that encloses the park was the scene (directly opposite No. 2) of a dramatic encounter between novelist-muckraker David Graham Phillips and one Fitzhugh Coyle Goldsborough, the neurotic scion of a wealthy Washington family, on January 23, 1911, as Phillips was on his way from his 19th Street apartment to the Princeton Club. Goldsborough had become obsessed with the idea that Phillips had used his sister as the target of sarcastic barbs in a recent novel. When the two met, Goldsborough drew a revolver and fired three shots, Phillips collapsed against the fence and later succumbed. The young man then pointed the gun at his own head and blew his brains out.

Lovely **Nos. 3** and **4,** with their lacy ironwork porches, were built in 1847 and are attributed to famed architect Alexander Jackson Davis. The pair of lanterns in front of No. 4 indicate that it was once a mayor's residence. James Harper, founder of the J. & J. Harper publishing house, was elected to the city's highest office in 1844, where he fought corruption and organized the Police Department. He bought the house in 1847, but after a fatal carriage accident in 1869 the house went to his children.

No. 10 was the site of the studio of painter **Robert Henri** (1865–1929). As a member of the group of artists known as The Eight, he was a progenitor of the Ashcan School of American Painting, and teacher of such famous artists as George Bellows, Rockwell Kent, and Edward Hopper. His final years were spent here, and his studio's huge north light is still intact.

Turning east at the corner, we see the large double brownstone mansion of the **National Arts Club** at 15 Gramercy Park South. Built in 1845, the two single houses were remodeled from about 1881 to 1884 by Calvert Vaux for Samuel J. Tilden (Vaux, with Frederick Law Olmsted, designed Central and Prospect parks). Although the brownstone façade has weathered badly and is deteriorating, it is nonetheless an engaging example of Ruskinian Gothic, inspired by the Medieval Revival style made famous by the 19th-century English author and artist John Ruskin. Tilden, an eminent lawyer and reformer, was governor of New York in 1875–76, but resigned the office to run as Democratic presidential contender against Rutherford B. Hayes. History records that he won the popular majority by a quarter of a million votes but lost the election—defeated by a group of Southern Republican electors. The National Arts Club purchased the landmark building in 1906.

The National Arts Club is private, but visitors are welcome to visit the art gallery on the second floor during the frequently changing exhibitions. Before entering the gallery, which once was Tilden's dining room, peek into the private rooms on the right and you will be transported back to the late 19th century! Vaux's superb remodeling was inspired by the Aesthetic Movement. Note how he made ample use of carved wood paneling and furniture, stained glass, and tiles. A photo on the wall shows the dining room as it was after the remodeling. The Club was founded in 1898, and early members were Robert Henri, Frederic Remington, and Daniel Chester French, as well as non-artists Woodrow Wilson and Theodore Dreiser.

Adjacent is **The Players,** 16 Gramercy Park South, built for a banker in 1845. It was later purchased by actor Edwin Booth, who in 1888 commissioned Stanford White to remodel it as a private club for the theatrical profession. The huge Tuscan stone porch and elaborate ironwork, including the two graceful lanterns, and high-relief sculptures, are some of White's additions. Not all the great "Players" were actors, however. The membership included such notables as Walter Damrosch, Thomas Nast, Mark Twain, Booth Tarkington, Stanford White, Winston Churchill, and even General William Tecumseh Sherman. But they were all *men,* as the Players' Club was until recently "no-woman's land."

"No-man's land," on the other hand, is still next door at **No. 17,** the **Salvation Army's Parkside Evangeline Residence Hall** for women, built in 1926.

Before crossing Irving Place, look through the park gates at the **statue of Edwin Booth** as Hamlet, sculpted by Edmond T. Quinn and unveiled in 1918.

No. 19 Gramercy Park South is the **Stuyvesant Fish House,** not to be confused with the Stuyvesant Fish residence on Stuyvesant Street [*see* page 144]. Built for Horace Brooks in 1845, it was acquired in 1887 by Stuyvesant Fish, wealthy socialite and president of the Illinois Central Railroad. The line had so many of the "400" on its board of directors that it was called the "Society Railroad." His wife, Mary "Mamie" Fish, succeeded Mrs. William Astor as the head of New York society. It is said that Mamie Fish curtailed the traditional dinner hour from a several-hour affair to a mere 50 minutes; she was also responsible for a new informality among members of society, by encouraging the use of guests' first names. The Fishes commissioned Stanford White to remodel the house in 1888. In 1909 the adjoining stable was demolished and rebuilt as No. 20 and connected to No. 19.

In 1931 the house was acquired by Benjamin Sonnenberg, the great public relations man, whose rise from "rags to riches" is vividly recounted in Rev. Stephen Garmey's seminal work, *Gramercy Park* (New York, 1984). The Sonnenbergs meticulously restored the house to its former grandeur and, as Garmey quotes Brendan Gill, it became "a work of art in its own right." No. 19, according to the author, "struck one as the coziest, most colorful, most opulent place one had ever seen." Sonnenberg died in 1978, and the house has changed hands several times, but it still remains the most beautiful on the Park.

No. 19 also figured in the historical novel *Time and Again,* by Jack Finney. In the thoroughly engaging story, which accurately portrays New York life and events in 1883, the building faced Gramercy Park and was a boarding house and the focus of the plot. (Read it and find out what happened there!)

No. 21, next door, built in 1853–54, was the residence of John Bigelow, author and diplomat. Bigelow was co-owner with William Cullen Bryant of the *New York Evening Post* from 1848 to 1861, when he gave up his newspaper business to become minister to France during the Civil War. He is credited with depriving the Confederacy of recognition by the French Government and with stopping the construction of rebel warships.

The **former Friends' Meeting House,** 144 East 20th Street, was designed by King & Kellum in 1859. It is a fine example of the dignified Italianate style so popular in the 1850s. For a time the fate of the Meeting House was uncertain, as the Friends had merged their meetings with the Stuyvesant Square congregation, selling the house to the United Federation of Teachers. There was even talk of demolition and the erection of a high-rise apartment house, in spite of its designation as a New York City Landmark. But early in 1975, the **Brotherhood Synagogue,** which had been sharing quarters with the Village Presbyterian Church on West 13th Street, purchased the building from the U.F.T. Under the direction of architect James Stewart Polshek, working pro bono, the beautifully proportioned building was painstakingly restored. Visit the lovely sanctuary—a space of great simplicity and classical elegance. Note the adjacent "Biblical Garden."

At the northeast corner of 20th Street is the turreted red-brick Victorian apartment house, **The Gramercy,** No. 34 Gramercy Park, erected in 1883 from plans by George DaCunha, and the first cooperative apartment house in New York City. Peek into its luxurious lobby! The foyer is adorned with stained glass and Minton tiles, and the building is equipped with Otis hydraulic elevators installed in 1883, and among the oldest of their kind still in service. Originally there was a Louis Sherry restaurant on the eighth floor, which, according to Rev. Garmey, was placed so high up in the building "so that residents would not be disturbed by kitchen smells. (Only servants' and bachelor quarters were above it.)"

No. 36, alongside (James Riely Gordon, 1909), in Francis I style, has a white terra-cotta façade replete with gargoyles and elaborate regal motifs; and guarding the entrance, a pair of knights in armor.

Return to Irving Place, walk south one block to 19th Street, and turn east.

9. The tree-lined and serene block between Irving Place and Third Avenue is known as the **"Block Beautiful."** Frederick Sterner was the prime mover in the rehabilitation of many of the old houses. Although none are particularly outstanding by themselves, they form a unity of "harmonious differences." Note the three "Gothic" conversions at **Nos. 127** (1854), **129** (1861), and **135** (1845). **No. 139**

The Academy of Music, built in 1854 at the corner of Irving Place and 14th Street, was New York's most popular and fashionable opera house until the advent of the Metropolitan Opera House in 1883. In 1926 it was razed to make way for Con Ed's new office building. Note the ad for Drake's Plantation Bitters painted on the curb. (The Consolidated Edison Company of New York)

(1842–43), in a Tuscan style, earned Sterner his initial popularity. **No. 141** (1843), with its jockey hitching posts, belonged to the late sportscaster Ted Husing. **No. 132** (1910) was the residence of silent film ingenue Theda Bara, and of Mrs. Patrick Campbell, who in 1912 created the role of Eliza Doolittle in Shaw's *Pygmalion.* It was also the home of "muckraker" Ida M. Tarbell, who wrote the highly critical two-volume *History of the Standard Oil Company.* The ceramic reliefs over the entrances of **Nos. 147–149** (1861) are the work of resident artist Robert Winthrop Chanler. Note also **Nos. 144** and **146.** It was in No. 146 that renowned painter George W. Bellows lived from 1910, when he purchased the house, until his death in 1925. The skylight of his third-floor studio is still visible.

Return to Irving Place and continue south to 18th Street.

10. Pete's Tavern, at 66 Irving Place, dating from 1864 when it was called "Healy's," boasts to be the oldest saloon in New York City. The assertion, however, is strongly disputed, although wrongly, by McSorley's Old Ale House, on East 7th Street, which opened ten years earlier. Pete's also claims to have been a favorite haunt of O. Henry; but, knowing his proclivities, almost any saloon could have earned that distinction! Legend (and a few faded newspaper clippings)

Tammany Hall, on the north side of 14th Street between Irving Place and Third Avenue in a ca. 1870 photograph. Chief Tamanend, above, presides over the Society, which was founded in 1789 as an outgrowth of the Sons of Liberty. Tammany became a political power through the efforts of Aaron Burr. (New-York Historical Society)

maintains that he wrote *The Gift of the Magi* in the second booth on the right (this is also disputed by a restaurant down the street at No. 55—in fact, they have a plaque on the building to "prove" it). Be that as it may, the Tavern has been a popular local landmark for many years. Anyway, author Ludwig Bemelmans *did* write his endearing *Madeline* in Pete's Tavern. Two old carriage houses in the rear have been absorbed into the expanded establishment, and much of the flavor of the gaslit era remains. Note the "O. Henry's Way" street sign.

11. Around the corner, **Nos. 135–143 East 18th Street** are a row of pre–Civil War houses (1855), each only two bays wide. Note the conspicuous hooded lintels over the windows. All but No. 141 retain their original cast-iron newels, balusters, and fences. **Nos. 145–151** date from the same period (1853–54).

12. No. 55 Irving Place is the site of William Sidney Porter's (O. Henry's) residence. Now an apartment house, little remains of the original building or the old Blue Bell Tavern at the corner (another purported "favorite" of the author). The plaque at the entrance to the restaurant claims *this* to be the location of the writing of *The Gift of the Magi*. (See the plaque over the entrance.)

13. The charming little red brick house on the southwest corner of 17th Street, **No. 49 Irving Place,** claims (on its bronze plaque) to have been the residence of Washington Irving. The house was actually built (ca. 1845) for his nephew, John T. Irving, but Washington Irving *was* a frequent visitor. (His home for a time was at 11 Commerce Street, in Greenwich Village.) From 1894 to 1911 the house was occupied by two remarkable women, Elsie de Wolfe and Elisabeth Marbury. Miss de Wolfe was considered "the best-dressed woman in town," and later shocked the interior design profession by becoming the first "lady decorator." Her friend Miss Marbury was a noted literary agent, representing authors such as Oscar Wilde and George Bernard Shaw. Their Sunday afternoon socials for the literary world were the talk of the town. In adjacent **No. 47,** Oscar Wilde spent time in 1883 for the performance of his first drama in America, *Vera.* It premiered in the Union Square Theater, but was a flop.

The house stands at the eastern edge of the diminutive **East 17th Street/Irving Place Historic District,** which extends for half a block, from Irving Place along the south side of East 17th Street, from No. 122 (49 Irving Place) to No. 104, offering a potpourri of late 19th-century architectural styles.

14. In front of Washington Irving High School, built in 1912, is an enormous bust of the school's namesake, executed by Friedrich Baer in 1885 and originally placed in Bryant Park.

15. A short detour to the right on East 15th Street reveals a pleasant architectural surprise, at Nos. 109–111, the **former Century Association Building,** now the **Century Association for the Performing Arts** (1996 conversion by Beyer Blinder Belle). The Association had acquired the venerable building in 1857, ten years after its founding, and in 1869 looked to two clubmember-architects to design a major reconstruction. The plans fell to the renowned Henry Hobson Richardson, who was assisted by Charles Gambrill. The result was a clubhouse in the then-fashionable neo-Grec style.

The Century Association, a social club dedicated to "promote the advancement of art and literature," was founded by William Cullen Bryant, and took its name from the 100 original male members [*see* Century Association Clubhouse, pages 337 and 340]. In 1891 the club moved to its present quarters on West 43rd Street. Until recently it had been assumed that their former building had long-since been demolished, but researchers discovered that the street had been renumbered, and it was the house bearing the old number that had disappeared. It now remains the only building in Manhattan by H. H. Richardson, as well as the oldest surviving private clubhouse. Adjacent No. 115 is also dedicated to the performing arts, and is the home of the **Lee Strasberg Theatre Institute.**

Return to Irving Place.

Occupying the entire block, from 15th to 14th streets, and Irving Place to Union Square, is massive **Zeckendorf Towers** (Davis, Brody & Assocs., 1987), a 670-unit condominium in four 29-story towers, topped by open-framework pyramids. The towers are set on a seven-story base that fills the triangular plot, while maintaining the orientation to the city street grid. [For further details, *see* Union Square section of Chapter 8.] On the west side of Irving Place, between West 15th and 16th streets, the **Amberg Theater** (demolished for the Zeckendorf project) was a favorite venue for devotees of avant garde foreign films. It had had a long history as legitimate theater, vaudeville house, and even as a site for X-rated movies.

16. Situated on the entire block to Third Avenue, between 15th and 14th streets, is the **headquarters of the Consolidated Edison Company of New York** ("Con Ed"). The main building was designed by Henry J. Hardenbergh (architect of the Plaza Hotel and the Dakota Apartments). Begun in 1911, the structure and its extensions developed in stages, and took 18 years to complete. The unique clock tower, a pleasing contribution to the cityscape, was planned by Warren & Wetmore (architects of Grand Central Terminal) and completed in 1926. The company's predecessor, the Manhattan Gas Light Company, was located near the corner of 14th Street from 1885 to 1910; and at the corner was the **Academy of Music,** built in 1854. Farther east in the block was Tammany Hall, and at the Third Avenue corner, the popular entertainment spot, Tony Pastor's Music Hall. The Academy of Music hosted such greats as Jenny Lind, Adelina Patti, Helena Modjeska, E. H. Sothern, Edwin Booth, and Julia Marlowe. When the Metropolitan Opera House opened at Broadway and West 39th Street in 1893, the Academy of Music soon declined, and for a number of years presented only vaudeville and silents. In 1926 it finally surrendered to the wrecker's ball, making way for the Consolidated Edison Company's main building extension. A description of the interior of the Academy of Music appears on the opening page of Edith Wharton's Pulitzer Prize–winning novel, *The Age of Innocence,* where she observes that "the world of fashion was still content to reassemble every winter in the shabby red and gold boxes of the sociable old Academy." (Look for the plaque on the 14th Street side of the Con Ed building indicating the exact site of the Academy of Music.)

17. Directly across the street, at 140 East 14th Street, is the New York University dormitory **Palladium Hall** (Davis Brody Bond, 1998), named for the movie theater formerly on the site. The Palladium was very popular with hip young people for its avant garde films and rock concerts. The late and lamented theater was built in the late 1920s, and was originally called the Academy of Music, a name that evoked considerable confusion with the recently departed (1926) *real* Academy of Music across the street.

No. 110 East 14th Street is another N.Y.U. high-rise dorm called **University Hall** (Davis Brody Bond, 1998) that occupies the **site of Lüchow's,** New York's most celebrated German restaurant. It rose to prominence when 14th Street became the heart of the entertainment district, as concertgoers from the Academy of Music and Steinway Hall (across the street) packed the mirrored and wood-paneled rooms, and the oompah bands played night after night, while the beer flowed like the Rhine. It was a mecca for the big names in the music world, and was frequented by Paderewski, Caruso, Fritz Kreisler, Victor Herbert, Cole Porter, Sigmund Romberg, Richard Rodgers, and Leonard Bernstein. Seen in earlier days were Lillian Russell, William Steinway, and even Theodore Roosevelt (who preferred venison to the traditional German fare). With the shift of the entertainment district uptown, the restaurant followed suit to a site near the Winter Garden, but having forsaken the very special ambiance of its 14th Street site, it failed to attract its old loyal clientele and closed in 1982. Efforts were made by community groups to preserve the old Victorian-style building, but not being a designated landmark, it fell victim the same year to the wrecker's ball.

End of tour. The Union Square subway station is one block west.

The Hippotheatron *was built in 1864 as an arena primarily for equestrian shows (*hippo = horse, *in Greek), and was one of several similar venues for horse shows in the city [see P. T. Barnum's Hippodrome, Franconi's Hippodrome, Hippodrome Theater, and Madison Square Garden]. The huge structure stood on the south side of 14th Street, directly opposite the Academy of Music, which had opened ten years earlier. Among other animal-related extravaganzas held on the site was P. T. Barnum's famous menagerie. The building's cast-iron construction, however, did not prevent its destruction in a disastrous fire in 1871. (Theater Collection, Museum of the City of New York)*

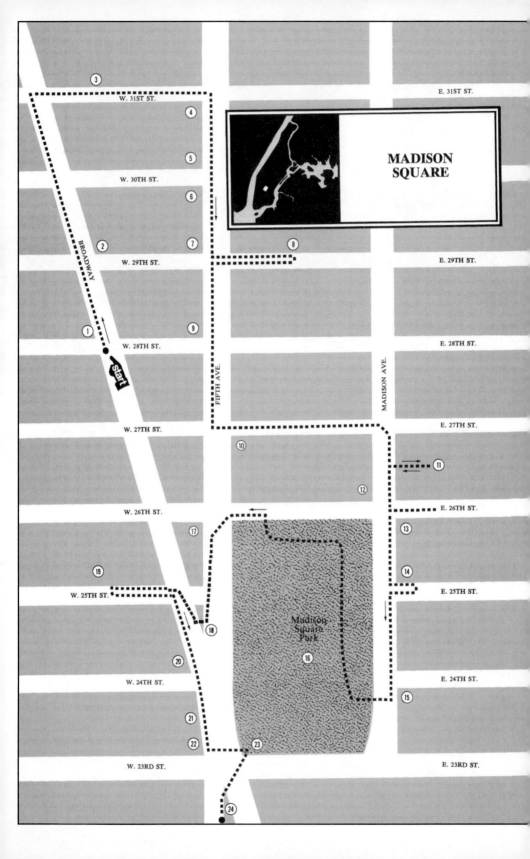

10. Madison Square

[Subways: N, R to 28th Street. Buses: M6, M7 to 28th Street.]

Along Broadway from 23rd to 42nd streets, during the 1880s and 1890s, was the Rialto of New York—the celebrated Great White Way. Keeping pace with the northward drive of the city, the theater district, in a series of moves up Broadway, now reached to Longacre Square (called Times Square after 1904). Our uniquely American theater idiom, the musical comedy, was coming into its own, and the heyday of songwriting had begun. Along 28th Street, music publishers and tunesmiths by the score worked around the clock in a cacophony of musical sounds, to give birth to the appropriately named Tin Pan Alley. Facing nearby Madison Square arose Stanford White's monumental "Garden" to present a variety of entertainment on a scale hitherto unheard of by American audiences. Competing with the live entertainment of Broadway came the infant motion-picture industry, grinding out its silent films in hastily constructed studios in the West 20s.

Gone now are the legitimate theaters and music halls, the budding film industry, and the opulent hotels, restaurants, and cafés that lined Fifth Avenue and Broadway. Gone, too, is the din, glitter, and excitement that drew the throngs of nightly visitors. Even lavish Madison Square Garden bade farewell to its namesake site in 1925 and moved (twice) to other locations.

Broadway and adjacent Madison Square have quite a different flavor now. The 20th century witnessed the development of a bustling business district, bringing with it some of the most imposing commercial structures in the city. The area now between 26th and 32nd streets is primarily an export-import center, with a wide variety of mostly wholesale businesses. The owners represent many of the recent larger immigrant groups—Koreans, Indians, Arabs, Africans, etc. Have you ever wondered where the ubiquitous street vendors obtain their merchandise? It is here in this colorful bazaar, which exudes a different sort of liveliness than did the theater district a century ago.

Shady Madison Square Park, however, still retains its quiet elegance—a refuge from the congestion and clamor of surrounding streets. And here and there, dwarfed by modern, multistoried neighbors, some architectural vestiges of the past still survive—mute reminders of that vibrant, exciting era of 90 years ago.

1. The tour begins at **West 28th Street and Broadway,** the former heart of "Tin Pan Alley," where most of the popular music publishers were located at the turn of the century. The sounds of tinkling pianos emanating from all the buildings in the block to Fifth Avenue gave rise to the name. Notice the typical turn-of-the-century skyscrapers, **No. 1170 Broadway** (DeLemos & Cordes, 1903) and **No. 1181,** The Baudoine Building (Alfred Zucker, 1896), in which architects still displayed that _horror vacui,_ or abhorrence of leaving any part of the building undecorated; hence the façades were usually divided into three distinct sections, similar to a Classic column: the "base," usually the first three or four stories; the "shaft," the tall, relatively unadorned center section; and the "capital," the top group of stories, frequently very ornate and topped with a projecting cornice. This "Tripartite" style of commercial building architecture remained popular until about 1910. Note the dome on No. 1170.

2. On the northeast corner of West 29th Street and Broadway is the charming **Gilsey House** (Stephen D. Hatch, 1869). Built of marble and cast iron, it is a splendid example of the French Second Empire style. It was a favored hotel of Oscar Wilde during his American lecture tours, and was also a frequent haunt of James Buchanan "Diamond Jim" Brady, the financier and _bon vivant_ of the Gay '90s. The hotel, built for Peter Gilsey, opened in 1871, and was the first in the city to boast a telephone. The sympathetic and precise restoration of this magnificent pile is a credit to the developer, who purchased a deteriorating commercial building and converted it into a profitable and desirable co-op.

At the southeast corner of West 31st Street is the **former Grand Hotel,** No. 1232–1238 Broadway. Built in 1868 from plans by Henry Engelbert, it was considered one of the great hostelries of New York. Erected when the theater district was moving uptown to Herald Square, the former glory of this now-commercial structure is evident in its French Second Empire style, with marble front, imposing mansard roof, pedimented dormers, ocular windows, large pavilion, and chamfered corners. Turn east on West 31st Street to the Herald Square Hotel.

3. The refurbished Herald Square Hotel, until recently the Hotel Clinton, is the **former home of Life Magazine.** Before its purchase by the Time-Life Corporation in 1936, _Life_ was a rather sophisticated humor weekly. Visible on the upper stone balcony is its name, as are groupings of L's on the ornate cast-iron balconies, together with the gilt sculptured cherub and the inscriptions of "Wit" and "Humor." The building, with its Classical façade, was designed in 1893 by the noted architectural firm of Carrère & Hastings. (Ignore the added upper two floors.)

4. **The Wolcott Hotel,** at 4–10 West 31st Street (John Duncan, 1904), is a fine example of Renaissance Eclectic–style hotel architecture so popular at the turn of the century. In its recent remodeling, the designers may have gone a bit far in re-creating the ornate _fin de siècle_ lobby. (Take a peek inside!) Now turn south on Fifth Avenue to the southwest corner of West 27th Street. (Fifth Avenue is the east-west dividing line of all numbered streets in Manhattan, from 8th Street north.)

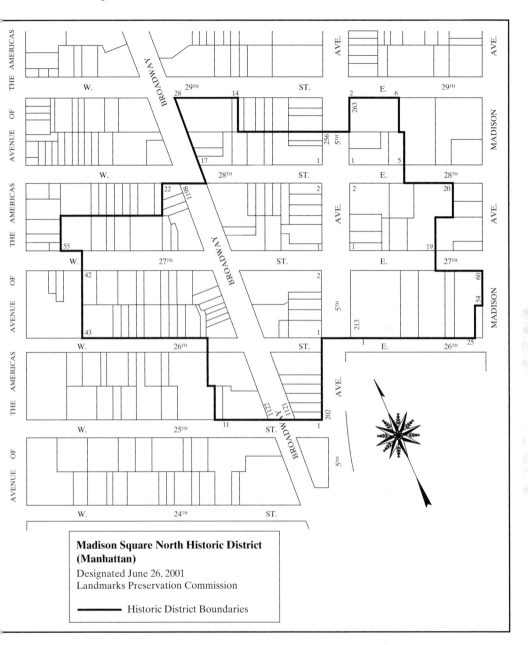

Madison Square North Historic District (Manhattan)

Designated June 26, 2001
Landmarks Preservation Commission

▬▬▬▬ Historic District Boundaries

5. The dark red brick apartment house across the street (284 Fifth Avenue, entrance on West 30th Street) is the **Wilbraham Apartments** (David & John Jardine, 1890). It was one of the first "French Flats," or residential apartments for the wealthy. Actress Lillian Russell occupied the top floor during the heyday of her career.

6. The building at 276 Fifth Avenue was **formerly the Holland House** (Harding & Gooch, 1891). Named for a similar hotel in the Kensington section of London, it was a gathering place for intellectuals and gourmets. The staircase of Siena marble and bronze and its famous restaurant made it a showplace until its closing in 1920. In its 1903 edition, *King's Views of New York* called it "the peer of any hotel in America...where the most fastidious people are its 'instant guests.'"

7. At the northwest corner of 29th Street is the well-known **Marble Collegiate Reformed Church,** where Dr. Norman Vincent Peale's Sunday sermons originated to reach a nationwide radio audience. Built in 1854 from plans by architect Samuel A. Warner, the church is a fine example of early Romanesque Revival style applied to what is essentially a Gothic Revival–style building. The congregation dates back to the founding of the Dutch Reformed Church in America in 1628. Note the huge bronze bell in front of the church. Cast in Holland, it summoned the faithful while it hung in the old North Church downtown on William Street in the 18th and 19th centuries.

8. Turn east on 29th Street to the landmark Episcopal Church of the Transfiguration. Known as the **"Little Church around the Corner,"** it dates from 1849–56, and is New York City's unique example of the Cottage Gothic style of the 14th century. It earned its nickname from an incident that occurred in 1870. When actor George Holland died and was refused burial rites at a nearby church, a friend, Joseph Jefferson, was informed that there was a *little church around the corner* that would perform the rites—and the name stuck. The church has been closely connected with the acting profession since that time. The lich-gate at the entrance recalls the custom of conducting a preliminary burial service outside the church (*lic* is the Anglo-Saxon word for "body"). The interior is unusually beautiful, with a quiet, intimate atmosphere. Look for the stained-glass window (in the south transept) of actor Edwin Booth as Hamlet, done by John LaFarge. The reredos of the *Last Supper,* as well as the lich-gate, were designed by architect Frederick Clarke Withers. Note also the Chantry with its Brides' Altar, the carved wooden screens at the entrance to the nave, the Joseph Jefferson Memorial Window, the Mortuary Chapel with stained-glass copy of Raphael's *Transfiguration,* and the little chapel dedicated to actor José María Muñoz. The church takes pride in its history of helping the less fortunate. During the Draft Riots of 1863, it sheltered runaway slaves, and in the depressions of 1907 and the mid-1930s, it operated bread lines. It is still very active in community service, and also supports a small professional theater company, appropriately called "The Jefferson Players." The Little Church around the Corner is both a New York City landmark and a National Historic Landmark, and listed as a "National Shrine of Church and Theater."

The first Madison Square Garden building was originally the Union Depot of the New York & Harlem Railroad at 28th Street and Madison Avenue. It served for a time as P. T. Barnum's Hippodrome, then in 1879 it became the "Garden." It lasted only until 1890, when Stanford White's great masterpiece replaced it. (New York Life Insurance Company)

Return to Fifth Avenue, where both sides of the Avenue, from between 28th and 29th streets to 26th Street, and from part of the west side of Madison Avenue to beyond Broadway, comprise the newly designated Madison Square North Historic District.

    9. 256 Fifth Avenue, above the ground floor, is pure fantasy—a mixture of Venetian Gothic, Moorish, and whatever; the builder of the early 1890s went "hog wild" with the new terra-cotta medium.

    250 Fifth Avenue (McKim, Mead & White, 1907) was built in Italianate style for the Second National Bank of the City of New York, and is not considered one of the firm's best designs. It is now a branch of the Broadway National Bank.

    Farther east on 27th Street is the **Prince George Hotel** (Howard Greenley, 1904). Once one of the city's most posh, it was the first with a private bath in every room, and catered to such flamboyant personalities as "Diamond Jim" Brady and Lillian Russell. In recent years, the once magnificent hotel, having deteriorated badly, sank to serving welfare clients for a time, and was then boarded up and offered for sale. It was ultimately purchased by the city and renovated by Common Ground Community H.D.F.C. into single-room furnished studios for low-income tenants. Return to Fifth Avenue and turn left (south).

10. The **former Brunswick Building** (Francis H. Kimball, 1907), No. 225 Fifth Avenue, on the southeast corner of 27th Street, is one of the city's most attractive commercial structures. Now a wholesale gift mart, it is notable for its red-brick façade and contrasting limestone trim, its splayed window lintels, swags and consoles, paired balconies, and ornate designs above the 10th floor's round-arch windows. An intricate wrought-iron balcony wraps around the building one floor higher, just below a verdigris cornice. The predecessor on the site, the fashionable Brunswick Hotel, was favored by the sporting crowd and particularly by the New York Coach Club, whose well-heeled members conducted an annual parade of their sumptuous horse-drawn carriages.

11. The New York Life Insurance Company Building, designed by Cass Gilbert and built in 1926–28, is a most imposing structure. Although of no particular architectural style, but with neo-Gothic ornamentation, the *AIA Guide to New York* refers to it as "Limestone Renaissance at the bottom, Birthday Cake at the top." The gilt pyramid that caps this mammoth structure is similar to the one Gilbert later designed for the top of the U.S. Court House on Foley Square and is illuminated at night. The splendid lobby of the New York Life Building is particularly attractive. Its coffered ceiling, enormous hanging lamps, and ornate doors and paneling—all of bronze—make it one of the great interiors of the city. The "grand staircase" leading to the subway station belies what is below. Compare

Planned at first to be the site for annual horse shows, Stanford White designed Madison Square Garden to include a theater, concert hall, roof-garden, and restaurant, graced with a dramatic tower—the second highest in the city—and surmounted by a gilt statue of Diana. (New York Life Insurance Company)

this lavish lobby with Cass Gilbert's treatment of his Woolworth Building, built 13 years before. (See the landmark plaque.)

This is the **site of the first two Madison Square Gardens.** Originally, the Union Depot of the New York & Harlem Railroad was built here after it had been moved uptown from its earlier location near City Hall. (The city fathers objected strenuously to the noise and air pollution of the old steam locomotives.) In 1871 the railroad terminal was shifted to the present site of Grand Central Terminal, and the Depot was sold to P. T. Barnum, who converted it into his popular Hippodrome. Nine years later it became the first Madison Square Garden.

In 1890, Stanford White designed the second Madison Square Garden, an imposing Spanish Renaissance–style structure, which occupied the entire block. Its central tower, modeled after the *Giralda* in Seville and topped by Augustus St. Gauden's statue of Diana, would be a dominant feature of the city skyline for 35 years. Complete with the largest amphitheater in the country, Garden Theater, Roof Garden, concert hall, café, and even an immense swimming pool, it was an immediate sensation. Among some of the events staged in the Garden were operatic concerts, prize fights (Jack Dempsey knocked out Bill Brennan), Wild West Shows, aquatic exhibitions, the first American automobile show, six-day bike races, and Barnum & Bailey's circus. Diana now resides in the Philadelphia Museum of Art.

Architect White had an eye not only for beautiful buildings, but for beautiful women as well. His two homes nearby were the scenes of frequent and wild all-night parties. Rumor had it that White had installed a high red-velvet swing on the top floor of his West 24th Street love nest, on which girlfriends were offered all manner of inducements to oscillate "in the altogether." One of these steady "swingers" was young Evelyn Nesbit, a former *Floradora* show girl who later married eccentric millionaire Harry K. Thaw. On the evening of June 25, 1906, Stanford White entered the Roof Garden theater and was observed by Thaw and his recent bride, who were dining at a nearby table. Evelyn whispered something about White to her husband that infuriated him; whereupon he leaped up from the table, stalked across the floor, drew a revolver, and fired three fatal shots at the architect. After nine years and three prolonged trials, Thaw was acquitted.

After its demolition in 1925, the Garden was rebuilt at West 50th Street and 8th Avenue, where it remained until 1968. Ironically, its present location at Eighth Avenue between 31st and 33rd streets is on the site of McKim, Mead & White's greatest architectural achievement—Pennsylvania Station—which fell victim to the wrecker's ball and civic short-sightedness in 1963–66!

12. No. 50 Madison Avenue was built in 1896 by Renwick, Aspinwall & Owens for the American Society for the Prevention of Cruelty to Animals (ASPCA).

13. The glistening **Merchandise Mart Building** (Emery Roth & Sons, 1974), on the southeast corner of 26th Street, is an unfortunate example of utter disregard for scale. It would appear that the designers cared not at all about the height, shape, and style of adjacent buildings when they planned this one. By acquiring the air rights from the Court House to the south, they were able to raise this enormous dark shaft to an eye-boggling height, thus overwhelming its neighbors, destroying a pleasing skyline, and casting a visual pall over the park below. To make the picture even more dismal, the former occupant of the site was the Leonard Jerome House (Jerome's daughter, Jennie, became Lady Randolph Churchill—Winston Churchill's mother). The attractive mansion, built in 1859, later became the Manhattan Club where, it is said, the Manhattan cocktail was invented. Demolition took place with indecent haste, just before the passage of the Landmarks Preservation Law, and New York suffered another irretrievable loss.

14. The Appellate Division, New York State Supreme Court is a Beaux Arts–style gem of a marble building, and is a tribute to its architect, James Brown Lord. Built of limestone in 1896–1900, this exceptional building miraculously escaped the fate of its ex-neighbor, the Jerome House, when public outcry prevented the Court's consolidation into the Foley Square complex.

The exterior, with its projecting Corinthian porticos, supports an astonishing display of sculpture by 16 artists, each figure representing a person noted for achievements in the history of law.

The elegant Leonard Jerome House, built in 1859, later the Manhattan Club, graced the southeast corner of 26th Street and Madison Avenue. Daughter Jennie Jerome later became Lady Randolph Churchill, mother of Sir Winston. The Landmark Law came too late to save the beautiful house, and in its place is the enormously out-of-scale Merchandise Mart Building. (New York Life Insurance Company)

"Dr. Parkhurst's Church," as the Madison Avenue Presbyterian Church was called, was built in 1853 when the neighborhood was entirely residential. On this peaceful site of the late 1880s—the corner of 23rd Street and Madison Avenue—now stands the Metropolitan Life Tower. (Metropolitan Life Insurance Company)

Madison Square has managed to escape most alterations made in the name of progress. The drinking fountains and pavilion are gone, but the trees remain, sporting the foliage of more than a century of growth since this 1901 photo was taken by Byron. (The Byron Collection, Museum of the City of New York)

The young boy drinking from the common cup was a participant in a Madison Square clean-up campaign sponsored by the Metropolitan Life Insurance Company in 1913. (Metropolitan Life Insurance Company)

An early 1900s sightseeing bus in front of No. 1 Madison Avenue. (Metropolitan Life Insurance Company)

The triangular site of the Flatiron Building, the intersection of Broadway and Fifth Avenue at 23rd Street, as seen from the Fifth Avenue Hotel in 1884. Note the white Broadway omnibus at left. (New-York Historical Society)

The expression "Twenty-Three Skidoo!" is said to have come from the efforts by Officer Kane, and others, stationed at Fifth Avenue and 23rd Street, to "shoo" away the young men who gathered at the breezy corner to catch a glimpse of a lady's ankle. (Metropolitan Life Insurance Company)

The 28th and 29th Street crosstown car was one of the last to exchange horsepower for electric. In this undated photo, a two-horse team passes in front of 45 East 29th Street on its way to the New Jersey ferry terminal at West 23rd Street. (Metropolitan Life Insurance Company)

Prim young ladies serving tempting desserts in Maillard's elegant confectionery shop, on the ground floor of the posh Fifth Avenue Hotel. (Photograph by Byron. The Byron Collection, Museum of the City of New York)

Take a moment or two to examine the sculpture:

Madison Square side:

Balustrade (left to right): *Confucius* (Philip Martiny), *Peace* group (Karl Bitter), *Moses* (William Couper)

Four caryatids: *The Four Seasons* (Thomas Shields Clarke)

25th Street Side:

Entrance: *Force* and *Wisdom* (Frederick Ruckstull)

Above portico windows: *Morning* and *Night, Noon* and *Evening* (Maximilian M. Schwartzott)

Pediment: *Triumph of Law* (Charles H. Niehaus)

Surmounting pediment: *Justice* flanked by *Power* and *Study* (Daniel Chester French)

Balustrade (left to right): *Zoroaster* (Edward C. Potter), *Alfred the Great* (Jonathan Scott Hartley), *Lycurgus* (George E. Bissell), *Solon* (Herbert Adams), *Louis IX* (John Donoghue), *Manu* (Augustus Lukeman), *Justinian* (Henry Kirke Bush-Brown), *vacant* (formerly *Mohammed,* Charles Albert Lopez; removed at the request of the Moslem community of New York City)

A visit to the interior is most rewarding (open weekdays only). The furniture was designed by the architectural and interior design firm of Herter Brothers, the cabinetry by George C. Flint Company, the sculpture of Charles O'Connor by James W. A. MacDonald, and the stained-glass windows by the Maitland Armstrong Company. There are also splendid murals painted by a number of famous American muralists. Nothing was spared in making the Appellate Court House an aesthetic, architectural masterpiece.

At the north end of the courthouse extension, and rising 27 feet above a 9½-foot base, is a six-sided marble half-column, the **Memorial to the Victims of the Holocaust** (Harriet Feigenbaum, 1990). The monument is designed to symbolize the horror of the Holocaust with flames incised into the column above an aerial view of the death camp at Auschwitz. The inscription reads "Indifference to Injustice is the Gate to Hell."

 15. The Metropolitan Life Insurance Company buildings complete the panorama of the east side of Madison Square. The original main building, at the corner of 23rd Street, was built in 1893. Its crowning glory, however, came in 1909 with the 700-foot tower addition, making it the tallest building in the world at the time, and the identifying symbol of the company—"the Light that Never Fails." Designed by the firm of Napoleon LeBrun & Sons, the tower is based on the *Campanile* of St. Mark's Square in Venice. Four years after its completion, its height record was surpassed by the 60-story Woolworth Building, downtown. In the mid-1950s, the original main building was demolished and the present 12-story structure erected in its place. The tower was given a "facelift" as part of the overall modernization project, with most of the ornamentation stripped off the façade. Only the four three-story-high clocks and the surmounting gilded lantern escaped the butchery. Yet the tower glitters like a jewel in its nighttime illumination. It is floodlit in a variety of colors corresponding to holidays—red, white, and blue on July 4th; green on St. Patrick's Day and at Christmas, when red lamps shine in the tower windows, simulating a holiday tree.

An interesting event in the history of the 50-story tower occurred on election night 1908, one year before its completion. The *New York Herald* installed a giant searchlight among the still-exposed girders near the top of the spire to signal the election results far and wide. A northward-swinging beam would indicate a majority for the Republican presidential candidate William Howard Taft, and a southward beam for Democrat William Jennings Bryan. As the first returns showed a plurality for Taft, the beacon moved slowly up and down in a northward direction. By a little after 8 P.M., as the telegraphed vote count gave a clear majority to the Republican, the searchlight's rays were held steadily northward. Thus New Yorkers and suburbanites for miles around were the first to get the election results transmitted from the tall tower's beacon.

The **former North Building,** known now only by its street address, No. 11 Madison Avenue, occupying the block between 24th and 25th streets, was designed by Wald, Corbett, & Angilly, and built in three stages from 1929 to 1950. A striking example of the Art Deco style, the massive Alabama limestone exterior was planned to conform to the city's building regulations requiring extensive setbacks on tall buildings. Their "stepped" arrangement, along with the interesting angular upper walls and chamfered corners, can best be appreciated from across the square. Arched

For a brief period in 1906 there were two Madison Square Presbyterian Churches standing side-by-side. Needing additional land to erect its famous tower, the Metropolitan Life Insurance Company bought and razed the older Gothic Revival–style church and built another for Dr. Charles H. Parkhurst's congregation. The neoclassic "temple," Stanford White's last major commission, survived only until 1919 when the Insurance Company again acquired the property to build its North Building. (Metropolitan Life Insurance Company)

loggias at the four corners provide entrance arcades that lead to central elevator halls, and the huge building is connected to the Home Office Building by a skywalk and a tunnel. The lobby walls are faced with handsome Italian cremo marble. Just before the outbreak of World War II the company stockpiled huge blocks of this marble for fear that a war might destroy the northern Italian quarries and prevent a uniform completion of the building's interior. The North Building holds the distinction of being the first commercial structure in New York City to have central air conditioning.

On the site of the adjacent **Metropolitan Life Tower** stood the brownstone Gothic Revival–style Madison Square Presbyterian Church, built in 1853. Its outspoken minister, the Reverend Charles H. Parkhurst, led a vociferous campaign from 1892 to 1894 against citywide crime and police corruption. Accused by angry Tammany politicians of being self-serving, Dr. Parkhurst documented his charges by personally visiting the dens of iniquity that City Hall denied existed and proving complicity and brutality by the police. After these revelations from Parkhurst's pulpit, the State Legislature convened the Lexow Committee, whose subsequent investigation corroborated Dr. Parkhurst's accusations and led to the defeat of Tammany Mayor Hugh Grant, a major shakeup in the Police Department, and the appointment of Theodore Roosevelt to the Board of Commissioners. The Metropolitan Life Insurance Company acquired the church property for needed building expansion, and in exchange for the corner plot, agreed to build a new house of worship across the street for Dr. Parkhurst's congregation. Stanford White was commissioned to design the new church, which was completed in 1906 in Italian Renaissance style. The bright, white granite New Madison Square Presbyterian Church was White's last public building and is considered by many authorities to be the most beautiful building he ever designed. In 1919, the ever-expanding company purchased the property and demolished the lovely church. (The parishioners had, for the most part, moved to more fashionable precincts uptown anyway, as the neighborhood by that time was almost exclusively commercial.) A "new" annex to the Home Office was erected, but it, too, was razed when the new North Building was designed.

16. Madison Square Park became the pleasant oasis it is now in 1870. At the time of the Revolution it was a swampy grassland traversed by a meandering stream, abounding with game. Later it became a paupers' burial ground. By the first decade of the 19th century, a military outpost was established as part of the defenses of the lower city at the junction of the Eastern Post Road and Bloomingdale Road—now Broadway—near the present intersection of Fifth Avenue. In 1811, the famous New York City Commissioners' Report officially designated the street pattern of much of Manhattan Island, and a "Parade" was laid out between 23rd and 34th streets and Third and Seventh avenues. A few years later it was greatly reduced in size and named in honor of the then fourth president, James Madison. In 1844 the Square was again reduced, to its present size. In its concept the plan was a forerunner of the one that subsequently gave us spacious Central Park. The park underwent a major restoration in the early 1990s. A significant change was in the park's paths, which are now aligned with the street grid, so that one can now walk from Madison to Fifth Avenue without a detour. The atmosphere in the renovated park now more closely evokes its gracious past.

Enter the Park at the Statue of Roscoe Conkling, at 23rd Street.

Elected as a Republican to the U.S. Senate in 1867, Conkling served the Empire State for 14 years. He resigned in 1881 after a dispute with President Garfield and retired to law practice. During the Great Blizzard of March 12, 1888, he was caught without transportation home from his downtown office, and set out on foot against the mounting drifts and sub-zero cold. He became lost in Madison Square, but was rescued and carried to his nearby home. The effects of the exposure, however, were fatal, and he died six weeks later. This bronze memorial statue, by sculptor John Quincy Adams Ward, was erected in 1893 through contributions by friends, and stands near the site where he was felled by the blizzard.

Walking north along the park path, we pass a towering **pin oak** brought from Montpelier, the Virginia estate of James Madison, and planted in 1936 to commemorate the centennial of both the year he died and the opening of Madison Avenue. (Note the plaque.) Then on to the north end under broad elms, ginkgos, and horse chestnuts, passing the novel and highly popular new children's playground, to the imposing **statue of Admiral David Glasgow Farragut,** dedicated in 1881. In a dramatic posture as a rugged sailor facing the wind, Farragut is memorialized as the great naval hero of the Civil War. His victories at New Orleans and Mobile Bay finally closed all Gulf ports to the Confederacy. One can almost hear him shout that celebrated order, "Damn the torpedoes, full speed ahead!" He is represented in one of the great 19th-century statues by famed sculptor Augustus St. Gaudens, with Stanford White as the designer of the beautifully rendered pedestal bench.

A short distance to the northeast is the **statue of Chester A. Arthur,** 21st president, who assumed the office after the assassination of James Garfield in 1881. The monument, by George E. Bissell, was unveiled in 1899 and was a gift of Catherine Lorillard Wolfe, who lived in a brownstone on the site of the Metropolitan Life Tower. For a quick snack, check out the ivy-covered Shake Shack.

Hansom cabs line the west side of Madison Square, across from the fashionable Fifth Avenue Hotel, as two young ladies stroll toward the camera of Percy C. Byron, 1905. (The Byron Collection, Museum of the City of New York)

Three types of horse-drawn carriages wait outside Delmonico's, at Fifth Avenue and 26th Street, in 1888, then the most fashionable dining place in town. A number of years later, the restaurant moved up Fifth Avenue to 44th Street where it finally closed in 1923. The restaurant on the site of Delmonico's first establishment, at Beaver and South William streets, seeks to preserve the name and tradition. (New-York Historical Society)

17. The southwest corner of Fifth Avenue and 26th Street marks the **site of Delmonico's restaurant,** between 1876 and 1902, before its ninth and final move uptown to 44th Street [*see* page 69]. When Charles, and son Lorenzo, Delmonico opened their newest dining salon, it achieved instant popularity with the "400" and became a formidable rival to the Café Brunswick, across the avenue. Its world-renowned chefs, lavish menus, impeccable service, and elite clientele made it the gourmet landmark *par excellence* well remembered to this day.

18. One block south is the **General William Jenkins Worth Monument.** Designed by James C. Batterson and erected in 1857, this 51-foot-tall granite obelisk marks one of the only two burial sites of a public figure under a Manhattan thoroughfare—the other is the General Ulysses S. Grant (with his wife) Tomb at West 122nd Street and Riverside Drive. Worth fought in the War of 1812 and the Seminole and Mexican wars, and the names of some of his famous battles are carved on the granite shaft. Although a downtown street is named for him, as is Lake Worth, Florida, he is perhaps more of a hero in the state of Texas, where the city of Fort Worth honors his memory. On the south face, above the seals of the State and City of New York, are sculptured 19th-century weaponry; while below, on a bronze tablet, is a high-relief sculpture of the General brandishing his sword on a rearing horse. He died in 1849, and his body lies beneath. The recently restored cast-iron fence, by the J. B. & W. W. Cornell Iron Works, consists of a row of swords that are replicas of a dress sword awarded General Worth by New York for his prowess in battle. The marble-faced structure directly behind is a water-metering station (1917), leading to Water Tunnel No. 1, part of the Catskill water supply system.

Along Fifth Avenue and adjacent Broadway stood many famous hotels of the gaslit era. On the southwest corner of Broadway and 26th Street stood the St. James Hotel, whose name is borne today by the neo-Gothic skyscraper on the site. Occupying the west side of Broadway between 24th and 25th streets was the Hoffman House, an elegant hostelry of the time, whose bar was also a noted art gallery. Remembered particularly is Adolphe Bouguereau's huge, somewhat risqué (at the time) painting, *Nymphs and Satyr,* which created quite a sensation in those Victorian days. The painting can be seen today, no longer causing a stir, at the Sterling and Francine Clark Art Institute, in Williamstown, Massachusetts.

19. Make a brief detour along West 25th Street to the **Serbian Orthodox Cathedral of St. Sava.** Designed in 1855 by Richard Upjohn, it was built in English Gothic style as the Trinity Protestant Episcopal Chapel, and was the site

Looking north on Fifth Avenue at Madison Square Park. In 1876 the arm of the Statue of Liberty was brought from Philadelphia's Centennial Exposition to New York as a means of raising money for the base and the costs of assembling France's gift to America. The statue was finally erected ten years later. (New-York Historical Society)

of Edith Wharton's wedding in 1885. Alongside is the 1860 **Parish House,** in Victorian Gothic style, by J. Wrey Mould. The buildings were purchased by the Serbian Church in 1943. In the alleyway between stands the statue of Serbian-born Michael Pupin (1858–1935), a noted physicist.

Return to Fifth Avenue.

20. The buildings occupying the entire block from 24th to 25th streets, as well as its neighbor to the south, are linked together not only by a skywalk, but by the same street number, **200 Fifth Avenue,** and are known as the **International Toy Center,** home for most of the city's wholesale toy manufacturers and distributors.

A few yards down 24th Street stood the Madison Square Theater, famous at the turn of the century for its hydraulically operated double stage.

Looking toward the center of the park, somewhat obscured by trees, is the **Star of Hope,** a five-pointed star on a 35-foot pole, set on an ornamental pedestal. Erected in 1916, it commemorates the country's first community Christmas tree that was lit in Madison Square Park on Christmas Eve, 1912, "as a gift to the less fortunate in the city." The annual tradition lives on with festivities sponsored by the 23rd Street Association and the Department of Parks and Recreation.

Across the street, at the edge of the park, is the **Eternal Light Flagpole.** Erected in 1924 from plans by Thomas Hastings (of the architectural firm of Carrère & Hastings) and Paul W. Bartlett, it honors the fallen of World War I. At a point just to the left, the arm of the Statue of Liberty was displayed from 1876 to 1884 while funds were being raised to pay for the base. The arm and torch were first sent by France to the Philadelphia Centennial Exposition, then brought to Madison Square Park. The arm was later returned to France for attachment to the statue, which was finally erected in New York Harbor in 1886. [*See* photo, page 286.]

21. The tall **sidewalk clock** in the next block is one of the last remaining on the streets of New York, a vestige of the days when wristwatches were unknown and pocket watches were for only the affluent. They were usually placed in front of a commercial establishment as an advertising gimmick. This cast-iron street clock, which still runs perfectly, was built by the Hecla Iron Works in the 1880s with a movement by Seth Thomas—the oldest surviving American clockmaker.

22. The plaque on the massive Italian Renaissance **Toy Center Building** (Maynicke & Franke, 1909), at the corner of 23rd Street, details the long and varied history of the site. **The Fifth Avenue Hotel** on the site was the most luxurious in the city when it was completed in 1859. Earlier in the 19th century, there was a post tavern used for changing horses, and later a road house, known as Corporal Thompson's Madison Cottage. The *New York Herald* of May 9, 1847, carried the following notice about the inn:

> MADISON COTTAGE—*This beautiful place of resort opposite Madison Square, corner of Twenty-Third Street and Broadway, is open for the season, and Palmer's omnibuses drive to the door. It is one of the most agreeable spots for an afternoon's lounge in the suburbs of our city. Go and see!*

In 1853, Franconi's Hippodrome replaced the Cottage, offering a variety of public entertainment in an open-air arena, which included chariot races and circus performances.

The elegant dining salon of the subsequent Fifth Avenue Hotel was a favorite gathering place for the financial and political bigwigs of the day. A nightly spectacle at the main entrance was the steady procession of flashy carriages with matched teams of horses, bringing such giants as Jay Gould, "Jim" Fisk, "Larry" Jerome, Commodore Vanderbilt, and "Boss" Tweed. The powerful politico "Tom" Platt—credited with Theodore Roosevelt's presidential victory in 1898—held court before a coterie of adulating yes-men near the bar, in his so-called "Amen Corner." O. Henry, in his *Voice of the City,* vividly described the life and spirit of the times. The Hotel was also frequented by Mark Twain, Edwin Booth, William Cullen Bryant, and Stanford White.

Cross Fifth Avenue to the park.

23. The Statue of William Henry Seward, by Randolph Rogers, was unveiled in 1876. As U.S. Senator from New York before the Civil War, and later as Lincoln's Secretary of State, Seward so distinguished himself as a statesman that President

Madison Square ca. 1916 is no longer dominated by the "Garden" but by the Metropolitan Life Insurance Company buildings rising on the east side. Horse-drawn vehicles are still plentiful, but the age of the motorcar has already begun. (Metropolitan Life Insurance Company.)

Andrew Johnson retained him in his own cabinet. A wise choice indeed, as Seward foresaw the importance of Alaska and was responsible for its purchase. The statue, however, was not well received. One critic proclaimed that "Mr. Seward was a man 'all head and no legs,' whereas the statue represents the statesman with unusual length and prominence,"—an observation that lent credence to the legend that the statue originally was not Seward, but *Abraham Lincoln Signing the Emancipation Proclamation!* However, this is only partially true, although the legend persists from one guidebook to another. When Rogers completed a statue of Lincoln for Philadelphia's Fairmount Park, there were striking similarities between the two figures, and gossipers claimed that to save money he used the same figure twice. The fact of the matter is that the subscription committee for the Seward statue was unable to come up with the sculptor's full fee. So, with a few changes in body details, some repositioning of limbs, and the alteration of the Emancipation Proclamation to fit the size of the Alaska Purchase agreement, including the signature pen, Rogers was able to recycle the statue. Seward was the first New Yorker to be honored with a public monument.

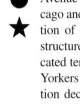

24. Directly across 23rd Street, in the triangle formed by the confluence of Fifth Avenue and Broadway, stands the striking **Flatiron Building.** Newly arrived from Chicago and his successful participation in the planning of the World's Columbian Exposition of 1893, Daniel H. Burnham designed this innovative and daring commercial structure in the Italian Renaissance style. With a towering steel framework and rusticated terra-cotta walls in the shape of an enormous flatiron, it startled even blasé New Yorkers when it was completed in 1902. Visitors at first shunned the rooftop observation deck, predicting that strong winds would soon topple "Burnham's Folly." With fears allayed by the passage of time, the panoramic view attracted crowds of sightseers. On a clear day, the New Jersey Palisades and Coney Island's beaches were easily visible. Although originally designated the Fuller Building, popular insistence on calling it by what it resembled forced the owners to yield and make the building's nickname official. It is now a designated landmark. Note the ornate yet restrained façade, whose undulating walls and sharp corners, topped by a classic cornice, result in a dramatic perspective. The protuberance on the ground floor extending toward 23rd Street was added a few years later, and was dubbed "the cow-catcher." Look up at the top where two stone cherubs look down on the street below. These are recent reproductions of the original pair that disappeared in 1988. The Landmarks Commission required that the present owners replace them, and the task fell to Betty Martin, an artist and theatrical set designer, who modeled her work on a fuzzy photograph from the 1920s.

The busy intersection in front of the Flatiron Building has always been a particularly windy spot, and in the era when skirts trailed on the ground, it was a favorite vantage point for girl-watchers hoping for a glimpse of a trim ankle. It is said that nearby traffic policemen would turn from their task of untangling the confusion of horsecars, omnibuses, wagons, and carriages, to shoo away these young voyeurs—hence the expression, "Twenty-Three Skidoo!"

End of tour. The N and R 23rd Street station is at the corner. The No. 6 line is two blocks east at 23rd Street and Park Avenue South.

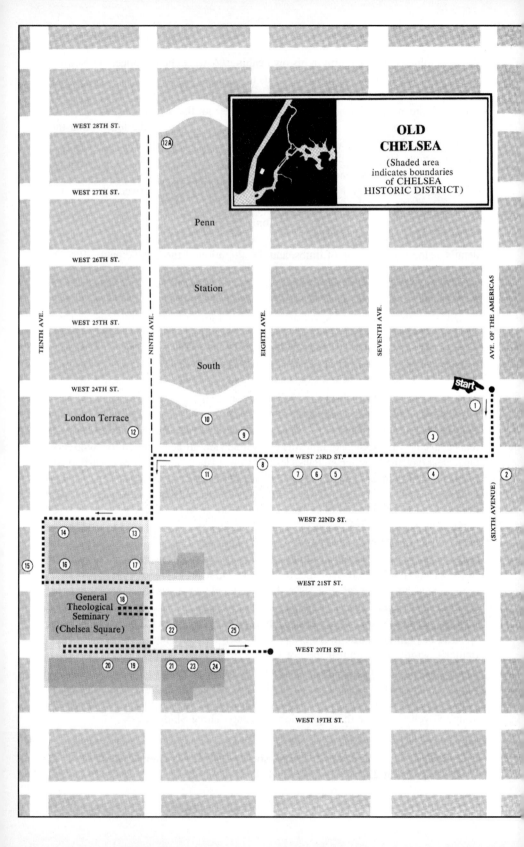

11. Old Chelsea

[Subways: 1, 2, F, V, PATH to 23rd Street. Buses: M5, M6, M7, M20 to 23rd Street.]

The neighborhood now encompassed by 14th to 30th streets and Avenue of the Americas to the Hudson River was rural farmland in 1750 when Captain Thomas Clarke bought a tract of land there and named it after the Chelsea Royal Hospital, an old soldiers' home built by Sir Christopher Wren in the Chelsea borough of London.

It was Clarke's grandson, however, who was to bring fame to Chelsea and immortality to himself. A professor of classics and biblical literature at General Theological Seminary, **Clement Clarke Moore** is remembered less for his scholarly *Compendious Lexicon of the Hebrew Language* than for his inspired poem, "A Visit from St. Nicholas," composed in 1822 while he was driving in a sleigh from the lower city, bringing goodies for the Christmas dinner. In addition to popularizing Santa Claus, Moore did much to influence the development and character of the neighborhood through foresight and wise urban planning. He served as vestryman at St. Luke's Church in Greenwich (Village), and was a founder of St. Peter's Church in Chelsea. He also donated the land for the General Theological Seminary and established guidelines for local residential zoning that in great measure contributed to the charming atmosphere of much of Chelsea today.

Moore is buried in uptown Trinity Church Cemetery (155th Street and Riverside Drive), where, every Christmas Eve, a candlelight procession of children carolers lays a wreath on the grave of the author of "'Twas the night before Christmas...." (Recent studies indicate that Moore may not have been the author of the revered poem.)

By the mid-19th century Chelsea had grown into a peaceful residential area. Only the chugging of the locomotives of the Hudson River Rail Road on Eleventh Avenue, and the rattling Eighth Avenue horsecar—Chelsea's first "rapid" transit—disturbed the quiet of the streets. But the tranquility of the neighborhood was shattered some 20 years later with the arrival of the city's liveliest entertainment district. Once-sedate 23rd Street now echoed to the sounds of music halls and late-night revelers. The Ninth Avenue El, the city's first overhead railway, pushed through the Chelsea district in 1871, and the noisy steam-driven trains competed with the furor of iron-tire dray wagons, horse-drawn omnibuses, and clanging bells of a proliferating network of horsecar lines. Along Sixth Avenue, a new and enormous shopping center was developing, as huge, palatial department stores opened their doors in what was to be the most popular retail district in the city. A year later the Sixth Avenue El added its roar to the growing clamor, and in the shadow of the El, at 30th Street, the "Haymarket" enjoyed the reputation of being the most-raided den of vice in the city's history.

As the century drew to a close, a new dimension was added to Chelsea with the birth of the motion-picture industry, as studios ground out silents in enormous, barnlike buildings east of Sixth Avenue.

Chelsea has become relatively quiet again. The music halls are all gone, the theaters have moved uptown, the great department stores either folded or relocated elsewhere, the film industry discovered Hollywood, and the Els were sent as scrap iron to Japan. And with the departure of commerce, the neighborhood began to decline. The lovely row houses deteriorated, and the area took on an air of neglect and decay. Then, at the last minute, Chelsea received a reprieve. With the shortage of housing and skyrocketing real-estate values, a new population entered the scene. Writers, actors, advertising executives, teachers, and other professionals discovered Chelsea and began buying up the aging town houses, restoring them with loving care. Overnight a "restoration revolution" began and the neighborhood has once again become an eminently desirable place to live—and just minutes from the heart of town. The designation by the Landmarks Commission of a part of Chelsea as a Historic District has added even greater impetus to maintaining the appearance and traditions of this charming quarter.

Many vestiges of the past are still to be seen: the old department store buildings, bits and pieces of the old theater district, several lovely churches, the delightful campus of the General Theological Seminary, and the row upon row of splendid town houses. But the special quality of Chelsea—still very much in evidence on almost every block—is the charming 19th-century atmosphere, all within the shadow of midtown Manhattan.

The tour begins at the corner of Avenue of the Americas (Sixth Avenue) and West 24th Street.

1. The small red brick building on the southwest corner (best seen from across the street) is all that remains of one of the most popular entertainment spots of the gaslit era, Koster & Bial's Concert Hall. The hall itself used to face 23rd Street, and is long since gone, but this structure, once the beer-garden annex, was known as **The Corner.** Its name still survives in the upper cornice, and is the sole reminder of a once frenetic entertainment career.

Koster & Bial's opened in 1879, and was probably the liveliest vaudeville house in town. Here Victor Herbert conducted his 40-piece orchestra, and between the music, the free-flowing liquor, and imported talent, the Concert Hall became *the* place during the "Naughty '90s." Seeking a larger theater and anticipating another uptown move by the entertainment district, Koster & Bial closed their popular establishment and entered into a short-lived partnership with impresario-composer Oscar Hammerstein at his 34th Street Manhattan Opera House (on the present site of Macy's). The relationship was tempestuous at best, and ended in a court battle that saw the exit from "show biz" of Koster & Bial, while Hammerstein's star continued to rise.

2. On the southeast corner of 23rd Street and Sixth Avenue from 1869 to 1883 stood the **Edwin Booth Theater,** with Booth himself as manager and frequent star performer. In spite of brother John Wilkes Booth's assassination of President Lincoln, Edwin remained one of the country's most popular actors. When James W. McCreery, known as the "Dean of the Retail Trade," acquired the site, he demolished the theater and erected his second department store. (The first still stands at Broadway and 11th Street, a cast-iron building converted into an apartment house.) In 1907 the firm moved uptown again, but his building remained until 1975. [For a detailed description of the department stores of the gaslit era, *see* Ladies' Mile.]

On the northeast corner stands the **Masonic Building** (Harry P. Knowles, 1911), a 19-story brick and limestone office building. The various commercial tenants help support the charitable works of the Masons, an international fraternal order with origins in the Middle Ages in England and Scotland. The first Masonic lodge in New York City was founded in 1739. Around the corner, on West 24th Street, is **Masonic Hall** (Harry P. Knowles, 1905; restored 1986–96).

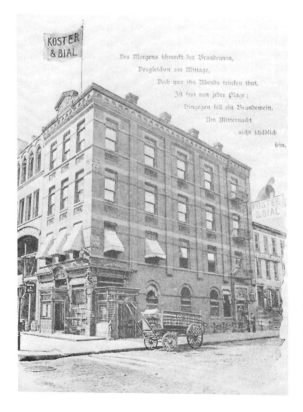

Koster & Bial's "The Corner," a beer-hall annex to the famous 23rd Street Music Hall, still stands at the southwest corner of Sixth Avenue and 24th Street. This photo was taken in 1904. (Museum of the City of New York)

Within are the Grand Lodge Room, an ornate auditorium, and twelve elaborately decorated ceremonial rooms. The Livingston Masonic Library is open to the public 8:30 A.M. to 4:30 P.M. Tours are available 11:00 A.M. to 3:00 P.M. Use the 71 West 23rd Street entrance.

Across the avenue, on the southwest corner, is a small cast-iron building that once housed **Riker's Drug Company** and was later absorbed into the Liggett Drug chain. When the building suffered a disastrous fire, it was rebuilt by the owners and restored (except for the cornice) to its original appearance.

Ehrich Brothers, another of the great emporiums, faced both 23rd Street and Sixth Avenue, surrounding Riker's corner. It gave up the ghost in 1911.

Cross to the north side of 23rd Street and walk west.

At. No. 118, the **Milan** apartment building (Der Scutt, 1988) presents an interesting break in the building line with its deeply recessed balconies and false gables.

3. At what is now No. 135 West was **Proctor's Twenty-Third Street Music Hall.** Another of the great vaudeville showplaces, Proctor's opened in 1888, in a large Flemish-style building, packing them in with such topflight stars as "Jersey Lily" Langtry; the inimitable Lillian Russell; Scotland's idol Harry Lauder; female impersonator Julian Eltinge; Eva Tanguay, the "I Don't Care" girl; and

Proctor's became the most famous music hall in the city when it opened in 1888, and featured only topflight entertainers. In this Byron photograph, taken ca. 1910, Lillian Russell is the starred performer. (The J. Clarence Davies Collection, Museum of the City of New York)

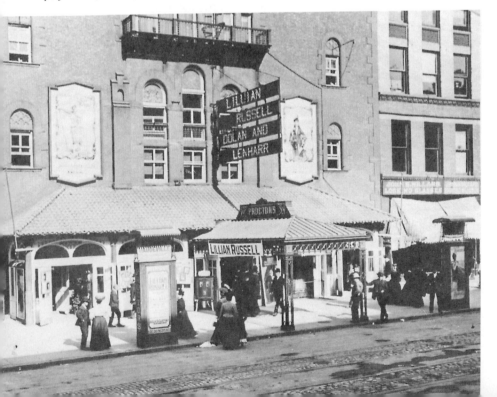

sparkling Lottie Collins, who never failed to stop the show cold with her rendition of "Ta Ra Ra BOOM De Ay!" E. F. Proctor later opened other theaters throughout the city as well as out of town, and when he died, his chain was sold to R.K.O. for a reported $16 million.

4. Continue west on 23rd Street, noting **No. 148–156,** a large Gothic Revival–style former commercial building, converted to a condo, named Chelsea Mews. Note the attractive façade of The **Traffic Building,** No. 163 (Abraham Fisher, 1927), with its diagonally laid bricks in a rich tapestry of orange, brown and umber, with complementary terra cotta.

The Muhlenberg Branch of the New York Public Library, at No. 209, was designed by Carrère & Hastings in 1906, and has served the Chelsea area for nearly a century. The three-story brick and limestone structure was built with funds given to the city by Andrew Carnegie and is named for William Augustus Muhlenberg, the first rector of the former Church of the Holy Communion, at Sixth Avenue and West 20th Street. [*See* Ladies' Mile, 14.] His personal collection of books formed the core of the library's first holdings. No. 215 is the recent site of the McBurney Branch of the Y.M.C.A., built in 1904 from plans by Parish & Schroeder. It was named for Robert Ross McBurney, a 19th-century Irish immigrant who became a leader in the Young Men's Christian Association movement. The "Y" moved in late 2002 to a spanking new facility at 125 West 14th Street. The present building is scheduled for conversion to condominiums.

5. On the south side of the street, midway between Seventh and Eighth avenues, is a proud survivor of the quarter's Golden Age—the striking **Hotel Chelsea** (No. 222). When opened in 1883 as a cooperative apartment house, it was a most luxurious address for those well-to-do artists who sought a quiet and elegant atmosphere to inspire creativity. In 1905 it became a hotel, and its guest register through the years reads like an artistic and literary *Who's Who*. Notice the bronze plaques honoring such greats as Mark Twain, Thomas Wolfe, Dylan Thomas, and Brendan Behan. Other notables who have graced the Hotel Chelsea are O. Henry, Sarah Bernhardt, Lillian Russell, Edgar Lee Masters,* John Sloan, Larry Rivers, James T. Farrell, Arthur Miller, Tennessee Williams, Virgil Thomson, Jackson Pollock, Willem de Kooning, and Yevgeny Yevtushenko. It was Andy Warhol, though, who brought the Chelsea to the world of moviegoers when he filmed artist Brigid Polk in her hotel room. This formed the basis for his screen classic, *The Chelsea Girls*, thought to be Warhol's best film and his first financial triumph. The hotel also figured in the British film *Sid and Nancy*.

Designed by Hubert, Pirsson & Company in a style that has been described as Queen Anne or Victorian Gothic, its outstanding architectural features are its exuberant roofline with dormers and tall chimneys, and its richly ornamented iron balconies and interior grand staircase. The labels at the base show that the iron was cast by the J. B. & J. M. Cornell Iron Works. When built, its 11 stories made

---

*Edgar Lee Masters, known mainly for his *Spoon River Anthology* (1915), also wrote a short poem entitled "The Hotel Chelsea":

> Today will pass as currents of the air that veer and die.
> Tell me how souls can be
> Such flames of suffering and of ecstasy.
> Then fare as the winds fare?

it one of the tallest structures in the city. Studios were added on the roof, making it the first such building to have duplexes. It also boasted the first penthouse in town. The lobby has been altered considerably and now doubles as a contemporary art gallery, presided over by managing director Stanley Bard, himself a patron of the arts. The broad iron staircase, which used to open with a wide sweep into the lobby, has been closed off at the ground-floor level because of fire laws. Its ten-story spiral ascent to the roof can, however, be admired from the second floor. Time has been kind to the old dowager. Its Edwardian charm still remains, just as faithfully as its worldwide devoted clientele.

6. The synagogue **Congregation Emunath Israel** ("Faith of Israel"), at No. 236–238, occupies the former house of worship of the Third Reformed Presbyterian Church. Founded in 1863 on West 18th Street, the Orthodox Jewish congregation ultimately relocated here in 1920. It plays an important role in the Chelsea Jewish community, offering counseling, meals, and job placement for the homeless.

7. No. 252–256, a **Cineplex Odeon theater,** sits on the **site of Cavanagh's Restaurant,** which opened in 1876. A favorite dining spot for the elite in the heyday of Chelsea's entertainment era, it hosted such personalities as Lillian Russell, "Diamond Jim" Brady, and John L. Sullivan. It was also the hangout of powerful turn-of-the-century Tammany Hall politicians. The exclusive establishment fell on hard times and closed its gaslit-era dining room in 1970.

8. The intersection of Eighth Avenue and West 23rd Street marks the approximate **site of the original Thomas Clarke house.** The farm, named "Chelsea," was situated between the Fitzroy Road (which ran parallel to and just west of Eighth Avenue) and the Hudson River, from 19th to 24th streets. The Fritzroy Road was the principal north-south thoroughfare and began about two blocks south, at Love Lane, between the present 21st and 22nd streets. Love Lane ran east to the Albany Post Road (later Bloomingdale Road; now Broadway), the only route to the lower city. When the Clarke house burned down in 1777, his widow had it rebuilt farther west, on a bluff overlooking the Hudson, between the present Ninth and Tenth avenues. Two years later, a grandson, Clement Clarke Moore, was born there.

9. When Pike's Opera House opened on the northwest corner in 1868 with a performance of Verdi's *Il Trovatore,* it was an instant success…so successful that financiers Jay Gould and Jim Fisk bought it within the year. They changed its name to **The Grand Opera-House** and enlarged its repertoire to include all kinds of theatrical entertainment. Some of the productions were tailor-made for the talents of Josie Mansfield, Fisk's mistress. Josie lived in an adjacent mansion, connected to the Opera-House by an underground tunnel. The two partners even moved the offices of their Erie Railway into the theater. Next year, when Fisk and Gould attempted to corner the gold market, causing the "Black Friday" panic, it is said that Fisk, himself in a panic, hid in the vault of the Opera-House to avoid the wrath of the surging crowds. In the meantime, Josie, tiring of "Jubilee" Jim, began taking up with a former partner of his, Edward S. Stokes. This led to a series of lovers' quarrels and a sensational lawsuit, all paraded across the front pages of New York's dailies. An angry Stokes then waylaid Fisk on the staircase of the old Grand Central Hotel on January 6, 1872, and shot him twice with a revolver. Fisk died the following day, and as one of the most influential politicos

The Grand Opera-House, on the northwest corner of 23rd Street and Eighth Avenue, was not only a theater, but also the headquarters of Jim Fisk's Erie Railway. After Fisk was shot by Edward S. Stokes over a lovers' quarrel and lawsuit in 1872, the Opera House was taken over by Jay Gould. The Grand Opera-House later featured silent films and degenerated into a second-rate movie house, falling under the wrecker's ball in 1960. (The J. Clarence Davies Collection, Museum of the City of New York)

in the city, was given a state funeral. Stokes was convicted after several trials and served four years in prison. Jay Gould continued to operate the theater for a number of years. During the first decade of the 20th century, the Opera-House inaugurated the "Subway Circuit," offering first-run productions shortly after their initial Broadway openings. By World War I, the theater, like so many of its contemporaries, switched to silent films with vaudeville, and continued as a movie house until 1960, when it was demolished to make way for the sprawling Penn Station South housing development.

10. Penn Station South (Eighth to Ninth avenues, 23rd to 29th streets) was built in 1962 from plans by Herman Jessor by the ILGWU (International Ladies' Garment Workers Union) as a middle-income housing co-op. Appropriately close to the Garment District, this mammoth urban-renewal project occupies 12 square blocks of former tenements and injected new life into the Chelsea area.

11. The solid-looking Classic-style building, **No. 322–324,** was built for the American Jersey Cattle Club. Look above for the stone escutcheons that represent the U.S. and the British island of Jersey. In recent years additional floors were added, and the building was converted to a condominium. A Citibank branch now occupies the ground floor.

The **Stribling, Wells & Gay (formerly James N. Wells) Real Estate Company,** at No. 340, is the oldest of its kind in Chelsea and dates back to 1819, when Wells began developing parts of Greenwich Village and later worked with Clement Clarke Moore on plans for Chelsea. He was also a skillful builder and was responsible for the construction of St. Luke's Church in Greenwich Village (where both Wells and Moore served as vestrymen). (More about James N. Wells later.) Step inside the entryway of this attractive, but much renovated 1849 brick row house to see a display of historic documents and photos.

12. Before the construction of the present **London Terrace Apartments** (occupying the entire block, Ninth to Tenth avenues, 23rd to 24th streets) in 1930, an earlier "London Terrace" stood on the site. Designed by famed architect Alexander Jackson Davis in 1845, the original row of Greek Revival buildings was set back from the street behind a shady garden and protected by an iron fence. A three-story-high colonnade ran the entire length of the row, giving the town houses an air of stately elegance. With the wealth of its prominent tenants, London Terrace was soon known as "Millionaires' Row." On the 24th Street side was a similar row of town houses, but only two stories high, called the Chelsea Cottages.

The new complex, built by Farrar & Watmaugh, is in reality two separate rows of interconnecting apartment buildings surrounding a central garden. In addition to the 1,670 units, there is a swimming pool, solarium, a number of stores, a bank, and a post office. When the new London Terrace opened in 1930, the doormen were uniformed as London "bobbies"—a touch of charming snobbery. After all, Chelsea was a London suburb, and this was thought to add upliftment to the area.

The **Clement Clarke Moore residence** stood alone in the block to the south until 1854 when land development forced the demolition of the large three-story house. (A plaque on No. 420 marks the site.) Dr. Moore spent his summers in Chelsea, his winters on Charlton Street in Greenwich Village, and occasionally stayed at a third home in the village of Newtown (now Elmhurst) in what is now the Borough of Queens.

The **Ninth Avenue Elevated,** which clattered overhead until 1940, was the first of three els erected over Manhattan streets and also the first to be razed. (The other two were erected over Second and Third avenues.) Originally constructed by Charles Harvey and his West Side and Yonkers Patent Railway Company in 1867, it employed a steam-driven cable system on a 30-foot-high elevated iron track over Greenwich Street, running first from Battery Park to Dey Street. The unreliable cables were soon replaced by tiny, but more efficient, steam locomotives by the newly organized New York Elevated Railway Company, and the line gradually pushed northward over Ninth Avenue. The system switched to electricity in 1902, extended up to 155th Street, and was acquired by the Interborough Rapid Transit (which constructed the first subway line) the following year.

12A. An optional side trip may be made to the landmark **Church of the Holy Apostles,** at Ninth Avenue and 28th Street. The church, designed by noted architect Minard Lafever in 1848–49, is quite handsome but fits into no particular architectural style; although some say it was a forerunner of the Italianate. Dominating the structure is the greatly oversized bronze and slate steeple, yet it is not incongruous among the towering apartment houses that surround it. Most attractive are the splendid stained-glass windows by William Jay Bolton, America's greatest stained-glass artisan of the time. The square glass panels with delicately painted circular medallions present a dazzling spectacle when brightened by the rays of a late afternoon sun. The transepts were added in 1858, and were designed by another well-known architect, Richard Upjohn (& Sons). For more than 20 years the church has been operating a soup kitchen for the poor.

In April 1990 the church suffered a devastating fire. Some of the magnificent Bolton stained-glass windows were lost and many were severely damaged, including the rose window. The church then undertook a major restoration project, including a careful replication of the missing glass. By the summer of 1993 work was completed, and once again the interior glistens in the afternoon sunlight.

A rare view of the original London Terrace, on West 23rd Street between Ninth and Tenth avenues, designed in 1845 by Alexander Jackson Davis, and known then as "Millionaires' Row." A year after this photo was taken in 1929, the "Row," no longer favored by millionaires, was demolished, and the new London Terrace Apartments were built. The old Ninth Avenue El in the background, as well as the crosstown trolley, are also gone. (The Consolidated Edison Company of New York)

The house of Clement Clarke Moore, author of "'Twas the Night before Christmas...," which stood alone on high ground between Ninth and Tenth avenues, 22nd to 23rd Street, until 1854, in a lithograph from Valentine's Manual *of the same year. (Museum of the City of New York)*

Return to 23rd Street and continue south. Turn west (right) on 22nd Street. The tour route now enters the Chelsea Historic District.

13. Nos. 400–412, built in 1856 in the Italianate style, are known as the **James N. Wells Row.** These narrow houses were each designed with an English basement and small entranceways, and form a harmonious unit with their original roof cornice. All but one still retain their dormer windows; No. 408 is probably the best in the row, except for its modified windows; however, only No. 404 has its original doors.

Nos. 419–421, on the north side, were also built in 1856.

No. 414 (1835) dates from the decade of the Greek Revival, and was the residence of James N. Wells. An elegant mansion in its heyday, it is the last surviving Greek Revival house with five bays (windows) in Manhattan. (Note plaque.) It was remodeled 1864–66 in Italianate style, and in 1875 it was sold to the Samaritan Home for the Aged. In the 1930s the Salvation Army acquired it for a women's shelter. It is now a nicely restored multiple-dwelling house.

No. 436 was the **residence of actor Edwin Forrest** [*see* East Village, 16, for more about Edwin Forrest and the Astor Place Riot]. Built in 1835 in Greek Revival style, it was bought by Forrest in 1839 together with the adjoining properties, Nos. 430–434. It was rumored that Forrest wanted the house as a sanctuary from his numerous in-laws who had moved in with him and his new bride when he lived downtown. Some years later the house was acquired by Christian Herter, the former Secretary of State. Sadly, the house has suffered too many "modernizations" through the years and is now barely a shadow of its former self.

No. 444 (1835–36) is a restored Greek Revival–style house, and was the property of Clement Clarke Moore. Note particularly the charming attic windows set in a wooden frieze (fascia) board below the cornice.

Nos. 446 and **448,** the Berrian-Walker Houses, were built in 1854 in the popular Italianate style of the middle decade of the 19th century. No. 448 unfortunately suffered a major renovation when its front wall was reconstructed with the addition of one bay per floor, as with No. 446.

No. 450 is a handsome Greek Revival house with a high stoop and typical basement windows. It has been very nicely refurbished and restored to its original appearance. It is gratifying to see a building correctly remodeled, rather than the more common "remuddled."

No. 453, across the street, is from the mid-1850s and has interesting ornate hooded lintels over the windows. **Nos. 457–477** are a splendidly restored row.

The L. Monette apartment building, **No. 454,** was built in 1897 in a neo-Renaissance style, and although a multifamily residence, is not an unpleasant addition to the street.

At the northeast corner of Tenth Avenue and West 22nd Street, the shiny chrome and black **Empire Diner** is an unmistakable presence. Unlike the original diners that were converted trolley-cars or railroad coaches that had evolved from horse-drawn working-class lunch wagons, according to historian Joyce Mendelsohn, this eatery was manufactured by the Fodero Dining Car Company and brought here in 1929, and boasts a history of celebrity patrons, including Franklin D. Roosevelt, Charles E. Lindbergh, Babe Ruth, Albert Einstein, Barbra Streisand, and Madonna. Look for the shiny winged clock above the counter, the trademark of the Fodero Company.

Actor Edwin Forrest purchased this stately town house (No. 436 West 22nd Street) four years after it was built in 1835, allegedly as a sanctuary from bothersome in-laws. In more recent times it was the home of former Secretary of State Christian Herter. Unfortunately, a series of mindless "modernizations" have all but obscured its original appearance. (Museum of the City of New York)

The interior of No. 436 West 22nd Street after Edwin Forrest's death, when it was owned by I. W. Drummond at the turn of the century. (Museum of the City of New York)

14. Clement Clarke Moore Park, on the southeast corner, was designed by landscape architect Paul M. Friedberg as a multilevel play park, opened in 1968.

Turn left (south) on Tenth Avenue.

Before the successive landfill projects of the 19th century, the Hudson River shoreline extended to where the east side of Tenth Avenue is now. As the streets and avenues were pushed through, the hills were leveled, and the earth was used to reclaim the land to the west.

15. The Guardian Angel Roman Catholic Church (John Van Pelt, 1930), known familiarly as the Shrine Church of the Sea, was built in a fanciful Italian Romanesque Revival style when the port of New York was much busier than it is now, and when much of the church's constituency came from the ships from far-flung parts of the world. It still serves a sea-oriented community. An earlier church, a grouping of three private houses, was built in 1888 on West 23rd Street west of Tenth Avenue. They were razed in 1929 for the construction of the New York Central Railroad (elevated) West Side Freight Line (now mostly demolished). In return, the railroad financed the construction of the present church complex. The city is now considering converting the old elevated freight line into a public promenade.

On the east side of the avenue, **No. 188–192** (Andrew Spence, 1891) is a well-kept small tenement built in the Queen Anne style, still preserving its original storefronts. Note the oversize spandrels running the full height of the building, which may have covered chimney flues.

Turn east (left) on West 21st Street, also called Chelsea Square North.

A pleasant feature of the north side of the street is the set-back arrangement of the houses, with a lush front yard complementing the dignified "halls of ivy" of the General Theological Seminary, across the street.

16. Nos. **473–465** are a well-preserved row of Greek Revival–style houses, built in the year 1853. **No. 471** is the best in the group, closest to the original design. Note the following architectural features of the houses: the bracketed entablature over the doorways, bracketed roof cornices, double-hung windows, the window lintels and window guards, cruciform paneled doors, and low stoops with cast-iron railings. Note the old Chelsea Square house numbers.

No. 463 was the first to be built on the block (1836) and dates from the Greek Revival period. Its brickwork is laid in Flemish bond (alternating short and long bricks, called "headers" and "stretchers"). Pedimented lintels cap the windows, and the attic windows are set in a wooden fascia board.

Nos. 461–459, two rowhouses converted to apartments, were built separately in 1854. The pair is called the William Cummings House after a descendant of the original owner of No. 461, Thomas Cummings, and both are typical brownstones in the Italianate style. Compare them with adjacent **457** and **455.** The latter two, built in the same year, are of a somewhat different style. Note the difference in height of the stoops. Thoughtless renovations over the years have destroyed the symmetry of the row of houses.

No. 453 (1857) still preserves its splendid entranceway. Crowning the stoop with its cast-iron railings is an arched doorway, above which a huge cornice slab rests on stuccoed consoles. The house has been listed on the National Register of Historic Places.

No. 445 (1898) is another neo-Renaissance–style apartment house. Built of Roman brick and stone, it is typical of the so-called Eclectic Period of the late 1890s. **No. 441** has been carefully restored and maintained.

The brownstone doorway of **No. 407** (1852) is well preserved, although little else on the façade is. Note the carved head in the keystone of the arch and the doorway pediment supported by a pair of ornate consoles.

No. 405, the last in the row of set-back houses, has been refaced with "brownstone" concrete which thoroughly destroyed all the former Italianate features. How this disaster escaped the watchful eye of the Landmarks Commission is a mystery, especially since the Commission had called it "one of the purest examples of this style in Chelsea."

17. Delightful No. 401, listed officially as **No. 183 Ninth Avenue,** was built in 1831–32, and is the second oldest house in the Historic District. It still preserves much of its original Federal-style appearance, and can best be viewed from across the street. The four-sided pitched roof, dormer windows, simple cornice above an equally simple fascia board, and side entrance are typical elements of the Federal style. The brickwork is in Flemish bond, the more expensive way of laying bricks, evidence of a wealthy original owner. Look up at the painted sign on adjacent No. 191 Ninth Avenue, advertising the James N. Wells & Son Real Estate firm. Wells lived in No. 183 in 1833–34 and maintained his office on the second floor, where his descendants carried on for many years. The sign itself is probably over 100 years old. The ground-floor store was incorporated into the building very early in 1835.

The three small wooden houses to the right, **Nos. 185, 187,** and **189,** were all built for Wells, No. 185 in 1856, the other pair in 1857. Wooden houses are now a rarity in Manhattan, and these three, while not as old as they appear, add considerable charm. In 1934 the Wells office moved to the 23rd Street site. Turn south on Ninth Avenue.

18. The General Theological Seminary, No. 175 Ninth Avenue, occupies the entire block from Ninth to Tenth avenues, and 21st to 20th streets. The plot, known as **Chelsea Square,** was donated to the seminary by Dr. Clement Clarke Moore, himself a professor of Biblical Learning at the institution. The lovely campus with its shady lawns and small-town college atmosphere is a veritable oasis in the city; it is open to the public Mon.–Fri. 12 P.M. to 3:00 P.M., Sat. 11 A.M. to 3:00 P.M., closed Sunday.

The modern building facing Ninth Avenue houses the administrative offices and the excellent St. Mark's Library; but one must first pass through the large entranceway into the inner quadrangle to appreciate the old-world quality of the campus.

Construction of the Episcopal Seminary began in 1825 with a Gothic-style East Building (now demolished), and was followed in 1836 by a counterpart on the west side, which still remains as a fine academic building. Early seminarians

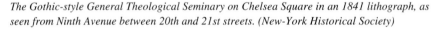

The Gothic-style General Theological Seminary on Chelsea Square in an 1841 lithograph, as seen from Ninth Avenue between 20th and 21st streets. (New-York Historical Society)

had an unobstructed view of the Hudson, as the riverbank reached the western edge of Chelsea Square. The completion of most of the seminary complex was accomplished during the brief period 1883–1902, when Eugene Augustus Hoffman, the third dean of the school, revolutionized the physical setting by engaging architect Charles Coolidge Haight to create a master plan for a campus equal to that of most American colleges of the day. Through Hoffman's own financial contributions and his ability to interest wealthy laymen, an endowment was established for professorships and the groundwork laid for the development of a great theological library.

The **St. Mark's Library,** which was completed in 1960, replaced Haight's original building and contains 210,000 volumes in its extensive reference collection. It is the **nation's greatest ecclesiastical library** and has the largest collection of Latin Bibles in the world! Among the Rare Book Room's treasures are a number of medieval manuscripts, prayer books, and psalters, and a unique Latin choir book that honors John Hus as a martyr.

Haight's plan called for an arrangement of buildings roughly in the shape of a letter "E" with the spine along West 21st Street. The style of construction was one that he himself pioneered, the English Collegiate Gothic. Centrally placed is the **Chapel of the Good Shepherd,** dominated by a 161-foot-high square **Bell Tower** modeled after that at Magdalen College, Oxford. Interestingly, the interior of the chapel is devoted mainly to choir stalls, since most of the communicants are postulants for Holy Orders. The spectacular bronze doors, by J. Massey Rhind, were executed in 1899, in memory of Dean Hoffman's son.

Sherred Hall, a three-story classroom building flanked by dormitories, was the first to be erected, and expresses beautifully the simple quality and uniform character sought by the architect. Its arched main entrance is especially noteworthy.

The culmination of the building plan came with the opening of handsome **Hoffman Hall,** the refectory-gymnasium building. The enormous dining hall, like a medieval knights' council chamber, re-creates an atmosphere of the Middle Ages. The huge fireplaces at each end, a musicians' gallery, a coffered barrel-vaulted ceiling, and a stained-glass bay window, combine to make it one of New York City's most beautiful interior spaces.

On leaving the Seminary grounds, turn right, and right again into West 20th Street.

19. No. 402, a Renaissance-style apartment house, was designed in 1897 by C. P. H. Gilbert, the architect of mansions for Felix Warburg (Jewish Museum), Joseph A. De Lamar (Polish Consulate), and Otto Kahn (Convent of the Sacred Heart), and a host of other well-heeled clients. The name "DONAC" is an acronym for the original land owner, Don Alonzo Cushman. Tenants have a pleasant view down West 20th Street through their large concave bay windows.

No. 404 is the oldest house in the Historic District. Built in 1829–30, it still retains one clapboard side wall. A Federal-style house, it later received a Greek Revival doorway, had its roof raised one story, and in the 1850s was modified with Italianate parlor-floor windows.

An 1854 engraving of Gothic Revival row houses that once lined 20th Street at the corner of Sixth Avenue before the arrival of the parade of Fashion Row department stores. (Museum of the City of New York)

20. Nos. 406–418, built for Don Alonzo Cushman in 1839–40, rank among the most beautiful Greek Revival rows of town houses in the country. Equal in many respects to "The Row" on Washington Square North [*see* Greenwich Village, 3, 5], this group of seven pristine houses, called **"Cushman Row,"** displays a wealth of architectural detail. The ten-foot front yards are a most agreeable complement to the greenery of the Seminary across the street. No. 408 has been nicely restored, except for the gable. Notice the pineapples atop the newels in front of Nos. 416 and 418, a traditional symbol of welcome. Exceptional are the charming attic windows encircled by cast-iron wreaths. Note, too, the well proportioned entablatures over the doorways, set on Doric pilasters, the molded window lintels and the six-over-six windows, typical elements of the Green Revival style. (Best seen from across the street.)

Don Alonzo Cushman (1792–1875) was a successful dry-goods merchant ("Don" *was* his first name, not a title) who became associated with Clement Clarke Moore and James N. Wells. He was a founder of the Greenwich Savings Bank—one of the first savings institutions in the city. With his later involvement in real estate, he helped influence the development and shape the character of the Chelsea neighborhood.

Return to Ninth Avenue.

21. The large Greek Revival–style house on the southeast corner, **No. 162 Ninth Avenue,** was a long-time residence of James N. Wells (he lived briefly at No. 414–416 West 22nd Street, and his offices were seen earlier at No. 183 Ninth Avenue). Built in 1834, it was one of the most imposing residences in Chelsea. Although somewhat modified, it still retains its original wide doorway, fluted Doric columns topped by a large entablature, and pedimented window lintels. The rambling, former *one*-family mansion is now a co-op occupied by many.

Cross Ninth Avenue and continue east on West 20th Street.

22. The group of four Italianate buildings on the north side of West 20th Street **(Nos. 361–355)** was built for Don Alonzo Cushman. No. 361 was built in 1860, the other three in 1858. Although somewhat altered, they present a fine row of houses. The late 19th-century ironwork on the stoops is very attractive, as are the rope moldings on the inner doorways. No. 353 still preserves its original ornate cast-iron railings. Note the dormers, too.

23. On the south side, another Italianate row **(Nos. 348–358)** was built in 1853–54 for the six children of James N. Wells. Each house is only two bays wide and set behind a small front yard. The Landmarks Commission describes it as "one of the longest and most charming of the rows of English basement houses to be found in Chelsea." It is unfortunate that each house has suffered some alteration; however, Nos. 348 and 352 are probably closest to the original design. Note the "ear panels" on the doors of No. 358. The entire row of buildings is unified by its original cornice line, which has survived unscathed.

24. The **St. Peter's Church group,** consisting of rectory, church, and parish hall, was, like its nearby neighbor the General Theological Seminary, built on land donated to the institution by Dr. Clement Clarke Moore. The cornerstone for the original chapel, which is now the **Rectory Building,** No. 349, was laid in 1832, making it the oldest church building in Chelsea and one of the oldest Greek Revival–style buildings in the city. It once had full-height Doric columns, but these were removed and replaced with unusual brick pilasters.

The **church building** was completed in 1838 in Gothic Revival style, and is considered a fine model of the English parish Gothic church—the first of its style in this country. Dr. Moore served as vestryman and organist for a number of years, and it is said that he was responsible for the selection of the church's design. Among the names on the cornerstone are those of Dr. Moore, James N. Wells, and architect-builder James W. Smith, himself a resident of Chelsea. The church building is virtually unchanged except for the loss of its beautiful Gothic wooden porches, which had to be removed because of rotting. The marks left by the old porches can still be seen on the church walls. Unlike the usual Gothic church built in cruciform shape, St. Peter's is built on the plan of a Greek temple. The pulpit, chancel rail, and lectern were presented as a memorial to Don Alonzo Cushman by members of his family.

The **Parish Hall,** called St. Peter's Hall, completes the group. It was designed in 1871 in the so-called Victorian Gothic style, and now houses the Atlantic Theater Company, founded in Chicago by David Mamet and William H. Macy. The ornamental **wrought-iron fence** that embraces the three buildings is from Trinity Church downtown and was a gift from Trinity Church in 1837. Two years later the downtown church was razed and the present Trinity Church erected.

25. No. 331, on the north side of the street, is a rather late Greek Revival house, built in 1846. The side door opens on a passageway leading to a rear building. Although it is the only one in the Historic District with such a feature, nearby Nos. 311 to 305 have similar passageways, the latter has a see-through gate. Occasionally called "horsewalks," they also provided access to rear stables.

End of tour. Walk to Eighth Avenue and turn left to West 23rd Street for the A and E. The Nos. 1 and 2 are one block east at Seventh Avenue. The F, V, and PATH are two blocks east at Sixth Avenue.

The campus of the General Theological Seminary, dating from 1825, as seen from above the tracks of the Ninth Avenue El, at West 22nd Street, ca. 1913. Three of the Collegiate, Gothic-style buildings in the foreground were demolished in 1960 for the construction of the Episcopal seminary's Main Building; however, the shady campus still retains its small-town-college ambiance. At right (No. 183 Ninth Avenue, 1831–32) is the still-extant house that once was the residence and office of the original developer of Chelsea, James N. Wells. The charming Federal-style building is said to be the second-oldest in the district. The Ninth Avenue El, a descendant of the original West Side Elevated Railway, begun in 1866, was razed in 1940. (General Theological Seminary)

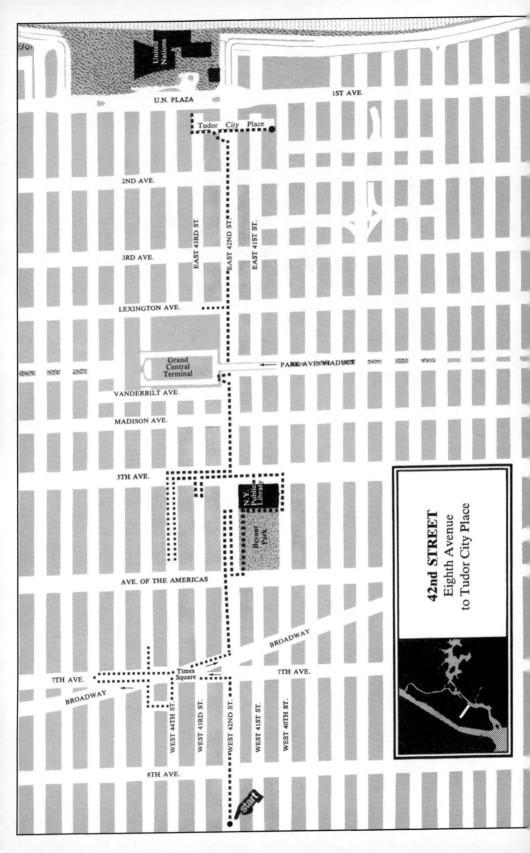

12. Forty-Second Street

Come and meet those dancing feet,
On the avenue I'm taking you to,
Forty-Second Street.
Hear the beat of dancing feet,
It's the song I love the melody of,
Forty-Second Street.

Little "nifties" from the Fifties, innocent and sweet,
Sexy ladies from the Eighties, who are indiscreet.
They're side by side,
They're glorified.
Where the underworld can meet the elite,
Naughty, bawdy, gawdy, sporty,
Forty-Second Street.*

[Words by Al Dubin, Music by Harry Warren]

[Subways: A, C, E to 42nd Street and Eighth Avenue. Buses: M42 crosstown to Eighth Avenue, buses from New Jersey to the Port Authority Bus Terminal.]

Few thoroughfares in the world are as well known or as widely diversified as 42nd Street—New York's major crosstown artery for almost three-quarters of a century. Considered by New Yorkers as the center of the city and, at its intersection with Broadway, the center of the world, it slices the middle of Manhattan horizontally from the Hudson to the East River. Although the street was opened officially in 1836 with the removal of squatters' shanties and the filling in of the

---

Construction of the Ninth Avenue El (the New York Elevated Railroad) station at 42nd Street, 1875–76. (Museum of the City of New York)

Grote Kil (Big Stream), the real history of 42nd Street begins late in the 19th century, and will be discussed block by block on the tour.

Before beginning the tour, you might want to take a quick stroll west on 42nd Street between Ninth and Tenth avenues. On the north side, the twin 45-story **Manhattan Plaza** towers (David Todd & Associates, 1977) provide federally subsidized rents to performing artists. Directly across the street is the off-Broadway **Theatre Row,** a group of ten playhouses carved out of former warehouses, sleazy tenements, and a few disreputable "entertainment" establishments. The project was created by the nonprofit 42nd Street Development Corporation, in cooperation with a group of theater pioneers, the City and State governments, private industry, and concerned citizens. The theaters are a bold experiment and a major phase in the revitalization of a once badly deteriorating neighborhood. Thus, with performing artists living in close proximity to a new and lively extension of the theater district, the contagion of this development can only spread, for the betterment of the entire area. Along the street are a number of theater-related restaurants and a theater bookshop.

The tour begins in front of the old McGraw-Hill Building, 330 West 42nd Street, west of Eighth Avenue.

New York's "green skyscraper," the **former McGraw-Hill Building,** was completed in 1931 from plans by architect Raymond M. Hood, in collaboration with Fouilhoux & Godley, in a unique variation of the Art Deco theme. The building's shape, with its series of setbacks, was dictated by the Zoning Resolution of 1916, and architect Hood exploited these requirements boldly and effectively. Unusual are the metallic bands of green, silver, and gold that encircle the ground floor and continue into the lobby; while on the façade above, row upon row of bluish-green terra-cotta bands continue the motif. Two other examples of Hood's ingenuity will be seen later. When the McGraw-Hill Publishing Company opened its new office skyscraper at 1221 Avenue of the Americas, fear was expressed for the future of the lovely green tower. However, in late 1974, Group Health Incorporated (GHI) took possession of it for its own corporate headquarters.

The Holy Cross Roman Catholic Church (Henry Engelbert, 1870), with its prominent verdigris dome, hearkens back to the time when the neighborhood was predominantly Irish and known as "Hell's Kitchen." An area of small factories and blocks of festering slums, it was one of the most notorious sections of the city, where even the police walked in fear and only in broad daylight. The church now ministers to a somewhat smaller, if more peaceful community. The simple exterior, in a transitional Byzantine style, belies the ornateness of the spacious interior. In a mixture of styles, primarily Italian Baroque, the architect has created an impressive nave and sanctuary. Observe the high barrel-vaulted ceiling, the wooden balcony, the fine paintings of Peter, Paul, and Jesus in the apse, and the Tiffany windows in the clerestory as well as the circular windows in the transept. The cupola was also decorated by Tiffany. This was famous Father Duffy's Church for many years—Francis P. Duffy, who worked so hard to uplift the old "Hell's Kitchen" neighborhood and break up the tough gangs that gave it such an unsavory reputation. It was Father Duffy who was closely associated with many theater personalities, and who served as chaplain of the "Fighting 69th" Division (actually the 165th Infantry Regiment) in the trenches of France during World War I. He served until his death in 1932, and an appreciative Broadway community erected a statue of him in Times Square.

A surviving row of tenement houses (ca. 1875) ends at No. 319 West, which is painted in "patriotic" colors to advertise **Kaufman's Army & Navy Store.** A local landmark since 1958, and the oldest business on West 42nd Street, its pair of World War I French Hotchkiss cannons guarding the door are about the only military surplus items not for sale.

The Port Authority Bus Terminal, the largest in the world, was opened in 1950, with the striking addition between 41st and 42nd streets completed in 1981 from plans by the architects and engineers of the Port Authority of New York & New Jersey Terminal Department. It has twin levels of bus ramps and serves 190,000 daily commuters from New Jersey, as well as long-distance bus riders. The upper levels are dominated by the dark brown steel trusses which project over sidewalk arcades. Walk up to the main ticketing area of the south wing to see sculptor George Segal's grouping of three white-painted bronze *Commuters* waiting for their bus (1980). (Segal, himself, is a bus commuter.)

The block between Eighth and Seventh avenues until the early 1990s was popularly referred to as "Sin Street," as both sides of the street were lined with X-rated movie houses, penny arcades, tawdry businesses, a succession of porno shops, and a proliferation of drug dealers, prostitutes, and panhandlers. In a transformation that no one ever thought possible, the entire street, as well as

neighboring Times Square, almost overnight became a center for newly renovated theaters, elegant hotels, glitzy office towers, upscale businesses, mega–
music stores, and fancy restaurants. A number of the movie houses—most of
them former legendary legitimate theaters—were renovated, and now offer topflight Broadway shows to standing-room-only audiences in the tradition of the
former famous Theater District. *(Walk along the north side.)*

On the northeast corner of Eighth Avenue, and extending to West 43rd Street,
is the **Westin New York (Hotel)** (Architectonica design architects, 2001), a multimedia extravaganza whose corner façade would make the hotelkeepers of
Atlantic City or Las Vegas salivate with envy. The split-sided multicolor base of
the structure supports an irregularly shaped skyscraper tower above. Within this
fantasy structure, and extending from the corner to the east, is the **E-Walk Complex** (D'Agostino Izzo Quirk with Gender Assocs. and Kupiec Koutsomitis
Architects, signage, 1999), a variety of showy enterprises, including restaurants
and a 13-screen theater. The iconoclastic building follows the lighting and design
prescriptions of architect Robert A. M. Stern and graphic designer Tibor Kalman
for a revitalized and exciting Times Square area.

The adjacent **Loews Theatre** with its tall arches is reminiscent of Ancient
Egypt. Walk inside and note the statue of four construction workers sitting on a
high steel beam. No. 229 West 42nd Street, once the Selwyn Theatre (George
Keister, 1918), has been transformed into the **42nd Street Rehearsal Studios,**

*The north side of 42nd Street
just west of Times Square,
ca. 1910, showing the Lyric
and Belasco theaters. Oscar
Hammerstein's Victoria
faces Times Square at right.
(Photograph by Byron. The
Byron Collection, Museum of
the City of New York)*

whose glass and aluminum walls are shielded from the sun by perforated steel louvres; and adjacent No. 227, into the **American Airlines Theater** with a new venue for the **Roundabout Theatre** (2001).

Return to Eighth Avenue, cross 42nd Street (carefully!) and walk east along the south side.

The **AMC Empire Theatre,** No. 234, was originally called the Eltinge, named for the great female impersonator Julian Eltinge. It survived several name changes and incarnations offering burlesque, comedy movies, and regular films. In addition to its Beaux Arts–style exterior, a new six-level interior with 25 movie theaters was added, in a blend of classical Egyptian, Greek, and Roman motifs. As part of the rejuvenation of 42nd Street, and in an unprecedented feat of engineering, the **landmark theater was moved 168 feet** on steel rails toward Eighth Avenue, on March 1, 1998 (at a cost of $588 per inch!). Through this major expansion, the entire project, by developer Bruce Ratner of the Forest City Ratner Theater & Store (Beyer Blinder Belle and the Rockwell Group, architects, 2000), created not only the new Empire, but swallowed up three other former theaters on the site, incorporating their façades into the exterior: the Harris (Willauer, Shape & Bready, 1914), the Liberty (Herts & Tallant, 1904), and the (original) Empire (Thomas W. Lamb, 1912).

Within the complex, and hidden by a two-story-high wall of fast-food signs, is the 44-story **Hilton Times Square Hotel** (No. 234, owned by the Forest City Ratner Companies). Except for the clock above the entrance, it can easily be missed. A new arrival, the Hilton, with a 44-story tower hidden behind, presents a number of little surprises, including an extensive exhibit of modern art. As you enter, note the small humorous bronze figures, the work of sculptor Tom Otterness. More than 60 of his signature bronze figures create a storybook world for the hotel's two marquees and inside the lower lobby, which displays an array of miniature New Yorkers, tourists, police officers, and piles of pennies in an engaging vignette called *Time and Money* that continues to the 41st Street lobby and climbs up the zany horizontal clock outside. [*See also* Otterness' work in Battery Park City, Chapter 1; and in the Eighth Avenue 14th Street subway station (A, C, E, L lines), a series of bronze sculptures of people and animals called *Life Underground*, representing the sculptor's perspective of the subway system as an underground world of its own.] Take the elevator to the 5th floor Sky Lobby to see more first-rate modern artworks plus a great view of the Times Square area.

Next door is New York's **Madame Tussaud's Wax Museum,** built on the skeleton of the Harris Theatre, whose sign and external elevator dangle from an enormous gilt hand, with a glass-enclosed exterior walkway above, and a few of Madame's fingers protruding below. The former Liberty Theatre's interior now embraces a shoe store.

Rising high above its neighbors is the **Candler Building,** No. 220 (Willauer, Shape & Bready, 1914), clad in gleaming white terra cotta. The imposing structure is named for the founder and owner of the Coca Cola Company, Asa G. Candler, who acquired the property in 1912 and had the building erected to house his offices. In 1999 a major renovation was completed by Swanke Hayden Connell.

The picturesque Casino Theater was built in 1882 on the southeast corner of Broadway and 39th Street as a concert hall, but played mostly comic operas. In this Byron photograph taken around 1900, shortly before it was acquired by the Shuberts, the Arabesque-style building is covered with advertisements for a long-forgotten musical. The Casino Theater survived until 1930. (The Byron Collection, Museum of the City of New York)

Posing for an unknown photographer in front of the Casino Theater entrance in 1924 is stage-door tender William Reilly. The gas lamp once stood in front of the Hoffman House Café, at Broadway and 26th Street; and was placed at the theater to recognize the 72-year-old Reilly's former career as a member of the city's once vast army of lamplighters. (The Consolidated Edison Company of New York)

Looking west on 42nd Street from in front of the original Grand Central Depot in the late 1890s. Just beyond is the newly opened Hotel Manhattan, at the corner of Madison Avenue. (Museum of the City of New York)

Looking across West 42nd Street, there are several theaters to note. No. 215, with an eye-catching colonnade, is the **Times Square Theatre** (De Rosa & Pereira, 1920), and to the right, **The Ford Center for the Performing Arts** (Beyer Blinder Belle, 1998), incorporating parts of the old Apollo (De Rosa & Pereira, 1920) and the Lyric (Victor Hugo Koehler, 1903). A passageway leads to the 43rd Street lobby.

At No. 209 is the **New Victory Theatre** (Albert E. Westover, 1899), beautifully restored in 1995 by Hardy Holzman Pfeiffer. Its impressive grand staircase is reminiscent of the entry to a 19th-century baroque opera house. Note the elegant lamp standards and other touches that enhance the building. If you have the opportunity, don't miss the spectacular interior. The date 1900 above refers to a renovation a year after construction (by J. B. McElfatrick) for impresario Oscar Hammerstein I, who renamed the theater the Republic. When producer David Belasco acquired it some years later, he renamed it for himself, and in the recent renovation, his name was removed, and the original name restored. [*See* photo, page 314.]

Again on the south side, near the corner of Seventh Avenue, is what many consider the "crown jewel" of the Theater District, **The New Amsterdam Theatre** (Herts & Tallant, 1903), No. 214 West. The first theater to be declared a landmark, its stunning and unique Art Nouveau interior (also a landmark) was a sensation. On October 26, 1903, the theater opened with Klaw and Erlanger's production of *A Midsummer Night's Dream*, and there followed a variety of mainly musical comedies. Florenz Ziegfeld acquired the theater in 1915 and for the next 15 years his *Ziegfeld Follies* packed the house. The theater was equipped with such amenities as specially carved furniture, a boudoir for ladies, a writing desk with current periodicals, a messenger service, and ornate promenades. The stage machinery and novel air-circulation system were far ahead of their time. Atop the narrow building is the **New Amsterdam Roof Theatre,** once a roof garden until acquired by Ziegfeld. He converted it into a small theater called the Aerial Gardens, where he introduced such hopefuls as Fanny Brice, Will Rogers, and Eddie Cantor.

The New Amsterdam was converted to a movie house in 1937, and closed in 1985. It was purchased by the city and the 42nd Street Development Project in 1995 and restored to its original splendor in a two-year project by the Walt Disney Company and Hardy Holzman Pfeiffer, with joint funding by the Empire State Development Corp., the New York City Economic Development Corp., and by the Port Authority of New York and New Jersey.

TIMES SQUARE

Known universally as "The Crossroads of the World," Times Square is the heart of the entertainment district, and has been for over a century. In the 1880s and 1890s, the two vertical triangles forming the "square" were lined with carriage dealers and called Longacre Square, after a London district. Then the Rialto arrived! The Metropolitan Opera House opened just to the south, at 39th Street and Broadway, in 1893; Charles Frohman built his large Empire theater across the street in 1894; Oscar Hammerstein (*père*) moved up from his 34th Street Manhattan Opera House site to open the dazzling Olympia Music Hall in 1895. The Olympia, looking for all the world like a Renaissance palace, occupied the entire Broadway blockfront from

Times Square in 1900—then called Longacre Square—looking south from 45th Street, with the New York and Criterion theaters at left, and Rector's famous restaurant and the Hotel Cadillac in the next block. (Photograph by Byron. The Byron Collection, Museum of the City of New York)

44th to 45th streets, with a roof garden, café, concert hall, and theater, and was the talk of the town. Hammerstein also built the lavish Victoria Theater on the northwest corner of 42nd Street, the site of the Reuters Building. Others soon followed, one more grandiose than the other, offering not only legitimate theater, but vaudeville, cabaret, and music-hall entertainment. Many even had roof gardens with luxurious restaurants. And to further satisfy the appetites of the new theater crowds came such establishments as Shanley's, Rector's, Churchill's, and the Café de l'Opéra. Broadway is still synonymous with the stage, with about three dozen legitimate theaters in the immediate Times Square area. Most are clustered in the blocks west of Broadway, between 44th and 52nd streets. Little Shubert Alley, connecting 44th and 45th streets, still evokes the glamour of "show biz," surrounded as it is by a number of theaters with brightly illuminated marquees.

With the rise of the film industry in the 1920s, enormous and opulent movie palaces opened along Broadway, displacing the "legit" theaters to the west. Who can forget such celebrated names as the Palace, Strand, Capitol, Paramount, Rialto, Rivoli, Warner (where in 1927 New Yorkers were treated to the first sound film, Al Jolson in *The Jazz Singer*), and the most lavish of them all, the Roxy? Some still remain, but mostly in name only.

The tour route around Times Square will be clockwise, going north on Seventh Avenue to West 48th Street, and returning south on Broadway to West 42nd Street.

Before touring Times Square, you might want to take a moment and descend into the renovated Times Square subway station to see the new **Roy Lichtenstein pop-art mural,** located on the mezzanine level between the Nos. 1, 2, and 3 lines and the Grand Central shuttle. The 6- × 53-foot porcelain-on-enamel work, commissioned by the Metropolitan Transit Authority **Arts for Transit Program** as a gift of the artist to the people of New York, portrays the skyline of a futuristic city. Nearby, on the stairway wall between the trains and the mezzanine is Jacob Lawrence's *New York in Transit* (2001), while on the wall of the 41st Street/Seventh Avenue mezzanine is Jack Beal's *The Return of Spring* (2001)—both glass mosaic murals.

In recent days the corner of West 42nd Street, where Seventh Avenue and Broadway intersect, has gained the sobriquet "Super Corner," for reasons that will be obvious. On the southwest corner, and due for completion in 2003, is the **Ernst & Young**

The Pabst Hotel, on 42nd Street, facing away from Longacre Square, now Times Square. The hotel and adjoining four-story buildings were demolished in 1903 to make way for the Times Tower. (Photograph by Byron. The Byron Collection, Museum of the City of New York)

Building, No. 5 Times Square, the latest behemoth to rise on this famous intersection. On the northwest corner is No. 3, the **Reuters Building** (Fox & Fowle, 2001), site of Hammerstein's lavish Victoria Theatre, later replaced by the Rialto Building (Thomas W. Lamb and Rosario Candela, 1935); and on the northeast corner, the astonishing **Condé Nast Building,** No. 4 (Fox & Fowle, 1999)—a building described as showing a "split personality." The north and west sides, clad in glass and metal, serve as hangers for huge advertising signs that integrate into the architecture of the building. An enormous cylinder supports the largest and most colorful (and most expensive) video screen on Times Square. The masonry-clad east side, on the other hand, is more staid and traditional. Visit the lobby to see Frank Gehry's undulating aluminum ceiling that extends from one entrance to the other.

No. 1 Times Square originally was the Times Tower, and later became the Allied Chemical Tower (Cyrus L. W. Eidlitz and Andrew C. MacKenzie; in 1966, major reconstruction by Smith, Smith, Haines, Lundberg & Waehler). With the arrival of New York's first subway line in 1904, *The New York Times* publisher Adolph Ochs astonished his contemporaries by moving out of "Newspaper Row" downtown [*see* Chapter 3] and erecting his wedged-shaped Times Tower on this site. Ochs persuaded the city fathers to name the new subway station after the *Times*, and soon Longacre Square became Times Square. Built of pink granite in Italian Renaissance style, the area's once-dominant landmark is known today only by its street address and for the annual New Year's Eve descent of the famous ball— a custom that began with a fireworks display on December 31, 1908. Even after the newspaper moved all of its operations into its former annex on West 43rd Street, and the Times Tower was reconstructed as the Allied Chemical Tower, the old custom was preserved. Another hallmark of the Times Tower is the five-foot-high **electric zipper** that encircles the building on a 379-foot-long trip, as it spells out the day's headlines from Dow Jones. The zipper, illuminated by 235,000 light-emitting diodes (LEDs), was designed and built by Artkraft Strauss Sign Corporation, the company responsible for many of Times Square's illuminated signs. The zipper can be set at variable speeds, with as many as nine letters zipping by every second. The original, dimmer Motogram, with its 12,400 30-watt incandescent bulbs that had become Times Square's signature, was inaugurated on election night 1928, announcing Herbert Hoover's presidential victory. It was replaced in 1966 in connection with the Allied Chemical renovation, and rebuilt again in 1984 to add computer controls. The new brighter zipper was installed in 1997, making it the fourth incarnation of this famous information display. Surrounding the building on all sides are layer upon layer of illuminated advertisements, converting the old Times Tower into little more than a monster signboard. Buildings on Times Square are *required* to display large flashy supersigns, as part of the plan to re-create Times Square's traditional glittering ambiance.

On the "island" in front is the New York Police Department booth, and nearby, the **U.S. Armed Forces Recruiting Station** (Parsons Brinckerhoff and Architecture Research Office, 1999), a most engaging glass, steel, and neon box, adorned with colorful fluorescent flags made of a reflective gel that glow day and night, and wrap the four sides of the diminutive building. This attractive addition to Times Square replaces an earlier recruiting station opened in 1946.

Continue north to No. 1501 Broadway, the **former Paramount Theatre Building** (C. W. Rapp & George L. Rapp, 1926). Best seen from a distance, the structure's nine ascending setbacks give the impression of a gargantuan set of children's building blocks assembled by some young Gulliver. The attractive globe and four-sided clocks are classical, but the rest is pure Art Deco. The setbacks were dictated by the Zoning Resolution of 1916. The once lavish and highly popular theater is long gone, replaced by a restaurant. The rest of the building is confined to commercial rentals.

Hotels also were built in the new theater district. For some 60 years the *grande dame* of them all, the **Hotel Astor,** was a familiar site on Times Square. Commissioned by William Waldorf Astor, it was built in an exuberant Beaux Arts style with a huge mansard roof, opening its doors in 1904 on the block between 44th and 45th streets. [*See* photo, page 329.] In 1969, it was replaced by the 53-story office tower,

The changing faces of the Times Tower: (left) as it appeared when built for The New York Times *in 1904; (center) as the Allied Chemical Building in 1964; (right) as it was planned to appear in 1976, sheathed in mirrors as One Times Square. The grandiose project was never carried out, and the building still looks much as portrayed in the middle photo. (Alex Parker)*

designed by Kahn & Jacobs for the now-defunct W. T. Grant Company. By changing its 1515 Broadway address to **Astor Plaza,** it keeps the old hotel's name alive. From a distance the odd concrete "wings" atop the structure add a gaudy and bizarre (and not wholly inappropriate) touch to the Times Square scene. The building houses the Minskoff Theatre, and it has the distinction of being the first structure to take advantage of the new zoning laws which permitted greater height in exchange for space set aside for a theater (it has a movie theater as well).

Take a short detour left into **Shubert Alley,** which many consider the heart of the Theater District. Here are a pair of distinguished landmark theaters: the **Sam S. Shubert** (Henry B. Herts, 1912) and the **Booth** (Henry B. Herts, 1913), both boasting some of the shows with the longest runs (among them, *A Chorus Line* at the Shubert and *You Can't Take It with You* at the Booth). In front of the offices of owners J. J. and Lee Shubert, in their namesake theater, aspiring actors would assemble with nervous anticipation when casting for new plays was announced.

Looking down West 44th and West 45th streets, the largest grouping of legitimate theaters in the city, if not the world, can be seen. On West 44th Street, called Rodgers and Hammerstein Row, are the **Helen Hayes, St. James, Broadhurst,** and **Majestic.** On West 45th Street are the **Plymouth, Royale, Golden, Music Box,** and the **former Martin Beck,** which was renamed on June 21, 2003, for the noted caricaturist and theater illustrator **Al Hirschfeld,** who was to have been honored on the occasion of his 100th birthday; unfortunately, he died five months before the event. Within Astor Plaza is the **Minskoff.** Return to Broadway on West 45th Street.

The first major hotel to be built on Times Square in more than 75 years was the **Marriott Marquis,** taking up the whole block between 44th and 45th streets. Designed by John Portman and completed in 1985, its concept created a storm of protest that continued for several years, as plans called for the demolition of five adjacent legitimate theaters—the Astor, Bijou, Gaiety, Helen Hayes (former), and Morosco playhouses that were revered by theatergoers and actors alike. Tumultuous demonstrations and repeated court challenges preceded the bulldozers, which finally leveled the site, including part of the Helen Hayes's façade that was supposed to be preserved. To prevent any similar occurrences, the Landmarks Commission then designated the exteriors (and some interiors) of 45 playhouses in the midtown area. The hotel, itself, became noted for its signature tall atrium and external elevators, a Portman touch duplicated in his hotels throughout the country.

Continue to West 46th Street and turn left.

The **Lunt-Fontanne Theatre,** 205 West 46th Street (Carrère & Hastings, 1909), was originally the Old Globe, but was rebuilt in 1958 (Roche & Roche) and renamed to honor the celebrated stage couple Alfred Lunt and Lynn Fontanne. The splendid Mediterranean palazzo was reopened in time for the exceptionally long run of *The Sound of Music.* Return to Broadway.

The traffic pattern in Times Square is much saner since the one-way routing was established. Before World War II, the scene was always one of bedlam, or at least total chaos. Adding to the confusion created by the number of intersecting streets were the trolley lines that crisscrossed Times Square on both Broadway and Seventh Avenue. The 42nd Street crosstown car, which either went west to the 42nd Street ferry or turned north on Broadway, contributed further to the disorder.

The upper "V" of Times Square is known as **Duffy Square** [*see* earlier description]. His statue (Charles Keck, 1937) in front of a Celtic cross stands close by that of **George M. Cohan** (Georg Lober, 1959), "giving his regards to Broadway." The adjacent **TKTS booth,** established in 1973, sells half-price tickets to Broadway shows to those who line up on the day of the performance. The attractive canvas and tubular-steel structure was designed by Mayers & Schiff.

At the northern end of Times Square, and virtually hidden by a tower of gaudy signs, is the new **Renaissance New York Hotel,** No. 714 Seventh Avenue (Mayers & Schiff, 1992). The dark-glass curtain-wall structure is best seen from the side.

Times Square looking north in 1934. To the right the Palace Theatre presents vaudeville, with its films and seats at 25 cents. The scene is a familiar one today with its proliferation of large, brash signs and the rows of movie marquees, plus the inevitable automobile traffic; but with the exception of the Palace Theatre, virtually not a single building still survives. (Author's collection)

The **"Great White Way,"** as Broadway's theater district has been called, is today brighter than ever. The name is attributed to outdoor-advertising executive O. J. Gude, who in 1901 conceived the idea of erecting very large electrical display signs to promote commercial products and theatrical performances. These signs were to be placed in the busiest and most conspicuous locations, and he settled on Times Square as the most appropriate site. Through the years the neon signs of Times Square have been one of its stellar attractions, particularly at night when the multicolored flashing advertisements create an almost magical atmosphere. Many of the designs were created by Douglas Leigh, who is responsible for the lovely floodlight illumination on many of New York's skyscrapers; and the builder and installer is the Artkraft Strauss Sign Corporation. The redevelopment guidelines established by the city for Times Square now require that any new building erected between 42nd and 50th streets devote the first 120 feet of its façade to illuminated signs. By keeping those colorful, blinking, and dazzling neon and laser signs, they continue to maintain the tradition of the bright lights and glitter that has made Times Square such a glamorous tourist attraction. Don't miss Coca-Cola's spectacular new sign at W. 47th Street and Broadway.

Times Square by night is a scene familiar to all, although there have been many changes since this photo was taken at the outbreak of World War II. Within a few months the bright lights would be dimmed for the duration of the war; gasoline rationing had already reduced the number of autos, leaving half-empty Broadway and Seventh Avenue to the trolleys and taxicabs. At left is the Hotel Astor, and across the Square is the famous Wrigley Chewing Gum sign atop the Criterion Theater. At the lower right, a billboard promotes the re-election campaigns of Mayor Fiorello H. LaGuardia and then–District Attorney Thomas E. Dewey. (Museum of the City of New York)

At the site of 1557 Broadway lies the ghost of **New York's first Automat.** Joseph V. Horn and Frank Hardart began operations in Philadelphia and came to New York in 1912. Then followed the ubiquitous chain of popular self-serve establishments that dispensed food at the turn of a knob, and drinks at the pull of a crank. In its heyday in 1922 there were 21 Automats in the city. By 1991 the last one, at 200 East 42nd Street, albeit an ersatz copy, closed its doors, and the city lost a great amenity.

On the northwest corner of West 47th Street is the massive **Morgan Stanley Building,** No. 1585 Broadway (Gwathmey Siegel & Assocs. with Emery Roth & Sons, 1990). The striking façade of mirrored glass, aluminum panels, and shiny stainless steel is dominated by three 140-foot-long electronic ticker tapes that tell "real-time" information using light-emitting diodes, while digital multi-time-zone clocks feature the major financial cities of the world. Take a moment to visit the very impressive lobby.

Turn right (east) on West 47th Street, and begin walking down the east side of Times Square.

At the southeast corner of 47th Street and Seventh Avenue is the **Doubletree Guest Suites** (formerly the Embassy Suites Times Square) (Fox & Fowle, 1990). An interesting feature is how this 43-story building was designed to accommodate the famous **Palace Theatre** (Kirchoff & Rose, 1913). Among the most famous of the early legitimate theaters, it was celebrated for its great theatrical performances, and for being the biggest and best vaudeville house in town. To preserve the landmark theater, the builders had to remove the outer structure and the lobby and incorporate the auditorium into the hotel's design. This unusual project was carried out through the installation of a 135-foot truss, 45 feet high, and set on four massive columns to span the theater like a bridge.

At the northeast corner of 46th Street and Seventh Avenue stands the **I. Miller Building** (Louis H. Friedland, 1927), virtually hidden by the massed supersigns. Once the showroom of the well-known women's shoe manufacturer, it boasts a splendid array of sculptures by Alexander Stirling Calder depicting famous actresses: Ethel Barrymore as *Ophelia*, Marilyn Miller as *Sunny*, Mary Pickford as *Little Lord Fauntleroy*, and Rosa Ponselle as *Norma*.

Occupying the entire block from 45th to 46th streets is the 44-story **Bertelsmann Building,** 1540 Broadway (Skidmore Owings & Merrill, 1987). A postmodern mixed-use building, it is sheathed in four contrasting bands of blue and green glass, and sports a novel 100-foot-high steel-frame spire. Within is the world's largest record store, Virgin, and four movie theaters. Its predecessor on the site was the famed Loews State Theatre Building, built in 1920 and dedicated to serving the film industry.

Detour briefly east on 45th Street to the elegant **Lyceum Theatre.** Built by Herts & Tallant in 1903 in a florid and strong Beaux-Arts style, it is the oldest legitimate house in the city, and arguably the most beautiful. Both the interior and exterior are designated landmarks. From its opening and for almost four decades the Lyceum was managed by impresario Daniel Frohman, who lived above the theater in a private suite, and often kept an eye on the stage below through a small trapdoor. The former Frohman suite is now the office of the **Shubert Archive,** said to be the largest theatrical collection housed under one roof.

The **former Lamb's Club Building,** No. 130 West 44th Street, is now home to the **Lamb's Theatre** and the **Manhattan Church of the Nazarene.** The neo-Georgian–style building was designed for this famous actors' club by Stanford White of the firm of McKim, Mead & White, in 1905. The southeast corner of 44th Street is the site of the Barrett House, where **playwright Eugene O'Neill** was born in 1888.

Return to Broadway. Walk one block south to West 43rd Street and turn left (east).

●   **Town Hall,** 123 West 43rd Street (McKim, Mead & White, 1919), was built for the League of Political Education, and designed in a Georgian Revival style, to be used for public meetings, lectures, and concerts. A popular site for political issues through the years, it was a favorite place for debates and forums. Among its many prominent figures were Theodore Roosevelt, Booker T. Washington, Jane Addams, and Henry James. With its superb acoustics, it has attracted such notable performers as Sergei Rachmaninoff, Richard Strauss, Joan Sutherland, and Dizzy Gillespie. Return to Broadway and turn left to West 42nd Street.

●   At the southeast corner of 42nd Street and Seventh Avenue is the **former Knick-erbocker Hotel,** 1462–1470 Broadway (Marvin & Davis and Bruce Price, 1902), commissioned by John Jacob Astor IV. Built two years before his Hotel Astor, it was

The 42nd Street crosstown horsecar makes its way eastbound across from Reservoir Square (now Bryant Park) in this 1889 photo. The tall building with the mansard roof is the Harmonie Club, the site of the present W. R. Grace Building. In the background the Sixth Avenue El and its 42nd Street station span the rather quiet thoroughfare. Forty-Second Street may again see rails running down the middle if plans are successful for the construction of a light-rail crosstown trolley line. (New-York Historical Society)

Looking north from the top of the just-completed Times Tower, 1905. To the left is the then brand-new Hotel Astor with its fashionable roof garden. (Museum of the City of New York)

the sole survivor of many Times Square hostelries built at the turn of the century, and was one of the most fashionable. Its King Cole Bar with Maxfield Parrish mural attracted many luminaries from the entertainment world, including George M. Cohan and Enrico Caruso, who often serenaded appreciative crowds from the balcony of his suite. Note the crowning mansard roof of this red-brick and limestone Renaissance Eclectic building. In a later incarnation it became the Newsweek Building, and now is a condominium. The Parrish mural was rescued and graces a bar with the same King Cole name at the St. Regis Hotel, at 2 East 55th Street.

Midway down the block, on the south side, stands the cathedrallike **former Bush Terminal Building** (No. 130 West), now the Bush Tower. It was erected in 1918 from plans by Helmle & Corbett; however, the architects seemed to have had a later tenant in mind when they designed this neo-Gothic–style building. For many years until the structure was renovated, it had been the home of the Wurlitzer Music Company. Although gone from New York, it is worthy of mention because of the firm's long and close association with the city. Founded in 1856 by Rudolph Wurlitzer, they made band instruments, and during the Civil War supplied the Union Army bands. They later specialized in keyboard instruments, and for a time also made juke boxes. In the 1930s they built the largest organ in the city, the "Mighty Wurlitzer" for Radio City Music Hall, and another almost as large for the Brooklyn Paramount Theater.

Forty-Second Street, looking east from Sixth Avenue in 1932. In the still undeveloped Bryant Park, a wooden replica of Federal Hall has been erected as part of that year's Washington Bicentennial Celebration. The view is much the same as today, except for the trolley cars and the Stern Brothers Department Store (extreme left), now replaced by the W. R. Grace Building. (The Consolidated Edison Company of New York)

Notice the *trompe l'oeil* effect on the side walls of the building, where vertical bands of tan and brown bricks are paired to give an illusion of depth. The sheer verticality of the structure is emphasized by its 480-foot height on a plot of ground only 50 feet wide.

Note the difference between the north and south sides of 42nd Street in this one block. Strangely, with all the high-rise construction in the midtown area, the north side remains a depressing sight. In the middle of the block can be seen the vestiges of a long-forgotten old bank, its beehive logo still barely visible above.

The gleaming white marble and black glass **New York Telephone Company Building,** now Verizon, at the southwest corner of Avenue of the Americas, is one of a number of skyscraper office towers erected by "Ma Bell" for local corporate headquarters. Completed in 1974 from plans by Kahn & Jacobs, it served as the "anchor" for a growing line of new "glass boxes" that sprang up along the avenue north of 42nd Street. The narrow plaza to the west of the building with its mini-waterfalls and tree plantings is a pleasant oasis between the tall towers—a concession to the zoning laws that require open space in proportion to building height. Above the subway entrance in the west lobby is an attractive and colorful mosaic mural by Richard Kirk (but why hidden away from the main entrance?).

Avenue of the Americas, popularly called Sixth Avenue, was renamed by former Mayor Fiorello H. LaGuardia. In spite of the decorative coats of arms of the Latin American nations mounted on the Avenue's lampposts, most New Yorkers rejected the mayor's flamboyant gesture, and still refer to the thoroughfare by its original name.

From 1878 until 1938 the Sixth Avenue El rattled overhead, keeping the busy avenue in perpetual twilight. The broad vistas from the old wooden platform cars, however, were superb.

You might want to make an optional detour to visit the midtown branch of the **International Center of Photography,** one block north at 1133 Avenue of the Americas (northwest corner of 43rd Street). At New York City's only museum dedicated exclusively to photography, there are frequently changing exhibitions on a variety of subjects, ranging from early vintage to avant garde prints, but the emphasis is on contemporary photographic art. (Hours: Tues., Wed., Thurs. 10:00 A.M. to 5:00 P.M., Fri. to 8:00 P.M., Sat., Sun. to 6:00 P.M. Admission $9.00, seniors $6.00, children under 12 free; Fri. after 5:00 P.M. voluntary contribution.)

One of the unusual additions to the city's ever-growing skyline is the slope-fronted **W. R. Grace & Company Building** (No. 43 West), completed in 1974. The revolutionary profile derives from the architects' (Skidmore, Owings & Merrill) interpretation of the zoning regulations, which stipulate the ratio of a building's verticality to the amount of horizontal setback. The façade is covered with travertine, and although the shape is controversial, it is a relief from the endless rows of unimaginative "glass boxes" erected during much of the second half of the 20th century. What is objectionable to many is the resultant destruction of the 42nd Street "street wall," considered an essential element in urban design.

The Grace Building occupies the **site of the Stern Brothers Department Store,** which stood on the L-shaped plot from 1913 to 1970. (Interestingly, Stern's first

The Avenue of the Americas today is a far cry from the dark and dingy Sixth Avenue 100 years ago. Looking north from 42nd Street, the Manhattan Elevated Railroad seems to cast a pall of gloom over the avenue. Not a vehicle, horsedrawn or other, is in sight. (New-York Historical Society)

store, an immense cast-iron building still in pristine condition, stands on the south side of West 23rd Street, between Fifth and Sixth avenues [*see* Ladies' Mile, 21].)

Adjacent No. 33 West, formerly a commercial office building, is now the **Optometric Center of the State University of New York.** The most striking feature is the renovation of the ground floor by architect Carl J. Petrilli, with its concrete cantilevered "canopy" and the open passageway to 43rd Street. The split-faced concrete walls of the passage are in sharp contrast to the exterior—one can almost forget that the building was erected in 1912 from plans by Warren & Wetmore. In the 1920s the building was famous for its third-floor concert hall, **Aeolian Hall** (note the lyres on the façade), and witnessed the premiere of George Gershwin's *Rhapsody in Blue.* The former Graduate Center was dedicated in 1970 after a three-year renovation and was the recipient of many awards for excellence in design. The Municipal Art Society awarded it a special prize "for improvement of the aesthetic quality of life in New York City," and former *New York Times* architecture critic Ada Louise Huxtable described the Center as "one of New York's most successfully recycled buildings."

No. 11 West, the **Salmon Tower** (York & Sawyer, 1927), is distinguished only in its elaborate entrance and luxurious lobby. Around the ornate arched entrance on both 42nd and 43rd streets are bas-relief sculptures of the months plus a row of classical figures above, representing the professions, and in the vaulted passage are marble walls and decorative bronze fixtures. Even the two mailboxes are adorned with low-relief bronze sculptures. The building also houses the **Midtown Center of New York University.** The "tower" section actually faces Fifth Avenue, as **No. 500 Fifth,** the two buildings being connected by a second-floor passageway. No. 500, completed in 1931 from plans by Shreve, Lamb & Harmon, was known as the Transportation Building, since it formerly housed the New York offices of virtually every important railroad in the country. In their stead today are numerous foreign airlines.

Cross 42nd Street at the corner of Fifth Avenue, and walk back (west) along Bryant Park to the midblock park entrance, but do not enter here.

Just to the left is the entrance to the No. 7 line subway. If you feel ambitious, you might want to go down and see the special **underground pedestrian passageway.** Built in 1973, it remains a point of unusual interest, with a brown ceramic-tiled corridor enlivened by eight vintage photomurals depicting Bryant Park, the Fifth Avenue Library, and old historic landmarks, plus Samm Kunce's wall mosaics entitled *Bryant Park* (2002). (But it will cost you a token!) If you choose to come back at another time, continue with the present tour, which is a must-see visit to Bryant Park: Walk ahead to the corner of Sixth Avenue, enter the park, sit down on a nearby bench, buy an ice-cream cone, and read the following information that will make your visit much more enjoyable:

Bryant Park Scenic Landmark has recently emerged from a four-year major restoration program. The landscaping was greatly enhanced with trees, shrubbery, and plantings; paths were relaid with bluestone paving; the statuary was rearranged and cleaned; new period lighting was installed; security upgraded; and incredibly, clean and functioning restrooms were opened. The design plan was eminently successful, as the junkies and undesirables have decamped, and it is once more a park for the people. Credit for the magnificent reconstruction goes to the firm of Hanna/Olin, Ltd. for the landscaping, and to Hardy Holzman Pfeiffer who designed the kiosks and restaurant. In addition, below the great lawn a two-story 120,000-square-foot underground structure was erected that houses 84 miles of stacks and 3.2 million books from the adjacent Central Research Library. The project was developed in 1980 by the Bryant Park Restoration Corporation, which was founded by the New York Public Library and the Rockefeller Brothers Fund, in cooperation with the City and the Department of Parks and Recreation.

HISTORICAL BACKGROUND. The site of Bryant Park was first set aside as a public property by the colonial government in 1686 when the area was still a wilderness and an Indian hunting ground. Almost a hundred years later, during the Revolutionary War, it witnessed the hasty retreat of General George Washington's army, as it withdrew up Manhattan Island to avoid superior British forces. From 1823 to 1840 it was used as a potter's field. Two years later the Croton Distributing Reservoir was constructed on the site, as a newly built aqueduct brought fresh water to the city for the first time. The reservoir was an enormous Egyptian-style stone enclosure that covered four acres, with walls 50 feet high and 25 feet thick, along the top of which there was a very popular public promenade. The reservoir was razed in 1911 to make way for the new library.

In 1853 New York City inaugurated the **Crystal Palace Exposition** on the site adjoining the reservoir. Modeled after London's famous exhibition of the same name two years earlier, it was an enormous domed cast-iron-and-glass pavilion, designed to display fine arts and industrial products from around the world. Like a gargantuan Victorian greenhouse, its pinnacles rose 76 feet above what was then called Reservoir Square. New York's first World's Fair lasted two years and was one of the most spectacular attractions ever to be presented in the city; but it was a financial failure, and five years later the pavilion was destroyed in a disastrous fire, as was the Latting Observatory Tower across 42nd Street, two years before.

During the Civil War the site was used as a drill field by the Union Army. In 1894 the name was changed to honor **William Cullen Bryant**—poet, orator, journalist, and editor of the *New York Evening Post*. But little was done to make the site parklike until 1933, when the city fathers conducted a competition for the development of Bryant Park. The successful entry was submitted by Lusby Simpson, an unemployed architect from Queens. Since the park's dedication, several pieces of fine sculpture have been installed, which can be seen on the brief tour below. Bryant Park has become a highly successful urban amenity—a source of rest and inspiration and a hub of cultural and educational activity.

A BRIEF TOUR OF BRYANT PARK. Notice the huge bronze lamp standards in turn-of-the-century style that surround the park. To the right (south) follow the path to the **Josephine Shaw Lowell Memorial Fountain.** The pink Stoney Creek granite fountain honors the pioneer social worker and philanthropist, and was designed by Charles A. Platt and presented to the city in 1912. Turn left and walk down the Great Lawn about halfway and turn left to the **statue of William Earle Dodge** by John Quincy Adams Ward (1885). Dodge was a merchant and philanthropist who founded the Y.M.C.A. The statue was moved from its original site in Herald Square in 1941 to make place for the James Gordon Bennett Memorial.

At the east end is the **Bryant Park Grill and Café** (Hardy Holzman Pfeiffer, 1995), with several dining choices, from snacks to more hearty fare. The outdoor café offers a particularly pleasant respite from walking. Behind it rises the imposing sculpture of the seated **William Cullen Bryant,** executed in 1911 by Henry Adams, and protected by a Roman-style arch designed by Thomas Hastings. A Beaux Arts–style comfort station is at the 42nd Street edge.

Continuing clockwise, we come to the bust of author **Gertrude Stein** (Jo Davidson, sculptor, 1923), and a few yards farther, the bust of **Johann Wolfgang von Goethe,** by Karl Fischer, presented to the city by the Goethe Society in 1932. Just beyond is one of the park's nicest amenities, especially for families with children, the **Carousel,** a re-creation of those ever-popular attractions seen in times past in virtually every amusement park in America. The calliope music is also authentic, but alas, no ring to catch. ($1.50 per ride.) In the southwest corner of the park is the statue of **José Bonifácio de Andrada e Silva** (José Lima, 1954), generally regarded as the chief founder of Brazil's independence.

The skyscraper panorama surrounding Bryant Park is striking. Look particularly south, to the West 40th Street side where, left to right, from Fifth Avenue, the following interesting buildings can be seen to good advantage:

The Republic National Bank Building, formerly the **Knox Building** (at the corner of Fifth Avenue). This ornate Classical showpiece with an imposing mansard roof was designed in 1902 by John H. Duncan for the Knox Hat Company. It

The burning of the Crystal Palace, October 5, 1858. The Exposition, which was held in 1853–54, is now the site of Bryant Park. (New-York Historical Society)

suffered some modifications in 1965, but still retains much of its charm. Wrapped around the landmark Knox Building on an L-shaped lot is the 27-story **Republic Tower,** world headquarters of the Republic National Bank (Eli Attia, 1982). Israeli-born architect Attia designed the glass-wall structure to serve as a backdrop for the older building, while at the same time preserving its own special geometric richness of form.

The **former Engineers Club,** No. 3 West 40th Street (Whitfield & King, 1906), was designed in a combination of Georgian and Renaissance Revival styles. With its huge Corinthian pilasters, it is harmonious with the Library opposite. It is now a co-op appropriately named The Columns. The fence on the parking lot farther down the street is also in harmony with the Library. Narrow No. 28 is a so-called "sliver" building, now called Metropolitan House. No. 32 is Beaux-Arts style below and Renaissance Revival above.

The **former American Standard Building,** originally the American Radiator Building, No. 40 West, has been given a new life as the **Bryant Park Hotel.** The management of this new "boutique" hotel has expressed pride in occupying and preserving this landmark. The building, designed in a bold, cubic massing of forms by architect Raymond M. Hood in 1923, is the undisputed beauty of the block. With its unique black-and-gold color scheme, it is most impressive. It has been said that its striking color combination, illuminated at night, gives it the appearance of an enormous glowing coal—ideal for the corporate headquarters of the former American Radiator Company. In 1926 Talbot Hamlin, the noted architectural historian, described it as "the most daring experiment in color in modern buildings yet made in America." Note how the tower's setbacks terminate in gold-colored cubistic masses—forms often associated with the Art Deco style. The arched and pinnacled form at the top of the tower is a delightful crown to this skyscraper.

No. 50 West 40th Street, **Daytop Village** (York & Sawyer, 1904), originally the Republican Club, is interesting for its massive segmented Tuscan columns, but for little else above.

No. 80 West, the **Bryant Park Studios,** formerly the Beaux Arts Studios (Charles A. Rich, 1901), was designed for artists' studios, offering two-story-high north-facing natural light. Appropriately named originally, the lavish façade is a textbook example of the style.

Note, too, the Beaux Arts–style former comfort stations at each end of the park, in complement to the style of the Library. Bryant Park, because of the high quality of its landscape architecture, its historical and aesthetic interest, and its splendid urban location, has been designated an official Scenic Landmark by the New York City Landmarks Preservation Commission.

Return to Fifth Avenue and make a brief detour 100 feet south to the bronze plaque set in a decorative niche of the Knox Tower, which depicts the 19th-century **John B. Wendel Mansion** that once occupied the site—one of many such houses of the affluent that lined Fifth Avenue.

Walk back up Fifth Avenue to the main entrance to the Library.

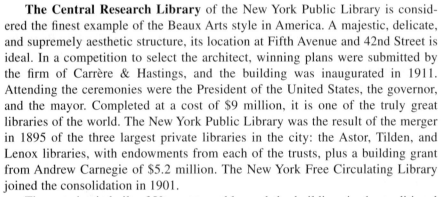

The Central Research Library of the New York Public Library is considered the finest example of the Beaux Arts style in America. A majestic, delicate, and supremely aesthetic structure, its location at Fifth Avenue and 42nd Street is ideal. In a competition to select the architect, winning plans were submitted by the firm of Carrère & Hastings, and the building was inaugurated in 1911. Attending the ceremonies were the President of the United States, the governor, and the mayor. Completed at a cost of $9 million, it is one of the truly great libraries of the world. The New York Public Library was the result of the merger in 1895 of the three largest private libraries in the city: the Astor, Tilden, and Lenox libraries, with endowments from each of the trusts, plus a building grant from Andrew Carnegie of $5.2 million. The New York Free Circulating Library joined the consolidation in 1901.

The exterior is built of Vermont marble, and the building, in the traditional Louis XVI Renaissance form, presents an ingratiating rather than imposing appearance. It is built around two inner courts with an immense central reading room occupying a half-acre of floor space. Dominating the grand entrance are the two famous lions designed by Edward C. Potter. The style of the majestic lions is from standard architectural forms, but they have been the source of humorous criticism since their installation, even to the unspeakable pun of "reading between the lions." The 95-foot tapered steel flagpoles are set on exquisite bronze bases designed by Raffaele Menconi and cast by the Tiffany Studios, and were installed in 1941 as a memorial to former reform Mayor John Purroy Mitchell. The sculpted figures on either side of the main entrance are by Frederick Mac-

Monnies: The man seated on a sphinx on the north side represents *Truth;* the woman seated on Pegasus on the south side represents *Beauty.* The six figures on the attic wall over the main entrance are by Paul Bartlett and are executed in Georgia marble for contrast. They depict, from left to right, *Philosophy, Romance, Religion, Poetry, Drama,* and *History.* The two groups in the pediment by George Gray Bernard represent *Art* and *History.*

Enter **Astor Hall** at the top of the stairs—a monumental white marble lobby whose high-arch bays rise on all sides to a segmental vault, flanked by twin grand staircases supported on flying arches leading to the upper floors. Statues of architects John Merven Carrère and Thomas Hastings are set in niches on the first landing. The walls of the third-floor Central Hall are of dark wood, above which are plaster-paneled barrel vaults. Notice how the ceiling extends over the cornice line at each end to permit light to enter from segmental arch windows. The fine murals were painted by Edward Laning, under the auspices of the Artists Program of the WPA, and were completed in 1940. The four arched murals represent the four stages in the development of the recorded word: *Moses with the Tablets of the Law, The Medieval Scribe, Gutenberg Showing a Proof to the Elector of Mainz,* and *The Linotype—Mergenthaler and Whitelaw Reid.* The murals in the lunettes above the square-headed doors are *Learning to Read* (west side), and *The Student* (east side). The aerial mural on the ceiling, with its *trompe l'oeil* effect, tells the story of *Prometheus Bringing Fire to Men.*

The main-floor **Gottesman Exhibition Hall** with white marble walls and Vermont marble columns is surmounted by a beautifully carved Renaissance-style oak ceiling. See also the **Celeste Bartos Forum,** the lecture hall downstairs, with its high elliptical glass dome.

Library hours: Mon., Thurs., Fri., Sat. 10:00 A.M. to 6:00 P.M.; Tues., Wed. 11:00 A.M. to 7:30 P.M. Free one-hour tours of the Library are conducted Monday through Saturday at 11:00 A.M. and 2:00 P.M.

Walk north on Fifth Avenue to the corner of 43rd Street.

The **J. P. Morgan Chase Building** (No. 510), formerly the Manufacturers Hanover Trust Company, on the southwest corner, was designed in 1954 by Skidmore, Owings & Merrill, and is an example of the early use of the "glass cage" as a building style. Look through the broad glass pane at the exposed bank vault door, now only for display.

Turn left (west) on West 43rd Street.

The **former Columbia University Club,** No. 4 West 43rd Street, originally the Hotel Renaissance, now the Headquarters of the Unification Church (Bruce Price with Howard, Cauldwell & Morgan, 1900), is a simple, unadorned Renaissance Revival–style palazzo, whereas across the street:

The **Century Association Clubhouse,** No. 7 West (McKim, Mead & White, 1889), is another, but far superior, example of Renaissance Revival. Since two partners of McKM&W were members (Stanford White and Charles Follen

The ruins of the Crystal Palace as depicted in Harper's Weekly, *October 16, 1858. (New-York Historical Society)*

The transept of the cast-iron-and-glass Crystal Palace Exposition Hall as seen from the gallery. Many nations were represented in this first American world's fair of science, industry, and art. (New-York Historical Society)

The height of satiety was reached in 1903 when C. K. G. Billings gave his famous Dinner on Horseback at Sherry's for a group of friends from his riding club. Diners were served on trays fastened to the horses' pommels by waiters in footman's livery. (Photograph by Byron. The Byron Collection, Museum of the City of New York)

The Latting Observatory Tower burned to the ground on August 30, 1856, a harbinger of the fate of the nearby Crystal Palace two years later. (New-York Historical Society)

McKim), one could have safely expected a certain extra touch—an assumption clearly vindicated in the design of this grand old Veronese *palazzo*. The Century was the first of the firm's many Renaissance-style clubs, and was begun in 1889 from plans by McKM&W architect William Kendall, and took two years to complete. Typical Renaissance features are the monumental arched doorway and Palladian window above the third-floor windows, which are skillfully joined to those below. Topping the building is a balustrade and ornate cornice. The Association dates from 1847 and was established "to promote the advancement of art and literature." The name "Century" refers to the original 100 members, among whom was William Cullen Bryant. The former clubhouse of the Century Association may be seen on East 15th Street. [*See* pages 264–265.]

No. 25 West 43rd Street, now an office building, was one of the city's most famous literary landmarks, the home of the *New Yorker* magazine. From 1925 to 1991 it occupied seven floors, and accommodated such luminaries as James Thurber, E. B. White, John Updike, John Cheever, Brendan Gill, Calvin Trilling, Peter Arno, and others. (Read the plaque.) A quirky provision in the lease required a manually operated elevator, to quiet the nerves of some who did not trust the self-operating kind.

Return to Fifth Avenue, turn left (north), stopping in front of the tall sidewalk clock in front of No. 522.

The 20-foot-high **Seth Thomas street clock** is probably the oldest artifact on the block. Built of cast iron, these sturdy timepieces were prevalent throughout the country from the 1880s until World War I, when the popularity of the wristwatch eliminated the need of a public clock. Most served as advertising gimmicks for the shops in front of which they were erected. Seth Thomas is still in business—the last survivor of dozens of 19th-century American clockmakers.

The southwest corner of 44th Street was the site of famed **Sherry's,** one of the most lavish and fashionable establishments at the turn of the century. A combination restaurant and residential apartments, it catered to New York's most affluent clientele for 21 years. The building, erected for owner Louis Sherry in 1898 by McKim, Mead & White, was later remodeled for the Guaranty Trust Company, and remained until the early 1950s when it was demolished to make way for the present successor bank.

No less extravagant was **Delmonico's,** Sherry's archrival, which, just six months before, moved up from its Madison Square location into an ornate Beaux Arts building designed by James Brown Lord on the northeast corner. The restaurant with its ballrooms and bachelor residences was closed in 1923, four years after the demise of Sherry's.

Turn left (west) on West 44th Street.

The General Society of Mechanics and Tradesmen of the City of New York (No. 20 West) was founded in 1785. It began as a technical institute offering free courses in the mechanical trades. The present building, formerly the Berkeley Preparatory School, was erected in 1891 from plans by Lamb & Rich. Note the equestrian frieze above the row of Ionic columns on its Renaissance Eclectic façade. Within is a library in a converted drill hall, but don't miss its unique **Mossman Collection of Locks** and see the mind-boggling Very Complicated Lock. (The building is open Mon.–Thurs., 9:00 A.M. to 7:00 P.M., Fri. 9:00 A.M. to 5:00 P.M. Closed weekends and holidays.)

The Harvard Club (No. 27 West) is a modest neo–Georgian-style building, designed by Charles Follen McKim, and completed in 1894. The red Harvard brick is laid in Flemish bond and the trim is in Indiana limestone. The club was extended through to West 45th Street in 1905 from plans by McKim, Mead & White, and was again enlarged in 1915. The interior Harvard Hall is an immense three-story Florentine-inspired "knights' chamber" with two great fireplaces.

No. 30 West, the **Penn (University of Pennsylvania) Club,** formerly the Yale Club, and more recently Touro College (Tracy & Swartwout, 1900), occupies an exuberant Georgian Revival–style clubhouse that at one time also served the Army and Navy Club of America.

The New York Yacht Club (No. 37 West) is one of the city's most romantic buildings. The bay windows imitate the sterns of baroque sailing vessels and are fancifully carved with garlands of shells and seaweed, sculpted waves, and dolphins. This neo-baroque version of Beaux Arts architecture with its striking limestone façade, was designed by Warren & Wetmore (who helped create Grand Central Terminal) in 1901. Founded in 1844, the New York Yacht Club is the patriarch of all American sailing clubs and the internationally famous "America's Cup Race" held every four years. The Cup was first won by the schooner *America* in 1851, and lost only once (to Australia in 1983), then regained by *Stars & Stripes* of the San Diego Yacht Club in 1987. The Club, now in its sixth home, was built on land donated by J. P. Morgan, the commodore from 1897 to 1899, and his 241-foot-long *Corsair II* became the club's flagship. The interior's Model Room, measuring almost 100 feet long, is surrounded by a balcony with galleon railings and covered by a splendid stained-glass ceiling. Hundreds of ship models are displayed, including every defender of the America's Cup. Interestingly, an ornate wooden pergola that once stood atop the building but was removed many years ago, has been replaced—a faithful reproduction of its turn-of-the-century predecessor and a charming final touch.

In stark contrast to the New York Yacht Club, the 30-story limestone and glass **Sofitel New York,** No. 45 West, is one of midtown's new, glitzy "boutique" hotels, and claims to offer a *"Mélange harmonieux du style Français et de l'esprit Américain."* Note the bronze adorned façade with flying geese above.

The Royalton Hotel, No. 44 West, once an "average behind Times Square hotel" was remodeled in 1988 (Philippe Starck and Gruzen Samton) into another French-influenced luxurious boutique hotel. In its early days it was home to George Jean Nathan, editor of *Smart Set* from 1914 to 1925, the major literary magazine of the day, and to writer and humorist Robert Benchley, who also maintained an apartment there. (Peek inside.)

The **Association of the Bar** (No. 42 West, adjacent to the Royalton Hotel) is a majestic structure, appropriate to its distinguished function. Two magnificent fluted Doric columns guard the portico of this Classic Eclectic limestone building, above which rise four pairs of Corinthian pilasters to an ornate cornice sup-

One of the New York Yacht Club's ornate windows that depict the elaborate stern of a 17th-century sailing ship. (Photo by author)

ported by finely detailed brackets. The Bar Association was founded in 1870 "for the purpose of maintaining the honor and dignity of the profession of the Law, of cultivating social relations among its members and increasing its usefulness in promoting the due administration of justice." The building was designed by Cyrus L. W. Eidlitz, and completed in 1895, and contains one of the largest law libraries in the country.

The **Hotel Algonquin** (Goldwyn Starrett, 1902), a Historic Hotel of America, has managed to maintain its *fin de siècle* elegance. The Algonquin, formerly the Puritan, has always been a favorite haunt of stage and literary personalities, though, alas, less so now. Enter and settle into one of the soft chairs in the oak-paneled lobby, order a drink, and imagine yourself a witness to the famous "Round Table" of the 1920s, when such figures as Alexander Woolcott, Robert Benchley, George S. Kaufman, Heywood Broun, Franklin P. Adams, Edna Ferber, Dorothy Parker, and others would gather and try to outdo each other in witty chatter, while pretending to act as the arbiters of the American cultural scene. Look, too, for Matilda, the hotel's live-in cat, who replaced a long line of cats named Hamlet.

At the corner of Sixth Avenue and extending to West 43rd Street stood the famous **Hippodrome Theater** (Frederick Thompson and Alfred S. Dundy, 1905), said to be the largest theater in the world. Its auditorium had a capacity of 5,300 and a projecting stage with two circus rings and an elliptical water tank. The building was a familiar sight with its twin corner towers and illuminated globes, and was known for its extravagant spectacles, with operas, performances by dancing elephants, boxing matches, and ballerinas disappearing into the huge tank (only to emerge across the street). The theater closed in 1939.

Return to Fifth Avenue, and cross and walk to the southeast corner of East 43rd Street.

The **Israel Discount Bank** (511 Fifth Avenue) remodeled the ground-floor space, preserving the remarkable character of the Renaissance façade and interior. Observe the splendid coffered ceiling. The building was originally the Postal Life Insurance Building, erected in 1917 from plans by York & Sawyer. The renovation in 1962 was designed by Luss, Kaplan & Associates.

Across 43rd Street on the northeast corner, from 1868 to 1927, stood **Temple Emanu-El,** the largest synagogue in the world. Its twin "Moorish" towers were conspicuous landmarks on Fifth Avenue for over half a century, until rising land values and the northward push of the business district forced relocation to the present site, 22 blocks north. It is still the world's largest.

Turn left (east) on 42nd Street to Madison Avenue.

The system of designating streets east and west of Fifth Avenue was inaugurated in 1838.

The **Lincoln Building** (No. 60 East 42nd Street) towers 53 stories above 42nd Street, and was built in 1929–30 from plans by the architectural firm of

Temple Emanu-El, at the northeast corner of Fifth Avenue and 43rd Street, with its twin Moorish towers, was the largest synagogue in the world when it occupied the corner from 1868 to 1927. It still maintains the distinction at its present site on East 65th Street and Fifth Avenue. (New-York Historical Society)

J. E. R. Carpenter. A product of the skyscraper building boom of the late 1920s, it was designed according to the setback requirements of the zoning law. In its 1929 prospectus it claimed that "No other office structure has ever been created where clear fresh air is more abundant or where radiant sunlight is more plentiful.... Other buildings are far enough away to give unimpeded ventilation to all floors." On the walls of the vestibule are quotes from speeches by Abraham Lincoln, and in the center of the lobby is a miniature bronze sculpture, *Seated Lincoln*, fashioned from Daniel Chester French's original model for the seated Lincoln at Washington's Lincoln Memorial.

The adjacent 26-story **Philip Morris Headquarters Building,** begun in 1981, blends harmoniously with the 42nd Street "street wall," since architects Ulrich Franzen and Associates chose to have their rough-textured precast gray granite-

(Photo, right) The same intersection forty years later, looking northeast, shows a new type of Fifth Avenue omnibus. The "double decker" open-top models ended service in 1946, the closed-top models in 1953. The building on the northeast corner, built ca. 1870 for Levi P. Morton who served as vice-president in the Benjamin Harrison administration (1889–93), survived until 1992! (Photograph by Alice Austen. Staten Island Historical Society)

Looking southwest across the intersection of Fifth Avenue and 42nd Street, ca. 1875, at the Croton Distributing Reservoir. (New-York Historical Society)

As late as 1902, Fifth Avenue and 44th Street still looked almost rural, with Henry H. Tyson's Fifth Avenue Market and Ye Olde Willow Cottage tavern. Temple Emanu-El is barely visible to the right. The photo was taken from in front of Sherry's. (New-York Historical Society)

paneled building face Park Avenue (No. 120), thus linking it to the axis of new skyscrapers that reach down Park Avenue to 32nd Street. The engaging three-story colonnade provides a covered pedestrian space, with access to street-level shops and a branch of the Whitney Museum. The site was formerly occupied by the noted Art Deco–style Airline Building, built in the late 1930s to serve as the in-town terminal for the newly opened LaGuardia Field. The **Whitney Museum of American Art at Philip Morris** features two public areas, a 42-foot-high sculpture court of 20th-century American works in a garden setting, a smaller gallery for changing exhibits, and a few shops. Take an espresso from the little bar, sit at one of the scattered tables, and enjoy the works of art. (The Sculpture Court is open Mon.–Sat. 7:30 A.M. to 9:30 P.M.; the Gallery, Mon.–Fri. 11:00 A.M. to 6:00 P.M., Thurs. to 7:30 P.M. The shops are closed on weekends. Admission free.)

    Grand Central Terminal, a magnificent Beaux Arts Eclectic structure of mammoth proportions, has provided a dramatic gateway into New York City since its completion in 1913. Designed by Whitney Warren and Charles D. Wetmore plus Charles A. Reed and Allen H. Stem, the master plan combined function, accessibility, and aesthetics, which resulted in a monumentally successful engineering and architectural achievement.

    Enter at the main entrance (under the Pershing Square Viaduct) and cross the Main Concourse Level, turning left at the Central Information Desk (with the four-sided clock), and walk to the staircase. Climb to the upper level, and view the arrival and departure signboards, the walls of smooth caen stone, the chandeliers, the broad windows at each end, the clerestory half-moon windows with carvings, and the lovely Sky Ceiling. After reading the following, explore this architectural masterpiece at leisure.

The exterior's south façade, with its triple arches, provides great expanses of glass to illuminate the interior. Crowning the center arch is the imposing **sculpture group by Jules Coutan,** representing Mercury, Hercules, and Minerva, set above a 13-foot-high clock. Below is a statue of the founder of the original railroad empire, Cornelius "Commodore" Vanderbilt (the statue, by Albert De Groot, is visible from the south side of 42nd Street). The terminal covers the three blocks to 45th Street, but below ground are 33.7 miles of track on two levels—66 tracks on the upper, and 57 on the lower level—a practical plan devised by railroad engineer William J. Wilgus. Reed and Stem's ingenious series of ramps connect the two levels with streets, subways, adjacent office buildings, and hotels, separating pedestrians from vehicular traffic, plus two recently opened passageways underground to 47th and 48th streets with four new entrances to the terminal that permit commuters convenient access from the trains to streets farther uptown.

The main concourse, one of the most awe-inspiring interior spaces in the country, is covered with a vaulted ceiling supported by 125-foot-high piers and

Commodore Vanderbilt's Grand Central Depot gave New York its first direct rail link. This sprawling Second Empire building, built in 1871, hid an enormous ground-level train shed. The station was enlarged in 1899 and replaced by the present multilevel terminal in 1913. (Museum of the City of New York)

hung from steel trusses. On the Sky Ceiling are fiber-optic illuminated constellations of the zodiac, painted by Charles Gulbrandsen when the terminal opened in 1913, and who, with some artistic license, painted the constellations his own way to fit the ceiling. Sunlight entering through the 75-foot-high windows casts long rays across the marble floor, augmenting the feeling of height and grandeur. The Main Concourse Level formerly served long-distance trains, and the lower, now the Dining Concourse Level, was used by the hundreds of commuter trains. With the shift of Amtrak service to Pennsylvania Station, the terminal now serves only the 125,000 daily Metro-North Railroad commuters, on both levels. Who can forget the names of such great trains as the "Empire State Express," the "North Shore Limited," or the "Commodore Vanderbilt"? Or the rolling out of the red carpet for the daily departure to Chicago of the "Twentieth-Century Limited"?

In 1983 Metro-North Railroad took over operation of both the rail lines and Grand Central Terminal from Conrail. Five years later it commissioned a master revitalization plan from Beyer Blinder Belle for the architectural design, and Williams Jackson Ewing, retail design specialists, for a master retail plan to address amenities and services in the terminal. Large-scale construction, however, did not begin until 1996. Two years later, the revitalized Grand Central Terminal was rededicated, and in 1999 Grand Central North, Grand Central Market, and the new Dining Concourse were opened. The former proliferation of shops and advertising displays that cramped the Main Concourse Level were removed, and the spacious waiting room was restored to its early 20th-century elegance. Even the splendid chandeliers and other fixtures were removed and restored. Among the new amenities on the Main Concourse Level is a branch of the **New York Transit Museum,** Mon.–Fri. 8:00 A.M. to 8:00 P.M., Sat., Sun. 10:00 A.M. to 6:00 P.M. On the Dining Concourse are almost two dozen food establishments. (Do look for the Guastavino tile vaulted ceilings in several locations, especially in the Oyster Bar.) At the east end of the Main Concourse Level is Grand Central Market, with vendors offering fresh produce and take-out food. The lovely Beaux Arts exterior was cleaned and now benefits from nighttime illumination to highlight the imposing façade. In 1994 the Metropolitan Transit Authority (MTA) gained control of Grand Central Terminal, but the trains continue to be operated by Metro-North.

BRIEF HISTORY. The New York & Harlem Railroad, which began chugging down Fourth Avenue in 1832, used a depot at 26th Street [the site of the first Madison Square Garden; *see* Madison Square, 11]. It then used horses to pull the coaches the rest of the way to the end of the line near City Hall. By 1858 the Common Council banned steam locomotives below 42nd Street because of the air and noise pollution, and in 1871 Commodore Vanderbilt had a huge cast-iron and glass terminal, designed by John B. Snook, built at the present site. The former route down Fourth Avenue (now Park Avenue) cut through Murray Hill to 32nd Street. This "cut" was taken over by the Metropolitan Street Railway for use by its horsecars and later trolleys, and was covered over and converted into a tunnel. Today it is used by automobiles only, and connects with an elevated viaduct that encircles the station on its way to upper Park Avenue. The viaduct also bypasses the huge MetLife (ex-Pan Am) Building and passes through the former New York Central Office Building,

The enormous cast-iron-and-glass train shed of Grand Central Depot, ca. 1872. Electrification did not come until 1902. (Museum of the City of New York)

which was later renamed the New York General Building, and in more recent times, the **Helmsley Building.** A short spur of the Third Avenue El that connected with Grand Central Terminal was demolished when the viaduct was built in 1919.

The old station was enlarged in 1899, but with the 1902 regulation banning steam trains altogether from the city, the company—now the New York Central Railroad—had the choice of either relocating outside the city limits, or doing what it so wisely did, electrifying its lines. The railroad then acquired the subsurface land rights for an underground terminal and yards, and began building the huge station. With the new land and air rights, the Central was able to build itself an attractive office building and two hotels, the Commodore (now the Grand Hyatt) and the Biltmore (rebuilt as the headquarters of the Bank of America). The new terminal also provided access to the heart of New York City for trains from New England of the New York, New Haven, and Hartford Railroad (now part of Amtrak).

For a short detour, cross the Main Concourse and take the escalator for a brief visit to the extravagant lobby of the **MetLife Building** (originally the Pan Am Building). Built in 1963 and designed by Walter Gropius, Emery Roth & Sons, and Pietro Belluschi, it did much to destroy the scale of Grand Central Terminal. The enormous office building provided more floor space than any other in the world, adding additional traffic and congestion to an already overcrowded area. Its precast curtain-wall construction made it one of the first of its kind in the city. It also created an outpouring of discontent, not diminished by the helicopter landing pad on the roof (since discontinued). Former Landmarks Commissioner Harmon H. Goldstone referred to the then–Pan Am Building's interruption of the broad view of Grand Central Terminal from upper Park Avenue as "a monstrous bland blanket." There was some regret at the loss of the familiar Pan Am logo atop the building. Some wags suggested that a more suitable logo for the Metropolitan Life Insurance Company, the building owner, would have been a giant Snoopy!

Some years ago the Penn Central Transporting Company (the merger of the New York Central, New Haven, and Pennsylvania railroads) sought to obtain permission to construct a 55-story tower above Grand Central Terminal. In denying the application, the Commission felt that such a tall tower would in effect destroy the landmark, reducing it to the status of a "curiosity." The Penn Central then had the temerity to suggest that the front of the terminal be demolished altogether! The Commission, of course, did not agree that this was an appropriate means of preserving the landmark. A major public outcry, supported by the Municipal Art Society and such public figures as Jacqueline Onassis, helped convince the courts that the destruction of Grand Central Terminal was really not in the best interest of the city or its citizens. However, the ultimate solution came with the transfer of the Terminal's air rights.

Before continuing on the tour, take a few minutes to explore the recently opened **Grand Central North** section of the terminal to enjoy the mosaic, bronze, and glass reliefs in Ellen Driscoll's *As Above, So Below*. The 13 major panels and associated reliefs present a round-the-world journey to the night sky above five different continents, recounting myths of their civilizations, the heavens, and the underworld. In the 45th and 47th streets Cross-Passages, the Northeast Passage, and the Escalator Wall, there are also many attractive panels. All are part of the Arts for Transit program, which, according to the MTA, are designed to "add a sense of comfort and security and reinforce the identity of individual stations," and "bring a vitality to travel that makes the experience inviting as well as convenient and quick." (For free descriptive brochures about the entire Program, call the MTA at 878-7250.) Exit from the Terminal and cross 42nd Street to the east side of Park Avenue and admire the restored south façade.

Although the name **Pershing Square** appears on the **Park Avenue Viaduct,** the square really no longer exists. A rectangular piece of land on the southeast corner of Park Avenue and East 42nd Street was cleared in 1914 after the demolition of the imposing Grand Union Hotel. Named for the Commander-in-Chief of the American Expeditionary Forces in World War I, the plot was acquired by the city for an open plaza. In 1920 the plaza plan was abandoned, and it was sold to a developer who three years later erected No. 100 East 42nd Street, naming it the **Pershing Square Building.** A large plaque in the lobby relates the history of the site.

The **former Bowery Savings Bank** (No. 110 East), now Cipriani's 42nd Street (catering hall), was built in 1923 from plans by York & Sawyer. Designed in a Romanesque basilica style, the imposing arch leads into the huge former banking room, 160 feet long and 65 feet high, with a beamed and coffered ceiling. The walls are of variegated limestone, interspersed with blocks of Ohio sandstone. On each side wall are six columns of different-colored marble, carrying five stone arches. Between the columns are panels of unpolished marble mosaic from quarries in France and Italy. The mosaic marble floors add to the artistic effect. The former massive bronze doors are hung for ornamentation on the east and west walls. Another dramatic interior space, it was cited for architectural merit by the Municipal Art Society and the Society of Architectural Historians. The Bowery Savings Bank, founded in 1834, was one of the city's oldest and boasted a magnificent Classic-style McKim, Mead & White landmark building in its 130 Bowery office downtown [*see* Lower East Side, 25]. The rich architectural detail has many lovely motifs, including the bull and bear of Wall Street, a rooster representing punctuality, a squirrel for thrift, and a lion for power. The sculpture is by Ricci & Zari. Many consider this the finest work of York & Sawyer. The bank was acquired in 1992 by Home Savings of America.

The 56-story Art Deco **Chanin Building** (No. 122 East), is a delightful addition to the city's panorama (enter on Lexington Avenue). Built in 1929 from designs by Sloan & Robertson, it came at a period when decoration was still considered an essential element of the architectural whole. Note the fossilized sea creatures in the black marble façade at the corner, the wide ornate bronze band on the third floor, with Art Deco motifs of birds and fish running the full length of the façade by Edward Trumbull, and the base of terra-cotta plant forms. The lobby is a gem of Art Deco styling. Bronze is used tastefully and artistically in the amazing convector grills, the low reliefs on the elevator doors and mailboxes, the "jeweled" clocks, and even in the "waves" on the floor at the 42nd Street entrance. One cannot help but rejoice at the excellent building maintenance and the lack of "modernization" which has helped keep the Chanin Building in pristine condition. Unfortunately, the top floor observation deck is now closed. A theater on the 50th floor is also closed, as is the former basement bus station of the Baltimore & Ohio Railroad train connection to Jersey City.

Facing, or rather reflecting, the Chanin Building, is the glistening **Grand Hyatt Hotel** (Gruzen & Partners, with Der Scutt, 1981). This glitzy member of the Hyatt chain in New York City is, alas, disturbingly out of context with its neighbor, Grand Central Terminal. The bronze-tone glass sheathing now covers the entire façade of what was once the Hotel Commodore, designed by architects Warren & Wetmore as part of the original Terminal project. As a hotel, the Hyatt is a vast improvement over its predecessor, which had declined badly in its later years. The striking Sun Garden cocktail lounge is cantilevered over 42nd Street, and although intrusive on the street wall, it provides a pleasant view with a tropical atmosphere. The plant-filled lobby, with its metal geometric sculptures and comfortable seating, is reached from the street entrance by an escalator gliding past a bubbling waterfall.

Perhaps the most unusually shaped building, and certainly one of the most beautiful, is the 1,048-foot-high **Chrysler Building** (No. 405 Lexington Avenue), on the northeast corner of Lexington Avenue. Its graceful vertical shaft tapering into a fine stainless-steel point gives it a distinctive and artistic position in New York's skyline. Designed by William Van Alen in 1929, it became, upon completion a year later, the tallest building in the world, only to be relegated to second place a few months later by the Empire State Building. Close examination of the lovely Art Deco façade readily indicates that this was planned as *the* automotive tower of the city. At each setback are stylized "motor" designs. The building flares out sharply at the fourth setback into what appears to be shiny radiator caps—for a 1929 Chrysler! At other levels are basket-weave designs and a band of abstract automobiles. The Chrysler Building was one of the first to have exposed metal as an essential part of the design. An interesting event in the history of its construction was the deception of a rival architect by Van Alen as the building neared completion. When they reached a height of 925 feet, everyone assumed that this was the maximum; and when the downtown "40 Wall Tower" (40 Wall Street) also reached that height, architects H. Craig Severance and Yasuo Matsui added another two feet to make *their* building "the tallest in the world." To their consternation the tall stainless-steel spire of the Chrysler Build-

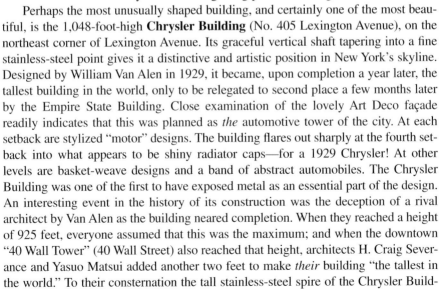

ing was secretly assembled, raised through the dome, and bolted into place, adding a victorious 123 feet. The elegant lobby is faced with African marble, and the ceiling is covered with what is considered the world's largest mural, 97 by 100 feet, depicting transportation themes. Artist Edward Trumbell used as models some of the men who had actually worked on the construction of the building. In its early years, the lobby served as a showroom for Chrysler Motors products. The lavish observation lounge has been closed and now houses electronic equipment; however, the installation of the spectacular illumination in the tower in the winter of 1981 (according to architect Van Alen's original plans, but with modern high-intensity light tubes) has added a brilliant touch to the nighttime city skyline. The successive rows of brightly lit inverted V's have been likened to some ethereal necklace suspended from the clouds.

After examining the unique lobby of the Chrysler Building, exit on the Lexington Avenue side. As you step outside, note the dazzling reflection of the building in the Grand Hyatt Hotel across the avenue. Then turn right and walk to the corner of 43rd Street. Diagonally across is the 33-story **Graybar Building** (Sloan & Robertson, 1927). Although relatively undistinguished architecturally, it was the largest office building in the world when completed. It also provides direct access into Grand Central Terminal, giving the impression that it is a part of the great station. What *is* unusual are the bright polychrome bas reliefs on the lower façade whose motifs are adapted from ancient mythology.

Note the steel canopy over the entrance to the passageway into the terminal. Supporting it from above are three cables designed to resemble ships' hawsers, with **iron rats** climbing the lines, including the usual rat-deflector cones, below.

Around the corner on 42nd Street (best viewed from the south side of the street), it will be noted that the east wall of the Chrysler Building's lower setback is not parallel to the north-south avenues. This is because the property line follows the route of the former East Post Road, which in the 18th century ran approximately between Lexington and Third avenues, wending its way up Manhattan Island. The Annex of the Chrysler Building, at its east end on 42nd Street, is a strange and mystifying confection. Attributed to Philip Johnson and Alan Ritchie, both distinguished architects, the first impression of the translucent and tilted panels is a disturbing re-creation of the crashing walls of the World Trade Center. (Hopefully an explanation will be forthcoming.)

The massive **former Mobil Building** (No. 150 East) occupies the entire block to Third Avenue. Unusual are the embossed stainless-steel panels that cover the entire building. Originally the Socony-Mobil Building, it was built in 1955 from plans by Harrison & Abramovitz. When opened it boasted three superlatives: the largest steel-sheathed building; the largest air-conditioning system; and on the second floor, the largest floor space in the world. The design of its steel panels prevents warping, and the projecting surfaces are cleansed by the wind.

Third Avenue has changed drastically since World War II. For over 70 years the avenue was darkened by the rattling Third Avenue El and, like so many of the El-covered thoroughfares, was lined with dingy tenements, saloons, and cheap little shops. When the El came down in 1955—the last survivor of Manhattan's once extensive overhead railway network—Third Avenue underwent a complete transformation. From 38th Street to 57th Street, modern office buildings were erected; and typical of the 1950s and early '60s, most were boring boxlike carbon copies of each other. **Second Avenue** was also relieved of its overhead El in 1942 and enjoyed a similar renaissance, albeit somewhat later.

On the southeast corner of Third Avenue, until 1990, stood New York's **last Automat.** Although a re-creation of the once ubiquitous fast-food Art Deco–style restaurants, it was a pleasant reminder of the days when tasty, low-cost food was dispensed from coin-operated see-through doors, and five-cent coffee flowed from brass dolphins' mouths at the turn of a crank. It was a gathering place that knew no social bounds and a homey amenity that is gone forever.

The adjacent **New York Helmsley Hotel** (Emery Roth & Sons, 1981) replaced the former Central Commercial High School, which had occupied the site since 1906. The lofty structure blends well with its modern neighbors, although it adds little architectural excitement to the streetscape. The porte-cochère, a novelty on 42nd Street, helps relieve some of the traffic congestion (unlike its rival, the Hyatt); and its two-story-high, dark-toned, mirrored-glass overhang, while breaking the "street wall," shifts attention from the monotonous verticality of the row of buildings. The Helmsley, newest of six New York City Helmsley hotels, is named for the late chairman of the board of the chain, real estate tycoon Harry Helmsley.

Step back across 42nd Street and notice the diminutive five-story Romanesque Revival–style structure **(No. 202)** tucked between the Helmsley and the corner building. Built in the mid-1880s, it became one of a number of "holdouts" in the city—buildings whose owners either refused to sell to site developers, or who held out for prohibitive sums, forcing architects and builders to work around them. An odd anachronism, this brick and masonry house gives some idea of the scale and type of building that lined the thoroughfare a hundred years ago.

The New York Daily News Building (No. 220 East) was completed in 1930, a year before architect Raymond M. Hood's opposite outpost, the McGraw-Hill Building. Differing sharply from it and from his American Radiator Building of seven years earlier, the News Building uses other means to stress its verticality. In cooperation with John Mead Howells, Hood resorted to rows of brown brick spandrels and windows to create an up-and-down stripe effect. In 1958, an addition was added by Harrison & Abramovitz, wisely following the original style. Not to be missed is the attractive lobby, designed as an educational exhibition. In the center is the world's largest interior globe, illuminated from within and rotating slowly on a recessed platform. An excellent geography lesson, the globe's details are constantly kept up to date. On the lobby floor are bronze lines pointing to cities around the world and to the relative positions of the planets. The back wall has various meteorological instruments. The *Daily News* does its printing in Brooklyn, Garden City, and Kearny, N.J., and at one time had the largest circulation of any newspaper in the country. The striking building was cited by the Municipal Art Society and the Society of Architectural Historians for "originality in design and influence on later work." The newspaper briefly became the *Daily Planet* when it was featured in the film *Superman* in 1978. The *News* has since abandoned the building in favor of more spacious quarters at 450 West 33rd Street.

The Ford Foundation Building, midway down the north side of 42nd Street, stands as a significant contribution to the quality of life in the city. The L-shaped

In the late 1920s, many rows of brownstones at the east end of 42nd Street were leveled to make way for Tudor City. This group of houses stood on the south side of 42nd Street near the present Tudor City Place before the thoroughfare was widened. (Fred F. French Investing Company)

building arranged around a 130-foot-high "greenhouse" was designed by Kevin Roche John Dinkeloo and Associates, and was completed in 1967. The architects' plan was "to provide a proper environment for the building's staff—a space that would allow them to enjoy the view, but at the same time, allow them to be aware of the existence of other members of the Foundation, people who share their common aims and purposes." They felt that their building should contribute something to the city, maintaining a low profile and observing "the lines and planes created by other buildings which form the surrounding street." The result was eminently successful. The 12-story glassed-in area is anchored by granite piers and side walls, and shelters a one-third-acre garden. The shrubbery is frequently changed and is centered about a terraced garden with 17 full-grown trees, thousands of ground-cover plants, and aquatic plants in a still pool. Each season brings its own bloomings, and the entire area is floodlit, adding to the natural effect of filtered sunlight. The "greenhouse" also serves the additional purpose of a waste air chamber and thermal buffer. Ada Louise Huxtable, former architecture critic of *The New York Times,* in praising its successful design, called the Ford Foundation Building "a splendid, shimmering Crystal Palace…one of the Foundation's more valid contributions to the arts." (The garden may be visited on weekdays. Enter on East 43rd Street.)

Across 42nd Street are the **Church of the Covenant,** 310 West; the **Crowne Plaza at The United Nations,** No. 304 West, formerly the Hotel Tudor, a 300-room "boutique" hotel; and the **Tudor City Historic District.** Not officially part of Tudor City, the Church (J. Cleveland Cady, 1871) fits harmoniously into the architectural style of the complex. Cady was a member of the congregation, and the church was one of his first commissions. Built as the Covenant Memorial Chapel to serve as a mission for the working-class neighborhood, it became a regular church in 1893. The interior has great charm, with antique glass, bright stained-glass windows, and delicately carved wood traceries. When 42nd Street was depressed for the construction of Tudor City, the church ended up a full story above street level, requiring the construction of the staircase for access to the entrance.

Climb the stairway on the north side of 42nd Street to Tudor City Place, which spans the street.

● **Tudor City** was developed in 1925–28 by the Fred F. French Company as a "self-contained city within walking distance of the city itself." There are 12 apartment houses with a total of 3,000 apartments, the 300-room hotel, shops, restaurant, post office, and private parks—all designed in a Tudor Gothic, or English Cottage, style to evoke the majesty of England's Tudor dynasty. From the north end of Tudor City Place there is a superb view of the United Nations.

The site has had a checkered history, beginning with the rural Winthrop Mansion, "Dutch Hill," in the 18th century. The house was later converted into a tavern and rest stop for the stagecoaches of the old East Post Road. By mid-19th century the area deteriorated badly and became the hangout for gangs of criminals. In the early 20th century, the rocky crags were taken over by the notorious "Rag Gang," led by archfelon Paddy Corcoran. The neighborhood surrounding "Corcoran's Roost" became industrialized with breweries, slaughterhouses, glue factories, and a gas works (which explains why there are so few windows in the east side of the Tudor City apartment houses that might offer unattractive views or admit unsavory odors). Tudor City has remained a staid and tranquil enclave, enhanced by the arrival of the U.N. in the early 1950s.

Toward the south end of Tudor City Place, turn right briefly into East 41st Street. Alongside the park is a solitary survivor of the mid-19th-century brownstone era. **No. 37,** a three-story plus basement Italianate residence, long a deserted hulk, was restored by its new owner to its original pristine beauty.

The two little shady parks on each side of the 42nd Street overpass had been the subject of a long-standing battle between the owners of Tudor City and the tenants. Plans were to erect additional high-rise apartment houses on each site, thus destroying the pair of parks. In 1987, after a fifteen-year struggle, the strong tenants' association negotiated with the general partnership that was converting seven Tudor City buildings to cooperative ownership, and the little parks were turned over to the not-for-profit tenants' group, Tudor Greens Inc., with development rights held by the Trust for Public Land, a national group. The rights can never be sold or transferred, and the trust also holds a conservation easement to the land, which means that it will forever remain a green oasis. [The United Nations is described at the beginning of the next tour, East River Panoramas.]

End of tour. The M42 and M104 42nd Street crosstown buses stop at the foot of the north stairs leading down from Tudor City Place.

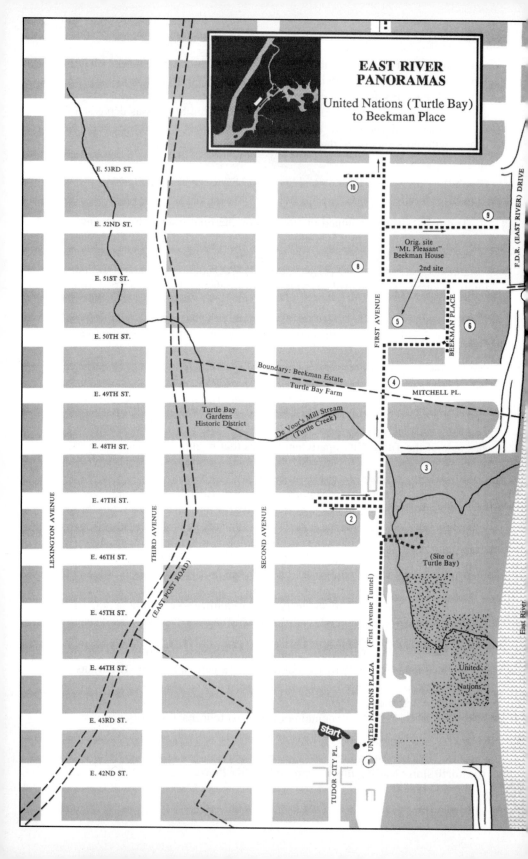

EAST RIVER PANORAMAS

United Nations (Turtle Bay)
to Beekman Place

E. 53RD ST.

E. 52ND ST.

E. 51ST ST.

E. 50TH ST.

E. 49TH ST.

Boundary: Beekman Estate
Turtle Bay Farm

Turtle Bay
Gardens
Historic District

De Voor's Mill Stream
(Turtle Creek)

E. 48TH ST.

E. 47TH ST.

E. 46TH ST.

E. 45TH ST.

E. 44TH ST.

E. 43RD ST.

E. 42ND ST.

Orig. site
"Mt. Pleasant"
Beekman House

2nd site

MITCHELL PL.

(Site of
Turtle Bay)

United
Nations

LEXINGTON AVENUE

THIRD AVENUE

(EAST POST ROAD)

SECOND AVENUE

FIRST AVENUE

BEEKMAN PLACE

F.D.R. (EAST RIVER) DRIVE

UNITED NATIONS PLAZA

(First Avenue Tunnel)

TUDOR CITY PL.

East River

start

⑩ ⑨ ⑧ ⑤ ⑥ ④ ③ ② ①

13. East River Panoramas and Roosevelt Island

[Subways: 4, 5, 6 lines or 42nd Street S Shuttle to Grand Central. Buses: First/ Second Avenue (M15) to East 42nd Street; 42nd Street crosstown (M42 or M104) to First Avenue.]

The walking tour begins at **United Nations Plaza,** opposite the U.N. Secretariat Building, in Ralph J. Bunche Park, just north of 42nd Street, on the west side of United Nations Plaza (First Avenue), and follows the East River shoreline (with some detours) to Gracie Mansion, ending at the Henderson Place Historic District at East 86th Street.

1. Ralph J. Bunche Park honors the peace efforts of the United States' first black U.N. official, who served as secretary to the Palestine Peace Commission in 1947 and was awarded the Nobel Peace Prize three years later. He was subsequently appointed Under-Secretary General for Political Affairs, a post he held until his death. The aluminum sculpture, *Peace Form One,* is by Los Angeles–born black artist Daniel LaRue Johnson.

The backdrop for the minipark is the **Isaiah Wall,** given by New York City to the United Nations. It bears the familiar lines from the Book of Isaiah, "They Shall Beat Their Swords into Plowshares...."

Climb the (Natan) **Shcharansky Steps** (named for the Soviet dissident) for a fine view of the U.N., then go back down and head north along the curbside **Raoul Wallenberg Walk** that honors the martyred Swedish diplomat who saved thousands of Hungarian Jews from the Nazis, only to be arrested by the Soviets and vanish. It is now believed that he was executed by the Russians in 1947.

The United Nations. After several years in temporary quarters on Long Island, at the City of New York Building in the Flushing Meadow Park 1939–40 World's Fair Grounds, and at the former Sperry Gyroscope Plant at Lake Success, the U.N. moved into its permanent headquarters on this Manhattan East River shorefront site in 1952. Technically outside the territorial jurisdiction of the United States, the U.N. complex consists of three main buildings: the 544-foot-high Secretariat, completed in 1950, the General Assembly Building (1952), and the Dag Hammarskjöld Library (1963).

The site that now appears so ideal for the location of the world body was formerly a depressing aggregation of slums, coal docks, factories, slaughterhouses, and breweries. The original plan called for a site north of the city in Westchester County, but a grant of $8.5 million from John D. Rockefeller made it possible to purchase a parcel of land that had already been accumulated by William Zeckendorf for private development. In the earlier Zeckendorf plan, all buildings east of Third Avenue between 46th and 49th Streets were to be razed. The revised proposal proved more practical and saved many beautiful houses from demolition, including the historic Turtle Bay Gardens.

The new plan was approved by Congress in record time, and the city rushed through all the enabling legislation, which included the waterfront rights and tax-

View of the United Nations site taken from Tudor City, looking north, December 1946. In the distance, the graceful Queensboro Bridge leaps across Welfare (now Roosevelt) Island. (Official United Nations Photo)

exempt status. An international team of renowned architects, led by America's Wallace K. Harrison, drew up the designs. Among the planners were Le Corbusier (France), Sven Markelius (Sweden), Oscar Niemeyer (Brazil), plus representatives from ten other countries. The library was designed by Harrison, Abramovitz & Harris. The pool was a gift from American schoolchildren; its freestanding stone sculpture is by England's Barbara Hepworth; and the Council Chambers, a gift from Norway, Sweden, and Denmark.

Along with the construction of the U.N., New York City diverted busy First Avenue, now United Nations Plaza, into a newly constructed five-block-long tunnel and widened East 47th Street into Dag Hammarskjöld Plaza. The flags of the 190 member nations (as of 2003) are displayed along the U.N.'s perimeter.

Visiting the United Nations. The entry gate is opposite East 45th Street. The U.N. is open weekdays, 9:00 A.M. to 4:45 P.M.; Sat., Sun., and holidays, 9:15 A.M. to 4:45 P.M. Guided tours are available all day. Last tour is at 4:45 P.M. Admission: adults $8.50, seniors $7.00, students $6.00, children 5–14 $5.00.

At the street entrance are two sculptures: *Twisted Pistol* by Carl Fredrik Reutersward, a gift from Luxembourg, and to the left, *Sphere within a Sphere* by Arnaldo Pomodoro, a gift from Italy. Enter the Secretariat Building and take the steps down to the lower concourse to the information desk. Hanging high above is a model of Sputnik, from the former Soviet Union, and to the right is a stained-glass mural by Marc Chagall, from France. The tour will include a wide assortment of artistic gifts presented to the U.N. from member nations. The grounds display many beautiful art objects, including the Peace Bell and Shrine from Japan and mosaics from Tunisia.

Many noteworthy sculptures can be seen in the North Garden (closed in winter). Take the path near the entrance gate and follow it clockwise. Among the more unusual are *Cast the Sleeping Elephant* (Mihail, 1998), a casting of a real live elephant—a symbol of the wildlife in Kenya, Namibia, and Nepal; a section of the Berlin Wall from Germany; an enormous stylized ship, entitled *Arrival,* by John Behan, from Ireland, commemorating the many Irish immigrants to the United States; facing the East River, the powerful male nude about to deliver a shattering blow to his sword, entitled *We Shall Beat Our Swords into Plowshares,* by Yevgeny Vuchetic, given by the USSR in 1959; and, dominating the lawn, the bronze, 16-foot-high equestrian *Monument to Peace,* on a 26-foot-high pedestal, by Antun Augustinčić, from Yugoslavia.

2. The west side of **United Nations Plaza** has its own panorama of modern architecture. Among the more interesting buildings are:

No. 771, the Herbert Hoover Building, headquarters of the **Boys and Girls Club of America** (1960).

No. 777, the **Church Center for the United Nations** (William Lascaze, 1962). The impressive stained glass in the sanctuary of this nondenominational church represents *Man's Struggle for Peace and Brotherhood,* by Henry L. Willet.

The Millenium Hotel, formerly One United Nations Plaza (Kevin Roche, John Dinkeloo and Associates, 1976), is a striking addition to the city skyline. This irregularly shaped aluminum and blue-green reflective-glass curtain-wall structure is a dramatic counterpart to the smooth, straight shaft of the U.N. Secre-

The "Old Store House at Turtle Bay, N.Y., 1852," now the site of the United Nations, in a lithograph from Valentine's Manual, *1857. The house was the site of a Liberty Boys' raid led by Marinus Willett, on the King's stores, just before the American Revolution. (Museum of the City of New York)*

tariat Building, and its gridiron skin looks for all the world like a sheet of misfolded graph paper, as it looms skyward from a street-level "skirt" to a sliced-off corner and 45-degree setbacks on the north side. It is a dizzying and exciting visual experience, and a welcome change from the traditional glass boxes of recent times.

No. 799, the **United States Permanent Mission to the United Nations** (Kelly & Gruzen and Kahn & Jacobs, 1959). It is an attractive, eye-catching building, and appropriate to the U.N.'s host country. The electric wires inside the precast concrete "honeycombs" were installed to shock pigeons into roosting on some other nation's edifice.

No. 809, originally the **Institute of International Education** (Harrison, Abramovitz & Harris, 1964). Architect Alvar Aalto designed the Edgar J. Kaufmann Conference Room in the penthouse.

No. 823 (345 East 46th Street), the **Anti-Defamation League of B'nai B'rith** (Harrison, Abramovitz & Harris, 1952), also Afro-American Institute. At No. 821, note the impressive **Turkish Center.**

On the north side of Dag Hammarskjöld Plaza:

No. 333 East 47th Street, the **Japan Society Building** (Junzo Yoshimuro and Gruzen & Partners, 1971). Funded by John D. Rockefeller III to the tune of $4.3 million, this striking example of modern Japanese architecture was inaugurated by Prince and Princess Hitachi and is the U.S. headquarters of the Society.

The Holy Family Roman Catholic Church (rebuilt in 1964 by George J. Sole) is dominated by its gray granite and aluminum bell tower. The church was built on the site of a brewery stable.

At the northwest corner of East 47th Street rises the **Trump World Tower, No. 845 United Nations Plaza** (Costas Kondylis, 2001), erected on the site of the United Engineering Center (Shreve, Lamb & Harmon, 1961). This enormous cloud-piercing monolith, at 90 stories, is the tallest residential building in the world and second in height in New York only to the Empire State Building.

Return to United Nations Plaza, and turn north to East 48th Street.

In the mid-17th century, the area along the river below the present East 49th Street was the **site of the Turtle Bay Farm.** The origin of "Turtle" is uncertain. Some claim it to come from the many turtles that were once common along the shore or Turtle Bay (where the U.N. is now); others attribute it to the early Dutch word *deutal,* a farm implement, which was later corrupted into "turtle." The original farm dated from 1639. Just before the Revolutionary War, the neighborhood figured in a bold act by a group of "Liberty Boys," under Marinus Willett, who sailed down from Greenwich, Connecticut, in a small sloop, seized a cache of arms from a British storehouse in the lower city, then attacked a small stone fort that stood at the foot of East 45th Street, surprising the guards and making off to Boston with a boatload of supplies for the new Continental Army.

Flowing deep below East 48th Street is **De Voor's Mill Stream,** later called Turtle Creek, which once emptied into Turtle Bay. Because of a cholera epidemic in 1854, the city fathers blocked the now polluted creek and channeled it into a culvert, which still empties into the East River under the present United Nations site.

On the northwest corner of 48th Street is the soaring tower of **100 United Nations Plaza** (Schuman, Lichtenstein, Claman & Efron, with Der Scutt, 1986). Its 52 stories of glass, stone, and steel rise to an eight-step pyramid, as each floor with its multiple wedge-shaped balconies gives the façade a striking texture.

3. On the east side, the twin monoliths of **Nos. 860 and 870 United Nations Plaza** (Harrison, Abramovitz & Harris, 1966) are luxury cooperative apartment houses. Originally they were planned to be the IBM World Trade Center, but now only the lower floors are used for commercial purposes.

4. The Beekman Tower (John Mead Howells, 1928), No. 3 Mitchell Place, was built as the Panhellenic Hotel, a national meeting place for Greek-letter sororities, and is now a residential hotel. It is a bold Art Deco shaft whose 26-story-high deep window recesses emphasize the feeling of verticality. The Top of the Tower lounge offers a spectacular view.

5. Beekman Hill. The high ground that dominated the area between 50th and 51st streets was the site of the James Beekman mansion, *Mount Pleasant.* Built in 1763, the beautiful Colonial mansion stood near East 51st Street, but was later moved one block south when First Avenue was opened.

Turn right to Beekman Place.

6. The Beekman Place District. The two blocks, East 50th Street to Beekman Place, and Beekman Place between 50th and 51st streets, were formerly cobblestoned, and consist mainly of town houses, remodeled in the 1920s. This delightful group of luxury residences on Beekman Place has a unique atmosphere of charm and tranquility, in striking contrast to the surrounding neighborhood. Although not startling architecturally, each house has a character of its own, reflecting the individual taste of the original owner and the imagination of its builder.

The town houses were favored particularly by great theater personalities Alfred Lunt and Lynn Fontanne, who lived in the house on the northeast corner of East 50th Street and Beekman Place. Among others who enjoyed Beekman Place addresses were Ethel Barrymore, Katherine Cornell, and Irving Berlin, as well as many diplomats. It was also home for members of the Rockefeller family and former Secretary of the Navy and Defense James Forrestal.

Some of the more interesting remodeled town houses on East 50th Street: **Nos. 405, 414–420, 417,** and **419.** On Beekman Place: **Nos. 19–21, 23** (look up at the modern superimposition!), **33** (note its storybook roof and dormers, and the ropelike twisted bronze rainspout), **32–34,** and **35.** Notice the old **bishop's crook lampposts** scattered throughout the historic district.

Turn right (east) on East 51st Street, pass through the little Peter Detmold Park, and down onto the footbridge over the East River Drive.

7. An excellent vantage point for a rear view of the Beekman Place District, the bridge is also a perfect site from which to view Cannon Point just to the north, where the Drive disappears under Sutton Place. Just to the south was a pleasant beach, where swimming was frequently enjoyed in the "altogether," and where Edgar Allan Poe came in 1846 to live with his young, sick wife, the former Virginia Clemm. Horace Greeley, the illustrious editor of the *Tribune,* came here to seek solace from the tragic loss of several children. Author Thomas Wolfe lived for a time on nearby First Avenue, and Yiddish novelist Sholem Asch described the neighborhood of the East 40s very vividly in his *East River,* published in 1946. The park is named for a murdered Turtle Bay activist.

To the north is the picturesque **Queensboro Bridge** (Gustav Lindenthal, engineer; Palmer & Hornbostel, architects), leapfrogging over Roosevelt Island. Completed in 1909, this intricately designed steel cantilever bridge connects Manhattan with Long Island City in Queens. The upper roadway once carried the wooden railway cars of the Second Avenue El, and a trolley line shared the lower level with vehicular traffic. The trolley, the last of the city's once-extensive network, shuttled back and forth at a five-cent fare, and was finally removed in 1955. The bridge also provided the backdrop for a number of movies in the 1930s and '40s, particularly the classic *Dead End,* which dealt with the conflicts between the wealthy of Beekman Place and the very poor of the tenements on adjoining dead-end streets.

The East River or **Franklin D. Roosevelt Drive,** begun in the late 1930s during the administration of New York's colorful Fiorello H. LaGuardia, was planned as a link in a projected "Circumferential Belt Parkway." It is built on landfill provided by the rubble of buildings destroyed during the World War II blitz on London and Bristol. Convoys of cargo ships returning from England during the war carried the broken masonry in their holds as ballast.

Return to East 51st Street and First Avenue.

8. On what is now the northwest corner of East 51st Street and First Avenue stood **James Beekman's mansion,** *Mount Pleasant,* from 1763 to 1874. During the American Revolution the house was used by the British for their military headquarters. Patriot Nathan Hale, captured on September 21, 1776, near Huntington, Long Island, was brought to the Beekman House, where he was condemned without trial and taken to the Dove Tavern (which stood on the site of the present Sign of the Dove restaurant, 1110 Third Avenue), where he was hanged as a spy. [*See* Statue of Nathan Hale near City Hall, Chapter 3.] And it was here four years later that Major John André received his instructions to meet General Benedict Arnold and obtain the plans to the fort at West Point. Intercepted by patriots in Tarrytown, André, too, was hanged for the same offense. With the signing of the Treaty of Paris in 1783, the British Commandant, Sir Guy Carlton, was permitted to rent the mansion to carry out the plans for the British evacuation of the port of New York. A frequent visitor in the following years was newly elected President George Washington. The Beekman family continued to occupy the house until the cholera epidemic of 1854, and it was demolished 20 years later. Fortunately, a number of furnishings were saved and the reconstructed parlor, a bedroom, and three mantelpieces can be seen at the New-York Historical Society (Central Park West at West 77th Street).

 The present building on the site was erected in 1892 as **Primary School 35** (George W. Debevoise, 1892), No. 931 First Avenue. This yellow brick and brownstone structure, in a mostly Romanesque Revival style, once served as the United Nations International School, for the children of U.N. delegates. The building has had a varied career: community center, nursery school, and shelter for homeless women; more recently, it was engulfed by the multistory Beekman Regent Condominium (Conklin & Rossant, 2000), which uses the school as its base.

Across First Avenue, at No. 940, is **Pisacane Mid-Town Sea Food,** an old-style fish market which replaced a similar establishment that had been on the site since the building was built, ca. 1860. Look inside; little has changed.

You have probably noticed that the east side of First Avenue, between 51st and 53rd streets, is virtually unchanged since the area was developed. The houses with straight window lintels were built in the 1860s, while those with the segmental-arc (curved) lintels date from the 1870s.

Turn east on East 52nd Street.

9. River House (Bottomley, Wagner & White, 1931), 435 East 52nd Street, enjoys one of the best panoramic views of the East River. A luxury cooperative apartment house, its facilities include tennis courts, a squash court, swimming pool, and ballroom, and at one time included a private dock for the convenience of visiting millionaires' yachts.

Return to First Avenue, go north one block, then west (left) on East 53rd Street.

10. Nos. 314 and **312 East 53rd Street** are surprising survivors from the days when the neighborhood was still semirural in character. The pair of wooden houses with their round-topped dormer windows and corbeled entrance hoods were built in 1866 and reflect the influence of the French Second Empire style, which became popular in this country after the Civil War. Only No. 312 has been designated a landmark, because No. 314's "wooden" slats are aluminum imitations.

Return to First Avenue, turn left (north) to East 55th Street.

On the northwest corner of East 55th Street is the Terence Cardinal Cooke Building of the **Catholic Center of New York,** 1011 First Avenue, erected in 1973, which houses, among other offices of the archdiocese, Catholic Charities. While the building is undistinguished, the **Church of St. John the Evangelist,** around the corner at No. 348 East 55th Street, is well worth a visit. The entrance façade has interesting low-relief sculpture work, and the sanctuary, which has seating on three sides, is dominated by a large carved mahogany reredos. Of special interest is the stained-glass mural *The Resurrection* by Serge Nouailhat. The organ, to the left, is free standing. This is the church's fifth building and the second on the site, replacing an earlier structure of 1881.

Turn right (east) on East 57th Street to Sutton Place, and walk one block north.

11. Sutton Place, named for late-19th-century land developer Effingham B. Sutton, was formerly called Avenue A (which now exists only between Houston and 14th streets). Lined with luxury apartment houses and elegant town houses, the street is another riverside bastion of the "upper crust," and continues north under the Queensboro Bridge approach, where it changes its name to York Avenue. Reminiscent of the Beekman Place district are the charming town houses along the short dead-ends on East 57th and 58th streets. **No. 1 Sutton Place North,** a lovely Georgian-style reproduction, was built in 1921 for Anne Morgan, daughter of J. P. Morgan. **No. 3** is the official residence of the Secretary General of the United Nations.

12. Turn right into little **Sutton Place Park** with its endearing bronze statue of the friendly wild boar and its tiny animal friends. The original, from ancient Greece, is in the Uffizi Gallery in Florence, Italy. Sculptor Pietro Tacca made two other copies—one stands in Florence's Straw Market, and the other is in Kansas City's Country Club Plaza. Years of children's caressing fingers have polished the protruding parts. Roosevelt Island is just across the East River.

Return to Sutton Place, and turn right (north).

13. The row of town houses on the east side of Sutton Place is particularly charming, each with its own engaging features. **No. 19** has a carved Medusa's head in the keystone, while in a niche on the second floor of **No. 21,** St. Francis cradles a little bird in his hands.

At the end of the delightful East 58th Street cul-de-sac called "Sutton Square," with cozy Sutton Place Park below, is another of New York City's seemingly endless source of surprises—secluded **Riverview Terrace,** one of the city's few remaining private streets. With its protective fence and entrance gate, and fronted by a lush sunken garden, the six fortunate town houses are quite removed

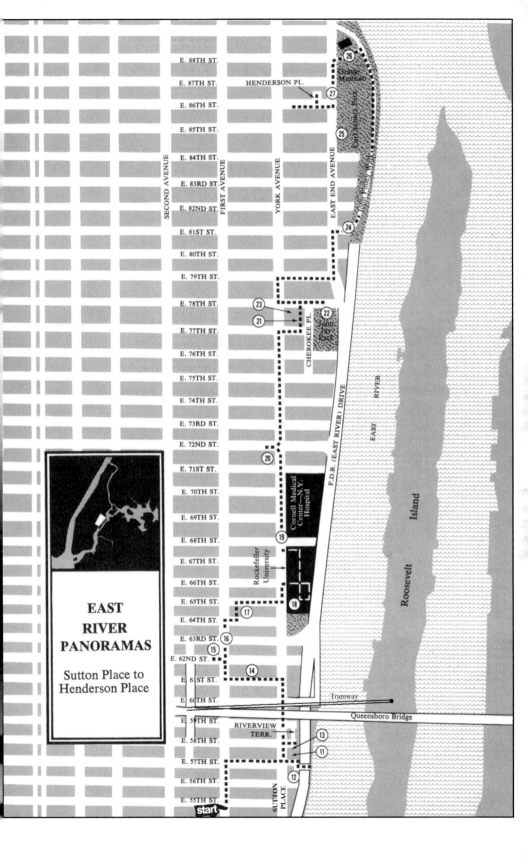

EAST
RIVER
PANORAMAS

Sutton Place to
Henderson Place

from the bustle of city life. The shady little lane, guarded by a pair of stone goats (with broken legs) and paved with Belgian blocks, extends north only to East 59th Street, where a stockade fence keeps out intruders. This is an excellent vantage point to view the Queensboro Bridge.

Continue north on Sutton Place (now York Avenue), and turn west (left) on East 61st Street.

Immediately to the right, on the north side, is **425 East 61st Street** (Liebman, Liebman & Associates, 1975), an office tower of unusual design. This block-through structure is "framed" between brownish-gray side walls, with the upper two floors successively cantilevered out (and commanding the best views of the bridge and highest rents). The side walls conceal the ventilation shafts for the floors and underground garage.

14. A delightful surprise is the **Mount Vernon Hotel Museum & Garden,** No. 421 East 61st Street, formerly the Abigail Adams Smith Museum. The property dates from a patent granted in 1676 and passed through many hands until 1795, when 23 acres were deeded to Col. William Stephens Smith who had served under George Washington during the American Revolution. Nine years earlier, Colonel Smith married Abigail Adams, daughter of John Adams, who later became the second president of the United States. They began building a country estate, which they named *Mount Vernon* after Washington's Virginia home. However, due to financial problems, their mansion was not completed, and in 1799 the estate was sold to William T. Robinson, a New York merchant who had prospered in the China trade, and who completed the structure. The Mount Vernon mansion, one of a number of fashionable residences along the East River, later passed into new ownership and became a hotel. According to an advertisement of the time, it boasted "excellent facilities for fishing, shooting, and salt-water bathing" (the East River shore was then only 50 feet from the door) and offered "every day in season soup made from the fine green turtles fattening in a crawl made for that purpose in the East River."

In 1823 the hotel was converted into a female academy that survived for only three years, when a disastrous fire consumed the building. The property was then divided and sold, and the undamaged stable, built of Manhattan schist, was remodeled as another hotel. One of the new proprietors, Joseph Coleman Hart, completely redesigned the old coach house; but in 1833 it was purchased by Jeremiah Towle, whose family lived in it for over 70 years. In 1905 his daughters sold it to the Standard Gas Light Company.

The lovely old house soon began to suffer from the encroachment of urban blight as the once fashionable rural neighborhood declined, with breweries and warehouses replacing the elegant riverside estates, and three enormous gas tanks rising up in the rear of the property. In 1919 the neglected house was leased by Jane Teller, president of the Society of American Antiquarians, who opened an antique and colonial crafts shop. Five years later the Colonial Dames of America, the nation's first patriotic women's organization, purchased and restored the house, and planted an 18th-century–style garden around it. They then assembled a collection of furniture and artifacts of the Federal period, which are displayed in nine period

The Abigail Adams Smith House, now the Mount Vernon Hotel Museum & Gardens, a museum maintained by the Colonial Dames of America, was built originally in 1799 as a stable for Col. William Stephens Smith. The site has been much improved with the removal of the gas tanks in the 1930s. (Museum of the City of New York)

rooms. The adjoining building, No. 417 East, has been remodeled in a matching Federal style and serves as the Headquarters of the Colonial Dames of America.

The purpose of the Mount Vernon Hotel is to re-create the years of the hotel, 1826 to 1833, and to help visitors understand and appreciate that era in New York City history. [Museum hours: Tues.–Sun. 11:00 A.M. to 4:00 P.M., Tues. eve. until 9:00 P.M. in June and July. Admission: adults, $4.00; seniors and students, $3.00; members and children under 12, free. Educational family programs all year. Tours available for walk-in visitors. (212) 838-6878.]

Continue west to First Avenue; turn north to East 62nd Street.

15. On the northeast corner is a typical multifamily residence of the late 19th century, with its ornate wood cornice and most of its details intact (except for the usual ground-floor renovations). These were never luxury apartments but were working-class tenements. Above 62nd Street are more and similar buildings.

16. First Avenue in the East 60s and 70s, once quietly residential and later a decaying commercial thoroughfare, has since the early 1960s enjoyed a renaissance as New York's "swingles" district, although of late it has lost some of its luster, and much of the "action" has moved to SoHo, Chelsea, and the Upper West Side. With upbeat bars and restaurants attracting the young (and not-so-young) "unattached" from all over town, the avenue "swings" every night, reaching a crescendo by Saturday evening, as lines form in front of the more popular spots. The rebirth of First Avenue has also encouraged an influx of expensive restaurants, flamboyant bars, boutiques, antique shops, plant stores, and exotic food emporiums.

17. Between East 64th and 65th streets, on the east side of First Avenue, are the **City & Suburban Homes Company, First Avenue Estate,** designed by James E. Ware & Philip H. Ohm, 1898–1915 as a low-cost multiple-dwelling complex. One of two mammoth (for the time) housing developments on the Upper East Side, these multifamily units were planned to have as much light and air as possible in the days before air conditioning. Walk through the alley between the buildings to East 65th Street, noting how the architect used the areaways both economically and practically for the comfort of the tenants and the services for the buildings. This model tenement complex, the largest built by the company, provided quality living far ahead of its time for working people.

The ornate Third Avenue Railway carbarn between 65th and 66th streets was erected some time before 1873, then rebuilt in 1896 in Victorian style from plans by architect Henry J. Hardenbergh. Today, no trace remains of the elaborate structure, its trolleys, or the Third Avenue El. (Photograph by Berenice Abbott for Federal Art Project "Changing New York," Museum of the City of New York)

Turn right on East 65th Street to York Avenue.

18. Rockefeller University, a research center for medical and related sciences, was founded by John D. Rockefeller in 1901 on the site of the former Schermer-horn estate. The shady campus is dominated by the Classic-style **Founders' Hall,** opened as a laboratory in 1903. Formerly known as the Rockefeller Institute for Medical Research, the name was changed in 1965, and in 1974 the institution was designated a National Historic Landmark by the National Park Service.

Ask permission of the guard (*on weekdays only*) at the 66th Street main entrance, and walk up the tree-lined hill. To the left, the incongruous hemisphere is the **Caspary Auditorium,** built in 1957 by the firm of Harrison & Abramovitz. Flanking Founders' Hall is the Hospital Building and Flexner Hall. Turn right at the sign that points to the ramp for the handicapped, and walk to the ramp overlooking the peaceful **Theodore H. Berlin Memorial Garden.** Descend the spiral staircase to the garden and walk north along the beautifully landscaped path, past the main entrance walk, exiting at the gate just beyond 67th Street. (If it is locked, you will have to return the way you came.)

Continue north on York Avenue.

19. York Avenue from Rockefeller University to East 72nd Street is devoted mainly to medical institutions:

Facing the University at 1233 York Avenue, between East 66th and 67th streets is the "glassy" **Sloane House Nurses' Residence of New York Hospital–Cornell Medical Center** (Harrison & Abramovitz, 1965).

Between East 67th and 68th streets is the **Arnold and Marie Schwartz International Hall of Science for Cancer Research,** formerly the Janes Ewing Memorial Building (Skidmore, Owings & Merrill, 1950); and around the corner at 444 East 68th Street, the main building of the **Memorial Sloan-Kettering Center** (James Gamble Rogers, Inc., 1935).

For the next two blocks, the cityscape is overwhelmed by the massive complex of **New York Hospital–Cornell Medical Center,** East 68th to East 71st streets, designed in 1933 by the firm of Coolidge, Shepley, Bulfinch & Abbott, of Boston. This powerful group of buildings displays a neo-Gothic motif in its pointed-arch windows that rise to the full height of the walls. The medical center also shelters the **city's oldest hospital.** In 1769, Dr. Samuel Bard of King's College (now Columbia University) pleaded to King George III for "an hospital for the sick poor of the Colony which would also serve as a medical training school." Two years later the monarch granted its charter.

The **Helmsley Medical Tower,** No. 1320 York Avenue (Schuman, Lichtenstein, Claman & Efron, 1987), a tall mixed-use tower, primarily for administration, retail space, and staff residencies, repeats the Gothic motifs of the Medical Center.

At the northwest corner of East 70th Street stands the towering **Laurence G. Payson House** (Frederick G. Frost, Jr. & Associates, 1966), a residence of the Medical Center which wraps around the attractive **Herman L. Stick Medical**

Building; and at 515 East 71st Street, around the corner, the **Cornell University Medical College S Building,** originally the Institute for Muscle Diseases (Skidmore, Owings & Merrill, 1961).

Between 71st and 72nd streets on the east side is **Sotheby's** auction gallery (founded in 1744). Once the Eastman Kodak warehouse, the building was given an $8 million face-lift in 1980, and it replaced the gallery's former Madison Avenue facility.

20. Occupying the block between 71st and 72nd streets, on the west side of York Avenue, is the **Mary Manning Home** (for the aged). It replaced the famous Murry and Leonie Guggenheim Children's Dental Clinic which had been on the block since 1930.

East 72nd Street ends in a terrace overlooking the East River and Roosevelt Island—a convenient place to relax on a park bench and observe Roosevelt Island, the Hell Gate Bridge (described later in the tour), and to the south, the tower of the old Williamsburgh Savings Bank, in Brooklyn.

Just north of East 72nd Street on the east side of York Avenue are a pair of five-story ca. 1870 buildings with **"Alfredo's Casinos"** emblazoned in the conspicuous cornices of Nos. 1364–1366. They were probably joined at street level as a dining saloon, or perhaps as a less-elegant tavern.

Continue north on York Avenue to East 77th Street, and turn right one block to Cherokee Place.

21. The Cherokee Apartments (Nos. 509–515, 517–527 East 78th Street and 506–526, 528–542 East 79th Street) is an enormous multifamily project designed by Henry Atterbury Smith, and is particularly interesting. Walk into one of the Guastavino tile vaulted tunnels leading to a central courtyard. Notice the separate entranceways grouped around the court, each with a semi-enclosed stairway leading six flights to the top. A central alley for building service splits the complex in half; side driveways slope down to the basement, with deep grooves in the pavement to keep horses from slipping. The exterior wrought-iron French balconies add a touch of elegance, as do the Spanish-style overhanging cornices and bronze lamp standards. The large windows are all triple-hung, making each apartment light and cheerful. The entire design is living-oriented—a visionary concept for 1910 when built as the Shively Sanitary Tenements.

22. John Jay Park, named for the nation's first chief justice, is the most popular recreational spot in the neighborhood. The swimming pool, picnic area, and athletic facilities on a site overlooking the river make this one of the most heavily used parks in the city. (Note the plaque on the east side of the remodeled auditorium and gymnasium.)

Return to York Avenue on East 78th Street.

23. Observe the old carved stone street sign on the wall of Public School 158, hearkening back to the days when this was still **Avenue A.** Note, too, the old boot-scrapers on the 78th Street entrance. This is a special school for the language and hearing impaired.

Across York Avenue, at No. 1465, is the **Webster Branch of the New York Public Library.** Built in 1905, it resembles a modest Italian Renaissance villa. The library until recently boasted an enormous Czech collection, as the neighborhood between East 71st and East 75th streets, east of Second Avenue, once was known as "Little Bohemia," but today only a dwindling number of Czechs and Slovaks still live in the area.

Look across the avenue at the three houses on the northwest corner of East 78th Street (Nos. 1477–1481 York Avenue), and notice the **sunburst designs** in the cornice pediments. This typical Victorian motif also appears on the adjoining houses around the corner on 78th Street.

Crossing York Avenue, and continuing a few steps farther west on East 78th Street, one is astonished by a pair of beautifully preserved survivors—two aging, two-story wooden buildings, numbered **450a** and **450b.** Once part of a row of five similar houses, they date from the 1850s when the area was completely rural. According to local legend, they were occupied by workers from an adjacent duck farm, and were not converted into stores until after the turn of the 20th century.

On the north side of East 78th Street, No. 425, **The Multi-Level Apartments** (William Gleckman, 1972), is a reconversion to end them all! Formerly a remodeled tenement, it was gutted and rebuilt with broad balconies (that double as fire escapes), an interesting lobby and entranceway, and apartments that are either true duplexes or "multi-level" with raised bedrooms or lowered living rooms. The whole building has been stuccoed over, giving it a warm, Mediterranean look. A precursor of many such dramatic reconversions throughout the city, it received the 1975 annual award for "excellence in modernization of a residential building" from the Building Owners & Managers Association.

Return to York Avenue, and walk north to East 79th Street. Turn right to East End Avenue.

●   **The City and Suburban Homes Company, Avenue A (York Ave.) Estate** antedate the apartment complex with a similar name seen earlier. From its construction in 1901–13 until the 1930s, the 14-building, 6-story complex was the largest low-income project in the country and was built with funds raised from New York's leading families. Profits were kept low so that high-quality apartments could be made available to the working classes. Yet it was the most successful of the privately financed limited-dividend developments of the time. The buildings, with restrained Beaux Arts and neo-Gothic details, were designed by Harde & Short, Percy Griffen, and Philip Ohm. After being declared a landmark in 1990 over the objections of the owner, the now-defunct Board of Estimate revoked the designation from the easternmost four buildings to allow the developer to erect a tower on the site. An appeal to the Appellate Court by residents, preservationists, and community activists two years later resulted in a reversal of the decision, reinstating landmark status. In 1993 an appeal to New York State's highest court reaffirmed the lower court's decision, and City and Suburban Homes' landmark status was sustained, ending an eight-year struggle to land-mark the complex and defend the designation.

East End Avenue, developed as an apartment-house row for the affluent at about the same time as Sutton Place, looks rather similar. Before the street became fashionable in the 1920s, it was named simply Avenue B.

No. 2 East End Avenue, a former electrical underwriters' factory building, was converted in 1979 to apartments under the provisions of the J-51 program, which provided for both property-tax abatements and the forgiveness of property taxes to encourage the renovation of run-down buildings.

At East 81st Street, turn right, then left into the promenade, called John Finley Walk.

24. This splendid promenade built over the East River Drive, with splendid panoramic views, is one of the great pedestrian walkways of the city. It is named most appropriately for **John Huston Finley** (1863–1940), past president of the City College of New York, state commissioner of education, and editor-in-chief of the *New York Times.* He was, in addition, a *great pedestrian,* who believed that "a good walk clears the mind and stimulates thinking." Finley walked to work daily until past the age of 70, and frequently hiked the 32 miles around Manhat-tan Island, declaring that he enjoyed the sights of the crowded city as much as the scenery of the open country.

Follow Finley Walk to Carl Schurz Park.

25. Carl Schurz Park, dramatically situated on rocky bluffs overlooking a bend in the East River, offers unsurpassed views of the Triborough and Hell Gate bridges, Ward's and Randall's islands, Astoria in Queens, plus an exciting parade of ships sailing close by in the river's deep-water channel. Just off 96th Street is treacherous Mill Rock.

The site during the Dutch Colonial period was known as Hoek van Hoorn ("Hoorn's Corner"), named for the Hanseatic town on the Zuyder Zee, but mis-translated from the Dutch as Hoorn's "Hook." Just before the American Revolu-tion, Jacob Walton built himself a house on the promontory, but his tenancy was short-lived, as the Continental Army set up a battery of nine guns and took over the house as part of the fortifications. Known as Thompson's Battery, it was knocked out of action by a cannonade from British men-of-war seeking to isolate the island of Manhattan as the war began in earnest in 1776. The Americans fled and the site became a British Army outpost. In more peaceful times it became East End Park, and was renamed in honor of Schurz in 1911.

The park has a wide range of recreational facilities distributed about the wooded and hilly terrain, and provides a verdant backdrop to New York City's most famous residence, Gracie Mansion.

Carl Schurz (1829–1906) is considered the most notable German immigrant of the 19th century. Fleeing the unsuccessful Revolution of 1848, he came to

The ferry Welfare *making its regular three-minute crossing between East 78th Street and Welfare Island, 1948. The elimination of this convenient service shortly thereafter virtually isolated the island for many years. (Gibbs Marine Photos)*

America in 1852, learned the language in an astonishingly brief time, and involved himself in politics. He settled in Watertown, Wisconsin, and practiced law there and in Milwaukee. Winning the confidence and respect of President Abraham Lincoln, he was appointed minister to Spain and, soon thereafter, a major general in the Union Army. He was also responsible for helping to shape the new liberal Republican party. After the war he was elected senator from Missouri, and in 1877 was named secretary of the interior in the Rutherford B. Hayes administration. Coming to New York he assumed the editorship of the *New York Evening Post* and wrote for *Harper's Weekly.* Schurz settled in the German community of Yorkville, where he remained until his death.

Continue following the promenade, and pause for a few moments at the flagpole marking the **site of "Hoorn's Hook."** The East River is usually rather turbulent at this point, as tidal currents flowing up from New York Bay meet those from Long Island Sound, causing eddies and rifts that are hazardous to small boats. The river makes an S-turn as it passes under the **Triborough** (suspension) **Bridge** (O. H. Ammann and Aymar Embury II, 1936) and the lovely arch of the **Hell Gate Bridge** (Gustav Lindenthal, engineer, and Henry Hornbostel, architect, 1917). Both bridges connect Queens with Ward's Island and the Bronx, with an extension of the Triborough to Manhattan. Hell Gate, once a graveyard of ships, was cleared of most of its rock outcroppings in 1885 by the Army Corps of Engineers. It is the supposed site of a sunken British treasure ship that was wrecked just before the Revolutionary War, and is still the object of occasional diving expeditions.

Hell Gate was also the site of the **General Slocum Disaster,** the second worst inland water catastrophe in American history. On June 15, 1904, the paddlewheel steamer *General Slocum* was sailing up the East River on a charter trip with over 1,300 passengers—mostly women and children—on a Sunday School picnic sponsored by the St. Mark's Evangelical Lutheran Church on East 6th Street. Just as the ship was passing opposite this point, fire broke out. Realizing that the fire was out of control, and seeing no favorable spot to beach the ship in the Hell Gate passage, the captain ordered full speed ahead in the hope of beaching his burning vessel on the Bronx shore. Lifesaving equipment proved inadequate, and the wind-fanned flames spread rapidly through the ship. In the ensuing panic, hundreds fell or jumped overboard to their deaths. By the time the *General Slocum* finally beached on North Brother Island, just off the Bronx, 1,021 lives were lost. A memorial service for the victims is conducted every year at the Trinity Lutheran Church of Middle Village, Queens, and a wreath-laying ceremony is held at the Slocum Monument in nearby Lutheran Cemetery. The Lower East Side German community was so stricken by the calamity that many moved out, settling uptown in the adjoining Yorkville neighborhood.

Take the stairs to the left and follow the path to Gracie Mansion.

26. Gracie Mansion. Built as a country manor house in 1799 by wealthy merchant Archibald Gracie, it is one of the best preserved and most striking examples of the Federal style, and is a place of gracious living. The Gracies entertained many famous guests, including Louis Philippe, later King of France; President John Quincy Adams; the Marquis de Lafayette; Alexander Hamilton; James Fenimore Cooper; Washington Irving; and John Jacob Astor.

In 1887, Gracie Mansion was purchased by the city. It was restored by the Parks Department in 1927 with early 19th-century antiques. Four years earlier, it had become the Museum of the City of New York, under the directorship of New York historian Henry Collins Brown. When the museum's new building was opened on Fifth Avenue and 103rd Street in 1932, the mansion lay dormant for a few years until selected by Mayor Fiorello H. LaGuardia to be the official mayor's residence. It now holds the distinction of being the only original county seat in Manhattan still occupied as a home. A ballroom and reception wing were added in 1966 in perfect harmony with the architectural style.

Until recently, the mayor's residence, although a national historic landmark, was "off limits" to all but official visitors. Now, however, the Gracie Mansion Conservancy gives tours on Wednesday only, at 10 A.M., 11 A.M., 1 P.M., and 2 P.M., by reservation only [phone (212) 570-4751]. Suggested admission: $5.00 general public, $4.00 seniors.

Before leaving the park make a short detour to the south of Gracie Mansion to the circular sunken seating area opposite East 87th Street, under the bridge to the charming **statue of Peter Pan** (Charles Andrew Hafner, 1928). The engaging figure once graced the lobby of the New York Paramount Theater on Times Square, and was moved to Carl Schurz Park in 1975, about 30 years after the theater closed.

Exit from the park at East 87th Street.

27. Occupying less than a half acre between East 87th and 86th streets is the charming **Henderson Place Historic District,** a group of 24 homogeneously designed town houses. Begun in 1881 from plans by Hugh Lamb and Charles A. Rich, the quaint little houses are built in what is described as the Queen Anne style.

Originally farmland, the property was acquired at the turn of the 19th century by Archibald Gracie and John Jacob Astor (who also had an estate nearby). After

East 86th Street (now Carl Schurz Park) ca. 1890. Barren of trees, Gracie Mansion stands out prominently at the far end. (Photograph by Jacob A. Riis. The Jacob A. Riis Collection, Museum of the City of New York)

some years it passed into the hands of John C. Henderson, a fur importer and hat manufacturer, who decided to expand into the real-estate business and build homes for "persons of moderate means."

Until the 1830s, the section had been part of the remote hamlet of **Yorkville,** surrounded by large country estates. With the arrival in 1834 of the New York & Harlem Railroad and a stagecoach line a year later, rapid development took place. Since the 1790s the neighborhood has been predominantly German but has been swelled by periodic waves of immigration—the largest moving up just after 1900 from the Tompkins Square area downtown. It has also been popular with immigrants from Austria, Hungary, and Czechoslovakia, and much evidence still survives throughout Yorkville of this intermingling of nationalities.

Walk around the corner of 86th Street to lovely **Henderson Place.** Observe how the design of the individual houses combines to create a uniform effect. A turret marks the corner of each block; roof gables, pediments, parapets, chimneys, and dormer windows are arranged symmetrically; doorways, stoops, and basement entrances are paired under broad arches. The building walls are of smooth red brick, joined by black mortar, rising to meet sloping gray slate roofs. Note, too, the typical bay windows and the double-hung sash, in which the lower is a solid pane, while the upper is divided into smaller squares. In its Designation Report for the Henderson Place Historical District, the Landmarks Commission describes the dwellings as having been "designed with the characteristics of the Elizabethan manor house with Flemish classic detail in a style developed in

A view of Gracie Mansion seen only by invited guests. The north side porch of this 1799 manor house, now the mayor's residence, enjoys a splendid East River panorama. (Museum of the City of New York)

England between the years 1870 and 1910, principally by Richard Norman Shaw." Although having little to do with Queen Anne who reigned from 1702 to 1714, Shaw developed the design to create a "comfortable and romantic domestic style." The so-called Queen Anne style achieved its greatest popularity here in the 1880s and '90s.

Unfortunately, the scale of little Henderson Place is severely damaged by the towering apartment house on the west side, for whose construction eight of these picturesque town houses were sacrificed. As a final indignity, the apartment house took the Henderson name for itself.

End of tour. The 86th Street crosstown bus (M86), at the northwest corner of York Avenue, connects with all Manhattan north-south subway lines.

ROOSEVELT ISLAND

[Aerial tram station at Tramway Plaza, on Second Avenue between East 59th and East 60th streets. Departs every 15 minutes, more frequently during rush hours, fare $1.50 each way. Subway: F line from Manhattan. Bus: The Queens Transit Q102 leaves from 59th Street and Second Avenue, but goes via the Queensboro Bridge to Long Island City first, then to Roosevelt Island where it circles the island.]

Roosevelt Island for many years was called Welfare Island. Prior to that, it was Blackwell's Island, and in Dutch Colonial times, Varcken Eylandt (Hog Island). Two miles long by no more than 800 feet wide, it was first acquired by Dutch Governor Van Twiller and used for pasturage for hogs. Some years later it was purchased by Captain John Manning, a British officer who surrendered New York back to the Dutch in 1673. It is said that he retired here in disgrace after having had his sword broken over his head for not resisting the invasion with more enthusiasm. Robert Blackwell took title to the island in 1686 after marrying Manning's stepdaughter, and lived here until his death in 1717. The old Blackwell House has been partially restored as part of the Roosevelt Island development. In the 19th and early 20th centuries, as Blackwell's Island, it was city property used for a hospital, penitentiary, "lunatic asylum," and "poor house." The notoriety of these institutions was so widespread that an investigation was

A Currier & Ives lithograph, 1862, showing Blackwell's (now Roosevelt) Island and the East River from 86th Street. (Museum of the City of New York)

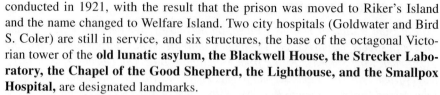

conducted in 1921, with the result that the prison was moved to Riker's Island and the name changed to Welfare Island. Two city hospitals (Goldwater and Bird S. Coler) are still in service, and six structures, the base of the octagonal Victorian tower of the **old lunatic asylum, the Blackwell House, the Strecker Laboratory, the Chapel of the Good Shepherd, the Lighthouse, and the Smallpox Hospital,** are designated landmarks.

In 1969, New York State's Urban Development Corporation (UDC) was granted a 99-year lease to develop the island. In the 1970s as part of the Federal Government's New Communities Program, Roosevelt Island became the "new town in town," and in 1973 the island was formally renamed in honor of President Franklin D. Roosevelt.

In 1984, the Roosevelt Island Operating Corporation (RIOC) was created as a state public-benefit corporation to run the island. RIOC runs the tram, sport facilities, minibuses, public safety, the Motorgate parking garage, and the grounds.

Connection to the city proper is by an aerial tramway that carries commuters in small cabins suspended from an overhead cable—much like a ski lift—to a terminal at Second Avenue and East 60th Street, and by a vehicular lift bridge from Ravenswood in Queens. Cars are restricted on the island and must be parked in a central garage near the bridge, where minibuses pick up passengers and make frequent trips on a fixed route around the island.

Roosevelt Island is a planned community of mixed income and multi-ethnic backgrounds, with a special quality of life, and has become one of the favored places to live in the city, as well as a prime tourist attraction. About 7,500 people live on the island in a dense massing of multistory buildings; with 2,864 units thus far completed, fewer than half the number originally projected.

The **Roosevelt Island Tramway** (station designed by Prentice & Chan, Ohlhausen, 1976) glides across the East River at 16 m.p.h., and is controlled automatically from the terminal on Roosevelt Island, although a cabin attendant can override the system if necessary. There is even a rescue car with its own power supply to prevent passengers from being stranded high overhead in case of a power failure. The Swiss-made tram consists of two opposing cabins that soar to a height of 250 feet alongside the Queensboro Bridge, providing a thrilling ride and spectacular river views, from this, the first aerial tramway to be used for urban mass transit. Be sure to see the operating mechanism in the tram dock.

There is a red minibus that runs frequently from Tramway Plaza north to Octagon Park (fare 10¢). The drivers are helpful and usually quite knowledgeable about the island and its facilities.

Whether you arrive by tram or subway, walk right (north) on the promenade past the subway station to the path that leads down to the **Seawall and Pier,** built in 1990, overlooking the West Channel of the East River. The "river" is actually an estuary connecting Upper New York Bay with Long Island Sound. Directly across are the buildings of Rockefeller University and the medical complex of New York Hospital–Cornell Medical Center. Just to the north are the **Meditation Steps,** which offer a peaceful setting for watching the river traffic or enjoying the panorama of Manhattan's East Side and its hospital complex. The **East River Walk,** popular

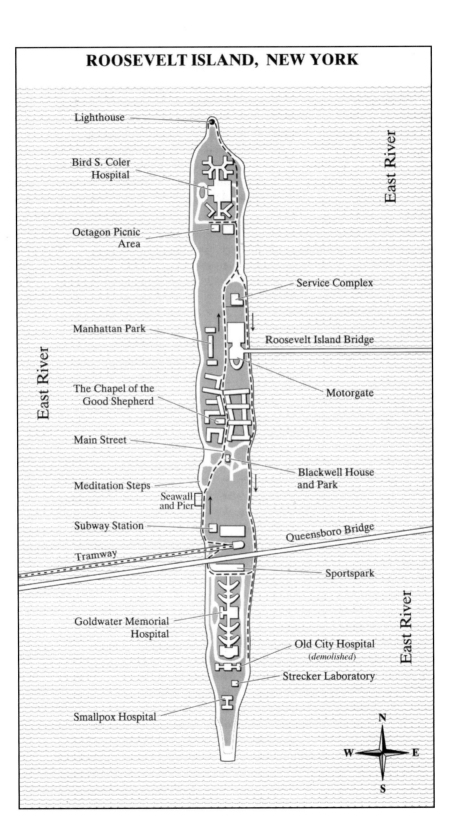

ROOSEVELT ISLAND, NEW YORK

Lighthouse

Bird S. Coler
Hospital

Octagon Picnic
Area

Service Complex

Manhattan Park

Roosevelt Island Bridge

The Chapel of the
Good Shepherd

Motorgate

Main Street

Blackwell House
and Park

Meditation Steps

Seawall
and Pier

Subway Station

Queensboro Bridge

Tramway

Sportspark

Goldwater Memorial
Hospital

Old City Hospital
(demolished)

Strecker Laboratory

Smallpox Hospital

East River

East River

East River

N
W E
S

The Roosevelt Island Aerial Tramway is the first to be used for urban mass transit. The twin cabins loft commuters across the west channel of the East River to the island's terminal at a speed of 16 m.p.h. The view is looking west toward the tramway's Manhattan terminal on Second Avenue near 59th Street. To the left are the approaches to the Queensboro Bridge. (Photo by author)

with strollers, cyclists, and joggers, provides additional opportunities for river viewing or just relaxing. To the right is The Commons, with various athletic fields.

Walk ahead to the next stairway. Go up, turn left, and follow the road. The wooden **Blackwell House** is on the right. The Blackwell House, named for James Blackwell who built it in 1796, is one of the few surviving farmhouses in New York City. When the island was purchased by the city in 1828, the house was acquired to serve as the residence for administrators of the various medical and penal institutions that were built on the island. By the 1970s it had become a derelict, but was restored in 1973 by preservation-architect Giorgio Cavaglieri, and in the same year the surrounding grounds were developed into **Blackwell Park,** and include playgrounds and basketball courts. (The house is temporarily closed.)

Continue north on Main Street, the island community's lifeline, into "town." On both sides of the street are the residential complexes plus a variety of convenience shops and facilities, including a bakery, delicatessen, three restaurants, a library, post office, etc. Note the charming brick paving and the sheer diversity of architecture that gives an integrated feeling to Main Street. The variety of buildings and massing suggests the scale of a European medieval town.

On the right is **Eastwood** (Sert, Jackson & Assocs., 1976), 510–580 Main Street, a Mitchell-Lama project (built with state subsidy) providing 1,003 apartments to low- and moderate-income tenants, plus specially designed units for

The 18th-century Blackwell farmhouse on Roosevelt Island before its restoration by architect Giorgio Cavaglieri as part of the development project for the island. (New York City Landmarks Preservation Commission)

seniors and the physically challenged. Just beyond, within Eastwood, is the Roosevelt Island Branch of the New York Public Library, and a bit farther, the **Youth Memorial Fountain.**

Across the street, on the left, is **Rivercross** (Johansen & Bhavani, 1975), 531 Main Street, a Mitchell-Lama cooperative with 377 units for moderate-income tenants.

For a pit stop or a meal, you might find "Trellis," at 549 Main Street, quite satisfactory.

The Good Shepherd Community Ecumenical Center, formerly the Chapel of the Good Shepherd (Frederick Clarke Withers, 1889), 543 Main Street, serves not only an active ecumenical congregation, but is a community center and town meeting hall. The lovely red-brick Victorian Gothic country chapel (restored in 1975 by Giorgio Cavaglieri) is the focal point of the town. The old bronze bell (read the inscription!) sits on the beautifully restored red-brick plaza like a piece of sculpture. It is said that the chapel bell rang each morning to wake the poor sleeping on their straw mattresses in the nearby alms-houses.

Just beyond the chapel on the left is **Island House** (Johansen & Bhavani, 1975), 551–575 Main Street, a Mitchell-Lama middle-income rental building with 400 apartments. The office of the RIOC is located at 591 Main Street.

Roosevelt Island's Northtown Main Street residential and business area has been compared in its massing, scale, and variety of architecture to a medieval European town. On the left is the Good Shepherd Community Ecumenical Center, formerly the Chapel of the Good Shepherd. (Photo by author)

Westview (Sert, Jackson & Assocs., 1976), 595–625 Main Street, is another Mitchell-Lama middle income rental building with 361 apartments and an indoor pool (visible at the rear).

Across the street is **Public School 217,** the island's innovative elementary school for grades pre-kindergarten to 8th grade (Michael Fieldman & Partners, 1992). After graduation, students must attend high school in Manhattan or elsewhere.

Manhattan Park (Gruzen Samton & Steinglass, 1989) is a five-building rental complex with 1,107 units. It was the final construction project of the second phase of the island's development. There are four market-rate buildings and one federally subsidized 222-unit building for seniors and low-income families. There is also a large auditorium and outdoor swimming pool with a formal European-style sitting park.

On the left is a decorative aluminum bridge that leads to the athletic fields. Walk across, but turn into the path toward **Octagon Park.** (There are restrooms in the strange metal building to the right.) Walk to the right around the extensive community gardens on the left, then go straight ahead. These lush, lovely gardens, designed in 1991 by Weintraub & di Domenico, landscape architects, are maintained by local resident volunteers.

Continuing farther, you arrive at one of the island's "nonlandmarks," the *site* of the **Octagon Tower,** once New York City's first mental institution, the Lunatic Asylum. [*See* photo, page 384.] Destroyed in a fire in the late 1980s, partially rebuilt, then razed for "safety reasons," little remains except the weed-strewn foundations of what was once an eight-sided marble structure with two wings, designed in 1839 by renowned architect Alexander Jackson Davis. Inside the rotunda was a cast-iron spiral staircase leading up to a large mansard roof. Charles Dickens visited it in 1841 on his famous tour of the United States and commented favorably on the architecture, but he lamented the "long, listless, madhouse air" and "the terrible crowd with which these halls and galleries were filled." In 1887, reporter Nellie Bly, with a $25 retainer from *New York World* publisher Joseph Pulitzer, had herself committed as an inmate, and she exposed its dreadful conditions as a "human rat trap, with some patients chained to their beds at night." In 1894, the Asylum became Metropolitan Hospital, and in 1955, the hospital was moved to Manhattan, and the Octagon was abandoned.

Before continuing north, take a brief detour at the intersection of the paths, and walk left along the river about 100 yards. Half hidden in the trees and virtually unknown by visitors and islanders alike is the **Christian Church of God** (International Chapel), an English Gothic–style country church built in 1922, and one of two Protestant houses of worship on Roosevelt Island. Return to the main road and walk north.

Directly ahead is **Bird S. Coler Hospital;** built in 1952, a many-winged complex with 1,045 beds, it is one of two remaining chronic care institutions on the island and is run by the New York City Health and Hospitals Corporation. Walk around the hospital on the west side and follow the promenade to the northern tip of the island.

The **Lighthouse,** a 50-foot octagonal Gothic Revival–style structure, was erected in 1872 from plans by the supervising architect for the city's Commission

The Lunatic Asylum in its final role as Metropolitan Hospital, as seen in an early-20th-century photograph. The building wing to the left was razed in 1970, leaving only the Octagon Tower, which has since been reduced to its foundations. (New-York Historical Society)

of Charities and Correction, James Renwick, Jr. (architect of St. Patrick's Cathedral and the Smallpox Hospital at the south end of the island). It is built of a locally quarried granite, called Fordham gneiss. When built, it stood on an islet just off the tip of the island but was later joined to the main island. The lighthouse and its site in **Lighthouse Park** are particularly romantic, with excellent views of the upper reaches of the East River and the swirling rifts of Hell Gate. Although an unofficial lighthouse when built, the U.S. Lighthouse Service provided a lamp until it was decommissioned some years ago. Note the lovely crocketed cornice—a tribute to Giorgio Cavaglieri's excellent restoration in 1975.

There is a legend connected with the construction of the lighthouse. Before work began, there was a small clay fort on the site constructed by John McCarthy, one of the inmates of the asylum, who feared an invasion by the British. After some negotiations, he was persuaded to demolish his fort and help build the lighthouse. Until recently, a plaque with the following inscription could be seen on the base:

> *This is the Work*
> *Was Done By*
> *John McCarthy*
> *Who Built The Light*
> *House From the Bottom to the*
> *Top. All Ye Who Pass By May*
> *Pray For His Soul When He Dies.*

Among the many municipal institutions on Blackwell's Island was the Hospital for Consumptives. Doctors, nurses, and patients pose for Percy C. Byron's camera on a summer afternoon in 1903. (The Byron Collection, Museum of the City of New York)

An interesting story, but no documented evidence exists to confirm it. Even the plaque has disappeared.

The huge **Motorgate Garage** provides visitors' parking and a ramp to the Roosevelt Island Bridge. The imposing glass-enclosed structure was designed by Kallmann & McKinnell in 1974. A new addition is a Sculpture Center where young, emerging sculptors can exhibit their work.

The **AVAC Complex and Fire House,** just to the north, is one of the unique features of the island. Designed by the same firm as the Motorgate, it houses the Automated Vacuum Collection system. Similar to the one in Disney World, it whisks all refuse from the island's residential buildings, at a speed of 55 m.p.h., to this building through underground tunnels. Here the garbage is efficiently compacted to one-fifth its original size, sealed in containers, and carted away by the city's Sanitation Department.

On foot, walk south past Octagon Park and bear to the left (west) and follow the road past Motorgate and under the **Roosevelt Island Bridge,** which links the island with Long Island City. Originally called the Welfare Island Bridge, it is a lift span erected in 1955, and provides the only motor vehicle access to the island. Across the east channel of the East River is Socrates Sculpture Park in Astoria and the prominent Adirondack Building, formerly the **Sohmer Piano factory** (1886) with its Second Empire cupola. Farther downriver is the gigantic

Ruins of the Smallpox Hospital, designed by James Renwick, Jr., in 1854–56. This Gothic Revival–style structure, with only a few walls remaining, was erected during a smallpox epidemic in the city and later served as City Hospital and a nurses' residence. (Photo by author)

Con Edison Ravenswood Generating Station, known as **"Big Allis."** Continue south past the steam plant, until you pass under the **Queensboro Bridge.** [For a description of the bridge, *see* East River Panoramas, 7.]

Just south of the bridge are a pair of tennis bubbles and the adjacent **Sportspark,** with an indoor swimming pool, squash courts, basketball court, and steam room.

Immediately below is the sprawling **Goldwater Memorial Hospital** (Isador Rosenfield, senior architect, NYC Department of Hospitals; Butler & Kohn, York & Sawyer, 1939, addition, 1971). This is the second chronic care hospital on the island, with a full-time staff of 1,800 to care for 900 patients. The hospital was designed with the patients in mind, with a series of chevron-shaped balconied wings extending from a central north-south hall, providing the long-term patients with panoramic views and sunlight.

At this writing, this is as far as the public can explore at the south end of the island. A tall fence extends from river to river because the structures below have deteriorated so badly as to pose a serious hazard. "The Ruins," as they are called, will some day be stabilized and accessible, but in the meantime you will have to settle for a brief description and photo.

In the middle of the island, just below the fence is the **site of the City Hospital,** formerly the Island Hospital, then the Charity Hospital, designed by James Renwick, Jr., in 1859. It was built of locally quarried stone by convicts from the nearby penitentiary (one of several prisons on the island). During the Civil War it was used as a military hospital for Union soldiers, and later an institution for the poor, as the name implies. Because of its advanced state of decay it was demolished in the late 1990s.

●   To the south and east is the **Smallpox Hospital** (James Renwick, Jr., 1854–56; south wing, York & Sawyer, 1903–04; north wing, Renwick, Aspinwall & Owen, 1904–05). [*See* photo, page 386.] This Gothic Revival–style structure, built of the familiar locally quarried granite, is now a stabilized ruin; it was constructed during a severe smallpox epidemic in the city. In 1875 it was converted to City Hospital, and in 1905 to a nursing school and residence, the third nursing school in the country. With binoculars the ruin can easily be seen from the Manhattan side of the river.

●   On the west side of the Smallpox Hospital is the **Strecker Laboratory** (visible from behind Goldwater Hospital from a rear porch), (Frederick Clarke Withers and Walter Dickson, 1892; third floor, William Flanagan, 1905). Originally built as the pathology laboratory for the adjacent Charity Hospital, the small Romanesque Revival–style structure of gray stone and orange brick is now overgrown and possibly even beyond stabilization. When opened in 1892, it was the city's premier laboratory for medical and bacteriological research.

   The 3½-acre southern tip of the island is planned as the **site of the Franklin D. Roosevelt Memorial Park.** Its location, directly opposite the United Nations, inspired the late architect Louis I. Kahn to produce a unique and unusual design; however, it is yet to be built.

End of tour. To return to the starting point, walk north along the west side promenade, past the Queensboro Bridge, to the Tram Dock. The subway station is a short distance further.

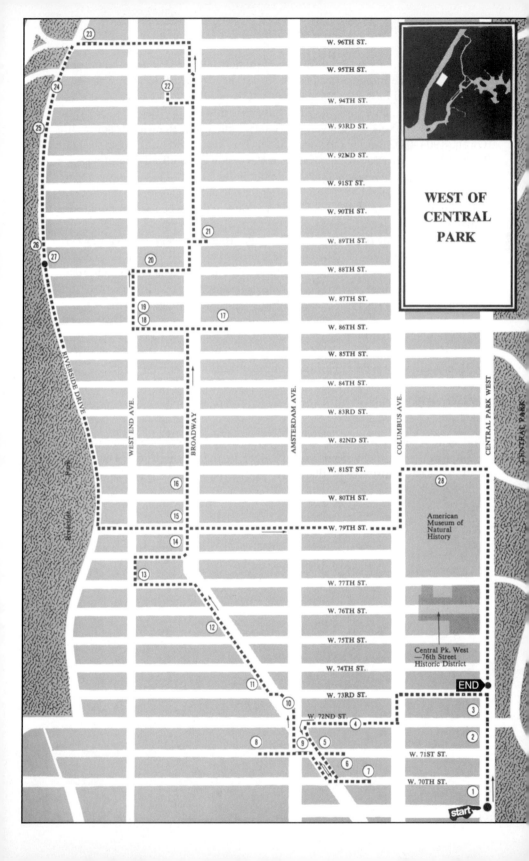

14. West of Central Park

[Subways: B, C lines to 72nd Street; 1, 2, 3 lines to 72nd Street. Buses: 72nd Street crosstown M72 to Central Park West, M10 Central Park West to West 72nd Street.]

The tour begins at Central Park West and West 70th Street.

Central Park, 59th Street to 110th Street, Fifth Avenue to Central Park West, is a tribute to the foresight of our early city fathers, and particularly to poet William Cullen Bryant, who pleaded the cause of a public park and recreation area close to the inner city. The land was acquired by the city in 1856, and a contest announced for the best plan of development. The winning entry, entitled "Greensward," was submitted by landscape architects Frederick Law Olmsted and Calvert Vaux, who spent the next 20 years supervising the creation of one of the most successful landscaped areas anywhere.

This charming piece of picturesque "country" includes several lakes, forest land, rocky hills, open meadows, secluded glens, a bird sanctuary, footpaths, bridle paths, extensive recreational facilities, an excellent zoo, and an array of artistic public sculpture. Central Park is listed in the National Register of Historic Places and has been designated a Scenic Landmark by the New York City Landmarks Preservation Commission.

Central Park West, from West 62nd Street to West 96th Street, with its extensive collection of distinguished buildings, is the backbone of the **Upper West Side–Central Park West Historic District.**

1. The Spanish & Portuguese Synagogue, Congregation Shearith Israel, at the southwest corner of West 70th Street, is the oldest Jewish congregation in the United States. Its first house of worship was erected in 1730 by the descendants of a group of 23 men, women, and children who arrived in Nieuw Amsterdam in 1654—refugees from the Inquisition in Brazil. After three successive moves uptown, this Classic Revival building was built in 1897 from plans by Brunner & Tryon. The interior is very impressive, and can be visited Sunday mornings or dur-

Central Park West (then called Eighth Avenue) in 1895, looking north toward the Hotel Majestic on 71st Street and the Hotel San Remo two blocks farther. The hotels have long since been replaced by luxury apartment houses that retain the old names. (Museum of the City of New York)

ing services on Friday evenings or Saturday mornings. The auditorium is arranged according to Sephardic tradition with the benches facing the centrally placed reading desk. The Little Synagogue, a small room in the rear of the building, is an accurate reconstruction of the Mill Street temple of 1730, with many of the original artifacts as well as some from subsequent buildings. Two huge millstones in the hall are from the old Dutch mill, which stood at the corner of Mill Lane and Mill Street (now South William Street), where services were conducted before the construction of the first synagogue. The congregation maintains the three Spanish & Portuguese cemeteries described on other tours [*see* Lower East Side, Supplementary Tour A; Greenwich Village, 32; and Ladies' Mile, 16]. The Synagogue still follows the Sephardic tradition handed down from the Jews of Spain and Portugal, and the ritual and Hebrew pronunciation differ somewhat from that of the Ashkenazic Jews, although Sephardic Hebrew is now the official language of Israel.

    2. The Majestic Apartments, 115 Central Park West, was built in 1930 from plans by Jacques Delemarre of the architectural firm of Irwin S. Chanin, and is a fine example of the Art Deco style that became the rage in the late 1920s and '30s. The avant-garde brickwork is particularly attractive, as are the pair of roof towers. (One of the towers hides unsightly water tanks.) One of four twin-tower apartment houses that enliven the cityscape of Central Park West, the Majestic is named for a

French Renaissance–style hotel that once occupied the site. [*See* photo, page 390.] The Majestic was originally planned as a 53-story apartment hotel, but the multiple-dwelling law, with its severe height restrictions, enacted just before construction was to begin, limited the number of stories to three times the width.

3. The Dakota, on the northwest corner of West 72nd Street, is the West Side's most prestigious address, and has been since it was completed in 1884. Designed by famed architect Henry Janeway Hardenbergh (Plaza Hotel, Con Edison Building, Hotel Martinique, Art Students' League Building, etc.) in a German Renaissance style, its picturesque setting facing Central Park has been the subject of many prints and photographs. The Dakota was the city's first luxury apartment house. Standing dark and dour for many years, the Dakota underwent a steam cleaning that revealed its original yellow brick with brownstone and terracotta trim. This massive ten-story edifice, which provided servants' quarters and laundry facilities on the eighth and ninth floors, plus a tenth-floor gymnasium and playroom, is considered one of the most notable buildings of its kind in the country. True to the architect's conception of a château, it is surrounded by a "moat," with access to the interior through a dramatic two-story segmental arch guarded by a sentry box. The entranceways to the building are in the four corners of the spacious courtyard, formerly a carriageway. On the south façade of the building are two end pavilions with semicircular oriel windows that extend from the ground

The Dakota forms a backdrop for the throngs of skaters on Central Park Lake, ca. 1890. (New-York Historical Society)

floor to the roof. The fanciful roof, with huge gables at each corner and in the center, is perforated with symmetrical dormer windows. The Dakota is indeed a fortress, as the load-bearing walls are several feet thick and each floor is separated by layers of thick concrete. When completed, the 85-apartment building had extensive facilities for an army of servants and boasted a private restaurant for the exclusive tenants. The eight hydraulic elevators, although modernized, are still in use and are operated from a huge pump room in the basement. The cast-iron fence that surrounds the building was made by the Hecla Iron Works in Brooklyn, in 1884.

The Dakota was built by Edward S. Clark, heir to the vast Singer Sewing Machine empire and manufacturer of "Clark's O. N. T. Thread." An unconfirmed and oft-quoted story claims that Clark's friends ridiculed the idea of his constructing a luxury house so far uptown and remarked that "it might just as well be in Dakota," which was then Indian territory. The name stuck, but "Clark's Folly" proved to be a sound investment. The Dakota, with its atmosphere of brooding hauteur, was the setting for Roman Polanski's film *Rosemary's Baby,* and for the historical science-fiction novel *Time and Again,* by Jack Finney. Home to such notables as Boris Karloff, Lauren Bacall, Rudolf Nureyev, and Leonard Bernstein, it was also the site of the tragic murder of former Beatle John Lennon, on December 8, 1980.

Clark's Dakota added great impetus to the growth of the neighborhood. Coinciding with its completion, the city changed the name of Eighth Avenue above 59th Street to Central Park West. Until that time the Eighth Avenue horsecar line and a stagecoach on the Bloomingdale Road (now Broadway) provided the only

In splendid isolation, the Dakota rises above Central Park West and 72nd Street, ca. 1890. Completed in 1884 from plans by Henry J. Hardenbergh, the huge apartment building was supposedly the subject of jibes for being "so far out of town...it might just as well be in Dakota!" (And the name stuck!) (Museum of the City of New York)

"rapid" transit, but in 1879 the Ninth Avenue El was pushed north on what is now Columbus Avenue, as far as 81st Street, affording quick access from downtown. However, it was not until the late 1880s that the great building boom began on the West Side.

The Langham, No. 135 (Clinton & Russell, 1904), one of the great luxury apartment residences of the first decade of the 20th century, displays many elegant touches typical of the era, including an elaborate cornice with ornate dormers. It was the second apartment house (after the Dakota) to be built on what was then Eighth Avenue.

Turn west on West 73rd Street.

Clark and Hardenbergh combined their talents in another project, the development of rental row houses on West 73rd Street. The street, the south edge of the former Central Park West–West 73rd–74th Street Historic District, now subsumed by the **Upper West Side–Central Park West Historic District,** is enlivened by these lovely polychrome beauties which are such a change from the unremitting rows of brownstones that lined the city's streets in the 1870s and '80s. Note **Nos. 15A–19** and **43–65** (1882–85). At the northwest corner of Columbus Avenue, **Nos. 101** and **103** (residences) are also the work of Hardenbergh (1879).

Turn south on Columbus Avenue to 72nd Street, then west.

4. Until the late 1940s **West 72nd Street** was one of the better addresses on the West Side. The **former Park & Tilford Building, No. 100 West,** was designed by the celebrated firm of McKim, Mead & White in 1892. It displays a prominent cornice above a rusticated limestone and brick façade. Some vestiges of former elegance can be seen in the building that was formerly the Hotel Hargrave (Frederick C. Browne, 1901) **(No. 112),** built in the typical Renaissance Revival style of architecture so favored during the so-called Eclectic Period at the turn of the century. **No. 118 West,** the **former Earlton Studios** (Buchman & Fox, 1914), is an impressive white glazed terra-cotta structure built on a narrow lot. **Nos. 129, 137, 139, 141, 145, 147,** and **149** were elegant town houses, and **No. 166** displays an ornate cornice. Alas, all have had their ground floors converted to commercial space. No. 174 was also a stately residence until the remodelers ("remuddlers"?) arrived. Note the pair of bishop's crook lampposts in front of Nos. 160 and 161.

Turn south on Broadway to West 71st Street.

5. No. 171 West 71st Street, the **Dorilton,** still maintains some pretense of luxury. Built in 1900 from designs by Janes & Leo, it is a grandiose French Beaux Arts–style structure. The original copper sheathing that adorned the roof has been replaced by shingles. Note the pair of sculptured figures on the Broadway façade, the handsome iron gateway on the 71st Street side, the high supporting arch, as well as the very ornate lobby. Because of its soundproof construction,

The Boulevard, now Broadway, looking north from 70th Street toward Sherman Square in 1907, showing some of the modes of transportation in use at the time. Somewhat blurred in the background is the newly completed Ansonia Hotel. To the right, the arched entrance of the Dorilton is clearly visible. (Photograph by Byron. The Byron Collection, Museum of the City of New York)

the Dorilton became a favorite residence for musicians. Note the two-and-a-half-story-high mansard roof (best seen from across Broadway).

   6. Farther down West 71st Street is the neo-Gothic–style **Church of the Blessed Sacrament** (Gustave Steinback, 1917). It is more noteworthy for its interior than for its somewhat disproportionately styled exterior. Note how the cleverly designed vaulted ceilings give the nave an impression of great height. Inside are very attractive stained-glass windows. The architect modeled the church after the smaller 14th-century French Gothic Sainte Chapelle in Paris.

Return to Broadway and turn south to West 70th Street.

   7. The former Knights of Pythias Temple, 135 West 70th Street, later a branch of the Borough of Manhattan Community College, now reconverted and named Pythian Apartments, was erected in 1926. Unfortunately, the developer stripped away most of the adornments. Architect Thomas W. Lamb drew on ancient Egyptian motifs for the styling of this fraternal organization's Grand Lodge. The polychrome designs, seated Pharaohs, ornate columns, and upper "temple" are straight out of Karnak! An Egyptian Revival style in architecture achieved brief popularity after the discovery in 1922 of the tomb of King Tutankhamen in Thebes.

Returning to Broadway, note the luxury apartment house at the northeast corner, **No. 155,** The Coronado. Interesting is the pair of huge metal griffins above the marquee.

Cross to the west side of Broadway (Sherman Square) and turn west (left) into West 71st Street.

8. The house, No. 213, is all that remains of the **former Christ Church.** The orange brick and terra-cotta trim of this Romanesque Revival–style old rectory gives some idea of the appearance of the church that was built in 1890 from plans by Charles C. Haight; the rectory three years later by Rose & Stone. The adjacent new high rise occupies the church site, while the corner office building stands on the former east end and bell tower of the church that was sold years before, in 1925.

The trio of adjacent town houses **(No. 215–219)** was built in 1891 in the Italianate style. Note how these brownstones are deceivingly painted to resemble marble. At Broadway there is an excellent view of the Dorilton.

9. At the intersection of Broadway and West 72nd Street, the **Subway Entrance** on the center "island" (Heins & LaFarge, 1904) is one of the last of such structures remaining in the city. Technically called "control houses," because subway riders were under the control of the transit system once they entered, they date from the original Interborough Rapid Transit subway line built

Backyard of the Jacob Harsen homestead at the corner of Tenth Avenue (now Amsterdam Avenue) and 70th Street, ca. 1888. The present intersection of Broadway and 72nd Street was the site of the hamlet of Harsenville during the 18th century. The house was built in 1701 for the Dyckman family, and survived until 1893. (New-York Historical Society)

in 1904, when many touches of elegance were included in our first underground railroad. The line's route began at City Hall, ran north to 42nd Street, crosstown to Times Square, then north on Broadway to 145th Street. A greatly enlarged subway station house has just been completed on the Verdi Square "triangle" to accommodate new subway entrances, elevators, and some retail space. The project also included a rehabilitation of Verdi Square.

The intersection is divided into **Sherman Square** to the south of West 72nd Street, and **Verdi Square** to the north.

At the beginning of the 19th century this busy confluence of major thoroughfares was the sleepy **hamlet of Harsenville,** named for farmer Jacob Harsen, whose house stood approximately at the present intersection. When the Bloomingdale Road was opened in 1701 from the lower city to the Hudson River, the area began to lose its bucolic flavor. Toward the end of the century, the Bloomingdale Road north of 59th Street was renamed the Boulevard. Moses King, in his *Handbook of New York City,* 1893 edition, described the Boulevard as "two capital roadways, separated by a central strip of lawns, trees, and flowers. When finished it will be one of the most beautiful driveways in the world, traversing as it does, the remarkably picturesque region between Central Park and the Hudson River, much of the way over high ground, commanding beautiful views." The Boulevard was renamed Broadway early in this century, making it Manhattan's longest traffic artery.

10. Verdi Square Scenic Landmark, named for the great Italian composer, provides a small patch of green along busy Broadway. The benches are usually filled with older adults from the neighborhood who meet to gossip, reminisce, or take in the sun in warmer weather, and who, unfortunately, must compete for space with drunks and undesirables. It was in this neighborhood that the late Nobel Prize winner, Isaac Bashevis Singer, spent most of his life in America. The **Statue of Giuseppe Verdi,** commissioned by New York's Italian community in 1906 and executed in marble by Pasquale Civiletti, stands on a granite pedestal over four life-size figures representing characters from Verdi's operas *Otello, Aïda, Falstaff,* and *La Forza del Destino.*

Dominating the north side of Verdi Square is the massive **former Central Savings Bank Building** (now Apple Bank for Savings). Its limestone façade, designed in the style of an enormous Italian Renaissance palace by York & Sawyer in 1928, creates an atmosphere of solid financial security—no doubt the intention of the builders. The wrought-iron window grilles and the large lanterns (by Samuel Yellin) add an artistic touch, while a handsome clock flanked by two lions decorates the 73rd Street entrance. The bank, built on a trapezoidal plot (although the interior is rectangular), is a well designed and dignified structure—a fitting backdrop to Verdi Square.

11. One of the city's truly magnificent buildings is the French Beaux Arts–style **Ansonia Hotel** (Graves & DuBoy) on the northwest corner of Broadway and 73rd Street. Begun in 1899 and completed five years later, it is the dominant landmark of the West Side. When the Ansonia opened, it was one of the most opulent hostelries in town. The builder, William Earl Dodge Stokes, a wealthy land developer and inheritor of the Phelps Dodge Company fortune, brought architect-sculptor Paul E. M. DuBoy from France to carry out his grandiose plans for a sumptuous hotel in the style of the elegant palaces along the Parisian *grands boulevards*. Although its 17 stories would have made it second only to the Eiffel Tower in Paris, its dramatic setting here on Broadway is quite appropriate.

The corner round towers, surmounted by cupolas and railings in harmony with the convex mansard roof, are the most striking feature of the building. Rows of delicately ornate balconies break up the overwhelming verticality caused by tier upon tier of windows, while a series of recessed courts on the Broadway and West 73rd Street sides give a feeling of depth and also provide a maximum of light and air.

Stokes, who owned the construction company, supervised every step in the building of the hotel. Thick masonry walls made it completely fireproof. The building also featured a roof garden, shops in the basement, and *two* swimming pools. The Ansonia is named indirectly for Stoke's maternal grandfather, Anson Greene Phelps, who founded the Ansonia Brass & Copper Company in his namesake town of Ansonia, Connecticut. In 1879, a subsidiary of the firm, the famous Ansonia Clock Company, moved its operations from the Connecticut town to Brooklyn, bringing the Ansonia name to the city 20 years ahead of the hotel. Stokes's most illustrious relative, however, was I. N. (Isaac Newton) Phelps Stokes, the architect-historian who wrote the definitive six-volume *Iconography of Manhattan Island.*

The fine reputation of the Ansonia through the years was due to its world-renowned clientele. Much the same way that the downtown Hotel Chelsea was

John C. van den Heuvel's country estate, ca. 1819, occupied the entire block now bounded by Broadway, West End Avenue, 78th and 79th streets. (The J. Clarence Davies Collection, Museum of the City of New York)

Pushed by a diminutive steam dummy (which was a locomotive encased in a boxlike structure to shield the machinery from public view for "cosmetic" reasons), a train of the newly opened New York Elevated Railroad (later the Ninth Avenue El) enters the 59th Street station. The name of "Ninth Avenue" above 59th Street was later changed to Columbus Avenue. (Museum of the City of New York)

the favorite of the *literati,* the Ansonia was the bastion of the musical world. The thick walls provided soundproofing that proved a most attractive feature. Among the "greats" who have stayed at the hotel were Enrico Caruso, Leopold Auer, Feodor Chaliapin, Mischa Elman, Geraldine Farrar, Lauritz Melchior, Ezio Pinza, Lily Pons, Yehudi Menuhin, Tito Schipa, Igor Stravinsky, Arturo Toscanini, and even Babe Ruth. It was for a time the favorite of Sol Hurok, Billie Burke, Florenz Ziegfeld, and Theodore Dreiser.

The Ansonia's glory days as a hotel are now in the past. After many years of neglect and decline, the building recently was given a multimillion-dollar restoration that restored its prominence as one of the city's most elegant buildings. The Ansonia, now a condominium, is once again a great lady!

Continue north on Broadway

On the east side of Broadway near West 75th Street is the **Beacon Theater** (Walter Ahlschlager, 1928). The splendid auditorium, a designated landmark, was saved from conversion to a disco by determined community residents, and now offers theatrical performances, rock concerts, etc. Across from the rear of the theater, the **Berkeley Garage,** 201 West 75th Street (C. Abbott French & Co., 1890), is a striking example of the Romanesque Revival style made popular by architect Henry Hobson Richardson in the 1880s and '90s. Once the stables of the New York Cab Company, the three huge half-round arches provided a grand entrance for the horses and carriages. The heavy stone base conflicts somewhat with the elaborate cornice, but it is nevertheless a worthy survivor. Look up at the west wall where a barely visible sign advertises an early "motor car" company. (A new owner, the Carousel Parking Corp., may have obliterated the Berkeley name.)

12. The Astor Apartments (Clinton & Russell, 1905), 235 West 75th Street, on the west side of Broadway, once a luxurious apartment house, was built by real-estate magnate William Waldorf Astor, who owned and developed much of the land in the neighborhood. Recent renovations have returned it (somewhat) to its former opulent state. Peek in and note the veined-marble lobby.

Continue north on Broadway to West 76th Street.

Walk a few steps west on West 76th Street to **No. 252,** whose well-preserved Renaissance Eclectic façade is an upliftment for the block.

At the southwest corner of Broadway and West 77th Street is the **Hotel Belleclaire** (Emery Roth, 1903), 250 West 77th Street. Its ornate, wildly eclectic façade, particularly on the 77th Street side, offers an endless variety of dormers, bay windows, balconies with wrought-iron railings, and unusual covered chimneys.

Walk west on West 77th Street to West End Avenue.

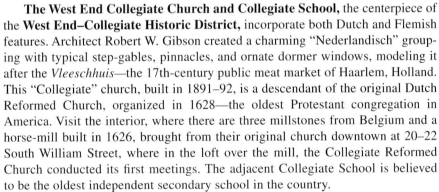

The West End Collegiate Church and Collegiate School, the centerpiece of the **West End–Collegiate Historic District,** incorporate both Dutch and Flemish features. Architect Robert W. Gibson created a charming "Nederlandisch" grouping with typical step-gables, pinnacles, and ornate dormer windows, modeling it after the *Vleeschhuis*—the 17th-century public meat market of Haarlem, Holland. This "Collegiate" church, built in 1891–92, is a descendant of the original Dutch Reformed Church, organized in 1628—the oldest Protestant congregation in America. Visit the interior, where there are three millstones from Belgium and a horse-mill built in 1626, brought from their original church downtown at 20–22 South William Street, where in the loft over the mill, the Collegiate Reformed Church conducted its first meetings. The adjacent Collegiate School is believed to be the oldest independent secondary school in the country.

13. West End Avenue was a "millionaires' row" of town houses until the early 20th century. When the New York Central Railroad freight line, one block to the west, was covered over and Riverside Drive opened, the affluent residents were lured away to the new street with its unrivaled vistas of the Hudson River. An apartment-house building boom on West End Avenue after World War I and through the 1930s again attracted the wealthy (and near-wealthy); and the street, which declined somewhat after World War II, is again a choice location.

Look at the **west side of West End Avenue, between West 77th and West 76th streets**—a complete blockfront of lively, exuberant town houses (Lamb &

Rich, 1891) that gives some sense of the first phase of development of the avenue. An engaging variety of gables, dormers, arches, and bay windows are on a row of houses that fortunately escaped the second phase.

14. The entire block, West End Avenue to Broadway and West 78th to West 79th streets, is occupied by the **Apthorp Apartments.** A dignified luxury apartment house, it still preserves its original old-world elegance, despite the less-than-elegant appearance of some of its neighboring streets. Built for William Waldorf Astor in 1906–08 from plans by Clinton & Russell, the enormous limestone structure is set around a broad central courtyard with fountain, access to which is through high vaulted passageways. The Broadway entrance is the grandest—a former carriageway whose bronze gates are reminiscent of the portcullis of some medieval castle. At each entrance, set in the spandrels of the façade, are two winged figures, and around the building runs a lovely ornate frieze. A cast-iron portico marks the entrance to each of the four separate units. Except for the addition of ground-floor shops on the Broadway side, the building remains virtually unchanged.

The apartment house is named for Charles Ward Apthorpe (*with an "e"*), who purchased the land in 1763. The property was passed to Apthorpe's son-in-law, Baron John C. van den Heuvel in 1792, and ultimately came into the Astor family in 1879.

The original building (1877) of the American Museum of Natural History at 77th Street and Central Park West. This photo, taken ten years later, shows a broad wasteland that was soon to be covered by many new wings of the Museum. (Museum of the City of New York)

Turn east on West 78th Street to Broadway, then north to West 80th Street.

15. The First Baptist Church, on the northwest corner of West 79th Street, was built in 1891 mainly in Romanesque Revival style from plans by George Keister. The asymmetry of its twin towers has Biblical-related symbolism. The taller tower is understood to represent Christ, the head of the church; the lower tower, which appears to be incomplete, was designed to represent the Church, which will remain incomplete until the return of Christ. The exterior, of Indiana limestone, is set on a base of Milford granite. This is the congregation's fourth church building. The first worship services were organized in 1745 in a rigging loft on Horse and Cart Street (now William Street), in lower Manhattan. In 1759 the congregation erected its first building on Gold Street, then moved to one on Broome and Elizabeth streets, and in 1882 to a Gothic structure at Park Avenue and East 39th Street, finally settling here in 1890.

16. Zabar's, at 2245 Broadway, is a *gourmet* landmark occupying more than half the block; known throughout the West Side (and by *cognoscenti* in all boroughs), it is a unique emporium whose mind-boggling variety of gustatory temptations defies cataloguing.

Directly across rises **The Broadway,** No. 2250, a condominium, with Staples occupying the retail space. Formerly the R.K.O. 81st Street (Thomas W. Lamb, 1914), it was converted in 1988 by Beyer Blinder Belle. The bright Palladian-style façade of glazed white terra cotta conceals the rather dull brown-brick tower behind. The entrance arcade, formerly the theater lobby, retains some of its former movie-palace charm.

The Broadway is typical of a spate of upscale high-rise condos that mushroomed along Broadway during the late 1980s, among which were **The Bromley,** 225 West 83rd Street (Costas Kondylis/Philip Birnbaum & Assocs., 1987); **The Boulevard,** No. 2373, at West 86th Street (Voorsanger & Mills, 1988); and **The Montana,** 247 West 87th Street (Gruzen Partnership, 1986).

The blocks along Broadway between 72nd and 96th streets are known unofficially as the **Broadway Mall.** The center islands have new plantings, and the corner benches have been restored.

At the southwest corner of Broadway and West 82nd Street, **No. 250 West** (Emery Roth, 1898) is a fine example of Italian Renaissance Revival style, in this first apartment house designed by the famous and ubiquitous architect.

Continue north on Broadway to West 86th Street.

Broadway and West 86th Street marks the **site of the village of Bloomingdale,** the largest settlement on the west side of Manhattan Island in the late 18th century. Its counterpart on the east side was the village of Haarlem (which subsequently dropped an "a" from the spelling).

17. Another massive luxury residence is the **Belnord Apartments,** located between Broadway and Amsterdam Avenue, from West 86th to West 87th streets, in a setting quite similar to that of its "cousin," the Apthorp. Completed in 1908, architect H. Hobart Weekes designed it for gracious living. Its porte-cochère, formal central garden, cast-iron lampposts, and ornate separate entranceways are reminders of the affluent lifestyle of its former tenants. One recent tenant was the late Isaac Bashevis Singer.

Cross Broadway again and walk west on West 86th Street to West End Avenue.

18. On the northeast corner of West 86th Street and West End Avenue is the **Church of St. Paul and St. Andrew** (R. H. Robertson, 1895–97). In its designation report, the Landmarks Preservation Commission called the church "…a brilliant exemplar of the eclecticism that spread through American architecture in the late 19th century." Designed in an unusual combination of Early Christian, German Romanesque, and early Italian Renaissance architectural styles, this striking edifice of yellow brick with buff-colored terra-cotta trim is one of the outstanding church buildings of the city. Built originally for St. Paul's Methodist Episcopal Church, the congregation merged in 1937 with nearby St. Andrew's M. E. Church, which since 1890 had been located on West 75th Street, between Amsterdam and Columbus avenues. (St. Andrew's old building, designed by J. Cleveland Cady, still stands, and is now a synagogue.)

The major features of the church are its bold octagonal campanile; the broad entrance porch with triple round-arched doorways, surmounted by ornate ocular windows flanked by terra-cotta reliefs of angels, and topped by a balustrade; a smaller tower with open belfry, set at a 45-degree angle to the façade; the tall clerestory on the 86th Street side with its odd round-arched flying buttresses; and a Spanish tile roof.

When erected, St. Paul's was a significant visual landmark in the area, until the advent of the tall apartment houses that supplanted the rows of town houses. The impact, however, is still quite apparent, and the landmark church is considered a key work in the career of the architect, Robert Henderson Robertson.

Turn north (right) on West End Avenue.

19. Adjacent **St. Ignatius of Antioch Episcopal Church** (1902), in Gothic Revival style, is another house of worship designed by architect Charles C. Haight, but not one of his better works. This "ecclesiastical block" provides a pleasant break in the monotony of the seemingly endless rows of apartment houses along West End Avenue. Across West End Avenue, at No. 555, is the Collegiate Gothic **Cathedral Preparatory Seminary** in attractive red brick and limestone. The building was built for St. Agatha's School (Boring & Tilton, 1907), and later became a branch of Cathedral College. The architects are known mainly for their plans for the major buildings at the Ellis Island Immigration Station (1897–1900) and for the Heights Casino (1905). [*See* page 436.]

Turn east (right) on West 88th Street.

20. Dominating the middle of the block is the imposing **Congregation B'nai Jeshurun,** designed by Henry B. Herts and Walter Schneider in 1918. A broad Moorish façade of orange granite and a highly ornate carved limestone portal in

Romanesque Revival style give this synagogue a stately and imposing appearance. The richly polychromed interior is well worth a visit. B'nai Jeshurun is the oldest Ashkenazic congregation in the city. It was founded in 1825 by a group of German and English Jews who split with the Spanish and Portuguese Synagogue and adopted the German ritual and language as opposed to the Sephardic Spanish-Portuguese.

Turn north (left) on Broadway to West 89th Street.

21. Another of the immense early 20th-century luxury multiple dwellings is the **Astor Court Apartments** (89th to 90th streets, east side of Broadway), designed by Charles A. Platt in 1916. The interior garden courtyard and ornate balconies add grace and charm, but its crowning glory is the superb copper-clad cornice.

Continue north on Broadway to West 94th Street and turn west (left). About 50 yards down the north side of the block is the entrance to Pomander Walk.

22. New York City presents an almost inexhaustible supply of architectural surprises, and delightful **Pomander Walk** is no exception. Constructed in 1921, this diminutive double row of charming houses was designed to imitate a small street in "Merrie England." The idea originated with the stage setting for the English play *Pomander Walk,* which opened in New York in 1911. In the play, the Walk was a small mews in the London suburb of Chiswick. Among the famous who lived here were Gloria Swanson, Rosalind Russell, and Humphrey Bogart.

Until recently it was possible to stroll through Pomander Walk to 95th Street. However, times being what they are, only residents may enter, but a good view may be had through the gate.

Return to Broadway.

At the southwest corner of 95th Street is **Symphony Space** (originally Astor Market, then the Symphony Theater). Since 1978 it has presented a wide variety of films and performing artists, including Garrison Keillor's "Prairie Home Companion" radio show—all at modest prices.

Continue north on Broadway to West 96th Street, and turn west (left) to Riverside Drive. Walk under the viaduct, turn right and climb up to the Drive.

23. The prominent **Cliff Dwellers' Apartments** are located at the west end of West 96th Street, on the north side, facing Riverside Drive. For the past hundred years or so, New Yorkers have been called "cliff dwellers" for reasons that are obvious. The architect of this otherwise undistinguished apartment house (Herman Lee Meader, 1914) displayed a keen sense of humor in the frieze that depicts motifs from the lives of the early Arizona Cliff Dwellers, with masks, buffalo skulls, mountain lions, and rattlesnakes. The interesting designs are more than symbolic of our contemporary "cliff dwellers."

Walk south on Riverside Drive along the west sidewalk.

● **24. Riverside Park and Riverside Drive** are both designated Scenic Land-marks. The park, designed by Frederick Law Olmsted, was originally established in 1865 to attract development and increase property values of the Upper West Side and was first laid out in 1870. Olmsted, following his plans for Central and Prospect parks, later designed the actual landscaping and scenic drive, taking advantage of the curves and hills of the natural topography.

Along Riverside Drive and West End Avenue, between West 94th and West 87th streets, and south to West 85th Street, is the irregularly shaped **Riverside–**
● **West End Historic District,** which encompasses a variety of elegant town houses, early luxurious apartment houses, the B'nai Jeshurun Synagogue on West 88th Street, and the Annunciation Greek Orthodox Church on West 91st Street.

Tree-lined Riverside Drive is one of the city's loveliest streets. Much of the dignity and elegance of yesteryear are gone, but the broad panoramic vistas are still unspoiled. As more affluent families moved into the area, elegant town houses and mansions were built, and it was not long before Riverside Drive challenged Fifth Avenue as one of the most fashionable addresses in town. By the 1930s it began to fade; but with the expansion of Riverside Park in 1937 when the adjacent New York Central Railroad tracks were covered, much of the charm returned. Vehicular traffic was then diverted to the new Henry Hudson Parkway, close to the riverbank. Riverside Drive was pushed north to West 129th Street by 1885, but the 96th Street viaduct was not built until 1902. Along the Drive can be seen the former opulent town houses and the newer luxury apartment houses that sprang up with the completion of the Park and Drive.

25. At West 93rd Street, on a slight crest overlooking Riverside Park, is the heroic **Joan of Arc Memorial Statue,** executed in 1915 by famed American sculptor Anna Vaughn Hyatt Huntington. The statue was commissioned by the Joan of Arc Statue Committee to commemorate the 500th anniversary of the birth of the Maid of Orleans, presumed to be in 1412. Her armor is historically accurate, having been researched by the Metropolitan Museum of Art's curator of armor. Sculptor Huntington has succeeded in capturing Joan of Arc's expression of intense fervor and sense of mission as she rode forth to lead the French troops in battle against the English and Burgundians. The bronze statue was cast by the well-known Gorham Company (which still is in business, but no longer casting huge statues). The Gothic-style pedestal of the monument was designed by architect John V. Van Pelt, and contains fragments from France's Rheims Cathedral (where in 1429 Joan of Arc reached the pinnacle of her career with the coronation of Charles VII) and stones from the Tower at Rouen (where she was burned at the stake two years later).

● **26.** At the corner of West 89th Street stands one of the West Side's most significant public sculptures, **The Soldiers' and Sailors' Monument.** Sculptor Paul E. M. DuBoy and architects Charles W. and Arthur A. Stoughton completed the marble Civil War memorial in 1902 (just after DuBoy put the final touches to his work on the Ansonia Hotel), patterning it after the Choragic Monument of Lysicrates in Athens, 335 B.C. The monument is surrounded by a ring of fluted Corinthian columns, and on the entrance pylons are carved the names of important Civil War battles.

27. The imposing mansion on the southeast corner of the Drive and West 89th Street is the **former Isaac L. Rice Residence** (Herts & Tallant, 1901), now the Yeshiva Ketana of Manhattan, a Jewish seminary. Rice, a lawyer, publicist, publisher, acclaimed chess player, and renowned pioneer in electric storage battery technology, named the house Villa Julia for his wife (who was the founder of an organization that would be much appreciated today, The Society for the Suppression of Unnecessary Noise). After Isaac's death, Julia Rice presented the city with a number of sports facilities, one of which survives in the Bronx, Rice Memorial Stadium. The mansion was acquired in 1908 by Samuel Schinasi, a partner in the Schinasi Brothers manufacturing firm. A year later, his brother, Morris, commissioned his own residence, which was erected about a mile north on the Drive, at West 107th Street. Coincidentally, these are the only two surviving free-standing mansions from the great number that once graced Riverside Drive. Although some alterations were made between 1906 and 1948, the maroon-colored brick, wildly eclectic house is a sheer delight! Note how the porte-cochère is partly recessed into the structure, and how the positioning of the house on its corner plot adds stature to the whole.

At the northeast corner of West 86th Street is **The Normandy,** No. 140 (Emery Roth, 1938), the last apartment house designed by Roth in a 40-year career that ran the gamut from Renaissance (his first, at No. 250 West 82nd Street), to the San Remo, the Beresford, and finally to this sleek and curvaceous Art Moderne structure.

Farther south, the apartment house at No. 110 was the **residence of baseball great, George Herman "Babe" Ruth** until his death in 1948.

Continue south to West 85th Street and turn east.

No. 350 West 85th Street, **The Red House** (Harde & Short, 1904), is a six-story romantic gem built of red brick and trimmed with white terra cotta, displaying Renaissance and French Gothic influences. Note the dragon and crown cartouche set high in the brickwork.

Return to Riverside Drive and turn south to West 84th Street.

In the park, just south of West 84th Street, is a prominent rock outcropping of Manhattan schist called **Mount Tom,** which Edgar Allan Poe found to be an attractive summer spot for contemplation of the river when he lived here in 1843–44. The site was also the original choice for the location of the Soldiers' and Sailors' Monument. For two blocks east, West 84th Street is called **Edgar Allan Poe Street,** although Poe actually lived in a house two blocks farther east.

You may want to take an optional brief detour one block east to West End Avenue, where on the southwest corner of the apartment house, No. 505, a bronze plaque proclaims the site of the **last residence of Sergei Rachmaninoff** (1873–1943). The Russian-born composer, pianist, and conductor, who never returned to his native land, ultimately became an American citizen and spent the last 17 years of his life in this building. The prolific musician, considered among the finest pianists of his day, produced an extensive repertoire—concertos, symphonies, vocal works, the familiar *Variations on a Theme of Paganini*, and *The Bells*, based on the poem of Edgar Allan Poe—many of which were written here. Return to Riverside Drive.

A few blocks south begins the **Riverside Drive–West 80th–81st Street Historic District** with a variety of large brick and stone row houses, many by noted architects Charles Israels and Clarence True, built mostly in the 1890s.

Turn left (east) on West 79th Street, and walk past Broadway one block to Amsterdam Avenue.

On the northwest corner is the surprising **Hotel Lucerne,** 201 West (Harry B. Mulliken, 1903). Built of plum-colored brick and brownstone, its baroque detailing, particularly on the massive entrance columns, presents a most engaging appearance. The building was spared the wrecker's ball through condominium conversion, and the neighborhood gained a splendid attraction.

Between Amsterdam and Columbus avenues, **Nos. 206–226** are a lovely row, with terra-cotta–adorned façades set on limestone bases, built of Roman brick, and many with bow fronts—individual homes for the wealthy and near-wealthy in 1894 (Thom & Wilson, architects).

At Columbus Avenue, turn left (north) to West 81st Street, and turn right.

Where once the Hayden Planetarium stood alone in its parklike setting, the spanking new **Frederick Phineas and Sandra Priest Rose Center** envelopes it in a glittering 90-foot-diameter sphere caged within an enormous glass cube (Polshek Partnership, with Ralph Applebaum Assocs., 2000). An astonishing sight, it is even more so after dark! In addition to the main floor exhibition hall, there are the Satellite and Planetarium shops, and of course, the world-famous Hayden Planetarium's frequently changing star shows with its Zeiss projector reproducing the heavenly skies. It is still the largest in the world. Not to be missed! [Hours: Sat.–Thurs. 10:00 A.M. to 5:45 P.M., Fri. 10:00 A.M. to 8:45 P.M. Planetarium *and* Museum admission: $19 adults, $14 seniors and students, $11.50 children; (212) 769-5100.]

Across West 81st Street are two buildings of more than casual interest: No. 11 West, the appropriately named **Hayden House** (Schickel & Ditmars, 1906), the unusual features of which include cast-iron balconies and a mansard roof replete with dormers; and at Central Park West, **The Beresford** (Emery Roth, 1928), one of several twin-tower luxury apartment houses that embellish the Central Park West skyline, but look—it has *three* towers, one facing south as well. The elegant apartment house replaced an earlier Hotel Beresford.

28. On Central Park West is the outstanding **American Museum of Natural History,** which houses one of the world's greatest scientific and gem collections with the largest number of dinosaur fossils, and is one of the most frequently visited places in town. The equestrian statue of Theodore Roosevelt flanked by an Indian chief and a Bantu was sculpted in 1939 by J. E. Frazer. The museum con-

An artist's conception of the completed American Museum of Natural History was not too far amiss when drawn for Moses King's Views of New York *in 1908. The central tower, however, was never built. (Author's collection)*

sists of a group of buildings occupying a four-block area formerly called Manhattan Square, whose construction began in 1873 with the original Jacob Wrey Mould and Calvert Vaux building (to be seen shortly). Adjacent to it in the rear is the power house and a wing by Charles Volz (1908). The Central Park West side is dominated by the rather pretentious Beaux Arts–style Theodore Roosevelt Memorial Wing (John Russell Pope, 1935), now the main entrance, with side wings by Trowbridge & Livingston (1924–33). The **West 77th Street side of the museum,** however, includes an impressive entrance and is one of the city's great examples of Romanesque Revival–style architecture. The massive structure of pink Vermont granite, with carriage entrance, arcaded porch, grand staircase, turrets, and corner towers, was erected between 1892 and 1899 under the supervision of J. Cleveland Cady, and later by his firm of Cady, Berg & See. Many feel that this should have remained the main entrance to this great institution. (The original red-brick building by Calvert Vaux and J. Wrey Mould can be seen by looking through the fence on Columbus Avenue and West 77th Street.) [Hours: Sat.–Thurs. 10:00 A.M. to 5:45 P.M., Fri. 10:00 A.M. to 8:45 P.M. Admission: $10.00 adults, $7.50 seniors and students, $6.00 children (suggested); (212) 769-5150.]

The New-York Historical Society, 2 West 77th Street (York & Sawyer, 1908; with wings added in 1937–38 by Walker & Gillette), was built in Classic style. The Society, founded in 1804, possesses a superb collection of books, prints, manuscripts, paintings, portraits, silver, and other historical memorabilia relating to the history of New York City and New York State, plus the original Audubon *Birds of America,* the McKim, Mead & White files, and a collection of Tiffany lamps. [Hours: Tues.–Sun. 11:00 A.M. to 6:00 P.M. Admission: $5.00 adults, $3.00 seniors and students, children under 12 free; (212) 873-3400.]

● ★ The two blocks between West 77th Street and West 75th streets mark the eastern edge of the **former Central Park West–76th Street Historic District** (now entirely within the Upper West Side–Central Park West Historic District), a grouping of 40 town houses of unified scale and general design, plus the New-York Historical Society Building; the neo-Gothic **Universalist Church of New York** (formerly called Church of the Divine Paternity, built in 1897 from plans by William A. Potter); and the Beaux Arts–style **Kenilworth Apartments** (Townsend, Steinle & Haskell, 1908). The church presents a varied and interesting façade with its pointed arch windows, buttresses, finials, and gables, plus two magnificent stained-glass windows. Take a brief detour along quiet, tree-lined **West 76th Street,** and notice the variety of architectural styles with their handsome details—so typical of the late 19th-century period of eclecticism.

● Continuing south, the two succeeding blocks are occupied respectively by the mammoth and luxurious twin-tower **San Remo Apartments,** 145 Central Park West (Emery Roth, 1930), a fine example of the architect's adaptation of the Italian Renaissance style to a high-rise apartment building and one of the most significant additions to the Central Park West skyline; and the previously mentioned ● stately **Langham** (Clinton & Russell, 1905), with its flamboyant roof line.

End of tour. B and C lines are at 72nd Street and Central Park West. Transfer at 59th Street–Columbus Circle for the A and D and the Nos. 1 and 2 lines.

Riverside Drive looking north from 72nd Street, ca. 1907. At the right is the extravagant French-Gothic–style Schwab Mansion, built on the site of the New York Orphan Asylum and completed in 1906. Architect Maurice Hébert adapted the style of three châteaux of France's Loire Valley (Blois, Chenonceaux, and Azay-le-Rideau) to suit the flamboyant taste of millionaire Charles M. Schwab. The pretentious and out-of-scale free-standing house and its surrounding gardens occupied the entire block between West 73rd and West 74th streets, completely overwhelming the neighboring elegant town houses visible to the north—most built between 1880 and 1900 by such eminent architects as Clarence True, Lamb & Rich, and C. P. H. Gilbert. The Schwab Mansion was razed in 1948 and replaced by a 16-story apartment building, ironically named Schwab House. Most of those charming town houses, however, still remain. Riverside Park, to the left, was originally designed by Frederick Law Olmsted in 1880. (Print Archives, Museum of the City of New York)

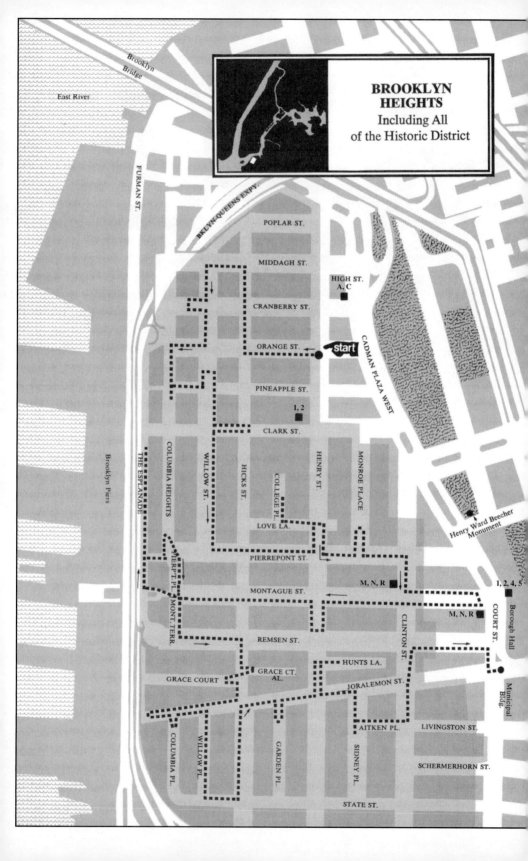

15. Brooklyn Heights and the Fulton Ferry Historic District

[Subways: A or C to High Street–Brooklyn Bridge (use the rear exit, and walk through Whitman Close town houses to Henry Street, turn left one block); Broadway–Seventh Avenue line to Clark Street–Brooklyn Heights. On exiting from the St. George Hotel, turn left to Henry Street, and left again two blocks to Orange Street.]

The section of Brooklyn known as Brooklyn Heights was **New York City's first suburb.** Situated on bluffs that rise steeply above New York Bay, the "Heights" was for over 250 years a relatively remote and rural area, undisturbed by the growth of the burgeoning port city across the East River. Before the arrival of the Dutch in 1626, the western portion of Long Island was inhabited by several tribes of the Algonkian Nation, particularly the Canarsees, who lived in long houses—some actually several blocks in length—on the high promontory facing Manhattan Island. When the first Dutch settlements were built, the Indians abandoned their village of Ihpetonga ("High Sandy Banks"), and in 1646 the village of Breukelen (named for a town in the Dutch province of Utrecht) was established by Dutch settlers from Manhattan. When the British captured New York, they changed the name to Brooklyn. The beginning of the Revolutionary War saw the crucial battle of Long Island lost by the patriots on August 27, 1776, as Washington's meager forces were overwhelmed by a superior British and Hessian army under Lord Howe. After their defeat at the Flatbush Pass (in the present Prospect Park) and the threat of total annihilation through a flanking maneuver, a

The Plymouth Church in a Civil War–era engraving, showing crowds gathering to hear the fiery oratory of abolitionist Henry Ward Beecher. Except for a later Tuscan-style porch, the barnlike building is unchanged. (Brooklyn Historical Society)

small regiment of Maryland Continentals fought a desperate delaying action at nearby Gowanus, as Washington successfully withdrew his army across the East River to Manhattan under cover of a heavy night fog.

Since Dutch colonial days, a small sail ferry operated from Peck Slip, in Manhattan, to the foot of the Old Ferry Road (now Fulton Street). A bell hung at each landing so that prospective "commuters" could summon the boat. However, the inauguration in 1814 of Robert Fulton's steam ferry *Nausau* signaled the beginning of the area's development as a residential community. Brooklyn Heights by 1820 was thickly settled, with much the same street layout as today. In 1834 the State Legislature granted a charter to the City of Brooklyn, and with its rapid growth and subsequent annexation of several other independent villages, by the mid-19th century it became the third largest city in the nation, with a population exceeding 85,000. Brooklyn has always been known as a city of churches and homes. It also has the distinction of having the most cemetery area in proportion to its size, which author Thomas Wolfe was keenly aware of when he said sardonically, "Only the dead know Brooklyn."

Laid out at right angles to the waterfront, the shady streets of Brooklyn Heights provided easy access to the river, and as late as the 20th century there were no fewer than three ferries operating to lower Manhattan (Wall Street to Montague Street, South Ferry to Atlantic Avenue, and the Fulton Ferry connecting both Brooklyn's and Manhattan's Fulton streets). With the rapid development of the City of Brooklyn (which did not merge with the City of New York until 1898) the "Heights" was bypassed and left undisturbed as land speculators and builders moved south and east. Thus, Brooklyn Heights today remains strikingly similar to its early appearance of more than 175 years ago. Of the approximately 1,100 houses in the neighborhood, more than 600 were built before 1860! The only major physical change was made in 1950 when the City of New York built the Brooklyn-Queens Expressway along the Brooklyn Heights waterfront, removing a number of old houses but substituting the magnificent Esplanade over the roadway, which provided residents with one of the most scenic panoramic views of New York Harbor. However, with the abandonment of the ferries and the construction of the new highway, the Heights is now permanently separated from the water. Its ties to Manhattan were greatly increased with the opening in 1883 of the Brooklyn Bridge; and by 1908 the first of several subway tunnels reached the Heights, although elevated trains had already been using the bridge for more than a decade. The arrival of the subway caused many of the patrician inhabitants to flee, and a number of their stately mansions were divided into small apartments. The neighborhood is still characterized by rows of lovely brick and brownstone houses—most with a uniform 50-foot height, representing virtually every architectural style of the 19th century. The Heights is also noted for several of its landmark churches designed by famous architects; but it is mainly regarded as one of the most charming and desirable residential sections of the city. In recognition of its aesthetic and historic value, Brooklyn Heights was designated in 1965 as the **City's first Historic District.**

Note: Brooklyn Heights is a rather extensive area with a great number of interesting and important sites. The chapter has therefore been divided into four sections, a **First Tour,** a **Second Tour,** and a **Brief Look at Brooklyn's Civic Center** followed by a **tour of the Fulton Ferry Historic District.**

All houses within historic districts are considered landmarks; hence, no specific landmark indications are inserted. However, buildings of singular significance, such as national historic landmarks, are indicated.

FIRST TOUR

The first tour begins at the corner of Henry and Orange streets (one block west of Cadman Plaza).

Orange Street and its two adjacent neighbors, Cranberry and Pineapple streets, were named by developers John and Jacob Middagh Hicks; or as a story goes, by one of their relatives, a Miss Middagh. Irked by wealthy neighbors who named the streets after themselves, she ripped down the immodest signs and replaced them with ones with botanical names. The city fathers promptly removed them, but after a protracted battle, the Board of Aldermen gave in and allowed her choices to remain. She is also credited with naming Poplar and Willow streets.

No. 69 Orange Street is one of the oldest houses in Brooklyn Heights. Built ca. 1829, it is typical of the wooden clapboard residences erected during the early development of the neighborhood. The mansard roof was added after 1870. Note the ornate brackets and consoles.

Alongside to the west is the famous **Plymouth Church of the Pilgrims.** Founded in 1847 by the fiery Henry Ward Beecher, its first minister, it was designed by architect Joseph C. Wells in an Italianate style and completed two years later. An austere, barnlike structure, it became one of the most influential churches in the nation. Beecher, an outspoken abolitionist, preached for many years and invited many noted public figures to share his pulpit. Among the antislavery agitators who shared his pulpit in passionate oratory were William Lloyd Garrison, Charles Sumner, and John Greenleaf Whittier. Abraham Lincoln worshipped here twice, and his pew, No. 89, where he worshipped the first time, is marked with a silver plaque. (On his second visit he sat in the balcony.) In 1867 Charles Dickens delivered an address on the occasion of his second visit to America; and through the years such greats as Horace Greeley, Mark Twain, and Booker T. Washington attended services here. In dramatic outpourings of rhetoric, Henry Ward Beecher fought with uncompromising vigor against slavery, and with equal grandiloquence campaigned for women's suffrage, temperance, and general reform. With typical dramatic flair, he once auctioned off a mulatto slave girl named Pinkie before an aghast congregation, using the money to purchase her freedom and arouse the attention of the entire country. Pinkie, actually Mrs. James Hunt, subsequently returned in 1927 to address the congregation from the very same platform where she had been "sold" almost 70 years before. Local Union Army units on their way south to southern battlefronts would stop for services at the Plymouth Church, and at the height of the Civil War, Beecher made a trip to England to win sympathy away from the Confederate cause. President Lincoln later honored Beecher by having him deliver a speech at the symbolic raising of the flag at Fort Sumter. (Incidentally, Beecher's sister, novelist Harriet Beecher Stowe, will always be remembered for her very influential but overimaginative *Uncle Tom's Cabin.*) Beecher, who in a few short years had become a national hero, was later involved in a sensational "page-one scandal," accused of having committed adultery with the wife of a former associate. Although the minister was subsequently acquitted by the jury, his reputation and career suffered irreparable damage.

The exterior of the church is virtually without ornamentation, in the tradition of the New England Congregational Church—even lacking the usual steeple. Inside, the sanctuary is simple, with pale green walls and woodwork. A balcony supported by cast-iron columns surrounds the hall, connecting with the organ in front. There are 19 stained-glass windows designed by Frederick Stymetz Lamb representing the "History of Puritanism and Its Influence Upon the Institutions and People of the Republic," with the broader theme of political, intellectual, and religious liberty. The chairs are contemporary copies of some brought from the Mount of Olives in 1868 by members of a trip to the Holy Land, the occasion made famous by Mark Twain in his *Innocents Abroad.* Adjoining the sanctuary is **Hillis Hall,** a social center, named for a turn-of-the-century pastor. Its middle stained-glass window on the north side is a magnificent representation of the Ascension into Heaven, one of five from the Tiffany Studios. The Church House (75 Hicks Street) was a gift from sugar and coffee magnate John Arbuckle, and

No. 68 Hicks Street, at the southwest corner of Cranberry Street, in 1920. Built 100 years before, most changes seem to have occurred in recent years. (Brooklyn Historical Society)

was built in 1913 in Classic Eclectic style from plans by Woodruff Leeming. In the connecting arcade is a fragment of the Plymouth Rock brought from Massachusetts in 1840, and portraits of the church's pastors, as well as a painting of Beecher with Pinkie. In the lovely arcade garden is a **statue of Beecher** by sculptor Gutzon Borglum. The church was seriously damaged by fire in 1849, and in the early 20th century a Tuscan porch was added; otherwise the structure is in original condition. The Plymouth Church was merged in 1934 with the Congregational Church of the Pilgrims (whose former building still stands on the corner of Henry and Remsen streets, now called Our Lady of Lebanon Maronite Cathedral).

Turn right (north) on Hicks Street.

Hicks Street is named for the family of the brothers John and Jacob Middagh Hicks, early residents and developers of the area.

No. 68 Hicks Street, at the southwest corner of Cranberry Street, is a two-and-a-half-story frame house topped by a gambrel roof, built ca. 1820. It was originally a grocery store and tavern. The clapboard walls are sympathetic modern replacements made of old wood. Note the Ionic colonnettes at the entranceway.

Brooklyn Heights was intimately involved in the life of poet **Walt Whitman.** In his childhood he lived on Cranberry Street almost directly behind the Plymouth Church, and some 30 years later his *Leaves of Grass* was printed in a shop just down the street at the corner of Fulton Street. "The Good Gray Poet" also served from 1846 to 1848 as editor of the Brooklyn *Daily Eagle,* whose offices were located a few steps farther north, close to the site of the old Fulton Ferry.

No. 59, diagonally across the intersection, another frame house of ca. 1820, was the residence and shop of a cooper (barrel maker). The building has also suffered the ravages of modernization, with a stucco front and replacement entrance door. Adjacent **No. 57,** built about five years later, was the home of a merchant. The mansard roof was added during the period of the popular French Second Empire style in the 1870s. Actually, the mansard roof fits rather harmoniously with a number of the revival styles, and, as will be seen later, lent itself quite well to the Italianate brownstone row house also.

No. 51, with arched dormer windows, belonged to a sea captain, and was built ca. 1831. The low front stoop was removed and the entrance door installed on the basement level. The original door lintel is still visible.

Across the street, **Nos. 60** and **56** have been altered considerably. No. 60, a two-and-a-half-story frame house with a gambrel roof, has dormer windows similar to No. 51. The arch of a former fanlight doorway is still visible. No. 56, a three-story frame building, was probably a boardinghouse when built, and has subsequently had an additional floor added. Both houses were constructed before 1829.

Turn left (west) into Middagh Street.

Middagh Street was probably named after early resident John Middagh, either by himself or by relatives John and Jacob Middagh Hicks. One speculates on what the cantankerous Miss Middagh would have said after her successful campaign for botanical street names, only to see a street named after *her* family.

Typical residences of middle-class merchants and artisans of the early 19th century are **Nos. 25–33** Middagh Street. **Nos. 31–33** are a dual house, built in 1820 (note plaque). The former was a "men's hairdressing parlor," the latter, a paint store. Doubtless, the rear and upper floors served as living quarters. **No. 29,** built ca. 1830, was the home of an engineer; the profession of **No. 27's** occupant is unknown, but the house dates from 1829; and the much-remodeled **No. 25,** a laborer's house, and smaller than the others, was built in 1824. It has suffered so many physical changes as to be almost unrecognizable (stuccoed front, lowered entrance, etc.).

Across Middagh Street, **No. 30,** a three-story frame house, was built in 1824, and has a street-level entranceway in Greek Revival style. Alas, the front wall has been defaced with asphalt shingles. Adjoining **No. 28** was erected ca. 1829 for a sea captain. Another unfortunate modernization has rendered this old house an aesthetic nonentity.

As if to make up for the architectural desecration committed on its neighbors, **No. 24 Middagh Street** is a delightful gem of a house! An amazingly well-preserved example of the Federal style, the **former Eugene Boisselet House,** built in 1820, is often referred to as "The Queen of Brooklyn Heights" and is said to be the oldest house in the neighborhood. The brickwork basement is laid in typical Flemish bond (rows of alternating long bricks, called "stretchers," and short bricks, called "headers"), while the walls are built of clapboard. Two stories plus an attic with dormers is very characteristic of the Federal style, although the roof of this house, rather than peaked, is gambrel. The doorway is artistically carved and flanked by Ionic colonnettes, with leaded-glass side lights (small windows), and surmounted by a transom and sculptured panel. On the attic level, visible from Willow Street, twin quarter-round windows enframe an arched window, and twin chimneys strike a harmonious balance. A board fence connects the house with a small rear-garden cottage, probably a former carriage house. The missing back porch would likely complete the beautifully proportioned building.

Turn left (south) on Willow Street.

Nos. 20 through 26 Willow Street form a pleasing row of simple Greek Revival–style houses, built 1846–48. **No. 22 was the residence of Henry Ward Beecher.** The entranceways are quite handsome, approached by stone stairs with ornate wrought-iron railings that terminate in a vertical swirl. Note the "Greek ears" on the door enframements, which are topped by a low-pitched pediment, and the recessed doors flanked by pilasters and side lights are surmounted by a transom. At the rear (not visible from Willow Street) are a pair of two-story open galleries on **Nos. 24** and **26,** facing the harbor, a typical and delightful addition to Brooklyn Heights houses facing the river. It's a shame the rest of the galleries were glassed-in.

Nos. 28 and **30** are a pair of Italianate brownstones, four stories high with a common cornice supported by brackets, and arched entranceways. No. 28 was built in 1858, its neighbor a year later.

At the corner of Cranberry and Willow streets stands one of the earliest apartment houses in the city, **"The Willows"** (No. 37). Elements of the Queen Anne style are evident in the high bay window with its classical swags and small broken pediment. This early multiple-dwelling house was designed by architect A. F. Norris and erected in 1886. Note the plaque.

Turn right (west) into Cranberry Street.

Nos. 13, 15, and **17** Cranberry Street show most of their original Federal-style details. No. 17 (now numbered No. 19), at the corner of Willow Street, was built in 1833, and still retains its paneled window lintels and arched doorways; however, the glass doors are later additions. Part of the original fence (with Greek Revival anthemion motifs) on the Willow Street side still remains. The cast-iron balustrade on the stoop and the romantic mansard roof were added later. The entrance to No. 13, flanked by paneled blocks, probably supported ornate cast-iron basket newels. The fanlight doorway is enframed by a lovely archway with matching panel blocks; and the cornice, typical of the Federal style, is supported by rows of consoles above a bead-and-reel board. The house dates from about 1829. No. 15 has suffered the most, with the loss of its stoop and cornice and the addition of the extra story.

Return to Willow Street and turn right (south).

Nos. 45, 55, and **57** Willow Street are a trio of Greek Revival–style houses; the first two were built ca. 1832, the latter ca. 1824. All have Flemish bond brickwork, indicative of more expensive construction. No. 57, a two-and-a-half-story house at the northeast corner of Orange Street, is known as the **Robert White House,** after the merchant who first occupied it. Note the handsome dormer windows, which luckily escaped the improvements that destroyed the entrance, railings, and windows. The original size of the windows can be seen in the "blind windows" on the Orange Street side. A lovely frieze with Greek key motif, tooled stone lintels above the windows and doors, and tall twin chimneys add to the charm.

Turn right (west) on Orange Street to the northeast corner of Columbia Heights.

The 12-story Margaret Apartments, 97 Columbia Heights (The Ehrenkrantz Group & Eckstut, 1988), was erected on the **site of the Hotel Margaret,** which was destroyed in a raging fire while under renovation in 1980. The old landmark hotel, designed by Brooklyn architect Frank Freeman in 1889, was a familiar and appreciated building, and had been the residence during the 1920s of etcher Joseph Pennell and novelists Sigrid Undset (Norwegian-born winner of the 1928 Nobel Prize) and Betty Smith, who wrote *A Tree Grows in Brooklyn* in 1943. The conflagration was compared to the one which consumed Underhill's Colonnade at almost the same location in 1853 [*see* engraving on the following page]. The new building was purchased by Jehovah's Witnesses, following a dispute with the city over the zoning laws, which limit new building height to 50 feet. Because the former hotel was taller and the developer feared economic loss, a compromise was reached on its ultimate bulk. Across the street is a sitting area with a splendid view of the harbor.

Turn left (south) on Columbia Heights.

On the left side of Columbia Heights, at No. 107, is the **Brooklyn Heights Residence of the Watchtower Bible and Tract Society,** commonly called Jehovah's Witnesses (Frederick G. Frost & Associates, 1959). The Witnesses have established their headquarters in Brooklyn Heights, and the residence, as well as the apartment house across the street, are some of their ever-increasing number of facilities. Erected before the passage of the Landmarks Law that limited the height of new buildings in this historic district, it overwhelms neighboring buildings. The garden and fountain do provide some relief.

Continue south on Columbia Heights to Pineapple Street, and turn left (east).

Halfway down the block on the north side is a peaceful country-style house, charming **No. 13 Pineapple Street.** Built around 1830, it is a large residence with an interior central transverse stair hall, whose rooms are arranged on either side. A third floor was added to the building in the mid-19th century, requiring a new bracketed cornice; and the front windows were then also enlarged. The stoop, too, is relatively new, as is the reproduction fanlight over the entrance. Nonetheless, it is a pleasant reminder of the past, enhanced by a spacious plot that breaks the monotony of the row houses.

Return to Columbia Heights and turn left (south).

On the southeast corner is a dormitory and library of the Jehovah's Witnesses, and part of the headquarters complex of their Watchtower Bible and Tract Society. Erected in 1970 the building's design won the approval of the Landmarks Commission only after several previous submissions had been rejected. The successful plans for the present structure, by Ulrich Franzen Associates, were accepted only because the Commission found them compatible with the style of the surroundings. (One of the rejected designs called for a 12-story tower, which the Landmarks Commission felt would have been totally out of scale with neighboring buildings.) An appealing aspect of the plan is the adaptation of the house fronts of the three adjacent brick houses to the south into the overall design, and the repetition of their bay-window motif in the theme of the office building's façade.

Across the street, **No. 138 Columbia Heights** is a lovely town house built ca. 1860 and a nice example of the Italianate style. In good condition are its delicate cornice consoles, the segmental arch windows, the frieze and cornice over the window and door enframements, and the curved pediment set on consoles over the doorway. But how did the owner get away with installing a window in the cornice?

Columbia Heights is named for the estate of early landowner Hezekiah Beers Pierrepont, whose mansion "Four Chimneys" and extensive property overlooked the harbor in the early 19th century. Pierrepont owned the Anchor Gin Distillery at the foot of Joralemon Street, which was operated by a large windmill and was conveniently close to the ferry. The wealthy merchant was also Robert

Underhill's Colonnade on the Heights, overlooking the harbor in the late 1830s. The engraving is from the letterhead of a fire insurance company, showing a house on fire (fanciful or otherwise), which was doubtless intended to serve as a graphic warning to those not insured. The Colonnade itself was consumed by fire in 1853. (Brooklyn Historical Society)

Fulton's chief financial backer, helping him establish the first steam ferry in the world. By mid-19th century, Columbia Heights (then Columbia Street) became one of the most fashionable strips in Brooklyn. A row of eight three-story, wooden, Greek Revival–style houses connected by a common colonnaded portico was erected in 1835 on the most prominent point on the Heights, between Cranberry and Middagh streets. Known as General Underhill's Colonnade Row, or simply **Underhill's Colonnade,** it was the area's most significant landmark until one cold December morning in 1853, when it was consumed in a spectacular conflagration. Occupying the east side of Columbia Heights between Pineapple and Clark streets from 1844 to 1904 was the sumptuous **Leavitt Bowen Mansion,** with a monumental Corinthian portico facing the harbor. Another long-vanished landmark was **Dr. Charles H. Shephard's Turkish Bath,** which occupied a Greek Revival house on the corner of Cranberry Street from 1863 until 1913.

Turn left (east) at Clark Street to Willow Street.

The **former Towers Hotel,** on the northeast corner of Clark and Willow streets was purchased by the Watchtower Bible and Tract Society to house staff members of its expanding world headquarters office. The Towers, a prominent feature of the Heights skyline since its opening in 1928, was one of Brooklyn's last luxury hotels. Designed by architects Starrett & Van Vleck, the building's four octagonal towers, illuminated at night, were a familiar landmark.

Continue east on Clark Street to Hicks Street and turn right (south).

Nos. 131 and **135 Hicks Street,** on the east side, are rare examples of brownstones in the Gothic Revival style. No. 131 is by far the better preserved of the pair, with its elaborate cornice still intact, and without the abominable penthouse that surmounts its twin. It is referred to as the **Henry C. Bowen House,** after the original merchant-owner who had the house built around 1848. Bowen was a founder of the Plymouth Church as well as the abolitionist newspaper, *The Independent,* which Henry Ward Beecher edited. Both houses share Tudor Gothic arched doorways and ornately carved spandrels, square-topped windows with sashes in imitation of casements, hood (or label) moldings over the windows, cast-iron railings and traceries. The cornice of No. 13 is set above a bead-and-reel molding, and only the missing cast-iron fence would complete this lovely house. (Perhaps the owner could make a deal with his neighbor in No. 135 to obtain its finials.) The Gothic Revival style was in vogue in Brooklyn Heights between 1844 and 1865. (Note the plaque.)

Returning to Clark Street, the **former Hotel St. George,** in a massing of several buildings of different styles and eras, occupies the entire block from Hicks to Henry and Clark to Pineapple streets. Built in 1885 by William Tunbridge, a retired sea captain, from plans by August Hatfield, it then grew piecemeal until 1929 and became the largest hotel in the city. The original section is still visible a few steps east of Hicks Street, split into two wings. Few old-timers will forget the once-famous Grand Ballroom; and just about anyone who grew up in Brooklyn in

The Congregational Church of the Pilgrims on Remsen and Henry streets still had its steeple in this ca. 1880 engraving. In 1934, the congregation moved to the Plymouth Church and the building now houses Our Lady of Lebanon Maronite Cathedral. (Brooklyn Historical Society)

Of these five unusual row houses on Clinton Street and Aitken Place, only two survive (Nos. 140 and 142). Most unusual are the cast-iron lintels, moldings, and cornices. (Brooklyn Historical Society)

Hezekiah Beers Pierrepont's Anchor Gin Distillery in 1823, near the present site of Joralemon and Furman streets, in a painting by an unknown artist. The windmill and boats are reminiscent of a 17th-century Dutch landscape. (Brooklyn Collection, Brooklyn Public Library)

The Fulton Ferry slip in 1746, showing the step-gabled Dutch-style house of the ferrymaster at right. (Author's collection)

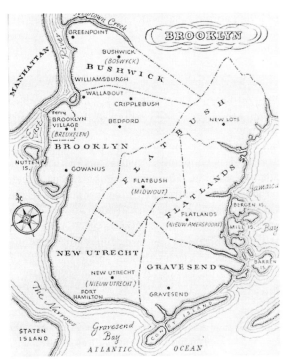

Map showing the five Dutch towns and the one English town (Gravesend), which during the 17th century constituted Kings County. The names of the original Dutch towns are in parentheses. (The Williamsburgh Savings Bank)

The first village map of Brooklyn showing the street patterns, which are virtually the same today, and the estates of the landowners, many of whom were not averse to having their names perpetuated in street designations. (Author's collection)

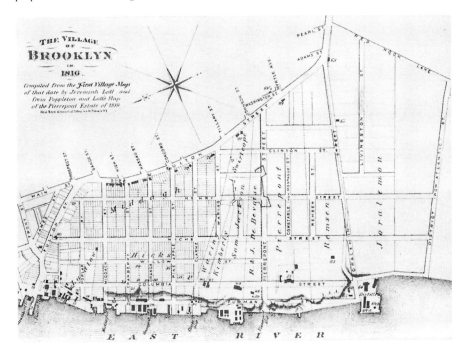

the '30s remembers swimming in the enormous saltwater pool and watching his floating reflection in the room-length ceiling mirrors. It was also the favorite hotel of the old Brooklyn Dodgers. Those were the halcyon days of the St. George as a hotel.

By the mid-1970s the hotel had deteriorated so badly that it became a source of serious concern to the community. But with the skyrocketing real-estate values of a few years later, along came the developers, and within a brief period the property was divided into several parcels and major renovation projects begun. The "Tower" section facing Hicks Street was converted into a co-op. The rear wings on Pineapple Street were rebuilt as cooperative apartments, with the late 19th-century façades sympathetically restored. The east wing on Henry Street, despite the hotel sign on the marquee to the contrary, was the last vestige of the hotel and was converted to a student residence. The former lobby with subway entrance is neglected and disgraceful. Walk counterclockwise around the hotel for a study in contrasts. No. 60 Pineapple Street, the north wing, still bears the hotel's name at the top. The red-brick center section—the oldest surviving part of the hotel (late 1880s)—was nicely restored as cooperative apartments; the newer building at the west end was similarly converted.

This charming residence, the Peck House, stood on the southwest corner of Clark and Willow streets until it was demolished ca. 1905. (Brooklyn Historical Society)

The lavish Bowen-Leavitt mansion was one of the area's most elegant. Razed over a half-century ago, it faced Columbia Heights at the northwest corner of Clark Street. (Brooklyn Historical Society)

The famed ballroom, however, which once echoed to the strains of society music and the din of gala celebrations, now reverberates to the thumps and thuds of two levels of squash and racquetball courts of the Eastern Athletic Club. The gargantuan, block-long tiled and mirrored swimming pool, destroyed through the intervening years by neglect and saltwater deterioration, was likewise divided into athletic facilities—large weight rooms and fitness centers. The upper ballroom is now the Grand Salon for group physical condition classes.

Walk back (west) one block to Willow Street and turn left.

Nos. 101 and **103 Willow Street** are a pair of Greek Revival–style houses, both with an added fourth story. No. 101, built in 1839, displays the characteristic (for Brooklyn Heights) pedestal blocks flanking the stairway with ornate wrought-iron railing and balusters that descend into ornate swirls. On No. 103, dating from ca. 1848, look for the "Greek ears" at the corners of the entrance door enframement.

Across the street is the **Danish Seamen's Church,** 102 Willow Street, a reminder of earlier days when the busy Brooklyn waterfront was crowded with sailors from many nations, and Brooklyn Heights and adjacent Cobble Hill had a large Scandinavian population. Its neighbor, **No. 104,** was built ca. 1829. A frame house, it has a rather high basement laid in Flemish bond, and was the home of a baker. **No. 106** was remodeled in neo-Grec style.

The best examples of the Queen Anne style in the Heights and in the city as well are the three houses **Nos. 108–112.** More a fashion than a revival, the basic characteristics of "Queen Anne" are the picturesque massing of different building materials (stone, brick, terra cotta, shingles, and slate) in a harmonious potpourri of gables, chimneys, bay windows, dormers, towers, rectangular and arched windows and entrances, balconies, and porches—combining elements of the Romanesque, Gothic, and Renaissance styles. The major advocate of the so-called Queen Anne style was English architect Richard Norman Shaw. Its popularity in America became fairly widespread after its introduction at the British Pavilion during the Philadelphia Centennial Exposition in Philadelphia in 1876, and lasted for about 20 years. Actually, Queen Anne of England died long before, in 1714; however, some of the Gothic and Renaissance elements popular during the reign of the last Stuart queen are evident in the design motifs. The 1883 date is on the south wall.

No. 151 Willow Street, set back from the street and occupying part of the site of a former house, is a nicely restored brick carriage house dating from the 1880s. The stars are the heads of tie rods, used to strengthen a brick bearing wall. The adjacent pleasant garden has a brick path leading to a side entrance. Playwright Arthur Miller lived here in the 1950s until he left to marry Marilyn Monroe.

A charming trio of Federal-style houses are **Nos. 155, 157,** and **159** (the latter having lost its dormers to a third-floor addition). All were built before 1829 and retain much of their original appearance. The articulated stone lintels above the windows and doorways are somewhat unusual. The trim buildings are laid in Flemish bond, have handsome entranceways framed by Ionic colonnettes and leaded-glass side lights and transom, and are topped by a peaked, or curb, roof with twin arched dormers set over a simple cornice. Note that the houses are not parallel to the street, as they were built in accordance with an earlier street pattern. (Love Lane [see map, page 423] formerly extended to Willow Street and emerged adjacent to No. 155.) A tunnel is supposed to lead from No. 159 to a former stable that was located at the site of No. 151. Look for the glass skylight imbedded in the pavement near the gate of No. 157.

Turn left (east) on Pierrepont Street.

Note: If you are taking only the First Tour, turn *right* on Pierrepont Street, and walk down to the Esplanade for a spectacular view of the Manhattan skyline. A description will be found in the Second Tour. After enjoying the view, follow the itinerary below:

Pierrepont Street, opened in 1832 and named for Hezekiah Beers Pierrepont, whose estate occupied the surrounding area, extends from Cadman Plaza West to the Esplanade. Before the construction of the Brooklyn-Queens Expressway, the western end dipped down to the waterfront. The two oldest houses on the street are Nos. 27 (at the corner of Willow Street) and 58, farther down the block. **No. 27,** one of the oldest Greek Revival houses in Brooklyn Heights, has suffered many alterations, including a dropped entrance and an added mansard roof. **Nos. 24–30** comprise a fine row of ca. 1890 town houses, with uniform L-shaped entrance stairways.

Brooklyn Union Gas Company emergency wagon leaving on a call for assistance, ca. 1900. (Brooklyn Union Gas Company)

Pierrepont Street is piled high in snowdrifts after a near-record blizzard on February 14, 1899. (Brooklyn Historical Society)

At the southwest corner of Hicks Street, No. 36 Pierrepont Street, is the **George Hastings House,** an attractive Gothic Revival–style residence. Built ca. 1844, it features the typical hood molds over lancet arches, trefoil and quatrefoil motifs, traceries, a handsome wrought-iron side balcony replete with Gothic designs and a balustrade to match.

No. 55, the **former Hotel Pierrepont,** was designed in 1928 by Herman I. Feldman and completed just before ornamentation on commercial buildings became passé. Look up at the griffin gargoyles and lion finials! The hotel ceased operations in 1975 and is now a senior citizens' residence.

Across the street, **No. 58** (previously mentioned) shares with No. 27 the distinction of being the oldest house on Pierrepont Street. Adjacent **No. 60** (ca. 1849) has a Greek Revival–style doorway with "Greek ears." Note the mansard roofs on the whole row. **No. 56** is a neo-Grec renovation.

No. 62 was built in 1911 as **The Woodhull,** a residential apartment house, from plans by George Fred Pelham, in a French Renaissance Eclectic style.

The **former Herman Behr House,** at the southwest corner of Henry Street, is an exquisite Romanesque Revival mansion, designed in 1890 by architect Frank Freeman. This massive style was popularized by Boston architect Henry Hobson Richardson in the early 1880s, and is characterized by heavy masonry walls, usually of rough-faced sandstone; low-relief carvings; a fortresslike design; restrained terra-cotta ornamentation, usually in wide bands or courses; tan-colored upper brickwork; tile or slate roofs with gables and chimneys; arched openings; rounded bays; substantial stone entranceways; and an overall pleasantly asymmetrical composition. This "Richardsonian Romanesque" was applied not only to large residences, but to public buildings as well—banks, offices, city halls, courthouses, and even railroad stations. The style remained popular until the turn of the century. The Behr house was enlarged with a six-story addition in 1919 and became the Hotel Palm. Declining fortunes compromised its former elegance, and according to local legend, "the Behr *House* was no longer a *Home.*" As if to redeem it from its life of sin, the mansion was acquired by nearby St. Francis College as a residence for novitiates. It was sold in 1976 for conversion into apartments.

Diagonally opposite the Behr House, on the northeast corner, is **No. 161 Henry Street,** a delightfully exuberant brick and limestone trim Renaissance Eclectic apartment house. Designed in 1906 by Schneider & Herts, it has a large mansard roof with a huge pediment over the attic windows, plus a monumental Baroque entranceway. (Look back at the fanciful roofline of the Behr House.)

Turn left (north) on Henry Street into Love Lane.

Love Lane was, as its name implies, a favorite path in Colonial times for young swains to promenade with their maidens fair. Earlier, it had been an Indian trail leading from a village to the water's edge. In 1822, the Brooklyn Collegiate Institute for Young Ladies was built on the site between Henry Street and the present **College Place.** The Institute later became a hotel called the *Mansion House,* and the former hotel stables on College Place now serve "horseless carriages." The neo-Federal supermarket at the entrance to Love Lane is a pleasant and appropriate reproduction.

Return to Pierrepont Street and turn left (east).

No. 104 Pierrepont Street, originally the Thomas Clark Residence, is a handsome four-story brownstone row mansion, built ca. 1857. The roof cornice is supported by ornate console brackets, with hoods similarly set on brackets over the windows and doorway. **No. 106** has an attractive bay window and entrance doors, both with art nouveau stained glass, and both surmounted by a decorative frieze.

Nos. 108 and **114** must be compared from across the street. The two were built as an identical pair around 1840 in Greek Revival style for Messrs. P. C. Cornell and George Cornell. Clay Lancaster, in *Old Brooklyn Heights,* calls the pair "the noblest residential building ever to grace Pierrepont Street." Today, only the right-hand half bears any resemblance to the original appearance, as No. 114 was completely remodeled in Romanesque Revival style around 1877 for Alfred C. Barnes. No. 108, the **P. C. Cornell House,** retains just one of its original Greek Revival elements, the pedimented entranceway with anthemion motif as an acroterium. Its former look-alike twin, No. 114, is now sheathed with brownstone, brick, and terra cotta, with typical Romanesque Revival features, including rounded bays, gables, a turret, and carved reliefs. In 1912, the George Cornell (or Alfred C. Barnes) House became the headquarters of the Brooklyn Women's Club. It was recently converted into co-op apartments.

Across Pierrepont Street is the **First Unitarian Church** (Minard Lafever, 1844). The lovely Gothic Revival–style church is the home of the oldest Unitarian Society in Brooklyn, organized in 1833. The tall pinnacles and high central gable emphasize the verticality of the sandstone edifice, while a broad roof extends beyond the nave over the side aisles, with small skylights illuminating the interior. In 1890 a new set of windows was installed from the studios of Louis Comfort Tiffany. Lafever, a trained carpenter and skilled architect whose buildings were executed almost always in the Greek Revival style, used the *Gothic* Revival exclusively for many churches. (Another of his fine churches will be seen shortly.) The church is on the approximate site of a British fort built here between 1780 and 1781.

On the northwest corner stands the **Appellate Division of the New York State Supreme Court,** designed by Slee & Bryson and built in 1938 in a simple Classic Revival style, and recently cleaned.

Walk up Monroe Place to **No. 46,** on the right side of the street. Set on a paneled pedestal block is a lovely wrought-iron basket urn, once fairly prevalent throughout the Heights, and now reduced to this last survivor. (The matching mate disappeared years ago.) The pineapple (a rare and luxurious fruit in the 19th century) atop the urn was a traditional symbol of hospitality. Both No. 46 and its neighbor No. 44 are Greek Revival–style houses laid in Flemish bond, and like the trio of houses on Willow Place (Nos. 155–159), are built askew from the street line. The houses were originally aligned with Love Lane, which in the early 19th century extended through to Fulton Street.

There is now a skyscraper where the Frank Freeman–designed Brooklyn Savings Bank stood at the northeast corner of Pierrepont and Clinton streets. A delightful Classic Eclectic building erected in 1893, it was taken down in 1962 when the bank built a modern structure around the corner on Montague Street. The site is now occupied by towering One Pierrepont Place. (The Brooklyn Savings Bank)

Monroe Place, once the widest street in Brooklyn Heights and, unlike others in the Heights, has the even-numbered houses on the *east* side. It also retains the original house-numbering system, which was abandoned on all other streets in 1871. The street is named for James Monroe, fifth president of the United States, who spent the last years of his retirement in New York City.

Continue east on Pierrepont Street to Clinton Street.

On the southwest corner is the **Brooklyn Historical Society,** formerly the Long Island Historical Society. Built for the Society between 1878 and 1880 from plans by George B. Post (architect of the New York Stock Exchange), it is a pleasing combination of Richardsonian Romanesque and Classical styles. Since its organization in 1863, the Society has amassed one of the finest historical collections in the country. Although now primarily concerned with the history of Brooklyn, it has extensive source material on New York City and New York State. Its Brooklyn Historical Gallery boasts a number of fascinating permanent exhibits: The Brooklyn Dodgers Baseball Hall of Fame, The Brooklyn Bridge, The Brooklyn Navy Yard, Coney Island, Famous Brooklynites, The TV "Honeymooners" Stage Set; plus regularly changing exhibits. The library contains over 125,000 volumes plus a collection of manuscripts, periodicals, pamphlets, newspapers, maps, paintings, photographs, prints, and other Brooklyn memorabilia. The library is considered one of the three best in the nation in the field of genealogy. Many paintings by famous American artists are displayed in the hall and reference room, and so extensive and valuable are its historical holdings that it was once called "Long Island's strongbox." Take time for a leisurely visit, and browse in the lovely library's reading room. A visit is a "must" (be sure to pick up a membership application!). On exiting, note the high-relief sculptures of the Viking and Indian in the spandrels of the entrance arch, as well as the rich façade with busts of Columbus and Franklin, and the earthy tones of red and brown in the terra-cotta adornments and Philadelphia pressed brick. The Latin inscription on the Clinton Street side is from Cicero, and means "History, the Witness of Time." [Hours: Tues.–Sat. 12:00 P.M. to 5:00 P.M. (Library closes at 4:45 P.M.) Admission: adults $2.50, seniors and children $1.00. Additional fee for library: adults $2.50, seniors and children $1.00. (718) 222-4111.]

On the northwest corner, **St. Ann's School** occupies the building of the **former Crescent Club,** one of a number of private athletic clubs that prevailed around the turn of the century. Designed in 1906 by architect Frank Freeman (of the Behr Mansion and the Hotel Margaret), it was the club's second building. Find the little stone crescents set in the upper section of the façade. Across Clinton Street on the northeast corner stood another Frank Freeman building—the Brooklyn Savings Bank—a splendid Classic Eclectic edifice with an extravagant oval interior. Built in 1893, it was lost to the wrecker's ball in 1962, and the bank moved into more modern quarters on Montague Street—the site now of **One Pierrepont Place** (Haines, Lundberg & Waehler, 1987) [*see* photo, page 430]. On the southeast corner, and extending to Montague Street, is the old **Brooklyn Trust Company Building,** now a branch of the J. P. Morgan Chase Bank. Designed in 1915 by the noted architects York & Sawyer, the exterior is said to be patterned after the Palazzo della Gran Guardia in Verona, and the interior possibly after the Tepidarium of the Roman Baths of Caracalla. The impressive granite-and-limestone Renaissance Revival–style *palazzo* was the home office of the Brooklyn Trust Company until 1950, when it was absorbed by the Manufacturers Hanover Trust Company, which in turn was merged with the Chemical Bank. And when you get to Montague Street, don't miss the splendid bronze lamp standards in whose delicately sculptured bases are griffins and turtles.

Turn right on Clinton Street to Montague Street.

Back to back with the Brooklyn Historical Society is the **Diocesan Church of St. Ann** and the **Holy Trinity, formerly the Holy Trinity Protestant Episcopal Church,** and another fine example of architect Minard Lafever's ecclesiastical work. Completed in 1847 in his customary Gothic Revival style, it is reminiscent, in its dark-red color, of an old English church. Unfortunately, the porous brownstone has weathered very badly. The interior is constructed of cast and painted terra cotta, a departure from the usual carved stone or plaster. The lovely windows were designed by William Jay Bolton, America's foremost stained-glass artist of the time, and are considered by art historians to be a national treasure. The church's tall spire was dismantled early in the 20th century when blasting for the new Montague Street tunnel of the former BMT subway made it unsafe. St. Ann and the Holy Trinity Church is now headquarters of the Episcopal Diocese of Brooklyn.

Underway for several years is a bold in-house restoration project aimed at returning the magnificent Gothic Revival–style treasure to its original flamboyant glory. In 1988, together with the World Monuments Fund, and supported by state and private grants, the church established the **American Heritage Center for Conservation and Training,** whose purpose is to establish apprenticeship programs in stained glass, sandstone, and wood preservation. The restoration of the glass is under the supervision of the renowned master stained-glass conservator, Mel Greenfield. New techniques for helping to preserve the deteriorating sandstone façade have been developed by the in-house conservation crew, and as each stone section is restored, completed windows are reinstalled, and light again enters the darkened church interior. Don't miss the elaborate wood-framed plaster vaults.

On entering the church vestibule, one is greeted by a bust of John Howard Melish, rector from 1904–49, by sculptor William Zorach. The reredos is by Frank Freeman. Above the altar is one of St. Ann's priceless treasures, the **Great Chancel Window.** The 20-by-40-foot stained glass masterpiece, *The Ascension*, is one of Bolton's crowning achievements and was restored in 1995. [*See* also page 299.]

Cross the intersection of Clinton and Montague streets to the corner diagonally opposite the church.

The block of Montague Street between Clinton and Court streets is considered part of the downtown Brooklyn business section and is known as **"Bank Row."** From left to right across Montague Street are:

The aforementioned J. P. Morgan Chase Bank, No. 177, in the building of the old **Brooklyn Trust Company,** erected in 1915. The structure occupies the site of the George Taylor residence, the home of a mid-19th-century congressman. His house was sold to the Brooklyn Trust Company in 1873, and was enlarged and altered through the years until 1914, when it was razed to make way for the present building.

The Citibank branch, No. 183, is in the **former People's Trust Company building,** designed as a reproduction of a Roman temple in 1904, by Mobray & Uffinger. It sports a large and impressive pediment complete with reclining classical figures, and rests on four huge Ionic fluted columns that frame what is known as an engaged tetra-style portico. The effect on the public must have been one of unquestioned security and solvency. An addition was designed in 1929 by Shreve, Lamb & Harmon, whose design for the Empire State Building was being carried out that same year.

Originally the National Title Guaranty Building, No. 185 is an imposing 15-story structure in a bold, three-dimensional Art Deco style, and was erected from plans by Helmle, Corbett & Harrison in 1929. The closely spaced stone piers rise dramatically in a group of rhythmic setbacks to create a strong sense of verticality. A mindless alteration in 1970 destroyed the entrance and lobby. The building has seen many banks as tenants through the years.

Adjacent to the right and totally unrecognizable in its present "glassy box" disguise is the nine-story **former Real Estate Exchange,** No. 189–191, erected in 1891. Built originally in a Renaissance Eclectic style, it was remodeled in 1911 by Brooklyn's most famous architect, Frank Freeman. Then, in 1916, 1953, and 1957, further modifications were made to the façade and interior; and finally, in 1972, the present bronze glass "skin" was attached. The ultimate indignity came with its renaming to the Montague Center.

The final group of bank buildings includes the former Brooklyn Union Gas Company, the National Westminster Bank, and the Brooklyn Savings Bank, all built between 1959 and 1962. The Gas Company's headquarters occupied the **site of the Mercantile Library** (Peter B. Wright, 1864), a modified High Victorian Gothic–style building that later became the home of the Brooklyn Library, until it merged with the Brooklyn Public Library in 1903. It then became the library system's main office until its central building was erected near Prospect Park in 1941; the building was then reduced to the Montague Street Branch, and was demolished in 1960. Although the name of the Brooklyn Union Gas Company still appears on some of the buildings, the company has moved its headquarters to the new MetroTech Center, a $1 billion commercial and academic complex on a 10-block site that includes eight new and three renovated buildings.

On the north side, the tall building halfway down the block on the south side is the **former Lawyers Title Insurance Company,** No. 188–190 (Helmle, Huberty & Hudswell, 1904), now the Atlantic Liberty Savings. Adjacent to the east stood another Frank Freeman building, the Title Guaranty & Trust Company, erected in 1905 in neoclassic style, and torn down in 1959. At the far end of the block, at the corner of Court Street, is one of Brooklyn's genuine skyscrapers, the **Montague-Court Building,** (H. Craig Severance, 1927). Rising 35 stories in a series of setbacks (as required by the 1916 zoning resolution), it is an imposing addition to the Brooklyn skyline.

Before the financial institutions came to Montague Street, this block had another distinction. It was the **most important cultural center in all of Brooklyn.** In addition to the library on the north side, the south side was the site of two famous institutions, one of which was the **Brooklyn Art Association.** In 1872, architect J. Cleveland Cady was hired to design an appropriate building for the Association, whose primary purpose was the promotion of the fine arts to Brooklyn residents. The result was an impressive High Victorian Gothic structure with lively use of polychromatic stone and brick whose façade dominated the block. The Art Association merged with the Brooklyn Institute of Arts & Science in 1899 to form one of the nation's greatest cultural institutions, the **Brooklyn Museum of Art.** With the completion of the museum's magnificent first building (designed by McKim, Mead & White) on Eastern Parkway near Prospect Park the same year, the Brooklyn Art Association abandoned its Montague Street home, and its name became only a memory. The building, however, survived until 1936, when all but a few interior walls were demolished.

The third cultural institution on the block was the **Brooklyn Academy of Music,** founded in 1859 as an outgrowth of the Brooklyn Philharmonic Society. Architect Leopold Eidlitz designed an enormous brick structure for the BAM, also in High Victorian style, at Nos. 176–190 Montague Street, just to the east of the site that would later be taken by the Brooklyn Art Association. Opening night was January 15, 1861, and Walt Whitman, writing in the *Brooklyn Standard,* described the building as "magnificent...on a scale commensurate with similar buildings, even in some of the largest and most polished capitals of Europe." The Academy remained as the center of all major cultural events in Brooklyn until it was destroyed in a fire in 1903. Five years later, a new Academy building arose a mile to the east and soon became one of New York City's major cultural centers. The mid-block Lawyers Title Insurance Company building now occupies the western end of the old Brooklyn Academy site.

Return to the corner of Clinton Street.

Completing the row of banks is the picturesque **Franklin Trust Company Building** on the southwest corner. With the invention of the elevator, the sky-scraper came into its own, and this charming Romanesque Revival château, complete with moat, is an outstanding example of the style applied to commercial buildings. Built in 1891 (see date in the pediment) from plans by George L. Morse, the bank presents a striking façade of limestone arches on a granite base, brick and terra-cotta piers, columns topped by arches, and a typical Spanish tile roof with dormer windows. Note the bishop's crook lamppost in front.

End of First Tour. To return to Manhattan, the Court Street station of the M, N, and R lines is here at the intersection of Montague and Clinton streets. For the 1, 2, 4, and 5 lines, walk one block east on Montague Street to Borough Hall. For the A, C, and F lines, walk two blocks east past Borough Hall.

SECOND TOUR

Continue west on Montague Street.

Montague Street is named for Lady Mary Wortley Montagu, née Pierrepont, the English author of wit and letters who died in 1762. (No one seems to know how Montague Street got its final "e.") It is the principal commercial thorough-fare of Brooklyn Heights and an appropriate place to stop for some refreshment. When the street was opened through to the riverfront around 1850, ferry service was begun to Wall Street in Manhattan.

In 1887 a cable car began operating the full length of Montague Street, pro-viding a convenient transportation link for Manhattan commuters who arrived on the brand-new Fulton Street El at the Court Street station and were then whisked down to the Wall Street Ferry. In 1909 the trolley was electrified, remaining in service until 1924 when the BMT's four-year-old Montague Street Tunnel ren-dered it obsolete.

The street has a variety of shops, boutiques, and ethnic restaurants. Along the south side, cast-iron stoops lead up to raised first-floor retail establishments

The "Penny Bridge" over Montague Street, ca. 1922, when the street sloped downhill to the Wall Street Ferry. In the background are the side-by-side Low and White Mansions (Nos. 3 and 2 Pierrepont Place) and the now-demolished Pierrepont Mansion. (Brooklyn Historical Society)

whose wares are displayed in large triple-bay windows. There is a pleasant, relaxed, continental atmosphere that adds charm to the lively street.

At Henry Street, turn left (south) one block to Remsen Street.

Our Lady of Lebanon Maronite Catholic Cathedral, originally the Congregational Church of the Pilgrims, was a radical departure for architect Richard Upjohn, renowned for his Gothic Revival–style churches, particularly Trinity Church in Manhattan; and this early Romanesque Revival church, built in 1846, is thought to be the first building of that style in this country. When the church merged with the Plymouth Church on Orange Street in 1934, the fragment of Plymouth Rock imbedded in the tower was brought along. The new church acquired the building in 1944 and serves a large and long-established Lebanese community, some of which is clustered along Atlantic Avenue in "Brooklyn's Middle East." Most of the Lebanese community has moved to Bay Ridge, but many still come back to worship here. The interior of the church is surprisingly delicate, with widely spaced slender columns and semicircular arches supporting the ceiling. Unfortunately, the steeple deteriorated and was removed. Newly installed windows detract from the overall effect. The west and south portals are made from metal panels rescued from the oceanliner, *Normandie,* which burned and capsized at its Hudson River pier in 1942, during World War II. Only a few of the circular door panels on the west side have religious motifs; on the south side there are three medieval castles, and a *steamship*!

Return to Montague Street and turn left (west).

Nos. 111–115 Montague Street are an interesting pair of Queen Anne–style apartment houses, built in 1885, with a particularly engaging common façade. The *Berkeley* and *Grosvenor* display a combination of building materials: red brick, brownstone, and ornamental terra cotta. The houses were designed by Parfitt Brothers, an important Brooklyn architectural firm of three English-born brothers. Both buildings have been converted to co-ops.

No. 105 Montague Street, by the same architects and from the same period, is another good example of the style. Look up at the sculptured figure in the gable. Built in 1890, it is now a condominium.

The Hotel Bossert, at the corner of Hicks Street, was built for lumber merchant Louis Bossert in 1909–12. Designed by architects Helmle & Huberty, the Bossert was a center of Brooklyn social life for many years; and its Marine Roof, decorated like a yacht, provided an unsurpassed view of the harbor. Alas, the Marine Roof and elegant ballroom are no more. Cross to the diagonally opposite corner of Montague Street and examine briefly the Beaux Arts lower section of the hotel. On the Hicks Street side are no fewer than twelve tall arches running the full length of the building, each with a carved lion's head in the keystone console. Above the columned main entrance is a balcony with filigree ironwork that includes the hotel's initials as a central design. The Bossert is now another trophy of the ever-expanding Jehovah's Witnesses, and serves as a residence for volunteer workers. While one might take issue with their insatiable quest for more properties, one still must commend them for the restoration and preservation of their historic buildings. When the Witnesses took over the hotel, the few remaining rent-controlled tenants were allowed to stay on. Peek into the spacious lobby with its massive columns and beautifully restored coffered ceiling. They have also done well with the preservation of the exterior. The Witnesses have acquired more than 30 buildings in Brooklyn Heights and seem always ready to gobble up more with plenty of ready cash—a temptation for homeowners and a source of deep concern to the community.

The Heights Casino, 75 Montague Street, an exclusive tennis and squash club, was designed by Boring & Tilton and opened in 1905. In front of the site of the Casino stood the H. B. Pierrepont Mansion, "Four Chimneys," built before the American Revolution and used briefly by General Washington as headquarters before the retreat to Manhattan. The mansion was razed in the mid-19th century when Montague Street was extended to the water's edge. At about the site of No. 63, the street began its descent to the harbor. The street was elevated in the late 1940s when the Esplanade was built. The architects of the Heights Casino also designed the U.S. Immigration Station on Ellis Island.

No. 76 Montague Street, originally **Sirius House,** a two-and-a-half–story Federal building with a severely modified storefront, was a ship broker's office and is now an audio-video showroom. The firm had taken its name from the paddle steamer *Sirius,* the first ship of its kind to cross the Atlantic in a westward direction, in 1838. A plaque illustrating the ship, which is named after the navigational star, is imbedded in the sidewalk; a 19th-century British Admiralty–type anchor, secured from a ship-breaker's yard in Staten Island, rests solidly in front. Brooklyn Heights was for many years the home of sea captains and shipping people, and the Sirius Brokers, Inc. found it appropriate to move here from Manhattan in 1981 and restore what was the oldest house on the block (1859) for their offices. (Those making the walking tour in the winter will appreciate that this building and the Brooklyn Union Gas Company's former headquarters are the only two in the Heights to have heated sidewalks, this one by electricity, and the Gas Company's, obviously, by gas.)

Continue west on Montague Street to just across the street from **No. 62,** an enormous red-brick apartment house of ca. 1885. Erected in a mixture of Queen Anne and what might be called "Edwardian" styles, it is an early example of the luxury multifamily residence, then called the French flat. The six-story oriel on the Montague Street side is overshadowed by the ten-story round tower that rises majestically, past nine levels of ornate iron fire escapes, to a pyramidal mansard roof.

From this point to the waterfront, Montague Street once dropped steeply to connect with the **Wall Street Ferry** (service discontinued in 1912). At this spot architect Minard Lafever built a charming but short-lived arch in 1855 that spanned Montague Street. And just ahead, where Pierrepont Place and Montague Terrace meet at street level, there was an iron footbridge over the then-depressed Montague Street, known as **The Penny Bridge,** which survived until 1946 when the land was filled in for the Brooklyn-Queens Connecting Highway. Some idea of the depth of the old street can be had by examining the wall and deep cellar of the last house on the left, just at the stop sign at Montague Terrace. [*See* photo, page 435.]

At the end of Montague Street, walk into the park.

Facing the end of Montague Street are **Nos. 3** and **2 Pierrepont Place,** considered to be the most elegant brownstone dwelling houses in the city. Designed by noted architect Richard Upjohn and built in 1856–57, they form a splendid pair of Italianate mansions situated in an ideal location. A third house, No. 1, whose empty plot now serves as a playground, was built for Henry E. Pierrepont, and was demolished in 1946. The twin mini-*palazzi* were built for Abiel Abbott Low, a tea merchant (No. 3), and for Alexander M. White, a fur dealer (No. 2). A. A. Low's son, **Seth Low,** served as mayor of Brooklyn from 1882 to 1886, then as president of Columbia University, and in 1901 was elected mayor of the City of New York. He is remembered for his vigorous campaigns to reform the police, finance, and education departments, and for the donation of his Library to Columbia University. No. 2 was later occupied by Alfred Tredway White, a wealthy businessman and philanthropist, and president of the Brooklyn Bureau of Charities. It was White who believed in "philanthropy plus 5%" when he built the

Riverside Houses on Columbia Place (to be seen shortly) and the Tower and Home Apartments in the Cobble Hill section.

Walk back around the south side of No. 3 to the Esplanade for a rear view of the lavish mansions and a lovely, tall gingko tree that stands in the southwest corner of the private garden. In the popular film *Prizzi's Honor,* No. 3 was the magnificent villa with surrounding gardens that was the home of Don Corrado. Before reaching the Esplanade, read the bronze tablet at the entrance that commemorates the mansion **"Four Chimneys."** The film *No Way to Treat a Lady* was also filmed here some years ago.

The Brooklyn Heights Promenade, or "Esplanade" (see plaques), provides one of the most unforgettable harbor panoramas, which can be enjoyed while relaxing on one of the convenient benches. Considered by many to be New York City's most breath-taking vantage point, its design is a commendable attempt at separation of vehicular and pedestrian traffic, and a tribute to the planning of our city fathers. Local civic groups such as the Brooklyn Heights Association cooperated with then Parks Commissioner Robert Moses in the planning, and the resultant cantilevered Esplanade over the Brooklyn-Queens Connecting Highway, completed in 1950, gave sudden impetus to the redevelopment of Brooklyn Heights. A somewhat better design would have duplicated the almost total sepa-

The Brooklyn Heights Esplanade provides one of the finest views in the country. This photo was taken in the early 1960s before the construction of the huge boxlike office buildings, which now obscure much of the traditional Manhattan skyline. The Singer Tower, demolished in 1968, is visible to the left of the tree; one of the former World Trade Center towers is visible to the right. (Brooklyn Union Gas Company)

ration of roadway from pedestrian mall that was achieved with the East River Drive on the Upper East Side of Manhattan, where traffic noise and fumes were almost completely eliminated. Spend a few minutes enjoying the magnificent view of the dramatic Lower Manhattan skyline.

Turn right on the Esplanade, and after a few minutes of contemplation, take the next right, exiting just beyond the two mansions. Turn left into Columbia Heights for a brief detour. Walk to No. 210, then turn back.

Nos. 210–220 Columbia Heights, a splendid row of Italianate brownstones (some painted white), were erected between 1857 and 1860. The entrance to No. 210 is flanked by a pair of Corinthian columns, and the doorway is framed by masonry blocks with alternating vermiform ("wormlike") rustication. No. 214's entrance was once as grand as the others. Nos. 216 and 218 are (fortunately) unpainted and show their warm brownstone color. Both had mansard roofs added in the 1870s when the Second Empire style became the rage. Look what was added to the roof of No. 220, giving it an Italian Renaissance *villa* appearance! **No. 222** is a harmonious modern replacement by resident architect Ian Bruce Eichner.

Continue south on Pierrepont Place (the extension of Columbia Heights), past Montague Street, where the street changes its name again to Montague Terrace.

Nos. 1–13 Montague Terrace, built ca. 1886, is an engaging English-style "terrace row" in almost pristine condition. Author Thomas Wolfe, while living at No. 5 in 1935, wrote *Of Time and the River.* Wolfe spent a number of years in the Heights and nearby Cobble Hill, and his novels are drawn from personal experiences. **No. 11** is the most authentic, having undergone the fewest alterations, and preserving its broad entrance stairway.

Turn left into Remsen Street.

Named for Henry Remsen, who lived nearby and opened the street in 1825, this shady, quiet thoroughfare is lined with interesting mid- and late-19th-century residences. The houses as far as Hicks Street date mostly from the 1850s to the last decade of the 19th century.

Turn right (south) into Hicks Street and left into Grace Court Alley.

Grace Court Alley, a charming little mews running eastward to a dead end, was formerly the stable alley for the patrician residents of Remsen Street. The stables and carriage houses, now considered very chic, are luxurious duplexes. Note particularly the solidly built **Nos. 2, 4, 12,** and **14** and the protruding hooks above that serve as hoists to lift bulky items to the second floor.

Cross Hicks Street and walk a few yards into **Grace Court** and look through the tall iron fence into the spacious backyards of the houses on Remsen Street.

Grace (Protestant Episcopal) Church of Brooklyn Heights, another Richard Upjohn work, was completed in 1848. In style, it is typical Gothic Revival, much like an English parish church, but rather low, long, and narrow. The side entrance court offers a pleasant spot of repose, tucked under a magnificent 85-foot-high elm. The boldly carved moldings, capitals, and brackets are highlighted against the textured wall surface with its pattern of varied tooled groovings. Inside, open wood-vaulted trusses support the roof, but matching wooden piers were replaced by stone during a 1909 restoration. At that time, the handsome J. Pierpont Morgan Memorial Doorway was installed. In the sanctuary are an alabaster altar and reredos surmounted by an artistic stained-glass window. The church boasts three Tiffany stained-glass windows in the nave and aisles. After years of patchwork repairs, the church underwent a complete stone-by-stone restoration of the exterior.

Turn right (west) into Joralemon Street.

Joralemon Street is named for Teunis Joralemon, who purchased the Philip Livingston estate in 1803. You have doubtless noticed the sudden change in the atmosphere of the neighborhood. While still very attractive, it is apparent that Joralemon Street cannot compare in elegance to the streets just visited. This area was originally a district of small merchants, artisans, and tradesmen. There are no mansions or fancy town houses here, just straightforward Greek Revival–style row houses. The street was opened in the 1840s after the Remsen farm was subdivided. Note, too, the "cobblestoned" street (properly called Belgian blocks) and the old bluestone sidewalks.

Nos. 29–75 Joralemon Street are 24 modified Greek Revival–style houses, built from 1844 to 1848 in neatly descending pairs, each about 30 inches lower than the next, and most still retain their pilastered entranceways and original iron fences. **No. 58** was converted unobtrusively into a **ventilation chamber and emergency exit for the Lexington Avenue line subway tunnel** far below the street.

At the southwest corner of Columbia Place are the remarkable **Riverside Houses,** model tenements built for Alfred Tredway White in 1890 by William Field & Son. These multiple dwellings followed on the heels of his revolutionary Tower and Home Apartments in the nearby Cobble Hill neighborhood, the first such project in America and a rare example (in public housing, anyway) of enlightened self-interest. His motto "Philanthropy plus 5%" actually did bring him a profit. These houses were aptly named, but in the construction of the expressway, the "river side" was demolished, along with a superb view of the harbor. A remnant of the original central garden, which was a major part of the plan to provide as much light and air as possible for the 280 apartments, is still visible between the remaining building and the expressway.

Turn left (south) into Columbia Place.

Across from Riverside Houses is a charming row of four clapboard frame houses, **Nos. 7–13 Columbia Place,** which were once part of the nine-unit "Cottage Row" built in the late 1840s.

Return to Joralemon Street, turn right one block, then right again into Willow Place.

Nos. 2–8 Willow Place are a most unusual row of Gothic Revival–style duplex houses, built about 1847. Among their interesting features are the coupled porches with clustered colonnettes, diamond-paned side lights, and transoms in the entranceways, Tudor arches with trefoils in the spandrels, recessed panels connecting the second and third floors with wooden "chevron" moldings (forerunners of the spandrels used on tall modern buildings), hood labels over the third-floor windows of No. 8, and an appropriate iron fence and stoop railings. Note the plaque on No. 6.

Farther down the street is the **former Willow Place Chapel** (Russell Sturgis, 1875), built as a mission church by the First Unitarian Church and closed in 1945. The diminutive Victorian Gothic–style building now serves as the Alfred T. White Community Center and St. Ann's Church, as well as a venue for theatrical productions by the Heights Players.

Buildings **Nos. 38–40, 44,** and **48,** erected in 1966, are an excellent example of the use of modern materials and techniques applied harmoniously in a more traditional environment. Designed by Joseph and Mary Merz, the arrangement of garage space and the use of special 8-by-8-inch cement blocks gives the houses a simple dignity and helps them blend well with their venerable neighbors.

Across the street is the **last surviving "Colonnade Row" in Brooklyn Heights, Nos. 43–49 Willow Place.** Designed ca. 1846 as a middle-class imitation of the elegant multicolumned row houses such as Underhill's Colonnade or the very sumptuous marble Colonnade Row on Manhattan's Lafayette Place, it is reminiscent of an antebellum Southern mansion. The two-story brick houses are revealed behind the twin-story porches whose square wooden columns support the entablature and cornice. Although the continuous portico is only a foot above ground level, the total effect is undiminished—even enhanced by the simple Greek Revival doorways flanked by pilasters. Across Willow Street, almost hidden by its neighbors and partly obscured by a small but lush garden, its wooden columns overgrown with ivy, is lovely **No. 46** in a fading shade of green and looking for all the world like a set from *Gone With the Wind*. In *Bricks and Brownstone,* author Charles Lockwood refers to the dignified wooden porch of the Willow Place Colonnade Row as "an easily forgivable architectural fraud…[which] holds great appeal today because of its modest scale and the naïveté of its conception and execution."

Turn left (east) on State Street to Hicks Street, then left again.

Nos. 284–276 Hicks Street are a row of five former carriage houses. Note the round and elliptical arches, and the carved woman's head on the dormer of **No. 276,** formerly the studio of sculptor William Zorach. Adjacent is **Engine Company 224,** in a Beaux Arts–style fire house, designed in 1903 by Adams & Warren, and set in perfect scale with its neighbors.

Across the street is the **former St. Charles Orthopaedic Clinic** (**No. 277** Hicks Street). This is the approximate site of the Philip Livingston house, built ca. 1764. It was in the Livingston House that George Washington, on August 29, 1776, planned the strategic withdrawal of his Continental Army to Manhattan, following the Battle of Brooklyn.

Nos. 270–262, built in 1887, add to the variety of the street with their romantic Queen Anne–style grouping of picturesque details.

Turn right (east) on Joralemon Street.

In the sidewalk in front of No. 88 is a circular **cast-iron coal chute cover** that dates from when coal for heating was delivered to homeowners' coal bins situated below.

Take a brief detour down **Garden Place,** laid out in 1842 and named for the garden that once graced the Philip Livingston estate. (Livingston was also one of the signers of the Declaration of Independence.) Note the Queen Anne style of **No. 26** and the storybook **converted carriage house** at **No. 21,** which, according to the plaque installed by its owners, was built ca. 1846. It was a garage with living quarters above between 1916 and 1936, then a single family residence until the present. Note also the atmosphere created by the row of London plane trees, which, since their planting in the early 1940s, have grown to provide a verdant umbrella for the street. See also Nos. 17, 19, and 19a.

Continue east on Joralemon Street to Henry Street, and turn left (north) for a brief detour to Hunts Lane.

Hunts Lane is another former stable alley, whose brick carriage houses were converted to duplexes, and which, like nearby Grace Court Alley, served the affluent homeowners on Remsen Street whose backyards abutted the Lane.

Return to Joralemon Street and continue east.

No. 129 Joralemon Street, the **former David Chauncey Mansion,** was designed by C. P. H. Gilbert in 1891 in an odd combination of Romanesque Revival and Colonial Revival details. A massive stone and yellow brick villa, it has been subdivided into apartments.

No. 135 always astonishes the visitor. Almost hidden between two overpowering neighbors, this delightful gem of a house is reminiscent of No. 24 Middagh Street, its "cousin" seen at the beginning of the tour. Built ca. 1833, and known as the **John Haslet House** (after its first owner, a U.S. Navy surgeon), it is the sole survivor of a row of similar residences that once lined the street and is an excellent example of Federal-style architecture. The ornate cast-iron porch was added in the mid-19th century, and the parlor-floor windows were lowered. Unfortunately, the house has been allowed to deteriorate badly and needs considerable restoration. Note the Flemish bond brickwork of the basement, the handsome entranceway with Ionic colonnettes, the neat clapboarding, simple cornice, twin dormers, and gambrel roof. The house, which until the early 1980s had been in a very poor state, was given a complete facelift, but sadly, time, weather, and probable lack of funds have prevented the long-time resident-owner from keeping up with necessary maintenance, and it is again taking on a woefully decrepit air.

Turn right into Sidney Place.

Sidney Place is even more varied than its neighbor Garden Place. It is named after Sir Philip Sidney, or Sydney (1554–86), an English author, statesman, and soldier who was a distinguished figure in the court of Queen Elizabeth. Most of the houses on the west side date from the 1840s. **No. 2,** the corner house, built about 1848, has a peculiar appendage facing Sidney Place in the form of a wooden two-story-high vestibule, with—lo and behold!—a delicate Greek Revival–style entryway. Twin Ionic colonnettes and wreathed side lights flank the door, with a transom and carved plaque above. It is said that the entranceway originally belonged to a house that was demolished to make way for the construction of the Towers Hotel. **No. 18,** a Greek Revival house of about 1838, has an attractive recessed doorway flanked by Doric columns. Some years later, three additional floors were added, making this doubtless the tallest Greek Revival house in the city.

Beyond Aitken Place, the row of houses on the east side is set back behind lush gardens and iron fences, adding to the cozy intimacy of the shady street. **Nos. 31–49,** a continuous row of Greek Revival–style houses, were all built about 1845. Most have suffered modifications, but **No. 35** is closest to the original appearance.

Framing the entrance to Aitken Place are the **St. Charles Borromeo (Roman Catholic) Church** (1869), and across the street, the Rectory (1920) and adjacent parish school (1916). The church, designed by that prolific architect of so many Catholic churches in the 19th century, Patrick C. Keely, is a simple modified Gothic Revival–style structure in dark-red painted brick, but in scale with its surrounding neighbors. Inside, the supporting arches and trim are in a delicate "carpenter Gothic" style. The plain, light-colored walls contrast strongly with the dark-brown ceiling. Rev. Ambrose S. Aitken was a former pastor of the congregation, and the adjoining street is named for him. Follow Aitken Place to Clinton Street.

Turn left on Clinton Street.

Clinton Street is named for De Witt Clinton (1769–1828) who served ten annual terms as mayor of New York City and two terms as governor. He was the guiding spirit behind the construction of the Erie Canal, ran unsuccessfully for president, was an amateur naturalist, and for his entire career a dedicated public servant.

At the corner, look to the right (south) down **Clinton Street.** Except for some modifications to the exteriors of the Greek Revival–style row houses, little has changed in the past 150 years. At the southeast corner is a row of four red brick houses, **Nos. 133–139 Clinton Street,** whose appearance is enhanced by the duo of gaslights. The corner house was once the home of the *Excelsiors,* an early Brooklyn baseball team and champions of the world in 1860. Read the plaque on No. 133 and learn who pitched the first curve ball, and how baseball is so closely tied to the history of Brooklyn. Across Livingston Street is the following:

The **former St. Ann's Episcopal Church,** closed in 1966 and merged with the Holy Trinity Church, is two blocks north. In a move to cut costs and help maintain their parochial school, the Episcopal Diocese of Brooklyn sold the church to the nearby Packer Collegiate Institute, and moved its headquarters along with its congregation to Holy Trinity. Designed in 1869 by famed architect James Renwick, Jr. (who planned St. Patrick's Cathedral as well as Manhattan's Grace Church), this is the only example in Brooklyn of the Ruskinian or Venetian Gothic style. Where this style differs from the more conventional Gothic Revival is in the use of polychromy in the façade. The arch blocks (voussoirs) are in alternating white and dark brown, while horizontal bands of white stone run across the full width of the exterior.

Nos. 142 and **140,** across Clinton Street from the church, are survivors of a row of five similar houses, built ca. 1855. Most unusual are the bracketed gables and the highly ornate black-painted cast-iron lintels set over the windows and entrances. [*See* photo, page 421.]

Walk north on Clinton Street to Joralemon Street.

To the right, on Clinton Street, is the **Packer Collegiate Institute,** designed in the "Collegiate" Gothic Revival style by Minard Lafever in 1854 and built on the site of the Brooklyn Female Academy that was destroyed by fire two years earlier. These lovely "halls of ivy" were endowed by Mrs. William S. Packer to honor her late husband's interest in women's education. The delightful exterior was published by Lafever in his *Architectural Instructor* and reflected his belief that churches as well as schools should be constructed in the medieval Gothic tradition. The Gothic-style wing at the east end was added in 1886.

Continue north on Clinton Street to Remsen Street, and turn right (east).

The little Gothic Revival–style brownstone church at the corner is the **former Spencer Memorial Church,** built in 1850–53 (architect unknown) for the First Church (Presbyterian) of Brooklyn. The church was closed in the early 1970s and was later sold to a developer and converted into 11 cooperative apartments. An alley to the left is called "Spencer Mews" and has entrances to some professional apartments. Other tenants enter at what were once the various doorways to the church. On the alley wall is a memorial tablet saved from the interior, honoring the former church's first pastor, Ichabod Spencer.

Just beyond the main building of **St. Francis College** is the tall Classic Revival–style building that housed the **former headquarters of the Brooklyn Union Gas Company** until their next structure was erected in 1962 on Montague Street. The building was designed in 1914 by Frank Freeman, and has been converted to classroom and office use by St. Francis College. Interesting is the Classic colonnade on the upper stories.

Immediately to the left, in what resembles a Greek temple, is the gem of the block, the **original headquarters of the Brooklyn Gas Light Company,** erected in 1857. The firm became the Brooklyn Union Gas Company in 1895, and remained in

Brooklyn's Civic Center at the turn of the century. To the left rear of Brooklyn's City Hall is the Court House (now the site of the Brooklyn Law School). Also gone are the trolley lines and the Brooklyn Rapid Transit Elevated on curving Fulton Street. The statue of Henry Ward Beecher in front of City Hall has been moved several hundred yards farther north. (Author's collection)

this diminutive white marble building until architect Freeman's plans for its new offices next door were executed twenty years later. Like its neighbor, it too has been incorporated into the St. Francis campus as the McGarry Library. Adjacent **No. 186** (ca. 1885) is a typical Romanesque Revival–style commercial building.

Continue to Court Street, turn right (south) one block to Joralemon Street, and cross to the opposite side of Court Street.

The tall commercial structure at the corner, the ornate **Temple Bar Building** (No. 44 Court Street), was the tallest in Brooklyn when completed in 1901 from plans by George L. Morse. Interesting are the ogee-shaped twin cupolas and the Classic Eclectic details of the façade. Court Street between Livingston and Pierrepont streets was once the major axis of Brooklyn's "Financial District"; however, a new commercial renaissance has taken place a half-mile farther east in such developments as MetroTech, Livingston Plaza, Renaissance Plaza, and Atlantic Center. Yet this area is still home to several universities, and serves as the civic hub of the borough, with nearby Borough Hall, the Brooklyn Municipal Building, and the various city, state, and federal courthouses, as well as the main Brooklyn Post Office, the Brooklyn Heights branch of the Brooklyn Public Library, the New York City Transit Authority, and the New York City Board of Education—all within a few blocks' radius.

End of Second Tour. At Borough Hall are the 1, 2, 4, and 5 lines, and at Montague Street, the Court Street station of the M, N, and R lines. For the A, C, and F lines, walk past Borough Hall to Fulton Street, then two blocks east to Jay Street.

A BRIEF LOOK AT BROOKLYN'S CIVIC CENTER

The **Brooklyn Municipal Building,** an immense and austere Indiana limestone structure, was designed in a modified Classic Eclectic style by McKenzie, Voorhees & Gmelin, and completed in 1926. The granite for the base came from Deer Island, Maine, and the interior marble was quarried in Vermont and Tennessee. The building houses most of the offices of borough government, including the files from the demolished Court House and Hall of Records, which stood just to the east.

Directly in front, and facing Cadman Plaza, is **Borough Hall, formerly the Brooklyn City Hall.** Said to be one of the most beautiful public buildings in the entire city, the old City Hall was built in 1836–49 in Greek Revival style, although its cupola is strictly Georgian, and was added in 1898. The Hall was originally planned to be a replica of Manhattan's City Hall, but instead the Greek Revival style was selected. The architect, Gamaliel King, was in fact a grocer and carpenter! An excellent view is from the Plaza where the splendid façade with its broad staircase gracefully ascending to the Ionic colonnade is seen to best advantage. Borough Hall houses the offices of the president of the borough of Brooklyn. The building underwent a major renovation in 1989.

From the colonnade of Borough Hall there is a broad perspective of **Cadman Plaza.** Named for Rev. S. Parkes Cadman, an active community leader and America's first radio preacher, the Plaza was the result of a major urban renewal in the 1950s, that included the razing of the Fulton Street El, which came over the Brooklyn Bridge and darkened Fulton Street for miles, also the removal of trolley tracks and the rebuilding of major traffic arteries. The Plaza, and Columbus Park in the center, act as a "buffer zone" between Brooklyn Heights and the rest of the borough.

To the right is the modern **New York State Supreme Court,** designed in 1957 by Shreve, Lamb & Harmon (architects of the Empire State Building). At its south end are **lamp standards from the old Hall of Records;** and to the east, the **Federal Building and Court House,** completed in 1961 from plans by Carson, Lundin & Shaw.

In front of the New York State Supreme Court Building is the imposing **statue of Christopher Columbus** (Emma Stebbins, base by A. Ottavino, 1867). The marble statue was originally placed in Central Park and has had the strange history of being removed from the park, then somehow "misplaced," rediscovered, restored, relocated here in 1971, and finally placed next to the formal garden that bears Columbus's name. Stebbins is best remembered for her *Angel of the Waters* sculpture atop Central Park's Bethesda Fountain. The nearby **bust of Senator Robert F. Kennedy,** by Anetta Duveen, was installed in 1972. Behind the bust of RFK is a plaque honoring **Washington Augustus Roebling,** son of

Brooklyn's Romanesque Revival–style Central Post Office is a designated landmark. Completed in 1891, it represents an unusually high standard of government-sponsored architecture. The tree-lined plot to the right was the site of the Brooklyn Eagle. *(Brooklyn Union Gas Company)*

Opening day of the Brooklyn Elevated Railroad with its special trainload of city officials, May 13, 1888, from an engraving in Leslie's Illustrated Newspaper *of the following week. (Brooklyn Historical Society)*

John A. Roebling, "father of the Brooklyn Bridge." When completed in 1883, it was the longest suspension bridge in the world. Farther west is an ornate three-tier **cast-iron fountain,** alongside of which is a historical plaque mounted on a light pole.

To the north, rising like a medieval château, is the **Brooklyn Central Office of the United States Post Office and Courthouse.** Designed in 1885 in Romanesque Revival style by Mifflin E. Bell, the work was later assumed by William A. Freret, supervising architect for the Treasury Department, and completed in 1891. A north section, in harmonious style, was designed by James A. Wetmore in 1933. The post office, built of granite while Brooklyn was still an independent city, represents a high standard of government-sponsored architecture, and with the great advances in stone-cutting techniques achieved late in the 19th century, it was possible to produce masonry buildings of great beauty. To the south of the post office stood the Brooklyn Eagle Building, built in 1893 and demolished in the late 1950s as part of the civic center redevelopment plan.

A half-block farther is the best piece of sculpture in the plaza, and one of the finest in the city, the extraordinary bronze **statue of Henry Ward Beecher,** by John Quincy Adams Ward, unveiled in 1891, with a black granite pedestal designed by Richard Morris Hunt. When Beecher died on March 8, 1887, Ward received a telegram urgently requesting that he make a death mask within four hours. Complying, he then received the commission for the eight-foot-high statue. In the completed monument an austere Beecher, in a simple knee-length Inverness cape, stands above three intimate figures of youngsters, a young black girl placing a palm frond in gratitude at the abolitionist's feet, and a young boy helping a girl climb the base to lay flowers at Beecher's feet—all three representing his love and devotion to children. The statue originally stood in front of Borough Hall, but was moved to its present site in 1959. In its praise for the Beecher Monument, the Metropolitan Museum of Art called it "public statuary at its best."

End of tour. (The following tour may be made by either walking the short distance indicated below, or by taking the three-minute bus ride.)

THE FULTON FERRY HISTORIC DISTRICT

Walk down Cadman Plaza to the waterfront (about a third of a mile) or take the B25 or B41 bus to the end of the line at Furman Street. (Cadman Plaza West becomes Old Fulton Street after the Expressway.)

The modern history of Brooklyn began at the waterfront hamlet of Fulton Ferry, which after the introduction of Robert Fulton's steam ferry in 1814 became the gateway not only to Brooklyn but to Long Island as well. (The first record of a ferry to Manhattan was Cornelis Dircksen's regular rowboat crossings in 1642. Crossings were later made with sailboats, and even with boats propelled by horses walking on treadmills.) Other ferries subsequently linked Manhattan and Brooklyn, and in 1872 as many as 1,200 daily crossings were recorded, but the Fulton Ferry was by far the most important. [*See* illustrations, page 457.] The little vil-

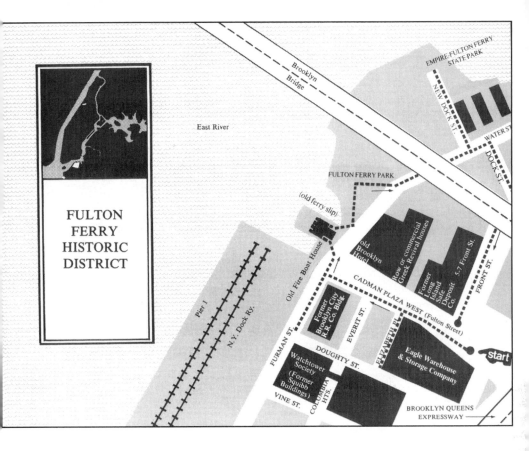

lage grew rapidly and soon boasted several hotels, a newspaper (the Brooklyn *Daily Eagle*, whose 100-year-old pages can be visited at *http//:eaglebrooklynpubliclibrary.org*), a bank, law offices, and a stagecoach terminal. With the opening of the Brooklyn Bridge in 1883, the Fulton Ferry district began a gradual decline, becoming an almost forgotten backwater by the 20th century. The ferry hung on, however, until 1924, after 110 years of service. After many years, work has been progressing slowly to restore many of the old landmarks and to re-create much of the early-19th-century atmosphere of the Village of Fulton Ferry, and the area has been designated a Historic District.

The tour begins on Old Fulton Street in front of the Eagle Warehouse and Storage Company building.

The Eagle Warehouse and Storage Company of Brooklyn engaged architect Frank Freeman to design this massive red brick "fortress" in 1893. Completed a year later, it became a notable example of his Romanesque Revival style. The arched main entrance with the company's bold lettering is particularly impressive. A stylized horse's head is mounted on a gooseneck post at the entry gate, which separates the vehicular entrance from the former office. Very impressive are the symmetrical façade and the heavy iron grilles on the windows. Above is a row of round arches surmounted by corbels that resemble the machicolations of a medieval castle. On the parapet is a clock flanked by the name of the establishment.

The Fulton Ferry terminal, built in 1871 in Victorian style, continued in operation until 1924. This 1891 view shows a steam train of the Brooklyn Elevated Railroad about to leave from the adjacent El station for its run on the Fulton Street line. (Brooklyn Historical Society)

Looking northeast on Fulton Street (now Cadman Plaza) in 1954 toward the old Brooklyn Eagle Building (demolished) and the extant Central Post Office Building. (Brooklyn Picture Collection, Brooklyn Public Library)

Once a warehouse for the storage of household furnishings and silverware, the enormous structure was renovated in 1980 and adaptively reused as a cooperative apartment building. In the lobby (if you can persuade the doorman or a tenant to let you peek inside) is an atrium in which "artifacts" from nearby demolished buildings are displayed on the walls. Unfortunately the building's former "birdcage" elevator has been removed and relegated to the roof. The lobby also has a colorful mural of Cadman Plaza West looking toward the river.

Walk around to the rear, on Elizabeth Place, and see if you can discover the old three-story brick building, with segmental-arc window lintels, that has been incorporated into the warehouse. This is the last physical vestige of the *Brooklyn Eagle's* first office, **its old pressroom.** Built in 1882 from a design by George L. Morse, it functioned until 1893 when the newspaper erected its new building next to the Brooklyn post office. The name of the warehouse was appropriated from the newspaper, as two of its directors were executives of the *Eagle.*

Up the hill to the south rise the prominent yellow-painted twin factory buildings that were once the **Squibb Pharmaceutical Company plant.** Connected by a "Bridge of Sighs" over Everit Street (whose name changes to Columbia Heights after one block), the once-busy drug manufacturing facility is now the printing plant of the Watchtower Bible & Tract Society, the Jehovah's Witnesses.

At No. 8 Old Fulton Street, at the corner of Furman Street, is the **former headquarters of the Brooklyn City Railroad Company,** the horsecar enterprise that began in 1853, replacing the stages and extending its ribbons of track throughout the city of Brooklyn, thus giving impetus to the development of many formerly isolated neighborhoods. (A portion of track is still visible protruding from under the gate on the west side. It is somewhat hidden, but it can be seen to the right of the entrance to the apartment house on Furman Street.) The structure was designed in Italianate style and is constructed of brick with granite trim. Completed in 1861, it occupies the riverfront site of the former Judge William Furman residence. From 1910 until the mid-1970s, the building housed a toilet-seat factory, and in 1975 it was converted to an apartment house by architect David Morton.

Across Old Fulton Street—which in the early 19th century was called Old Ferry Road—is a **row of commercial structures in Greek Revival style,** built between 1836 and 1839.

Notice the painted names of merchants and their wares fading from the façades of the row of buildings. These four-story houses retain much of their original appearance and are significant as one of the few surviving examples in the city of commercial Greek Revival architecture.

At the end of the commercial row, at the corner of Water Street, the **old Franklin House,** now a tavern called Pete's Downtown, was the most important dining saloon and hotel in the district during the 19th century. Its prime location at the Fulton Ferry made it a favored stop for commuters for over sixty years.

Ahead, at the river's edge, the small wood-frame building with hipped roof and tower is the **former Marine Fire Boat Station.** Erected in 1930 on the site of the old Victorian-style Ferry Terminal, it served the harbor firefighting patrol until the station became obsolete in the late 1970s. (The tower was used to hang the fire hoses to dry.) The former fireboat pier occupies the site of the old Fulton

Ferry slip. A recent occupant of the old fireboat station is the Brooklyn Ice Cream Factory, a good place for a cooling and refreshing pit stop.

A **plaque** on a nearby boulder marks the spot where Gen. George Washington escaped with his Continental Army to Manhattan on the night of August 29, 1776. Anchored to the left is **"Bargemusic,"** formerly the Erie-Lackawanna R.R. Coffee Barge 375, which was acquired in 1977 and converted into a floating chamber music concert hall. In this unique ambiance, gifted soloists perform year round on Sunday afternoons at 4:00 and Thursday evenings at 7:30 [reservations: (718) 624–4061].

Just to the right and in the shadow of the Brooklyn Bridge is a tranquil little sitting park built by the adjacent River Café and open to the public. The privately owned restaurant, set on a barge, offers diners a panoramic but pricey view of the harbor.

Follow Water Street under the bridge to the first street on the left, New Dock Street. The old red brick structure was built in the early 1860s as the **Tobacco Inspection Warehouse**, No. 25–39 Water Street. It was used until well after the turn of the 20th century for the storage of tobacco and as a customs inspection center for tobacco imports, since 90 percent of Brooklyn's tobacco trade was carried on here.

Reaching the corner, turn left into New Dock Street, and walk to the entrance of **Empire–Fulton Ferry State Park** (*closed in winter*). To the left, an open "cobblestoned" plaza offers dramatic views of the Lower Manhattan skyline and the ships of the South Street Seaport, framed by the towers of the Brooklyn Bridge. A plaque describes the Bridge and its two neighbors to the north, the Manhattan and Williamsburg bridges. In the park itself, follow the boardwalk, relax and watch the passing parade of East River ship traffic, or turn around and enjoy the lush green lawn, designed to be walked on.

To the right of the Manhattan Bridge, is the **Clocktower Building** (William Higginson, 1886) with the hipped roof and four-sided clock. Erected for pioneer corrugated box manufacturer Robert Gair, it was originally called the **Gair Building.** It and a group of about a dozen similar structures were among the first reinforced-concrete buildings in America, and all were named Gair, but with separate numbers. This one was Gair No. 7. The building was renovated in 1986 by Beyer Blinder Belle, and converted to a co-op.

The backdrop of the park, and its main feature, is the **Empire Stores,** a monumental row of seven connected brick warehouses with long rows of similar round-arched windows and doors. Erected in two stages, the first group to the west was built in 1870, and the eastern section in 1885, by architect Thomas Stone, and share a unified façade. Loading hoists project from the flat roofs under corbelled roof cornices, and the doors and windows have heavy iron shutters that swing on pintle-type hinges. Metal tie-rod caps in the shape of stars reinforce the walls and add a decorative touch. In front of the Stores and leading to the water's edge were once railroad sidings to accommodate freight cars brought on car floats from the various railroad terminals around the city. The Empire Stores were used originally for the general storage of such raw materials as coffee beans, animal hides, grains, raw sugar and molasses, brought from points all over the world. They were just one of many such warehouses that lined the Brooklyn waterfront for miles, earning the borough the sobriquet "the walled city." No

In the shadow of the Brooklyn Bridge, the Long Island Safe Deposit Company building, erected in 1869 in a Venetian Gothic style, is a remarkably well-preserved example of cast-iron construction. The original bank closed in 1891, but the building has managed to survive, having served a variety of clients through the years. (Photo by author)

longer in use, they were acquired in 1963 by Con Edison, and later by the city for development by some as yet undecided institution, such as a museum. Return to the park entrance and walk back along New Dock Street to Front Street.

Turn left on Water Street, then right on Dock Street to Front Street, and turn right again.

No. 7 Front Street is a small Greek Revival structure built in 1834 for the **Long Island Insurance Company,** and it may be the earliest example of an office building that still survives in the entire city. The insurance company lasted until 1867, when the building was sold to the bank that erected its office two years later at the corner to the left. Note the original iron hand-railings, ornamented with scrolls and acorns, which are preserved at the central doorway. The façade above the first floor is in Flemish-bond brickwork, with alternating long bricks (stretchers) and short bricks (headers), a fashion typical of better buildings erected during the Federal and Greek Revival periods. Stone windowsills and cap-molded lintels and a brick fascia below the roof cornice are typical of the era. It is now a tavern.

At the northwest corner of Old Fulton and Front Streets is a highly ornate cast-iron-front building erected in 1869 for the **Long Island Safe Deposit Company.** Designed by William Mundell at a time when cast iron had come into vogue as a successful building medium, the highly decorative façade is modeled after a Venetian Renaissance palace. The company's safety-deposit vaults were once visible on the first floor of the bank, set in their own granite foundations. The bank closed in 1891, and the building has since served a wide variety of owners. At this writing it is vacant.

The cast-iron façade is unique in this area, and its delicate detailing is worth a few minutes' examination. The first-floor round-arched windows are protected by iron window guards with fleur-de-lis cresting, and are separated by pilasters with egg-and-dart capitals. The second-story windows are even more ornate and recall the style of the Venetian Renaissance *palazzi*. All details, both of the exterior as well as the interior, were rendered in cast iron, since it was its fireproofing qualities that attracted the original owners. The old bank is on the site of the 19th-century Abraham Remsen home and dry-goods store, which had replaced the original 17th-century stone farmhouse of the Rapelje family.

A BRIEF NOTE ABOUT THE BROOKLYN BRIDGE. Construction began on January 3, 1870, and was completed 13 years later, providing the vital link to Manhattan that ultimately led to the consolidation of Brooklyn into the City of New York in 1898. The monumental bridge represented the largest leap across an open space to that date—1,595.5 feet—and is still considered by many to be the most beautiful span ever built. Engineer John Augustus Roebling had few architectural precedents to draw upon and had to test his designs on the spot. He had built three previous smaller bridges—the Suspension Bridge at Niagara Falls, in 1852, the still-extant Delaware & Hudson Aqueduct Bridge at Lackawaxen, Pennsylvania, and the Ohio River Bridge in Cincinnati. The Delaware bridge originally carried canal boats across the Delaware River and now is used by vehicular traffic. The Cincinnati bridge is also still in active service and a beloved local landmark. In planning the bridge, Roebling wisely anticipated the oscillation caused by aerodynamic instability and was a great pioneer in the use of structural steel. He is ranked with Joseph Paxton, who designed London's Crystal Palace Exposition Hall in 1851, and with Alexandre Gustave Eiffel, whose great Tower was erected in Paris in 1889. The Brooklyn Bridge cost in excess of $16 million, some of which ended up in the pockets of "Boss" Tweed and his Ring.

Roebling suffered a fatal accident in the early stages of the bridge's construction. His foot was crushed by a wooden piling as the Fulton ferryboat was docking, and he died of tetanus a few weeks later. His son, Washington Augustus Roebling, carried on the project, and proved himself as capable an engineer as his father. He, too, was struck down by the bridge, suffering a disabling attack of caisson disease (the bends) from a too-rapid ascent from the underwater pressure chambers, and he directed the remaining work from the window of his sickroom, several blocks away on Columbia Heights. He was assisted by his wife Emily, who even taught herself advanced mathematics to be able to better help her husband. Little was known then of nitrogen narcosis, and the dangerous construction job

City dignitaries gathered to inspect the cables of the Brooklyn Bridge in 1873. Judging from engineer Roebling's warning sign, the terrifying hike on the Bridge's catwalk across the river must have been fairly commonplace. (Brooklyn Union Gas Company)

The Bridge Promenade has always been a popular attraction. In warm weather, hundreds of commuters from Brooklyn Heights still use it daily. (Brooklyn Historical Society)

A two-cent ticket to walk across the Brooklyn Bridge after it was opened to the public in 1883. (Brooklyn Union Gas Company)

Traffic was already heavy on the Brooklyn Bridge in 1905. (Brooklyn Historical Society)

An 1814 newspaper advertisement announcing the commutation fares for Robert Fulton's new steam ferry service to Brooklyn. (Brooklyn Historical Society)

New-York and Brooklyn Ferry.

SUCH persons as are inclined to compound, agreeable to law, in the Steam Ferry-Boat, Barges, or common Horse Boats, will be pleased to apply to the subscribers, who are authorized to settle the same.

GEORGE HICKS, Brooklyn,
JOHN PINTARD, 52 Wall-st

Commutation for a single person not
transferable, for 12 months, $10 00
Do.   do.   8 months,   6 67
May 3, 1814.   6m.

The ferry from the tip of lower Manhattan entering its slip at the foot of Atlantic Avenue, Brooklyn, ca. 1830. (South Street Seaport Museum)

took the lives of many workers. Opening day caused some furor among the Irish population of the city, as the date coincided with Queen Victoria's birthday. Shortly thereafter, a tragedy occurred that took the lives of a number of bridge pedestrians caught in an unexplained panic at the Manhattan end. Newspaper accounts attributed the crush to an organization of pickpockets who spread confusion to facilitate their criminal activities. To date 45 people have leaped from the bridge, of whom only 11 survived, including a Bowery saloonkeeper named Steve Brodie, whose claim of having survived the plunge may have been a publicity stunt. For many years the bridge carried cable cars, then the trains of the Brooklyn Elevated Railway, as well as trolley cars. The trolleys and trains were removed in the early 1940s and replaced by additional traffic lanes. More supporting cables were added later, but the strength and beauty of the bridge remains an enduring monument to the genius and skill of the Roeblings. A few years ago the twin Gothic-style stone piers were sandblasted, and to everyone's surprise, the original color of the granite was revealed to be pink!

The view of the Manhattan skyline at dusk, framed in the dark arches and gossamerlike cables of the great span, is a never-to-be-forgotten experience. Thomas Wolfe, in *Of Time and the River,* extolled the beauty of the bridge "whose wing-like sweep" reached across to the "shining city, far-flung and blazing into tiers of jeweled light."

Walk back on the left side of Old Fulton Street to where the Expressway crosses overhead.

Look carefully along the base of the bridge for the minipark called **Anchorage Plaza,** where steel sculptures of John, Washington, and Emily Roebling (by Keith Godard) point to the bridge they created. The figures were installed as part of the Brooklyn Bridge Centennial Celebration in 1983. Within the walls is the Anchorage itself, a cavernous space where the bridge's great anchor chains disappear underground. Until recently, it was used for public exhibits and performances but is temporarily closed for security reasons.

End of tour. To reach the A or C line, follow Old Fulton Street into Cadman Plaza West. The station entrance is opposite Cranberry Street, adjacent to the Whitman Close town houses, where the first Brooklyn Heights tour began.

Recommended Reading: New York City Architecture and History

ALBION, ROBERT GREENHALGH. *The Rise of New York Port (1815–1860)*. New York: Charles Scribner's Sons, 1967.

ANDREWS, WAYNE. *Architecture in New York*. New York: Atheneum, 1969. Reprint, New York: Harper & Row Icon Books, 1973.

———. *Architecture, Ambition and Americans*. New York: The Free Press, 1964.

ASBURY, HERBERT. *All Around the Town*. New York: Knopf, 1929.

———. *The Gangs of New York*. Garden City, N.Y.: Garden City Publishing Co., 1927.

BALDWIN, CHARLES C. *Stanford White*. New York, 1931. Reprint with introduction by Paul Goldberger. New York: DaCapo Press, 1976.

BARAL, ROBERT. *Turn West on 23rd*. New York: Fleet Press, 1965.

BARLOW, ELIZABETH. *Frederick Law Olmsted's New York*. With an illustrative portfolio by William Alex. In association with the Whitney Museum of American Art. New York: Praeger, 1972.

BATTERBERRY, MICHAEL and ARIANE BATTERBERRY. *On the Town in New York, from 1776 to the Present*. New York: Charles Scribner's Sons, 1973.

BELLE, JOHN and MAXINNE RHEA LEIGHTON. *Grand Central: Gateway to a Million Lives*. New York: W. W. Norton, 1999.

BERGER, MEYER. *Meyer Berger's New York*. New York: Random House, 1960.

BERMAN, MIRIAM. *Madison Square—The Park and Its Celebrated Landmarks*. Salt Lake City: Gibbs Smith Publishers, 2001.

BETTMAN, OTTO L. *The Good Old Days—They Were Terrible!* New York: Random House, 1974.

BIXBY, WILLIAM. *South Street, New York's Seaport Museum*. New York: David McKay, 1972.

BLACK, MARY, ed. *Old New York in Early Photographs*. From the collection of the New-York Historical Society. New York: Dover, 1973.

BLIVEN, BRUCE, JR. *The Battle for Manhattan*. Baltimore: Penguin Books, 1965.

———. *Under the Guns—New York: 1775–1776*. New York: Harper & Row, 1972.

BOTKIN, B. A., ed. *New York City Folklore*. New York: Random House, 1956.

BOYER, M. CHRISTINE. *Manhattan Manners, Architecture and Style, 1850–1900*. New York: Rizzoli, 1985.

BROWN, HENRY COLLINS, ed. *Valentine's Manual of the City of New York, 1916–1928* (New Series) 12 vols. published annually. New York: The Valentine Co., 1916–1928.

BULLATY, SONJA, PAUL GOLDBERGER, and ANGELA LOMEO. *The World Trade Center Remembered*. New York: Abbeville Press, 2001.

BURNHAM, ALAN, ed. *New York Landmarks*. Middletown, Conn.: Wesleyan University Press, 1963.

BURROWS, EDWIN G. and MIKE WALLACE. *Gotham: A History of New York City to 1898*. New York: Oxford University Press, 2001.

CABLE, MARY. *The Blizzard of '88*. New York: Atheneum, 1988.

CANTOR, MINDY, ed. *Around the Square, 1830–1890*. New York: New York University, 1982.

CAPLOVICH, JUDD. *Blizzard! The Great Storm of '88*. Vernon, Conn.: VeRo Publishing Co., 1987.

CHASE, W. PARKER. *New York 1932: The Wonder City* (facsimile edition). Introduction by Paul Goldberger. New York: New York Bound, 1983.

CHRISTMAN, HENRY M., ed. *Walt Whitman's New York*. New York: Macmillan, 1963.

COHEN, BARBARA, SEYMOUR CHWAST, and STEVEN HELLER, eds. *New York Observed. Artists and Writers Look at the City*. New York: Harry N. Abrams, 1987.

CONDIT, CARL W. *American Building*. Chicago: University of Chicago Press, 1968.

———. *The Port of New York*, Vol. 1: *A History of the Rail and Terminal System from the Beginnings to Pennsylvania Station*, Vol. 2: *A History of the Rail and Terminal System from the Grand Central Electrification to the Present*. Chicago: University of Chicago Press, 1980, 1981.

CONDON, THOMAS J. *New York Beginnings: The Commercial Origins of New Netherland*. New York: New York University Press, 1968.

CROMLEY, ELIZABETH COLLINS. *Alone Together: A History of New York's Early Apartments*. Ithaca: Cornell University Press, 1990.

CUDAHY, BRIAN. *Under the Sidewalks of New York: The Story of the Greatest Subway System in the World*. Brattleboro, Vt.: The Stephen Greene Press, 1979.

DELANEY, EDMUND T. *New York's Greenwich Village*. Barre, Mass.: Barre Publishers, 1965.

———. *New York's Turtle Bay—Old and New*. Barre, Mass.: Barre Publishers, 1965.

DIAMONSTEIN, BARBARALEE. *The Landmarks of New York*. New York: Harry N. Abrams, 1988.

DICKENS, CHARLES. *American Notes*. Philadelphia: Lippincott, 1885.

DIEHL, LORRAINE B. and MARIANNE HARDART. *The Automat. The History, Recipes, and Allure of Horn & Hardart's Masterpiece*. New York: Clarkson Potter/Publisher, 2002.

DINER, HASIA. *Lower East Side Memories: A Jewish Place in America*. Princeton: Princeton University Press, 2000.

DOLKART, ANDREW S. *Guide to New York City Landmarks*. New York: John Wiley & Sons, 1998.

———. *Texture of TriBeCa*. New York: TriBeCa Community Assn., 1989.

———. *Touring the Upper East Side: Walks in Five Historic Districts*. New York: New York Landmarks Conservancy, 1999.

——— and STEVEN WHEELER. *Lower Manhattan: Three Walks in New York's Historic Downtown*. New York: New York Landmarks Conservancy, 2000.

DUNLAP, DAVID. *On Broadway: A Journey Uptown over Time*. New York: Rizzoli, 1990.

——— and JOSEPH J. VECCHIONE. *Glory in Gotham*. New York: New York City & Co. Guide, 2001.

DUNSHEE, KENNETH HOLCOMB. *As You Pass By: Old Manhattan Through the Fire Laddies' Eyes*. New York: Hastings House, 1962.

EDMISTON, SUSAN and LINDA D. CIRINO. *Literary New York—A History and Guide*. Boston: Houghton Mifflin, 1991.

ELLIS, EDWARD ROBB. *The Epic of New York City*. New York: Coward-McCann, 1966.

Fabos, Julius Gy, Gordon T. Milde, and V. Michael Weinmayr. *Frederick Law Olmsted, Sr.* Amherst, Mass.: University of Massachusetts Press, 1968.

Finney, Jack. *Time and Again.* New York: Simon & Schuster, 1970, 1978.

Fischler, Stan. *Uptown, Downtown: A Trip Through Time on New York's Subway.* New York: Hawthorn Books, 1976.

Fleming, John, Hugh Honour, and Nikolaus Pevsner, eds. *The Penguin Dictionary of Architecture.* Baltimore: Penguin Books, 1966.

Fletcher, Ellen. *Walking Around in South Street: Discoveries in New York's Old Shipping District.* New York: South Street Seaport Museum; revised edition, in association with Leete's Island Books, Stony Creek, Conn., 1999.

Fried, Frederick and Edmund V. Gillon, photographer. *New York Civic Sculpture—A Pictorial Guide.* New York: Dover, 1976.

Friedman, Joe and Richard Berenholts, photographer. *Inside New York: Discovering New York's Classic Interiors.* New York: Harper Collins, 1992.

Garmey, Stephen. *Gramercy Park.* Foreword by Paul Goldberger. New York: Balsam Press Rutledge Books, 1984.

Gayle, Margot, ed. and Edmund V. Gillon, Jr., photographer. *Cast-Iron Architecture in New York.* New York: Dover, 1974.

——— and Michele Cohen. *A Guide to Manhattan's Outdoor Sculpture.* The Art Commission and the Municipal Art Society. New York: Prentice Hall, 1988.

Gill, Brendan. *Flatiron: A Photographic History of the World's First Steel Frame Skyscraper.* Washington: AIA Press, 1990.

Ginter, Val. *Manhattan Trivia: The Ultimate Challenge.* Boston: Quinlan Press, 1985.

Glueck, Grace and Paul Gardner. *Brooklyn: People and Places, Past and Present.* New York: Harry N. Abrams, 1991.

Gold, Joyce. *From Trout Stream to Bohemia.* New York: Old Warren Road Press.

———. *From Windmills to the World Trade Center.* New York: Old Warren Road Press.

Goldberger, Paul. *The City Observed: New York. A Guide to the Architecture of Manhattan.* New York: Vintage Books, 1979.

———. *On the Rise: Architecture and Design in a Postmodern Age.* New York: Times Books, 1983.

———. *The Skyscraper.* New York: Knopf, 1981.

Goldstone, Harmon and Martha Dalrymple. *History Preserved: A Guide to New York City Landmarks and Historic Districts.* New York: Simon & Schuster, 1974.

Golway, Terry. *So Others Might Live: A History of New York's Bravest—The FDNY from 1700 to the Present.* New York: Basic Books, 2002

Greenthal, Kathryn. *Augustus Saint-Gaudens, Master Sculptor.* New York: Metropolitan Museum of Art, 1985.

Haas, Richard. *An Architecture of Illusion.* New York: Rizzoli, 1981.

Hamlin, Talbot. *Greek Revival Architecture in America.* New York: Oxford University Press, 1944. Reprint, New York: Dover, 1964.

Headley, Joel Tyler. *The Great Riots of New York, 1712–1873.* A facsimile of the 1873 edition. New York: Dover, 1971.

Hendrickson, Robert. *The Grand Emporiums: The Illustrated History of America's Great Department Stores.* New York: Stein & Day, 1979.

Huxtable, Ada Louise. *Architecture, Anyone?* New York: Random House, 1986.

———. *Classic New York: Georgian Gentility to Greek Elegance.* Garden City, N.Y.: Doubleday Anchor Books, 1964.

Irving, Washington. *Knickerbocker's History of New York.* New York, 1809.

Jackson, Kenneth T., ed. *The Encyclopedia of New York City.* New Haven: Yale University Press, 1995.

JOHNSON, HARRY and FREDERICK S. LIGHTFOOT. *Maritime New York in Nineteenth-Century Photographs.* New York: Dover, 1980.

KAHN, ALAN PAUL. *The Tracks of New York, 1907: The Metropolitan Street Railway.* New York: Electric Railroaders' Association, 1973.

KAMIL, SETH, et al. *The Big Onion Guide to New City: Ten Historic Walking Tours.* New York: New York University Press, 2002.

KAUFMANN, EDGAR, JR., ed. *The Rise of an American Architecture.* Henry-Russell Hitchcock, Albert Fein, Winston Weisman, Vincent Scully, contributors. In association with The Metropolitan Museum of Art. New York: Praeger, 1970.

KIDNEY, WALTER C. *The Architecture of Choice: Eclecticism in America, 1880–1930.* New York: George Braziller, 1974.

KING, MOSES, ed. *King's Handbook of New York City.* A facsimile of the 1896 edition. New York: Arno Press, 1974.

———. *King's Views of New York 1896–1915, and Brooklyn 1905.* A facsimile of editions published between 1896 and 1915. Introduction by A. E. Santaniello. New York: Benjamin Blom, 1974.

KLOTZ, HEINRICH. *New York Architecture, 1970–1990.* New York: Rizzoli, 1989.

KOUWENHOVEN, JOHN A. *The Columbia Historical Portrait of New York.* New York: Doubleday, 1953. Reprint, New York: Harper & Row Icon Books, 1972.

KREITLER, PETER GWILLIM. *Flatiron.* Washington: AIA Press, 1992.

LAAS, WILLIAM. *Crossroads of the World—The Story of Times Square.* New York: Popular Library, 1963.

LAMB, MRS. MARTHA J. *History of the City of New York.* 2 vols. New York: A. S. Barnes, 1877.

LANCASTER, CLAY. *Old Brooklyn Heights.* Rutland, Vt.: Charles E. Tuttle, 1961. Reprint, New York: Dover, 1979.

LEDERER, JOSEPH and ARLEY BONDARIN, photographer. *All Around the Town: A Walking Guide to Outdoor Sculpture in New York City.* New York: Charles Scribner's Sons, 1975.

LOCKWOOD, CHARLES. *Bricks and Brownstones: The Row House, 1783–1929: An Architectural and Social History.* New York: McGraw-Hill, 1972.

———. *Manhattan Moves Uptown: An Illustrated History.* Boston: Houghton Mifflin, 1976.

LOWE, DAVID GARRARD. *Stanford White's New York.* New York: Doubleday, 1992.

LYMAN, SUSAN. *The Story of New York: An Informal History of the City from the First Settlement to the Present Day.* New York: Crown Publishers, 1975.

——— and ANDREAS FEININGER, photographer. *The Face of New York: The City as It Was and as It Is.* New York: Crown Publishers, 1954.

MARCUSE, MAXWELL F. *This Was New York! A Nostalgic Picture of Gotham in the Gaslit Era.* New York: LIM Press, 1969.

Master Builders: A Guide to Famous American Architects. Washington: The Preservation Press of the National Trust for Historic Preservation, 1985.

MAYER, GRACE M. *Once Upon a City.* New York: Macmillan, 1958.

McCABE, JAMES D., JR. *Lights and Shadows of New York Life, or The Sights and Sensations of the Great City.* A facsimile of the 1872 edition. New York: Farrar, Straus & Giroux, 1970.

———. *New York by Gaslight.* Introduction by Gerard R. Wolfe. A facsimile of the 1882 edition. New York: Crown Publishers, 1984.

McCAUSLAND, ELIZABETH, ed. *New York in the Thirties as Photographed by Berenice Abbott.* Formerly titled *Changing New York,* New York, 1939. New York: Dover, 1963.

McCULLOUGH, DAVID. *The Great Bridge, The Epic Story of the Building of the Brooklyn Bridge.* New York: Simon & Schuster, 1972. Reprint, New York: Avon, 1976.

MENDELSOHN, JOYCE. *The Lower East Side—Remembered and Revisited.* New York: The Lower East Side Press, 2001.

————. *Walks in Four Historic Neighborhoods: Madison Square, Gramercy Park, Ladies' Mile, Chelsea.* New York: New York Landmarks Conservancy, 1998.

MENT, DAVID with ANTHONY ROBINS and DAVID FRAMBERGER. *Building Blocks of Brooklyn,* "A Study of Urban Growth." Brooklyn: Brooklyn Rediscovery, Brooklyn Educational & Cultural Alliance, 1979.

MIDDLETON, WILLIAM D. *Grand Central: The World's Greatest Railway Terminal.* New York: Golden West Books, 2000.

MILLER, TERRY. *Greenwich Village and How It Got That Way.* New York: Crown Publishers, 1990.

A Monograph of the Works of McKim, Mead & White, 1879–1915. Introduction by Leland Roth. First published in 1915. New York: Benjamin Blom, 1973. Reprint, New York: Arno Press, 1977. Student's Edition, with introduction by Allan Greenberg and Michael George, New York: Architectural Publishing Co., 1981.

MOORE, MARGARET and TRUMAN MOORE, photographer. *End of the Road for Ladies' Mile?* Foreword by David Garrard Lowe. New York: The Drive to Protect the Ladies' Mile District, 1986.

MORRIS, LLOYD. *Incredible New York.* New York: Random House, 1951.

MORRONE, FRANCIS. *An Architectural Guide to Brooklyn.* Salt Lake City: Gibbs Smith Publishers, 2001.

———— and JAMES ISKA, photographer. *The Architectural Guidebook to New York City.* Salt Lake City: Gibbs Smith Publishers, 1998.

MOSCOW, HENRY. *The Book of New York Firsts.* New York: Collier Books, 1982.

————. *The Street Book: An Encyclopedia of Manhattan's Street Names and Their Origins.* New York: Hagstrom, 1978.

NEVINS, ALLAN, ed. *The Diary of George Templeton Strong, 1835–1875.* New York: Macmillan, 1952.

————, ed. *The Diary of Philip Hone, 1828–1851.* 2 vols. New York: Dodd, Mead, 1936.

New York City Guide. Guilds' Committee for Federal Writers' Publications, Works Progress Administration. New York: Random House, 1939.

PATTERSON, JERRY E. *The City of New York: A History Illustrated from the Collections of the Museum of the City of New York.* New York: Harry N. Abrams, 1978.

PLOTCH, BATIA, ed. with JOHN MORSE, with various contributors. *New Yorkwalks.* New York: Henry Holt, 1992.

POPPELIERS, JOHN, S. ALLEN CHAMBERS, and NANCY B. SCHWARTZ. *What Style Is It?* Washington: The Preservation Press of the National Trust for Historic Preservation, 1983.

REED, HENRY HOPE. *The Golden City.* New York: W. W. Norton, 1971.

————. *The New York Public Library: Its Architecture and Decoration.* New York: W. W. Norton, 1986.

———— and EDMUND V. GILLON, JR., photographer. *Beaux-Arts Architecture in New York: A Photographic Guide.* New York: Dover, 1988.

REIER, SHARON. *The Bridges of New York.* New York: Dover Publications, 2000.

REYNOLDS, DONALD MARTIN. *The Architecture of New York City: Histories and Views of Important Structures, Sites, and Symbols.* New York: John Wiley & Sons, 1994.

RIFKIND, CAROLE. *A Field Guide to American Architecture: The Periods, the Styles, the Form and Function of Historical Buildings from Colonial Times to Today.* New York: New American Library Plume Books, 1980.

RIIS, JACOB. *How the Other Half Lives—Studies Among the Tenements of New York.* New York: Charles Scribner's Sons, 1890. Reprint, New York: Dover, 1971.

ROBERTO, JOSEPH J. and BAYRD STILL, eds. *Greenwich Village: A Brief Architectural and Pictorial Guide.* New York: New York University, 1981.

ROBINSON, CERVIN and ROSEMARY HAAG BLETTER. *Skyscraper Style: Art Deco New York.* New York: Oxford University Press, 1975.

ROFF, SANDRA, ANTHONY CUCCHIARA, and BARBARA DUNLAP. *From the Free Academy to CUNY— Illustrating Public Higher Education in New York City, 1847–1997.* New York: Fordham University Press, 2002.

ROSEN, LAURA. *The Top of the City: New York's Hidden Rooftop World.* New York: Thames & Hudson, 1982.

RUTTENBAUM, STEVEN. *Mansions in the Clouds: The Skyscraper Palazzi of Emery Roth.* New York: Balsam Press, 1986.

SALWEN, PETER. *Upper West Side Story.* New York: Abbeville Press, 1989.

SANDERS, RONALD. *The Downtown Jews—Portraits of an Immigrant Generation.* New York: Harper & Row, 1969.

———— and EDMUND V. GILLON, JR., photographer. *The Lower East Side—A Guide to Its Jewish Past in 99 New Photographs.* New York: Dover, 1979.

SCHLICHTING, KURT C. *Grand Central Terminal: Railroads, Engineering, and Architecture in New York City.* Baltimore: Johns Hopkins University Press, 2001.

SHANOR, REBECCA READ. *The City That Never Was.* New York: Viking, 1988.

SHARP, LEWIS I. *John Quincy Adams Ward, Dean of American Sculpture.* Newark, Del.: University of Delaware Press, 1985.

———— and DAVID W. KIEHL, eds., *New York Public Sculpture by 19th Century American Artists.* New York: Metropolitan Museum of Art, 1974.

SHEPARD, RICHARD F. *Broadway, from the Battery to the Bronx.* New York: Harry N. Abrams, 1987.

SHOPSIN, WILLIAM C. and MOSETTE BRODERICK. *The Villard Houses: Life Story of a Landmark.* Foreword by Henry-Russell Hitchcock, introduction by Brendan Gill, prologue by Sarah Bradford Landau. In cooperation with the Municipal Art Society of New York. New York: Viking Press, 1980.

SILVER, NATHAN. *Lost New York.* Boston: Houghton Mifflin, 1967. Reprint, New York: Schocken, 1971.

SIREFMAN, SUSANNA and KEITH COLLIE. *New York: A Guide to Recent Architecture.* London: Ellipsis London, Ltd., 2001.

SKINNER, PETER. *The World Trade Center.* New York: Metro Books, 2002.

SMALL, VERNA. *Nineteenth Century Dwelling Houses of Greenwich Village.* New York: Landmarks Committee. Association of Village Homeowners, 1968.

SMITH, THOMAS E. V. *The City of New York in the Year of Washington's Inauguration, 1789.* A reprint of the 1889 Trow's edition. Introduction by Joseph Veach Noble. In cooperation with the U.S. Department of the Interior, National Park Service. Riverside, Conn.: Chatham Press, 1972.

STARR, TAMA and EDWARD HAYMAN. *Signs and Wonders: The Spectacular Marketing of America.* New York: Doubleday & Co., 1998.

STEIN, LEON. *The Triangle Fire.* Philadelphia: Lippincott, 1962.

STEIN, SUSAN R., ed. *The Architecture of Richard Morris Hunt.* Chicago: University of Chicago Press, 1986.

STERN, ROBERT A. M., GREGORY GILMARTIN and JOHN MASSENGALE. *New York: 1900.* New York: Rizzoli, 1983.

———— and THOMAS MELLINS. *New York: 1930.* New York: Rizzoli, 1987.

STILES, HENRY R., ed. *History of the County of Kings and the City of Brooklyn, N.Y., 1684–1884.* 3 vols. Brooklyn, 1884.

STILL, BAYRD. *Mirror for Gotham.* New York: New York University Press, 1956.

STOKES, ISAAC NEWTON PHELPS. *The Iconography of Manhattan Island, 1498–1909.* 6 vols. New York: Robert H. Dodd, 1915. Reprint, New York: Arno Press, 1971.

Sturges, Walter Knight, ed. *Origins of Cast Iron Architecture in America.* Daniel D. Badger's "Illustrations of Iron Architecture" (1865), and James Bogardus's "Cast Iron Buildings, Their Construction and Advantages" (1856). A facsimile edition. New York: DaCapo Press, 1970.

Sturm, James L. and James Chotas, photographer. *Stained Glass from Medieval Times to the Present: Treasures to Be Seen in New York.* New York: E. P. Dutton, 1982.

Tauranac, John. *Essential New York: A Guide to the History and Architecture of Manhattan's Important Buildings, Parks, and Bridges.* New York: Holt, Rinehart, Winston, 1979.

———— and Christopher Little. *Elegant New York: The Builders and the Buildings, 1885–1915.* New York: Abbeville Press, 1985.

Trager, James. *Park Avenue: Street of Dreams.* New York: Atheneum, 1990.

Trent, George D., ed. *The Gentle Art of Walking.* A compilation from *The New York Times.* New York: Arno Press/Random House, 1971.

Tunick, Susan. *Apartment Building Architecture: An Illustrated Overview Providing a Simple Way to Identify Building Parts, Styles and Materials.* New York: Friends of Terra Cotta/ New York, 1986.

Vlack, Don. *Art Deco Architecture in New York, 1920–1940.* New York: Harper & Row, 1974.

von Essen, Thomas. *Strong of Heart. Life and Death in the Fire Department of New York.* New York: Regan Books/Harper Collins, 2002.

von Pressentin Wright, Carol. *Blue Guide Museums and Galleries of New York.* New York: W. W. Norton, 1996.

————. *Blue Guide New York.* New York: W. W. Norton, 1990.

Waite, John G., ed. *Iron Architecture in New York City.* The Edgar Laing Stores and the Cooper Union. Albany: New York State Historic Trust in conjunction with the Society for Industrial Archeology, 1972.

Wharton, Edith. *The Age of Innocence.* New York: D. Appleton & Co., 1921, (reprinted).

Whiffen, Marcus. *American Architecture Since 1870: A Guide to the Styles.* Cambridge: M.I.T. Press, 1969.

White, Norval and Elliot Willensky. *The AIA Guide to New York City,* 4th ed. New York: Three Rivers Press, 2000.

Whitehouse, Roger. *New York Sunshine and Shadow: A Photographic Record of the City and Its People from 1850–1915.* New York: Harper & Row, 1974.

Willensky, Elliot. *When Brooklyn Was the World, 1920–1957.* New York: Harmony Books, 1986.

Willis, Carol. *Form Follows Function. Skyscrapers and Skylines in New York and Chicago.* New York: Princeton Architectural Press, 1995.

Wolfe, Gerard R. *Chicago: In and Around the Loop—Walking Tours of Architecture and History.* New York: McGraw-Hill, 1996.

————. *42nd Street: River-to-River Guide.* New York: 42nd Street E.T.C., Inc., 1991.

————. *The House of Appleton: The History of a Publishing House and Its Relationship to the Cultural, Social, and Political Events that Helped Shape the Destiny of New York City.* Metuchen, N.J.: Scarecrow Press, 1981.

———— and Jo Renée Fine, photographer. *The Synagogues of New York's Lower East Side.* New York: New York University Press, 1978.

Index